Street by Stre

G000022123

SOUTH ESSEX

PLUS CHESHUNT, ROMFORD, WALTHAM ABBEY

Enlarged Areas Basildon, Chelmsford, Harlow, Southend-on-Sea

1st edition May 2001

© Automobile Association Developments Limited 2001

This product includes map data licensed from Ordnance Survey® with the permission of the Controller of Her Majesty's Stationery Office. © Crown copyright 2000. All rights reserved. Licence No: 399221.

Published by AA Publishing (a trading name of Automobile Association Developments Limited, whose registered office is Norfolk House, Priestley Road, Basingstoke, Hampshire, RG24 9NY. Registered number 1878835).

Mapping produced by the Cartographic Department of The Automobile Association.

A CIP Catalogue record for this book is available from the British Library.

Printed in Italy by Printer Trento srl

The contents of this atlas are believed to be correct at the time of the latest revision. However, the publishers cannot be held responsible for loss occasioned to any person acting or refraining from action as a result of any material in this atlas, nor for any errors, omissions or changes in such material. The publishers would welcome information to correct any errors or omissions and to keep this atlas up to date. Please write to Publishing, The Automobile Association, Fanum House, Basing View, Basingstoke, Hampshire, RG21 4EA.

Ref: MD029

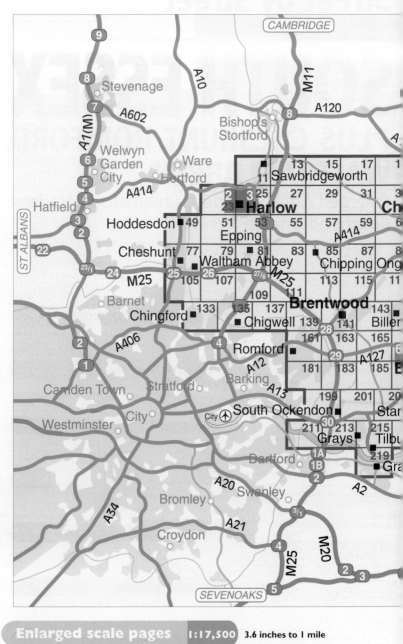

CAMBRIDGE

Stevenage

A10

M11

A602

A120

A1(M)

Bishop's
Stortford

8

Welwyn
Garden
City

Ware

Hertford

A414

13 15 17 1

11 Sawbridgeworth

Hatfield

ST ALBANS

Hoddesdon

Cheshunt

M25

Barnet

Chingford

2 3 25 27 29 31 3

23 Harlow Ch

49 51 53 55 57 59 6

Epping A414

77 79 81 83 85 87 8

Waltham Abbey Chipping Ong

105 107 109 113 115 11

133 135 137 Brentwood 143

Chigwell 139 141 Biller

22

23/1 24 25 26 27/6 M25 111

Romford

A406

4

A12

Barking

A13

Camden Town

Stratford

City

Westminster

City

South Ockenden

28 161 163 165

29 A127 6

181 183 185 E

199 201 20

Star

30 211 213 215

Grays Tilb

219

Gra

Dartford

1A

1B

2

A20 Swanley

A2

Bromley

A21

A34

Croydon

3/1

M25 M20

4

2 3

5

SEVENOAKS

Enlarged scale pages 1:17,500 3.6 inches to 1 mile

0 1/2 miles 1

0 1/2 1 kilometres 1 1/2

BURY ST EDMUNDS

IPSWICH

ntree

A120

Colchester

A12

A133

Brightlingsea

Witham

West Mersea

A12

Clacton-on-Sea

21

35 | **37** | **39** | **41** | **43** | **45** | **47**

nsford

Maldon

5 | A414 | **67** | **69** | **71** | **73** | **75**

63

91 | **93** | **95** | **97** | **99** | **101** | **103**

Sth Woodham Ferrers

119 | **121** | **123** | **125** | **127** | **129** | **131**

A430

Burnham-on-Crouch

147 | **149** | **151** | **153** | **155** | **157** | **159**

Wickford

169 | **171** | **173** | **175** | **177** | **179**

Rayleigh

ildon

191 | **193** | **8** | **9** | **197**

189

SOUTHEND-ON-SEA

205 | **207** | **209**

d le Hope | Canvey Island

Grain

Sheerness

send

A228

MARGATE

Gillingham

2

Chatham

Sittingbourne

3

4 | S

5

6 | **7**

M2

MAIDSTONE

2.5 inches to 1 mile   **Scale of main map pages 1:25,000**

| 0 | 1/2 | miles | 1 | 1 1/2 |

| 0 | 1/2 | 1 | kilometres | 1 1/2 | 2 |

Junction 9	Motorway & junction	**P+**	Park & Ride
Services	Motorway service area		Bus/coach station
	Primary road single/dual carriageway		Railway & main railway station
Services	Primary road service area		Railway & minor railway station
	A road single/dual carriageway		Underground station
	B road single/dual carriageway		Light railway & station
	Other road single/dual carriageway	++++++++	Preserved private railway
	Restricted road	LC	Level crossing
	Private road	•—•—•	Tramway
← ←	One way street	----------	Ferry route
	Pedestrian street	....	Airport runway
	Track/footpath	— · — · —	Boundaries-borough/district
	Road under construction	◢◢◢◢◢◢◢	Mounds
	Road tunnel	**93**	Page continuation 1:25,000
P	Parking	**7**	Page continuation to enlarged scale 1:17,500

River/canal lake, pier		Toilet with disabled facilities
Aqueduct lock, weir		Petrol station
465 Winter Hill — Peak (with height in metres)		PH Public house
Beach		PO Post Office
Coniferous woodland		Public library
Broadleaved woodland		Tourist Information Centre
Mixed woodland		Castle
Park		Historic house/ building
Cemetery		Wakehurst Place NT — National Trust property
Built-up area		Museum/ art gallery
Featured building		Church/chapel
City wall		Country park
A&E Accident & Emergency hospital		Theatre/ performing arts
Toilet		Cinema

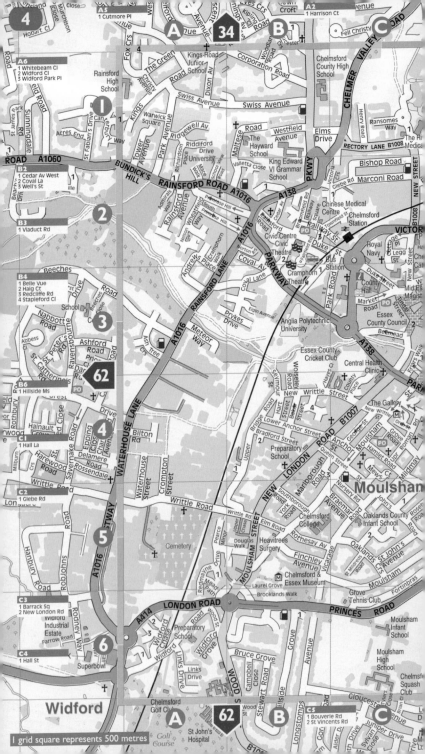

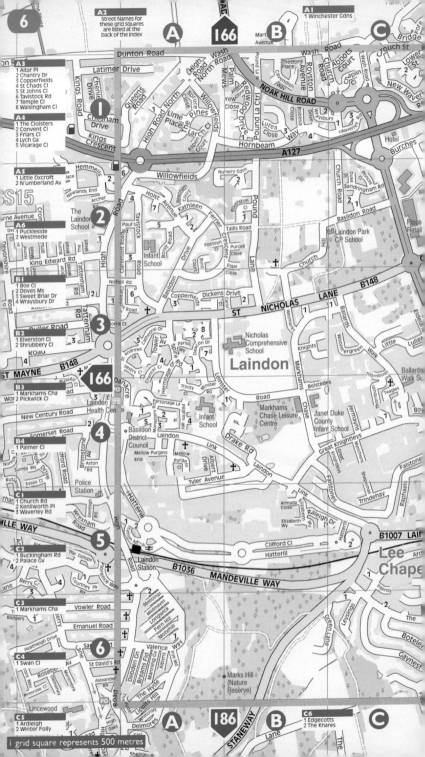

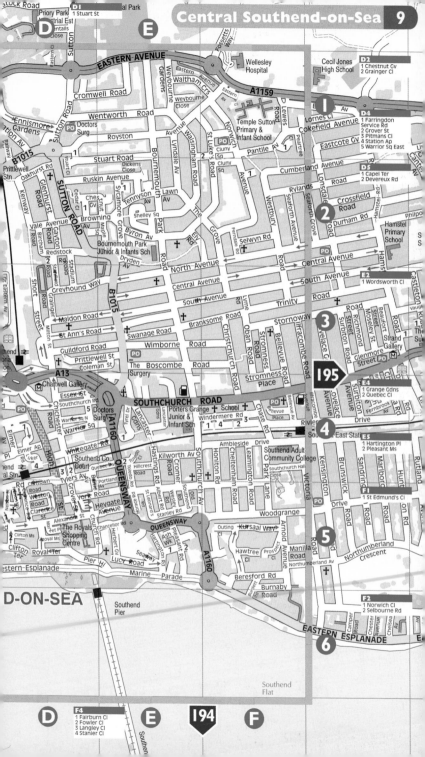

10

A   B   C   D   E

I

Hardings

Bearnfield Road

2

Gangies
Gangies Hill

Carters

Hoskins

Fryars

Actons
Farm

The Manor of
Groves Golf Club

3

Jeffs

Great
Pennys
Farm

High Wych Lane

Bakers
Farm

4

Sayes Park
Farm

High Wych Lane

5

Overhall
Farm

Channocks
Farm

6

High Wych Road

Redricks Lane

Redericks
Farm

7

Gilston
Park

Pole Hole
Farm

8

Vine Grove

Eastwick Road

Gilston

CM20

River

astwick

A   B   **24**   C   D   E   Temple
Fields

Eastwick Lo
Farm

Eastwick Road

Mead
Industrial

Sherwo
Industri
Estate

WEST ROAD

Virgin
Cinemas

WEST ROAD

I grid square represents 500 metres

F G H J K

I

2

3

4

16

5

6

7

8

F G H 29 J K

DUNMOW

B184

New
Hall

Poplars
Farm

Aythorpe
Roding

Roundb
Green

Drury
Lane

Walkers
Farm

Three Forests Way

Langlands

Lucas
Farm

The
Rodings

Rodings Central
Primary School

Roding or
Roothing

A1060

Brownlows
Close

New House
Farm

STORTFORD

ROAD

A1060

Mascallsbury
Farm

Three Forests Way

B184

Hales
Farm

Anchor Lane

Berwick
Hall

Green Hill
Farm

Nether
Street

Abbess
Roding

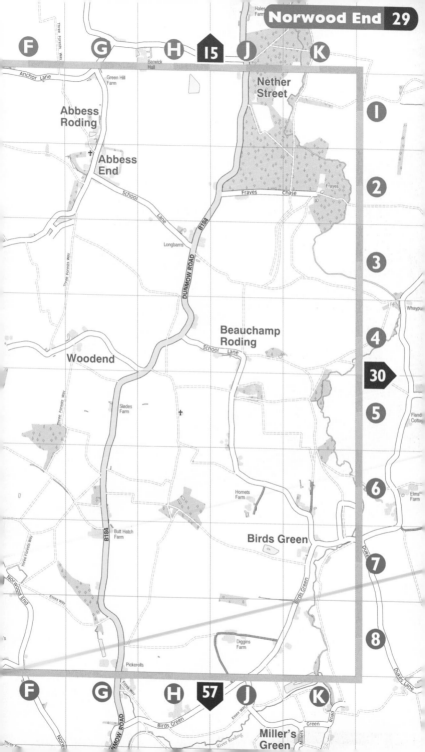

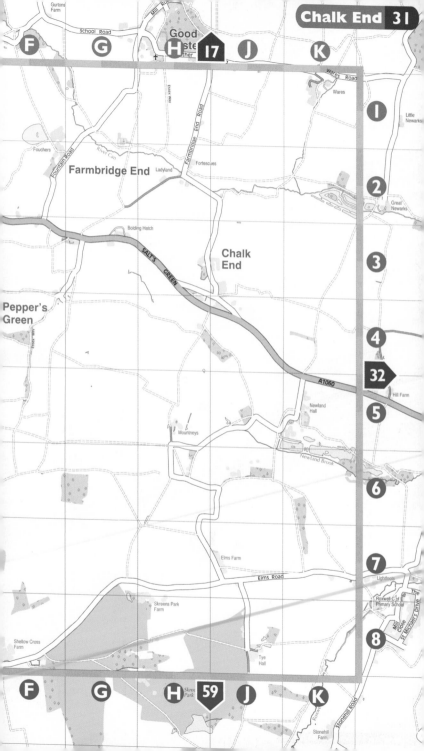

F G H 17 J K

Gurtons Farm
School Road

Good
ste
ther

Wares Road
Wares

I
Little Newarks

2
Great Newarks

Fouchers
River Can

Fountain Road

Farmbridge End
Ladyland
Fortescues

Farmbridge End Road

3

Bolding Hatch

SALTS GREEN

Chalk End

4

Pepper's Green

Essex Way

A1060

32

Hill Farm

5
Newland Hall

Mountneys

Newland Brook

6

Elms Farm

Elms Road

7
Lightfoots
The
Roxwell C of E Primary School

8
Mill Close
St Michael's Drive

Skreens Park Farm

Shellow Cross Farm

Tye Hall

F G H 59 J K

Skreens Park

Stonehill Farm

Stonehill Road

F5
1 Wavell Cl

F7
1 Lawn La

F6
1 Ashurst Dr
2 Briarswood
3 Eridge Cl
4 Matfield Cl
5 Perriclose

F8
1 Springfield Pl
2 Tavistock Rd
3 Torquay Rd

G5
1 Saddle Ri

G6
1 Forsythia Cl
2 Montgomery Cl
3 Snowdrop Cl
4 Tulip Cl

36

G7
1 Sidmouth Rd

H5
1 Goldenacres

H6
1 Hunters Wy
2 Vermeer Ride

Springfield

H8
1 Dahlia Cl
2 Lavender Ct
3 Wallasea Gdns

63

I8
1 Sprfield Lyons Ap

H7
1 Bouchers Mead
2 Camellia Ct
3 Heather Ct
4 Wallflower Ct

D4
1 Hurrell Down
2 Shearers Wy

C5
1 Howards Cl
2 The Larches

C4
1 Armonde Cl
2 Cleves Ct
3 Gwyn Cl

A **B** **C** **D** **E**

1

2

3

4

35

5

6

7

8

Boreham

Generals Lane

Waltham Road

Chantry Farm

Chantry

A12(T)

MAIN ROAD

B1137

Plantation Road

St Andrews Road

Clavpits Road

Allens Close

Gwyn Wy

Butterfield Road

Haselfoot Road

Juniper Road

Boreham County Primary School

The Laurels Surgery

Church Road

Tyssen Mead

The Chase

The Lodge

Old Hall

Boreham Hall

Old Forest

Villers Fence

Bulls Lodge

Circle

Circle

Circle

A130

A130

A12(T)

A12(T)

B1137

MAIN ROAD

COLCHESTER ROAD

A138

Sheepcotes

Centenary Circle

Hammonds Road

Culton Hall

A12(T)

A **B** **64** **C** **D** **E**

I grid square represents 500 metres

Totham
Hill

F

G

H

J

Office Lane

K

The

STREET

Sawyer's

Road

Chelmer Drive

Post Office

Cherry Close

Chelmer Close

Green Lane

1

Little Totham

Vine Farm

Voucher's Farm

Park

Wood

Lane

Moor's Farm

Whitehorse Farm

2

Jepcrack's Farm

Church Road

Sheepcoates Lane

Moor's Lane

School Road

Beckingham

STREET

3

Little Renters Farm

Spickets Brook

Sheepcoates Farm

Church Lane

Little Totham Hall

Wash Lane

Little To

ROAD

4

Clarks Farm

42

Sains Hall

Church

Lane

5

Scraley Road

Chigborough Road

Little London Farm

6

Blind

Slough House Farm

Lofts

Chappel Farm

7

Heybridge Swifts Football Club

Chigborough Road

Rook Hall

Cobb's Farm

MALDO

Drapers Sports Club

Chigborough Farm

Wash Lane

8

Gardener's Farm

Salcote Hall

F

GRANGER ROAD

G

Basin Road

Wharf Road

H

69

J

Vaulty Manor

K

GOLDHA

ROAD

B1026

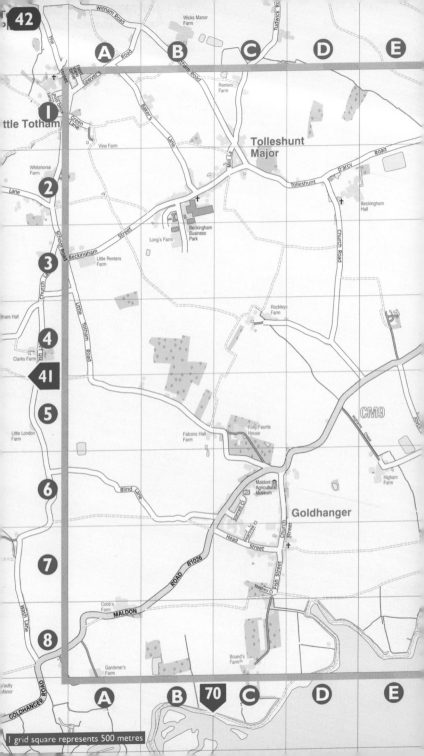

1 grid square represents 500 metres

1 Vicarage Cl

Limesbrook

F   G   H   J   K

Frame Farm

Chase Hl

Tolleshunt D'Arcy

Salter's Meadow

NORTH STREET

SOUTH STREET

Chapel Road

D'ARCY WAY

I

Hill Farm

Beckingham Road

Festival Gdns

Church St

Tolleshunt Darcy C of E Primary School

B1023

TOLLESBURY ROAD

Guisnes Court

Cemetery

B1026

Gorwell Hall

2

Tolleshunts Farm

MALDON ROAD

3

Brook House Farm

D White House Farm

4

1026

Hyde Farm

44

Pyes Lane

5

Wycke Farm

6

Joyce's Farm

Lauriston Farm

Joyce's Creek

7

8

Gore Saltings

Goldhanger Creek

A B C D E

1

Mersea
Quarters

Quarters
Spit

2

North Channel

Great Cob
Island

3

South Channel

Shinglehead
Point

4

45

5

6

7

Bradwell
Nuclear Power
Station

8

Pewet
Island

A B 74 C D E

Bradwell Quay
Yacht Club

Bradwell
Waterside

Bosom Fleet

Cobmarsh
Island

West Mersea
Museum

Meadow
Lane

I grid square represents 500 metres

F G H J K

I

2

3

4

5

6

Sales
Point

7

Tip
Head

8

East Hall
Farm

Eastend

Road

Eastlands

F G H **75** J K

Eastend Road

E3
1 Ramsay Cl
2 Willoughby Cl

E2
1 Hickman Cl
2 Overlord Cl

D8
1 The Links

Hoddesdonpark Wood

HO

A   **B**   **C**   **D**   **E**

Cock Lane

1

E6
1 Priory Cl

2

E7
1 The Canadas
2 Nunsbury Dr
3 Nursery Rd

Pembridge Lane

Paradise
Wildlife
Park

3

E8
1 Brickcroft
2 Perram Cl
3 Robertson Cl

Cold
Hall

Wood House Lane

Bass Hill

Bass Manor
Farm

Alamein
Close

Norris Cr

Gold
Close

Bass Hill
Close

Bell

Emanuel
Pollards

4

Carneles
Green

Wormley
West End

West End Road

EN10

Church Lane

Wormley
JMI Sch

5

Wormleybury

Park Lane   High Cross Hill

Wormley

Beaumont Road

6

Thunderfield
Cross

Factory Farm

Huntington Clo

The Oval

7

Paradise

A10(T)

Canada
Lane

Turnford

Prescott
Close

8

Thunderfield

Cheshunt
Park

Broxbourne
Borough
Council

Broxbourne
Business
Centre

Hotel

HALFHIDE LANE

A10 GREAT CAMBRIDGE ROAD

B156

Old Road

The

Hillview Gardens

Herongate Road

CHESHUNT WASH

A   **B**   **76**   **C**   **D**   **E**

Debenham Rd

St Pauls
Roman Catholic
JMI School

Fairfields Junior
Middle & Infant
School

Moretor

OXFIELD LANE WEST

Prescott
Road

Endeavour
Road

F1
1 The Spinney

F2
1 Bassingbourne Cl
2 Monson Rd
3 Richmond Ct
4 St Augustines Cl

Hoddesdon
Health Centre
Lowewood
Museum

Spitalbrook

St David's Drive
New Road
Springfield

St Michael's
Friarscroft

Grosvenor Road

Broxbourne
Station

Broxbourne B194
STATION ROAD

Mill Lane

Broxbourne
Sports Club

Broxbourne
C of E JMI
School

Winford Drive

Cozens Lane East
Lily
Park CP
School

Doctors
Surgery

Fairfield Dr

Spencer's Lane

Slipe Lane

Wharf Road

King's
Weir

Nazeing
Marsh

Langridge

Keysers
Estate

Green Lane

Riverside Avenue

Hillgrove
Business
Park

Old Nazeing Road

Lower
Nazeing

Tatsfield Avenue

Nursery Road

Elizabeth Close

St Leonards Road

St Leonard's

Coleman's Lane

Nazeing
Mead

Broxbourne
Sailing Club
Meadgate

Meadgate Road

Blythe Road
Derby Road
Weir Road

I

F3
1 Ashbourne Rd
2 Royce Cl

2

F4
1 Caldecot Wy
2 Lichfield Wy
3 The Sidings

3

F5
1 Fern Cl
2 The Square
3 Virgil Dr
4 Wormley Ldg Cl

North Road
Shooters Dri
Western Road

4

50

Mayflower
Close

Nazeing
CP School

Barnas
Acres

5

F6
1 Orchard Sq
2 Shirley Cl
3 Westlea Cl

6

F7
1 Farmhouse Cl
2 Felton Cl
3 Juniper Cl

7

F8
1 Farriers End
2 Helens Ga
3 Shire Cl

8

Marsh Hill
House

MARSH HILL B194

K4
1 Nazeingbury Cl

G2
1 Courtfield Cl
2 Stafford Dr

G1
1 Hallmores
2 St Cross Ct
3 Westcroft Ct

Lee Valley
Park

F G H 27 J K

I

Start Farm

Moreton Mill

2

Ashlings Cottages

Crispins

Weald Lodge

Maltings Hill

Scotts Farm

The Hoppitt

Moreton C of E Primary School

Maltings

Nether Hall

Church Road

Moreton

Upper Hall

3

Pedlars End

Gould Close

Bridge End

Pedlars

Ashlyns Lane

Bovinger Lodge

Ashlyns

Moreton Road

Moreton Bridge

New Farm

4

Clatterford Brook

Moreton

56

Newhouse Lane

Road

Gainsthorpe

od Farm

5

Road

Bobbingworth

Stony Lane

Hobban's Farm

Bridgefield

Mill

Blake Hall

6

Bovinger

EPPING ROAD

Stony Lane

Lower Bobbingworth Green

A414 EPPING ROAD

Blake Hill Road

7

Perills

Water End Farm

8

Bilsdens Farm

A414

St Pr

EPPIN

F G H 83 J K Pennon's

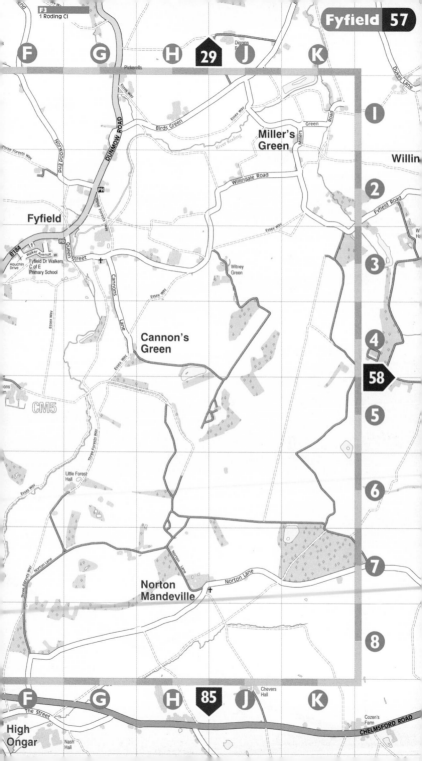

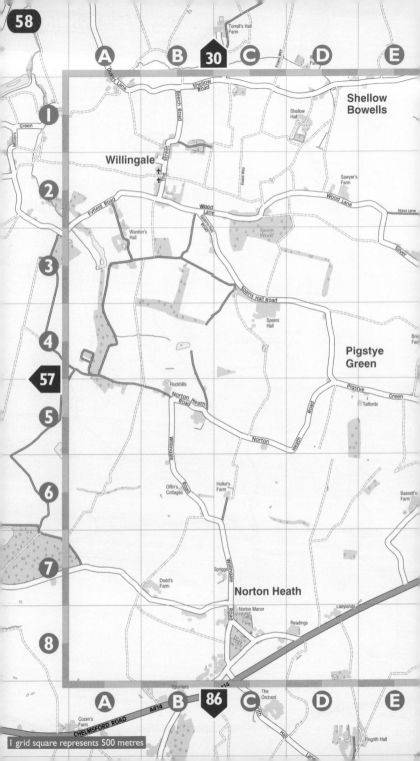

Shellow
Bowells

Willingale

Pigstye
Green

Norton Heath

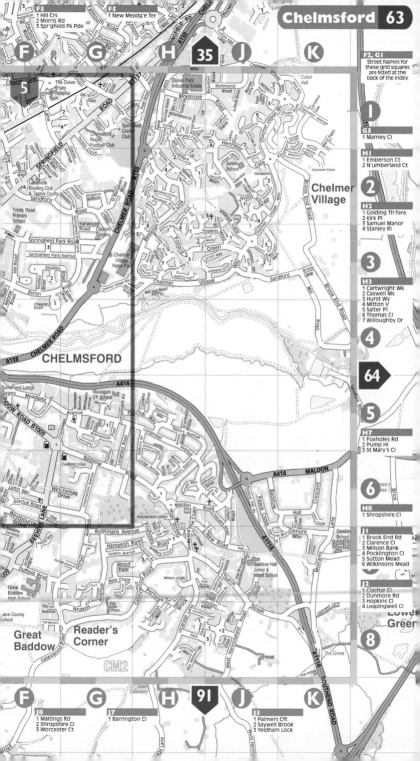

Chelmer Village

CHELMSFORD

Great Baddow

Reader's Corner

CM2

F G H 39 J K

Manor Farm

Woodlands

Beeleigh Grange Farm

I

Hop Gardens Lane

Manor Road

Cut-A-Thwart Lane

Cut-A-Thwart Lane

Abbey Turning

Beeson Chase

A414

2

Whitehouse Farm

Curling Tye Lane

Beeleigh Farms

Cemetery

London Road

Maldon All Saints C of E Primary School

Cherry Gardens

Curling Tye Green

Curling Tye Lane

Brook Farm

St Giles Crescent

3

London Road

A414

ROAD

4

Wood Corner

West Station Road

West Station Yard

Old London Road

WYCKE HILL

A414 Spital

68

Wycke Hill Business Park

Longship Way

5

Narvik Close

B1018

LIMEBROOK

A414 SPITAL ROAD

6

Hall Farm

MALDON ROAD

A414

Limebrook Farm

Brookhead Farm

Lodge Road

7

Rectory Lane

Hill Farm

Elms Farm

8

HAM

ROAD

B1010

Hazeleigh

Lane

Hazeleigh

Cemetery

F G H 95 J K

Rectory Lane

B1010

68

40

67

96

MALDON

I grid square represents 500 metres

G1
1 Saltcote Maltings

G2
1 Maritime Av
2 Spinnaker Dr

F G H **41** J K

Gardener's
Farm

Salcote
Hall

B1026

Vaulty
Manor

HANGER ROAD

B1026 GOLDHANGER ROAD

Wharf Road

Basin Road

I

**Heybridge
Basin**

Blackwater
Sailing
Club

2

The Sidings

Burnham Place

Lock Hill

Deep Drive

Chapel Lane

Hilly
Pool Point

Collier's
Reach

Ousel Road

Decoy
Point

3

River Blackwater

Northey
Island

CM9

4

70

5

Southey
Creek

6

Limbourne Creek

7

Iltney
Farm

Bramble
Hall Farm

New Hall Lane

8

Garlands

F G H **97** J K

Blackwater
Farm

White
House
Farm

Brookmead
Farm

Mundon Wash

F G H 43 J K

Goldhanger Creek

Gore S...

❶

❷

❸

Osea
Island

East Point

❹

72

Stansgate Abbey
Farm

❺

Ramsey
Marsh

❻

Steeple
Creek

❼ Steeple
Wick

❽

Stansgate Road

Cannery
Road

...nd Creek

Canney Road

F G H **45** J K

Pewet
Island

Br
Ya

I

Bradwell

Westwick
Farm

2

3

ON ROAD

4

74

Maldon Road

5

Highfield

Bradwell
Hall

Bradwell
Wick

6

Bradwell Brook

Byhams

ROAD

7

BRADWELL

Sampsons

Blackbirds

8

East
Hyde

Lawrence

St Lawrence Road

Brook Road

ST NICHOLAS Road

NORTH STREET

F G **101** J K

West
Hyde

Lane

Tillingham St Nicholas
C of E Primary School

Vicarage Lane

Casey
Lane

Stowe's Lane

Stows
Farm

chapel La

Birch R

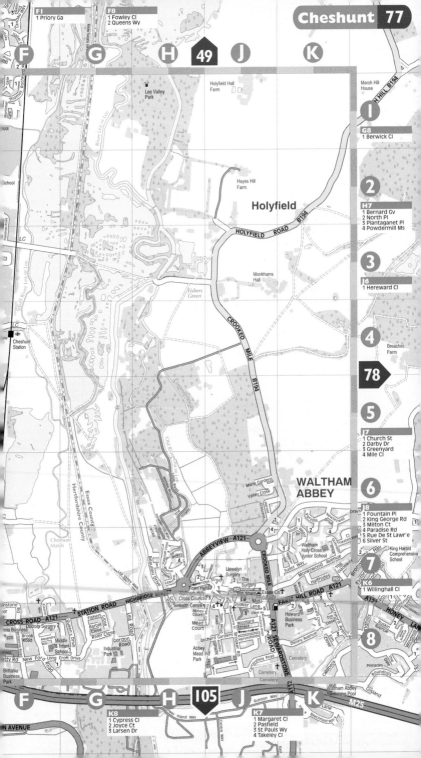

F1
1 Priory Ga

F8
1 Fowley Cl
2 Queens Wy

F   G   H   49   J   K

Marsh Hill
House

1

G8
1 Berwick Cl

2

H7
1 Bernard Gv
2 North Pl
3 Plantaganet Pl
4 Powdermill Ms

Hayes Hill
Farm

Holyfield

HOLYFIELD ROAD B194

Lee Valley
Park

Holyfield Hall
Farm

3

J6
1 Hereward Cl

Monkhams
Hall

Fishers
Green

4

Breaches
Farm

78

CROOKED MILE B194

Cheshunt
Station

5

J7
1 Church St
2 Darby Dr
3 Greenyard
4 Mile Cl

6

J8
1 Fountain Pl
2 King George Rd
3 Milton Ct
4 Paradise Rd
5 Rue De St Lawr'e
6 Silver St

**WALTHAM
ABBEY**

Marie Gardens

Valley Close

Cheshunt
Marsh

Waltham
Holy Cross
Junior School

King Harold
Comprehensive
School

7

K6
1 Willinghall Cl

ABBEYVIEW A121

Llewelyn
Surgery

The
Surgery

CROSS ROAD A121   STATION ROAD   HIGHBRIDGE STREET

Doctors Surgery

Brook
Road

Middle
School

Gordon
Road

Industrial
Park

Cross Council
Health Centre

Abbey
Court

Mead
Court

Orchard Gardens

Abbey
Mead and
Park

Quaker Lane

Woollard
Street

Harveyfields

Howard
Business
Park

Denny Avenue

Cemetery

Cemetery
Cemetery

Honey Lane

Quaker
Avenue

Waltham Abbey
Swimming Pool

F   G   H   105   J   K   M25

K8
1 Cypress Cl
2 Joyce Ct
3 Larsen Dr

K7
1 Margaret Cl
2 Pasfield
3 St Pauls Wy
4 Takeley Cl

N AVENUE

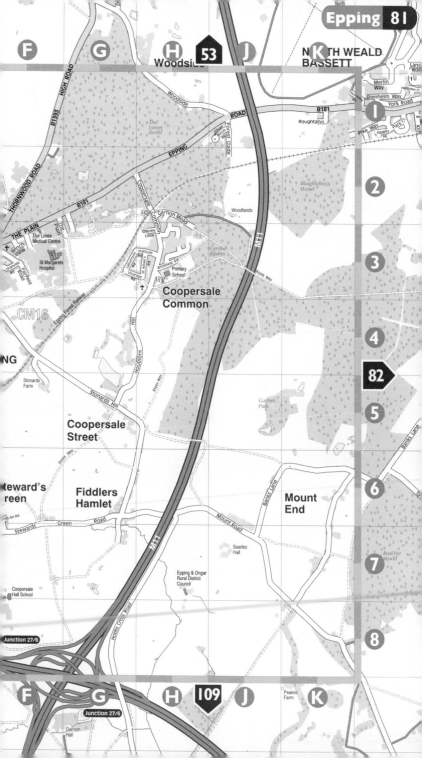

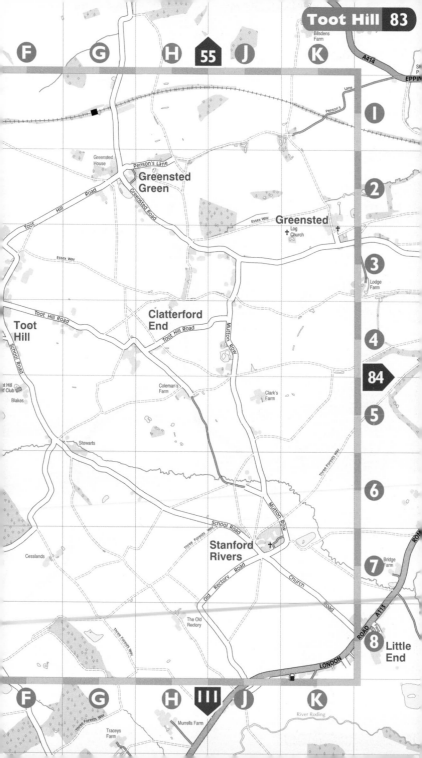

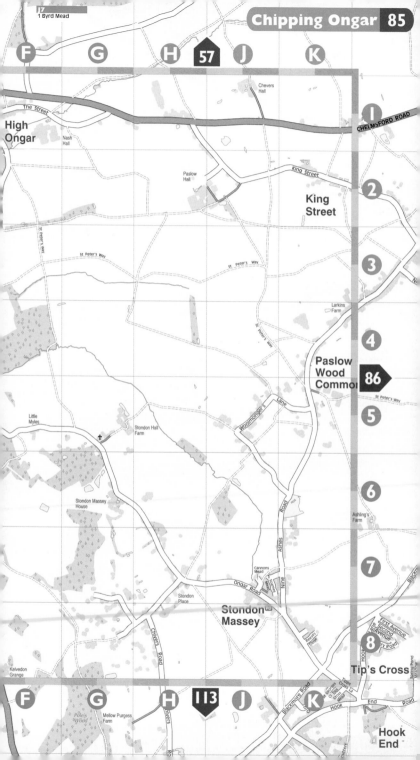

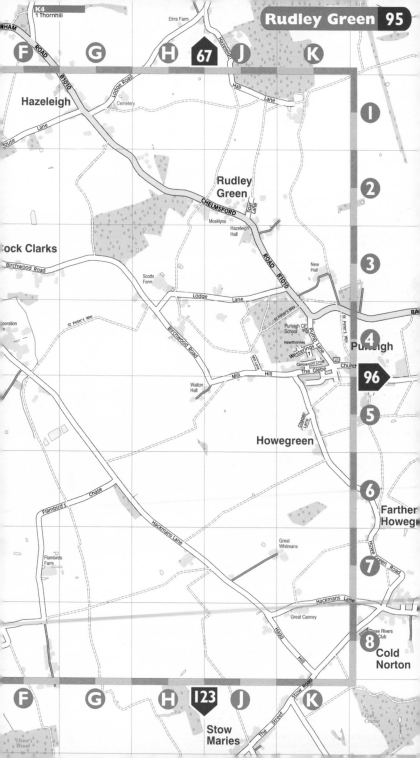

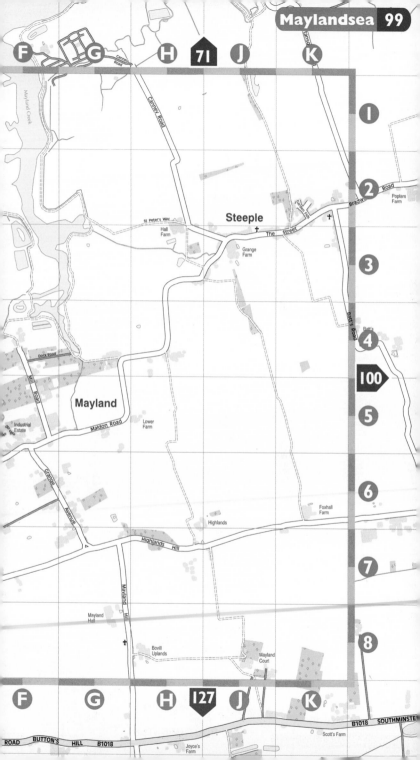

Marshhouse
Outfall

F G H 75 J K

I

2

Marshhouse
Decoy Pond

Tillingham Marshes

House

Howe
Farm

3

4

Grange Outfall

5

6

Round Barn

7

Fieldham Brook

8

Bridge
Arts Centre

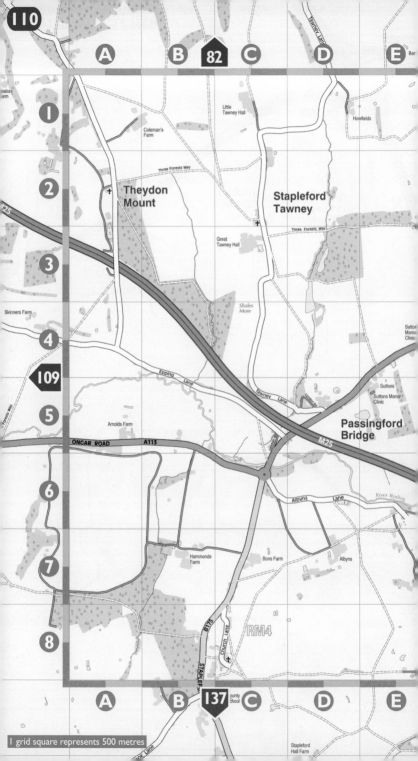

A   **B**   86   **C**   Ha **D** Green   **E**

Stubbers Farm

First Avenue
Second Avenue
Nursery Road

Tip's Cross

1

Blackmore Road
Deartree Close
Outing's

Hook End Road   Hay Green Lane

Mill Lane

The Robins
Beehive
Whitelands

Hook End

Church Lane
Willbrook

2

All Saints

Doddinghurst County Infant School

Rectory Chase

Watt's Green Road

Watts Grn La

Swallows Cross

Brook

Peartree Green

Brook

Pettits Lane

Wyatt's Green Road

Doddinghurst C of E Jun

3

Doddinghurst

Dagwood Lane

Middle Green
Harpers
Parsonage Field

Peartree Lane
Lime Grove
Apple Tree Crescent
Yellow Close
Peartree Close
Park Meadow

Mountnessing Lane

Mountnessing Road

4

Dave Lane

Park Farm

Park Woods

River Wid

▼ 113

5

America Farm

CM15

Heard's Farm

6

Wishfields Farm

Doddinghurst Road

Heard's Lane

7

Sumner's Farm

Palmer's Farm

Hall Lane

Hall Lane

8

Pilgrims Hatch

Brickhouse Farm

Canterbury Tye Hall

Lascelles Close

Hatch Road

Church Road

Lilac Close

Balmoral Way

Honeysuckle

A   **B**   141   **C**   A12th **D**   **E**

CHELM

Shell Sport Oliver

Rochford

89
118
144

F8, G8
Street Names for
these grid squares
are listed at the
back of the index

F   G   H   J   K

I

H8
1 Blacksmith Cl
2 W'bourne Gdns

2

J7
1 Princes Ct
2 Princes Ms

3

Thornton
Place

K3
1 Austen Dr
2 Cambridge Cl

4

5

K8
1 Martingale Cl
2 Moore Cl

6

7

8

F   G   H   J   K

sbury

Tyrrells

Brocks
Farm

Ingatestone Road

Lilystone
Hall

Honeypot Lane

Small Gains

Little
Blunts

Great
Blunts

The Vale

Buckwyns Chase

Queen's
Park

Queens Park Avenue

Norsey View Drive

Tylers Avenue

Mayflower
Comprehensive
School

Newlands Road

Norsey Wood
(Nature
Reserve)

122

94

121

149

C6
1 Connaught Dr
2 Raymonds Cl

B7
1 Treebeard Copse
2 White Tree Ct

B5
1 Meadow Ms

C5
1 Coral Cl
2 Fengates
3 Tanners Wy
4 Tythe Barn Wy

Chapel Row

Woodham Ferrers

C7
1 Butterbur Cha
2 Goldberry Mead

D4
1 Fremantle Cl
2 Redshank Crs

D5
1 Algars Wy
2 Bakers Cl
3 The Cedars
4 Clements Pl
5 Hither Blakers
6 Longhams Dr
7 Rookery Mead

D6
1 Cimarron Cl

D7
1 Ashmans Rw
2 Ch'berlains Ride
3 Charlotte Ct

E4
1 Chadwick Rd

E5
1 Bridgend Cl
2 Foulgar Cl
3 King Edward's Rd
4 Millars Cl

D8, E7
Street Names for these grid squares are listed at the back of the index

E6
1 Akenfield Cl
2 Crouch Beck
3 Merchant St
4 Roding Leigh
5 Tutors Wy

E8
1 Quarter Ga
2 Starboard Vw

1 grid square represents 500 metres

THE STREET

NORTON ROAD

Crofton

Snoreham
Gardens

Heritage

tchingdon

F **G** **H** **97** **J** **K**

B1018

Red Lyons
Farm

Purleigh
Barns

I

Snoreham
Hall

Rectory Lane

2

Rosed
Farm

London
Hayes

Scatterbrook
Farm

Marsh House
Farm

3

WER BURNHAM ROAD

Ulehams
Farm

Stamfords Farm

4

126

LC

5

Bridgemarsh Creek

6

Bridgemarsh
Island

7

Landsend
Point

River Crouch

8

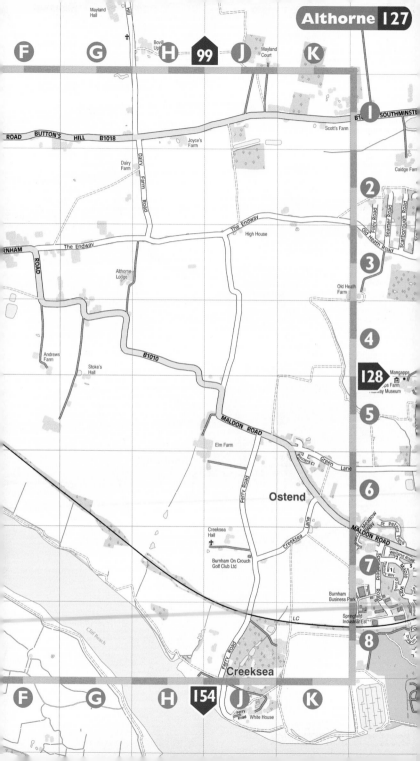

F G H **99** J K

I SOUTHMINSTER

ROAD BUTTON'S HILL B1018

Mayland Hall

Bovill Upt

Mayland Court

Scott's Farm

Caidge Farm

Joyce's Farm

Dairy Farm

Dairy Farm Road

2

Old Ferry Road

Seamer Road

Scarborough Road

Old Heath Road

The Endway

High House

3

rnham ROAD

The Endway

Althorne Lodge

Old Heath Farm

4

128 Mangapps
ps Farm
way Museum

Andrews Farm

Stoke's Hall

B1010

5

MALDON ROAD

Elm Farm

Green Lane

Pinners Cl

6

Ostend

Ferry Road

adow
St Peter's Rd

MALDON ROAD

Creeksea Hall

Burnham On Crouch Golf Club Ltd

Creeksea Lane

welland road

7

Di

Maple Way

LC

Burnham Business Park

Springfield Industrial Est

8

Cliff Reach

Ferry Road

Creeksea

F G H **154** J White House K

Ferry Road

130

A　　B　102　C　　D　E

Brook
Farm

Bridgewick

Brid

I

2

3

Middle
Wick

Turncole Farm

4

129

5

Old
Turncole

Montsale

6

Deal
Hall

7

Coney
Hall

Marsh Road

East
Wick

Redward

8

Holliwell Farm

A　　B　157　C　　D　　E

1 grid square represents 500 metres

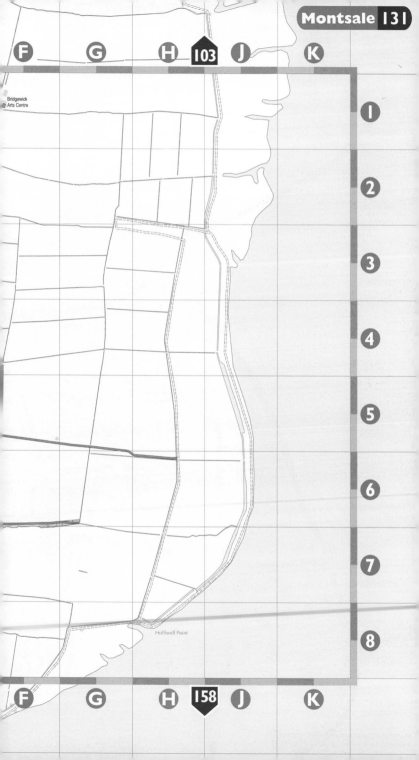

F G H 103 J K

Bridgewick
Arts Centre

1
2
3
4
5
6
7
8

Holliwell Point

G8
1 Conifer Av

RM4

F G H **110** J K

1

2

3

4

138

5

6

7

8

Stapleford Abbotts County Primary School

Stapleford Hall Farm

Grove House

Gutteridge Lane

High House Farm

Knolls Hill Farm

Brook Farm Industrial Estate

Stapleford Abbotts

Nuper's Hatch

Tyseahill Farm

The Paddocks

TYS

Tysea Hill

Hook Lane

STAPLEFORD ROAD

Church Lane

Bournebridge Lane

Crown Park Farm

OAK HILL ROAD

Park Farm

Bower Farm

Bower Farm Road

Dame Tipping School

Wellington Avenue

B175 NORTH ROAD

Havering-6-Bower

River Rom

Carter Drive

Havering Country Park

Pinewood Road

CHANGE TREE HILL

B175

Bower House

Bower House

Bedfords Park

Thrustdene Av

Pinewood Primary School

Craven Gdns

Cornell Way

Oates Road

Wensley

Portmore Gdns

Firbank Road

Saint Johns Road

Warden Av

Bonmoor Road

Citherce Road

Hunter's Grove

Silvermere Rd

Victoria Avenue

Kingshill

Lane

Avenue

Hengon Gdns

Highfield

Mount Pleasant Rd

Belle Vue Road

Azhvale Gdns

Havering Court Nursing Home

Bower Park School

Immanuel School

Merino Gdns

Merino Close

ROAD

B1459

Chase Cross

F G H J K

RM5

Lodge Lane

Udall Gardens

Ascension Rd

Clockhouse Junior School

Burland Road

Campbell Close

Nevis Rd

138

A B III C D E

E8
1 Bridgwater Wk
2 Chip'ham Gdns
3 Newbury Wk

E7
1 Woodbridge Cl

Curtis Mill Lane

Brook
Farm

ld Lane

Jenkins Farm

Horseman Side

Wat

1
Tyseahill Farm

The Paddocks

Tysea Hill

Watton's
Green

M25

2

Navestock
Common

Nuper's
Hatch

3

Tysea Hill

Asheton
Farm

Goatswood

Lane

Church

4

HILL

ROAD

Essex County
Havering

137

Paternoster Row

5

ROAD

Home Farm

Widdrington
Farm

B175

NEW

The Tipping
ool

6

Havering-
atte-Bower

Broxhill Road

Cummings Hall La

Greenbank

Wellington
Avenue

The Mount

Castle
Close

Wincanton Road

Preston Rd

B175

7

Ingrebourne CP
School

NGE TREE HILL

8

Bedfords
Park

Nork Hill Road

Straight Road

Applesby Dr

Hallsham

Lewes
Rd

Stephens Cl

HITCHIN

Barnstable Road

Aylsham

Longtown
Road

Carsdale
Close

Darlington
Gardens

Montgomery

Avenue

Troopers Dr

Appley Dr

Harnel
Road

Havering Court
Nursing Home

Immanuel School

Bower
Park
School

Chase
Cross

A B 160 C

St Ursulas
Junior and
Infant
School

Stanwyck
Gardens

Dawley Rd

Hildene

Hildene
Crescent

Grange
End

Bridgwater

Davenham

D

Chippenham

E

Chatteris

Dunstan
Rd

Erickley
Rd

Dudley

Grange
Road

Hildene
Junior and Infant
School

Archway

Myrtle

Tulip

Lucerne
Dr

Coltsfoot Pth

Broom
Prim
Scho

Brae
Primary
School

St Nevis

1 grid square represents 500 metres

F3
1 Rushdene Rd

F4
1 Mayfield Gdns
2 Wingway

F · G · H · 114 · J · K

I
F5
1 Crown St
2 Regency Ct

2
F6
1 King Edward Rd
2 The Mount
3 Rose Va
4 White Lyons Rd

3
F8
1 Hampden Crs
2 Pompadour Cl

4 Hutton Mount

142

5
G4
1 Alfred Rd

6
G8
1 Blackthorn Wy

7
J3
1 Margaret Av

8

Shenfield

Brentwood

K7
1 The Broadw'k (S)

K6
1 The Broad Wk (N)
2 Grangewood Cl
3 Norman Crs
4 Wingfield Cl

J6
1 The Limes
2 Maple Cl
3 Oaktree Cl
4 Rowan Gn East
5 Rowan Gn West

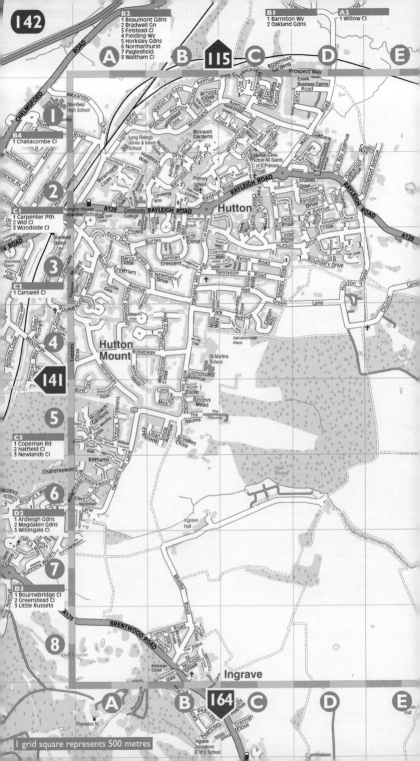

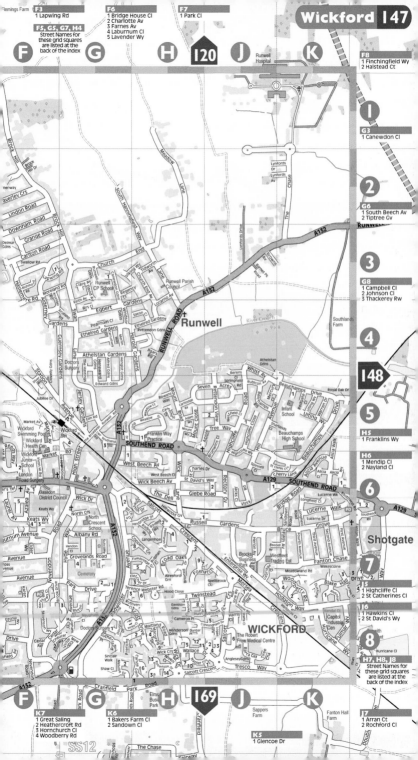

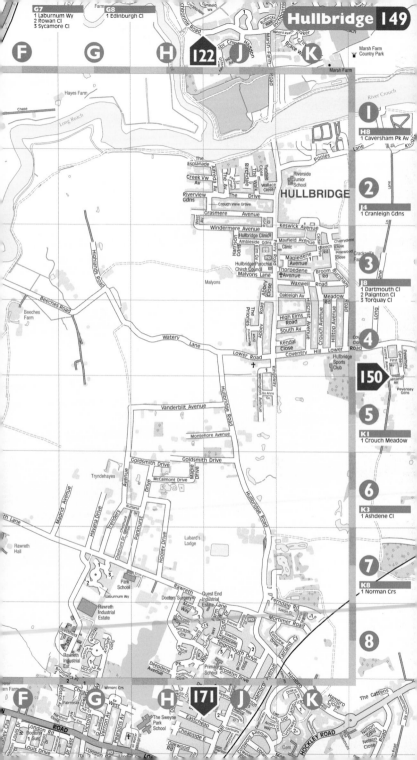

F
G
H
124
J
K

I

2

3

4

152

5

ASHINGDON

6

7

8

South Fambridge

Pemberton Field

Brickhouse Farm

Fambridge Road

Brenham Farm

Beckney Farm

Lovedown

Lower Road

Lowlands Farm

Lower Road

Ashingdon School

Ashingdon Road

Canewdon Rd

Fambridge Road

Canewdon Vie

Branksome Avenue

Malvern Road

Tonbridge Rd

Orchard Avenue

Cornhill Av

Oak Walk

Greensward College

Greensward Surgery

Greensward Lane

Crouch Vw

The Chase

The Chase

Stanley Road

Clifton Road

York Road

Alexandra Road

Albert Road

Wedgwood

Doulton

Church Rd

Hockley Station

Broad Walk

Chestnut Close

Roach Valley Way

Durham Road

Lincoln

Magnolia Road

Rectory Avenue

Lascelles Gardens

Ashingdon Surgery

Princess Gardens

Harwood Avenue

Central Avenue

HEND N RD

MAIN ROAD

HAWKWELL

Victor Gardens

Harrow Cl

Park Gardens

Doctors Surg

Hawkwell Park Drive

Hazelwood

Rectory Road

F
G
H
173
J
K

Hawkwell Hall Farm

Ironwell Lane

Belchamps

Poplars Av

Holyoak Lane

F   G   H   126   J   K

I

2

3

4

154

5

6

7

8

Old Fleet

Easter
Reach

Upper
Raypitts
Farm

Roach Valley Way

Canewdon

Roach Valley Way

Butts   Paddock
Canewdon Hall Close
High Street

Cays Lane

Mill

New
Hall

Lambourne

Lambourne
Hall

Canewdon Endowed
Primary School

Ash Green   Anchor
Sycamore Way   Rowan   Way
Willow Way

Gardeners   Lane

Hall   Road

Lark Hill Road   Anchor Lane

White House
Farm

Scott's Hall Road

Creeksea Ferry Road

Saltings

Loftmans
Farm

West
Hall

Scott's
Hall

Ballards Gore
Golf Club

Ballards Gore

Apton Hall Road   Gore Road   Paglesham Road

Biggins Farm

SS4

Stanbridge Road

Stewards
Elm Farm

Wheatfields

Stambridge Road

PO
Cagefield Rd

Cross Elms
Farm Lane

Brick House

Bampstone

F   G   175   H   J   K

**Great
Stambridge**

Hampton Barns

River

154

A · B · **127** · C · D · E

Creeksea

1

Cliff Reach

Ferry Road

LC

White House

Ferry Road

2

River Crouch

Link Wharf

3

Saltings

Creeksea Ferry Road

Creeksea Ferry Road

Ferry Road

Creeksea

Paglesham Creek

Lambourne Hall

4

Road

153

Sea Ferry Road

5

Loftmans Farm

Clements Marsh

6

West Hall

Paglesham Churchend

PH

Roach Valley Way

East Hall

7

Road

Ingulls

Biggins Farm

8

South Hall

Pagle

A · B · **176** · C · D · E

Roach Valley Way

St

I grid square represents 500 metres

ON-CROUCH

HI
1 The Quay
2 Riverside Rd
3 Shore Rd

F **G** **H** **128** **J** **K**

Wick Road
Burnham Wick

Crouch Yacht Club

HIGH STREET
Museum

Old Club House
Royal Corinthian Yacht Club

Belvedere Road

I

2

River Crouch

Ringwood Bar

Grapnells

3

4

156
Wallasea Island

5

Paglesham Pool

6

7

lesham tend

Waterside Road

8

Potton Point

F **G** **H** **177** **J** **K**

River Roach

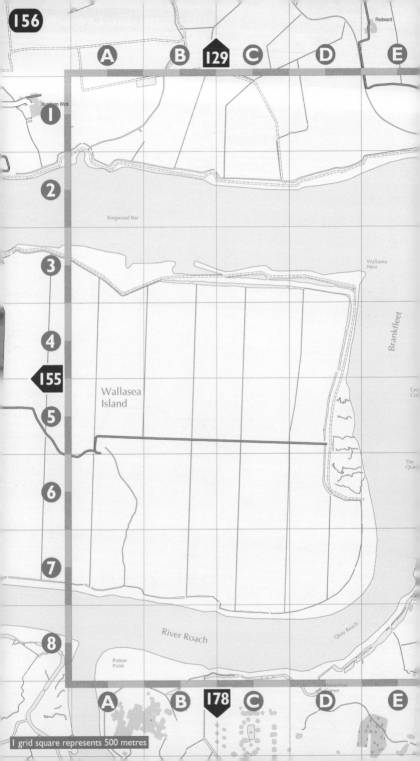

A　　B　129　C　　D　　E

Redward

1 Burnham Wick

2

Ringwood Bar

3

Wallasea
Ness

Brankfleet

4

155

Wallasea
Island

5

The
Qua

6

7

River Roach

Quay Reach

8

Potton
Point

Horseshoe
Corner

A　　B　178　C　　D　　E

1 grid square represents 500 metres

F G H 130 J K

Holliwell Farm

I

River Crouch   River Crouch 2

3

Clark's Hard

4

158

Nase Wick   5

Monkton Barn

6

Lodge Farm

†

PO Churchend   Foulness Island 7

Priestwood

8

East Wick

Rugwood Farm

F G H 179 J K

Foulness
Point

F G H J K

1

2

3

4

5

6

7

8

F G H J K

138

180

Havering Court
Nursing Home

Chase
Rise

Rise
Park

Gidea
Park

Gallows
Corner

Ardleigh
Green

OMFOR

Heath
Park

Rush

1 grid square represents 500 metres

A **B** **C** **D** **E**

St Ursulas
Junior and
Infant
School

Gidea Park
Sports Ground

Gidea Park
Station

Frances Bardsley
School for Girls

Frances Bardsley
School for Girls

Romford
Ice Rink

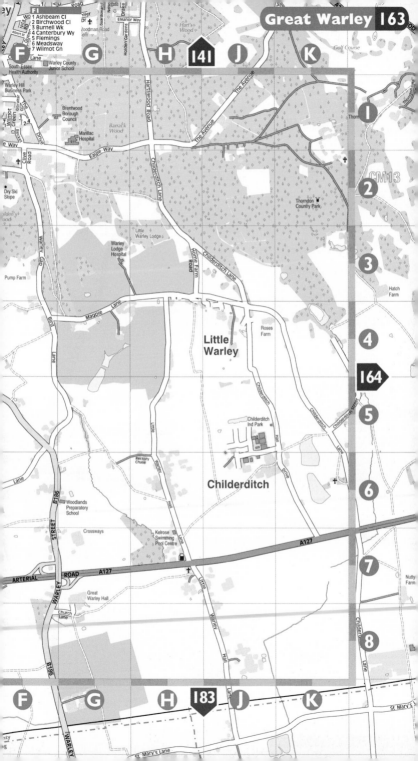

164

A128

C2
1 Cricketers Rw

B8
1 Sanderson Cl

B1
1 Meadows Cl

A · B **142** C · D · E

Ingrave

Heron Hall

I

C8
1 Burntwood Cl
2 Lombards Cha
3 Witham Gdns

Thorndon N.

CM13

Ingrave
Johnstone
C of E School

2

Thorridon

D2
1 Glebe Gdns
2 Rectory La

3

Hatch
Farm

Billericay Road

Herongate

Park
House

Thorndon S.

4

163

5

Cockridden
Farm Industrial
Estate

A128

6

Hotel
Halfway
House

A127

Ea
Ho

7

SOUTHEND ARTERIAL ROAD A127

A127

Nuttys
Farm

West
Horndon
CP School

8

**West
Horndon**

Cadogan Avenue

Station Road

Morndon
Ind Park

West
Horndon
St

A · B **184** C · D · E

St Mary's Lane

Blue
Ho

I grid square represents 500 metres

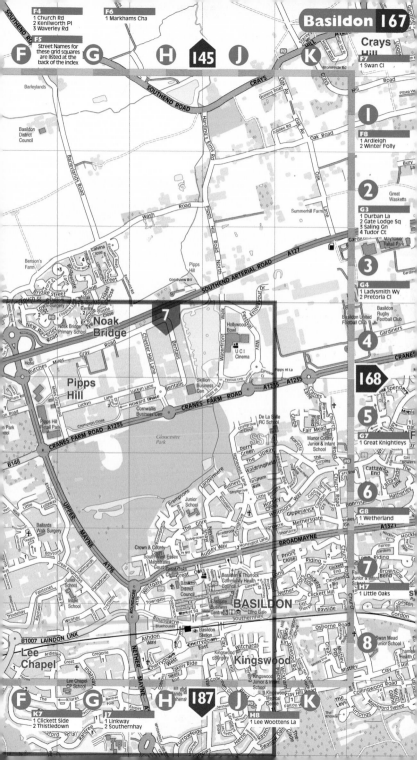

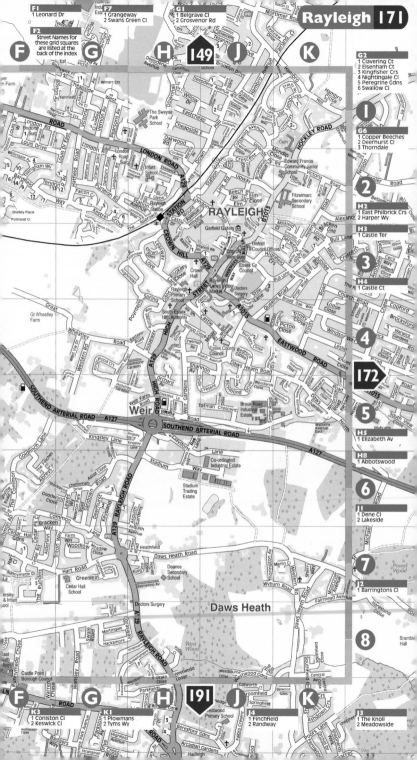

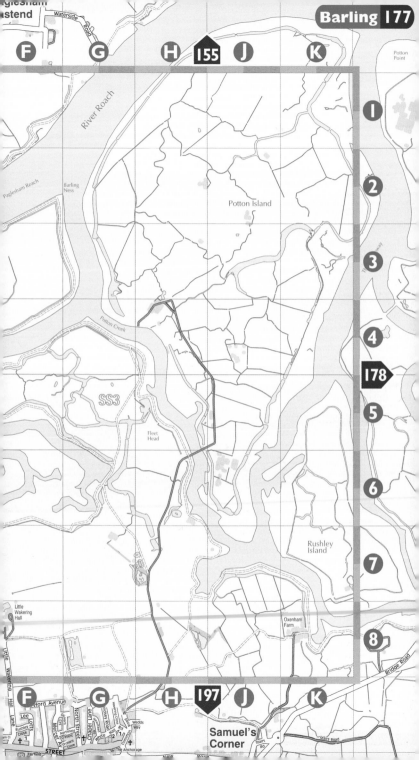

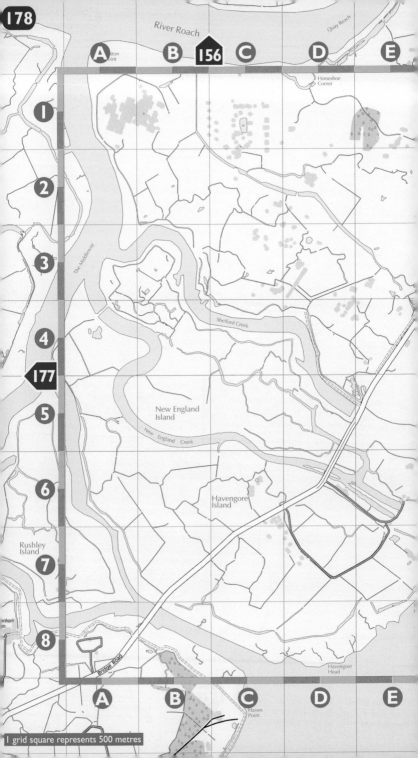

River Roach

 156

Quay Reach

tton Point

Horseshoe Corner

The Middleway

Shelford Creek

177

New England Island

New England Creek

Havengore Island

Rushley Island

nham m

Bridge Road

Havengore Head

Haven Point

I grid square represents 500 metres

F G etwood H **157** J K East Wick

Rugwood Farm

I

2

Great
Burwood Farm

3 Rugwood Head

4

Asplins
Head

5

Shelford
Head

6

7

8

F G H J K

F G H **163** J K

Church
Lane

Warley
Hall
Lane

ditch
Lane

St. Mary's Lane

1

B186

WARLEY

STREET

Monks
Farm

St. Mary's Lane

Old Englands
Farm

2

Dunnings Lane

Puddle
Dock

Warley

3

Bury
Farm

CLAY TYE

Clay Tye Farm

Thurrock
Havering

4

184

5

Mar Dyke

ROAD

RM14

Home Farm

6

B186

White
Post Farm

Corner
Farm

Fen Lane

Fen Lane

7

Havering
Thurrock

Fen Farm

8

OCKENDON ROAD

B186

NORTH

ROAD

F G H **200** J K

West
Horndon

Cadogan Avenue

Station Road

TILBURY

Childerditch Lane

A

Horndon
Ind
Park

B

164

Dunmow Gdns

C

West
Horndon
Station

D

E

ROAD

Brentwood Road

A128

Blue
Hou

St Mary's Lane

I

Dunnings Lane

2

Tillingham
Hall

Field House

3

Peartree Lane

4

Slose

Bulphan
Primary School

183

Fen Lane

5

Blankets
Farm

Hatch Farm

Drift

Church

Victor

Home Farm

6

Mar Dyke

Stone
Hall

The
Elms Farm

Church Lane

orner
arm

Fen Lane

7

Fen Farm

8

Parker's Farm La

A

B

201

C

D

E

Parker's Fa

K1
1 Woodview

F G H **165** J K

Church Road

Dunton Hall

Church Road

Essex County
Thurrock

Lower Dunton Road

Lower Dunton Hall

I

Forest

Great
Berry CP
School

Lake View

2

3

Brentwood Road

Noke
Hall Farm

Doesgate Lane

Doesgate
Farm

Doesgate Lane

Little
Malgraves

Little
Malgraves Inn

4

Church Road

186

Lower Dunton Road

Manor
House

Kirkham Road

Kirkham

5

6

BRENTWOOD ROAD

A128

Ongar
Hall Farm

7
Malgraves

Wyfields
Farm

8

F G H **202** J K

Lorking
Farm

Black

Robinson Road

North Hill
Business Park

Oxford Road

**Horndon on
the Hill**

Bowers
Gifford

LONDON ROAD A13

B1464

LONDON ROAD

F **G** **H** **169** A13 **J** **K**

West G

Malwood Road

Bouldrewood Road

Saxonville
The Spin

Elmhurst Avenue

Cemetery

Primary School
nut Grove

I

Limetree Avenue

HIGH ROAD

Wavertree Road

Bowers Hall

High Beeches

Spendon

Elm View Road

B1006

2

Church Road

Cem

Jotmans Hall Farm

Perry Road

Park Road

CANVEY WAY

A130

Jotmans Lane

Wartington Road

Philmead Road

Appleton

Tyrrell Road

Rd

3

Church Road

Lotem

Woodham Road

Rave Driv

Brackendale Avenue

4

Bowers Marshes

190

5

6

7

East Haven Creek

8

Northwick

F **G** **H** **206** **J** Nor **K** Road

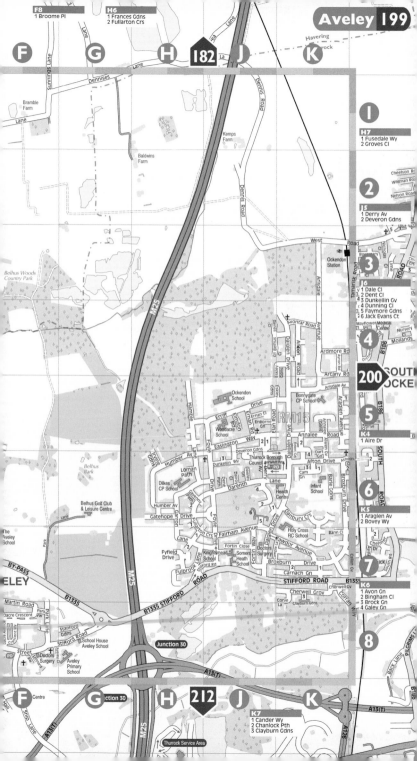

F8
1 Broome Pl

H6
1 Frances Gdns
2 Fullarton Crs

182

H7
1 Fusedale Wy
2 Groves Cl

J5
1 Derry Av
2 Deveron Gdns

Ockendon Station

J6
1 Dale Cl
2 Dent Cl
3 Dunkellin Gv
4 Dunning Cl
5 Faymore Gdns
6 Jack Evans Ct

200 SOUTH OCKE

K4
1 Aire Dr

K5
1 Araglen Av
2 Bovey Wy

K6
1 Avon Gn
2 Bingham Cl
3 Brock Gn
4 Galey Gn

212

K7
1 Cander Wy
2 Chanlock Pth
3 Clayburn Gdns

Thurrock Service Area

Havering
Thurrock

A4
1 Quince Tree Cl
2 Tamarisk Rd

A3
1 Benyon Pth
2 Bradd Cl
3 Copper Beech Rd
4 Tamarisk Rd
5 Tyssen Pl
6 Whitebeam Dr

A2
1 Peartree Cl

A **B** **183** **C** **D** **E**

1

A6
1 Elwick Rd
2 Foxglove Rd
3 Verbena Cl

2

A7
1 Broxburn Dr
2 Colne Cl
3 Stifford Rd

Cheelson Road
Wilsman Road
Nelson Road

South
Ockendon Hall

Benyon
CP School

Peartree
Surgery

West   Road

3

B3
1 Cherry Tree Dr

Rosemary
ICI
Larkspur
ICI
Viola Cl
Celandine
Brandon

Birch Crescent
Ash Wk
Hazel Dr
Groves
Birch Cl

4

wontar Road
Ardmore

Aveley Garth Rd
Mayflower
Cline
Nursery
Mollands

Sycamore Way
Lane

Holly Drive

Magnolia

Poplar

Cedar Drive

Mollands
La

199

**SOUTH
OCKENDON**

Bonnygate
CP School

5

B4
1 Cedar Ri
2 Laburnum Gv
3 Maple Dr
4 Nordmann Pl
5 Redwood Cha

Oaklands

Buckles   Lane

6

C3
1 Rosewood Cl

Infant
School

Holy Cross
RC School

Bann Cl

Stifford
Farm

7

urn   Drive
Carnach Gn

STIFFORD ROAD   B1335
C4
1 Lavender Cl
2 Medlar Dr
Clayburn Gdns

well Gv
Cullen

**North
Stifford**

Hotel

8

Black Lane
PILGRIMS La

Corner Way

Stifford

Stifford   Hill

Ardale
Sch

High   Road

A13(T)

A1012

A **B** **213** **C** **D** **1306** **E**

ARTERIAL ROAD NORTH STIFF
1 Silverwood Cl
2 Stifford Clays Rd

E8
1 Hogarth Rd
2 Simmons Pl
3 Westland Vw

A13(T)

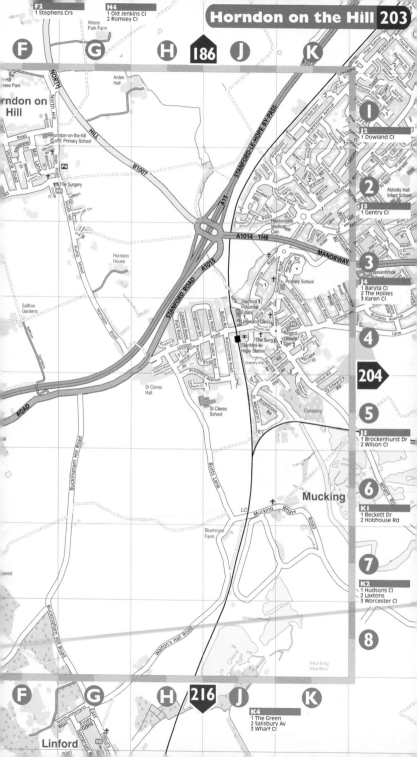

F2
1 Stephens Crs

H4
1 Old Jenkins Cl
2 Romsey Cl

Wrens
Park Farm

F

G

H

186

J

K

NORTH

Arden
Hall

orndon on
Hill

NORTH HILL

Horndon-on-the-hill
CofE Primary School

B1007

Road

Stephens Crs

Hillcrest

Victoria Road

High Road

Mill Lane

PH

The Surgery

PO

South Hill

South Hill Crs

Horndon
House

Saffron
Gardens

Pump Street

ROAD

Buckingham Hill Road

Saffron
Gardens

STANFORD ROAD

A1013

STANFORD-LEHOPE BY-PASS

A13

A1014 – THE

MANORWAY

A1014 – THE

I
1 Dowland Cl

1

2

Abbots Hall
Infant School

2

3

1 Gentry Cl

Hassenbrook
Medical
Cen

Hassenbrook
School

Haven

3
4

1 Baryta Cl
2 The Hollies
3 Karen Cl

Burgess Avenue

4

Primary School

Victoria Road

Roundmead

Caldwell Road

Kingsman Road

Butts Rd

Runnymede Road

Park Road

Stanford
Industrial
Estate

Lingwood Clinic

Church Hill

Regent
Leisure
Cen

The Surg
Stanford-le-
Hope Station

Chantry Crs

Grove Rd

Cemetery

St Margarets Rd

Brockenhurst Rd

Corringham

Cottingham

204

5

J5
1 Brockenhurst Dr
2 Wilson Cl

6

K1
1 Beckett Dr
2 Hobhouse Rd

7

Wharf Rd

London
Road

Bexley
Road

Oxford Road

Robin Road

Warley

Prospect Avenue

Corth Cl

St Cleres
Hall

St Cleres
School

Butts Lane

Buckingham Hill Road

Mucking

LC

Mucking
Wharf

Mucking
Wharf
Road

Bluehouse
Farm

Walton's Hall Road

K2
1 Hudsons Cl
2 Laxtons
3 Worcester Cl

8

Mucking
Marshes

wood

F

G

H

216

J

K

Linford

Northumberland
Road

Essex
Gdns

Somerset
Road

PO

K4
1 The Green
2 Salisbury Av
3 Wharf Cl

A B 189 C D E

I

2

3 A1014 THE MANORWAY

4 Coryton

205

5

6

7

8

Northwick

Northwick Road

Holehaven Creek

Lower Horse

She Poi

Oil Refinery

Shell Haven

Coryton Wharves

Thames Haven

Thurrock
Medway Towns

Blythe Sands

A B C D E

River Thames

1 grid square represents 500 metres

G2
1 Arjan Wy
2 Cambria Cl

H1
1 St Andrews Cl
2 St James Cl
3 St Lukes Cl
4 St Peters Rd

190
Dutch Village

H2
1 Palmerstone Rd
2 Village Hall Cl

J1
1 Central Av

J2
1 Beechcroft Rd
2 The Redwoods

CANVEY ISLAND

Hole Haven

Sea Reach

River Thames

Essex County
Medway Towns

208

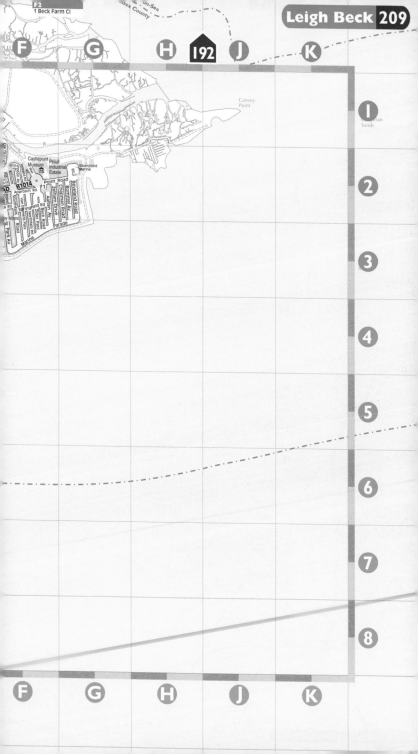

192

Canvey
Point

Croman
Sands

Castlepoint
Museum
Prout
Industrial
Estate
Silverpoint
Marine

Approach Rd
Point Road
Beveland Road
B1014
Chapman Rd
Alston Rd
Beck Road
Aldham Drive
Roosevel Road
Denham Rd
Northwic Rd
Newlands Pass
Sydervelt Road
Tiptree Road
Parade
Marine
Park Av
Jones Island Road

210

A6
1 Fairview

A5
1 Aveley Cl

A4
1 Bexley Rd

C6
1 Dabbling Cl
2 Lapwing Cl
3 Moorhen Cl
4 Stevenson Cl
5 Sunset Cl
6 Webber Cl

C7
1 Watermeadow Cl

Coldharbour

Erith Rands

Havering
Bexley

Crayford
Ness

Erith

DA8

Manford
Industrial
Estate

Slade Green

North End

Crayford
Marshes

Kent County

1 grid square represents 500 metres

Abbess End 29 G2
Abbess Roding 29 F1
Abridge 109 G7
Aimes Green 78 B2
Althorne 126 E3
Ardleigh Green 160 D5
Ardley End 13 H4
Asheldham 101 H6
Ashingdon 152 A6
Aveley 199 F7
Aythorpe Roding 15 K2
Baddow Park 91 G3
Baker Street 201 K6
Ballards Gore 153 J7
Balstonia 204 B1
Barling 176 D6
Barstable 168 A7
Basildon 7 F5
Battlesbridge 148 C3
Beauchamp Roding 29 J4
Beggar Hill 87 J6
Bell Common 80 B6
Bentley 113 G7
Berners Roding 30 C5
Bicknacre 93 K3
Biggin 215 H5
Billericay 144 C4
Birds Green 29 J7
Blackmore 86 D5
Blasford Hill 34 D2
Bobbingworth 55 K5
Boreham 36 C5
Bournes Green 196 A3
Bovinger 55 F6
Bowers Gifford 169 H8
Boyton Cross 32 B6
Bradwell on Sea 74 D3
Bradwell Waterside 74 B1
Brandy Hole 150 B1
Brays Grove 24 E6
Breeds 19 K7
Brimsdown 104 E6
Broadley Common 51 F2
Broad's Green 20 A8
Broad Street Green 40 E5
Brock Hill 119 K8
Brook Street 140 B7
Broomfield 34 D3
Broxbourne 49 G2
Buckhurst Hill 133 K6
Bulls Cross 104 A2
Bulphan 184 E4
Bumble's Green 50 C6
Burnham-on-Crouch ... 128 D8
Burnt Mills 169 F3
Bury Green 76 B5
Buttsbury 116 E3
Butt's Green 92 D2
Cambridge Town 196 B7
Campions 11 K8
Canewdon 153 G3
Cannon's Green 57 H4
Canvey Island 207 J3
Carter's Green 26 E3
Chadwell St Mary 214 E2
Chalk End 31 J3
Chalkwell 193 H5
Chalvedon 168 D7
Chapel Row 94 A8
Chatham Green 21 F2
Chelmer Village 63 K2
Chelmsford 5 E4
Cheshunt 76 B4
Chignall Smealy 33 F2
Chignall St James 33 F5
Chigwell 134 E5
Chigwell Row 136 A5
Childerditch 163 J6
Chingford 132 D5
Chingford Green 132 D4
Chingford Hatch 133 F7
Chipping Ongar 84 D3
Churchend 157 H7
Churchgate 76 B3
Churchgate Street 25 K1
Church Langley 25 H5
Clatterford End 17 F6
Clatterford End 56 E3
Clatterford End 83 H4
Claverhambury 78 D1
Clifftown 8 B5
Coalhill 120 C6
Cock Clarks 95 F3
Coldharbour 210 B3

Cold Norton 96 A8
Colliers Hatch 82 C4
Cooksmill Green 59 K4
Coopersale Common 81 H3
Coopersale Street 81 G5
Copthall Green 79 F7
Corbets Tey 181 J6
Corringham 204 C1
Coryton 206 A4
Courtsend 158 C5
Coxtie Green 140 A1
Cranham 182 B1
Crays Hill 146 A8
Creeksea 127 J8
Crow Green 113 J7
Curling Tye Green 67 G2
Curtismill Green 111 F7
Danbury 65 H6
Danbury Common 65 J8
Daws Heath 171 J8
Debden Green 108 A4
Dengie 102 A5
Denton 219 K5
Doddinghurst 113 K3
Downham 146 B1
Dry Street 187 G3
Dutch Village 207 H1
East End 74 D2
Eastend 23 G4
East Hanningfield 93 G6
East Horndon 164 E6
East Tilbury 216 D6
Eastwick 23 K1
Eastwood 173 F8
Edney Common 60 C8
Elkins Green 86 D5
Elm Park 180 C6
Emerson Park 161 F8
Enfield Highway 104 C6
Enfield Lock 105 F3
Enfield Wash 104 E4
Epping 80 E4
Epping Green 51 J6
Epping Upland 52 A8
Erith 210 A4
Eversley 168 E6
Fanner's Green 19 H8
Farmbridge End 31 G2
Farther Howegreen 96 A6
Feimore 168 D5
Fiddlers Hamlet 81 G6
Flamstead End 76 B2
Fobbing 205 F1
Foster Street 25 K6
Four Wantz 30 D2
Fox Hatch 113 H4
Freezy Water 104 E2
Friday Hill 132 E6
Fryerning 88 A8
Fryerns 168 A5
Fyfield 57 F2
Galleyend 90 E2
Galleywood 90 E3
Gallows Corner 160 E3
Gay Bowers 66 A8
Gidea Park 160 A4
Gilston 10 B8
Gilston Park 10 A7
Gilwell Park 105 J7
Goldhanger 42 D6
Good Easter 17 H8
Goosebury Green 143 K8
Gravesend 219 H4
Grays 213 K6
Great Baddow 63 F8
Great Berry 186 B1
Great Burstead 144 D8
Great Claydons 92 E4
Great Malgraves 186 A7
Great Oxney Green 61 F4
Great Parndon 2 A5
Great Stambridge 175 H1
Great Totham 40 C1
Great Wakering 197 H2
Great Waltham 20 A6
Great Warley 162 D3
Greensted 83 J2
Greensted Green 83 H2
Green Street 115 H1
Hacton 181 F6
Hadleigh 191 K2
Hallsford Bridge 84 D4
Halls Green 22 E7
Handley Green 88 D5

Hare Street 2 B1
Harlow 3 D2
Harold Hill 139 F8
Harold Park 161 J1
Harold Wood 161 H5
Hastingwood 53 K8
Hatfield Heath 13 H2
Havering-atte-Bower .. 138 A6
Hawkwell 151 H8
Hay Green 86 D6
Hazeleigh 95 F1
Heath Park 160 C8
Herongate 164 D2
Heybridge 40 D7
Heybridge 116 B3
Heybridge Basin 69 F2
High Beach 106 D8
High Easter 17 G2
High Houses 19 K8
High Laver 27 H7
High Ongar 85 F1
The High 2 C4
High Wych 11 F4
Hobbs Cross 26 A4
Hobbs Cross 109 H2
Hockley 150 D6
Holyfield 77 J2
Hook End 114 A1
Hope's Green 190 B5
Hornchurch 180 E3
Horndon on the Hill ... 203 F1
Horne Row 65 G7
Horseman Side 112 A8
Housham Tye 26 D6
Howe Green 92 A2
Howegreen 95 J6
Howe Street 20 A3
Hullbridge 149 K2
Hutton 142 B2
Hutton Mount 142 A4
Hyde Chase 94 D1
Ingatestone 116 C2
Ingrave 142 C8
Ivy Chimneys 80 C6
Jack's Hatch 51 K3
Katherines 23 G6
Keeres Green 16 B4
Kelvedon Hatch 113 F3
Keysers Estate 49 H7
Kings Farm 219 H8
Kingsmoor 52 A2
King Street 85 K2
Kingswood 7 F5
Laindon 6 B3
Lakeside 212 D2
Lambourne 109 H6
Lambourne End 136 B3
Langdon Hills 186 B1
Langford 39 K8
Latchingdon 97 J6
Latton Bush 52 E1
Leaden Roding 16 B5
Lee Chapel 6 C5
Leigh Beck 208 E2
Leigh-on-Sea 193 F2
Linford 216 A2
Lippitts Hill 106 B6
Little Baddow 65 H1
Little Burstead 166 B1
Little End 84 A8
Little Laver 28 B6
Little Mascalls 91 J4
Little Oxney Green 60 D8
Little Parndon 2 B2
Little Thurrock 214 B3
Little Totham 41 J1
Little Wakering 176 D2
Little Waltham 20 E5
Little Warley 163 J4
Loughton 107 H5
Loves Green 60 A4
Lower Bobbingworth Green . 55 H4
Lower Green 64 A2
Lower Green 90 E2
Lower Nazeing 49 K8
Lower Sheering 12 A4
Low Street 216 A2
Loyter's Green 27 F2
Magdalen Laver 26 D6
Maldon 68 C2
Manwood Green 14 A2
Marden Ash 84 B4
Margaret Roding 16 B8
Margaretting 89 G2

Margaretting Tye	89 H6	
Mark Hall North	24 E2	
Mark Hall South	24 E3	
Mashbury	32 C1	
Matching	27 G1	
Matching Green	27 K2	
Matching Tye	27 F2	
Mayland	99 G5	
Maylandsea	98 C4	
Miller's Green	57 J1	
Mill Green	87 K6	
Mill Hill	150 C6	
Milton	219 J4	
Minnow End	20 C6	
Montsale	130 D5	
Moreton	55 J3	
Moulsham	4 C5	
Mount Bovers	172 E2	
Mount End	81 K6	
Mountnessing	115 H5	
Mowden	37 H4	
Mucking	203 K6	
Mundon	97 G3	
Navestock Heath	111 J6	
Navestock Side	112 E6	
Nazeing	50 D4	
Nazeing Gate	50 E7	
Nazeing Long Green	50 C7	
Nazeing Mead	49 K1	
Needham Green	14 C1	
Nether Street	29 J1	
Netteswell	3 E2	
Nevendon	169 F2	
New House	218 D7	
Newman's End	13 F8	
Newney Green	60 B3	
New Thundersley	170 C6	
Nine Ashes	86 B4	
Noak Bridge	7 D1	
Noak Hill	139 F5	
Noak Hill	166 D1	
North Benfleet	169 J5	
North End	210 A7	
Northend	100 D8	
North Fambridge	124 C6	
Northfleet	218 B3	
North Ockendon	182 E6	
North Shoebury	196 E4	
North Stifford	200 C7	
North Weald Bassett	53 K8	
Norton Heath	58 C7	
Norton Mandeville	57 H7	
Norwood End	28 E8	
Nounsley	38 A3	
Nuper's Hatch	137 K3	
Old Harlow	25 G1	
Orsett	202 B5	
Orsett Heath	214 E1	
Ostend	127 J6	
Padham's Green	116 B6	
Paglesham Churchend	154 C6	
Paglesham Eastend	155 F6	
Parrock Farm	219 J8	
Parsonage Green	34 C5	
Paslow Wood Common	85 K4	
Passingford Bridge	110 D5	
Passmores	3 D6	
Peartree Green	114 B3	
Pedlars End	55 H3	
Pepper's Green	31 F4	
Perry Street	218 E5	
Piercing Hill	108 B1	
Pilgrims Hatch	113 K8	
Pinnacles	2 A3	
Pipps Hill	7 D2	
Pitsea	168 E8	
Pleshey	18 E3	
Potter Street	25 H7	
Prittlewell	8 B1	
Purfleet	211 H5	
Purleigh	96 A4	
Queen's Park	117 G7	
Radley Green	59 G6	
Ramsden Bellhouse	146 B4	
Ramsden Heath	146 A1	
Ramsey Island	72 B5	
Rawreth	148 D6	
Rawreth Shot	148 B6	
Rayleigh	171 J2	
Reader's Corner	63 G8	
Rettendon	121 F4	
Rochford	174 D3	
Rosherville	218 E3	
Roundbush	96 C5	
Roundbush Green	16 A3	
Roxwell	32 B7	
Roydon	22 D4	
Roydon Hamlet	50 E1	
Rudley Green	95 J2	
Runsell Green	66 A6	
Runwell	147 H4	
Sabine's Green	111 K6	
St Lawrence	73 F8	
St Vincent's Hamlet	139 H4	
Samuel's Corner	197 J2	
Sandon	64 A7	
Sawbridgeworth	11 F3	
Sewardstone	105 K6	
Sewardstonebury	133 F1	
Sheering	12 D5	
Shelley	56 C6	
Shellow Bowells	58 D1	
Shenfield	141 H3	
Shoeburyness	197 F7	
Shotgate	148 A7	
Slade Green	210 B8	
South Benfleet	190 D2	
Southchurch	195 H5	
Southend-on-Sea	8 C6	
South Fambridge	151 J1	
Southfields	202 D7	
South Green	144 E6	
South Hanningfield	120 B5	
Southminster	128 B1	
South Ockendon	200 A4	
South Stifford	213 G4	
South Weald	140 B5	
South Woodham Ferrers	123 F4	
Spitalbrook	49 G1	
Springfield	35 F7	
Stagden Cross	17 K3	
Stanford-le-Hope	204 B3	
Stanford Rivers	83 J7	
Stanstead Abbots	22 A1	
Stapleford Abbotts	137 J2	
Stapleford Tawney	110 C2	
Steeple	99 J2	
Stewards	52 C2	
Steward's Green	81 F6	
Stondon Massey	85 J8	
Stonebridge	175 J7	
Stoneyhills	128 C6	
Stow Maries	123 J1	
Stroud Green	173 J3	
Sumners	51 J1	
Sunken Marsh	191 H8	
Sunnymede	144 E3	
Swallows Cross	114 D3	
Tarpots	170 B8	
Temple Fields	24 E1	
Theydon Bois	108 B3	
Theydon Garnon	109 G2	
Theydon Mount	110 A2	
Thornwood Common	53 F7	
Thorpe Bay	196 A6	
Threshers Bush	26 A6	
Thundersley	170 D6	
Tilbury	215 F7	
Tilegate Green	26 D7	
Tillingham	102 B1	
Tip's Cross	86 A8	
Tollesbury	44 C4	
Tolleshunt D'Arcy	43 G1	
Tolleshunt Major	42 C1	
Toot Hill	83 F4	
Turnford	48 D7	
Tye Common	144 A6	
Tye Green	3 D5	
Tye Green	17 J7	
Tyler's Green	54 D6	
Ulting Wick	38 C6	
Upminster	181 K3	
Upshire	78 E6	
Vange	188 B1	
Waltham Abbey	77 K6	
Waltham Cross	76 C7	
Warley	140 E8	
Waterhales	138 E2	
Watton's Green	138 C2	
Weir	171 H5	
Wennington	198 A7	
Westcliff-on-Sea	193 K6	
West Court	219 K7	
West Hanningfield	119 K1	
West Horndon	164 B8	
Westley Heights	186 D3	
West Thurrock	212 D4	
West Tilbury	215 K5	
White Roding or White Roothing	14 E6	
Wickford	147 J8	
Widford	62 A7	
Willingale	58 A2	
Winter Gardens	190 D8	
Woodend	29 G4	
Woodford Wells	133 J6	
Wood Green	78 E8	
Woodham Ferrers	122 A1	
Woodham Mortimer	66 D8	
Woodham Walter	66 C3	
Woodhill	65 F7	
Woodside	53 H8	
Wormley	48 B6	
Wormleybury	48 B5	
Wormley West End	48 A4	
Writtle	61 G5	

USING THE STREET INDEX

Street names are listed alphabetically. Each street name is followed by its postal town or area locality, the Postcode District, the page number, and the reference to the square in which the name is found.

Example: Abbey Cl ROM RM1...................... 160 B8 1

Some entries are followed by a number in a blue box. This number indicates the location of the street within the referenced grid square. The full street name is listed at the side of the map page.

GENERAL ABBREVIATIONS

ACC............ACCESS	GA............GATE	PL............PLACE
ALY............ALLEY	GAL............GALLERY	PLN............PLAIN
AP............APPROACH	GDN............GARDEN	PLNS............PLAINS
AR............ARCADE	GDNS............GARDENS	PLZ............PLAZA
ASS............ASSOCIATION	GLD............GLADE	POL............POLICE STATION
AV............AVENUE	GLN............GLEN	PR............PRINCE
BCH............BEACH	GN............GREEN	PREC............PRECINCT
BLDS............BUILDINGS	GND............GROUND	PREP............PREPARATORY
BND............BEND	GRA............GRANGE	PRIM............PRIMARY
BNK............BANK	GRG............GARAGE	PROM............PROMENADE
BR............BRIDGE	GT............GREAT	PRS............PRINCESS
BRK............BROOK	GTWY............GATEWAY	PRT............PORT
BTM............BOTTOM	GV............GROVE	PT............POINT
BUS............BUSINESS	HGR............HIGHER	PTH............PATH
BVD............BOULEVARD	HL............HILL	PZ............PIAZZA
BY............BYPASS	HLS............HILLS	QD............QUADRANT
CATH............CATHEDRAL	HO............HOUSE	QU............QUEEN
CEM............CEMETERY	HOL............HOLLOW	QY............QUAY
CEN............CENTRE	HOSP............HOSPITAL	R............RIVER
CFT............CROFT	HRB............HARBOUR	RBT............ROUNDABOUT
CH............CHURCH	HTH............HEATH	RD............ROAD
CHA............CHASE	HTS............HEIGHTS	RDG............RIDGE
CHYD............CHURCHYARD	HVN............HAVEN	REP............REPUBLIC
CIR............CIRCLE	HWY............HIGHWAY	RES............RESERVOIR
CIRC............CIRCUS	IMP............IMPERIAL	RFC............RUGBY FOOTBALL CLUB
CL............CLOSE	IN............INLET	RI............RISE
CLFS............CLIFFS	IND EST............INDUSTRIAL ESTATE	RP............RAMP
CMP............CAMP	INF............INFIRMARY	RW............ROW
CNR............CORNER	INFO............INFORMATION	S............SOUTH
CO............COUNTY	INT............INTERCHANGE	SCH............SCHOOL
COLL............COLLEGE	IS............ISLAND	SE............SOUTH EAST
COM............COMMON	JCT............JUNCTION	SER............SERVICE AREA
COMM............COMMISSION	JTY............JETTY	SH............SHORE
CON............CONVENT	KG............KING	SHOP............SHOPPING
COT............COTTAGE	KNL............KNOLL	SKWY............SKYWAY
COTS............COTTAGES	L............LAKE	SMT............SUMMIT
CP............CAPE	LA............LANE	SOC............SOCIETY
CPS............COPSE	LDG............LODGE	SP............SPUR
CR............CREEK	LGT............LIGHT	SPR............SPRING
CREM............CREMATORIUM	LK............LOCK	SQ............SQUARE
CRS............CRESCENT	LKS............LAKES	ST............STREET
CSWY............CAUSEWAY	LNDG............LANDING	STN............STATION
CT............COURT	LTL............LITTLE	STR............STREAM
CTRL............CENTRAL	LWR............LOWER	STRD............STRAND
CTS............COURTS	MAG............MAGISTRATE	SW............SOUTH WEST
CTYD............COURTYARD	MAN............MANSIONS	TDG............TRADING
CUTT............CUTTINGS	MD............MEAD	TER............TERRACE
CV............COVE	MDW............MEADOWS	THWY............THROUGHWAY
CYN............CANYON	MEM............MEMORIAL	TNL............TUNNEL
DEPT............DEPARTMENT	MKT............MARKET	TOLL............TOLLWAY
DL............DALE	MKTS............MARKETS	TPK............TURNPIKE
DM............DAM	ML............MALL	TR............TRACK
DR............DRIVE	ML............MILL	TRL............TRAIL
DRO............DROVE	MNR............MANOR	TWR............TOWER
DRY............DRIVEWAY	MS............MEWS	U/P............UNDERPASS
DWGS............DWELLINGS	MSN............MISSION	UNI............UNIVERSITY
E............EAST	MT............MOUNT	UPR............UPPER
EMB............EMBANKMENT	MTN............MOUNTAIN	V............VALE
EMBY............EMBASSY	MTS............MOUNTAINS	VA............VALLEY
ESP............ESPLANADE	MUS............MUSEUM	VIAD............VIADUCT
EST............ESTATE	MWY............MOTORWAY	VIL............VILLA
EX............EXCHANGE	N............NORTH	VIS............VISTA
EXPY............EXPRESSWAY	NE............NORTH EAST	VLG............VILLAGE
EXT............EXTENSION	NW............NORTH WEST	VLS............VILLAS
F/O............FLYOVER	O/P............OVERPASS	VW............VIEW
FC............FOOTBALL CLUB	OFF............OFFICE	W............WEST
FK............FORK	ORCH............ORCHARD	WD............WOOD
FLD............FIELD	OV............OVAL	WHF............WHARF
FLDS............FIELDS	PAL............PALACE	WK............WALK
FLS............FALLS	PAS............PASSAGE	WKS............WALKS
FLS............FLATS	PAV............PAVILION	WLS............WELLS
FM............FARM	PDE............PARADE	WY............WAY
FT............FORT	PH............PUBLIC HOUSE	YD............YARD
FWY............FREEWAY	PK............PARK	YHA............YOUTH HOSTEL
FY............FERRY	PKWY............PARKWAY	

POSTCODE TOWNS AND AREA ABBREVIATIONS

ABR/ST............Abridge/Stapleford Abbotts	CDW/CHF............Chadwell St Mary/ Chafford Hundred	DAGE............Dagenham east
BARK/HLT............Barkingside/Hainault		DART............Dartford
BCAYE............Billericay east	CHDH............Chadwell Heath	ED............Edmonton
BCAYW............Billericay west	CHES/WCR............Cheshunt/Waltham Cross	EMPK............Emerson Park
BKHH............Buckhurst Hill	CHESW............Cheshunt west	EN............Enfield
BOC............Burnham-on-Crouch	CHIG............Chigwell	ENC/FH............Enfield Chase/Forty Hill
BROX............Broxbourne	CHING............Chingford	EPP............Epping
BRW............Brentwood	CHLM/GWD............Chelmsford/Galleywood	ERITH............Erith
BRWN............Brentwood north	CHLM/WR............Chelmsford/Writtle	GPK............Gidea Park
BSDN............Basildon	CHONG............Chipping Ongar	GRAYS............Grays
BXLYHN............Bexleyheath north	CRW............Collier Row	GRH............Greenhithe
	CVI............Canvey Island	GTDUN............Great Dunmow

GVE	Gravesend east
GVW	Gravesend west
HARH	Harold Hill
HCH	Hornchurch
HERT/BAY	Hertford/Bayford
HLW	Harlow
HLWE	Harlow east
HLWS	Harlow south
HLWW/ROY	Harlow west/Roydon
HOC/HUL	Hockley/Hullbridge
HOD	Hoddesdon
HOO/HM	Hoo St Werburgh/Higham
ING	Ingatestone
KIR/NAC	Kirton/Nacton
LAIN	Laindon
LOS	Leigh-on-Sea
MAL	Maldon
MEO	Meopham
MHAD	Much Hadham
PEND	Ponders End
PIT	Pitsea
PUR	Purfleet
RAIN	Rainham (Gt Lon)
RAYL	Rayleigh
RBRW/HUT	Rural Brentwood/Hutton
RBSF	Rural Bishop's Stortford
RCFD	Rochford
RCHLM	Rural Chelmsford
ROM	Romford
ROMW/RG	Romford west/Rush Green
SBF/HAD	South Benfleet/Hadleigh
SBN/FI	Shoeburyness/Foulness Island
SBW	Sawbridgeworth
SLH/COR	Stanford-le-Hope/Corringham
SOCK/AV	South Ockendon/Aveley
SOS	Southend-on-Sea
SOSN	Southend-on-Sea north
SWCM	Swanscombe
TIL	Tilbury
UED	Upper Edmonton
UPMR	Upminster
VGE	Vange
WAB	Waltham Abbey
WARE	Ware
WCHMH	Winchmore Hill
WFD	Woodford
WICKE	Wickford east
WICKW	Wickford west
WIT	Witham
WOS/PRIT	Westcliff-on-Sea/Prittlewell
WTHK	West Thurrock

Aal - Alm

Index - streets

A

Aalten Av CVI SS8 .... 209 F2
Abbess Cl CHLM/WR CM1 .... 62 A3
ROM RM1 .... 160 B8 1
Abbey Ct WAB EN9 .... 77 H8
Abbey Dale Cl HLWE CM17 .... 25 G6
Abbey Flds WICKE SS11 .... 93 F6
Abbey Rd CHES/WCR EN8 .... 76 B8 1
BCAYW CM12 .... 144 A4
GVE DA12 .... 219 K6
HOC/HUL SS5 .... 149 J4
Abbey Turning MAL CM9 .... 67 G2
Abbeyview WAB EN9 .... 77 H7
Abbingdon Ct PIT SS13 .... 168 D4 1
Abbots Cl BRWN CM15 .... 141 K4
Abbots Ct LAIN SS15 .... 6 C1
Abbotsleigh Rd RCHLM CM3 .... 122 C6
Abbotsmead MAL CM9 .... 40 B8
Abbots Ride BCAYE CM11 .... 144 D3 1
Abbots Wk SBN/FI SS3 .... 196 B5
Abbotsweld HLWS CM18 .... 3 D6
Abbotswood SBF/HAD SS7 .... 171 H8 1
Abbotts Cl LOS SS9 .... 173 F8
Abbotts Crs CHING E4 .... 132 C7
Abbotts Dr SLH/COR SS17 .... 204 A3
WAB EN9 .... 78 C3
Abbotts Hall Cha SLH/COR SS17 .... 204 A3
Abbs Cross Gdns HCH RM12 .... 180 D2
Abbs Cross La HCH RM12 .... 180 D4
Abell Wy CHLM/GWD CM2 .... 63 K1
Abenberg Wy RBRW/HUT CM13 .... 141 K5
Abensburg Rd CVI SS8 .... 191 J8 1
Abercrombie Dr EN EN1 .... 104 A5 1
Abercrombie Wy HLWW/ROY CM19 .... 2 C5
Aberdare Rd PEND EN3 .... 104 C8
Aberdeen Gdns LOS SS9 .... 192 B3
Abingdon Ct PIT SS13 .... 168 D4 1
Abreys Gr SBN/FI SS3 .... 171 F6
Abridge Cl CHIG IG7 .... 135 H2
Abridge Rd CHIG IG7 .... 108 C3
EPP CM16 .... 108 C3
Acacia Av HCH RM12 .... 180 A3
Acacia Dr MAL CM9 .... 68 A3
SOS SS1 .... 195 K6
UPMR RM14 .... 181 H5
Acacia Gdns UPMR RM14 .... 182 C1
Acacia Rd PIT SS13 .... 169 H5
Acorn Cl CHING E4 .... 132 C8 1
Acorn Pl VGE SS16 .... 166 B8
The Acorns HOC/HUL SS5 .... 151 F6
Acres Av CHONG CM5 .... 56 B8
Acres End CHLM/WR CM1 .... 62 A1
The Acres SLH/COR SS17 .... 204 B2
Acton Cl CHES/WCR EN8 .... 76 E5 1
Adalia Crs LOS SS9 .... 192 C3
Adalia Wy LOS SS9 .... 192 C3
Adams Gld RCFD SS4 .... 152 A7
Adams House HLWE CM20 .... 3 D2 1
Adams Rd SLH/COR SS17 .... 204 A4
Adam Wy WICKE SS11 .... 147 H5
Addie Cl CHLM/WR CM1 .... 104 D5 1
Addison Gdns GRAYS RM17 .... 214 B3 1
Addison Rd PEND EN3 .... 104 C5
Adelaide Gdns SBF/HAD SS7 .... 190 C4 1
Adelaide Rd TIL RM18 .... 214 E7
Adelphi Crs HCH RM12 .... 180 B3
Adelsburg Rd CVI SS8 .... 208 C1
Aden Rd PEND EN3 .... 104 E8
Admirals Wk CHLM/WR CM1 .... 4 A1
HOD EN11 .... 49 G1
SBN/FI SS3 .... 196 C8
Admiral Ms WOS/PRIT SS0 .... 193 K6
Adnams Wk RAIN RM13 .... 180 B7 1
Adstock Wy GRAYS RM17 .... 213 J3
Advice Av CDH/CHF RM16 .... 213 K1
Afton Dr SOCK/AV RM15 .... 199 K6
Agister Rd CHIG IG7 .... 135 K8
Agnes Av LOS SS9 .... 192 C3
Ailsa Rd WOS/PRIT SS0 .... 193 K5
Ainslie Wood Crs CHING E4 .... 132 C8 2
Ainslie Wood Gdns CHING E4 .... 132 C7
Ainslie Wood Rd CHING E4 .... 132 B8
Aintree Cl GVE DA12 .... 219 G8
Aintree Gv UPMR RM14 .... 181 G4 1
Aire Dr SOCK/AV RM15 .... 199 K4 1
Airfield Wy HCH RM12 .... 180 C7
Akenfield Cl RCHLM CM3 .... 122 E6 1
Alamein Cl BROX EN10 .... 48 D2
Alamein Rd BOC CM0 .... 155 H1
CHLM/WR CM1 .... 34 B7
Alanbrooke GVE DA12 .... 219 H5
Alan Cl LOS SS9 .... 173 F7
Alan Gv LOS SS9 .... 173 F7
Albany Av WOS/PRIT SS0 .... 8 B3
Albany Cl CHLM/WR CM1 .... 34 A8
Albany Ct EPP CM16 .... 80 D4
Albany Park Av PEND EN3 .... 104 C5
Albany Rd BRWN CM15 .... 140 E2
HCH RM12 .... 180 B2
PEND EN3 .... 104 D3
RAYL SS6 .... 172 B4
TIL RM18 .... 215 F7
WICKW SS12 .... 147 G7
Albany Vw BKHH IG9 .... 133 H4
Albemarle Av CHES/WCR EN8 .... 76 C2
Albemarle Cl GRAYS RM17 .... 213 K1
Albert Av CHING E4 .... 132 B7
Albert Cl CDH/CHF RM16 .... 214 B2
RAYL SS6 .... 172 A3
RCFD SS4 .... 151 K6
Albert Crs CHING E4 .... 132 B7 1
Albert Dr LAIN SS15 .... 6 A4
Albert Gdns HLWE CM17 .... 25 H6
Albert Murray Cl GVE DA12 .... 219 H5 1
Albert Rd BKHH IG9 .... 134 A5
BOC CM0 .... 155 H1
RAYL SS6 .... 172 A3
RCFD SS4 .... 151 K7
RCHLM CM3 .... 122 C6
ROM RM1 .... 160 A8 1
SBF/HAD SS7 .... 170 A7
SOS SS1 .... 9 E5
UPMR RM14 .... 184 E5
Albert St BRW CM14 .... 141 F8
Albion Cl LAIN SS15 .... 6 B1
Albion Hl LOU IG10 .... 133 K1
Albion Pk LOU IG10 .... 133 K1
Albion Rd GVE DA12 .... 219 H5
SBF/HAD SS7 .... 190 B1
WOS/PRIT SS0 .... 8 B3
Albion Ter SBW CM14 .... 219 H4
Albury Grove Rd CHES/WCR EN8 .... 76 D4
Albury Ride CHES/WCR EN8 .... 76 D5
Albury Wk CHES/WCR EN8 .... 76 C4
Albyns Vgl SS16 .... 166 A6
Albyns La ABR/ST RM4 .... 110 D6
Alcotes BSDN SS14 .... 168 C4
Aldborough Rd UPMR RM14 .... 181 G3
Aldbrough Pl WFD IG8 .... 133 H7
Aldeburgh Wy CHLM/WR CM1 .... 35 F8
Alder Av UPMR RM14 .... 181 G6
Alderbury Lea RCHLM CM3 .... 93 K4 1
Alder Cl LAIN SS15 .... 6 B1
Alder Dr CHLM/GWD CM2 .... 62 D7
SOCK/AV RM15 .... 200 A4
Alderleys SBF/HAD SS7 .... 171 F7
Alderman's Hl HOC/HUL SS5 .... 150 C8
Alderman Wk SLH/COR SS17 .... 187 F8
Alderney Gdns WICKE SS11 .... 147 F3
Alderney Rd ERITH DA8 .... 210 B6
Alders Wk SBW CM21 .... 11 J3
Alderton Cl BRWN CM15 .... 140 E1
LOU IG10 .... 107 J8
Alderton Hall La LOU IG10 .... 107 J8
Alderton Hl LOU IG10 .... 134 C1
Alderton Ri LOU IG10 .... 107 J8
Alderton Rd CDH/CHF RM16 .... 202 D6
Alderton Wy LOU IG10 .... 134 C1
Alderwood Dr ABR/ST RM4 .... 109 F7
Alderwood Wy SBF/HAD SS7 .... 191 H2
Aldham Gdns RAYL SS6 .... 170 E2
Aldingham Gdns HCH RM12 .... 180 B6 1
Aldria Rd SLH/COR SS17 .... 187 F8 1
Aldridge Av PEND EN3 .... 105 G4
Aldridge Cl CHLM/GWD CM2 .... 63 J1
Aldrin Cl SLH/COR SS17 .... 204 A3
Aldrin Wy LOS SS9 .... 173 H7
Aldwych Cl HCH RM12 .... 180 B3 1
Alexander La BRWN CM15 .... 141 K1
Alexander Ms CHLM/GWD CM2 .... 92 B3
Alexander Rd VGE SS16 .... 186 C5
Alexandra Cl CDH/CHF RM16 .... 215 G1
Alexandra Rd BOC CM0 .... 128 B8
ERITH DA8 .... 210 A5
GVE DA12 .... 219 K5
LOS SS9 .... 193 F5 1
PEND EN3 .... 104 D8
RAYL SS6 .... 171 K2
RCFD SS4 .... 151 K7
ROM RM1 .... 160 A8 1
SBF/HAD SS7 .... 190 C3
SBN/FI SS3 .... 197 F2
SOS SS1 .... 8 C5
TIL RM18 .... 214 E8 1
Alexandra St SOS SS1 .... 9 D5
Alexandra Wy CHES/WCR EN8 .... 77 F8
TIL RM18 .... 216 C3
Alexandria Dr RAYL SS6 .... 171 F1
Alfreda Av HOC/HUL SS5 .... 149 J2
Alfred Gdns WICKE SS11 .... 147 G4
Alfred Pl GVW DA11 .... 218 E6
Alfred Rd BKHH IG9 .... 134 A5
BRW CM14 .... 141 G6 1
GWW DA11 .... 219 G7
SOCK/AV RM15 .... 198 E8 1
Alfred St GRAYS RM17 .... 214 B5
Algars Wy SLH/COR SS17 .... 187 H4
Algers Cl LOU IG10 .... 134 A1
Algers Rd LOU IG10 .... 134 B1
Alghers Md LOU IG10 .... 134 A1
Alicia Av WICKE SS11 .... 147 K6
Alicia Cl WICKE SS11 .... 147 K6
Alicia Wk WICKE SS11 .... 147 K6
Alicia Wy WICKE SS11 .... 147 K6
Allandale SBF/HAD SS7 .... 171 F6
Allandale Rd EMPK RM11 .... 180 A1
PEND EN3 .... 104 D2
Allard Wy BROX EN10 .... 48 E3
Allenby Crs GRAYS RM17 .... 214 A4
Allenby Dr EMPK RM11 .... 181 F2
Allens Cl RCHLM CM3 .... 36 C4
Allens Rd BCAYE CM11 .... 118 E3 1
Allensway SLH/COR SS17 .... 204 B2
Allerton Cl RCFD SS4 .... 151 K7 1
Alley Dock LOS SS9 .... 192 E5
Alleyn Pl WOS/PRIT SS0 .... 193 K4
Allison Cl WAB EN9 .... 78 C7
Allistonway SLH/COR SS17 .... 204 B2
Allmains Cl WAB EN9 .... 50 D7
Allnutts Rd EPP CM16 .... 80 E7
All Saints Cl BRWN CM15 .... 113 K2
CHIG IG7 .... 136 A6
CHLM/WR CM1 .... 5 F1
All Saints' Rd GVW DA11 .... 218 E6
Alma Av HCH RM12 .... 181 F4
Alma Cl SBF/HAD SS7 .... 192 A3
WICKW SS12 .... 146 D7
Alma Rd SBF/HAD SS7 .... 192 B3
Almere SBF/HAD SS7 .... 190 C1
Almond Av WICKW SS12 .... 146 E6
Almond Cl CDH/CHF RM16 .... 215 F2
Almonds Av BKHH IG9 .... 133 H5
Almond Wk CVI SS8 .... 207 K1
Almshouse La EN EN1 .... 104 B3 1

Ainwick Cl VGE SS16 ... 166 A8 1
Alpha Cl PIT SS13 ... 169 J7
Alpha Rd BOC CM0 ... 128 C8
  CHING E4 ... 132 B6
  PIT SS13 ... 169 J7
Alresford Gn WICKW SS12 ... 147 H7
Altar Pl LAIN SS15 ... 6 A3
Altham Gv HLW CM20 ... 3 E1
Althorne Cl PIT SS13 ... 168 E4
Althorne Wy RCFD SS4 ... 153 H3
Althorpe Cl HOC/HUL SS5 ... 150 E7
Alton Gdns SOSN SS2 ... 174 B8
Aluric Cl CDH/CHF RM16 ... 215 G3
Alverstoke Rd HARH RM3 ... 161 F2
Alwen Gv SOCK/AV RM15 ... 199 K5
Alwyne Av BRWN CM15 ... 141 J2
Alyssum Cl CHLM/WR CM1 ... 35 H7
Amberley Rd BKHH IG9 ... 133 K4
Ambleside EPP CM16 ... 80 E5
  WICKE SS11 ... 148 A1
Ambleside Av HARH RM12 ... 180 C6
Ambleside Crs PEND EN3 ... 104 D7
Ambleside Dr SOS SS1 ... 9 F4
Ambleside Gdns HOC/HUL SS5 ... 149 J3
Ambleside Wk CVI SS8 ... 207 K1
Amcotes Pl CHLM/GWD CM2 ... 5 D5
Ameland Rd MAL CM9 ... 68 C3
America St MAL CM9 ... 68 C3 1
Amersham Av VGE SS16 ... 166 A8 2
Amersham Cl HARH RM3 ... 161 G1
Amersham Rd HARH RM3 ... 161 F1
Amersham Wk HARH RM3 ... 161 G1
Amery Gdns GPK RM2 ... 160 E5
Amesbury WAB EN9 ... 78 C6
Amesbury Dr CHING E4 ... 132 C2 1
Amesbury Rd EPP CM16 ... 80 D5
Amid Rd CVI SS8 ... 191 H8
Amoss Rd CHLM/GWD CM2 ... 63 H5
Ampers End BSDN SS14 ... 168 A7 1
Amwell Ct WAB EN9 ... 78 A7
The Anchorage SBN/FI SS3 ... 19 G1
Anchor Cl CHES/WCR EN8 ... 76 D2
Anchor La CHONG CM5 ... 28 D1
  MAL CM9 ... 40 C8
  RCFD SS4 ... 153 G4
Anchor Reach RCHLM CM3 ... 122 E8
Anchor St CHLM/GWD CM2 ... 4 C4
Anders Fall LOS SS9 ... 173 H7
Anderson Av CHLM/WR CM1 ... 34 B8
Andersons SLH/COR SS17 ... 204 B3
Andrea Av CDH/CHF RM16 ... 213 J1
Andrew Cl SLH/COR SS17 ... 203 K1
Andrews Cl BKHH IG9 ... 133 K5
Andrew's La CHESW EN7 ... 76 A2
Andrews Pl CHLM/WR CM1 ... 4 A3
Andyk Rd CVI SS8 ... 208 E2
Anerley Rd WOS/PRIT SS0 ... 8 A4
Angel Cl VGE SS16 ... 188 A2
Angle Rd WTHK RM20 ... 213 G5
Anglesea Rd GVE DA12 ... 219 G4
  GVW DA11 ... 219 G4
Anglesey Gdns WICKW SS12 ... 147 J8
Anglesey Rd PEND EN3 ... 104 B8
Anjou Gn CHLM/WR CM1 ... 35 J6
Annabell Av CDH/CHF RM16 ... 202 D6
Annalee Gdns SOCK/AV RM15 ... 199 K5
Annalee Rd SOCK/AV RM15 ... 199 K5
Ann Boleyn Dr RCFD SS4 ... 174 C6
Anson Cha SBN/FI SS3 ... 196 D5
Anson Cl RCHLM CM3 ... 122 E7
Anstey Cl LOS SS9 ... 172 E6
Antelope Av CDH/CHF RM16 ... 213 K2
Anthony Cl BCAYE CM11 ... 144 E7 1
Anthony Dr SLH/COR SS17 ... 204 A1
Antlers CVI SS8 ... 207 K3
Antlers Hl CHING E4 ... 132 D1
Anton Rd SOCK/AV RM15 ... 199 K4
Antony Cl CVI SS8 ... 191 G8
Antrim Rd SBN/FI SS3 ... 196 C6
Anvil Wy BCAYW CM12 ... 117 H8
  CHLM/WR CM1 ... 35 G8
Apeldoorn SBF/HAD SS7 ... 170 A6 1
Aperfield St ERITH DA8 ... 210 A5
Apollo Cl HCH RM12 ... 180 C3 1
  VGE SS16 ... 166 A8
Appleby Dr HARH RM3 ... 138 D8
  VGE SS16 ... 166 A8
Appledene Cl RAYL SS6 ... 171 J1
Appledore SBN/FI SS3 ... 196 B4
Appledore Cl HARH RM3 ... 160 D3
Apple Ga BRW CM14 ... 140 C1
Applerow LOS SS9 ... 173 G7
Appleton Cl HLWW/ROY CM19 ... 2 C4
Appleton Rd LOU IG10 ... 107 K7
  SBF/HAD SS7 ... 190 A2
Appleton Wy HCH RM12 ... 180 E2
Appletree Cl HOCN SS12 ... 195 H2
Apple Trees Crs BRWN CM15 ... 114 A4
Apple Tree Wy WICKE SS11 ... 147 J5
Apple Wy CHLM/GWD CM2 ... 63 F7
Appleyard Av HOC/HUL SS5 ... 151 F5
Appold St ERITH DA8 ... 210 A5
Approach Rd BCAYE CM11 ... 146 A8
  CVI SS8 ... 209 F2
The Approach EN EN1 ... 104 B6 1
  RAYL SS6 ... 171 H3

UPMR RM14 ... 181 J4
Apton Hall Rd RCFD SS4 ... 152 D7
Arabia Cl CHING E4 ... 132 D3
Araglen Av SOCK/AV RM15 ... 199 K5 1
Aragon Cl SOSN SS2 ... 194 B1
Arbor Cl CHING E4 ... 132 E6
Arbour Cl CHLM/WR CM1 ... 5 E1
Arbour La CHLM/WR CM1 ... 5 E1
Arbour Rd PEND EN3 ... 104 D8
Arbour Wy HARH RM12 ... 180 O6
Arcadian Gdns SBF/HAD SS7 ... 191 H1
Arcadia Rd CVI SS8 ... 208 D2
Arcany Rd SOCK/AV RM15 ... 199 K4
Archates Av CDH/CHF RM16 ... 213 K2
Archer Av SOSN SS2 ... 195 H2
Archer Cl SOSN SS2 ... 195 H2
Archer Rd LAIN SS15 ... 166 C5
Archers EPP CM16 ... 51 K2 1
Archers Cl BCAYW CM12 ... 144 B5
Archers Dr PEND EN3 ... 104 O6 1
Archers Flds PIT SS13 ... 168 E4
Archers Fields Cl PIT SS13 ... 168 D4
Archibald Rd HARH RM3 ... 161 H3
Archway HARH RM3 ... 160 C1
Ardleigh VGE SS16 ... 6 C5 1
Ardleigh Cl EMPK RM11 ... 160 E5
Ardleigh Ct BRWN CM15 ... 141 J3
Ardleigh Gdns RBRW/HUT CM13 ... 142 D2 1
Ardley Crs RBSF CM22 ... 13 H3
Ardley Wy RAYL SS6 ... 171 J1
Ardmore La BKHH IG9 ... 133 J4
Ardmore Rd SOCK/AV RM15 ... 199 K4
Argent St GRAYS RM17 ... 214 A6
  WTHK RM20 ... 213 H6
Argyle Gdns UPMR RM14 ... 182 A4
Argyle Rd BOC CM0 ... 155 J1
Argyll Rd GRAYS RM17 ... 213 K4
  WOS/PRIT SS0 ... 8 A4
Arisdale Av SOCK/AV RM15 ... 199 K3
Arjan Wy CVI SS8 ... 207 G2 1
Ark Av CDH/CHF RM16 ... 213 K2
Ark La RCFD SS4 ... 173 H4
Arkwright Rd TIL RM18 ... 215 F8
Arkwrights HARH RM3 ... 3 F2
Arlington Crs CHES/WCR EN8 ... 76 B8
Arlington Gdns HARH RM3 ... 161 F3
Arlington Rd SOSN SS2 ... 195 H4
Arlington Wy BCAYW CM12 ... 117 F8
Armada Cl LAIN SS15 ... 6 B5
Armadale CVI SS8 ... 207 K1
Armagh Rd SBN/FI SS3 ... 196 C6
Armath La VGE SS16 ... 186 A1
Armitage Rd SOS SS1 ... 195 K4
Armonde Cl RCHLM CM3 ... 56 C4 1
Armor Rd PUR RM19 ... 212 A3
Armoury Dr GVE DA12 ... 219 H5
Armstrong Cl RCHLM CM3 ... 65 K5 1
  SLH/COR SS17 ... 204 A3
Armstrong Rd SBF/HAD SS7 ... 170 C6
Arne Cl SLH/COR SS17 ... 203 K2
Arne Ct LAIN SS15 ... 6 A2 1
Arne Ms LAIN SS15 ... 6 A2 1
Arnheim Rd BOC CM0 ... 155 H1
Arnhem Av SOCK/AV RM15 ... 198 E8
Arnhem Rd CHLM/WR CM1 ... 34 A7
Arnold Av SOS SS1 ... 9 F5
Arnold Av East PEND EN3 ... 105 F4 1
Arnold Pl TIL RM18 ... 215 H7
Arnold Rd GVE DA12 ... 219 H7
Arnolds Av RBRW/HUT CM13 ... 142 B1
Arnolds Cl RBRW/HUT CM13 ... 142 B1
Arnolds Farm La RBRW/HUT CM13 ... 115 J7
Arnolds Wy RCFD SS4 ... 151 K6
Arnold Wy CHLM/GWD CM2 ... 90 E2
Arrowsmith Rd CHIG IG7 ... 135 J8
Artemis Cl GVE DA12 ... 219 K5
Arterial Road North Stifford
  CDH/CHF RM16 ... 213 H1
Arterial Road Purfleet PUR RM19 ... 211 K3
Arterial Road West Thurrock
  WTHK RM20 ... 212 C2
Artesian Cl ROM RM1 ... 180 A1 1
Arthur Ct CHLM/WR CM1 ... 34 B8 1
Arthur St ERITH DA8 ... 210 A6
  GRAYS RM17 ... 214 B5
  GVW DA11 ... 219 F5
Arthy Cl RCHLM CM3 ... 38 A1
Artillery Rw GVE DA12 ... 219 H5
Arun TIL RM18 ... 216 D3
Arun Cl CHLM/WR CM1 ... 34 E8
Arundel Cl CHES/WCR EN8 ... 76 B2
Arundel Dr SLH/COR SS17 ... 204 C1
Arundel Gdns RAYL SS6 ... 149 G8
  WOS/PRIT SS0 ... 195 H2
Arundel Rd HARH RM3 ... 161 G2
  SBF/HAD SS7 ... 170 A6
  WICKE SS11 ... 147 F4
Arundel Wy BCAYW CM12 ... 117 J7
Arwen Gv RCHLM CM3 ... 122 C7
Ascot Cl SBF/HAD SS7 ... 171 G6

Ascot Gdns HCH RM12 ... 181 F1
  PEND EN3 ... 104 C8
Ascot Rd GVW DA11 ... 219 G6
Ashanti Cl SBN/FI SS3 ... 196 E6
Ashbeam Cl RBRW/HUT CM13 ... 163 F1
Ashbourne Rd BROX EN10 ... 49 F3
  HARH RM3 ... 138 D7
Ashburnham Gdns UPMR RM14 ... 181 J2
Ashburnham Rd SOS SS1 ... 8 C6
Ashby Cl CDH/CHF RM16 ... 202 E6
  EMPK RM11 ... 181 H2
Ash Cl BRWN CM15 ... 140 C5
  RCHLM CM3 ... 38 A1
Ashcombe RCFD SS4 ... 174 A3
Ashcombe Cl LOS SS9 ... 172 C5
Ashcombe Wy HARH RM3 ... 172 A4
Ashdene Cl HOC/HUL SS5 ... 149 H3
Ashdon Cl RBRW/HUT CM13 ... 142 B5
  SOCK/AV RM15 ... 199 K6
Ashdon Wy VGE SS16 ... 7 E6
Ashdown Crs CHES/WCR EN8 ... 76 E2
  SBF/HAD SS7 ... 191 K5
Ashdown Rd PEND EN3 ... 104 C6
Ashfield RAYL SS6 ... 170 E2
Ashfield Farm Rd MAL CM9 ... 38 D6
Ashfields LOU IG10 ... 107 H1
  PIT SS13 ... 169 F6
Ashford Av BRW CM14 ... 140 E4
Ashford Crs PEND EN3 ... 104 C8
Ashford Rd CHLM/WR CM1 ... 62 A3
Ash Gn RCFD SS4 ... 153 G3
Ash Gv BOC CM0 ... 128 B8
  CHLM/GWD CM2 ... 5 D7
  MAL CM9 ... 40 D7
Ash Groves SBW CM21 ... 12 A4
Ashingdale Cl CVI SS8 ... 208 C3
Ashingdon Cl CHING E4 ... 132 D6
Ashingdon Rd HOC/HUL SS5 ... 151 J7
Ashleigh Cl SLH/COR SS17 ... 191 F7
Ashleigh Dr LOS SS9 ... 193 G3
Ashleigh Gdns UPMR RM14 ... 182 A3
Ashley Cl SLH/COR SS17 ... 204 C2
Ashley Gdns CDH/CHF RM16 ... 201 G1
Ashley Gn RCHLM CM3 ... 93 F7
Ashley Rd CHING E4 ... 132 B6
  PEND EN3 ... 104 C6
Ashlyn Gv EMPK RM11 ... 160 E8
Ashlyns PIT SS13 ... 168 C6
Ashlyns La CHONG CM5 ... 55 F7
Ashlyns Rd EPP CM16 ... 80 D4
Ashmans Rw RCHLM CM3 ... 122 D7
Ashmore Gdns GVW DA11 ... 218 C8
Ash Rd CVI SS8 ... 208 C2
  SBF/HAD SS7 ... 191 K5
Ashton Pl CHLM/GWD CM2 ... 63 J3
Ashton Rd HARH RM3 ... 160 E1
  PEND EN3 ... 104 E4
Ash Tree Ct RCFD SS4 ... 175 G3
Ash Tree Crs CHLM/WR CM1 ... 4 A4
Ash Tree Fld HLW CM20 ... 2 A2
Ashurst Av SOSN SS2 ... 195 J2
Ashurst Dr CHLM/WR CM1 ... 35 F6
Ashvale Dr UPMR RM14 ... 182 B3
Ashvale Gdns CRW RM5 ... 137 J2
  UPMR RM14 ... 182 B3
Ash Wk SOCK/AV RM15 ... 200 B2
  SOS SS1 ... 9 E3
Ash Wy HOC/HUL SS5 ... 151 F5
Ashway Cl SLH/COR SS17 ... 187 J4
Ashwells Rd BRWN CM15 ... 115 H2
Ashwood Rd CHING E4 ... 132 E2
Ashworths Pl HLWE CM17 ... 25 H4
Ashworths CVI SS8 ... 191 F7
  RCFD SS4 ... 151 K6
Askews Farm GRAYS RM17 ... 213 H5
Aspdin Rd GVW DA11 ... 218 C2
Aspen Cl CVI SS8 ... 207 J2
  LAIN SS15 ... 6 A4
Aspen Ct UPMR RM14 ... 181 H2
Aspen Wy PEND EN3 ... 104 D2
Asquith Av SBF/HAD SS7 ... 171 H1
Asquith Gdns SBF/HAD SS7 ... 171 H1
Assandune Cl RCFD SS4 ... 152 A6
Aster Cl CHLM/WR CM1 ... 35 H7
Astley GRAYS RM17 ... 213 K4
Aston Rd LAIN SS15 ... 166 C5
Astra Cl RAIN RM13 ... 180 C7
Athelstan Cl HARH RM3 ... 161 G1
Athelstan Gdns WICKE SS11 ... 147 G5
Athelstan Rd HARH RM3 ... 161 G1
Atherstone Ct CVI SS8 ... 208 C2
Atherstone Rd CVI SS8 ... 208 C2
Atherton End SBW CM21 ... 11 J2
Atherton Gdns CDH/CHF RM16 ... 215 H5
Athos Rd CVI SS8 ... 191 H8
Atridge Cha BCAYW CM12 ... 144 B6
Attlee Ct GRAYS RM17 ... 213 K4
Attwoods Cl CHLM/GWD CM2 ... 90 D1
Aubrey Cl CHLM/WR CM1 ... 34 D7
Aubrietia Cl HARH RM3 ... 161 F3
Auckland Cl CHLM/WR CM1 ... 34 A8
  EN EN1 ... 104 B5
  TIL RM18 ... 215 F7
Audley Gdns LOU IG10 ... 108 A1

WAB EN9 .... 77 J8
Audleys Cl SOSN SS2 .... 174 B8 1
Audley Wy BSDN SS14 .... 7 E4
Audwick Cl CHES/WCR EN8 .... 76 D2
Augustine Gdns GVE DA12 .... 219 H5
Augustine Wy RCHLM CM3 .... 93 K3
Aukingford Gdns CHONG CM5 ..... 84 B1 1
Aukingford Gn CHONG CM5 .... 84 B1 2
Austen Cl LOU IG10 .... 108 B7 1
TIL RM18 .... 215 H8 1
Austen Dr CM4 .... 117 K3 1
Austin Rd GVW DA11 .... 218 E6
Austral Dr EMPK RM11 .... 180 E1
Austral Wy RCHLM CM3 .... 126 E2
Autumn Cl EN EN1 .... 104 B6
Avebury Rd WOS/PRIT SS0 .... 8 B3 1
Aveley By-pass SOCK/AV RM15 .. 198 C3
Aveley Cl ERITH DA8 .... 210 A5 1
Aveley Rd UPMR RM14 .... 181 J8
Aveley Wy MAL CM9 .... 68 B5
Avenue Rd BRW CM14 .... 141 F7 1
CHLM/GWD CM2 .... 5 E8
EPP CM16 .... 108 B2
HARH RM3 .... 161 G2
HOD EN11 .... 49 K1
ING CM4 .... 116 B2
LOS SS9 .... 193 F5
SBF/HAD SS7 .... 190 D2
WOS/PRIT SS0 .... 8 B4
Avenue Ter WOS/PRIT SS0 .... 8 B4
The Avenue BCAYW CM12 .... 144 B3
CVI SS8 .... 208 B2
GVW DA11 .... 219 F6
HCH RM12 .... 180 E3
HOC/HUL SS5 .... 149 J2
HOD EN11 .... 49 F1
LOU IG10 .... 134 B2
RBRW/HUT CM13 .... 163 H1
RCHLM CM3 .... 65 K7
RCHLM CM3 .... 124 C6
SBF/HAD SS7 .... 191 K2
SLH/COR SS17 .... 188 A8
WAB EN9 .... 50 E7
Avey La LOU IG10 .... 106 B3
Aviation Wy SOSN SS2 .... 173 K6
Avila Cha CHLM/GWD CM2.......... 40 EB 1
Avocet Wy MAL CM9 .... 40 EB 1
Avon Cl GVE DA12 .... 219 J7
RCFD SS4 ....
Avondale Av LOU IG10 .... 134 C3
RAYL SS6 .... 172 A3
Avondale Crs PEND EN3 .... 104 E7
Avondale Dr LOS SS9 .... 193 G1
LOU IG10 .... 134 C2
Avondale Gdns SLH/COR SS17 .. 187 F8
RAYL SS6 .... 172 A3
SBF/HAD SS7 .... 190 C2
VGE SS16 .... 188 D1
Avon Gn SOCK/AV RM15 .... 199 K6 1
Avon Rd CHLM/WR CM1 .... 61 K1
CVI SS8 .... 208 A2
UPMR RM14 .... 161 K8
Avontar Rd SOCK/AV RM15 .... 199 K4
Avro Rd SOSN SS2 .... 174 A7
Aylands Rd PEND EN3 .... 104 D2
Aylesbeare SBN/FI SS3 .... 195 C5
Aylesbury Dr VGE SS16 .... 166 A8
Aylets Fld HLWS CM18 .... 3 E6
Aylett Cl CVI SS8 .... 208 C1 1
Aylett Rd UPMR RM14 .... 181 K3 1
Ayletts CHLM/WR CM1 .... 34 D2
Ayloffs Cl EMPK RM11 .... 161 F7 1
Ayloff's Wk EMPK RM11 .... 161 F7
Aylsham La HARH RM3 .... 138 D7
Aynsley Gdns HLWE CM17 .... 25 G5
Ayron Rd SOCK/AV RM15 .... 199 K4
Azalea Av WICKW SS12 .... 147 F6

B

Baardwyk Av CVI SS8 .... 208 E2
Baas Hl BROX EN10 .... 48 D3
Baas Hill Cl BROX EN10 .... 48 E3
Baas La BROX EN10 .... 48 E3
Babington Rd HCH RM12 .... 180 C2
Back La CDH/CHF RM16 .... 200 A8
ING CM4 .... 88 A8
ING CM4 .... 117 J3
PUR RM19 .... 212 B3
RBSF CM22 .... 12 C5
RCFD SS4 .... 174 A3
RCHLM CM3 .... 18 E3
RCHLM CM3 .... 20 E8
RCHLM CM3 .... 92 E6
WAB EN9 .... 50 E5
WIT CM8 .... 40 B1
Back Rd CHLM/WR CM1 .... 61 F4
MAL CM9 .... 44 B1
Bacons Cha BOC CM0 .... 74 C4

Badburgham Ct WAB EN9 .... 78 B7
Baddow Hall Av CHLM/GWD CM2 .. 63 J6
Baddow Hall Crs CHLM/GWD CM2 .. 63 J6
Baddow Place Av CHLM/GWD CM2 .. 63 J7
Bader Av GVW DA11 .... 218 D8
Bader Wy RAIN RM13 .... 180 B7
Badger Hall Av SBF/HAD SS7 .... 191 F1
Badgers Cl CHLM/GWD CM2 .... 90 D4
WOS/PRIT SS0 .... 193 J1 1
Badgers Cft BROX EN10 .... 48 E3
Badgers Keep BOC CM0 .... 128 B5 1
Badgers Mt CDH/CHF RM16 ...... 214 E1
HOC/HUL SS5 .... 150 D6
The Badgers VGE SS16 .... 186 B1
Badminton Pl BROX EN10 .... 48 E2
Bag La ING CM4 .... 115 J1
Bailey Cl PUR RM19 .... 212 A3
Bailey Rd LOS SS9 .... 192 C3
The Bailey SS6 .... 171 H3
Baird Rd EN EN1 .... 104 B7
Baker Av RCHLM CM3 .... 38 A2
Bakers Cl RCHLM CM3 .... 122 D5 2
Baker's Ct BSDN SS14 .... 168 D3
Bakers Farm Cl WICKE SS11 ..... 147 K6 1
Bakers Fld ING CM4 .... 117 K3
Bakers La CHLM/GWD CM2 .... 90 A2
EPP CM16 .... 80 D4
ING CM4 .... 116 B1
MAL CM9 .... 42 A1
RCHLM CM3 .... 65 J8
Bakers Md RCHLM CM3 .... 20 B6 1
Bakers Meadow BRWN CM15 ..... 114 A3
Bakers Rd CHESW EN7 .... 76 B4
Baker St CDH/CHF RM16 .... 201 J6
CHLM/GWD CM2 .... 4 B4
Bakery Cl BOC CM0 .... 102 A2
HLWW/ROY CM19 .... 22 E5
Baldocks Rd EPP CM16 .... 108 C1
Baldwin's Hl LOU IG10 .... 107 H5
Balfour Cl WICKW SS12 .... 147 H8 1
Balfour Rd GRAYS RM17 .... 214 B3
Balgonie Rd CHLM/GWD CM2 ...... 63 K1
Balgores Crs GPK RM2 .... 160 C5
Balgores La GPK RM2 .... 160 C6
Balgores Sq GPK RM2 .... 160 C6 1
Balliol Av CHING E4 .... 132 E7
Balmerino Av SBF/HAD SS7 .... 171 H7
Balmoral Av SLH/COR SS17 .... 204 A2
Balmoral Cl CHES/WCR EN8 .... 76 D8
BCAYE CM11 .... 145 F4
Balmoral Gdns HOC/HUL SS5 .... 150 C1 1
Balmoral Rd BRWN CM15 .... 140 E2
GPK RM2 .... 160 C3
HCH RM12 .... 180 C4
PEND EN3 .... 104 D2
WOS/PRIT SS0 .... 8 B3 2
Balstonia Dr SLH/COR SS17 ...... 187 F8
Baltic Av SOS SS1 .... 9 D4
Bamford Cl CHLM/GWD CM2 .... 63 J6
Bampton Rd HARH RM3 .... 161 F2
Bancrofts Rd RCHLM CM3 .... 122 E5
Bandhills Cl RCHLM CM3 .... 122 D5
Banes Down WAB EN9 .... 50 A4
Bankart La CHLM/GWD CM2 .... 63 H1
Bankside GVW DA11 .... 218 B4
Bankside Cl RCHLM CM3 .... 122 E4
Banks La EPP CM16 .... 81 J6
Bank St GVE DA12 .... 219 G4 1
Bann Cl SOCK/AV RM15 .... 199 H7
Banner Cl PUR RM19 .... 212 A3
Bannister Dr RBRW/HUT CM13 .. 142 B2
Bannister Gn WICKW SS12 .... 147 H7 1
Banson's La CHONG CM5 .... 84 C2
Bansons Wy CHONG CM5 .... 84 C2
Banton Cl EN EN1 .... 104 B6
Banyards EMPK RM11 .... 161 F6 1
Banyardway RCFD SS4 .... 173 K3
Barbara Av CVI SS8 .... 207 K2
Barbara Cl RCFD SS4 .... 174 A2
Barbel Cl CHES/WCR EN8 .... 77 G8
Barberry Rd HARH RM3 .... 160 E2 1
Barbrook Wy RCHLM CM3 .... 93 J4
Barclay Cl CHLM/GWD CM2 .... 63 J1
Barclay Ov WFD IG8 .... 133 H7
Barclay Rd PIT SS13 .... 169 H4
Barclay Wy WTHK RM20 .... 212 C4
Bardell Cl CHLM/WR CM1 .... 34 D7
Bardenville Rd CVI SS8 .... 208 E2
Bardeswell Cl BRW CM14 .... 141 F5
Bardfield VGE SS16 .... 168 B8
Bardfield Wy RAYL SS6 .... 171 F2
Barfields LOU IG10 .... 107 J8
Barge Pier Rd SBN/FI SS3 .... 196 B8
Barington Ct RBRW/HUT CM13 .. 142 B2
Bark Burr Rd CDH/CHF RM16 .... 213 J1
Barkis Cl CHLM/WR CM1 .... 33 K1
Barle Gdns SOCK/AV RM15 .... 199 K6
Barley Cl RBSF CM22 .... 14 A3
VGE SS16 .... 186 B2
Barleycorn Wy EMPK RM11 .... 161 G8

Barley Cft HLWS CM18 .... 52 B1
Barley Fld BRWN CM15 .... 113 H3
Barleylands Rd LAIN SS15 .... 167 G2
Barley Md RCHLM CM3 .... 66 B7
Barling Rd SBN/FI SS3 .... 176 B7
Barlow's Reach CHLM/GWD CM2 .. 63 J1
Barnaby Rudge CHLM/WR CM1 .... 34 B6
Barnaby Wy CHIG IG7 .... 134 D6
Barnard Acres WAB EN9 .... 50 A5
Barnard Cl VGE SS16 .... 188 B2
Barnard Rd CHLM/GWD CM2 .... 90 E3
EN EN1 .... 104 B6
LOS SS9 .... 192 C3
SBW CM21 .... 11 J2
Barnards Av CVI SS8 .... 208 D1
Barncombe Cl SBF/HAD SS7 ..... 170 C7
Barncroft Cl LOU IG10 .... 134 D1 1
Barncroft Gn LOU IG10 .... 134 D1
Barncroft Rd LOU IG10 .... 134 D1
Barnes Farm Dr RCHLM CM3 ..... 126 C3
Barnet Park Rd WICKE SS11 ..... 147 J3
Barnett Cl ERITH DA8 .... 210 A8
Barnfield EPP CM16 .... 80 E2
GVW DA11 .... 219 F7
Barnfield Cl WAB EN9 .... 50 B4
Barnfield Ms CHLM/WR CM1 .... 34 C7
Barn Gn CHLM/WR CM1 .... 35 G6
Barn Hl HLWW/ROY CM19 .... 50 D1
Barn Md BRWN CM15 .... 114 A2
HLWS CM18 .... 3 E6
Barnmead Wy BOC CM0 .... 128 B6
Barns Ct EPP CM16 .... 51 K2
Barnsley Rd HARH RM3 .... 161 G2 1
Barnstable Cl SOS SS1 .... 195 K5
Barnstaple Rd HARH RM3 .... 138 D8
SOS SS1 .... 196 A5
Barnston Wy RBRW/HUT CM13 .. 142 B1 1
Barnwell Dr HOC/HUL SS5 .... 150 E7
The Barnyard VGE SS16 .... 186 B1
Baron Rd RCHLM CM3 .... 122 E6
Baron's La RCHLM CM3 .... 96 A4
Barons Wy VGE SS16 .... 186 C1
Barrack La RCHLM CM3 .... 20 A5
Barrack Rd CHLM/WR CM1 .... 18 A7
Barrack Rw GVW DA11 .... 219 F4 1
Barrack Sq CHLM/GWD CM2 .... 4 C3 1
Barra Gld WICKW SS12 .... 147 J8
Barrington Cl BSDN SS14 .... 168 C5 1
CHLM/GWD CM2 .... 63 J7 1
SBN/FI SS3 .... 196 D4 1
Barrington Gdns BSDN SS14 ..... 168 C5
Barrington Gn LOU IG10 .... 108 A8
Barrington Pl ING CM4 .... 116 B2
Barrington Rd LOU IG10 .... 108 A8
Barringtons Cl RAYL SS6 .... 171 J2 1
Barron's Cl CHONG CM5 .... 84 B1
Barrow Hall Rd SBN/FI SS3 .... 176 B8
Barrowsand SOS SS1 .... 196 A7
Barrows Rd HLWW/ROY CM19 ..... 23 H5
Barry Cl CDH/CHF RM16 .... 215 F2
Barstable Rd SLH/COR SS17 ..... 203 K3
Bartholomew Dr HARH RM3 ...... 160 E4
Bartlett Cl RCHLM CM3 .... 98 D4
Bartlett Rd GVW DA11 .... 219 F6
Bartley Cl SBF/HAD SS7 .... 170 A7
Bartley Rd SBF/HAD SS7 .... 170 A7
Bartlow End PIT SS13 .... 168 E5
Bartlow Side PIT SS13 .... 168 E5
Barton Cl CHIG IG7 .... 135 F5
RCHLM CM3 .... 122 D4
Barton Rd HCH RM12 .... 180 B2
Baryta Cl SLH/COR SS17 .... 203 J4 1
Basildon Dr LAIN SS15 .... 6 A3
Basildon Rd LAIN SS15 .... 6 C2
Basin Rd MAL CM9 .... 69 G1
Bassenthwaite Rd SBF/HAD SS7 .. 170 D7
Bassett Gdns EPP CM16 .... 54 B8
Bassett's La CHONG CM5 .... 59 F5
MAL CM9 .... 66 A1
Bassingbourne Cl BROX EN10 .... 49 F2 1
Bata Av TIL RM18 .... 216 C4
Batavia Rd CVI SS8 .... 207 H1
Bate-dudley Dr BOC CM0 .... 74 D2
Bates Rd HARH RM3 .... 161 H2
MAL CM9 .... 68 C1
Bath St GVW DA11 .... 219 G4 2
Baton Cl PUR RM19 .... 212 A3
Battleswick BSDN SS14 .... 168 B4
Batt's Rd BOC CM0 .... 99 K4
Baxter Av SOSN SS2 .... 8 C3
Baxters RCHLM CM3 .... 66 A6 1
Bay Cl CVI SS8 .... 208 B3
Bayleys Md RBRW/HUT CM13 .... 142 B6
Bay Manor La WTHK RM20 .... 212 C5
Baymans Wd BRWN CM15 .... 141 H5
Baynes Cl EN EN1 .... 104 A5
Bay Vw BOC CM0 .... 72 C5
Baywood Sq CHIG IG7 .... 136 A7
Beach Av LOS SS9 .... 193 H5
Beach Cl SBN/FI SS3 .... 197 H2
Beaches Cl HOC/HUL SS5 .... 151 G7
Beach House Gdns CVI SS8 .... 208 E3
Beach Rd CVI SS8 .... 208 D1
SBN/FI SS3 .... 196 E8

Beach's Dr CHLM/WR CM1 .... 61 K2
Beachway CVI SS8 .... 208 B3
Beachy Dr BOC CM0 .... 72 C5
Beaconfield Av EPP CM16 .... 80 D3
Beaconfield Rd EPP CM16 .... 80 D3
Beaconfield Wy EPP CM16 .... 80 E3
Beacon HI BRW CM14 .... 112 E3
MAL CM9 .... 68 A3
PUR RM19 .... 211 J4
Beacon Hill Rd BRW CM14 .... 112 E3
Beacon Rd ERITH DA8 .... 210 C6
Beaconsfield Rd PEND EN3 .... 104 C3
The Beacons LOU IG10 .... 107 J4
Beads Hall La BRWN CM15 .... 113 K8
Beambridge PIT SS13 .... 168 D7
Beamish CI EPP CM16 .... 54 C7
Beams Wy BCAYE CM11 .... 144 D5
Beanfield Rd SBW CM21 .... 10 E1
Beardsley Dr CHLM/WR CM1 .... 35 G6
Bearing CI CHIG IG7 .... 135 K7
Bearing Wy CHIG IG7 .... 135 K7
Bearsted Dr PIT SS13 .... 169 F8
Beatrice Av CVI SS8 .... 208 B1
Beatrice CI HOC/HUL SS5 .... 150 E7
Beatrice Gdns GVW DA11 .... 218 D5
Beatty La BSDN SS14 .... 168 B7
Beatty Ri RCHLM CM3 .... 123 F7
Beatty Rd CHES/WCR EN8 .... 77 F8
Beauchamps BOC CM0 .... 128 B5
Beauchamps Dr WICKE SS11 .... 147 K6
Beaufort CI CDH/CHF RM16 .... 213 J2
EPP CM16 .... 82 A1
Beaufort Rd BCAYW CM12 .... 144 A3
CHLM/GWD CM2 .... 63 J1
Beaufort St SOSN SS2 .... 195 G4
Beaulieu Dr CHLM/WR CM1 .... 35 H6
Beaulieu Dr WAB EN9 .... 77 H7
Beaumont CI GPK RM2 .... 160 D4
Beaumont Crs RAIN RM13 .... 180 B7
Beaumont Dr GVW DA11 .... 218 D5
Beaumont Gdns
  RBRW/HUT CM13 .... 142 B2
Beaumont Pk RCHLM CM3 .... 65 G7
Beaumont Park Dr
  HLWE/ROY CM19 .... 22 D5
Beaumont Rd GVW DA11 .... 218 D5
Beaumont Wy MAL CM9 .... 68 D5
Beazley End WICKW SS12 .... 147 H2
Bebington CI BCAYW CM12 .... 144 B2
Beccles Ct WICKE SS11 .... 147 G5
Beecham CI LAIN SS15 .... 6 A2
Beech Av BKHH IG9 .... 133 J5
RAYL SS6 .... 171 J2
RBRW/HUT CM13 .... 141 J6
UPMR RM14 .... 181 J4
Beech CI BOC CM0 .... 128 B7
HCH RM12 .... 180 C4
LOU IG10 .... 107 K1
Beechcombe SLH/COR SS17 .... 187 J8
Beechcroft Rd CVI SS8 .... 207 J2
Beech Dr SBW CM21 .... 11 G6
Beeches CI CHLM/WR CM1 .... 62 A3
Beeches Rd CHLM/WR CM1 .... 40 B8
MAL CM9 .... 148 D3
WICKE SS11 .... 148 D3
The Beeches BRW CM14 .... 140 E6
TIL RM18 .... 215 G8
Beechfield SBW CM21 .... 11 K3
Beechfield WK WAB EN9 .... 105 K1
Beech Gv SOCK/AV RM15 .... 211 K1
Beech Hill Gdns WAB EN9 .... 106 D3
Beechmont Gdns SOSN SS2 .... 194 B1
Beech PI EPP CM16 .... 80 D5
Beech Ri RCHLM CM3 .... 38 A1
Beech Rd BSDN SS14 .... 168 B8
  CHONG CM5 .... 58 B1
  HOC/HUL SS5 .... 149 K3
  SBF/HAD SS7 .... 191 F7
Beech Tree Gld CHING E4 .... 133 G4
Beechwood Dr WFD IG8 .... 133 G8
Beecroft Crs CVI SS8 .... 207 J1
Beedell Av WICKE SS11 .... 147 J7
  WOS/PRIT SS0 .... 8 A2
Beehive Cha BRWN CM15 .... 114 B1
Beehive Ct RBSF CM22 .... 13 G2
Beehive La CHLM/GWD CM2 .... 90 D1
Beeleigh Av VGE SS16 .... 186 D2

Beeleigh Cha MAL CM9 .... 67 K1
Beeleigh CI SOSN SS2 .... 8 B1
Beeleigh Cross BSDN SS14 .... 168 B6
Beeleigh East BSDN SS14 .... 168 B6
Beeleigh Link CHLM/GWD CM2 .... 63 H3
Beeleigh Rd MAL CM9 .... 68 D2
Beeleigh West BSDN SS14 .... 168 A5
Beeston Dr CHES/WCR EN8 .... 76 D1
Beggarhill ING CM4 .... 87 H6
Begonia CI CHLM/WR CM1 .... 35 H7
Beke Hall Cha North RAYL SS6 .... 170 D1
Beke Hall Cha South RAYL SS6 .... 170 D2
Bekeswell La CHLM/GWD CM2 .... 90 B2
Belchamps Rd WICKE SS11 .... 147 J5
Belchamps Wy HOC/HUL SS5 .... 151 F8
Belchers La WAB EN9 .... 50 E6
Belfairs CI LOS SS9 .... 192 E3
Belfairs Dr LOS SS9 .... 192 E3
Belfairs Park CI LOS SS9 .... 172 D8
Belfairs Park Dr LOS SS9 .... 172 C8
Belgrave Av GPK RM2 .... 160 D5
Belgrave CI CHLM/GWD CM2 .... 5 E6
  LOS SS9 .... 172 C7
  RAYL SS6 .... 171 G1
Belgrave Rd BCAYW CM12 .... 144 A1
  LOS SS9 .... 172 C7
Bellamy Rd CHES/WCR EN8 .... 76 E3
Bell Av HARH RM3 .... 160 C3
Bell Common EPP CM16 .... 80 C6
Belle Staines Pleasaunce
  CHING E4 .... 132 B5
Belle Vue CHLM/GWD CM2 .... 4 B4
Bellevue Av SOS SS1 .... 9 F4
Bellevue PI SOS SS1 .... 9 F4
Bellevue Rd BCAYW CM12 .... 144 A3
  EMPK RM11 .... 181 G2
  SOSN SS2 .... 9 F3
Bellfield VGE SS16 .... 188 B2
Bellfield Gdns HLWE CM17 .... 25 G6
Bell HI RCHLM CM3 .... 65 G6
Bell Hill Rd VGE SS16 .... 187 J3
Bellhouse Crs LOS SS9 .... 172 E8
Bellhouse La BRW CM14 .... 140 B1
  LOS SS9 .... 192 E1
Bellhouse Rd LOS SS9 .... 172 E7
Bellingham La RAYL SS6 .... 171 J3
Bell La BROX EN10 .... 48 E3
  PEND EN3 .... 104 D4
Bellmaine Av SLH/COR SS17 .... 204 B1
Bellman Av GVE DA12 .... 219 K6
Bellmead CHLM/GWD CM2 .... 4 C3
Bell Md ING CM4 .... 116 B2
  SBW CM21 .... 11 J3
Bells Cha CHLM/GWD CM2 .... 63 G7
Bells Hill Rd VGE SS16 .... 187 J3
Bell St CHLM/GWD CM2 .... 63 H7
  SBW CM21 .... 11 J3
Bell WK WOS/PRIT SS0 .... 194 A1
Belmonde Dr CHLM/WR CM1 .... 35 F6
Belmont Av UPMR RM14 .... 181 G3
  WICKW SS12 .... 146 D7
Belmont CI CHING E4 .... 132 B8
  CHLM/WR CM1 .... 35 G6
  WFD IG8 .... 133 J7
  WICKW SS12 .... 146 E6
Belmont Rd GRAYS RM17 .... 213 J4
  HCH RM12 .... 180 E4
Belsteads Farm La CHLM/WR CM1 .... 35 F3
Belstedes LAIN SS15 .... 6 B4
Beltinge Rd HARH RM3 .... 161 G6
Beltona Gdns CHES/WCR EN8 .... 76 D1
Belton Br LOS SS9 .... 192 E5
Belton Gdns LOS SS9 .... 192 E5
Belton Wy East LOS SS9 .... 192 D5
Belton Wy West LOS SS9 .... 192 C5
Belvawney CI CHLM/WR CM1 .... 34 A7
Belvedere CI HOC/HUL SS5 .... 150 D7
Belvedere CI GVE DA12 .... 219 H6
  RCHLM CM3 .... 65 K6
Belvedere PI MAL CM9 .... 68 B5
Belvedere Rd BOC CM0 .... 155 H2
  BRW CM14 .... 140 C5
  RCHLM CM3 .... 65 K6
  RCHLM CM3 .... 66 A6
The Belvoir RCHLM CM3 .... 116 A2
Benbow Dr RCHLM CM3 .... 122 E7
Bencroft CHESW EN7 .... 48 A8
Benderloch CVI SS8 .... 207 J1
Benedict Dr CHLM/WR CM1 .... 62 A3
Benets Rd EMPK RM11 .... 181 G2
Benfleet Park Rd SBF/HAD SS7 .... 190 A2
Benfleet Rd SBF/HAD SS7 .... 191 F3
Benford Rd HOD EN11 .... 49 F1
Benhurst Av HCH RM12 .... 180 C4
Benjamin CI EMPK RM11 .... 160 B8
Bennett's Av RCHLM CM3 .... 120 D2
Bennett Wy RCHLM CM3 .... 38 A1
Bennions CI HCH RM12 .... 180 E7
Bennison Dr HARH RM3 .... 160 A4
Benskins La ABF/ST RM4 .... 138 E4
Benson Rd GRAYS RM17 .... 214 A5
Bentalls BSDN SS14 .... 7 E2
Bentalls CI SOSN SS2 .... 194 B1
Bentley Dr HLWE CM17 .... 23 G6
The Bentleys LOS SS9 .... 173 G6

Bentley St GVE DA12 .... 219 H4
Bentley Wy WFD IG8 .... 133 H6
Benton Gdns SLH/COR SS17 .... 187 G8
Benvenue Av LOS SS9 .... 173 G6
Benyon Pth SOCK/AV RM15 .... 200 A3
Berberis CI VGE SS16 .... 186 A5
Berdens VGE SS16 .... 168 A8
Berecroft HLWS CM18 .... 52 B2
Beredens La RBRW/HUT CM13 .... 162 C4
Berens CI WICKE SS11 .... 147 J8
Beresford CI SBF/HAD SS7 .... 191 J1
Beresford Ct BCAYW CM12 .... 117 F8
Beresford Dr WFD IG8 .... 133 K7
Beresford Gdns SBF/HAD SS7 .... 191 H1
Beresford Rd CHING E4 .... 133 F4
  GVW DA11 .... 218 D5
  SOS SS1 .... 9 F5
Berg Av CVI SS8 .... 191 J8
Berkeley Ct UPMR RM14 .... 181 J3
Berkeley Dr BCAYW CM12 .... 117 G8
  EMPK RM11 .... 181 H2
Berkeley Gdns LOS SS9 .... 192 B4
Berkeley La CVI SS8 .... 208 A3
Berkely Dr CHLM/GWD CM2 .... 63 H3
Berkley Av CHES/WCR EN8 .... 76 D8
Berkley HI SLH/COR SS17 .... 204 A1
Berkley Rd GVE DA12 .... 219 G3
Berkshire CI LOS SS9 .... 172 D8
Berkshire Wy EMPK RM11 .... 161 H7
Bermuda Rd TIL RM18 .... 215 F8
Bernard Gv WAB EN9 .... 77 H7
Bernard St GVE DA12 .... 219 G4
Berners Wy BROX EN10 .... 49 F5
Berriwell Rd CHING E4 .... 133 F6
Berrybank CI CHING E4 .... 132 D5
Berry CI HCH RM12 .... 180 E6
  VGE SS16 .... 166 C8
  WICKW SS12 .... 146 E7
Berry La LOS SS9 .... 186 C1
Berry V RCHLM CM3 .... 122 E7
Bersham La GRAYS RM17 .... 213 J3
Berther Rd EMPK RM11 .... 181 F1
Bertram Rd EN EN1 .... 104 A8
Berwick Av CHLM/GWD CM2 .... 34 C5
Berwick CI CHES/WCR EN8 .... 77 G8
Berwick La CHONG CM5 .... 82 E7
Berwick Pond Rd RAIN RM13 .... 198 A2
  UPMR RM14 .... 181 G7
Berwood Rd SLH/COR SS17 .... 204 B2
Betjeman CI CHESW EN7 .... 76 A2
  RAYL SS6 .... 172 A2
Betjeman Wy CHONG CM5 .... 56 B8
Betony Crs BCAYW CM12 .... 117 F8
Betoyne Av CHING E4 .... 133 F7
Betsham Rd ERITH DA8 .... 210 A6
Bett's La HOC/HUL SS5 .... 150 E7
  WAB EN9 .... 50 E3
Beulah Rd EPP CM16 .... 80 D3
  HCH RM12 .... 180 D4
Bevan Wy HCH RM12 .... 181 G4
Beveland Rd CVI SS8 .... 209 G2
Beverley Av CVI SS8 .... 207 K2
Beverley CI CDH/CHF RM16 .... 202 D1
  EMPK RM11 .... 181 G1
Beverley Gdns EMPK RM11 .... 181 F1
  SOSN SS2 .... 194 B1
Beverley Ri BCAYW CM12 .... 144 D4
  SOSN SS2 .... 194 B1
Beverly CI BROX EN10 .... 48 E3
Bewley CI CHES/WCR EN8 .... 76 D5
Bexhill Dr GRAYS RM17 .... 213 H5
Bexley Rd ERITH DA8 .... 210 A4
Bibby CI SLH/COR SS17 .... 204 C2
Bickenhall SBN/FI SS3 .... 196 C5
Bickerton Point RCHLM CM3 .... 123 F7
Bicknacre Rd RCHLM CM3 .... 65 H8
Biddenden Ct PIT SS13 .... 169 F7
Bideford CI HARH RM3 .... 160 D3
  WOS/PRIT SS0 .... 173 H8
Bideford Rd PEND EN3 .... 105 F4
Biggin La GRAYS RM17 .... 215 G6
The Bight RCHLM CM3 .... 123 F8
Billericay Rd RBRW/HUT CM13 .... 164 D2
Billet La EMPK RM11 .... 180 D2
  SLH/COR SS17 .... 204 A4
Bilton Rd CHLM/WR CM1 .... 4 A4
  SBF/HAD SS7 .... 191 K2
Bilton Wy PEND EN3 .... 105 F5
Bingham CI SOCK/AV RM15 .... 199 K8
Binley Rd CHLM/GWD CM2 .... 9 D2
Bircham Rd SOSN SS2 .... 134 A6
Birch CI BKHH IG9 .... 207 K2
  CVI SS8 .... 171 H2
  RAYL SS6 .... 153 H4
  RCFD SS4 .... 170 A6
  SBF/HAD SS7 .... 200 B4
  SOCK/AV RM15 .... 161 F6
Birch Crs EMPK RM11 .... 200 B3
  SOCK/AV RM15 .... 149 J2
Birchdale HOC/HUL SS5 .... 193 F1
Birche CI RCHLM CM3 .... 54 B8
The Birches EPP CM16 .... 141 H6
  RBRW/HUT CM13 .... 170 B5
  SBF/HAD SS7 .... 90 C3
Birches WK CHLM/GWD CM2 .... 90 C3

irchfield Rd CHES/WCR EN8	76 B3
irch Gn WICKW SS12	147 G6
irch La ING CM4	118 B2
irch Rd BOC CM0	102 A1
irchwood SBF/HAD SS7	170 A6
irchwood Cl RBRW/HUT CM13	163 F1 2
irchwood Dr LOS SS9	193 H3
irchwood Rd RCHLM CM3	95 F3
SLH/COR SS17	187 J8
irdbrook Cl RBRW/HUT CM13	142 A2
ird La RBRW/HUT CM13	163 F4
UPMR RM14	182 A7
irds Gn CHONG CM5	57 H1
irkbeck Rd RBRW/HUT CM13	142 C2
irkdale Av HARH RM3	161 H2 1
irkdale Ri RCHLM CM3	38 B1
iros Rd BCAYE CM11	118 E8
irs Cl WICKE SS11	147 G4
iscay SOSN SS2	173 H6
ishop Rd CHLM/WR CM1	4 C2
ishops Cl EN EN1	104 B6
PIT SS13	168 D3
ishopscourt Gdns	
CHLM/WR CM1	5 F1 1
ishopsfield HLWS CM18	3 D6
ishop's Hall Rd BRWN CM15	140 E2
ishops Rd SLH/COR SS17	204 B2
WICKW SS12	169 G2
ishopsteignton SBN/FI SS3	196 B5
ishops Wk BRWN CM15	141 J5
isley Cl CHES/WCR EN8	76 D7
lackacre Rd EPP CM16	108 C3
lack Bush La CDH/CHF RM16	202 D1
lackbush Spring HLW CM20	24 E4
lackdale CHESW EN7	76 A1
lack Ditch Rd WAB EN9	105 J2
lack Ditch Wy WAB EN9	105 H2
lackgate Rd SBN/FI SS3	197 F6
lackhorse La EPP CM16	54 D7
lack Lion La HLWE CM17	25 G1
lacklock CHLM/GWD CM2	63 J2
lackmore Av CVI SS8	208 B3 1
lackmore Cl WAB EN9	78 C7
lackmore Md ING CM4	86 D5 1
lackmore Rd BKHH IG9	134 B3 1
BRWN CM15	113 K3
GRAYS RM17	214 B4 1
ING CM4	86 A7
lackmores LAIN SS15	165 K7
lackshots La CDH/CHF RM16	201 G7
lacksmith Cl BCAYW CM12	117 H8 1
CHLM/WR CM1	35 G6
lacksmiths Aly ING CM4	86 C5
lacksmiths Wy SBW CM21	11 F4 1
lackthorn Cl CHLM/WR CM1	61 G4 1
lackthorn Ct VGE SS16	186 B1
lackthorn Dr CHING E4	132 E7
lackthorne Rd CVI SS8	208 C2
lackthorn Rd CDH/CHF RM16	201 F8
HOC/HUL SS5	151 G5 1
lackthorn Wy BRW CM14	141 G8 1
lackwall Br CHLM/WR CM1	32 B8
lackwater SBF/HAD SS7	190 E1 1
lackwater Rd BOC CM0	128 C3 1
CHLM/WR CM1	34 E7
MAL CM9	69 G2
SBN/FI SS3	196 D4 2
lackwood Chine RCHLM CM3	122 E7
lake Hall Dr WICKE SS11	147 K7
lake Hall Rd CHONG CM5	55 G8
landford Crs CHING E4	132 D3
latches Cha VGE SS16	172 E2
lenheim Cha LOS SS9	193 F2
lenheim Cl HOC/HUL SS5	93 K3
SBW CM21	11 F5
UPMR RM14	182 B2 1
lenheim Crs LOS SS9	193 F2
lenheim Gdns RCHLM CM3	98 E4
SOCK/AV RM15	198 D8
lenheim Ms LOS SS9	193 F2
lenheim Park Cl LOS SS9	193 G1
lenheim Rd BRWN CM15	140 D2
lenheim EPP CM16	82 A1
ligh Rd GVW DA11	219 F4
lind La BCAYW CM12	143 G7
CHLM/GWD CM2	91 H8
CHLM/GWD CM2	92 C1
MAL CM9	42 A6
MAL CM9	96 D3
lindman's La CHES/WCR EN8	76 B3
lockhouse Rd GRAYS RM17	214 B5 1
lountswood Rd HOC/HUL SS5	150 B6
lower Cl RAYL SS6	172 A2
lue Anchor La TIL RM18	215 K3
luebell Wd BCAYW CM12	143 J1
lue House Farm Cha	
RCHLM CM3	124 D3
luehouse Rd CHING E4	133 F6
luehouses LAIN SS15	7 E5
luemans EPP CM16	54 D6
luemans End EPP CM16	54 D6
lue Mill La MAL CM9	66 D1
lunts Wall Rd BCAYW CM12	143 K4
Blyth Av SBN/FI SS3	196 B6
Blythe Rd HOD EN11	49 K1
SLH/COR SS9	204 A1 1
Blythe Wy MAL CM9	68 C5
SBF/HAD SS7	170 B6
Blyth Wk UPMR RM14	182 B1
Blyton Cl WICKW SS12	147 G8
Boardman Av CHING E4	132 C1
Bobbing Rd RCFD SS4	174 C3
Bobbingworth MI CHONG CM5	55 G6
Bockingham Gn PIT SS13	168 D5
Bodell Cl CDH/CHF RM16	214 A1
Bodley Cl EPP CM16	80 D4
Bodmin Rd CHLM/WR CM1	35 F8
Bohemia Cha LOS SS9	172 D8
Boleyn Av EN EN1	104 B5
Boleyn Cl BCAYW CM12	117 G8 2
CDH/CHF RM16	213 J2 1
LOS SS9	172 D6
Boleyn Ct BKHH IG9	133 H4
BROX EN10	48 E3
Boleyn Gdns RBRW/HUT CM13	141 K6
Boleyn Wy RCHLM CM3	36 D4
Bolney Dr LOS SS9	172 D6
Bommel Av CVI SS8	209 G2
Bonchurch Av LOS SS9	192 E3
Bond St CHLM/WR CM1	5 D3
GRAYS RM17	214 B5
Bonington Cha CHLM/WR CM1	35 G7
Bonington Rd HCH RM12	180 E6 2
Bonks HI SBW CM21	11 H4
Bonner Wk CDH/CHF RM16	213 J2 2
Bonney Gv CHESW EN7	76 A4
Bonningtons RBRW/HUT CM13	142 A6
Bonnygate BSDN SS14	167 K6
Bootham Cl BCAYW CM12	144 A4
Bootham Rd BCAYW CM12	144 A4
Borda Cl CHLM/WR CM1	34 C8
Border's La LOU IG10	39 J1
Boreham Rd WICKE SS11	148 A8 1
Boreham Rd RCHLM CM3	21 K2
Borman Cl LOS SS9	173 H7 1
The Borough CHONG CM5	84 B3
Borrell Cl BROX EN10	48 E2
Borrett Av CVI SS8	208 A1
Borrowdale Cl SBF/HAD SS7	170 E7
Borrowdale Rd SBF/HAD SS7	170 E6
Borwick La BCAYE CM11	168 B1
WICKW SS12	168 E1
Boscombe Av EMPK RM11	180 E1
GRAYS RM17	214 C3
WICKW SS12	146 C5
Boscombe Rd SOSN SS2	9 E3
Bosgrove CHING E4	132 D4
Boston Av RAYL SS6	171 G1
SOSN SS2	8 C3
Boswell Av RCFD SS4	152 A8
Boswells Dr CHLM/WR CM1	5 D3
Bosworth Cl HOC/HUL SS5	173 G1
Bosworth Crs HARH RM3	160 D1
Bosworth Rd LOS SS9	172 D6
Botany Wy PUR RM19	211 J4
Botelers VGE SS16	6 C6
Boteley Cl CHING E4	132 E5
Botney Hill Rd BCAYW CM12	165 H1
Boucher Gv DA11	218 E8
Bouchers Md CHLM/WR CM1	35 H7 1
Bouldrewood Rd SBF/HAD SS7	170 A8
The Boulevard RCFD SS4	174 C2
Boulter Gdns RAIN RM13	180 B7
Boult Rd LAIN SS15	6 A2
Boundary Dr RBRW/HUT CM13	142 D3
Boundary Rd LOS SS9	172 C5
ROM RM1	160 B8 3
UPMR RM14	181 H4
Boundary St ERITH DA8	210 A6
Bounderby Gv CHLM/WR CM1	34 A7 1
Bourne Av LAIN SS15	166 B5
Bournebridge Cl	
RBRW/HUT CM13	142 D3 1
Bournebridge La ABR/ST RM4	137 G3
Bourne Cl BROX EN10	49 F2
LAIN SS15	166 B5
Bourne End EMPK RM11	181 H1
Bourne Gdns CHING E4	132 C7
Bournemouth Park Rd SOSN SS2	9 E1
Bournes Green Cha SBN/FI SS3	196 B3
SOS SS1	196 A4
Bouvel Dr BOC CM0	128 B5
Bouverie Rd CHLM/GWD CM2	4 C5 1
Bouvier Rd PEND EN3	104 C4
Bovey Wy SOCK/AV RM15	199 K5 2
Bovinger Wy SOS SS1	195 J4
Bowbank Cl SBN/FI SS3	196 E4
Bowden Dr EMPK RM11	181 F2 1
Bower Farm Rd ABR/ST RM4	137 H6
Bower Gdns MAL CM9	69 B2
Bower HI EPP CM16	80 E6
Bower La BSDN SS14	168 B5
Bowerman Rd CDH/CHF RM16	215 F3
Bowers Court Dr PIT SS13	169 J8
Bowers Rd SBF/HAD SS7	170 C8
Bower V EPP CM16	80 E6
Bowes Dr CHONG SS5	84 B3
Bowfell Dr VGE SS16	166 B8
Bowhay RBRW/HUT CM13	142 A5
Bowles Gn EN EN1	104 B2
Bowman Av LOS SS9	172 C7
Bowmont Cl RBRW/HUT CM13	142 A2
Bown Cl TIL RM18	215 G8 1
Bowness Wy HCH RM12	180 B6 2
Bowood Rd PEND EN3	104 D6
Box Cl LAIN SS15	6 B1 1
Boxford Cl RAYL SS6	170 E2 2
Boxmoor Rd CRW RM5	137 H8
Boxted Cl BKHH IG9	134 B4
Boyce Gn SBF/HAD SS7	190 C3
Boyce Hill Cl LOS SS9	172 C8
Boyce Rd SBN/FI SS3	197 G5
SLH/COR SS17	203 J2
Boyce View Dr SBF/HAD SS7	190 A3
Boyd Ct WICKW SS12	147 J8 1
Boyden Cl SOSN SS2	195 J3
Boyne Dr CHLM/WR CM1	35 F7
Boyton Cl SBF/HAD SS7	170 E8
Boytons LAIN SS15	6 C4
Brabant Rd CHLM CM3	124 C6
Brabner Gdns BCAYE CM11	145 K1
Bracelet Cl SLH/COR SS17	187 G8 3
Brace Wk RCHLM CM3	122 E8
Bracken Cl LOU IG10	107 K5
Brackendale BCAYE CM11	144 E2
Brackendale Av PIT SS13	189 F1
Brackendale Cl HOC/HUL SS5	151 F6 1
Brackendale Gdns UPMR RM14	181 K5
Bracken Dell RAYL SS6	171 K3
Brackenden Dr CHLM/WR CM1	35 F6
Brackens Dr BRW CM14	141 G8
The Brackens CHING E4	132 D5
Bracken Wy SBF/HAD SS7	171 F6
Brackley Crs PIT SS13	168 D4
Bradbourne Rd GRAYS RM17	214 A5 1
Bradbourne Wy PIT SS13	169 F8 1
Bradd Cl SOCK/AV RM15	200 A3 2
Bradford Bury LOS SS9	172 D7
Bradford St CHLM/GWD CM2	4 B4
Bradleigh Av GRAYS RM17	214 B3
Bradley Av SBF/HAD SS7	190 E1
Bradley Cl CVI SS8	191 F8
SBF/HAD SS7	170 E8
Bradley Link SBF/HAD SS7	170 E8 1
Bradley Rd PEND EN3	104 E4
Bradley Wy RCFD SS4	174 B4
Bradshaw Rd CDH/CHF RM16	200 E8
Bradwell Cl HCH RM12	180 C7 2
Bradwell Gn RBRW/HUT CM13	142 B2 1
Bradwell Rd BKHH IG9	134 B4
BOC CM0	72 E7
BOC CM0	74 A8
BOC CM0	100 A2
Brady Av LOU IG10	108 A6
Braemar Av CHLM/GWD CM2	4 B5
Braemar Crs LOS SS9	192 B3
Braemar Gdns EMPK RM11	161 H8
Braemore CVI SS8	190 B8 1
Brairwood Cl LOS SS9	172 E8
Braiswick Pl LAIN SS15	166 C5
Braithwaite Rd PEND EN3	105 F7
Bramble Cl LOS SS9	172 C6
Bramble Crs SBF/HAD SS7	172 B8
Bramble La UPMR RM14	198 E1
Bramble Ri HLW CM20	2 C2
Bramble Rd CVI SS8	208 C1
LOS SS9	172 C6
SBF/HAD SS7	172 A7
The Brambles CHES/WCR EN8	76 D5
BOC CM0	128 D2 1
Bramble Tye LAIN SS15	7 D1
The Bramblings CHING E4	132 E7
Bramerton Rd HOC/HUL SS5	150 E7
Bramfield Rd East RAYL SS6	172 B3
Bramfield Rd West RAYL SS6	172 A3 1
Bramley Gdns LAIN SS15	6 A2 3
Bramleys SLH/COR SS17	203 K2
Bramley Shaw WAB EN9	78 B7
The Bramleys RCFD SS4	152 A8 1
Bramley Wy RCHLM CM3	98 E4
Brampstead LAIN SS15	166 B7 2
Brampton Cl CHESW EN7	76 A2
SLH/COR SS17	187 H8
WOS/PRIT SS0	193 H1
Bramston Cl CHLM/GWD CM2	63 H5
Bramston Link LAIN SS15	165 K6
Bramston Wy LAIN SS15	165 K7
Bramwoods Rd CHLM/GWD CM2	5 F5
Branch Rd BARK/HLT IG6	136 A8
SBF/HAD SS7	191 K3
Brancroft Wy PEND EN3	104 E5
Brandenburg Rd CVI SS8	191 J8
Brandon Cl BCAYW CM12	117 G8
Brandon Groves Av	
SOCK/AV RM15	200 A3
Brandon St GVW DA11	219 G6
Branfill Rd UPMR RM14	181 J3
Branksome Av HOC/HUL SS5	151 F5
SLH/COR SS17	203 K1
WICKW SS12	146 C6
Branksome Rd SLH/COR SS17	203 J2
Branksome Rd SOSN SS2	9 E3
Branscombe Gdns SOS SS1	196 A5

Branscombe Sq SOS SS1 .... 196 A4
Branscombe Wk SOS SS1 .... 196 A4 1
Braxted Cl RCFD SS4 .... 173 K1
Braybrooke BSDN SS14 .... 7 F4
Bray Ct SBN/FI SS3 .... 196 D3
Brayers Ms RCFD SS4 .... 174 C4 1
Brays La RCFD SS4 .... 152 B8
Brays Md HLWS CM18 .... 3 F5
Braziers Cl CHLM/GWD CM2 .... 90 E2
Breach Rd WTHK RM20 .... 212 C5
Break Egg HI BCAYE CM11 .... 144 E2
Breams Fld VGE SS16 .... 6 A6
Brecon Cl PIT SS13 .... 169 F5 1
Brecon Rd PEND EN3 .... 104 C8
Bree HI RCHLM CM3 .... 122 C7
Brempsons BSDN SS14 .... 7 E3
Brendans Cl UPMR RM11 .... 181 F2 2
Brendon Dr CHLM/WR CM1 .... 62 A4 1
Brendon Wy WOS/PRIT SS0 .... 173 H8
Brennan Rd TIL RM18 .... 215 G8
Brent Av RCHLM CM3 .... 122 D4
Brentwood Pl BRWN CM15 .... 141 G4
Brentwood Rd CDH/CHF RM16 .... 202 C3
  CHONG CM5 .... 84 C5
  GPK RM2 .... 160 D7
  RBRW/HUT CM13 .... 142 A8
  ROM RM1 .... 160 A8
  UPMR RM14 .... 185 F4
Bressey Av EN EN1 .... 104 A5
Bressingham Gdns RCHLM CM3 .... 122 C6
Brettenham Dr SOS SS1 .... 195 H5
Brevet Cl PUR RM19 .... 212 A3
Brewhouse Yd GVE DA12 .... 219 G4 1
Brewster Ct CHLM/GWD CM2 .... 62 D7
Brian Cl CHLM/GWD CM2 .... 62 D7
  HCH RM12 .... 180 C5 1
Briar Cl CHES/WCR EN8 .... 76 C3
  BCAYE CM11 .... 144 E6 1
  BKHH IG9 .... 134 A5
  HOC/HUL SS5 .... 173 G1
Briarleas Gdns UPMR RM14 .... 182 B5
Briarley Cl BROX EN10 .... 49 F4
Briar Md LAIN SS15 .... 166 C6
Briar Rd HARH RM3 .... 160 D2
The Briars CHES/WCR EN8 .... 76 E5
  HLWS CM18 .... 3 E6 1
Briars Wk HARH RM3 .... 161 F4
Briarswood CHLM/WR CM1 .... 35 F6 2
  CVI SS8 .... 191 F8
Briar Vw BCAYE CM11 .... 144 E6 2
Briarwood BRWN CM15 .... 113 H3
Briarwood Dr LOS SS9 .... 172 E8
The Briary WICKW SS12 .... 146 E6 1
Briceway SLH/COR SS17 .... 204 B1 2
Brickcroft BROX EN10 .... 48 E8 1
Brickfield Cl VGE SS16 .... 188 A3
Brickfield Rd EPP CM16 .... 181 H3
  VGE SS16 .... 188 A3
Brickfields Rd RCHLM CM3 .... 122 E6
Brickfields Wy RCFD SS4 .... 174 D4
Brick House La RCHLM CM3 .... 36 C4
Brick Kiln Rd CHLM/GWD CM2 .... 64 A6
Brick La EN EN1 .... 104 B6
  PEND EN3 .... 104 C6
Brickwall Cl BOC CM0 .... 155 G1
Bridge Av UPMR RM14 .... 181 H4
Bridge Cl EN EN1 .... 104 B5 1
  RBRW/HUT CM13 .... 141 H6
  SBN/FI SS3 .... 196 D6
Bridgecote La LAIN SS15 .... 167 G3
Bridge Cft RCHLM CM3 .... 20 B3
Bridge HI EPP CM16 .... 80 D7
Bridge House Cl WICKW SS12 .... 147 F6 1
Bridgemans Gn RCHLM CM3 .... 97 J7
Bridgemarsh La RCHLM CM3 .... 126 D6
Bridgend Cl RCHLM CM3 .... 122 E5 1
Bridgend Rd EN EN1 .... 104 C1
Bridge Rd CHONG CM5 .... 55 J3
  ERITH DA8 .... 210 B7
  GRAYS RM17 .... 214 A5
  SBN/FI SS3 .... 178 A8
  WICKE SS11 .... 147 K6
Bridge St CHLM/WR CM1 .... 61 H4
  LAIN SS15 .... 167 F3
Bridgewick Rd BOC CM0 .... 102 C5
Bridgwater Dr LOS SS9 .... 173 G8
  WOS/PRIT SS0 .... 193 H1
Bridgwater Rd HARH RM3 .... 138 D8
Bridgwater Wk HARH RM3 .... 138 D8 1
Bridle Cl PEND EN3 .... 105 F3
Bridleway CHLM/WR CM1 .... 35 F8
Bridon Cl RCHLM CM3 .... 93 F7 1
Bridport Rd CHLM/WR CM1 .... 35 F8
Brierley Cl EMPK RM11 .... 160 D8
Brighten Rd WOS/PRIT SS0 .... 8 C4
Brighton Av SOS SS1 .... 195 G4
Brightside BCAYW CM12 .... 143 K1
Brightside Cl BCAYW CM12 .... 143 K1
The Brightside PEND EN3 .... 104 D5
Brightwell Av WOS/PRIT SS0 .... 8 A2
Brimfield Rd PUR RM19 .... 212 A3
Brimsdown Av PEND EN3 .... 104 E5
Brimstone Av LAIN SS15 .... 166 C7
Brindles CVI SS8 .... 207 K1

EMPK RM11 .... 161 F6
Brindles Cl RBRW/HUT CM13 .... 142 B5
  TIL RM18 .... 216 B3
Brindwood Rd CHING E4 .... 132 B6
The Bringey CHLM/GWD CM2 .... 62 B8
Brinkworth La HOC/HUL SS5 .... 151 G7 1
Brinley Cl CHES/WCR EN8 .... 76 D5
Brinsmead Rd HARH RM3 .... 161 H4
Briscoe Rd PIT SS13 .... 168 E6
Bristol Av RAYL SS6 .... 149 H8
Bristol Rd GVE DA12 .... 219 J8
  SOSN SS2 .... 174 A7
Bristowe Av CHLM/GWD CM2 .... 63 J8
Bristowe Dr CDH/CHF RM16 .... 202 D6
Britannia Gdns WOS/PRIT SS0 .... 193 K5
Britannia La CHES/WCR EN8 .... 77 F8
  BRW CM14 .... 141 FB
  WOS/PRIT SS0 .... 193 K5
British Legion Rd CHING E4 .... 133 G6 1
Britten Cl VGE SS16 .... 166 B8
Britten Crs CHLM/GWD CM2 .... 63 H5
Brittons La ING CM4 .... 118 B5
Brixham Cl RAYL SS6 .... 149 J8
Broad Cl HLW CM20 .... 151 F7
Broadclyst Av LOS SS9 .... 172 E8
Broadclyst Cl SOS SS1 .... 195 K4 1
Broadclyst Gdns SOS SS1 .... 196 A4 1
Broadfield HLW CM20 .... 3 E2
Broadfield Cl ROM RM1 .... 160 A7 1
Broadfields SBW CM21 .... 11 F4
Broadfield Sq EN EN1 .... 104 B7
Broadfield Wy BKHH IG8 .... 133 K6
Broadgate WAB EN9 .... 78 B7
Broadhope Rd SLH/COR SS17 .... 203 J5
Broadlands GRAYS RM17 .... 213 J4
  SBF/HAD SS7 .... 170 E7
Broadlands Av HOC/HUL SS5 .... 151 G6
  PEND EN3 .... 104 B7
  RAYL SS6 .... 171 J2
Broadlands Cl PEND EN3 .... 104 C7 1
Broadlands Rd HOC/HUL SS5 .... 151 G7
Broadlawn LOS SS9 .... 192 D1
Bradley Rd HLWW/ROY CM19 .... 51 H1
Broadmayne BSDN SS14 .... 167 K7
Broad Meadow BRWN CM15 .... 113 H4
Broad Oak WFD IG8 .... 133 J8
Broadoak Av PEND EN3 .... 104 D1
Broad Oak Cl CHING E4 .... 132 B8
Broadoaks EPP CM16 .... 80 D6
Broad Oaks WICKW SS12 .... 147 H7
Broadoak Wy RAYL SS6 .... 171 K3
Broad Pde HOC/HUL SS5 .... 151 G7 2
Broadstone Rd HCH RM12 .... 180 B3 2
Broad Street Green Rd MAL CM9 .... 40 E5
Broadstrood LOU IG10 .... 107 J4
Broadview Av CDH/CHF RM16 .... 214 C1
Broad Wk HOC/HUL SS5 .... 151 G7
The Broad Wk (North)
  RBRW/HUT CM13 .... 141 K6 1
The Broadwalk (South)
  RBRW/HUT CM13 .... 141 K7 1
Broadwater Gn LAIN SS15 .... 166 A7 1
Broad Wy HOC/HUL SS5 .... 151 G6
Broadway GPK RM2 .... 160 B5
  GRAYS RM17 .... 214 B5
  LOS SS9 .... 193 F5
  TIL RM18 .... 214 E2 2
Broadway Av HLWE CM17 .... 25 F1
The Broadway HCH RM12 .... 180 C5
  LOU IG10 .... 108 A7
  SOS SS1 .... 195 K7
  WICKW SS12 .... 147 G6
Broadway West LOS SS9 .... 192 E5 1
Brockenhurst Dr SLH/COR SS17 .... 203 J5 1
Brockenhurst Wy RCHLM CM3 .... 93 K4
Brocket Cl CHIG IG7 .... 135 J7
Brockett Rd CDH/CHF RM16 .... 215 G2 1
Brocket Wy CHIG IG7 .... 135 H8
Brock Gn SOCK/AV RM15 .... 199 K6 3
Brock HI WICKE SS11 .... 119 K8
Brock Hill Dr WICKE SS11 .... 147 F2
Brockles Md HLWW/ROY CM19 .... 52 A1
Brockley Gv HLWW/ROY CM13 .... 141 K4
Brockley Rd CHLM/GWD CM2 .... 5 E3
Brocksford Av RAYL SS6 .... 172 A4
Brocksparkwood
  RBRW/HUT CM13 .... 142 A6
Brockton Cl ROM RM1 .... 160 A6 1
Brodie Rd CHING E4 .... 132 B4
  SBN/FI SS3 .... 197 G4
Brodie Wk WICKW SS12 .... 147 J8 2
Brograve Cl CHLM/GWD CM2 .... 91 F2
Bromefield Ct WAB EN9 .... 78 C7 1
Bromfelde Rd BCAYE CM11 .... 145 K8
Bromfords Cl WICKW SS12 .... 146 E8
Bromfords Dr WICKW SS12 .... 146 E8
Bromleigh Cl CHES/WCR EN8 .... 76 E2 1
Bromley GRAYS RM17 .... 213 J5 1
Bromley Ms RAYL SS6 .... 171 F2 1
Brompton Cl BCAYW CM12 .... 117 G8 3
Brompton Dr ERITH DA8 .... 210 C6
Brompton Gdns MAL CM9 .... 68 A5 1
Bronte Cl TIL RM18 .... 215 H8
Bronte Vw GVE DA12 .... 219 H6
Brook Cl GPK RM2 .... 160 A3

MAL CM9 .... 40 C?
MAL CM9 .... 66 D3
RCFD SS4 .... 174 D?
Brook Crs CHING E4 .... 132 B?
Brookdale Av UPMR RM14 .... 181 H?
Brookdale Cl UPMR RM14 .... 181 J4
Brook Dr SLH/COR SS17 .... 187 K
  WICKW SS12 .... 147 F
Brook End SBW CM21 .... 11 H
Brook End Rd CHLM/GWD CM2 .... 63 J1
Brooke Rd GRAYS RM17 .... 213 H
Brooker Rd WAB EN9 .... 77 J?
Brooke Sq MAL CM9 .... 68 C4
Brookfield EPP CM16 .... 53 G
Brookfield Cl RBRW/HUT CM13 .... 142 B?
Brookfield Gdns CHES/WCR EN8 .... 76 D
Brookfield La CHES/WCR EN8 .... 76 C?
Brookfield La East CHES/WCR EN8 .... 76 D
Brookfield La West CHES/WCR EN8 .... 76 C
Brookfields CHONG CM5 .... 56 B
  LOS SS9 .... 172 E
  PEND EN3 .... 104 D
  SBW CM21 .... 11 H
Brookfields Cl LOS SS9 .... 172 E
Brook Gdns CHING E4 .... 132 C
Brook HI RCHLM CM3 .... 20 D
Brookhouse Gdns CHING E4 .... 133 F7
Brookhurst Cl CHLM/GWD CM2 .... 5 E2
Brooklands WICKW SS12 .... 146 E
Brooklands Av LOS SS9 .... 173 F
Brooklands Gdns EMPK RM11 .... 159 F
Brooklands Pk LAIN SS15 .... 166 A
Brooklands Sq CVI SS8 .... 207 J?
Brooklands Wk CHLM/GWD CM2 .... 4 B
Brooklane Fld HLWS CM18 .... 25 F
Brooklyn Av LOU IG10 .... 107 G
Brooklyn Dr RAYL SS6 .... 149 J
Brookman's Av CDH/CHF RM16 .... 201 G
Brookmans Cl UPMR RM14 .... 182 B
Brookmans Rd ING CM4 .... 117 K
Brook Md LAIN SS15 .... 166 A
  RCHLM CM3 .... 20 A
Brook Ri CHIG IG7 .... 134 D
Brook Rd CHES/WCR EN8 .... 77 F
  BKHH IG9 .... 133 H
  BOC CM0 .... 73 K
  BRW CM14 .... 140 C
  EPP CM16 .... 80 E
  GPK RM2 .... 160 A
  GVW DA11 .... 218 D
  LOU IG10 .... 134 B
  RAYL SS6 .... 171 H
  SBF/HAD SS7 .... 190 B
  SBW CM21 .... 11 H
Brookside BCAYE CM11 .... 117 J
  CVI SS8 .... 191 F8
  EMPK RM11 .... 161 F
  HLWW/ROY CM19 .... 23 H
  HOC/HUL SS5 .... 173 G?
  WAB EN9 .... 78 A6
Brookside Av SBN/FI SS3 .... 197 H
Brookside Gdns EN EN1 .... 104 B
Brook St BRW CM14 .... 140 B
  CHLM/WR CM1 .... 4 C
Brook Vw CHLM/GWD CM2 .... 64 A
Brook Wy CHIG IG7 .... 134 D
Broome Pl SOCK/AV RM15 .... 199 F?
Broome Rd BCAYE CM11 .... 117 K
Broomer Pl CHES/WCR EN8 .... 76 C
Broomfield HLW CM20 .... 3 F?
  SBF/HAD SS7 .... 191 J
Broomfield Av BROX EN10 .... 48 E
  LOS SS9 .... 173 G
  LOU IG10 .... 134 C
  RAYL SS6 .... 171 F2
Broomfield Gn CVI SS8 .... 190 E
Broomfield Rd CHLM/WR CM1 .... 4 B
Broomfields PIT SS13 .... 168 D
  RBSF CM22 .... 13 G
Broomfords Dr WICKW SS12 .... 146 E
Broomhall Cl CHLM/WR CM1 .... 34 D3
Broomhall Rd CHLM/WR CM1 .... 34 C
Broomhills Cha BCAYW CM12 .... 144 B8
Broom Rd HOC/HUL SS5 .... 149 K
Broomstick Hall Rd WAB EN9 .... 78 A
Broomways SBN/FI SS3 .... 197 H
Broomwood Gdns BRWN CM15 .... 140 D
Broomwood La ING CM4 .... 118 C
Broseley Gdns HARH RM3 .... 139 F
Broseley Rd HARH RM3 .... 139 F
Brougham Cl SBN/FI SS3 .... 197 F
Broughton Rd RCHLM CM3 .... 122 E
  SBF/HAD SS7 .... 191 J
Browne Cl BRW CM14 .... 140 E
Browning Av SOSN SS2 .... 174 E
Browning Cl MAL CM9 .... 68 C
Brownings Av CHLM/WR CM1 .... 34 C
Brownlow Bend BSDN SS14 .... 168 A
Brownlows Cl GTDUN CM6 .... 16 A
Brown Rd GVE DA12 .... 219 H

rowns Av WICKE SS11 .... 147 J3
roxburn Dr SOCK/AV RM15 .... 199 K6
SOCK/AV RM15 .... 200 A7 1
roxhill Rd ABR/ST RM4 .... 138 B6
roxted Dr WICKW SS12 .... 147 H7
ruce Av HCH RM12 .... 180 D3
ruce Gv CHLM/GWD CM2 .... 4 B6
WICKE SS11 .... 147 K7
ruce Rd CHLM/WR CM1 .... 61 H4
ruces Wharf Rd GRAYS RM17 ...... 213 K5
ruce Wy CHES/WCR EN8 .... 76 D7
ruges CVI SS8 .... 208 C3 3
rundish PIT SS13 .... 168 D8
runel CI TIL RM18 .... 215 G8
runel Rd LOS SS9 .... 172 D6
SBF/HAD SS7 .... 170 C6
WFD IG8 .... 134 C8
runel Wy RCHLM CM3 .... 122 C6
runswick Av UPMR RM14 .... 182 B1
runswick PI RAYL SS6 .... 149 F8
runswick Rd SOS SS1 .... 195 G5
WAB EN9 .... 105 G4
runswick Wk GVE DA12 .... 219 J4 1
ryant Av HARH RM3 .... 160 E4
SOS SS1 .... 195 H7
ryant's La MAL CM9 .... 66 D6
ryn Farm CI BSDN SS14 .... 167 K5
ryn-y-mawr Rd EN EN1 .... 104 A8
ryant Av CVI SS8 .... 190 E8
runwins CI WICKE SS11 .... 147 J6
russum Rd CVI SS8 .... 208 D3 1
ruton Av WOS/PRIT SS0 .... 173 H8
ryanstone Rd CHES/WCR EN8 ..... 77 F8
ryanston Rd TIL RM18 .... 215 H8
ryant Av HARH RM3 .... 160 E4
SOS SS1 .... 195 H7
uchanan CI SOCK/AV RM15 .... 198 E8 2
uchanan Gdns WICKW SS12 .... 147 H8 2
uchanan Wy RCHLM CM3 .... 97 J8
uckeridge Wy BOC CM0 .... 74 D2 1
uckerills PIT SS13 .... 168 D8
uckhatch La RCHLM CM3 .... 93 H8
uckhurst Wy BKHH IG9 .... 134 A6
uckingham CI EMPK RM11 .... 160 E7 1
uckingham Ct CHLM/GWD CM2 .... 63 H1
uckingham Hill Rd
CDH/CHF RM16 .... 203 F8
uckingham Rd GVW DA11 .... 218 C5 1
HOC/HUL SS5 .... 150 E7
LAIN SS15 .... 6 C2 1
uckland SBN/FI SS3 .... 196 B4
ucklebury Heath RCHLM CM3 ..... 122 C7
ucklers CI BROX EN10 .... 49 F4
ucklers Ct BRW CM14 .... 141 F8
uckles La SOCK/AV RM15 .... 200 A5
uckley CI DART DA1 .... 210 A8
SLH/COR SS17 .... 187 G8
uckleys CHLM/GWD CM2 .... 63 H6
uckrell Rd CHING E4 .... 132 E5
ucks Cross Rd GVW DA11 .... 218 E8
uckwyns Cha BCAYW CM12 .... 116 E7 1
uckwyns Ct BCAYW CM12 .... 144 A1 1
udna Rd CVI SS8 .... 190 E8
uglers Ri CHLM/WR CM1 .... 61 H5
ulbecks Wk RCHLM CM3 .... 122 D8
ull CI CDH/CHF RM16 .... 213 J1 1
VGE SS16 .... 168 B8
uller Rd LAIN SS15 .... 166 C6
RCHLM CM3 .... 124 C4
ullfields SBW CM21 .... 11 J2
ull La HOC/HUL SS5 .... 150 D7
MAL CM9 .... 68 B2
RAYL SS6 .... 149 G8
ull's Cross ENC/FH EN2 .... 104 A2
ulls Cross Ride CHESW EN7 .... 76 A8
ullsmoor CI CHES/WCR EN8 ...... 104 C1 1
ullsmoor Gdns CHES/WCR EN8 . 104 C1 3
ullsmoor La EN EN1 .... 104 B1
PEND EN3 .... 104 D1
ullsmoor Ride CHES/WCR EN8 ... 104 C1 2
ullsmoor Wy CHES/WCR EN8 ..... 104 B1
ullwell Crs CHES/WCR EN8 .... 76 E1
ullwood Ap HOC/HUL SS5 .... 150 C8
ullwood Hall La HOC/HUL SS5 .... 172 B1
ullwood Rd HOC/HUL SS5 .... 150 E8
ulow Av CVI SS8 .... 208 B2 1
ulphan By-pass UPMR RM14 ...... 185 F3
ulphan CI WICKW SS12 .... 147 H7
ulwark Rd SBN/FI SS3 .... 196 D5
umbles Green La WAB EN9 .... 50 D7
umfords La RCHLM CM3 .... 38 A6
undick's HI CHLM/WR CM1 .... 62 A2
unters Av SBN/FI SS3 .... 196 B7
unting La RCHLM CM3 .... 124 D3
urbage Ct CHES/WCR EN8 .... 76 E5
urches LAIN SS15 .... 6 C1
urches Md SBF/HAD SS7 .... 171 F6
urches Rd SBF/HAD SS7 .... 170 E5
urdett Av WOS/PRIT SS0 .... 8 B4
urdett Rd SOS SS1 .... 9 F6
ure TIL RM18 .... 216 D2
uren Av CVI SS8 .... 208 E2
urfield CI SOS SS9 .... 173 G7
urfield Rd LOS SS9 .... 173 G7
urges Rd EMPK RM11 .... 161 G8
SOS SS1 .... 196 B3
urges Rd SOS SS1 .... 195 K7

Burgess Av SLH/COR SS17 .... 204 A4
Burgess Fld CHLM/GWD CM2 ...... 63 H1
Burges Ter SOS SS1 .... 195 J7
Burghley Rd CDH/CHF RM16 ...... 213 F2
Burghstead CI CHLM/GWD CM2 ... 144 B4 1
Burgundy Gdns PIT SS13 .... 168 E5 1
Burland Rd BRWN CM15 .... 141 G4
Burleigh CI BCAYW CM12 .... 117 H8
Burleigh Rd CHES/WCR EN8 .... 76 E1 1
Burleigh Sq CHLM/WR CM1 .... 196 A5 1
Burlescoombe CI SOS SS1 .... 195 K5 1
Burlescoombe Leas SOS SS1 .... 196 A4 2
Burlescoombe Rd SOS SS1 .... 196 A4
Burley CI CHING E4 .... 132 B8 1
Burley HI HLWE CM17 .... 25 H6
Burlington Ct PIT SS13 .... 168 E5
Burlington Gdns SBF/HAD SS7 ... 192 A2
Burlington PI WFD IG8 .... 133 H6
Burnaby Rd GVW DA11 .... 218 D5
SOS SS1 .... 9 F5
Burncroft Av PEND EN3 .... 104 C6 4
PEND EN3 .... 104 D6 1
Burne Av WICKW SS12 .... 146 E7 1
Burnell Ga CHLM/WR CM1 .... 35 J6
Burnell Wk RBRW/HUT CM13 ..... 163 F1 3
Burnett Pk HLWW/ROY CM19 .... 51 K2 2
Burnett Rd ERITH DA8 .... 210 E5
Burney Dr LOU IG10 .... 108 A7
Burnham Av RCHLM CM3 .... 96 C8
Burnham Rd BOC CM0 .... 128 C3
CHING E4 .... 132 A8
CHLM/WR CM1 .... 35 H7
HOC/HUL SS5 .... 149 K3
LOS SS9 .... 192 D4
MAL CM9 .... 67 F8
RCHLM CM3 .... 98 B8
RCHLM CM3 .... 122 B5
WICKE SS11 .... 148 D2

Burnham Road (Summerhill)
RCHLM CM3 .... 126 D1
Burnley Rd WTHK RM20 .... 212 C7
Burns Av PIT SS13 .... 168 E8
Burns CI ERITH DA8 .... 210 A7
MAL CM9 .... 68 C4 2
Burns Crs CHLM/GWD CM2 .... 4 C5
Burnside CVI SS8 .... 191 F8 2
SBW CM21 .... 11 H3
Burnside Crs CHLM/WR CM1 ...... 34 D6
Burns PI TIL RM18 .... 215 G7
Burns Wy RBRW/HUT CM13 ...... 142 A3
Burnthouse La ING CM4 .... 115 K4
Burntmill CI HLW CM20 .... 24 A2 1
Burntmill La HLW CM20 .... 24 A2
Burnt Mills Rd PIT SS13 .... 168 D5
Burntwood Av EMPK RM11 .... 160 E8
Burntwood CI BCAYW CM12 .... 144 A3
RBRW/HUT CM13 .... 164 C8
Burnway EMPK RM11 .... 181 F1
Burr CI VGE SS16 .... 165 K8
Burr Hill Cha WOS/PRIT SS0 ...... 8 B1
Burrow Av CHIG IG7 .... 135 J8
Burrow Rd CHIG IG7 .... 135 K8
Burrows Wy RAYL SS6 .... 171 H4
Burr's Wy SLH/COR SS17 .... 204 D1
Burrswood PI MAL CM9 .... 69 F2
Bursland Rd PEND EN3 .... 104 D8
Burstead Dr BCAYE CM11 .... 144 E6
Burton CI SLH/COR SS17 .... 187 G8
Burton PI CHLM/GWD CM2 .... 63 H1
Burwell Av CVI SS8 .... 190 E8
Bury Farm La BCAYE CM11 .... 168 A2
Bury Green Rd CHESW EN7 .... 76 A5
Bury Holme BROX EN10 .... 49 F5
Bury La EPP CM16 .... 80 B4
RCHLM CM3 .... 19 K5
Bury Rd CHING E4 .... 105 K8
EPP CM16 .... 80 C5
HLWE CM17 .... 25 G1
Bushbarns CHESW EN7 .... 76 A3
Bushby Av BROX EN10 .... 49 F4
Bush Elms Rd EMPK RM11 .... 180 D1
Bushey CI CHING E4 .... 132 D6
RCHLM CM3 .... 122 E6
Bushey Cft HLWS CM18 .... 3 E3
Bushfields LOU IG10 .... 134 D1
Bush Hall Rd BCAYW CM12 .... 117 H8
Bush Rd BKHH IG9 .... 134 D3
Bushy Md LAIN SS15 .... 166 C5
Butlers CI CHLM/WR CM1 .... 34 D3
Butlers Dr CHING E4 .... 105 J4
Butlers Gv VGE SS16 .... 186 C2 2
Butneys BSDN SS14 .... 7 F3
Butterbur Cha RCHLM CM3 .... 122 C7 1
Buttercross La EPP CM16 .... 80 E4 1
Buttercup CI BCAYW CM12 .... 144 B1 1
HARH RM3 .... 160 E3 2
Buttercup Wy BOC CM0 .... 128 C2
Butterfield Rd RCHLM CM3 .... 36 C5
Buttersweet Ri SBW CM21 .... 11 J4 1
Butterworth Gdns WFD IG8 .... 133 H8 1
Butterys SOS SS1 .... 195 H5
Butt La MAL CM9 .... 68 C3
Buttondene Crs BROX EN10 ...... 49 H4

Button Rd CDH/CHF RM16 .... 213 J3
Buttsbury ING CM4 .... 116 E4
Butt's Green Rd CHLM/GWD CM2 . 92 D1
EMPK RM11 .... 160 E8
Butts La RCHLM CM3 .... 65 J6
SLH/COR SS17 .... 203 J6
Butts Paddock RCFD SS4 .... 153 G3
Butts Rd SLH/COR SS17 .... 203 J4
The Butts BROX EN10 .... 48 E6
Butts Wy CHLM/GWD CM2 .... 90 A2
Buxton Av LOS SS9 .... 192 B2
Buxton CI LOS SS9 .... 192 B2
Buxton Link LAIN SS15 .... 165 K7
Buxton Rd CDH/CHF RM16 .... 214 D1
CHING E4 .... 132 E3
EPP CM16 .... 108 C2
WAB EN9 .... 78 C6
Buxton Sq LOS SS9 .... 192 B2
Buyl Av CVI SS8 .... 191 G8
Byfield LOS SS9 .... 173 G6
Byfletts VGE SS16 .... 188 C1
Byford Rd RAYL SS6 .... 171 K2
Bynghams HLWW/ROY CM19 .... 23 H7
By-pass Rd SLH/COR SS17 .... 203 G3
Byrd CI LAIN SS15 .... 6 A2
Byrd Md BRWN CM15 .... 85 J7 1
Byrne Dr SOSN SS2 .... 174 B8
Byron Av SOSN SS2 .... 9 E2
Byron CI CVI SS8 .... 208 C1
Byron Ct LAIN SS15 .... 166 C7 1
Byron Gdns TIL RM18 .... 215 H7
Byron Rd CHLM/GWD CM2 .... 5 E3
RBRW/HUT CM13 .... 142 C3
Byron Wy HARH RM3 .... 160 D3
Bywater CI RCHLM CM3 .... 122 C7

C

Cabborns Crs SLH/COR SS17 ..... 203 K5
Cabinet Wy LOS SS9 .... 172 D7
Cadmore La CHES/WCR EN8 ..... 76 E2
Cadogan Av RBRW/HUT CM13 ... 164 C8
Caernarvon CI EMPK RM11 .... 181 H2 2
HOC/HUL SS5 .... 150 E7 2
Cagefield Rd RCFD SS4 .... 175 H1
Caister Dr PIT SS13 .... 168 E7
Caladonia La WICKW SS12 .... 147 H8 3
Calbourne Av HCH RM12 .... 180 C6
Calcott CI BRW CM14 .... 140 E4
Calcutta Rd TIL RM18 .... 214 E8
Caldbeck WAB EN9 .... 77 K8
Caldecot Wy BROX EN10 .... 49 F4 1
Caldwell Rd SLH/COR SS17 ...... 203 H4
Callan Gv SOCK/AV RM15 .... 200 A7
Callowood Cft RCHLM CM3 .... 95 K4
Calmore CI HCH RM12 .... 180 D6
Calshot Av CDH/CHF RM16 .... 213 J1
Calvert Dr PIT SS13 .... 169 F4 1
Calvina CI LAIN SS15 .... 167 G3
Camborne Av HARH RM3 .... 161 F2
Camborne Wy HARH RM3 .... 161 G2 2
Cambria CI CVI SS8 .... 207 G2 2
Cambrian Gv GVW DA11 .... 219 F5
Cambridge Av GPK RM2 .... 160 D5
Cambridge CI CHES/WCR EN8 ... 76 C3 1
ING CM4 .... 117 K3 2
VGE SS16 .... 166 A8 3
Cambridge Gdns
CDH/CHF RM16 .... 215 F3 1
EN EN1 .... 104 A6 1
RCFD SS4 .... 151 K8 2
Cambridge Rd CHING E4 .... 132 E4 1
CVI SS8 .... 207 K2
HLW CM20 .... 11 G3
SOS SS1 .... 8 C5
Camden CI CDH/CHF RM16 .... 215 G3
GVW DA11 .... 218 B6
Camden Rd CDH/CHF RM16 ...... 213 H2
Camellia CI CHLM/WR CM1 .... 35 H7 2
HARH RM3 .... 161 F3 2
Camelot CI CHLM/WR CM1 .... 34 B8 2
Camelot Gdns PIT SS13 .... 169 F5
Cameron CI BRW CM14 .... 141 F7
ING CM4 .... 116 B2
LOS SS9 .... 192 D3
SLH/COR SS17 .... 187 F7
Cameron Dr CHES/WCR EN8 ..... 76 D8
Cameron PI WICKW SS12 .... 147 H8
Cam Gn SOCK/AV RM15 .... 199 K6
Camomile Dr WICKE SS11 .... 147 H5
Campbell CI CHLM/GWD CM2 ..... 4 B6
HLWE CM17 .... 25 F6 1
WICKW SS12 .... 147 G8 1
Campbell Rd GVW DA11 .... 218 E6
Camperdown Rd CVI SS8 .... 191 H8 1
Camper Rd SOS SS1 .... 195 G7
Campfield Rd SBN/FI SS3 .... 196 D7 2
Campine CI CHES/WCR EN8 ...... 76 D2 1
Campion Gdns WFD IG8 .... 133 H8
Campions LOU IG10 .... 107 J4
Cample La SOCK/AV RM15 .... 199 J7
Canada La BROX EN10 .... 48 E7

Canada Rd ERITH DA8 .... 210 O5
The Canadas BROX EN10 .... 48 E7 1
Canal Basin GVE DA12 .... 219 J4
Canal Rd GVE DA12 .... 219 J4
Canberra Cl CHLM/WR CM1 ...... 34 A8
  HCH RM12 .... 180 D5 1
Canberra Sq TIL RM18 .... 215 F8 1
Can Bridge Wy CHLM/GWD CM2... 5 D4
Cander Wy SOCK/AV RM15 .... 199 K7 1
The Candlemakers SOSN SS2 .... 174 D8
Candover Rd HCH RM12 .... 180 C2
Candytuft Rd CHLM/GWD CM2 .... 35 H7
Cane Hl HARH RM3 .... 160 E4
Canes La HLWE CM17 .... 53 J4
Canewdon Cl WICKE SS11 .... 147 G3
Canewdon Gdns WICKE SS11 ..... 147 G3
Canewdon Hall RCFD SS4 .... 153 G3
Canewdon Rd RCFD SS4 .... 151 K5
  WOS/PRIT SS0 .... 8 A4
Canewdon View Rd RCFD SS4 .... 152 A7
Canford Av WICKW SS12 .... 146 C5
Canford Cl CHLM/GWD CM2 .... 5 F6
Canney Rd BOC CM0 .... 71 G8
Cannon Leys CHLM/GWD CM2 .... 90 G2
Cannon Ms WAB EN9 .... 77 H7
Cannons La CHONG CM5 .... 57 G3
Cannons Md BRWN CM15 .... 85 J7
Canon Cl SLH/COR SS17 .... 204 B3
Canons Brook HLWW/ROY CM19 .. 2 A3
Canons Cl RCHLM CM3 .... 93 J4 1
Canons Ga CHES/WCR EN8 .... 49 F8
  HLW CM20 .... 2 A1
Canonsleigh Crs LOS SS9 .... 193 F4
Canterbury Av SOSN SS2 .... 195 H2
  UPMR RM14 .... 182 C2
Canterbury Cl BSDN SS14 .... 168 C5 2
  CHIG IG7 .... 135 J6
  RAYL SS6 .... 149 H8
Canterbury Rd GVE DA12 .... 219 H7 1
Canterbury Wy CHLM/WR CM1 ... 62 A1
  RBRW/HUT CM13 .... 163 F1 4
  WTHK RM20 .... 212 B6
The Canters SBF/HAD SS7 .... 171 G8
Canuden Rd CHLM/WR CM1 ...... 62 A4
Canute Cl RCFD SS4 .... 153 H3
Canvey Rd CVI SS8 .... 190 O6
  LOS SS9 .... 192 C4
  PIT SS13 .... 169 J7
Canvey Wk CHLM/WR CM1 .... 35 G2
Canvey Wy CVI SS8 .... 190 B6
  SBF/HAD SS7 .... 189 K2
Capadocia St SOS SS1 .... 195 H7
Capel Cl CHLM/WR CM1 .... 34 D6
  SLH/COR SS17 .... 204 A3
Capel Rd EN EN1 .... 24 B1
Capel Ter SOS SS1 .... 9 D5 1
Capon Cl BRW CM14 .... 140 E4
Capons La RCHLM CM3 .... 66 A7
Captains Wood Rd MAL CM9 ...... 40 C3
The Caravan Site SOCK/AV RM15 . 212 A4
Caravel Cl CDH/CHF RM16 .... 213 J2
Carbis Cl CHING E4 .... 132 E4 2
Carbury Cl HCH RM12 .... 180 D7
Cardiff Rd PEND EN3 .... 104 B8
Cardigan Av WOS/PRIT SS0 ...... 193 K2
Card's Rd CHLM/GWD CM2 .... 64 A7
Carfax Rd HCH RM12 .... 180 A5
Carisbrooke Cl EMPK RM11 ...... 181 H2 3
  PIT SS13 .... 168 E7 1
Carisbrooke Dr RCHLM CM3 ..... 122 C6
  SLH/COR SS17 .... 204 C1
Carisbrooke Rd BRWN CM15 ..... 140 E2
  WOS/PRIT SS0 .... 8 B3
Carleton Rd CHES/WCR EN8 ..... 76 D1
Carlina Gdns WFD IG8 .... 133 J8
Carlingford Dr WOS/PRIT SS0 .... 193 K2
Carlisle Av ROM RM1 .... 160 A7
Carlisle Cl PIT SS13 .... 168 E7
Carlisle Wy PIT SS13 .... 168 E7
Carlton Av WOS/PRIT SS0 .... 193 K1
Carlton Cl UPMR RM14 .... 181 J3
Carlton Dr LOS SS9 .... 193 G4
  SBF/HAD SS7 .... 191 H1
Carlton Rd CDH/CHF RM16 .... 214 E1
  GPK RM2 .... 160 B7
  PIT SS13 .... 169 H5
  WICKE SS11 .... 147 F3
Carlyle Gdns BCAYW CM12 .... 117 F8
  WICK RM8 .... 147 H8
Carmania Cl SBN/FI SS3 .... 196 E4
Carnaby Rd BROX EN10 .... 48 E2
Carnach Gn SOCK/AV RM15 ...... 199 K7
Carnarvon Rd SOSN SS2 .... 8 C3
Carnation Cl CHLM/WR CM1 ...... 35 H8
Carnforth Gdns HCH RM12 .... 180 B6
Carnival Cl BSDN SS14 .... 7 F1
Carol Cl LAIN SS15 .... 6 B3
Caroline's Cl SOSN SS2 .... 174 B8 2
Caro Rd CVI SS8 .... 208 C2
Carpenter Cl BCAYW CM12 .... 144 A4
Carpenter Pth
  RBRW/HUT CM13 .... 142 C1 1
Carpenters SBN/FI SS3 .... 176 C7
Carpenters Arms La EPP CM16.... 53 F7
Carpenters Rd EN EN1 .... 104 C2
Carriage Dr CHLM/WR CM1 .... 35 G6

Carroll Hl LOU IG10 .... 107 H7
Carron Md RCHLM CM3 .... 123 F7
Carruthers Dr WICKE SS11 .... 147 G4
Carsey Cl BCAYE CM11 .... 145 K1
Carson Rd BCAYE CM11 .... 117 K8
Carswell Cl RBRW/HUT CM13 .... 142 C2 1
Carte Cl PUR RM19 .... 212 A3
Carte Pl VGE SS16 .... 166 B8
Carter Dr CRW RM5 .... 137 G2
Carterhatch La EN EN1 .... 104 A6
  PEND EN3 .... 104 C6 5
Carterhatch Rd PEND EN3 .... 104 E6
Cartersfield Rd WAB EN9 .... 77 J8
Carters La EPP CM16 .... 51 K6
Carters Md HLWE CM17 .... 25 F6
Cart La CHING E4 .... 133 F4
Cartlodge Av WICKE SS11 .... 147 H5
Cartwright Rd SBF/HAD SS7 ..... 170 C6
Cartwright Wk CHLM/GWD CM2 .. 63 H3 1
Carvers Wd BCAYE CM11 .... 144 D6 1
Cascade Rd BKHH IG9 .... 134 A5
Casey La BOC CM0 .... 102 A1
Cashiobury Ter SOS SS1 .... 8 C5 1
Cashmere Wy VGE SS16 .... 188 A2
Cassandra Ga CHES/WCR EN8 ... 77 F1
Cassel Av CVI SS8 .... 191 J3
Cassino Rd CHLM/WR CM1 .... 34 A7 2
Castellan Av GPK RM2 .... 160 C5
Castell Rd LOU IG10 .... 108 A5
Castle Av SBF/HAD SS7 .... 191 J4
Castle Cl HARH RM3 .... 138 D6
  RAYL SS6 .... 171 H4
  SBN/FI SS3 .... 197 G1
Castle Cl RAYL SS6 .... 171 H4 1
Castle Dr LOS SS9 .... 192 C5
  RAYL SS6 .... 171 H2
Castle La SBF/HAD SS7 .... 191 K3
Castle Rd GRAYS RM17 .... 213 H5
  PEND EN3 .... 104 E5
  RAYL SS6 .... 171 H4
  SBF/HAD SS7 .... 191 K3
Castle St CHONG CM5 .... 84 C3
Castle Ter RAYL SS6 .... 171 H3 1
Castleton Rd SOSN SS2 .... 195 H4
Castle View Rd CVI SS8 .... 191 F7
Caswell Cl SLH/COR SS17 .... 204 C1
Caswell Ms CHLM/GWD CM2 ..... 63 H3 2
Catalina Av CDH/CHF RM16 ...... 213 J1
Catchpole La MAL CM9 .... 40 C1
Caterham St WAB EN9 .... 78 B8
Cater Wd BCAYW CM12 .... 144 C2
Catharine Cl CDH/CHF RM16 .... 213 J1
Cathedral Dr LAIN SS15 .... 6 A3
Catherine Cl BRWN CM15 .... 140 D1
Catherine Rd GPK RM2 .... 160 C7
  PEND EN3 .... 104 E6
  SBF/HAD SS7 .... 190 C1
Catisfield Rd PEND EN3 .... 104 E3
Cattawade End BSDN SS14 ...... 168 A6
Cattawade Link BSDN SS14 ...... 168 A6
Caulfield Rd SBN/FI SS3 .... 196 B6
Causeway Br SOCK/AV RM15 .... 212 B2
The Causeway CHLM/GWD CM2 .. 63 H1
  CHLM/WR CM1 .... 60 D7
  MAL CM9 .... 38 D7
  MAL CM9 .... 68 C1
Caustonway RAYL SS6 .... 171 J1
Cavell Rd BCAYE CM11 .... 144 B4
Cavendish Av CDH/CHF RM16 ... 180 C2
Cavendish Crs RAIN RM13 .... 180 C7
Cavendish Gdns CHLM/GWD CM2 . 62 B1
  WOS/PRIT SS0 .... 193 H3
Cavendish Rd HOC/HUL SS5 ..... 151 H4
Cavendish Wy CHLM/GWD CM2 .. 62 B1
Cavenham Gdns EMPK RM11 .... 160 D7
Caversham Av SBN/FI SS3 .... 196 D4
Caversham Park Av RAYL SS6 ... 149 H8 1
Cawdor Av SOCK/AV RM15........ 199 J3
Cawkwell Cl CHLM/GWD CM2 .... 63 H1
Cecil Av CDH/CHF RM16 .... 213 J1
  EMPK RM11 .... 161 F5
Cecil Ct CHES/WCR EN8 .... 76 D6
Cecil Rd CHES/WCR EN8 .... 76 D6
  GVV DA11 .... 218 E6
Cecil Wy RAYL SS6 .... 172 A3
Cedar Av CHES/WCR EN8 .... 76 D7
  CHLM/WR CM1 .... 4 B2
  PEND EN3 .... 104 C6
  UPMR RM14 .... 181 H5
  WICKW SS12 .... 147 F8
Cedar Av West CHLM/WR CM1 ... 4 B2 1
Cedar Cha MAL CM9 .... 40 A8
Cedar Cl BKHH IG9 .... 134 A5
  RAYL SS6 .... 172 A5 1
  RBRW/HUT CM13 .... 142 A3
  SBW CM21 .... 11 J4
  SOSN CM21 .... 9 D2
Cedar Dr HOC/HUL SS5 .... 149 K3
  LOU IG10 .... 107 K6
Cedar Gv BOC CM0 .... 128 B7
Cedar Hall Gdns SBF/HAD SS7 ... 171 F7
Cedar Ms HOC/HUL SS5 .... 150 D7
Cedar Park Cl SBF/HAD SS7 ..... 171 F7

Cedar Ri SOCK/AV RM15 .... 200 B4
Cedar Rd CDH/CHF RM16 .... 215 F
  CVI SS8 .... 207 K
  ERITH DA8 .... 210 B
  HCH RM12 .... 180 D
  RBRW/HUT CM13 .... 142 C
  SBF/HAD SS7 .... 171 F
Cedars SLH/COR SS17 .... 204 A3
The Cedars BKHH IG9 .... 133 H
  RCHLM CM3 .... 122 D6
  SBN/FI SS3 .... 197 G1
Cedar Wk RCFD SS4 .... 153 G
Celadon Cl PEND EN3 .... 104 E
Celandine Cl BCAYW CM12 .... 144 A1
  SOCK/AV RM15 .... 200 A
Celeborn St RCHLM CM3 .... 122 C
Celedon Cl CDH/CHF RM16 .... 213 H
Cement Block Cottages
  GRAYS RM17 .... 214 B
Centaur Wy MAL CM9 .... 68 C
Centenary Cir CHLM/GWD CM2 .. 90 D
  CHLM/WR CM1 .... 34 B
  CHLM CM3 .... 35 J
Centenary Wk EPP CM16 .... 80 A
  LOU IG10 .... 133 J
Central Av CHES/WCR EN8 .... 76 E
  BCAYW CM12.................... 117 J
  CVI SS8 .... 190 D
  CVI SS8 .... 207 J1
  EN EN1 .... 104 Be
  GVE DA12 .... 219 G
  HOC/HUL SS5 .... 150 A
  RCFD SS4 .... 152 A
  SBF/HAD SS7 .... 171 K
  SLH/COR SS17 .... 187 F
  SOCK/AV RM15 .... 211 K
  SOSN SS2 .... 9 E
  TIL RM18 .... 215 F
  WTHK RM20 .... 212 C
Central Cl SBF/HAD SS7 .... 191 K
Central Dr HCH RM12 .... 181 F
Central Rd HLW CM20 .... 24 E
  SLH/COR SS17 .... 203 K
Central Wall CVI SS8 .... 191 F
Central Wall Rd CVI SS8 .... 191 G
Centre Av EPP CM16 .... 80 D
Centre Dr EPP CM16 .... 80 D
Centre Gn EPP CM16 .... 80 D6
Centre Wy WAB EN9 .... 105 J
Centurion Cl SBN/FI SS3 .... 196 E
Centurion Wy PUR RM19 .... 211 G
Ceylon Rd WOS/PRIT SS0 .... 8 A
Chadacre Rd SOS SS1 .... 196 A
Chadfields TIL RM18 .... 215 F
Chadwell Av CHES/WCR EN8 ..... 76 C
Chadwell By-pass GRAYS RM17 .. 215 F
Chadwell Hl CDH/CHF RM16 ..... 215 G
Chadwell Rd GRAYS RM17 .... 214 D
Chadwick Av CHING E4 .... 132 E7
Chadwick Cl GWW DA11 .... 218 D
Chadwick Dr HARH RM3 .... 160 E4
Chadwick Rd RCHLM CM3 .... 122 E4
  WOS/PRIT SS0 .... 193 K
Chaffinch Cl SBN/FI SS3 .... 196 D5
Chafford Gdns RBRW/HUT CM13 . 164 C0
Chafford Wy CDH/CHF RM16 .... 200 E
Chaingate Av SOSN SS2 .... 195 H
Chalfont Cl LOS SS9 .... 192 E
Chalfont Gdns GPK RM2 .... 160 C
Chalice Cl BSDN SS14 .... 168 B
Chalk End PIT SS13 .... 168 D
Chalklands CHLM/GWD CM2 ..... 92 B
Chalk La HLWE CM17 .... 26 A
Chalk Rd CVI SS8 .... 191 F7
Chalks Av SBW CM21 .... 11 H
Chalk St RCHLM CM3 .... 120 D
Chalkwell Av WOS/PRIT SS0 ..... 193 J
Chalkwell Esp WOS/PRIT SS0 .... 193 J
Chalkwell Park Dr LOS SS9 ...... 193 G
Challacombe SBN/FI SS3 .... 196 B
Challacombe Cl
  RBRW/HUT CM13 .... 142 B4
Challinor HLWE CM17 .... 25 J
Challock Lees PIT SS13 .... 169 F8 1
Chalvedon Av PIT SS13 .... 168 E
Chamberlain Av CVI SS8 .... 208 C
  SLH/COR SS17 .... 187 H
Chamberlain Cl HLWE CM17 ..... 25 G
Chamberlains Ride RCHLM CM3 .. 122 D7
Champion Cl SLH/COR SS17 ..... 204 A
  WICKW SS12 .... 147 G
Champion Rd UPMR RM14 .... 181 J
Champions Wy RCHLM CM3 ..... 122 C
Champlain Av CVI SS8 .... 190 E
Chance Cl CDH/CHF RM16 .... 213 J
Chancel Cl BOC CM0 .... 102 A
  LAIN SS15 .... 6 A
  SBF/HAD SS7 .... 170 E
Chancellor Av CHLM/GWD CM2 .. 63 K
Chancellor Rd SOS SS1 .... 9 D
Chancery Av CHLM/WR CM1 ..... 61 H
Chandler Rd LOU IG10 .... 107 K
Chandlers Cl BOC CM0 .... 128 A
Chandlers Wk BRWN CM15 ...... 113 G
Chandlers Wy SOSN SS2 .... 174 C

Chandos Cl BKHH IG9 .... 133 J5
Chandos Pde SBF/HAD SS7 .... 192 A2
Chanlock Pth SOCK/AV RM15 .... 199 K7 2
Channing Cl EMPK RM11 .... 181 G1 1
Chanton Cl LOS SS9 .... 172 E6 1
Chantreywood RBRW/HUT CM13 .. 141 K6
Chantry Crs SLH/COR SS17 .... 203 J4
Chantry Dr ING CM4 .... 116 B2
  LAIN SS15 .... 6 A3 1
The Chantry HLW CM20 .... 24 E2 1
Chantry La RCHLM CM3 .... 36 E2
Chapel Cl WTHK RM20 .... 212 E5
Chapel Ct BCAYE CM11 .... 144 C3
Chapel Cft ING CM4 .... 116 B1 2
Chapel Dr RCHLM CM3 .... 20 D7
Chapel Flds CHLMW CM17 .... 25 G7
Chapel La BOC CM0 .... 102 A1
  CHIG IG7 .... 135 J6
  CHLM/WR CM1 .... 59 K4
  HLWE CM17 .... 25 G2
  MAL CM9 .... 69 G3
  RCHLM CM3 .... 65 F2
  RCHLM CM3 .... 191 H3
  SBF/HAD SS7 .... 191 H3
  SBN/FI SS3 .... 197 G1
Chapel Rd BOC CM0 .... 155 H1
  EPP CM16 .... 80 D4
  MAL CM9 .... 43 J1
  SBN/FI SS3 .... 196 E7
Chapel St BCAYW CM12 .... 144 B3
Chaplaince Gdns EMPK RM11 ...... 181 F2 3
Chaplin Cl CHLM/GWD CM2 .... 90 D3
  LAIN SS15 .... 6 C1
Chapman Rd CVI SS8 .... 209 G2
Chapmans Cl LOS SS9 .... 192 C4
Chapmans Wk LOS SS9 .... 192 C4
Charcroft Gdns PEND EN3 .... 104 D8
Charfinch Crs BCAYE CM11 .... 144 D4
Charfleets Cl CVI SS8 .... 207 H2
Charfleets Rd CVI SS8 .... 207 G2
Charfleets Service Rd CVI SS8.. 207 G2
Charity Farm Cha BCAYW CM12 .... 144 A2
Charlbury Cl HARH RM3 .... 160 D1 1
Charlbury Crs HARH RM3 .... 160 D1
Charles Cl WOS/PRIT SS0 .... 173 H8
Charles St EPP CM16 .... 80 C5
  GRAYS RM17 .... 214 A5
Charleston Av PIT SS13 .... 169 F4
Charleston Cl PIT SS13 .... 169 F4 2
Charlotte Av WICKW SS12 .... 147 F6 2
Charlotte Ct RCHLM CM3 .... 122 D7 3
Charlotte Pl WTHK RM20 .... 212 E5
Charlton Cl PIT SS13 .... 169 F6
Charlton St WTHK RM20 .... 213 G5
Charnwood Av CHLM/WR CM1 ...... 62 A4
Charnwood Rd EN EN1 .... 104 B2 1
Charters Cross HLWS CM18 ...... 5 D6 1
Chartwell Cl WAB EN9 .... 78 A7
Chase Cl SBF/HAD SS7 .... 170 E8
Chase Dr RCHLM CM3 .... 122 C5
Chase End RAYL SS6 .... 172 A3
Chase Gdns CHING E4 .... 132 B7
  WOS/PRIT SS0 .... 8 A1
Chase House Gdns EMPK RM11 .... 161 G7 2
Chase La CHIG IG7 .... 135 K6
Chase Rd BRW CM14 .... 141 F6
  SLH/COR SS17 .... 204 C2
  SOS SS1 .... 9 F4
Chaseside RAYL SS6 .... 171 K5
Chaseways SBW CM21 .... 11 F5
The Chaseway ING CM4 .... 116 C4
Chatham Hall La RCHLM CM3 ...... 20 C3
Chatsworth SBF/HAD SS7 .... 190 C4
Chatsworth Gdns HOC/HUL SS5 .. 150 E7 3
Chatterris Av HARH RM3 .... 160 D1
Chatton Cl WICKW SS12 .... 147 H8 4
Chaucer Cl MAL CM9 .... 68 C5
  TIL RM18 .... 215 H8

Chaucer Rd CHLM/GWD CM2 ...... 5 E4
  GWW DA11 .... 218 C8
  HARH RM3 .... 160 C2
Chaucer Wk WICKW SS12 .... 147 F8
Cheapside East RAYL SS6 .... 171 H1
Cheapside West RAYL SS6 .... 171 G1
Cheddar Av WOS/PRIT SS0 .... 173 H1
Chedington SBN/FI SS3 .... 196 B4
Cheelson Rd SOCK/AV RM15 ...... 200 A2
Cheldon Barton SBN/FI SS3....... 196 B5
Chelmer Av RAYL SS6 .... 171 H4
  RCHLM CM3 .... 20 D8
Chelmer Cl MAL CM9 .... 41 K1
Chelmer Dr RBRW/HUT CM13 ...... 142 D2
  SOCK/AV RM15 .... 200 A7
Chelmer Lea CHLM/GWD CM2 ...... 5 F6
Chelmer Pl CHLM/WR CM1 .... 5 E2 2
Chelmer Rd CDH/CHF RM16 ...... 215 F4 1
  CHLM/GWD CM2 .... 5 E4
  UPMR RM14 .... 162 A8
Chelmer Ter MAL CM9 .... 68 D3 1
Chelmerton Av CHLM/GWD CM2 .... 5 F6
Chelmer Valley Rd CHLM/WR CM1 .. 4 C1
Chelmer Village Wy
  CHLM/GWD CM2 .... 5 F3
Chelmer Wy BOC CM0 .... 128 A7 1
  SBN/FI SS3 .... 196 B6
Chelmsford Av SOSN SS2 .... 8 C3
Chelmsford Dr UPMR RM14 .... 181 G4
Chelmsford Rd BRWN CM15 .... 115 G2
  CHLM/WR CM1 .... 61 A4
  CHONG CM5 .... 84 D1
  GTDUN CM6 .... 30 D1
  ING CM4 .... 86 C4
  MAL CM9 .... 68 O6
  RBSF CM22 .... 13 H3
  RCHLM CM3 .... 20 C6
  RCHLM CM3 .... 95 H2
  WICKE SS11 .... 148 D5
Chelsea Av SOS SS1 .... 195 G7
Chelsea Gdns HLWE CM17 .... 25 J6
Chelsworth Cl SOS SS1 .... 195 H5
Chelsworth Crs SOS SS1 .... 195 H5
Chelsworth Dr HARH RM3 .... 161 F3
Cheltenham Dr LOS SS9 .... 193 G3
  SBF/HAD SS7 .... 171 G6
Cheltenham Gdns LOU IG10 .... 190 C4
Cheltenham Rd HOC/HUL SS5 ...... 151 G6 1
  SOS SS1 .... 9 F4
Chelwater CHLM/GWD CM2 .... 5 E5
Chelwood Cl CHING E4 .... 132 C2 2
Chemsford Rd WICKE SS11 .... 148 D4
Chenies Dr LAIN SS15 .... 166 C4
Chepstow Av HCH RM12 .... 181 F4
Chepstow Cl BCAYE CM11 .... 117 K8
Chequers BKHH IG9 .... 133 J4
Chequers La MAL CM9 .... 68 C2 1
Chequers Rd ABR/ST RM4 .... 139 F5
  CHLM/WR CM1 .... 61 F4
  LOU IG10 .... 134 D1
The Cherries CVI SS8 .... 208 B4 1
Cherry Av RBRW/HUT CM13 .... 141 K6
Cherry Blossom La RCHLM CM3 ... 96 B8
Cherrybrook SOS SS1 .... 196 B4
Cherry Cl CVI SS8 .... 207 J1
  HOC/HUL SS5 .... 151 F6
Cherrydene Cl HOC/HUL SS5 ...... 149 K3
Cherrydown CDH/CHF RM16...... 201 H8
  RAYL SS6 .... 171 J1
Cherrydown Av CHING E4 .... 132 A6
  LOS SS9 .... 132 A6
Cherrydown Cl CHING E4 .... 132 A6
Cherrydown East VGE SS16 .... 7 E5
Cherrydown West VGE SS16 .... 7 E5
Cherry Garden La RCHLM CM3 .... 66 A6
Cherry Garden Rd MAL CM9 .... 68 A3
  RCHLM CM3 .... 20 A6
Cherry Gdns BCAYW CM12 .... 143 K1
  SBW CM21 .... 11 J1
Cherry La WICKE SS11 .... 147 J6
Cherrymeade SBF/HAD SS7 .... 191 F1
Cherry Orch SOS SS0 .... 128 E1
Cherry Orchard La RCFD SS4 ...... 173 J5
Cherry Orchard Wy RCFD SS4 ... 173 J5
  SOSN SS2 .... 173 J6
Cherry Rd PEND EN3 .... 104 C4
Cherrytree Cha SBN/FI SS3 .... 197 H4
Cherry Tree Dr SOCK/AV RM15 .... 200 B3 1
Cherry Tree Ri BKHH IG9 .... 134 A7
Cherrytrees BCAYW CM12 .... 144 A5
Cherry Wk CDH/CHF RM16 .... 215 F2
Chertsey Cl SBN/FI SS3 .... 196 C4
Cherwell Dr CHLM/WR CM1 .... 33 J8
Cherwell Gv SOCK/AV RM15 .... 199 K7
Chesham Dr LAIN SS15 .... 166 C4
Cheshire Cl EMPK RM11 .... 161 H7 1
  DR RAYL SS6 .... 149 G7
Cheshunts PIT SS13 .... 168 D7
Cheshunt Wash CHES/WCR EN8 ... 76 E1
Chester Av SOS SS1 .... 195 G7
  UPMR RM14 .... 182 B3
Chesterfield Av SBF/HAD SS7 ...... 170 C2
Chesterfield Crs LOS SS9 .... 172 E7
Chesterfield Rd PEND EN3 .... 104 B3
Chesterford Gdns BSDN SS14 ...... 168 C5 3
Chester Hall La BSDN SS14 .... 7 E1

Chester Pl CHLM/WR CM1 .... 34 C8 1
Chester Rd CHIG IG7 .... 134 D6
  LOU IG10 .... 108 A5
Chestnut Av BCAYW CM12 .... 144 A3
  BKHH IG9 .... 134 A6
  CDH/CHF RM16 .... 214 A1
  HCH RM12 .... 180 A3
  MAL CM9 .... 40 E7
  RCHLM CM3 .... 38 A2
Chestnut Cl BKHH IG9 .... 134 A5 1
  BOC CM0 .... 128 A8
  GWW DA11 .... 218 E4 1
  HCH RM12 .... 180 D5 2
  HOC/HUL SS5 .... 151 G7
Chestnut Ct VGE SS16 .... 188 D1
Chestnut Farm Dr RCHLM CM3 .... 126 C3
Chestnut Gln HCH RM12 .... 180 A3
Chestnut Gv BRW CM14 .... 141 F5
  SBF/HAD SS7 .... 190 A1
  SOSN SS2 .... 9 D2 1
Chestnut Rd PEND EN3 .... 104 E2
  VGE SS16 .... 188 D1
Chestnuts RBRW/HUT CM13 .... 142 A4
The Chestnuts RAYL SS6 .... 171 K1
Chestnut Wk CHLM/WR CM1 .... 34 C8
  EPP CM16 .... 51 K6 1
  RCHLM CM3 .... 65 J4
Chestwood Cl BCAYW CM12 .... 144 C1
Chevely Cl EPP CM16 .... 81 H3
Chevening Gdns HOC/HUL SS5 ... 150 D7 3
Chevers Pawen PIT SS13 .... 168 D8
Chevington Wy HCH RM12 .... 180 E5
Cheviot Dr CHLM/WR CM1 .... 33 K8
Cheviot Rd EMPK RM11 .... 180 B1
Cheyne Ct WICKW SS12 .... 169 H1 1
Chichester Cl BSDN SS14 .... 168 C5
  CVI SS8 .... 208 A3 1
  SOCK/AV RM15 .... 198 B8
Chichester Dr CHLM/WR CM1 .... 5 D1
Chichester Rd SOS SS1 .... 9 D4
Chichester Wy MAL CM9 .... 68 D5 1
Chieftan Dr PUR RM19 .... 211 H3
Chiffinch Gdns GVW DA11 .... 218 D8
Chigborough Rd MAL CM9 .... 41 H6
Chignall Rd CHLM/WR CM1 .... 61 K1
The Chignalls LAIN SS15 .... 166 B7 4
Chigwell La CHIG IG7 .... 135 F2
  LOU IG10 .... 108 A8
Chigwell Park Dr CHIG IG7 .... 134 D7
Chigwell Ri CHIG IG7 .... 134 D5
Childerditch Hall Dr
  RBRW/HUT CM13 .... 163 J5
Childerditch La RBRW/HUT CM13... 163 K5
Childerditch St RBRW/HUT CM13... 163 K5
The Childers WFD IG8 .... 134 C8
Childs Cl EMPK RM11 .... 160 D8
Chilham Cl PIT SS13 .... 169 F8
Chiltern Cl RAYL SS6 .... 171 J2
Chiltern Gdns HCH RM12 .... 180 D4
Chiltern Rd GVW DA11 .... 218 D8
The Chilterns CVI SS8 .... 207 K1
Chiltern Wy WFD IG8 .... 133 H6
Chilton Cl CHLM/GWD CM2 .... 5 E6
Chilton Rd CDH/CHF RM16 .... 215 F2
Chilworth Ga BROX EN10 .... 49 F4
The Chimes SBF/HAD SS7 .... 190 D1
Chimney Pot La RCHLM CM3 .... 94 E2
China La UPMR RM14 .... 184 C5
Chinchilla Rd SOS SS1 .... 195 G4
Chindit Cl BROX EN10 .... 48 D2
Chindits La RBRW/HUT CM13 .... 141 F8
Chingdale Rd CHING E4 .... 133 F6
Chingford Av CHING E4 .... 132 C6
Chingford La WFD IG8 .... 133 F7
Chingford Mount Rd CHING E4 ... 132 B8
Chippenham Gdns HARH RM3 .... 138 C8 2
Chippenham Rd HARH RM3 .... 160 E1
Chipperfield Cl UPMR RM14 .... 182 B2
Chippingfield HLWE CM17 .... 25 G2
Chisholm Ct WICKW SS12 .... 147 H8 5
Chislett Rw CHLM/GWD CM2 .... 5 D5
Chittock Ga BSDN SS14 .... 168 B7
Chittock Md BSDN SS14 .... 168 B7
Chivers Rd BRWN CM15 .... 85 H8
  CHING E4 .... 132 C6
Chorley Cl VGE SS16 .... 166 A8
Christchurch Av WICKW SS12 .... 146 D5
Christ Church Rd GVE DA12 .... 219 H5 3
Christchurch Rd SOSN SS2........ 9 F3
Christie Cl BROX EN10 .... 49 F3
Christopher Cl HCH RM12 .... 180 E5 1
Christopher Martin Rd
  BSDN SS14 .... 168 B3 1
Christy Av CHLM/WR CM1 .... 4 A1
Christy Wy LAIN SS15 .... 165 K6
Chudleigh Rd HARH RM3 .... 160 E1
Church Av CHLM/WR CM1 .... 34 C3
Church Cha RCHLM CM3 .... 121 G8
Church Cl BRW CM14 .... 113 F3
  BRWN CM15 .... 115 J5
  CVI SS8 .... 207 K2
  SBN/FI SS3 .... 196 C7
  SLH/COR SS17 .... 203 F2
Church Cnr SBF/HAD SS7 .... 190 C4

Church Crs BRWN CM15 .... 115 J5
  SOCK/AV RM15 .... 200 A3
Church End HLWW/ROY CM19 ...... 2 A5
Church End Av WICKE SS11 ...... 147 H3
Church End La WICKE SS11 ...... 147 G3
Churchfield HLW CM20 .... 24 E3
Church Field Pth CHES/WCR EN8 .. 76 C3
Churchfields BROX EN10 .... 49 G2
  LOU IG10 .... 107 G8 1
  SBN/FI SS3 .... 196 D3
Churchfields La BROX EN10 ...... 49 G2
Churchgate CHES/WCR EN8 ...... 76 B4
Churchgate Rd CHES/WCR EN8 .. 76 B3
Churchgate St HLWE CM17 ...... 25 J1
Church Gn CHLM/WR CM1 ...... 32 B8
  RCFD SS4 .... 153 G4
Church HI EPP CM16 .... 80 E3
  LAIN SS15 .... 6 B3
  LOU IG10 .... 107 H7
  MAL CM9 .... 66 D3
  RCHLM CM3 .... 20 E7
  RCHLM CM3 .... 95 K4
  SLH/COR SS17 .... 203 J4
Church Hollow PUR RM19 ...... 211 H4 1
Churchill CI CHONG CM5 ...... 84 C1
Churchill Crs SLH/COR SS17 .... 204 A1
Churchill Ri CHLM/WR CM1 ...... 35 G6
Churchill Rd GRAYS RM17 ...... 214 C5
  GVW DA11 .... 218 E6
Church Langley Wy HLWE CM17 .. 25 G5
Church Leys HLWS CM18 ...... 3 F4
Church Ms LAIN SS15 .... 166 C8 1
Church Pde CVI SS8 .... 190 D8
Church Park Rd PIT SS13 ...... 168 E8
Church Pth GVW DA11 ...... 218 B4
Church St ABR/ST RM4 ...... 111 K5
  ABR/ST RM4 .... 138 E4
  BCAYE CM11 .... 145 K1
  BOC CM0 .... 128 B7
  BRW CM14 .... 112 E3
  BSDN SS14 .... 167 K6
  CHLM/WR CM1 .... 119 H1
  CHONG CM5 .... 55 J3
  CHONG CM5 .... 83 K7
  HARH RM3 .... 161 H2
  HLWE CM17 .... 25 G8
  HOC/HUL SS5 .... 150 C6
  LAIN SS15 .... 6 C1 1
  LOU IG10 .... 106 C7
  MAL CM9 .... 38 C7
  MAL CM9 .... 41 F3
  MAL CM9 .... 42 D3
  PIT SS13 .... 169 H8
  RAYL SS6 .... 171 K3
  RBRW/HUT CM13 .... 115 J5
  RBRW/HUT CM13 .... 165 H8
  RCFD SS4 .... 151 K6
  RCHLM CM3 .... 36 C5
  RCHLM CM3 .... 38 A2
  RCHLM CM3 .... 124 B6
  SBF/HAD SS7 .... 170 B7
  SBF/HAD SS7 .... 191 K2
  SBN/FI SS3 .... 176 D6
  SBN/FI SS3 .... 196 B7
  SLH/COR SS17 .... 204 D2
  SOS SS1 .... 9 D5
  TIL RM18 .... 214 D7
  TIL RM18 .... 215 K5
  UPMR RM14 .... 184 E5
  VGE SS16 .... 189 H2
  WICKE SS11 .... 148 C8
Church St BCAYE CM11 ...... 144 D8
  BCAYW CM12 .... 144 C8
  CHLM/GWD CM2 .... 63 J7
  GRAYS RM17 .... 214 B5
  GVW DA11 .... 219 G4
  ING CM4 .... 86 C5

MAL CM9 .... 42 C7
MAL CM9 .... 43 H1
MAL CM9 .... 44 D4
MAL CM9 .... 68 D3
SBW CM21 .... 11 J3
WAB EN9 .... 77 J7 1
Church Vw BROX EN10 ...... 49 F2
  SOCK/AV RM15 .... 211 K1
  UPMR RM14 .... 181 J3
Church View Rd SBF/HAD SS7 .. 170 D7
Church Wk GVE DA12 ...... 219 J5
  SBW CM21 .... 11 K3
Churchway SBF/HAD SS7 ...... 192 A3
Chuzzlewit Dr CHLM/WR CM1 .. 34 A6 1
Cimarron Cl RCHLM CM3 ...... 122 D6 1
Civic Sq TIL RM18 .... 215 F8
Clachar Cl CHLM/GWD CM2 .. 63 J2 1
Claire Cl RBRW/HUT CM13 ...... 141 K7
Clairvale EMPK RM11 .... 181 F1
Clare Av WICKE SS11 .... 147 G3
Clare Ms CHONG CM5 .... 56 C8
Claremont Cl CDH/CHF RM16 .. 214 B2 1
  WOS/PRIT SS0 .... 8 B3
Claremont Dr VGE SS16 ...... 188 C1
Claremont Gdns UPMR RM14 .. 182 A2
Claremont Rd EMPK RM11 ...... 160 B8
  LAIN SS15 .... 6 A3
  WOS/PRIT SS0 .... 8 A3
Clarence Av UPMR RM14 ...... 181 H3
Clarence Cl CHLM/GWD CM2 .. 63 J1
  SBF/HAD SS7 .... 190 C1
Clarence Pl GVE DA12 ...... 219 G6
Clarence Rd BRWN CM15 ...... 140 E2
  GRAYS RM17 .... 213 K5
  PIT SS13 .... 169 J6
  RAYL SS6 .... 172 B4
  SBF/HAD SS7 .... 190 C1
  SLH/COR SS17 .... 204 E1
  SOS SS1 .... 9 D5
Clarence Rd North SBF/HAD SS7 . 190 C1
Clarence Rw GVE DA12 ...... 219 G6
Clarence St SOS SS1 .... 9 D5
Clarendon Rd CHES/WCR EN8 .. 76 D3
  CVI SS8 .... 208 C1
  GVE DA12 .... 219 H4
  PIT SS13 .... 169 F6
Clare Rd SBF/HAD SS7 ...... 169 K7
Clarkbourne Dr GRAYS RM17 .. 214 C5
Clark Cl ERITH DA8 .... 210 B7
Clarke Ri RCHLM CM3 ...... 96 B8
Clarkhill HLWS CM18 .... 52 C1
Clarks Farm Rd RCHLM CM3 .. 65 K5 1
Clarks La EPP CM16 .... 80 D5
Clark Wy CHLM/WR CM1 ...... 34 C4 1
Claters Cl BSDN SS14 ...... 195 J3
Clatterfield Gdns WOS/PRIT SS0 193 H3
Claudian Wy CDH/CHF RM16 .. 215 G2
Claughton Wy RBRW/HUT CM13 142 C2
Claverhambury Rd WAB EN9 .. 78 B3
Clavering Ct RAYL SS6 ...... 171 G2 1
Clavering Gdns RBRW/HUT CM13 164 C8
Clavering Wy RBRW/HUT CM13 142 B2
Claybrick Av HOC/HUL SS5 ...... 150 E8 1
Clayburn Cir BSDN SS14 ...... 168 A7
Clayburn Gdns SOCK/AV RM15 199 K7 3
Claydon Crs BSDN SS14 ...... 167 K8
Claydons La SBF/HAD SS7 ...... 171 H5
Claygate Cl HCH RM12 ...... 180 B5 1
Clay Hill Rd VGE SS16 ...... 7 F5
  VGE SS16 .... 168 B8
  VGE SS16 .... 188 B1 1
Claypit HI WAB EN9 .... 106 E2
Claypits Rd RCHLM CM3 ...... 36 D4
Clayspring Cl HOC/HUL SS5 .. 150 E6
Clayton Av UPMR RM14 ...... 181 J6
Clayton Wy MAL CM9 .... 68 C5
Clay Tye Rd UPMR RM14 ...... 183 F4
Cleall Av WAB EN9 .... 77 J8
Cleland Pth LOU IG10 ...... 107 K6
Clematis Cl HARH RM3 ...... 160 D2
Clematis Gdns WFD IG8 ...... 133 H8
Clement Rd CHES/WCR EN8 .. 76 E1 1
Clements Cl CHLM/GWD CM2 .. 63 K2
Clements Gdns HOC/HUL SS5 .. 151 H8
Clements Green La RCHLM CM3 122 D5
Clements Hall La HOC/HUL SS5 151 H8
Clements Hall Wy HOC/HUL SS5 171 H1
Clements Pl RCHLM CM3 ...... 122 D5 4
Clement Wy HCH RM12 ...... 181 J3
Clerks Piece LOU IG10 ...... 107 H7
Cleveland Dr WOS/PRIT SS0 .. 8 A1
Cleveland Rd BSDN SS14 ...... 167 K7
  CVI SS8 .... 208 B3
Cleves Av BRW CM14 ...... 140 E4
Cleves Ct RCHLM CM3 ...... 36 C4 2
Clevis Dr RCHLM CM3 ...... 123 F8
Clickett End BSDN SS14 ...... 167 K7
Clickett HI BSDN SS14 ...... 167 K7
Clickett Side BSDN SS14 ...... 167 K7
Clieveden Rd SOS SS1 ...... 195 J7
Cliff Av WOS/PRIT SS0 ...... 8 B3
Cliff Gdns LOS SS9 .... 193 H5
  WOS/PRIT SS0 .... 193 H5
Clifford Cl LAIN SS15 ...... 6 B5

Clifford Rd CDH/CHF RM16 .... 213 J1
Cliff Pde LOS SS9 .... 193 F5
Cliff Pl SOCK/AV RM15 ...... 200 A3
Cliff Rd LOS SS9 .... 193 H5
Cliffsea Gv LOS SS9 ...... 193 G5
Clifftown Pde SOS SS1 ...... 8 C5
Clifftown Rd SOS SS1 ...... 9 D5
Clifton Av SBF/HAD SS7 ...... 190 B1
Clifton Cl CHES/WCR EN8 ...... 76 E1
  SBF/HAD SS7 .... 190 C1
Clifton Dr WOS/PRIT SS0 ...... 8 A1
Clifton Gv GVW DA11 ...... 219 G2
Clifton Hatch HLWS CM18 .... 24 E8
Clifton Marine Pde GVW DA11 218 E4
Clifton Ms SOS SS1 .... 9 D4
Clifton Rd CVI SS8 .... 208 E2
  EMPK RM11 .... 160 B8
  GVW DA11 .... 219 F4
  LOU IG10 .... 107 G8 2
  PIT SS13 .... 169 J6
  RCFD SS4 .... 151 K6
Clifton Ter SOS SS1 .... 9 D5
Clifton Wy RBRW/HUT CM13 .. 142 C2
  SBF/HAD SS7 .... 190 B3
Climmen Rd CVI SS8 .... 191 G8
Clinton Cl RCHLM CM3 ...... 93 G6
Clinton Rd CVI SS8 .... 207 H2
Clipped Hedge RBSF CM22 .... 13 G5
Clitheroe Rd CRW RM5 ...... 137 H8
Cliveden Cl BRWN CM15 ...... 141 J2
  CHLM/WR CM1 .... 62 A1
Clivedon Rd CHING E4 ...... 133 F8
Clive Rd EN EN1 .... 104 A4
  GPK RM2 .... 160 C2
  GVW DA11 .... 219 G2
  RBRW/HUT CM13 .... 163 F2
Clive Wy EN EN1 .... 104 A4
Clockhouse La CDH/CHF RM16 200 B8
Clock House Rd BCAYW CM12 .. 143 K8
Cloisters SLH/COR SS17 ...... 204 A3
The Cloisters LAIN SS15 ...... 6 A4
The Close BRW CM14 ...... 141 G8
  CDH/CHF RM16 .... 214 A7
  RBSF CM22 .... 13 G5
Cloudberry Rd HARH RM3 ...... 160 E1
Cloudesley Rd ERITH DA8 ...... 210 A3
Clova Rd LOS SS9 .... 193 G3
Clovelly Gdns WICKE SS11 .... 147 F5
Clover Cl VGE SS16 .... 188 B2
Clover Fld HLWS CM18 ...... 24 E8
Clover Leas EPP CM16 ...... 80 D6
Cloverley Rd CHONG CM5 ...... 84 C4
Clover Wy VGE SS16 .... 188 B2
Clunas Gdns GPK RM2 ...... 160 E2
Cluny Sq SOSN SS2 .... 9 F1
Clyde TIL RM18 .... 216 D2
Clyde Crs CHLM/WR CM1 ...... 61 K1
  RAYL SS6 .... 171 H4
  UPMR RM14 .... 162 B4
Clyde Rd HOD EN11 .... 49 K1
Clydesdale PEND EN3 ...... 104 D6
Clydesdale Rd EMPK RM11 .... 180 A3
Clyfton Cl BROX EN10 ...... 49 F2 1
Coach La MAL CM9 .... 68 B2
Coach Ms BCAYE CM11 ...... 117 K6
Coalport Cl HLWE CM17 ...... 25 G8
Coates Cl MAL CM9 .... 68 D1 5
Cobbett Cl PEND EN3 ...... 104 C2
Cobbin's Br EPP CM16 ...... 80 B1
Cobbins Cha BOC CM0 ...... 128 B8
Cobbins Cl BOC CM0 ...... 128 B8
Cobbinsend Rd WAB EN9 ...... 79 F5
The Cobbins BOC CM0 ...... 128 B8
  WAB EN9 .... 78 A4
Cobbins Wy HLWE CM17 ...... 25 J1
The Cobbles BRWN CM15 ...... 141 H6
  UPMR RM14 .... 182 C5
Cobham CDH/CHF RM16 ...... 214 A3
Cobham Rd WOS/PRIT SS0 .... 193 K6
Cobham St GVW DA11 ...... 219 F5
Cobill Cl EMPK RM11 ...... 160 D6
Coburg La VGE SS16 ...... 186 A1
Coburg Pl RCHLM CM3 ...... 122 D7
Cockerell Cl PIT SS13 ...... 168 E2
Cocker Rd EN EN1 .... 104 B2
Cockethurst Cl WOS/PRIT SS0 . 193 H1
Cock La BROX EN10 .... 48 C4
  CHLM/WR CM1 .... 87 K7
Codenham Gn VGE SS16 ...... 7 F8
Codenham Straight VGE SS16 .. 7 F8
Codham Hall La RBRW/HUT CM13 . 162 E7
Cohen Cl CHES/WCR EN8 ...... 76 B1
Cokefield Av SOSN SS2 ...... 9 F1
Coker Rd CVI SS8 .... 207 H5
Colam La MAL CM9 .... 65 G4
Colbert Av SOS SS1 .... 195 H4
Colbourne Cl SLH/COR SS17 .. 204 B2
Colchester Cl WOS/PRIT SS0 .. 194 C4
Colchester Rd CHLM/GWD CM2 . 35 J1
  HARH RM3 .... 161 F2
  MAL CM9 .... 40 D6
  SOSN SS2 .... 8 C2
Coldham Gv PEND EN3 ...... 104 E3
Coldharbour Rd GVW DA11 .... 218 D2
  HLWW/ROY CM19 .... 2 A4

old Norton Rd RCHLM CM3 .... 97 F8
ole Av CDH/CHF RM16 .... 215 H3
olebrook Gdns LOU IG10 .... 107 K6 1
olebrook La LOU IG10 .... 107 K6
ole HI RCHLM CM3 .... 21 K1
olemans Av WOS/PRIT SS0 .... 194 A1
olemans La RCHLM CM3 .... 65 H6
WAB EN9 .... 49 K8
oleman St SOSN SS2 .... 9 D3
oleridge Rd HARH RM3 .... 160 C2
MAL CM9 .... 68 C4
TIL RM18 .... 215 H8
oleridge Wk RBRW/HUT CM13 .. 142 B3
oles CI CHONG CM5 .... 56 C8
oles Gn LOU IG10 .... 107 K5
olet Rd RBRW/HUT CM13 .... 142 B1
ollard Av LOU IG10 .... 108 A6
ollege Av GRAYS RM17 .... 214 A3
ollege Ct CHES/WCR EN8 .... 76 C4 1
ollege Gdns CHING E4 .... 132 C3
ollege Rd CHES/WCR EN8 .... 76 D4
CHESW EN7 .... 76 B4
GRAYS RM17 .... 214 B3
GVW DA11 .... 218 A3 1
ollege Sq HLW CM20 .... 3 D3 1
ollege Wy SOS SS1 .... 8 C4
ollet CI CHES/WCR EN8. .... 76 C2
olley Rd CHLM/GWD CM2 .... 63 J7
he Colliers MAL CM9 .... 69 G2
ollindale CI CVI SS8 .... 208 D1
ollington Rd GVW DA11 .... 218 D5 1
ollingwood SBF/HAD SS7 .... 190 D1 1
ollingwood Rd RCHLM CM3 .... 123 F7
VGE SS16 .... 188 A1
ollingwood Wk VGE SS16 .... 168 A8 1
ollingwood Wy SBN/FI SS3 .... 196 D4
ollins CI SLH/COR SS17 .... 204 A3
ollins Meadow HLWW/ROY CM19 .. 2 B3
ollins Wy LOS SS9 .... 173 H7
RBRW/HUT CM13 .... 142 D1
ollinwood Av PEND EN3 .... 104 C7
olman CI SLH/COR SS17 .... 203 K2
olmore Rd PEND EN3 .... 104 C8
olne TIL RM18 .... 216 D2
olne CI RCHLM CM3 .... 122 D6
SOCK/AV RM15 .... 200 A7 2
olne Dr HARH RM3 .... 161 G1
SBN/FI SS3 .... 196 D4
olne PI VGE SS16 .... 167 K8
olne Va UPMR RM14 .... 162 B8
he Colonnade CHES/WCR EN8 .. 76 D2 2
olson Pth LOU IG10 .... 107 J8
olson Rd LOU IG10 .... 107 K8
oltishall CI WICKE SS11 .... 148 A7 1
oltishall Rd RBRW/HUT CM13 ... 180 D7
oltsfoot Ct GRAYS RM17 .... 214 A5
oltsfoot Pth HARH RM3 .... 160 E2
olumbia Wharf Rd GRAYS RM17 .. 213 K5
olumbine Wy HARH RM3 .... 161 F3
olvers HLWE CM17 .... 27 J3
olville Ct SLH/COR SS17 .... 187 G8
olville Ms CHLM/GWD CM2 ...... 117 F8 2
olvin Cha CHLM/GWD CM2 .... 90 D4
olvin Gdns CHES/WCR EN8 ...... 104 D1
CHING E4 .... 132 D6
olwall Gdns WFD IG8 .... 133 H8 2
olworth St SBF/HAD SS7 .... 191 J1
olyer Rd GVW DA11 .... 218 C2
olyers Reach CHLM/GWD CM2 ... 63 J3
omet CI PUR RM19 .... 211 H3
omfrey Ct GRAYS RM17 .... 214 C5
ommercial PI GVE DA12 .... 219 H4
ommercial Rd WOS/PRIT SS0 ...... 8 A1
ommon Ap SBF/HAD SS7 .... 171 F7
ommon Rd ING CM4 .... 118 A3
ommonhall La ING CM4 .... 118 A3 1
MAL CM9 .... 66 B3
RCHLM CM3 .... 95 J6 1
SBF/HAD SS7 .... 171 F6
ommon Rd ING CM4 .... 118 A2
RBRW/HUT CM13 .... 142 B8
SBN/FI SS3 .... 197 G1
WAB EN9 .... 51 G3
ommonside Rd HLWS CM18 .... 52 D1
he Common RCHLM CM3 .... 65 J7
RCHLM CM3 .... 93 F5 1
SBF/HAD SS7 .... 171 F6
ompton Av GPK RM2 .... 160 C5
RBRW/HUT CM13 .... 142 B4
ompton Ct CVI SS8 .... 208 D3 2
ompton PI ERITH DA8 .... 210 A6
omyns Rd CHLM/WR CM1 .... 61 H4 1
oncord PI CHLM/WR CM1 .... 61 H4 1
onduit La HLW CM20 .... 66 E7
oney Burrows CHING E4 .... 133 F5 1
oney Gn SBW CM21 .... 11 H2
onference Ct CHING E4 .... 133 D6 2
ongreve Rd WAB EN9 .... 78 A7
onifer Av CRW RM5 .... 137 G8 1
onifer Dr BRW CM14 .... 141 K6
onifers SBF/HAD SS7 .... 191 K2
oniston LOS SS9 .... 173 H6
oniston Av UPMR RM14 .... 181 K5
oniston CI RAYL SS6 .... 171 K3 1

Coniston Rd CVI SS8 .... 208 A2
SBF/HAD SS7 .... 170 D6
Coniston Wy RCHLM CM3 .... 180 B6
CHING E4 .... 132 E3
LOU IG10 .... 107 F8
Connaught Dr RCHLM CM3 .... 122 C6 1
Connaught Gdns SBN/FI SS3 ...... 196 B3
Connaught HI LOU IG10 .... 107 F8
Connaught Rd CHING E4 .... 133 F3 1
HCH RM12 .... 180 E4
RAYL SS6 .... 172 C5
Connaught Wy BCAYW CM12 .... 117 F8
Connington Crs CHING E4 .... 132 E6 1
Connop Rd PEND EN3 .... 104 D4
Conquerors CI RCHLM CM3 .... 38 B2 1
Conrad CI CDH/CHF RM16 .... 214 A1
Conrad Gdns CDH/CHF RM16 ... 213 K1
Conrad Rd SLH/COR SS17 .... 204 A3
Consort CI BRW CM14 .... 141 F8
Constable Dr GVW DA11 .... 218 D8
Constable Wy SBN/FI SS3 .... 196 E5
Constance CI CHLM/WR CM1 ...... 34 D2 1
Constitution HI GVE DA12 .... 219 H6
SBF/HAD SS7 .... 190 C2
Convent CI LAIN SS15 .... 6 A4 2
Convent Rd CVI SS8 .... 208 B2
Con Wy SBF/HAD SS7 .... 190 C2
Conway Av SBN/FI SS3 .... 197 G2
Conway CI RAIN RM13 .... 180 B8 1
Conway Gdns GRAYS RM17 ...... 214 A6
Conway's Rd CDH/CHF RM16 ... 202 A1
Conybury CI WAB EN9 .... 78 C6
Conyer CI MAL CM9 .... 68 B5
Conyers HLW CM20 .... 2 C1
Conyers Wy LOU IG10 .... 107 K7
Cookham CE SBN/FI SS3 .... 196 D3 1
Cook PI CHLM/GWD CM2 .... 53 H2
Cooks Gn PIT SS13 .... 169 F4 3
Cooks Spinney HLW CM20 .... 24 E3
Coolgardie Av CHIG IG7 .... 134 D6
CHING E4 .... 132 E8
Coombe Dr VGE SS16 .... 186 D4
Coombes Gv RCHLM CM3 .... 174 D3
Coombewood Dr SBF/HAD SS7 .. 170 D8
Coopersale Common EPP CM16 .. 81 H2
Coopersale La EPP CM16 .... 108 E3
Coopersales LAIN SS15 .... 166 A7
Coopers CI CHIG IG7 .... 136 A5
Coopers Dr BCAYE CM11 .... 144 D7
Cooper Shaw Rd TIL RM18 .... 215 J6
Coopers HI CHONG CM5 .... 84 C3
Cooper's Rd GVW DA11 .... 218 D6
Copdoek BSDN SS14 .... 167 K6
Copeland La CHLM/WR CM1 .... 34 C7
Copeland Rd SLH/COR SS17 ...... 203 K4
Copeman Rd RBRW/HUT CM13 .. 142 C3 1
Copford Av RAYL SS6 .... 172 A4
Copford Rd BCAYE CM11 .... 144 D3 3
Copland CI CHLM/GWD CM2 ...... 63 H5
CHLM/WR CM1 .... 34 C4
Copland Rd SLH/COR SS17 .... 203 K4
Coppens Gn WICKW SS12 .... 147 G7
Copper Beech CI GVE DA12 .... 219 J5 1
Copper Beech Rd
SOCK/AV RM15 .... 200 A3 1
Copperfield BCAYE CM11 .... 144 E7 2
Copperfield Gdns BRW CM14 ... 140 E4
Copperfield Rd CHLM/WR CM1 ... 33 H8
Copperfields LAIN SS15 .... 6 A3 1
Copperfields Wy HARH RM3 ..... 160 E3 2
Coppice La CHLM/GWD CM2 .... 7 D1
Coppice Pth CHIG IG7 .... 136 A3
Coppice Rw EPP CM16 .... 108 B2
Coppins CI CHLM/WR CM1 .... 5 F1
Copse HI HLWW/ROY CM19 .... 2 B6
The Copse BCAYW CM12 .... 144 B1
CHING E4 .... 133 G4
Copshall CI HLWS CM18 .... 52 C1
Coptfold CI SOS SS1 .... 195 J4 1
Coptfold Rd BRW CM14 .... 141 F5
Copt HI RCHLM CM3 .... 65 J7
Copthorne BROX EN10 .... 49 F2
Copthorne Gdns EMPK RM11 ..... 161 H7
Coral CI RCHLM CM3 .... 122 C5 1
Coram Gn RBRW/HUT CM13 .... 142 C2
Corans BRWN CM15 .... 140 E2
Corbets Av UPMR RM14 .... 181 J5
Corbets Tey Rd UPMR RM14 ..... 181 J4
Cordelia Crs RAYL SS6 .... 171 H2
Cordell CI CHES/WCR EN8 .... 76 E2 2
The Cordwainers SOSN SS2 .... 174 D8
Cornec Av LOS SS9 .... 172 C7
Cornec Cha LOS SS9 .... 172 D7

Cornelius V CHLM/GWD CM2 ...... 63 K1
Cornell Wy CRW RM5 .... 137 G8
Corner Meadow HLWS CM18 ...... 52 E1
Corner Rd BCAYE CM11 .... 146 A7
Cornfields RCHLM CM3 .... 122 C5
Cornflower Dr CHLM/WR CM1 .... 35 H8
Cornflower Gdns BCAYW CM12 .. 117 F8
Cornflower Wy HARH RM3 .... 161 F3
Cornhill Av HOC/HUL SS5 .... 151 F6
Cornhill Dr PEND EN3 .... 104 E3 2
Cornish Gv RCHLM CM3 .... 122 E7
Cornsland BRW CM14 .... 141 G6
Cornwall CI CHES/WCR EN8 ...... 76 E7
EMPK RM11 .... 161 H6 1
Cornwall Crs CHLM/WR CM1 ...... 34 C6
Cornwall Gdns RCFD SS4 .... 151 K8
Cornwallis CI ERITH DA8 .... 210 A5
Cornwallis Dr RCHLM CM3 .... 123 F6
Cornwall Rd CHLM/WR CM1 .... 140 E1
PIT SS13 .... 169 J6
Cornwell Av GVE DA12 .... 219 H8
Cornwell Crs SLH/COR SS17 ..... 204 A2
Cornworthy SBN/FI SS3 .... 196 B5
Corona Rd CVI SS8 .... 191 H8
VGE SS16 .... 186 C2
Coronation Av TIL RM18 .... 216 C3
Coronation CI SBN/FI SS3 .... 196 E1
Coronation Dr HCH RM12 .... 180 C6
Coronation HI EPP CM16 .... 80 D4
Corporation Rd BOC CM0 .... 155 G1
Corran Wy SOCK/AV RM15 .... 199 K2
Corringham Rd SLH/COR SS17 .. 203 K4
Corsel Rd CVI SS8 .... 208 E2 1
Corve La SOCK/AV RM15 .... 199 K2
Cory Dr RBRW/HUT CM13 .... 142 A3
Cosgrove Av LOS SS9 .... 192 C2
Cossington Rd WOS/PRIT SS0 ...... 8 B5
Costead Manor Rd BRW CM14 .. 140 E4
Coteford Ct LOU IG10 .... 107 K6
Cotelands VGE SS16 .... 188 C2
Cotswold Av RAYL SS6 .... 171 J2
Cotswold Crs CHLM/WR CM1 ...... 33 K7
Cotswold Gdns RBRW/HUT CM13 .. 142 B3
Cotswold Rd GVW DA11 .... 218 D8
HARH RM3 .... 161 G4
WOS/PRIT SS0 .... 8 A4
Cottage Gdns CHES/WCR EN8 .... 76 C3
Cottage PI CHLM/WR CM1 .... 4 C2
Cottesmore CI CVI SS8 .... 208 A3
Cottesmore Gdns LOS SS9 .... 192 B4
Cottis CI VGE SS16 .... 186 B2
Coulde Dennis RCHLM CM3 .... 93 F6 1
Coulton Av GVW DA11 .... 218 D5
Council Av GVW DA11 .... 218 B4
County PI CHLM/GWD CM2 .... 4 C4
Courage CI EMPK RM11 .... 160 D6 1
Courtauld Rd PIT SS13 .... 168 E3 2
Court Av HARH RM3 .... 161 H2
Courtenay Dr CDH/CHF RM16 .. 213 J2 3
Courtenay Gdns UPMR RM14 .... 181 K3
Courtfield CI BROX EN10 .... 49 G2 1
Courtland Av CHING E4 .... 133 G5
Courtland Dr CHIG IG7 .... 135 F6
Courtland Ms MAL CM9 .... 68 B5 1
Courtland PI MAL CM9 .... 68 B5
Courtlands BCAYW CM12 .... 143 K3
CHLM/WR CM1 .... 34 C7
Courtney Park Rd VGE SS16 ..... 166 C8 1
Courtney Rd CDH/CHF RM16 .... 215 H1
Court Rd CHLM/WR CM1 .... 34 C2
The Courts MAL CM9 .... 171 K2
Court Vw ING CM4 .... 115 K4 1
Court Wy HARH RM3 .... 161 F4
Coval Av CHLM/WR CM1 .... 4 B2
Coval La CHLM/WR CM1 .... 4 B2 2
Covenbrook RBRW/HUT CM13 .. 141 K6
Coventry CI HOC/HUL SS5 .... 150 A4
Coventry Hill Lower Rd
HOC/HUL SS5 .... 149 K4 1
Coverley CI RBRW/HUT CM13 ... 163 F1
The Coverts CHLM/WR CM1 .... 61 H4
RBRW/HUT CM13 .... 141 K4
Cowdray Wy HCH RM12 .... 180 B5
Cowell Av CDH/CHF RM16 .... 34 A8
Cowland Av PEND EN3 .... 104 C8
Cowley Rd HARH RM3 .... 160 C2
Cowlins HLWE CM17 .... 25 H1 1
Cowper Av TIL RM18 .... 215 G7
Cowlins HLWE CM17 .... 25 H1 1
Cow Watering La CHLM/WR CM1 .. 61 F2
Coxbridge Ct BCAYW CM12 ...... 144 B3
Coxes CI SLH/COR SS17 .... 203 K2
Coxes Farm Rd BCAYE CM11 ... 145 F6
Cox Ley RBSF CM22 .... 13 G2
Coxs CI RCHLM CM3 .... 122 E5
Coxtie Green Rd BRW CM14 ..... 112 D8
Cozens La East BROX EN10 .... 49 F4
Cozens La West BROX EN10 ...... 37 K4
Crabb's HI RCHLM CM3 .... 20 E1
Craftsmans Sq SOSN SS2 .... 174 D8
Craigdale Rd ROM RM1 .... 160 A8
Craigs Wk CHES/WCR EN8 .... 76 D2
Craiston Wy CHLM/GWD CM2 .... 63 H8
Crammavill St CDH/CHF RM16 .. 200 E3 1
Cramphorn Wk CHLM/WR CM1 .... 4 A2

D

anesfield SBF/HAD SS7 .... 190 A3
anesleigh Gdns LOS SS9 .... 192 E1
ane St SBN/FI SS3 .... 197 F7
'arcy Av BRWN CM15 .... 140 C1
aniel Cl CDH/CHF RM16 .... 213 H1
CDH/CHF RM16 .... 215 G2
aphne Gdns CHING E4 .... 132 D6 2
'arcy Av MAL CM9 .... 68 D4
arby Dr WAB EN9 .... 77 J7 2
'arcy Av MAL CM9 .... 68 D4
arcy Cl CHES/WCR EN8 .... 76 E5
BOC CM0 .... 128 C7
RBRW/HUT CM13 .... 142 A3
'arcy Wy MAL CM9 .... 43 J1
areli Wy BCAYE CM11 .... 144 E4 1
arenth Cl SOCK/AV RM15 .... 199 J6
arenth Rd LOS SS9 .... 192 C4
arinel Valley Pth DART DA1 ..... 210 E7
ark La BRW CM14 .... 162 D2
CHESW EN7 .... 76 A5
SBF/HAD SS7 .... 171 F7
arlinghurst Gv LOS SS9 .... 193 H3
arlington Ct BRWN CM15 .... 140 D2 1
arlington Gdns HARH RM3 .... 138 E8
arlton Cl DART DA1 .... 210 A8
arnet Rd MAL CM9 .... 44 E4
arnley Rd GRAYS RM17 .... 214 A5 2
GVW DA11 .... 219 F4 2
arnley St GVW DA11 .... 219 F5
arrell Cl CHLM/WR CM1 .... 34 D7
art Cl UPMR RM14 .... 162 A8 1
artfields HARH RM3 .... 160 E1
art Gn SOCK/AV RM15 .... 199 K6
artmouth Cl RAYL SS6 .... 149 J8 1
art Gn SOCK/AV RM15 .... 199 K6
artmouth Rd CHLM/WR CM1 ... 35 G3 7
artview Cl GRAYS RM17 .... 214 D3
arwin Rd TIL RM18 .... 214 E7
he Dashes HLW CM20 .... 3 E2
ashwood Rd GVW DA11 .... 219 F6
atchet Dr SBN/FI SS3 .... 196 D3
avenants PIT SS13 .... 168 E5
avenport Dr LAIN SS15 .... 6 A3
aventry Gdns HARH RM3 .... 138 D8
aventry Rd HARH RM3 .... 138 D8
avid Av WICKE SS11 .... 147 G3
avid Cl CHLM/WR CM1 .... 61 F4
avid Dr HARH RM3 .... 161 H1
avidson Gdns WICKW SS12 ..... 147 K8
avid's Wk BCAYE CM11 .... 144 D3 4
avis Av GVW DA11 .... 218 D6
avison Cl CHES/WCR EN8 .... 76 D6
avison Dr CHES/WCR EN8 .... 76 D2
avis Rd CDH/CHF RM16 .... 213 J2
SOCK/AV RM15 .... 199 F8
awn Cl CHLM/WR CM1 .... 61 F4
aws Heath Rd RAYL SS6 .... 171 J4
SBF/HAD SS7 .... 171 F7
aws Hl CHING E4 .... 105 J7
aylop Dr CHIG IG7 .... 136 A6
ays Cl CHLM/WR CM1 .... 34 D5
ays La BRWN CM15 .... 113 J8
ayton Dr ERITH DA8 .... 210 E4
eacon Dr LAIN SS15 .... 6 A3
eadman's La CHLM/GWD CM2 ... 90 C1
ealtree Cl BRWN CM15 .... 113 H1
earsley Rd EN EN1 .... 104 A7
ebden Gn SES16 .... 6 A6
ebden La LOU IG10 .... 107 K4
ebden Rd LOU IG10 .... 107 J4
ebden Wy BOC CM0 .... 128 A7 2
e Beauvoir Cha BCAYE CM11 ... 146 A2
ebenham Rd CHESW EN7 .... 76 B1
edham Cl BCAYE CM11 .... 144 D3
edham Rd BCAYE CM11 .... 144 D3
ee Cl UPMR RM14 .... 162 A8
eefe Pk HLWW/ROY CM19 .... 2 A6
eefoe Rd CDH/CHF RM16 .... 215 G2
eirdre Av WICKW SS12 .... 146 B6
eirdre Cl WICKW SS12 .... 146 B6
elafield Rd GRAYS RM17 .... 214 C4
elamare Rd CHES/WCR EN8 ..... 77 F3
elamere Rd CHLM/WR CM1 ...... 62 A4
elargy Cl CDH/CHF RM16 .... 215 G2
elaware Crs SBN/FI SS3 .... 196 B6
elaware Rd SBN/FI SS3 .... 196 B6
elder Av CVI SS8 .... 208 D3
elft Rd CVI SS8 .... 208 A1

Delfzul Rd CVI SS8 .... 208 A1
Delgada Rd CVI SS8 .... 208 D2
Delhi Rd PIT SS13 .... 169 F7
Delimands LAIN SS15 .... 7 D4
Dell Cl WFD IG8 .... 133 J6
Dell Rd GRAYS RM17 .... 214 A3
PEND EN3 .... 104 C4
Dells Cl CHING E4 .... 132 C3
The Dell BRW CM14 .... 162 E1
CHLM/GWD CM2 .... 63 H6
VGE SS16 .... 187 J2
WFD IG8 .... 133 J6
WICKE SS11 .... 147 H3
Delmar Gdns WICKE SS11 .... 147 F3
Delmores VGE SS16 .... 186 D2
Delta Rd RBRW/HUT CM13 ...... 142 C2
Delview CVI SS8 .... 190 E8
Delvins PIT SS13 .... 168 D5
De Mandeville Ga EN EN1 .... 104 A8
Denbigh Cl EMPK RM11 .... 161 G6
Denbigh Rd LAIN SS15 .... 166 C3
Denby Gra HLWE CM17 .... 25 J5
Dencourt Crs BSDN SS14 .... 168 C8
Dendridge Cl EN EN1 .... 104 B3
Dene Cl RAYL SS6 .... 171 J1 1
Dene Ct CHLM/WR CM1 .... 33 K8
Denecroft Gdns GRAYS RM17 .. 214 C2
Dene Gdns RAYL SS6 .... 171 J1
Dene Holm Rd GVW DA11 .... 218 C8
Denehurst Gdns VGE SS16 .... 185 K1
WFD IG8 .... 133 J7
Dene Pth SOCK/AV RM15 .... 199 J6
Dene Rd BKHH IG9 .... 134 B4
Denesmere SBF/HAD SS7 .... 190 B1 1
Deneway VGE SS16 .... 188 A3
Dengayne BSDN SS14 .... 168 A7
Denham Rd CVI SS8 .... 208 A1
Denham V RAYL SS6 .... 171 F2 3
Denholme Wk RAIN RM13 .... 149 J8
Denner Rd CHING E4 .... 132 B5
Dennises La UPMR RM14 .... 182 C3
Dennis Rd GVW DA11 .... 219 F8
UPMR RM14 .... 199 J1
Denny Av WAB EN9 .... 77 K8
Denny Ga CHES/WCR EN8 .... 77 F1
Denton Av WOS/PRIT SS0 .... 173 K8 1
Denton Av WOS/PRIT SS0 .... 173 K8
Denton Cl WOS/PRIT SS0 .... 173 K8
Denton Court GVE DA12 .... 219 K6
Denton St GVE DA12 .... 219 K5
Denver Cl PIT SS13 .... 169 F4
Denys Dr BSDN SS14 .... 168 A5
Derby Av UPMR RM14 .... 181 G4
Derby Cl BCAYE CM11 .... 117 K8
RCHLM CM3 .... 98 D4
VGE SS16 .... 186 A1 2
Derbydale RCFD SS4 .... 151 K7
Derby Rd HOD EN11 .... 49 K1
Derby Road Br GRAYS RM17 ... 214 A4
Derek Cl LAIN SS15 .... 6 A3
Derham Gdns UPMR RM14 .... 181 K4
Dering Crs LOS SS9 .... 172 E5
Derry Av SOCK/AV RM15 .... 199 J5 1
Derventer Av CVI SS8 .... 191 F7
Derwent Av WAB EN9 .... 171 K3
Derwent Pde SOCK/AV RM15 .. 199 J6
Derwent Wy HCH RM12 .... 180 C6 1
Detling Cl HCH RM12 .... 180 D6 1
Detling Rd GVW DA11 .... 218 C6
De Vere Av MAL CM9 .... 68 D4
De Vere Cl RCHLM CM3 .... 38 B2
Devereux Cl CDH/CHF RM16 .... 213 J2
SOS SS1 .... 9 D5 2
Devereux Rd BCAYW CM12 ...... 117 F8
Deveron Gdns SOCK/AV RM15 . 199 J5 2
Devon Cl BKHH IG9 .... 133 J5
Devon Gdns RCFD SS4 .... 151 K8
Devonshire Cl LAIN SS15 .... 166 B5
Devonshire Gdns SLH/COR SS17 216 B2
Devonshire Rd BOC CM0 .... 128 B8
CDH/CHF RM16 .... 213 H3
GVW DA11 .... 219 G6
HCH RM12 .... 180 C3
LAIN SS15 .... 166 B5
Devon Wy CVI SS8 .... 191 F8
Dewgrass Gv CHES/WCR EN8 .. 104 D3 2
Dewhurst Rd CHES/WCR EN8 ... 76 C3
Dewsbury Gdns HARH RM3 ...... 160 E1 2
Dewsbury Rd HARH RM3 .... 161 F1 1
Dewsgreen VGE SS16 .... 186 A2
Dewyk Rd CVI SS8 .... 208 A1
Dexter Cl GRAYS RM17 .... 213 K2
Deyncourt Gdns UPMR RM14 ... 181 K3
Diamond Cl CDH/CHF RM16 ..... 213 J1
Diana Cl CDH/CHF RM16 .... 213 J2
Diban Av HCH RM12 .... 180 C5
Dickens Av TIL RM18 .... 215 G7
Dickens Cl SOSN SS2 .... 9 E2
Dickens Dr LAIN SS15 .... 6 A3
Dickens Ri CHIG IG7 .... 134 D6
Dickens Rd GVE DA12 .... 219 K6
Dickins Cl CHESW EN7 .... 76 A1
Dicky Moors RCHLM CM3 .... 20 B6

Digby Rd SLH/COR SS17 .... 187 J8
Dilston RCHLM CM3 .... 66 A7
Dinant Av CVI SS8 .... 190 D8
Disney Cl ING CM4 .... 116 B1
Dison Cl PEND EN3 .... 104 D5 2
Disraeli Rd RAYL SS6 .... 172 C5
Ditton Court Rd WOS/PRIT SS0 .... 8 A4
Dixon Av CHLM/WR CM1 .... 4 A1
Dobsons Cl LOS SS9 .... 193 G3
RAYL SS6 .... 171 K4
Dock Approach Rd
CDH/CHF RM16 .... 201 K8
GRAYS RM17 .... 214 D4
Docklands Av ING CM4 .... 116 C1
Dock Rd GRAYS RM17 .... 214 C5
RCHLM CM3 .... 99 F4
TIL RM18 .... 214 D7
Dockwra La CDH/CHF RM16 .... 65 K6
Doddinghurst Rd BRWN CM15 .. 114 A3
BRWN CM15 .... 141 F1
Doesgate La UPMR RM14 .... 185 G4
Doeshill Dr WICKW SS12 .... 147 H6
Doggetts Cha RCFD SS4 .... 152 C7
Doggetts Cl RCFD SS4 .... 174 C2
Dog Kennel La ING CM4 .... 88 B6
Dolby Ri CHLM/GWD CM2 .... 63 H3
Doliant Av RCFD SS4 .... 208 A2
Dolphin Ap ROM RM1 .... 160 A6
Dolphin Gdns BCAYW CM12 ..... 117 F8 3
Dolphins WOS/PRIT SS0 .... 174 A8
Dombey Cl CHLM/WR CM1 .... 34 B6
Domsey La RCHLM CM3 .... 35 G2
Donald Thorn Cl WICKW SS12 .. 147 G7 2
Donald Wy CHLM/GWD CM2 .... 5 D6
Doncaster Wy UPMR RM14 ...... 181 G4
Donkey La EN EN1 .... 104 A6
Donovan's Gdn RBRW/HUT CM13 .. 164 D2
Dorchester Gdns CHING E4 ...... 132 B7 2
Dorchester Rd BCAYW CM12 .... 117 G8 4
GVE DA12 .... 219 J8
Dorian Rd HCH RM12 .... 180 B2
Doric Av RCFD SS4 .... 152 A8
Dorking Ri HARH RM3 .... 138 E7
Dorking Rd HARH RM3 .... 138 E7
Dorking Wk HARH RM3 .... 138 E7
Dorkins Wy UPMR RM14 .... 182 B1
Dorothy Farm Rd RAYL SS6 ..... 172 BA 1
Dorothy Gdns SBF/HAD SS7 ..... 170 E8
Dorrington Gdns HCH RM12 ..... 180 E2
Dorset Av CHLM/GWD CM2 .... 63 F7
Dorset Cl CHLM/GWD CM2 .... 63 G7
Dorset Gdns RCFD SS4 .... 151 K8
Dorset Rd BOC CM0 .... 155 H1
MAL CM9 .... 68 B4
Dorset Wy BCAYW CM12 .... 117 G8
Doubleday Dr MAL CM9 .... 40 B8
Doubleday Rd LOU IG10 .... 108 A7
Doublegate La WICKE SS11 ...... 148 B8
WICKW SS12 .... 170 A1
Doublet Ms BCAYE CM11 .... 117 K8
Douglas Av HARH RM3 .... 161 F4
Douglas Cl CDH/CHF RM16 ...... 213 H2
CHLM/GWD CM2 .... 91 F2 1
Douglas Dr WICKW SS12 .... 147 G8
Douglas Rd CHING E4 .... 133 F3
ROM RM1 .... 160 A8
SBF/HAD SS7 .... 192 A2
Douglas Wk CHLM/GWD CM2 ..... 4 B5
Doug Siddons Ct GRAYS RM17 . 214 B5 2
Doulton Cl HLWE CM17 .... 25 J6
Doulton Wy RCFD SS4 .... 151 K7
Dovecote SBN/FI SS3 .... 196 D4 3
Dovedale Cl CVI SS8 .... 191 J8 3
Dovedale Cl BCAYE CM11 .... 145 K1 1
VGE SS16 .... 186 B1
Dove Dr SBF/HAD SS7 .... 190 A3
Dovehouse Cft HLW CM20 .... 24 E3 1
Dove House Gdns CHING E4 ..... 132 B5 2
Dove La CHLM/GWD CM2 .... 62 C7
Dovercliff Rd CVI SS8 .... 208 B2
Dover Rd GVW DA11 .... 218 C5
Dover Rd East GVW DA11 .... 218 D5
Dovervelt Rd CVI SS8 .... 191 G8
Dover Wy PIT SS13 .... 168 E7
Dovesgate SBF/HAD SS7 .... 190 A1 1
Doves Ms LAIN SS15 .... 6 B1 2
Dow Ct BOC CM0 .... 128 C1
Dowding Cl RAIN RM13 .... 180 C8
Dowland Cl SLH/COR SS17 .... 203 J2 1
The Downage GVW DA11 .... 219 F7
Downer Rd SBF/HAD SS7 .... 190 C1
Downer Rd North SBF/HAD SS7 170 D8
Downesway SBF/HAD SS7 .... 190 C2
Downey Cl BSDN SS14 .... 167 K6
Downfield Rd CHES/WCR EN8 .... 76 E5
Downhall Rd RAYL SS6 .... 171 J1
Downhall Park Wy RAYL SS6 .... 171 H1
Down Hall Rd RAYL SS6 .... 171 H2
Downhall Rd RBSF CM22 .... 13 H7
Downham Rd BCAYW CM11 ...... 119 F8
CVI SS8 .... 208 A2
ING CM4 .... 118 C1
WICKE SS11 .... 147 F3
Downlands WAB EN9 .... 78 A8 1
Downleaze RCHLM CM3 .... 122 E5

Downs Gv VGE SS16 .... 188 B2
Downsland Dr BRW CM14 .... 141 F6
Downs Rd MAL CM9 .... 68 C2
The Downs HLW CM20 .... 3 E3
Downsway CHLM/WR CM1 .... 35 F6
Dowsetts La BCAYE CM11 .... 118 D5
Dragon Cl BOC CM0 .... 128 A8
Drake Av RCHLM CM3 .... 98 E5
Drake Cl BRW CM14 .... 141 G8
SBF/HAD SS7 .... 191 H1
Drake Ms RAIN RM13 .... 180 B8 ⓘ
Drake Rd CDH/CHF RM16 .... 213 H6
LAIN SS15 .... 165 K6
WOS/PRIT SS0 .... 193 K5
Drakes Cl CHES/WCR EN8 .... 76 D2 ⓘ
Drakes La RCHLM CM3 .... 21 H6
The Drakes SBN/FI SS3 .... 196 D5
Drakes Wy RAYL SS6 .... 171 K1
Drapers Cha MAL CM9 .... 69 F1
Drapers Rd RCHLM CM3 .... 122 E5
Drayson Cl WAB EN9 .... 77 K6
Drayton Av LOU IG10 .... 134 C2
Drayton Cl MAL CM9 .... 68 C4 ⓘ
Drewsteignton SBN/FI SS3 .... 196 C5
Driftway VGE SS16 .... 188 C2
The Drive BKHH IG9 .... 133 K3
CHING E4 .... 132 E3
CHLM/WR CM1 .... 34 C7
CHESW EN7 .... 76 B2
HARH RM3 .... 161 F3
HLW CM20 .... 3 E2
HOC/HUL SS5 .... 149 J2
LOU IG10 .... 107 G7
RAYL SS6 .... 172 C5
RBRW/HUT CM13 .... 163 F1
RCFD SS4 .... 174 C3
RCHLM CM3 .... 98 D5
SBW CM21 .... 11 J5
WOS/PRIT SS0 .... 193 J5
The Driveway CVI SS8 .... 208 B3
Droitwich Cl SOSN SS2 .... 195 G4 ⓘ
Drood Cl CHLM/WR CM1 .... 34 B6
Drummond Cl CVI SS8 .... -
Drummond Pl WICKW SS12 .... 147 H8 ⓘ
The Drummonds EPP CM16 .... 80 E4 ⓘ
Drury La GTDUN CM6 .... 15 K3
Dryden Av SOSN SS2 .... 9 E2
Dryden Cl MAL CM9 .... 68 C5 ⓘ
Dryden Pl TIL RM18 .... 215 G2
Drysdale Av CHING E4 .... 132 C2
Dry St VGE SS16 .... 186 D3
Drywoods RCHLM CM3 .... 122 D8 ⓘ
Duarte Pl CDH/CHF RM16 .... 213 J2
Dubarry Cl SBF/HAD SS7 .... 190 E1
Ducker's La CHLM/WR CM1 .... 18 C6
Ducketts Md HLWW/ROY CM19 .... 22 D4
RCFD SS4 .... 153 G3
Duck La EPP CM16 .... 53 G8
Duck Lees La PEND EN3 .... 104 E8
Duckling La SBW CM21 .... 11 J3 ⓘ
Dudbrook Rd BRW CM14 .... 112 C4
Dudely Rd GVW DA11 .... 218 D5
Dudley Av CHES/WCR EN8 .... 76 D6
Dudley Cl CDH/CHF RM16 .... 213 H1
RCHLM CM3 .... 36 C4
Dudley Rd HARH RM3 .... 160 E1
Duffield Cl CDH/CHF RM16 .... 213 J2
Duffield Rd CHLM/GWD CM2 ...... 63 F7
Duffries Cl RCHLM CM3 .... 20 A6
Duke Pl LAIN SS15 .... 6 C2
Dukes Av BOC CM0 .... 128 D2
CDH/CHF RM16 .... 213 K2
EPP CM16 .... 108 C1
Dukes Cl EPP CM16 .... 82 B1
Dukes Farm Cl BCAYW CM12 ..... 117 J8
Dukes Farm Rd BCAYW CM12 .... 144 C1
Dukes La CHLM/GWD CM2 .... 63 H1
CHONG CM5 .... 30 A7
Dukes Rd BCAYE CM11 .... 114 D1
Dulverton Av WOS/PRIT SS0 ...... 193 H1
Dulverton Cl WOS/PRIT SS0 ...... 173 H8
Dulverton Rd HARH RM3 .... 160 E1
Dumbarton Av CHES/WCR EN8 .... 76 D8 ⓘ
Dunbar Pl WICKW SS12 .... 147 H8
Duncan Cl WICKW SS12 .... 147 J8 ⓘ
Dundee Av LOS SS9 .... 192 C3
Dundee Cl LOS SS9 .... 192 D3
Dundee Ct BSDN SS14 .... 168 C5
Dundee Wy PEND EN3 .... 104 E2
Dundonald Dr LOS SS9 .... 193 G4
Dunfane BCAYW CM12 .... 117 J8
Dungannon Cha SOS SS1 .... 196 A7 ⓘ
Dungannon Dr SOS SS1 .... 196 A7
Dunkellin La SOCK/AV RM15 ...... 199 J6 ⓘ
Dunkellin Wy SOCK/AV RM15 ..... 199 J6
Dunkirk Rd BOC CM0 .... 155 H1
Dunlin Cl MAL CM9 .... 40 E8 ⓘ
RCHLM CM3 .... 122 D4
Dunlop Rd TIL RM18 .... 214 E7
Dunmore Rd CHLM/GWD CM2 ..... 63 J2 ⓘ
Dunmow Cl LOU IG10 .... 134 B2
Dunmow Gdns RBRW/HUT CM13 .. 164 C8
Dunmow Rd CHONG CM5 .... 29 H4
Dunning Cl SOCK/AV RM15 .... 199 J6 ⓘ
Dunningford Cl HCH RM12 .... 180 A6 ⓘ
Dunnings La RBRW/HUT CM13 .... 184 A3

Dunstable Rd HARH RM3 .... 160 E1
SLH/COR SS17 .... 203 J2
Dunstalls HLWW/ROY CM19 ...... 51 J1
Dunster Av WOS/PRIT SS0 .... 173 H8
Dunster Crs UPMR RM14 .... 181 H3
Dunton Rd RBRW/HUT CM13 ..... 165 J4
Durants Park Av PEND EN3 .... 104 D8
Durants Rd PEND EN3 .... 104 C8
Durban La LAIN SS15 .... 167 G3 ⓘ
The Durdans VGE SS16 .... 186 C1
Durham Av GPK RM2 .... 160 D6
WFD IG8 .... 134 A8
Durham Cl SBW CM21 .... 11 G4 ⓘ
RCFD SS4 .... 151 J8
SOSN SS2 .... 195 J5
Durham Wy RAYL SS6 .... 149 J8
Durian Wy ERITH DA8 .... 210 C6
Durley Av WICKW SS12 .... 146 C5
Durley Cl SBF/HAD SS7 .... 190 D1
Durnell Wy LOU IG10 .... 107 J7
Durrington Cl LAIN SS15 .... 167 K8
Dury Falls Cl EMPK RM11 .... 181 G2 ⓘ
Duxford WICKE SS11 .... 147 K7
Duxford Cl HCH RM12 .... 180 C7
Dyer's Rd MAL CM9 .... 68 C3
Dyers Wy HARH RM3 .... 160 B2
Dyke Crs CVI SS8 .... 207 H1
Dykes Cha MAL CM9 .... 68 A2
Dymoke Rd ROM RM1 .... 180 A4
Dynevor Gdns LOS SS9 .... 192 C4
Dysons Cl CHES/WCR EN8 .... 76 D7

E

Eagle Cl PEND EN3 .... 104 C8
RAIN RM13 .... 180 C7
WAB EN9 .... 78 C8
Eagle La BRWN CM15 .... 113 G3
Eagle Wy RBRW/HUT CM13 ...... 163 F1
SBN/FI SS3 .... 196 D5
Earl Mountbatten Dr
BCAYW CM12 .... 144 A2 ⓘ
Earl Rd GVW DA11 .... 218 D7
Earlsfield Dr CHLM/GWD CM2 .... 63 H2
Earls Hall Av SOSN SS2 .... 9 J2
Earls Hall Pde SOSN SS2 .... 194 B1
Earl's Pth LOU IG10 .... 106 E7
Earlswood SBF/HAD SS7 .... 190 C1
Easedale Dr HCH RM12 .... 180 C6
Easington Dr SOCK/AV RM15 ..... 199 J5
Eastbourne Gv WOS/PRIT SS0 .... 193 K2
Eastbrook Rd WAB EN9 .... 78 A7
Eastbrooks PIT SS13 .... 168 E6
Eastbury Av RCFD SS4 .... 174 A1
Eastcheap RAYL SS6 .... 171 H1
Eastcote Gv SOSN SS2 .... 195 G2
East Crs CVI SS8 .... 207 K1
East Dene Dr HARH RM3 .... 138 E8
East Dr SBW CM21 .... 11 J4
Eastend Rd BOC CM0 .... 74 D3
Eastern Av BOC CM0 .... 128 C7
GRAYS RM17 .... 214 C3 ⓘ
RAYL SS6 .... 171 G5
ROM RM1 .... 160 A7
Eastern Av East GPK RM2 .... 160 A3
Eastern Cl SOSN SS2 .... 9 D1
Eastern Crs CHLM/WR CM1 ...... 34 B8
SOS SS1 .... 9 F6
WTHK RM20 .... 212 C4
Eastern Av East GPK RM2 .... 160 A3
Eastern Rd BOC CM0 .... 128 C7
GRAYS RM17 .... 214 C3 ⓘ
RAYL SS6 .... 171 G5
ROM RM1 .... 160 A7
Eastern Wy GRAYS RM17 .... 213 K5
Eastfield Rd CHES/WCR EN8 ..... 77 F6
BRW CM14 .... 141 G8
CVI SS8 .... 191 J8
LAIN SS15 .... 167 G3
PEND EN3 .... 104 D4
East Ga HLW CM20 .... 3 D2
East Glebe Dr RAYL SS6 .... 171 H2
East Ham Crs RBRW/HUT CM13 .. 141 K7
East Hanningfield Rd
CHLM/GWD CM2 .... 92 C2
RCHLM CM3 .... 121 F4
East Kent Av GVW DA11 .... 218 B4
Eastleigh Rd SBF/HAD SS7 ...... 190 D5
Eastley SS16 .... 7 E6
East Mayne BSDN SS14 .... 168 D3
PIT SS13 .... 168 C6
East Milton Rd GVE DA12 .... 219 F3
Easton End LAIN SS15 .... 166 B7 ⓘ
East Pk HLWE CM17 .... 25 C2
SBW CM21 .... 11 J4
East Philbrick Crs RAYL SS6 ..... 171 H2 ⓘ
East Rd HLW CM20 .... 25 F1
PEND EN3 .... 104 C4
East St LOS SS9 .... 193 F5

MAL CM9 .... 44 D
RCFD SS4 .... 174 C
SOSN SS2 .... 213 H
WTHK RM20 .... 213 H
East Ter GVE DA12 .... 219 H
East Thorpe BSDN SS14 .... 167 K
East Thurrock Rd GRAYS RM17 .. 214 A
East Tilbury Rd SLH/COR SS17 .. 216 E
East Vw CHING E4 .... 132 C
CHLM/WR CM1 .... 61 F
Eastview Dr RAYL SS6 .... 149 J
East Wy WAB EN9 .... 105 K
Eastways CVI SS8 .... 190 D
Eastwick Rd HLW CM20 .... 23 K
Eastwood Bvd WOS/PRIT SS0 .... 193 H
Eastwoodbury Cl SOSN SS2 ..... 174 A
Eastwoodbury Crs SOSN SS2 .... 174 E
Eastwoodbury La SOSN SS2 ..... 173 J
Eastwood La South
WOS/PRIT SS0 .... 193 J
Eastwood Old Rd LOS SS9 ...... 172 C
SBF/HAD SS7 .... 172 E
Eastwood Park Dr LOS SS9 ..... 173 F
Eastwood Ri LOS SS9 .... 172 C
Eastwood Rd LOS SS9 .... 192 E
RAYL SS6 .... 171 K
Eastwood Rd North LOS SS9 .... 192 E
Eaton Cl BCAYW CM12 .... 117 C
Eaton Rd LOS SS9 .... 192 D
UPMR RM14 .... 182 B
Eatons Md CHING E4 .... 132 B
Eccleston Gdns BCAYW CM12 ... 117 C8
Echo Ct GVE DA12 .... 219 H
Echo Hts CHING E4 .... 132 C4
Eckersley Rd CHLM/WR CM1 .... 5 D
Eden Gn SOCK/AV RM15 .... 199 K
Edenhall Rd HARH RM3 .... 138 D
Eden Pl GVE DA12 .... 219 C
Edgecotts VGE SS16 .... 6 C6
Edinburgh Av LOS SS9 .... 192 C
SLH/COR SS17 .... 204 B
Edinburgh Cl RAYL SS6 .... 149 G8
Edinburgh Crs CHES/WCR EN8 .. 76 E
Edinburgh Ms TIL RM18 .... 215 G8
Edinburgh Pl HLW CM20 .... 24 E
Edinburgh Wy HLW CM20 ...... 25 F
HLWE CM17 .... 11 G8
PIT SS13 .... 168 E
Edington Rd PEND EN3 .... 104 C6
Edison Av HCH RM12 .... 180 A
Edison Cl HCH RM12 .... 180 A
Edison Rd PEND EN3 .... 105 F
Edith Cl CVI SS8 .... 207 H
Edith Rd CVI SS8 .... 207 H
SOSN SS2 .... 8 C
Edith Wy SLH/COR SS17 .... 187 H
Edmund Rd CDH/CHF RM16 .... 213 C
Edridge Cl HCH RM12 .... 180 E6
Edward Av CHING E4 .... 132 C
Edward Cl BCAYW CM12 .... 117 F8
GPK RM2 .... 160 D5
RCFD SS4 .... 151 K7
Edward Ct WAB EN9 .... 78 B
Edward Dr CHLM/GWD CM2 .... 5 D
Edward Gdns WICKE SS11 ...... 147 C
Edwards Cl RBRW/HUT CM13 ... 142 D
Edwards Wy RBRW/HUT CM13 .. 142 D
Edwin Hall Vw RCHLM CM3 .... 122 C
Edwin's Hall Rd RCHLM CM3 ... 122 C
Edwin St GVE DA12 .... 219 C
Egbert Gdns WICKE SS11 ...... 147 C
Egerton Dr VGE SS16 .... 165 K
Egg Hall EPP CM16 .... 80 E
Eglington Rd CHING E4 .... 132 E
Eisenhower Rd LAIN SS15 ..... 166 B7
Elan Rd SOCK/AV RM15 .... 199 J
Elbert Cl SOSN SS2 .... 195 H3
Eldeland LAIN SS15 .... 6 C
Elder Av WICKW SS12 .... 146 E
Elderbeck Cl CHESW EN7 ..... 76 A
Elderberry Cl VGE SS16 ...... 166 C8
Elderfield HLWE CM17 .... 25 H
Elderstep Av CVI SS8 .... 208 E2
Elderton Rd WOS/PRIT SS0 .... 8 A
Elder Wy WICKW SS12 .... 147 F
Eldon Rd HOD EN11 .... 49 K
Eldon Wy HOC/HUL SS5 ...... 150 E
Eldred Gdns UPMR RM14 ..... 182 B
Eleanor Cha WICKW SS12 .... 147 F
Eleanor Cross Rd CHES/WCR EN8 76 E
Eleanor Rd CHES/WCR EN8 .... 76 B
Eleanor Wy CHES/WCR EN8 ... 77 F
Electric Av WOS/PRIT SS0 .... 193 K
Eleven Acre Ri LOU IG10 ..... 107 H
Elgar Cl BKHH IG9 .... 134 A
LAIN SS15 .... 6 B
SBF/HAD SS7 .... 170 A
Elgar Gdns TIL RM18 .... 215 F
Elgin Av CHLM/WR CM1 ...... 4 B
HARH RM3 .... 161 J
Elgin Rd CHES/WCR EN8 ..... 76 E
BROX EN10 .... 49 F
Elham Dr PIT SS13 .... 169 F
Eliot Wy MAL CM9 .... 68 C

zabeth Av RAYL SS6 .... 171 H5
zabeth Cl HOC/HUL SS5 .... 173 F1
  TIL RM18 .... 215 G8
  WAB EN9 .... 49 K5
zabeth Dr EPP CM16 .... 108 C2
  WICKW SS12 .... 146 E5
zabeth Rd BRWN CM15 .... 113 J8
  CDH/CHF RM16 .... 213 J2
zabeth Wy HLW CM20 .... 2 A1
  HLWW/ROY CM19 .... 23 H6
  LAIN SS15 .... 6 B5
  MAL CM9 .... 40 C8
  RCHLM CM3 .... 38 A1
  SBF/HAD SS7 .... 191 H1
enbrook Cl LOS SS9 .... 193 F2
esmere Rd CVI SS8 .... 207 J2
iott Cl RCHLM CM3 .... 123 F7
iott Gdns HARH RM3 .... 160 C5
iott St GVE DA12 .... 219 J5
is Cl CDH/CHF RM16 .... 202 D6
more Cl HARH RM3 .... 160 C3
m Av MAL CM9 .... 40 D8
  UPMR RM14 .... 181 J4
mbridge HLWE CM17 .... 25 K2
m Cl BKHH IG9 .... 134 A5
mfield Rd CHING E4 .... 132 D5
m Gdns EPPK CM16 .... 54 B8
m Gn PIT SS13 .... 168 D8
m Green La RCHLM CM3 .... 65 C5
m Gv EMPK RM11 .... 161 F8
  HOC/HUL SS5 .... 149 J3
  SOS SS1 .... 195 K5
mhurst Av SBF/HAD SS7 .... 190 A1
mhurst Dr EMPK RM11 .... 180 D1
mhurst End PEND EN3 .... 104 C3
mhurst Wy LOU IG10 .... 134 C3
more Rd PEND EN3 .... 104 D5
mores LOU IG10 .... 107 J7
m Park Av RCHLM CM12 .... 180 C5
m Rd CHLM/GWD CM2 .... 4 B5
  CVI SS8 .... 208 C2
  ERITH DA8 .... 210 B7
  GRAYS RM17 .... 214 B5
  GVE DA12 .... 219 H8
  LOS SS9 .... 193 F4
  PIT SS13 .... 169 H4
  RCHLM CM3 .... 122 C5
  SBF/HAD SS7 .... 191 J3
  SBN/FI SS3 .... 196 B6
  SOCK/AV RM15 .... 199 F8
  WICKE SS11 .... 147 G5
ms Dr CHLM/WR CM1 .... 4 B1
ms Farm Rd HCH RM12 .... 180 E5
msleigh Dr LOS SS9 .... 193 F2
ms Rd CHLM/GWD CM2 .... 4 B5
ns Rd CHLM/WR CM1 .... 31 J7
este Rd SLH/COR SS17 .... 187 J8
e Elms CHONG CM5 .... 84 C4
m Ter WTHK RM20 .... 212 E5
ntree Av VGE SS16 .... 188 C3
ntree Rd BRWN CM15 .... 113 H3
n View Rd SBF/HAD SS7 .... 190 A2
n Wk GPK RM2 .... 160 B5
n Wy BRW CM14 .... 140 D6
nway CDH/CHF RM16 .... 201 G7
n Wy RCHLM CM3 .... 36 C4
nwood SBW CM21 .... 11 K4
nwood Av HOC/HUL SS5 .... 173 F1
rington Rd WFD IG8 .... 133 H8
ounda Ct SBF/HAD SS7 .... 190 C1
ronds Rest RCHLM CM3 .... 122 C7
sden Cha BOC CM0 .... 128 D1
senham Crs BSDN SS14 .... 168 C7
singe EN EN1 .... 104 B2
sinor Av CVI SS8 .... 191 F7
verston Cl LAIN SS15 .... 6 B2
vet Av HARH RM3 .... 160 D6
wick Rd SOCK/AV RM15 .... 200 A6
wood HLWE CM17 .... 25 J6
y Cl BOC CM0 .... 128 D1
  ERITH DA8 .... 210 A8
  RAYL SS6 .... 171 H1
y Pl WFD IG8 .... 134 D8
y Rd SOS SS9 .... 9 E2
ysian Gdns MAL CM9 .... 44 C4
manuel Rd VGE SS16 .... 186 C1
nberson Ct CHLM/GWD CM2 .... 63 H1
nberson Wy EPP CM16 .... 54 B8
nerson Dr EMPK RM11 .... 180 E1

Emmaus Wy CHIG IG7 .... 134 D8
Empress Rd GVE DA12 .... 219 K5
Enborne Gn SOCK/AV RM15 .... 199 J5
Endeavour Cl MAL CM9 .... 44 D5
Endeavour Dr BSDN SS14 .... 7 K1
Endeavour Rd CHES/WCR EN8 .... 76 D1
Endlebury Rd CHING E4 .... 132 D5
Endway SBF/HAD SS7 .... 191 K3
The Endway RCHLM CM3 .... 127 C3
Enfield Rd WICKE SS11 .... 148 B6
Engayne Gdns UPMR RM14 .... 181 J2
England's La LOU IG10 .... 107 J6
Englefield Cl HOC/HUL SS5 .... 173 H1
Englefields BOC CM0 .... 102 A2
Ennerdale Av HCH RM12 .... 180 B6
Ennismore Gdns SOSN SS2 .... 9 D1
Ensign Cl LOS SS9 .... 193 H4
Enterprise Wy WICKW SS12 .... 147 J7
Epping Old CHING E4 .... 132 D2
Epping La ABR/ST RM4 .... 7 H4
Epping New Rd BKHH IG9 .... 133 J5
  LOU IG10 .... 107 F4
Epping Wy CHING E4 .... 132 C2
Epsom Wy HCH RM12 .... 181 G5
Erick Av CHLM/WR CM1 .... 34 D6
Eric Rd PIT SS13 .... 169 J7
Eridge Cl CHLM/WR CM1 .... 35 F6
Erith Ct PUR RM19 .... 211 H3
Erith High St ERITH DA8 .... 210 A5
Ermine Cl CHESW EN7 .... 76 B5
Ernan Cl SOCK/AV RM15 .... 199 J5
Ernan Rd SOCK/AV RM15 .... 199 J5
Ernest Rd EMPK RM11 .... 161 F8
Erriff Dr SOCK/AV RM15 .... 199 J5
Errington Cl CDH/CHF RM16 .... 215 G2
Erroll Rd ROM RM1 .... 160 A6
Erskine Pl WICKW SS12 .... 147 H7
Esdaile Gdns UPMR RM14 .... 182 A1
Eskley Gdns SOCK/AV RM15 .... 199 J5
Esmond Cl RAIN RM13 .... 180 C8
Esplanade Gdns WOS/PRIT SS0 .... 193 K5
The Esplanade HOC/HUL SS5 .... 149 H2
  RCHLM CM3 .... 65 C3
Essex Av SBF/HAD SS7 .... 190 A1
Essex Cl CVI SS8 .... 208 A3
  LAIN SS15 .... 166 C3
  RAYL SS6 .... 172 A4
Essex Gdns EMPK RM11 .... 161 H7
  LOS SS9 .... 193 F1
  SLH/COR SS17 .... 216 B1
Essex Regiment Wy RCHLM CM3 .... 20 C3
Essex Rd BOC CM0 .... 128 C3
  CHING E4 .... 133 F4
  CVI SS8 .... 208 C1
  GVW DA11 .... 219 F6
  MAL CM9 .... 68 B4
  WTHK RM20 .... 212 D5
Essex St SOS SS1 .... 4 C6
Essex Wy CHONG CM5 .... 31 F4
  CHONG CM5 .... 58 C2
  EPP CM16 .... 80 E6
  EPP CM16 .... 82 C3
  RBRW/HUT CM13 .... 165 F1
  SBF/HAD SS7 .... 170 B2
Estate Rd SBF/HAD SS7 .... 192 A2
Estella Md CHLM/WR CM1 .... 34 A6
Estuary Ms MAL CM9 .... 44 D3
Estuary Rd SBN/FI SS3 .... 197 H3
Ethelburga Rd HARH RM3 .... 161 G3
Ethelred Gdns WICKE SS11 .... 147 H4
Ethel Rd RAYL SS6 .... 172 A5
Etheridge Rd LOU IG10 .... 108 A7
Eton Cl CVI SS8 .... 191 J4
Eton Wk SBN/FI SS3 .... 196 D4
Etton Cl HCH RM12 .... 181 F5
Euclid Wy WTHK RM20 .... 212 C5
Eugene Cl GPK RM2 .... 160 D6
Evelyn Rd HOC/HUL SS5 .... 151 F8
Evelyn Sharp Cl GPK RM2 .... 160 E5
Everard Rd BSDN SS14 .... 168 C7
Everest RAYL SS6 .... 149 J8
Everest Cl GVW DA11 .... 218 D8
Everest Rd BCAYW CM12 .... 144 A4
Everest Wy MAL CM9 .... 40 D8
Eversleigh Gdns UPMR RM14 .... 182 A2
Eversley Rd PIT SS13 .... 169 J5
  SBF/HAD SS7 .... 170 A6
Eves Cnr RCHLM CM3 .... 65 J6
Eves Crs CHLM/WR CM1 .... 34 C8
Evesham Rd GVE DA12 .... 219 J1
Ewan Cl LOS SS9 .... 192 B2
Ewanrigg Ter WFD IG8 .... 133 K8
Ewan Rd HARH RM3 .... 160 E4
Ewan Wy SBF/HAD SS7 .... 192 B2
Exeter Cl BSDN SS14 .... 168 C6
  SBN/FI SS3 .... 196 E4
Exeter Rd CHLM/WR CM1 .... 35 G8
  GVE DA12 .... 219 J8
  PEND EN3 .... 104 D7

Exford Av WOS/PRIT SS0 .... 173 H8
Exhibition La SBN/FI SS3 .... 196 E1
Exley Cl INC CM4 .... 116 B1
Exmoor Cl CHLM/WR CM1 .... 61 K4
Exmouth Dr RAYL SS6 .... 149 J8
Exmouth Rd GRAYS RM17 .... 214 A5
Eyhurst Av HCH RM12 .... 180 B4
Eynesham Wy PIT SS13 .... 168 D4
Eyre Cl GPK RM2 .... 160 C6

F

Factory Rd GVW DA11 .... 218 B4
Fairbank Cl CHONG CM5 .... 84 B3
Fairburn Cl SOS SS1 .... 9 F4
Fairfax Av PIT SS13 .... 169 F5
Fairfax Dr WOS/PRIT SS0 .... 193 K3
Fairfax Md CHLM/GWD CM2 .... 63 H3
Fairfax Rd GRAYS RM17 .... 214 A4
  TIL RM18 .... 214 E7
Fairfield INC CM4 .... 116 C1
  SBN/FI SS3 .... 197 F2
Fairfield Av CDH/CHF RM16 .... 201 G8
  UPMR RM14 .... 181 K4
Fairfield Cl HCH RM12 .... 180 B2
  PEND EN3 .... 104 E8
Fairfield Crs LOS SS9 .... 173 G6
Fairfield Dr BROX EN10 .... 49 F6
Fairfield Gdns LOS SS9 .... 173 F6
Fairfield Ri BCAYW CM12 .... 144 A5
Fairfield Rd BRW CM14 .... 141 F6
  CHLM/WR CM1 .... 4 B2
  CHONG CM5 .... 84 B3
  EPP CM16 .... 81 F3
  LOS SS9 .... 173 F6
Fairford Cl HARH RM3 .... 161 J1
Fairford Wy HARH RM3 .... 161 J1
Fairham Av SOCK/AV RM15 .... 199 J7
Fairholme Av GPK RM2 .... 160 B7
Fairholme Gdns UPMR RM14 .... 182 C1
Fairkytes Av EMPK RM11 .... 180 E2
Fairland Cl RAYL SS6 .... 149 K8
Fairlands Av BKHH IG9 .... 133 H5
Fairlawn Gdns SOSN SS2 .... 174 B8
Fairlawns Cl EMPK RM11 .... 181 G1
Fairleads RCHLM CM3 .... 65 K5
Fairleigh Av PIT SS13 .... 169 G8
Fairleigh Dr LOS SS9 .... 192 E4
Fairleigh Rd PIT SS13 .... 169 G8
Fairley Wy CHESW EN7 .... 76 B2
Fairlight Av CHING E4 .... 132 E5
Fairlight Cl CHING E4 .... 132 E5
Fairlight Rd SBF/HAD SS7 .... 191 H2
Fairlop Av CVI SS8 .... 208 A1
Fairlop Cl HCH RM12 .... 180 C7
Fairlop Gdns BSDN SS14 .... 168 A7
Fair Md BSDN SS14 .... 167 K5
Fairmead RAYL SS6 .... 171 G1
Fairmead Av SBF/HAD SS7 .... 171 K8
  WOS/PRIT SS0 .... 193 K3
Fairmead Rd LOU IG10 .... 106 D8
Fairmeads LOU IG10 .... 107 K6
Fairoaks Gv PEND EN3 .... 104 D3
Fairview BCAYW CM12 .... 144 B4
  CVI SS8 .... 190 E8
  ERITH DA8 .... 210 A6
Fairview Av RBRW/HUT CM13 .... 142 D3
  SLH/COR SS17 .... 203 J4
Fairview Cha SLH/COR SS17 .... 203 J5
Fairview Cl CHIG IG7 .... 135 H7
  SBF/HAD SS7 .... 170 B6
Fairview Crs SBF/HAD SS7 .... 170 B6
Fairview Dr CHIG IG7 .... 135 H8
  WOS/PRIT SS0 .... 193 K1
Fairview Gdns LOS SS9 .... 192 D3
Fairview Rd BSDN SS14 .... 168 B7
  CHIG IG7 .... 135 H7
Fairway Dr BOC CM0 .... 128 B8
Fairway Gdns LOS SS9 .... 172 B8
Fairway Gardens Cl LOS SS9 .... 172 B8
Fairways CHES/WCR EN8 .... 48 C8
The Fairways RCHLM CM3 .... 96 B8
The Fairway GVW DA11 .... 219 F7
  HLWS CM18 .... 3 F6
  LOS SS9 .... 172 B8
  SBF/HAD SS7 .... 170 B6
  UPMR RM14 .... 181 K1
Falbro Crs SBF/HAD SS7 .... 191 J2
Falbro Cresent SBF/HAD SS7 .... 191 J1
Falcon Av GRAYS RM17 .... 214 A6
Falcon Cl LOS SS9 .... 173 F8
  RAYL SS6 .... 171 G2
  SBW CM21 .... 11 G4
Falconer Rd BARK/HLT IG6 .... 136 A8
Falconers Pk SBW CM21 .... 11 H4
Falcon Flds MAL CM9 .... 68 B5

Falcon Ms *GVW* DA11 .... 218 D6 🔲
  MAL CM9 .... 68 B5 🔲
Falcon Pk *BSDN* SS14 .... 7 D2
Falcon Rd *BOC* CM0 .... 128 C1
Falcon Wy *CHLM/GWD* CM2 .... 62 C7
  VGE SS16 .... 187 K1
Falkenham End *BSDN* SS14 .... 167 K6
Falkenham Ri *BSDN* SS14 .... 167 K5
Falkenham Rw *BSDN* SS14 .... 167 K6
Falkirk Cl *EMPK* RM11 .... 181 H2
Falkland Cl *RCHLM* CM3 .... 36 C5
Falklands Rd *BOC* CM0 .... 128 B8 🔲
Falkner Cl *CHJG* CM4 .... 118 B2
Fallow Cl *CHIG* IG7 .... 135 J8
Fallowfield *SBN/FI* SS3 .... 196 C4
Fallow Flds *LOU* IG10 .... 134 A3
The Fallows *CVI* SS8 .... 190 E7
Falmouth Av *CHING* E4 .... 132 E8
Falmouth Rd *CHLM/WR* CM1 .... 35 G8
Falstones *LAIN* SS15 .... 6 B4
Fambridge Cl *MAL* CM9 .... 68 C4
Fambridge Dr *WICKW* SS12 .... 147 H7
Fambridge Rd *MAL* CM9 .... 68 B3
  RCFD SS4 .... 151 J2
  RCHLM CM3 .... 124 E1
  RCHLM CM3 .... 126 D3
Fane Rd *SBF/HAD* SS7 .... 170 C5
Fanns Ri *PUR* RM19 .... 211 H3
Fanshawe Cre *EMPK* RM11 .... 160 E4
Fanshawe Rd *CDH/CHF* CM16 ...... 215 F2 🔲
Fanton Av *WICKW* SS12 .... 169 J3
Fanton Cha *WICKW* SS11 .... 147 K7
Fanton Gdns *WICKE* SS11 .... 148 A7
Fanton Wk *WICKE* SS11 .... 148 A6
Faraday Cl *LOS* SS9 .... 172 C7
Faringdon Av *HARH* RM3 .... 160 D3
Farlow Cl *GVW* DA11 .... 218 E8
Farmbridge End Rd
  CHLM/WR CM1 .... 31 H2
Farm Cl *CHES/WCR* EN8 .... 76 C4
  BKHH IG9 .... 133 K6
  RBRW/HUT CM13 .... 142 B3
Farm Crs *RCHLM* CM3 .... 148 D1
Farmcroft *GVW* DA11 .... 219 F7
Farm End *CHING* E4 .... 133 F1
Farmer Ct *WAB* EN9 .... 78 C7
Farm Hill Rd *WAB* EN9 .... 77 K8
Farmhouse Cl *BROX* EN10 .... 49 F7
Farm La *WTHK* RM20 .... 213 H5
Farm Rd *CDH/CHF* RM16 .... 214 E1
  CVI SS8 .... 191 G8
  TIL RM18 .... 216 D3
Farm Vw *RAYL* SS6 .... 149 J8
Farm Wy *BKHH* IG9 .... 133 K7
  HCH RM12 .... 180 C5
  SBF/HAD SS7 .... 171 G7
Farnes Av *WICKW* SS12 .... 147 F6 🔲
Farnes Dr *GPK* RM2 .... 160 D4
Farnham Cl *SBW* CM21 .... 11 G4
Farnham Rd *HARH* RM3 .... 138 E8
Farnley Rd *CHING* E4 .... 133 F3
Farriers Dr *BCAYW* CM12 .... 117 G8 🔲
Farriers End *BROX* EN10 .... 49 F8 🔲
Farriers Wy *SOSN* SS3 .... 174 C3
Farringdon Service Rd *SOS* SS1 ...... 9 D4 🔲
Farrow Gdns *CDH/CHF* RM16 ...... 201 F8
Farthingale La *WAB* EN9 .... 78 C8
Farthings Cl *CHING* E4 .... 133 F6
Fastnet *SOSN* SS2 .... 175 H6
Fauners *VGE* SS16 .... 7 E5
Faverolle Gn *CHES/WCR* EN8 .... 76 D2 🔲
Faversham Av *CHING* E4 .... 133 F4
Faversham Cl *CHIG* IG7 .... 136 A5
Fawkner Cl *CHLM/GWD* CM2 .... 63 H3
Fawn Rd *CHIG* IG7 .... 135 J8
Fawters Cl *RBRW/HUT* CM13 .... 142 C2
Faymore Gdns *SOCK/AV* RM15 .... 199 J6 🔲
Featherby Wy *RCFD* SS4 .... 174 D4
Feeches Rd *SOSN* SS2 .... 174 A8
Feenan Hwy *TIL* RM18 .... 215 G6
Feering Dr *BSDN* SS14 .... 168 C3
Feering Gn *BSDN* SS14 .... 168 C3
Feering Rd *BCAYE* CM11 .... 144 D3
Feering Rw *BSDN* SS14 .... 168 C3 🔲
Felicia Wy *CDH/CHF* RM16 .... 215 G3
Felipe Rd *CDH/CHF* RM16 .... 213 F3
Fell Christy *CHLM/WR* CM1 .... 34 D8
Felmongers *HLW* CM20 .... 25 F5
Felmores *PIT* SS13 .... 168 D5
Felstead Cl *RBRW/HUT* CM13 ...... 142 B2 🔲
  SBF/HAD SS7 .... 190 C1
Felstead Rd *CHES/WCR* EN8 .... 76 E6
  LOU IG10 .... 134 B3
  SBF/HAD SS7 .... 190 C1
Felsted Rd *BCAYE* CM11 .... 144 D3 🔲
Felton Cl *BROX* EN10 .... 49 F7
Fen Cl *BRWN* CM15 .... 115 G8
  UPMR RM14 .... 184 E5
Fengates Rd *RCHLM* CM3 .... 122 C5 🔲
Fen La *CDH/CHF* RM16 .... 201 K4
  UPMR RM14 .... 183 G6
Fenn Cl *RCHLM* CM3 .... 122 C5
Fennells *HLWW/ROY* CM19 .... 51 K2
Fenner Rd *CDH/CHF* RM16 .... 213 F3
Fenners Wy *PIT* SS13 .... 168 D3 🔲

Fennfields Rd *RCHLM* CM3 .... 122 B5
Fentiman Wy *EMPK* RM11 .... 181 F2
Fenton Gra *HLWE* CM17 .... 25 G6
Fenton Rd *ERITH* DA8 .... 210 E4
Fenton Wy *LAIN* SS15 .... 166 A6
Fenwick Wy *CVI* SS8 .... 191 F7
Ferguson Av *GPK* RM2 .... 160 D4
Ferguson Ct *GPK* RM2 .... 160 E4
Fermoy Rd *SOS* SS1 .... 195 K6
Fernbank *BCAYW* CM12 .... 144 A4
  IG9 .... 133 J4
Fernbank Av *HCH* RM12 .... 180 D5
Fernbrook Av *SOS* SS1 .... 195 G5
Ferndale *BCAYW* CM12 .... 144 A4 🔲
  BROX EN10 .... 49 F5
  ERITH DA8 .... 210 C7
Ferndale Cl *LAIN* SS15 .... 166 C7 🔲
Ferndale Crs *CVI* SS8 .... 208 B3
Ferndale Rd *GVE* DA12 .... 219 G7
  PEND EN3 .... 104 E3
  RAYL SS6 .... 149 J7
  SOSN SS2 .... 9 F2
Ferndown *EMPK* RM11 .... 161 H8
Ferndown Wy *RCHLM* CM3 .... 38 B1
Fernhall La *WAB* EN9 .... 79 F5
Fernhill *HLWS* CM18 .... 52 C1
Fern Hl *VGE* SS16 .... 6 A6
Fern Hill La *HLWS* CM18 .... 52 D1
Fernlea Rd *BOC* CM0 .... 128 B8
  SBF/HAD SS7 .... 190 D2
Fernleigh Dr *LOS* SS9 .... 193 H4
Ferns Cl *PEND* EN3 .... 104 E2 🔲
Fernside *BKHH* IG9 .... 133 J4
Fernside Cl *SLH/COR* SS17 .... 187 J8 🔲
  BROX EN10 .... 49 F5
Fernwood *SBF/HAD* SS7 .... 191 K1
Ferrers Rd *RCHLM* CM3 .... 122 C5
Ferris Av *RCHLM* CM3 .... 96 B8
Ferrymead *CVI* SS8 .... 190 E8
Feryby Rd *BOC* CM0 .... 127 J8
  HOC/HUL SS5 .... 149 J3
  RCHLM CM3 .... 124 C6
  SBF/HAD SS7 .... 190 C5
  TIL RM18 .... 215 F8
Fesants Cft *HLW* CM20 .... 25 F2
Festival Cl *ERITH* DA8 .... 210 A6
Festival Gdns *MAL* CM9 .... 43 H1
Festival Link *BSDN* SS14 .... 7 F1
Festival Wy *BSDN* SS14 .... 7 F1
Fetherston Rd *SLH/COR* SS17 ..... 203 K3
Field Cl *ABR/ST* RM4 .... 109 F7
  BKHH IG9 .... 133 K6
The Fielders *CVI* SS8 .... 207 K3
Fieldfare *BCAYW* CM12 .... 144 D5
Field Gdns *CHONG* CM5 .... 84 A8
Fielding Av *TIL* RM18 .... 215 G7
Fieldings Rd *CHES/WCR* EN8 .... 77 F3
Fielding Wy *RBRW/HUT* CM13 .... 142 B2 🔲
Field Kiln *BRW* CM15 .... 114 B1
Field Kiln *SOCK/AV* RM15 .... 198 E8
Fieldway *CDH/CHF* RM16 .... 200 E8
  PIT SS13 .... 188 E1
  WICKW SS12 .... 169 G2
Fifth Av *CHLM/WR* CM1 .... 34 D7
  CVI SS8 .... 207 J1
  WICKE SS11 .... 147 K7
  WTHK RM20 .... 212 D5
Fifth Avenue Allende Av
  HLW CM20 .... 3 D2
Filey Rd *BOC* CM0 .... 128 A3
Fillebrook Av *LOS* SS9 .... 193 H5
Finches Cl *SLH/COR* SS17 .... 187 K8
The Finches *SBF/HAD* SS7 .... 171 J4 🔲
Finchfield *RAYL* SS6 .... 171 J4 🔲
The Finchingfields *BRW* CM15 .... 113 G3 🔲
Finchingfield Wy *WICKW* SS12 ... 147 F8 🔲
Finchland Vw *RCHLM* CM3 .... 122 D7
Finchley Av *CHLM/GWD* CM2 .... 4 B5
Finchley Rd *GRAYS* RM17 .... 214 A5
  WOS/PRIT SS0 .... 193 K5
Finchmoor *HLWS* CM18 .... 3 H5
Fingrith Hall La *ING* CM4 .... 86 C1
Finucane Gdns *RAIN* RM13 .... 180 B7
Firbank Rd *CRW* RM5 .... 137 G8
Firecrest Rd *CHLM/GWD* CM2 .... 62 E8
Firfield Rd *SBF/HAD* SS7 .... 171 H7
Firham Park Av *HARH* RM3 .... 161 H2 🔲
The Firle *VGE* SS16 .... 186 D2
Firmans *VGE* SS16 .... 186 C2
Fir Pk *HLWW/ROY* CM19 .... 2 B6
Firs Dr *CHLM/WR* CM1 .... 61 H4
  LOU IG10 .... 107 J5 🔲

HLWE CM17 .... 25 F
The Firs *BRWN* CM15 .... 140 C
  CDH/CHF RM16 .... 201 C
  CVI SS8 .... 190 E
Firs Wk *WFD* IG8 .... 133 H
Fir Tree La *RCHLM* CM3 .... 65 H
Fir Tree Ri *CHLM/GWD* CM2 .... 62 C
Fir Trees *ABR/ST* RM4 .... 109 F
Fir Tree Wk *MAL* CM9 .... 40 E8
Fishermen's Hl *GVW* DA11 .... 218 A3
Fishers Cl *CHES/WCR* EN8 .... 77 C
Fish St *MAL* CM9 .... 42 C
Fitches Crs *MAL* CM9 .... 68 C
Fitzilian Av *HARH* RM3 .... 161 C
Fitzroy Cl *BCAYW* CM12 .... 144 B
Fitzwalter La *RCHLM* CM3 .... 65 H
Fitzwalter Pl *CHLM/WR* CM1 .... 62 A2
Fitzwalter Rd *RCHLM* CM3 .... 36 C
Fitzwarren Rd *SBF/HAD* SS7 .... 196 C
Fitzwilliams Ct *HLWE* CM17 .... 25 J7
Five Acres *HLWS* CM18 .... 3 H
  RCHLM CM3 .... 93 K3
Fiveash Rd *GVW* DA11 .... 218 E
Five Oaks *SBF/HAD* SS7 .... 191 C
Flagstaff Cl *WAB* EN9 .... 77 H
Flagstaff Rd *WAB* EN9 .... 77 H
Flambird's Cha *RCHLM* CM3 .... 95 F
Flamboro Cl *LOS* SS9 .... 172 E
Flamingo Wk *RAIN* RM13 .... 180 B8
Flamstead End Rd *CHES/WCR* EN8 .. 76 E
Flaxen Cl *CHING* E4 .... 132 C6
Flaxen Rd *CHING* E4 .... 132 C
Fleet Av *UPMR* RM14 .... 162 E
Fleet Cl *UPMR* RM14 .... 162 E
Fleethall Gv *CDH/CHF* RM16 ...... 200 E8
Fleethall Rd *RCFD* SS4 .... 174 C
Fleet Rd *GVW* DA11 .... 218 E
  SBF/HAD SS7 .... 190 C
Fleetwood Av *WOS/PRIT* SS0 ...... 193 H
  CHING E4 .... 132 A8
Fleming Gdns *HARH* RM3 .... 160 E4
Fleming Rd *CHESW* EN7 .... 96 C
  TIL RM18 .... 215 H
Fleming Rd *CDH/CHF* RM16 .... 213 F
Flemings *RBRW/HUT* CM13 .... 163 F1
Flemings Farm Rd *LOS* SS9 .... 172 E
Flemming Av *LOS* SS9 .... 192 E
Flemming Crs *LOS* SS9 .... 192 E
Fletcher Dr *WICKW* SS12 .... 147 C
Fletcher Rd *CHIG* IG7 .... 135 J
Fletchers *VGE* SS16 .... 6 D
Fletchers Sq *SOSN* SS3 .... 174 D1
Flex Meadow *HLWW/ROY* CM19 .... 23 F
Flint Cl *VGE* SS16 .... 166 A8
Flint St *WTHK* RM20 .... 212 E
Flintwich Mnr *CHLM/WR* CM1 .... 34 A
Florence Cl *HCH* RM12 .... 181 F3
  HLWE CM17 .... 25 C
  SBF/HAD SS7 .... 191 C
  WTHK RM20 .... 213 H
Florence Gdns *SBF/HAD* SS7 ...... 191 H
Florence Rd *CVI* SS8 .... 208 C
Florence Wy *VGE* SS16 .... 166 C
Flux's La *EPP* CM16 .... 80 B
Fobbing Farm Cl *VGE* SS16 .... 187 F
Fobbing Rd *SLH/COR* SS17 .... 204 B
Fodderwick *BSDN* SS14 .... 7 C
Foksville Rd *CVI* SS8 .... 208 C
Fold Cft *HLW* CM20 .... 2 C
Folkes La *UPMR* RM14 .... 162 C
Folly Cha *HOC/HUL* SS5 .... 150 C
Folly La *HOC/HUL* SS5 .... 150 C
Fontayne Av *CHIG* IG7 .... 135 F
Fonteyn Cl *LAIN* SS15 .... 6 C
Fontwell Park Gdns *HCH* RM12 ... 181 F5
Forbes Cl *HCH* RM12 .... 180 C
Fordhams Rw *CDH/CHF* RM16 .... 202 E
Ford La *RAIN* RM13 .... 180 A
Ford Rd *GVW* DA11 .... 218 A3 🔲
Fordson Rd *CHLM/GWD* CM2 .... 35 K
Fordyce Cl *EMPK* RM11 .... 181 H
Forebury Av *SBW* CM21 .... 11 C
The Forebury *SBW* CM21 .... 11 C
Forefield Gn *CHLM/WR* CM1 .... 35 C
Foremark Cl *BARK/HLT* IG6 .... 135 J8
Forest Ap *CHING* E4 .... 133 C
Forest Av *CHIG* IG7 .... 133 C
  CHING E4 .... 133 C
Forest Cl *WAB* EN9 .... 106 C
  WFD IG8 .... 133 J7
Forest Ct *CHING* E4 .... 133 C
Forest Dr *CHLM/WR* CM1 .... 62 C
  EPP CM16 .... 108 C
Forest Edge *BKHH* IG9 .... 133 C
Forest Gld *CHING* E4 .... 81 C
  EPP CM16 .... 108 C
  VGE SS16 .... 186 A1
Forest La *CHIG* IG7 .... 134 C
Fore St *HLWE* CM17 .... 167 H
  LAIN SS15 .... 167 C
Forest Rd *CHES/WCR* EN8 .... 76 C
  ERITH DA8 .... 210 C

LOU IG10 .... 107 F8
PEND EN3 .... 104 E2
WFD IG8 .... 133 H6
orest Side BKHH IC9 .... 133 J4
CHING E4 .... 133 G3
EPP CM16 .... 80 B7
orest Vw CHING E4 .... 132 E3
orest View Dr LOS SS9 .... 192 B2
orn Wy HLWE CM17 .... 26 C3
HLWE CM17 .... 53 F1
LOU IG10 .... 106 E4
WAB EN9 .... 79 G5
WFD IG8 .... 133 J7
orfar CI LOS SS9 .... 192 C3
orrest CI RCHLM CM3 .... 122 C6
orsythia CI CHLM/WR CM1 .... 35 G6
ortescue Cha SOS SS1 .... 195 J4
orth Rd UPMR RM14 .... 162 A8
ortinbras Wy CHLM/GWD CM2 ...... 4 C6
ortin CI CHLM/WR CM1 .... 31 F2
ortin Wy RCHLM RM15 .... 199 J7
ortin Wy SOCK/AV RM15 .... 199 J7
ort Rd TIL RM18 .... 219 G2
ortrye CI GVW DA11 .... 218 D7
he Fortunes HLWS CM18 .... 3 F5
ossetts Wy SOSN SS2 .... 193 F1
ostal CI LOS SS9 .... 193 F1
oster CI CHES/WCR EN8 .... 76 E4
MAL CM9 .... 40 C1
osters CI CHLM/WR CM1 .... 61 F4
oster St HLWE CM17 .... 25 K7
oulgar CI RCHLM CM3 .... 122 E5
oundry La BOC CM0 .... 128 A8
ountain Farm HLWS CM18 .... 3 E5
ountain PI WAB EN9 .... 77 J8
ountain Rd CHLM/WR CM1 .... 31 F2
ountain Wk GVW DA11 .... 218 D4
he Four Acres SBW CM21 .... 12 A3
our Sisters CI LOS SS9 .... 173 G8
our Sisters Wy LOS SS9 .... 173 G7
ourth Av CHLM/WR CM1 .... 34 C8
HLW CM20 .... 2 C2
HLWW/ROY CM19 .... 2 A3
SLH/COR SS17 .... 187 F8
WICKE SS11 .... 147 K7
WTHK RM20 .... 212 D5
he Four Wents CHING E4 .... 132 E5
owler CI SOS SS1 .... 9 F4
owler Rd BARK/HLT IG6 .... 136 B8
owley CI CHES/WCR EN8 .... 77 F8
oxborough Cha ING CM4 .... 90 C6
ox Burrow Rd CHIG IG7 .... 136 C7
ox Burrows La CHLM/WR CM1 ...... 61 H3
ox CI CRW RM5 .... 137 G8
SBF/HAD SS7 .... 170 E7
ox Crs CHLM/WR CM1 .... 4 A1
oxes CI CDH/CHF RM16 .... 215 F1
oxes Gv RBRW/HUT CM13 .... 143 G3
oxfield CI HOC/HUL SS5 .... 151 H7
oxfield Dr SLH/COR SS17 .... 187 F8
oxglove Rd SOCK/AV RM15 ...... 200 A6
he Foxgloves BCAYW CM12 ...... 144 A4
oxglove Wy CHLM/WR CM1 .... 35 H7
oxhall Rd BOC CM0 .... 100 B6
UPMR RM14 .... 181 K6
ox Hatch BRWN CM15 .... 113 C4
oxhatch WICKE SS11 .... 147 H7
oxhills Rd CDH/CHF RM16 .... 201 H8
oxholes Rd CHLM/GWD CM2 .... 63 H7
oxleigh BCAYW CM12 .... 144 B5
ox Manor Wy WTHK RM20 .... 213 G5
oxmeadows SBF/HAD SS7 .... 170 E7
oxton Rd WTHK RM20 .... 213 G5
oxwood Gv GVW DA11 .... 218 D6
oxwood PI LOS SS9 .... 192 E3
oyle Dr SOCK/AV RM15 .... 199 J5
oys Mdw BCAYW CM12 .... 144 D6
rampton Rd BSDN SS14 .... 168 D4
EPP CM16 .... 80 E2
rances Gdns SOCK/AV RM15 .... 199 H6
rances Ga CHLM/WR CM1 .... 35 J6
rancis CI SLH/COR SS17 .... 203 F2
rancisco CI CDH/CHF RM16 ...... 213 F2
rancis Ms MAL CM9 .... 68 D5
rancis Wk RAYL SS6 .... 171 H3
rancombe Gdns ROM RM1 .... 160 B8
rankland CI WFD IG8 .... 133 K8
rankland Rd CHING E4 .... 132 B8
ranklin Av CHEW EN7 .... 76 A4
ranklin Rd HCH RM12 .... 180 D7
RCHLM CM3 .... 124 D5
ranklins Wy WICKE SS11 .... 147 H5
rank Martin CI CHESW EN7 .... 76 A4
ranmil Rd EMPK RM11 .... 180 A1
raser CI CHLM/GWD CM2 .... 5 D5
LAIN SS15 .... 165 K7
SBN/FI SS3 .... 196 E4
raser CI CHES/WCR EN8 .... 76 E2
rayes Cha CHONG CM5 .... 29 J2
razer CI ROMW/RG RM7 .... 180 A1
rederica Rd CHING E4 .... 132 E3

Frederick Crs PEND EN3 .... 104 C6
Freeborne Gdns RAIN RM13 ...... 180 B7
Freeland Wy ERITH DA8 .... 210 B7
Freeman CI SLH/COR SS17 .... 204 B2
Freeman Rd GVE DA12 .... 219 K8
Freeman Wy EMPK RM11 .... 161 F8
Fremantle SBN/FI SS3 .... 196 C8
Fremantle Rd RCHLM CM3 .... 122 D4
The Fremnells BSDN SS14 .... 168 A4
French Rd RCHLM CM3 .... 124 B4
Frerichs CI WICKW SS12 .... 147 G8
Freshfields Av UPMR RM14 .... 181 J6
Freshwater Crs MAL CM9 .... 68 C1
Freshwater Dr VGE SS16 .... 188 C2
Freshwaters HLW CM20 .... 3 E2
Freshwell Gdns RBRW/HUT CM13 164 C8
Frettons BSDN SS14 .... 168 B8
Friar's Av BRWN CM15 .... 141 K5
Friar's CI BRWN CM15 .... 141 K3
CHING E4 .... 132 D6
Friarscroft BROX EN10 .... 49 G2
Friars Gate CI WFD IG8 .... 133 H7
Friars La CM9 .... 68 B3
RBSF CM22 .... 13 H4
Friars St SBN/FI SS3 .... 196 E6
The Friars CHIG IG7 .... 135 H7
Friars Wk CHLM/GWD CM2 .... 4 C4
Friary La WFD IG8 .... 133 H7
Friday HI CHING E4 .... 133 F6
Friday HI East CHING E4 .... 133 F6
Friday HI West CHING E4 .... 133 F5
Friends Av CHES/WCR EN8 .... 76 D6
Friern Gdns WICKW SS12 .... 146 E6
Friern PI WICKW SS12 .... 146 E7
Friern Rd WICKW SS12 .... 146 E6
Frimley Av EMPK RM11 .... 181 H2
Frithwood BCAYW CM12 .... 144 A6
Frithwood La BCAYW CM12 .... 144 A5
Frobisher Rd ERITH DA8 .... 210 B6
Frobisher Wy SBN/FI SS3 .... 196 D4
Froden Brook BCAYE CM11 .... 144 D6
Froden CI BCAYE CM11 .... 144 D7
Frog St BRWN CM15 .... 113 G5
Frome TIL RM18 .... 216 D3
Front La UPMR RM14 .... 182 B3
Fry CI CRW RM5 .... 137 F8
Fryerning La ING CM4 .... 116 B1
The Fryth BSDN SS14 .... 168 B5
Fulbrook La SOCK/AV RM15 ...... 199 H7
Fulcher Av CHLM/GWD CM2 .... 63 H7
Fulford Dr LOS SS9 .... 173 H7
Fullarton Crs SOCK/AV RM15 .... 199 H6
Fullbridge MAL CM9 .... 68 C2
Fullers CI WAB EN9 .... 78 B7
Fullers Md HLWE CM17 .... 25 G6
Fulmar Rd RAIN RM13 .... 180 C7
Fulmar Wy WICKE SS11 .... 147 K8
Fulton Rd SBF/HAD SS7 .... 170 C6
Furlongs VGE SS16 .... 188 B1
The Furlongs ING CM4 .... 116 B2
Furness CI CDH/CHF RM16 .... 215 G4
Furness Wy HCH RM12 .... 180 B6
Furrowfelde VGE SS16 .... 7 E6
Further Meadow CHLM/WR CM1 .. 61 G5
Furtherwick Rd CVI SS8 .... 208 B3
Furze Gld VGE SS16 .... 166 C8
Furze La ING CM4 .... 118 C5
Fusedale Wy SOCK/AV RM15 ..... 199 H7
Fyefields PIT SS13 .... 169 F5
Fyfield Av WICKW SS12 .... 147 F5
Fyfield CI RBRW/HUT CM13 .... 164 C8
Fyfield Dr SOCK/AV RM15 .... 199 H7
Fyfield Rd CHONG CM5 .... 56 B2
CHONG CM5 .... 56 B2
CHONG CM5 .... 58 A2

G

Gabion Av PUR RM19 .... 212 A3
Gablefields CHLM/GWD CM2 .... 64 A7
The Gables PIT SS13 .... 168 E5
SBF/HAD SS7 .... 172 B6
Gadsden CI UPMR RM14 .... 162 B8
Gaffzelle Dr CVI SS8 .... 208 A3
Gaiger CI CHLM/WR CM1 .... 35 F6
Gainsborough Av CVI SS8 .... 208 E3
TIL RM18 .... 215 F7
Gainsborough CI BCAYW CM12 .. 144 C4
Gainsborough Crs CHLM/GWD CM2 5 F2
Gainsborough Dr GVW DA11 ...... 218 C3
WOS/PRIT SS0 .... 8 B1
Gainsborough PI
RBRW/HUT CM13 .... 142 C4
Gains CI CVI SS8 .... 208 D1
Gainsthorpe Rd CHONG CM5 .... 55 K5
Galadriel RCHLM CM3 .... 122 B7
Galahad CI BOC CM0 .... 128 B8
Galey Gn SOCK/AV RM15 .... 199 K6
Galleons Hill Vicarage Rd
CHLM/WR CM1 .... 32 B8
Galleydene SBF/HAD SS7 .... 191 H2

Galleyhill Rd WAB EN9 .... 78 A6
Galleywood Rd CHLM/GWD CM2 .. 90 C1
Galliford Rd MAL CM9 .... 68 C1
The Gallops VGE SS16 .... 166 C8
Galloway CI BROX EN10 .... 49 F8
Galsworthy Rd TIL RM18 .... 215 H7
Galton Rd WOS/PRIT SS0 .... 193 J5
Gambleside CI VGE SS16 .... 188 B2
Gandalf's Ride RCHLM CM3 .... 122 C7
Ganels CI BCAYE CM11 .... 144 D6
Ganels Rd BCAYE CM11 .... 144 D6
Gangies HI SBW CM21 .... 10 E2
Gant Ct WAB EN9 .... 78 B8
Garbutt Rd UPMR RM14 .... 181 K3
Garden CI CHING E4 .... 132 B8
RCHLM CM3 .... 126 D1
Garden End ING CM4 .... 118 B3
Gardeners CHLM/GWD CM2 .... 63 F8
Gardeners La RCFD SS4 .... 153 H4
Garden Fld RCHLM CM3 .... 37 K1
Garden Flds BOC CM0 .... 99 K2
Gardenia Wy WFD IG8 .... 133 H8
Garden Rw GVW DA11 .... 218 E3
The Gardens BRWN CM15 .... 113 K2
Garden Terrace Rd HLWE CM17 ... 25 G1
Garden Wy LOU IG10 .... 107 J4
Gardiners CI BSDN SS14 .... 168 A4
Gardiners La North BCAYE CM11 146 A8
Gardiners La South BSDN SS14 .. 168 B3
Gardiners Link BSDN SS14 .... 168 A3
The Gardiners HLWE CM17 .... 25 F6
Gardiners Wy BSDN SS14 .... 168 A3
Gardner Av SLH/COR SS17 .... 187 G8
Garfield Rd CHING E4 .... 132 E4
PEND EN3 .... 104 C8
Garland CI CHES/WCR EN8 .... 76 E5
Garland Wy EMPK RM11 .... 161 F6
Garner Dr BROX EN10 .... 48 E8
Garnon Md EPP CM16 .... 81 J3
Garrettlands CHLM/GWD CM2 ..... 64 D7
Garrick St GVW DA11 .... 219 G4
Garron La SOCK/AV RM15 .... 199 H6
Garth Rd SOCK/AV RM15 .... 200 A4
Gascoigne Av BCAYE CM11 .... 144 E3
Gascoyne CI HARH RM3 .... 160 E3
Gatehope Dr SOCK/AV RM15 ..... 199 H6
Gatehouse Ms ING CM4 .... 116 B2
Gate Lodge Sq LAIN SS15 .... 167 G3
Gate Lodge Wy LAIN SS15 .... 167 G3
Gate St MAL CM9 .... 68 B2
Gate Street Ms MAL CM9 .... 68 B2
Gatscombe CI HOC/HUL SS5 ..... 150 E7
The Gattens RAYL SS6 .... 172 A1
Gatwick Rd GVE DA12 .... 219 G7
Gatwick Vw BCAYW CM12 .... 144 C5
Gavenny Pth SOCK/AV RM15 ..... 199 H6
Gay Bowers BSDN SS14 .... 168 A6
HOC/HUL SS5 .... 150 C7
Gay Bowers La RCHLM CM3 .... 65 K7
Gay Bowers Rd RCHLM CM3 .... 93 J1
Gayleighs RAYL SS6 .... 171 J1
Gaylor Rd TIL RM18 .... 214 D7
Gaynes Ct UPMR RM14 .... 181 J5
Gaynesford VGE SS16 .... 6 C6
Gaynes Park Rd UPMR RM14 ..... 181 J5
Gaynes Rd UPMR RM14 .... 181 J5
Gays La RCFD SS4 .... 153 H3
Gayton Rd SOSN SS2 .... 9 D2
Gaywood LAIN SS15 .... 166 B6
Gaywood Av CHES/WCR EN8 .... 76 D4
Geary Dr BRW CM14 .... 141 F4
The Geerings SLH/COR SS17 ..... 204 C2
Geesh Rd CVI SS8 .... 191 H8
Geisthorp Ct WAB EN9 .... 78 C7
The Generals Wk PEND EN3 ...... 104 E3
Genesta CI MAL CM9 .... 44 D3
Genesta Rd WOS/PRIT SS0 .... 193 K5
Genever CI CHING E4 .... 132 B8
Genk CI CVI SS8 .... 191 G8
Gennep Rd CVI SS8 .... 191 G8
Gentry CI SLH/COR SS17 .... 203 J3
Geoffrey Av HARH RM3 .... 161 H1
George Avey Cft EPP CM16 .... 54 B8
George Cardnell Wy RCHLM CM3 . 98 C4
George CI CVI SS8 .... 190 E7
Georges Dr BRWN CM15 .... 140 C1
George St CHLM/GWD CM2 .... 4 C4
GRAYS RM17 .... 213 K5
ROM RM1 .... 160 A8
SBN/FI SS3 .... 197 F7
Gepps CI CHLM/WR CM1 .... 17 H3
Gerald Rd GVE DA12 .... 219 K5
Gernon CI CHLM/WR CM1 .... 34 D2
Gernons VGE SS16 .... 7 D6
Gerpins La UPMR RM14 .... 198 B2
Gerrard Crs BRW CM14 .... 141 F6
Gew's Cnr CHES/WCR EN8 .... 76 D3
Geylen Rd CVI SS8 .... 208 D1
Ghyllgrove BSDN SS14 .... 7 F4
Ghyllgrove CI BSDN SS14 .... 7 F2
Gibb Cft HLWS CM18 .... 52 C1
Gibbs CI CHES/WCR EN8 .... 76 D3
Gibcracks BSDN SS14 .... 168 B7
Gibraltar CI RBRW/HUT CM13 .... 163 F1
Gibson CI EPP CM16 .... 54 C7

GVW DA11 .... 218 E8
Gidea Av GPK RM2 .... 160 B5
Gidea Cl GPK RM2 .... 160 B5
Gideons Wy SLH/COR SS17 .... 203 K2
Gifford Cl PIT SS13 .... 168 E8
Gifford Rd SBF/HAD SS7 .... 170 C8
Giffords Cross Av SLH/COR SS17 ... 204 C1
Giffords Cross Rd SLH/COR SS17 ... 204 C2
Giffordside CDH/CHF RM16 .... 215 G4
Gifhorn Rd CVI SS8 .... 208 E2
Gilbert Cl RAYL SS6 .... 172 A3
Gilbert Dr VGE SS16 .... 166 B8
Gilbert Rd CDH/CHF RM16 .... 213 F2
ROM RM1 .... 160 A6
Gilbert St PEND EN3 .... 104 C3
Gildborne Cl SLH/COR SS17 .... 188 A8
Gilden Cl HLWE CM17 .... 25 J1
Gilden Wy HLWE CM17 .... 25 H2
Gilders SBW CM21 .... 11 H3
Gillam Wy RAIN RM13 .... 180 B7
Gill Cl MAL CM9 .... 40 B7
Gill Crs GVW DA11 .... 218 E8
Gillian Crs CVI SS8 .... 208 C1
Gills Av CVI SS8 .... 208 C1
The Gill SBN/FI SS3 .... 171 J8
Gilman Dr SBN/FI SS3 .... 196 B6
Gilmore Wy CHLM/GWD CM2 .... 63 K7
Gilmour Cl ENC/FH EN2 .... 104 A1
Gilmour Ri BCAYW CM12 .... 144 A4
Gilroy Cl RAIN RM13 .... 180 A7 ②
Gilsland WAB EN9 .... 106 A1
Gilwell Cl CHING E4 .... 105 H8
Gilwell La CHING E4 .... 105 K8
Gippeswyck BSDN SS14 .... 167 K6
Gipson Park Cl LOS SS9 .... 172 E7
Gipsy La GRAYS RM17 .... 214 B5
Girton Ct CHES/WCR EN8 .... 76 E4
Gladden Cl HLWS CM18 .... 52 C1 ②
Gladden Flds RCHLM CM3 .... 122 C7
The Glade RBRW/HUT CM13 .... 141 K4
UPMR RM14 .... 181 K6
VGE SS16 .... 187 K1
WFD IG8 .... 133 J6
The Gladeway WAB EN9 .... 77 K7
Gladstone Gdns RAYL SS6 .... 172 A3 ②
Gladstone Rd BKHH IG9 .... 133 K4
HOC/HUL SS5 .... 151 F8
Glamis Cl CHESW EN7 .... 76 A3
Glamis Dr EMPK RM11 .... 181 F2
Glanmead BRWN CM15 .... 141 H4
Glanmire BCAYE CM11 .... 117 K7
Glanthams Rd BRWN CM15 .... 141 J5
Glanville Dr EMPK RM11 .... 181 G2
Glasseys La RAYL SS6 .... 171 H5
Glastonbury Cha WOS/PRIT SS0 ... 173 J3 ②
Glebe BSDN SS14 .... 167 K5
Glebe Cl RAYL SS6 .... 171 H2
SBN/FI SS3 .... 197 J2
SOS SS1 .... 195 H5
Glebe Crs CHLM/WR CM1 .... 34 C4
Glebe Dr RAYL SS6 .... 171 H2
Glebefield Rd RCHLM CM3 .... 38 B1 ②
Glebe Gdns RBRW/HUT CM13 ..... 164 D2 ②
Glebelands CHIG IG7 .... 136 A6
HLW CM20 .... 24 D2
SBF/HAD SS7 .... 170 A8
Glebe La BOC CM0 .... 101 K4
Glebe Meadow RCHLM CM3 .... 20 A6
Glebe Rd BCAYE CM11 .... 146 B5
CHLM/WR CM1 .... 4 C2 ②
CHONG CM5 .... 84 B3
GVW DA11 .... 218 E6
MAL CM9 .... 40 E8
WICKE SS11 .... 147 H6
The Glebe RCHLM CM3 .... 95 K4
Glebe Wy BOC CM0 .... 128 B7
EMPK RM11 .... 181 F1
SBF/HAD SS7 .... 192 A2
Glebeway WFD IG8 .... 133 K8
Glenbervie Dr LOS SS9 .... 193 G5 ②
Glencoe Dr WICKE SS11 .... 147 K5 ②
Glencree BCAYE CM11 .... 117 K7
Glendale RCHLM CM3 .... 122 E4
Glendale Cl BRWN CM15 .... 141 H4
Glendale Gdns LOS SS9 .... 192 E4
Glendale Rd BOC CM0 .... 128 C7
Glendower Rd CHING E4 .... 132 E4 ②
Gleneagles SBF/HAD SS7 .... 170 A8
Gleneagles Cl HARH RM3 .... 161 G2 ②
Gleneagles Rd LOS SS9 .... 172 D8 ②
Gleneagles Wy RCHLM CM3 ...... 38 B1 ②
Glen Faba Rd HLWW/ROY CM19 ... 22 B2
Glenfield Rd SLH/COR SS17 .... 187 J8 ②
Glen Hazel BRWN CM15 .... 114 A3 ②
Glenhurst Rd SOSN SS2 .... 9 D2
Glenloch Rd PEND EN3 .... 104 C6
Glenmere VGE SS16 .... 188 A3
Glenmere Park Av SBF/HAD SS7 ... 191 G2
Glenmore St SOSN SS2 .... 195 G4
Glenridding SBF/HAD SS7 .... 170 C8 ②
Glen Rd LOS SS9 .... 193 H5
SBF/HAD SS7 .... 170 D8
Glenside BCAYE CM11 .... 144 E3
The Glen RAYL SS6 .... 171 K5

SLH/COR SS17 .... 204 B2
VGE SS16 .... 188 D1
Glen Vw GVE DA12 .... 219 H6
Glenwood BROX EN10 .... 49 F1
Glenwood Av HOC/HUL SS5 .... 151 G8 ②
LOS SS9 .... 172 C6
WOS/PRIT SS0 .... 8 A2
Glenwood Dr GPK RM2 .... 160 B7
Glenwood Gdns VGE SS16 .... 185 K1
Gleten Rd CVI SS8 .... 208 D1
Globe Rd EMPK RM11 .... 160 B8
Gloucester Av CHES/WCR EN8 .... 76 E2
CDH/CHF RM16 .... 214 B1 ②
CHLM/GWD CM2 .... 62 D7
EMPK RM11 .... 161 H7
MAL CM9 .... 68 B5
RAYL SS6 .... 172 B5
TIL RM18 .... 216 D4
Gloucester Crs CHLM/WR CM1 .... 34 C5
Gloucester Pl BCAYW CM12 .... 117 C8
Gloucester Rd BRWN CM15 .... 140 E1
Gloucester Ter SOS SS1 .... 195 J7
Glovers Fld BRWN CM15 .... 113 H3
Glovers La HLWE CM17 .... 53 J2
Glynde Wy SOSN SS2 .... 195 J4
Glynn Rd BOC CM0 .... 128 B7
Glyn Rd PEND EN3 .... 104 C8 ②
Goat Hall La CHLM/GWD CM2 ..... 90 B2
Goat House La RCHLM CM3 .... 94 E2
Goatsmoor La BCAYE CM11 .... 118 A8
Goatswood La ABR/ST RM4 .... 138 C3
Gobions VGE SS16 .... 7 E6
Goddard Rd CDH/CHF RM16 ...... 200 E8
Goddard Wy CHLM/GWD CM2 ..... 63 H5
Godman Rd CDH/CHF RM16 ...... 215 G2
Godwin Cl CHING E4 .... 105 J4
Goirle Av CVI SS8 .... 208 C1
Goldace GRAYS RM17 .... 213 J5 ②
Goldberry Md RCHLM CM3 .... 122 C7 ②
Gold Cl BROX EN10 .... 48 E2
Goldcrest Dr BCAYE CM11 .... 144 D4
Goldenacres CHLM/WR CM1 ...... 35 H5 ②
Golden Cross Rd RCFD SS4 .... 152 A7
Golden Manor Dr SBF/HAD SS7 ... 170 E8
Goldfinch La SBF/HAD SS7 .... 171 F6
Goldhanger Cl RAYL SS6 .... 171 F2 ②
Goldhanger Cross BSDN SS14 ..... 168 B6
Goldhanger Rd MAL CM9 .... 68 E1
Golding Crs SLH/COR SS17 .... 204 A2
Goldingham Av LOU IG10 .... 108 A6
Goldings Crs VGE SS16 .... 188 B2
Golding's Hl LOU IG10 .... 107 H4
Goldings Ri LOU IG10 .... 107 J5
Goldings Rd LOU IG10 .... 107 J5
Golding Thoroughfare
CHLM/GWD CM2 .... 63 H2 ②
Goldington Crs BCAYW CM12 ..... 117 F8
Goldlay Av CHLM/GWD CM2 ...... 5 D5
Goldlay Rd CHLM/GWD CM2 ...... 5 D4 ②
Goldmer Cl SBN/FI SS3 .... 196 B5
Goldsands Rd BOC CM0 .... 128 E3
Goldsborough Crs CHING E4 ...... 132 D5 ②
Goldsdown Cl PEND EN3 .... 104 E6
Goldsdown Rd PEND EN3 .... 104 D6
Goldsmith GRAYS RM17 .... 213 J5 ②
Goldsmith Dr RAYL SS6 .... 149 G6
Goldsmiths Av SLH/COR SS17 .... 204 C2
Goldsworthy Dr SBN/FI SS3 ...... 197 H5
Golf Ride SBF/HAD SS7 .... 190 C2
Goodview Rd LAIN SS15 .... 167 H5
Goodwin Ct CHES/WCR EN8 ...... 76 E2 ②
Goodwood Av HCH RM12 .... 181 F4
PEND EN3 .... 104 C3
RBRW/HUT CM13 .... 142 E2
Goodwood Rd SBF/HAD SS7 ...... 171 F6
Goodwood Cl SBF/HAD SS7 ...... 171 F6 ②
Gooshays Dr HARH RM3 .... 161 F1
Gooshays Gdns HARH RM3 .... 180 A3
Gordon Av HCH RM12 .... 180 D7
Gordon Cl BCAYW CM12 .... 144 A2
TIL RM18 .... 216 E6
Gordon Pl GVE DA12 .... 219 H4 ②
SOS SS1 .... 9 G4
Gordon Rd CHES/WCR EN8 .... 77 G8
BRWN CM15 .... 141 K4
BSDN SS14 .... 168 A8
CDH/CHF RM16 .... 214 D1
CHING E4 .... 133 F3
CHLM/GWD CM2 .... 62 C7
GVW DA11 .... 218 D5
LOS SS9 .... 192 C3
SLH/COR SS17 .... 204 B2
SOS SS1 .... 8 C4
Gordons PIT SS13 .... 168 D8 ②
Gore Rd RCFD SS4 .... 153 H7
The Gore BSDN SS14 .... 167 H8
Gosfield Cl RAYL SS6 .... 171 F2 ②
Goshawk Dr CHLM/GWD CM2 .... 63 H5 ②
The Goslings SBN/FI SS3 .... 197 F6
Gosport Dr HCH RM12 .... 180 D7 ②
The Gossetts GTDUN CM6 .... 30 C1
Gouge Av GVW DA11 .... 218 D6
Gough Rd EN EN1 .... 104 B6
Gould Cl CHONG CM5 .... 55 J3
Goulton Rd CHLM/WR CM1 .... 34 C4
Gourney Gv CDH/CHF RM16 ...... 201 F7

Government Rw PEND EN3 .... 105 G2
Gowan Brae SBF/HAD SS7 .... 170 A8
Gowan Cl SBF/HAD SS7 .... 170 A8
Gowers Av CHLM/GWD CM2 ...... 63 G3
Gowers La CDH/CHF RM16 .... 214 E2
The Gowers HLW CM20 .... 24 E4
Goya Ri SBN/FI SS3 .... 197 F5
Graces La RCHLM CM3 .... 65 F1
Grace's Wk RCHLM CM3 .... 64 D3
Grafton Pl CHLM/GWD CM2 ...... 63 J7
Grafton Rd CVI SS8 .... 208 C2
Graham Av BROX EN10 .... 48 E3
Graham Cl BCAYW CM12 .... 117 H4
HOC/HUL SS5 .... 151 F3
RBRW/HUT CM13 .... 142 B7
SLH/COR SS17 .... 203 K2
Grainger Cl SOSN SS2 .... 9 D2
Grainger Rd SOSN SS2 .... 9 D1
Crampian Gv CHLM/WR CM1 ..... 33 K7
The Granaries WAB EN9 .... 78 A7 ②
Granary Cl RCHLM CM3 .... 97 K5
The Granary HLWW/ROY CM19 ... 22 D4
Granby Rd GVW DA11 .... 218 C2
Grand Dr LOS SS9 .... 193 G5
Grand Pde LOS SS9 .... 193 G5
Grandview Rd SBF/HAD SS7 ...... 170 E8
Grange Av LOS SS9 .... 172 B5
RCHLM CM3 .... 99 F8
WICKW SS12 .... 146 E3
Grange Cl LOS SS9 .... 193 F5
RBRW/HUT CM13 .... 142 B7
Grange Ct WAB EN9 .... 77 J4
Grange Crs CHIG IG7 .... 135 G2
Grange Gdns RAYL SS6 .... 171 G5
SOS SS1 .... 9 E4
Grange La HLWW/ROY CM19 ..... 22 E4
Grange Park Av LOS SS9 .... 193 G5
Granger Av MAL CM9 .... 68 B3
Grange Rd BCAYE CM11 .... 144 D4
BOC CM0 .... 102 B3
GRAYS RM17 .... 214 A3
GVW DA11 .... 219 F7
HARH RM3 .... 160 C5
LOS SS9 .... 192 D5
PIT SS13 .... 169 H1
RCHLM CM3 .... 18 E3
SBF/HAD SS7 .... 170 D7
SOCK/AV RM15 .... 198 E1
WICKE SS11 .... 147 K5
WIT CM8 .... 39 G5
Granger Wy EMPK RM11 .... 160 B8
Grange Wy ERITH DA8 .... 210 C1
Grangeway SBF/HAD SS7 .... 171 F7
WFD IG8 .... 133 K7 ②
Grangewood Av CDH/CHF RM16 ... 214 E2
Grangewood Cl
RBRW/HUT CM13 .... 141 K6
Granites Cha BCAYE CM11 .... 145 G2
Grant Cl WICKW SS12 .... 147 H8 ②
Grantham Wy CDH/CHF RM16 .... 200 E8
Granton Av HCH RM12 .... 181 C2
Granville Cl BCAYW CM12 .... 117 F8
SBF/HAD SS7 .... 190 D7
Granville Rd EPP CM16 .... 81 F7
GVW DA11 .... 218 E8
Grapnells VGE SS16 .... 188 C3
Grasmere Av LOS SS9 .... 193 G3
Grasmere Av HOC/HUL SS5 ...... 149 J4
Grasmere Cl LOU IG10 .... 107 H1
Grasmere Rd CVI SS8 .... 208 D1
SBF/HAD SS7 .... 170 D7
Grassmere Rd EMPK RM11 .... 161 C6
Gratmore Gn VGE SS16 .... 188 B3
Gravel Cl CHIG IG7 .... 135 K5
Gravel La CHIG IG7 .... 135 K5
Gravelly La CHLM/WR CM1 .... 60 E5
Gravel Rd LOS SS9 .... 172 C5
Gray Gdns RAIN RM13 .... 180 D5
Grays Av RAIN RM13 .... 186 D5
Grays Av VGE SS16 .... 186 D5
Grays End Cl CDH/CHF RM16 .... 213 K4
Graysons Cl RAYL SS6 .... 171 K2
Grays Wk RBRW/HUT CM13 ...... 142 C7
Great Berry Farm Cha VGE SS16 ... 186 B1
Great Berry La VGE SS16 .... 186 B8
Great Brays HLWS CM18 .... 24 E1
Great Burches Rd SBF/HAD SS7 ... 171 F7
Great Cambridge Rd CHES/WCR EN8 76 C1
BROX EN10 .... 48 E2
Great Cob CHLM/WR CM1 .... 35 G4
Great Eastern Rd BRW CM14 .... 141 J1
HOC/HUL SS5 .... 151 H5
Great Fox Meadow BRWN CM15 ... 113 J4
Great Gardens Rd EMPK RM11 ... 160 C6
Great Gibcracks Cha RCHLM CM3 ... 92 E3
Great Godfreys CHLM/WR CM1 ... 61 F7
Great Gregorie VGE SS16 .... 7 D7
Great Gregories La EPP CM16 .... 80 C7
Great Hays LOS SS9 .... 172 D7
Greathouse Cha SLH/COR SS17 ... 187 H7
Great Knightleys LAIN SS15 ...... 7 D4
Great Lawn CHONG CM5 .... 84 C2
Great Leighs Wy PIT SS13 .... 169 F4 ②
Great Leylands HLWS CM18 ...... 24 E2
Great Meadow BROX EN10 .... 49 G5
Great Mistley VGE SS16 .... 167 G7

...eat Nelmes Cha *EMPK* RM11...... 161 G7
...eat Oaks *BSDN* SS14 .... 7 E4
...*CHIG* IG7 .... 135 F7
...*RBRW/HUT* CM13 .... 142 A2
...eat Owl Rd *CHIG* IG7 .... 134 D6
...eat Plumtree *HLW* CM20 ...... 3 F1
...*eat Ranton PIT* SS13............ 169 F5
...eat Ropers La *BRW* CM14 .... 162 D1
...eat Snials *WICKE* SS11 ...... 147 K7 ▣
...eat Spenders *BSDN* SS14 .... 122 C9
...eat Warley St *RBRW/HUT* CM13 .. 162 D5
...eat Wheatley Rd *RAYL* SS6 .. 171 F4
...ebe Cl *RCHLM* CM3 .... 98 C5
...ebe Crest *WTHK* RM20 .... 212 D3
...reding Wk *RBRW/HUT* CM13.... 142 A5
...eenacre La *ING* CM4 .... 118 A5
...eenacre Ms *LOS* SS9 .... 193 F5
...eenacres *EPP* CM16 .... 80 D2 ▣
...*SBF/HAD* SS7 .... 191 K2
...eenall Cl *CHES/WCR* EN8 .... 76 E4
...eenbank *CHESW* EN7 .... 76 B2
...eenbank Cl *CHING* E4 .... 132 D5
...*HARH* RM3 .... 138 E6
...eenbanks *LOS* SS9 .... 193 H3
...*UPMR* RM14 .... 182 B3 ▣
...een Cl *CHES/WCR* EN8 .... 76 E6
...*CHLM/WR* CM1 .... 5 E1
...*EPP* CM16 .... 51 K6
...*RCHLM* CM3 .... 98 C2
...eendyke *CVI* SS8 .... 190 B9
...eenfields *BCAYW* CM12 ...... 144 B5
...*LOU* IG10 .... 107 J8
...eenfields Cl *BCAYW* CM12 .... 144 A5
...eenfield St *WAB* EN9 .... 77 J8
...een Gld *EPP* CM16 .... 108 C3
...een Glades *EMPK* RM11 ...... 161 G8
...eenhill *BKHH* IG9 .... 133 K4
...eenhill Rd *GVW* DA11 .... 218 E7 ▣
...eenhills *HLW* CM20 .... 3 E3
...eenlands *RCFD* SS4 .... 174 A1
...een La *BCAYW* CM12 .... 165 H1
...*BCAYW* CM12 .... 166 B2
...*BOC* CM0 .... 127 K6
...*BROX* EN10 .... 49 H5
...*BRW* CM14 .... 113 F5
...*BRW* CM14 .... 140 D4
...*BRWN* CM15 .... 141 F2
...*CDH/CHF* RM16 .... 201 C5
...*CHIG* IG7 .... 135 H6
...*CHLM/WR* CM1 .... 60 B1
...*CVI* SS8 .... 207 K2
...*HLWE* CM17 .... 26 B6
...*LOS* SS9 .... 172 E6
...*MAL* CM9 .... 42 A1
...*RBRW/HUT* CM13 .... 162 D2
...*RCHLM* CM3 .... 98 E7
...*VGE* SS16 .... 6 B6
...*WAB* EN9 .... 107 F1
...eenleas *SBF/HAD* SS7 .... 171 C7
...een Md *RCHLM* CM3 .... 122 C6
...eenmoor Rd *PEND* EN3 .... 104 C6
...eenoaks *SBF/HAD* SS7 .... 190 D2
...een Rd *SBF/HAD* SS7 .... 190 D2
...e Green *CHES/WCR* EN8 ...... 76 C2
...*CDH/CHF* RM16 .... 202 A5
...*CHLM/WR* CM1 .... 4 A1
...*CHLM/WR* CM1 .... 61 H8
...*EPP* CM16 .... 108 C3
...*ING* CM4 .... 86 C5
...*LOS* SS9 .... 173 F6
...*SLH/COR* SS17 .... 203 K4 ▣
...een Trees *EPP* CM16 .... 80 E5
...een Trees Av *RCHLM* CM3 .... 96 B8
...een Wk *CHONG* CM5 .... 84 B4
...e Green Wk *CHING* E4 .... 132 E4 ▣
...eenway *BCAYE* CM11 .... 144 E4
...*HARH* RM3 .... 161 J1
...*HLWW/ROY* CM19 .... 23 C5
...*RBRW/HUT* CM13 .... 141 K3
...eenways *CHLM/WR* CM1 ...... 34 D7
...*CVI* SS8 .... 190 E8 ▣
...*MAL* CM9 .... 68 B3 ▣
...*RCFD* SS4 .... 174 C3
...*SBF/HAD* SS7 .... 190 A3
...*SOS* SS1 .... 195 H6
...e Greenway *PEND* EN3 .... 104 D1 ▣
...*WICKE* SS11 .... 147 F2
...eenwood Av *CHESW* EN7...... 76 B5

PEND EN3 .... 104 E5
SBF/HAD SS7 .... 190 C4
Greenwood Cl *CHESW* EN7 .... 76 B5 ▣
Greenwood Dr *CHING* E4 ...... 132 E8 ▣
Greenwood Rd *CHING* IG7 .... 136 A7
Greenyard *WAB* EN9 .... 77 J7 ▣
Gregory Cl *HOC/HUL* SS5 .... 173 G3 ▣
Grenfell Av *HCH* RM12 .... 180 A2
Grennan Cl *RBRW/HUT* CM13 .. 164 C1
Grenville Av *BROX* EN10 .... 49 F3
Grenville Cl *CHES/WCR* EN8 .. 76 D6
Gresham Ct *BRW* CM14 .... 141 F6
Gresham Rd *BRW* CM14 .... 141 F6
Greyfriars *RBRW/HUT* CM13 .. 142 A3
Greygoose Pk *HLWW/ROY* CM19 .. 2 B6 ▣
Greyhound La *CDH/CHF* RM16 .. 215 F1
Greyhound Wy *SOSN* SS2 ...... 9 D5
Grey Ladys *CHLM/GWD* CM2 .... 90 D2
Grey Towers Av *EMPK* RM11 .. 180 C2
Grey Towers Gdns *EMPK* RM11 .. 180 D1 ▣
Gridiron Pl *UPMR* RM14 .... 181 J3
Grieves Rd *GVW* DA11 .... 218 E8
Griffin Av *CVI* SS8 .... 191 H8
UPMR RM14 .... 162 B8
The Griffins *CDH/CHF* RM16 .. 214 A1
Grifon Cl *CDH/CHF* RM16 ...... 213 F2 ▣
Grifon Rd *CDH/CHF* RM16 ...... 213 F2
Griggs Gdns *HCH* RM12 .... 180 D6 ▣
Grimshaw Wy *ROM* RM1 .... 160 A7 ▣
Grimston Rd *BSDN* SS14 .... 168 C4
Groom Rd *BROX* EN10 .... 49 F8
Grosvenor Cl *CHLM/GWD* CM2 .... 5 E6
LOU IG10 .... 107 K5
Grosvenor Dr *EMPK* RM11 .... 180 D2
LOU IG10 .... 107 K6
Grosvenor Gdns *BCAYW* CM12 .. 144 B1
UPMR RM14 .... 182 A3
Grosvenor Ms *WOS/PRIT* SS0 .. 193 K6
Grosvenor Rd *BROX* EN10 ...... 49 F2
CDH/CHF RM16 .... 202 D6
RAYL SS6 .... 171 G1 ▣
SBF/HAD SS7 .... 190 D4
WOS/PRIT SS0 .... 193 K6
Grove Av *VGE* SS16 .... 186 C2
Grove Cl *RAYL* SS6 .... 172 A3
Grove Ct *RAYL* SS6 .... 172 B4
WAB EN9 .... 77 H7
Grove Gdns *PEND* EN3 .... 104 D5
Grove Hl *LOS* SS9 .... 172 C6
Grovelands Rd *WICKW* SS12 .. 147 G7
Grovelands Wy *GRAYS* RM17 .. 213 J4
Grove La *CHIG* IG7 .... 135 J6
EPP CM16 .... 80 E4 ▣
Grove Rd *BCAYW* CM12 .... 144 A3
CHING E4 .... 132 D6
CHLM/GWD CM2 .... 4 C4
CVI SS8 .... 208 C1
GRAYS RM17 .... 214 B5
GVW DA11 .... 218 A3
RAYL SS6 .... 172 A3
SBF/HAD SS7 .... 190 A3
SLH/COR SS17 .... 203 K5
Grove Rd West *PEND* EN3 ...... 104 C5
Grover St *SOS* SS1 .... 9 D4 ▣
Groves Cl *SOCK/AV* RM15 ...... 199 H7 ▣
Groveside Rd *CHING* E4 .... 133 F6
The Grove *BCAYE* CM11 .... 117 J8
BRW CM14 .... 140 C7
CHLM/GWD CM2 .... 63 K8
GVE DA12 .... 219 G5
RCHLM CM3 .... 93 K4
SOSN SS2 .... 9 E2
UPMR RM14 .... 181 H5
Grove Wk *SBN/FI* SS3 .... 196 D6 ▣
Grovewood Av *LOS* SS9 .... 172 E6
Grovewood Cl *LOS* SS9 .... 172 C6
Guardian Cl *HCH* RM12 .... 180 C5
Guardsman Cl *BRW* CM14 .... 141 G8
Gubbins La *HARH* RM3 .... 161 G3
Guernsey Gdns *WICKE* SS11 .. 147 F4
Guildford Rd *HARH* RM3.......... 161 F1
SOSN SS2 .... 9 D3
Guild Rd *ERITH* DA8 .... 210 A6
The Guilfords *HLWE* CM17 .... 11 H8
Guinevere Gdns *CHES/WCR* EN8 .. 76 E4 ▣
Gumley Rd *WTHK* RM20 .... 213 G5
Gunfleet Cl *GVE* DA12 .... 219 K5
Gun Hl *TIL* RM18 .... 215 J5
Gun Hill Pl *VGE* SS16 .... 167 K8
Gunners Gv *CHING* E4 .... 132 D6
Gunners Rd *SBN/FI* SS3 .... 197 F6
Gustedhall La *HOC/HUL* SS5 .. 173 F3
Gutteridge La *ABR/ST* RM4 .... 137 H2
Gutters La *CHLM/WR* CM1 ...... 34 D6
Guys Farm Rd *RCHLM* CM3 .... 122 D6
Gwendalen Av *CVI* SS8 .... 208 D1
Gwyn Cl *RCHLM* CM3 .... 36 C4 ▣
Gwynn Rd *GVW* DA11 .... 218 B7

H

Haarlem Rd *CVI* SS8 .... 207 H1

Haarle Rd *CVI* SS8 .... 208 D3 ▣
Haase Cl *CVI* SS8 .... 191 F7
Habgood Rd *LOU* IG10 .... 107 G7
Hackamore *SBF/HAD* SS7 ...... 171 G8
Hackmans La *RCHLM* CM3 ...... 94 E2
Hacton Dr *HCH* RM12 .... 181 F5
Hacton La *HCH* RM12 .... 181 G3
UPMR RM14 .... 181 G6
Haddestoke Ga *BROX* EN10 .... 49 F8
Haddon Cl *RAYL* SS6 .... 171 F2
Haddon Md *RCHLM* CM3 .... 122 D8
Hadfield Rd *SLH/COR* SS17 .... 203 K4
Hadleigh Ct *BROX* EN10 .... 49 F4
Hadleigh Park Av *SBF/HAD* SS7 .. 191 H2
Hadleigh Rd *LOS* SS9 .... 192 D4
WOS/PRIT SS0 .... 8 B5
Hadley Gra *HLWE* CM17 .... 25 G6
Hadrians Wy *MAL* CM9 .... 40 C8
Hagg Hl *RCHLM* CM3.............. 95 J8
Haig Cl *CHLM/GWD* CM2 .... 4 B4 ▣
Haig Gdns *GVE* DA12 .... 219 H5
Haig Rd *CDH/CHF* RM16 .... 215 F2
Hailsham Cl *HARH* RM3 .... 138 D8
Hailsham Rd *HARH* RM3 .... 138 D8
Hainault Av *RCFD* SS4 .... 173 K1
WOS/PRIT SS0 .... 8 A2
Hainault Cl *SBF/HAD* SS7 ...... 191 K1
Hainault Gv *CHIG* IG7 .... 135 F7
CHLM/WR CM1 .... 62 A4
Hainault Rd *CHIG* IG7 .... 135 F7
RCHLM CM3 .... 124 C4
Halcyon Wy *EMPK* RM11 .... 181 G2
Haldane Gdns *GVW* DA11 ...... 218 B6
Hale Cl *CHING* E4 .... 132 D6
Hale End *HARH* RM3 .... 160 C1
Halesworth Cl *HARH* RM3 ...... 161 F1 ▣
Halesworth Rd *HARH* RM3...... 161 F1
Halfhide La *CHES/WCR* EN8 .... 48 D8
Halfhides *WAB* EN9 .... 77 K7
Half Moon La *EPP* CM16 .... 80 D5 ▣
Halfway Ct *PUR* RM19 .... 211 H3
Halidon Ri *HARH* RM3 .... 161 J1
Hallam Cl *BRWN* CM15 .... 113 K3
Hallam Ct *BCAYW* CM12 .... 144 A1 ▣
Hall Av *SOCK/AV* RM15 .... 198 E8
Hall Bridge Ri *MAL* CM9 .... 68 E1
Hall Cl *CHLM/GWD* CM2 .... 63 J7
SLH/COR SS17 .... 204 A1
Hall Crs *SBF/HAD* SS7 .... 191 J2
SOCK/AV RM15 .... 211 K1
Hallet Rd *CVI* SS8 .... 208 E2
Hall Farm Cl *SBF/HAD* SS7 .... 190 C4
Hall Farm Rd *SBF/HAD* SS7 .... 190 C3
Hall Gdns *CHING* E4 .... 132 A7
Hall Green La *RBRW/HUT* CM13 .. 142 C3
Hallingbury Rd *SBW* CM21...... 12 A1
Halling Hl *HLW* CM20 .... 3 F2
Hall La *BRWN* CM15................ 141 J2
CHING E4 .... 132 A8
CHLM/GWD CM2 .... 64 A7
CHLM/GWD CM2 .... 91 F8
CHLM/WR CM1 .... 4 C1 ▣
HARH RM3 .... 161 K4
ING CM4 .... 116 C3
UPMR RM14 .... 161 K7
Hallmores *BROX* EN10 .... 49 G1 ▣
Hallowell Down *RCHLM* CM3 .. 122 E7
Hall Park Av *WOS/PRIT* SS0 .... 193 J5
Hall Park Rd *UPMR* RM14 ...... 181 K6 ▣
Hall Rd *BOC* CM0 .... 101 H6
GPK RM2 .... 160 C5
GVW DA11 .... 218 C7
HOC/HUL SS5 .... 173 H3
MAL CM9 .... 40 D2
MAL CM9 .... 44 D4
MAL CM9 .... 68 D1
RCFD SS4 .... 174 A4
SOCK/AV RM15 .... 211 K1
Halt Cl *CHLM/GWD* CM2 .... 4 C4 ▣
Hall Ter *SOCK/AV* RM15.......... 212 A1
Hallwood Crs *BRWN* CM15 .... 141 H3
Halstead Ct *WICKW* SS12 ...... 147 F8 ▣
Halstead Wy *RBRW/HUT* CM13 .. 142 A2
Halston Pl *MAL* CM9 .... 68 B5
Halstow Wy *PIT* SS13 .... 169 F8
Halt Dr *TIL* RM18 .... 216 B3
Halton Rd *CDH/CHF* RM16 .... 215 G2
Haltwhistle Rd *RCHLM* CM3 .. 122 C5
Halyard Reach *RCHLM* CM3.... 122 D8
Hamberts Rd *RCHLM* CM3 .... 122 D4
Hamble La *SOCK/AV* RM15 .... 199 H5
Hamble Wy *BOC* CM0 .... 128 A7 ▣
Hamboro Gdns *LOS* SS9 .... 192 C4
Hambro' Av *RAYL* SS6 .... 171 J1
Hambro Cl *RAYL* SS6 .... 171 K1
Hambro Hl *RAYL* SS6 .... 149 K8
Hambro Rd *BRW* CM14 .... 141 G5
Hamburgh Ct *CHES/WCR* EN8 .. 76 D2 ▣
Hamerton Rd *GVW* DA11 ...... 218 A3 ▣
Hamilton Cl *LOS* SS9 .... 192 B3
Hamilton Crs *BRW* CM14 .... 141 F8
Hamilton Dr *HARH* RM3 .... 161 F8
Hamilton Gdns *HOC/HUL* SS5 .. 151 F6
Hamilton Ms *RAYL* SS6 .... 172 A2
Hamilton Rd *GPK* RM2 .... 160 C7

Hamlet Court Ms *WOS/PRIT* SS0 .... 8 B3 🄰
Hamlet Court Rd *WOS/PRIT* SS0 .... 8 A4
Hamlet HI *HLWG/ROY* CM19 .... 50 E1
Hamlet Rd *CHLM/GWD* CM2 .... 4 C4
   SOS SS1 .... 8 C5
Hamley CI *SBF/HAD* SS7 .... 170 A7
Hammarskjold Rd *HLW* CM20 .... 2 C2
Hammond Rd *EN* EN1 .... 104 B7
Hammonds La *BCAYE* CM11 .... 144 D6 🄰
   RBRW/HUT CM13 .... 162 E1 🄰
Hammonds Rd *CHLM/GWD* CM2 .... 64 B4
Hampden CI *EPP* CM16 .... 82 A1
Hampden Crs *BRW* CM14 .... 141 F8 🄰
   CHESW EN7 .... 76 B5
Hampden Rd *GRAYS* RM17 .... 214 A4
Hampshire Gdns *EMPK* RM11 .... 161 H6 🄰
Hampstead Gdns *HOC/HUL* SS5 .... 151 G6
Hampton CI *SOSN* SS2 .... 194 B1
Hampton Ct *HOC/HUL* SS5 .... 150 E7 🄰
Hampton Gdns *GVE* DA12 .... 219 K7
Hampton Gdns *SBW* CM21 .... 11 F6
   SOSN SS2 .... 194 B1
Hampton Rd *CHIG* E4 .... 132 A8
   CHLM/GWD CM2 .... 63 C8
Hamstel Rd *HLW* CM20 .... 2 B1
   SOSN SS2 .... 195 G3
Hanbury CI *CHES/WCR* EN8 .... 76 D4
Hanbury Rd *CHLM/WR* CM1 .... 62 A5
Handel Crs *TIL* RM18 .... 215 F6
Handel Rd *CVI* SS8 .... 208 D3
Hand La *SBW* CM21 .... 11 C4
Handleys Cha *LAIN* SS15 .... 167 G3
Hanford Rd *SOCK/AV* RM15 .... 198 E8 🄰
Hanging Hill La *RBRW/HUT* CM13 ...... 142 A6
Haning Hill La *RBRW/HUT* CM13 .... 142 B2
Hanlee Brook *CHLM/GWD* CM2 .... 63 H8
Hannah CI *CVI* SS8 .... 191 F7 🄰
Hannards Wy *CHIG* IG7 .... 136 A3
Hannett Rd *CVI* SS8 .... 208 E2
Hanningfield CI *RAYL* SS6 .... 171 F2 🄰
Hanover CI *BSDN* SS14 .... 168 B8 🄰
Hanover Dr *BSDN* SS14 .... 168 B8
Hanover Ms *HOC/HUL* SS5 .... 150 E7 🄰
Hansells Md *HLWW/ROY* CM19 .... 22 C5
Hanson Dr *LOU* IG10 .... 108 A6
Harberts Rd *HLWW/ROY* CM19 .... 2 B4
Harberts Wy *RAYL* SS6 .... 149 H8
Harbourer Rd *BARK/HLT* IG6 .... 136 A8
Harcourt Av *SOSN* SS2 .... 160 A7 🄰
Harcourt Ms *ROM* RM1 .... 161 J3
Hardie Rd *GVW* DA11 .... 218 E2
Hardie Rd *SLH/COR* SS17 .... 205 K3
Harding Rd *CDH/CHF* RM16 .... 215 F2
Harding's Elms Rd *BCAYE* CM11 .... 167 J1
Harding's La *ING* CM4 .... 87 K6
Hardley Crs *EMPK* RM11 .... 160 E6
Hardwick CI *RAYL* SS6 .... 171 J4
Hardy Av *GVW* DA11 .... 218 D7
Hardys Wy *CVI* SS8 .... 191 F7
Harebell CI *BCAYW* CM12 .... 144 A1
Harebell Wy *HARH* RM3 .... 160 E2
Harefield *HLW* CM17 .... 24 E4
Hare Hall La *GPK* RM2 .... 160 C6 🄰
Hares Cha *BCAYW* CM12 .... 144 A4
Haresland CI *SBF/HAD* SS7 .... 172 A8
Hare St *HLWW/ROY* CM19 .... 2 B3
Hare Street Springs
   HLWW/ROY CM19 .... 2 C3 🄰
Harewood Rd *RCFD* SS4 .... 151 K8
Harewood HI *EPP* CM16 .... 108 C1
Harewood Rd *BRWN* CM15 .... 140 E2
   CHLM/WR CM1 .... 62 A4
Harford CI *CHING* E4 .... 132 C3
Harford Rd *CHING* E4 .... 132 C3
Harfred Av *MAL* CM9 .... 69 G2
Hargreaves Av *CHESW* EN7 .... 76 C5
Hargreaves CI *CHESW* EN7 .... 76 B5 🄰
Harkness CI *HARH* RM3 .... 139 G8
Harlech Rd *PIT* SS13 .... 168 E8
Harlesden CI *HARH* RM3 .... 161 G2
Harlesden Rd *HARH* RM3 .... 161 G1
Harley St *LOS* SS9 .... 192 D4
Harlings Gv *CHLM/WR* CM1 .... 4 C2
Harlow Common *HLWE* CM17 .... 25 H8
Harlow Rd *CHONG* CM5 .... 55 J2
   HLWE CM17 .... 12 B6
   HLWW/ROY CM19 .... 22 E4
   SBW CM21 .... 11 G5
Harman CI *CHING* E4 .... 132 E7 🄰
Harmer St *GVE* DA12 .... 219 H4
Harness CI *CHLM/WR* CM1 .... 35 G6
Harold Court Rd *HARH* RM3 .... 161 J1
Harold Crs *WAB* EN9 .... 77 J6
Harold Gdns *WICKE* SS11 .... 147 G4
Harold Rd *CHING* E4 .... 132 D6
Harolds Rd *HLWW/ROY* CM19 .... 23 H6
Harold Vw *HARH* RM3 .... 161 G4
Haron CI *CVI* SS8 .... 208 B2
Harpers La *BRWN* CM15 .... 144 A5
Harper Wy *RAYL* SS6 .... 171 H2 🄰
Harrap Cha *GRAYS* RM17 .... 213 J4
Harridge CI *LOS* SS9 .... 193 F2
Harridge Rd *LOS* SS9 .... 193 F2
Harrier CI *RAIN* RM13 .... 180 C7 🄰
Harrier Wy *WAB* EN9 .... 78 C8

Harriescourt *WAB* EN9 .... 78 C6
Harris CI *GVW* DA11 .... 218 D8
   SLH/COR SS17 .... 204 D1
   WICKW SS12 .... 147 J8
Harrison CI *RBRW/HUT* CM13 .... 142 C1
Harrison Ct *CHLM/WR* CM1 .... 4 A2 🄰
Harrison Dr *EPP* CM16 .... 54 B8 🄰
Harrison Gdns *HOC/HUL* SS5 .... 149 J5
Harrisons Whf *PUR* RM19 .... 211 H4
Harrison Wk *CHES/WCR* EN8 .... 76 D4
Harrods Ct *BCAYE* CM11 .... 145 F3 🄰
Harrogate Dr *HOC/HUL* SS5 .... 151 G5
Harrogate Rd *HOC/HUL* SS5 .... 151 G6
Harrowby Gdns *GVW* DA11 .... 218 D7 🄰
Harrow CI *HOC/HUL* SS5 .... 151 H8
Harrow Crs *HARH* RM3 .... 160 C2
Harrow Dr *EMPK* RM11 .... 180 C1
Harrow Gdns *HOC/HUL* SS5 .... 151 H8
Harrow Rd *CVI* SS8 .... 169 K3
   WICKW SS12 .... 147 H8
Harrow Vw *CHLM/GWD* CM2 .... 63 J7
Harston Dr *PEND* EN3 .... 105 G4
Hart CI *SBF/HAD* SS7 .... 171 F7
Hart Crs *CHIG* IG7 .... 135 J8
Hatfield PI *GVW* DA11 .... 171 C5 🄰
Hartford End *PIT* SS13 .... 168 D8 🄰
Hartington PI *SOS* SS1 .... 9 E5 🄰
Hartington Rd *SOS* SS1 .... 9 E5
Hartland CI *LOS* SS9 .... 172 E6
Hartland Rd *CHES/WCR* EN8 .... 76 D4
   EPP CM16 .... 80 E5
   HCH RM12 .... 180 B3
Hartley CI *CHLM/GWD* CM2 .... 63 J1
Hartmoor Ms *PEND* EN3 .... 104 D3 🄰
Hart Rd *HLWE* CM17 .... 11 C8
   SBF/HAD SS7 .... 170 E7
Harts Gv *WFD* IG8 .... 133 H8
Hartshill Rd *GVW* DA11 .... 218 E2
Hart St *BRW* CM14 .... 141 F5
   CHLM/GWD CM2 .... 4 B4
Hartsway *PEND* EN3 .... 104 B8
Hartswood CI *BRW* CM14 .... 141 H7
Hartswood Rd *BRW* CM14 .... 141 H7
Harty CI *CDH/CHF* RM16 .... 201 F8
Harvest CI *CHLM* CM2 .... 122 D6
Harvest La *LOU* IG10 .... 134 A3
Harvest Rd *CVI* SS8 .... 191 C8
Harvest Wy *MAL* CM9 .... 40 B8
Harvey CI *CDH/CHF* RM16 .... 214 A1
Harveyfields *WAB* EN9 .... 77 J8
Harvey Gdns *LOU* IG10 .... 107 K7
Harvey Rd *MAL* CM9 .... 40 C1
   PIT SS13 .... 168 E3
Harwater Dr *LOU* IG10 .... 107 H6
Harwood Av *EMPK* RM11 .... 161 F5
Harwood Hall La *UPMR* RM14 .... 181 J7
Haselfoot Rd *RCHLM* CM3 .... 36 D5
Haskins *SLH/COR* SS17 .... 204 B3 🄰
Haslemere Av *WICKE* SS11 .... 147 F3
Hasler Rd *MAL* CM9 .... 44 D3
Hassell Rd *CVI* SS8 .... 208 D2
Hassenbrook Rd *SLH/COR* SS17 .... 205 K3
Hastings CI *WTHK* RM20 .... 213 H5
Hastings Rd *GPK* RM2 .... 160 C7
   SOS SS1 .... 9 F4
The Hastings *WICKE* SS11 .... 147 G4
Hastingwood Rd *HLWE* CM17 .... 53 J2
Hatches Farm Rd *BCAYW* CM12 .... 143 J8
Hatchfields *RCHLM* CM3 .... 20 B6
Hatch La *CHING* E4 .... 132 E7
Hatch Rd *BRWN* CM15 .... 140 D1
Hatch Side *CHIG* IG7 .... 134 D8 🄰
The Hatch *PEND* EN3 .... 104 D5
Hatchwoods *WFD* IG8 .... 133 G7 🄰
Hatfield CI *HCH* RM12 .... 180 E6 🄰
   RBRW/HUT CM13 .... 142 E3 🄰
Hatfield Dr *BCAYE* CM11 .... 144 E3 🄰
Hatfield Gv *CHLM/WR* CM1 .... 61 K4
Hatfield Rd *MAL* CM9 .... 39 H6
   RAYL SS6 .... 171 G2
Hatfields *LOU* IG10 .... 107 K7
Hathaway Av *GRAYS* RM17 .... 214 A2
Hathingleigh Wy *HARH* RM3 .... 160 E3 🄰
The Hatherley *BSDN* SS14 .... 168 A6
Hatley Gdns *SBF/HAD* SS7 .... 170 B8
Hatterill *LAIN* SS15 .... 6 B5
Hatton CI *CDH/CHF* RM16 .... 213 G2
   GVW DA11 .... 218 D8
Havana CI *RAYL* SS6 .... 149 G7
Havelock St *GVW* DA11 .... 218 E6
Haven CI *CVI* SS8 .... 207 H2
   VGE SS16 .... 188 B2
Havengore *CHLM/WR* CM1 .... 35 C8
   PIT SS13 .... 169 F5
Havengore Av *GVE* DA12 .... 219 K5
Haven PI *CDH/CHF* RM16 .... 214 B1
Haven Ri *BCAYE* CM11 .... 144 E7
Haven Rd *CVI* SS8 .... 207 H3
Havenside *SBN/FI* SS3 .... 176 D8
The Haven *GRAYS* RM17 .... 214 E4 🄰
Haverhill Rd *CHING* E4 .... 132 D4
Havering Rd *SBN/FI* SS3 .... 197 C1
Havisham Wy *CHLM/WR* CM1 .... 33 K6

Havis Rd *SLH/COR* SS17 .... 204 A3
Hawes La *WAB* EN9 .... 105 J3
Hawkbush Gn *PIT* SS13 .... 168 E4 🄰
Hawk CI *WAB* EN9 .... 78 C8 🄰
Hawkdene *CHING* E4 .... 132 C7
Hawkenbury *HLWW/ROY* CM19 .... 2 A7
Hawkesbury Bush La *VGE* SS16 .... 187 H1
Hawkesbury CI *CVI* SS8 .... 207 J2
Hawkesbury Rd *CVI* SS8 .... 207 J3
Hawkes CI *GRAYS* RM17 .... 214 A5 🄰
Hawk HI *WICKE* SS11 .... 148 B3
Hawkhurst CI *CHLM/WR* CM1 .... 62 A1
Hawkinge Wy *HCH* RM12 .... 180 D7 🄰
Hawkins CI *RCHLM* CM3 .... 94 E1
   WICKE SS11 .... 147 J6 🄰
Hawk La *WICKE* SS11 .... 148 C1
Hawkridge *SBN/FI* SS3 .... 196 B3 🄰
Hawks CI *RCHLM* CM3 .... 66 A6
Hawks HI *EPP* CM16 .... 82 A1
Hawk La *HOC/HUL* SS5 .... 151 F7
Hawksmead CI *PEND* EN3 .... 104 D1 🄰
Hawksmoor Gn *RBRW/HUT* CM13 ..... 142 C7
Hawksmouth *CHING* E4 .... 132 C7
Hawksway *VGE* SS16 .... 7 F7
Hawkswood Rd *BCAYE* CM11 .... 119 H6
Hawkwell Cha *HOC/HUL* SS5 .... 173 F4
Hawkwell Park Dr *HOC/HUL* SS5 ..... 151 G2
Hawkwell Rd *HOC/HUL* SS5 .... 151 F7
Hawkwood CI *RCHLM* CM3 .... 122 E8
Hawkwood Crs *CHING* E4 .... 132 C2
Hawsted *BKHH* IG9 .... 133 J5 🄰
Hawthorn Av *RBRW/HUT* CM13 .... 141 J7
Hawthorn CI *CHLM/GWD* CM2 .... 62 E7 🄰
   HOC/HUL SS5 .... 151 G8 🄰
Hawthorne Av *CHESW* EN7 .... 76 B3
Hawthorne CI *CHESW* EN7 .... 76 B3
Hawthorne Gdns *HOC/HUL* SS5 .... 150 C6
Hawthorne Rd *SLH/COR* SS17 .... 204 B8 🄰
Hawthornes *RCHLM* CM3 .... 95 K4
Hawthorn Rd *BKHH* IG9 .... 133 K3
   CVI SS8 .... 208 C2
Hawthorns *HLWS* CM18 .... 52 D3
   LOS SS9 .... 193 F1 🄰
   SBF/HAD SS7 .... 190 B1 🄰
   WFD IG8 .... 133 H8
The Hawthorns *RCHLM* CM3 .... 66 A6 🄰
   SLH/COR SS17 .... 204 B8
Hawthorn Wk *RCHLM* CM3 .... 122 E8
Hawthorn Wy *RAYL* SS6 .... 172 A5 🄰
Hawtree CI *SOS* SS1 .... 9 F7
Hayburn Wy *HCH* RM12 .... 180 A4
Haydens Rd *HLWW/ROY* CM19 .... 2 C7 🄰
Haydock CI *HCH* RM12 .... 181 C2
Hayes Barton *SOS* SS1 .... 196 B5
Hayes Cha *RCHLM* CM3 .... 121 K5
   WICKE SS11 .... 148 E1
Hayes CI *CHLM/GWD* CM2 .... 4 B3
   WTHK RM20 .... 213 F5
Hayes Dr *RAIN* RM13 .... 180 C2
Hayes La *CVI* SS8 .... 207 K2
Hay Gn *RCHLM* CM3 .... 114 B3
   ING CM4 .... 86 D1
Hayle *TIL* RM18 .... 216 D2
Haynes Rd *EMPK* RM11 .... 160 E8
   GVW DA11 .... 218 E2
Hayron's La *CHLM/WR* CM1 .... 17 H4
Haywards CI *RBRW/HUT* CM13 .... 142 D1 🄰
Hayword Ct *WAB* EN9 .... 78 B1
Hazel CI *HCH* RM12 .... 180 C4 🄰
   LAIN SS15 .... 167 G3
   LOS SS9 .... 192 D5 🄰
   SBF/HAD SS7 .... 192 A5 🄰
Hazeldene *CHES/WCR* EN8 .... 76 E3
Hazeldon CI *RCHLM* CM3 .... 20 E7 🄰
Hazel Dr *ERITH* DA8 .... 210 B3
   SOCK/AV RM15 .... 200 A6
Hazeleigh *RBRW/HUT* CM13 .... 142 A6
Hazeleigh Gdns *WFD* IG8 .... 134 B6
Hazeleigh Hall La *MAL* CM9 .... 67 J2
Hazel Gdns *CDH/CHF* RM16 .... 214 D2
Hazelmere *PIT* SS13 .... 188 C5
Hazelmere Gdns *EMPK* RM11 .... 160 C5
Hazel Ri *EMPK* RM11 .... 160 D5
Hazel Rd *ERITH* DA8 .... 210 B8
Hazelwood *HOC/HUL* SS5 .... 173 C5
   SBF/HAD SS7 .... 170 A6 🄰
   TIL RM18 .... 216 B3
Hazelwood Ct *MAL* CM9 .... 40 D7
Hazelwood Gdns *BRWN* CM15 .... 140 D2
Hazelwood Gv *LOS* SS9 .... 173 F1
Hazelwood Park CI *BARK/HLT* IG6 ... 135 K2
Hazlemere Rd *SBF/HAD* SS7 .... 170 C5
Headcorn CI *PIT* SS13 .... 169 F2
Headley Cha *BRW* CM14 .... 141 F7
Headley Rd *BCAYE* CM11 .... 144 D3
Head St *MAL* CM9 .... 42 C4
Heard's La *BRWN* CM15 .... 114 D4
Hearn Rd *ROM* RM1 .... 160 A4
Hearsail Av *CHLM/WR* CM1 .... 34 C3
   SLH/COR SS17 .... 204 A1
Heath CI *BCAYW* CM12 .... 144 A4
   GPK RM2 .... 160 E6
Heathcote Gdns *HLWE* CM17 .... 25 J7
Heathcote Gv *CHING* E4 .... 132 A1

Heath Dr *CHLM/GWD* CM2 .... **62** D7
  EPP CM16 .... **108** C1
  GPK RM2 .... **160** B3
Heather Bank *BCAYE* CM11 .... **144** D3
Heather Cl *BRWN* CM15 .... **140** E1
Heather Ct *CHLM/WR* CM1 .... **35** H7
Heathercroft Rd *WICKE* SS11 .... **147** K7
Heather Dr *SBF/HAD* SS7 .... **192** A3
Heathfield *CHLM* E4 .... **132** D6
  SBF/HAD SS7 .... **171** H7
Heathfield Rd *CHLM/WR* CM1 .... **34** D5
Heathleigh Dr *VGE* SS16 .... **186** C1
Heath Park Rd *GPK* RM2 .... **160** B7
Heath Rd *BCAYE* CM11 .... **145** F1
  CDH/CHF RM16 .... **201** K8
Heath View Gdns *CDH/CHF* RM16 .. **214** B1
Heath View Rd *CDH/CHF* RM16 ... **214** B1
Heathway *WFD* IG8 .... **133** K7
Heaton Av *HARH* RM3 .... **160** C2
Heaton Cl *CHING* SE4 .... **132** D6
  HARH RM3 .... **160** D2
Heaton Grange Rd *GPK* RM2 ..... **160** A3
Heaton Wy *HARH* RM3 .... **160** D2
Hedgehope Av *RAYL* SS6 .... **171** J1
Hedge La *SBF/HAD* SS7 .... **191** J1
Hedgerows *SBW* CM21 .... **11** K3
The Hedgerows *GVW* DA11 .... **218** D7
Hedingham Rd *EPP* CM16 .... **108** C1
Hedley Av *WTHK* RM20 .... **180** A1
Hedworth Av *CHES/WCR* EN8 .... **76** D7
Heeswyk Rd *CVI* SS8 .... **191** J8
Heidelburg Rd *CVI* SS8 .... **191** H8
Heighams *HLWW/ROY* CM19 ..... **23** H8
The Heights *LOU* IG10 .... **107** H6
  RCHLM CM3 .... **65** G6
  WAB EN9 .... **50** D7
Heilsburg Rd *CVI* SS8 .... **191** J8
Helden Av *CVI* SS8 .... **191** G8
Helena Cl *HOC/HUL* SS5 .... **151** G6
Helena Ct *RCHLM* CM3 .... **122** D7
Helena Rd *RAYL* SS6 .... **171** K3
Helens Rd *EMPK* RM11 .... **160** E5
Helens Cl *CHES/WCR* EN8 .... **49** F8
Helford Wy *UPMR* RM14 .... **162** A8
Helions Rd *HLWW/ROY* CM19 .... **2** B3
Hellendoorn Rd *CVI* SS8 .... **208** C3
Helmons La *CHLM/GWD* CM2 ..... **119** J1
Helmores *LAIN* SS15 .... **166** A7
Helmsdale *CVI* SS8 .... **190** E8
Helpeston *BSDN* SS14 .... **168** A8
Helston Rd *CHLM/WR* CM1 .... **35** G8
Hemley Rd *CDH/CHF* RM16 .... **202** D6
Hemmells *LAIN* SS15 .... **166** C5
Hemmings St *MAL* CM9 .... **68** A5
Hemnall St *EPP* CM16 .... **80** D5
Hempstead Cl *BKHH* IG9 .... **133** H5
Henderson Gdns *WICKE* SS12 .... **147** H8
Hendersons Cl *HCH* RM12 .... **180** C3
Hendon Cl *WICKW* SS12 .... **147** G7
Hengist Gdns *WICKE* SS11 .... **147** G4
Henham Cl *BCAYE* CM11 .... **144** E3
Henley Crs *WOS/PRIT* SS0 .... **194** A1
Henney Cl *RCHLM* CM3 .... **96** B7
Henniker Ga *CHLM/GWD* CM2 ... **63** J2
Henry Dr *LOS* SS9 .... **192** C3
Henry Rd *CHLM/WR* CM1 .... **4** C1
Henry's Av *WFD* IG8 .... **133** G8
Henry St *GRAYS* RM17 .... **214** B5
Henson Av *CVI* SS8 .... **208** E2
Herbage Park Rd *MAL* CM9 .... **66** C4
Herbert Gv *SOS* SS1 .... **9** E5
Herbert Rd *CVI* SS8 .... **208** C1
  EMPK RM11 .... **181** F1
  SBN/FI SS3 .... **196** B7
Herd La *SLH/COR* SS17 .... **204** E1
Hereford Ct *CHLM/GWD* CM2 ..... **63** H8
Hereward Cl *WAB* EN9 .... **77** J6
Hereward Gdns *WICKE* SS11 ..... **147** G4
Hereward Rd *LOU* IG10 .... **108** A5
Herga Hyll *CDH/CHF* RM16 .... **202** A5
Herington Av *RBRW/HUT* CM13 .. **141** K3
Heriot Av *CHING* E4 .... **132** B3
Heriot Wy *MAL* CM9 .... **40** D1
Heritage Wy *RCFD* SS4 .... **174** B3
  RCHLM CM3 .... **97** K8
Hermes Dr *BOC* CM0 .... **128** B8
Hermes Wy *SBN/FI* SS3 .... **196** E5
Hermitage Av *SBF/HAD* SS7 ...... **191** F1
Hermitage Ct *SBF/HAD* SS7 .... **191** F1
Hermitage Dr *LAIN* SS15 .... **6** A4
Hermitage Rd *WOS/PRIT* SS0 ..... **8** B4
Hernen Rd *CVI* SS8 .... **191** G8
Hernshaw *RBRW/HUT* CM13 ...... **164** C2
Heron Cl *WICKE* SS11 .... **147** J7
Heron Cha *RBRW/HUT* CM13 ..... **164** D2
Heron Cl *BKHH* IG9 .... **133** H4
  RAYL SS6 .... **171** G3
  SBW CM21 .... **11** H4
Heron La *BSDN* SS14 .... **168** A7
Heron Flight Av *RAIN* RM13 .... **180** C8
Heron Gdns *RAYL* SS6 .... **171** G2
Herongate *SBF/HAD* SS7 .... **190** A1
  SBN/FI SS3 .... **196** D5
Herongate Rd *CHES/WCR* EN8 ... **76** D7

Herons La *CHONG* CM5 .... **56** E4
Herons Wd *HLW* CM20 .... **2** B1
Heron Wy *MAL* CM9 .... **40** E8
Heron Wy *RCHLM* CM3 .... **98** E5
  UPMR RM14 .... **182** B2
  WTHK RM20 .... **212** E4
Herschell Rd *LOS* SS9 .... **192** D3
Hertford Dr *SLH/COR* SS17 .... **187** K4
Hertford Rd *CVI* SS8 .... **207** K2
  PEND EN3 .... **104** D1
  PEND EN3 .... **104** C4
  PEND EN3 .... **104** C4
Hertford Road High St
  PEND EN3 .... **104** C8
Hesselyn Rd *RAIN* RM13 .... **180** C8
Hester Pl *BOC* CM0 .... **128** C8
Hetzand Rd *CVI* SS8 .... **209** F2
Hever Cl *HOC/HUL* SS5 .... **150** E7
Heybridge Ap *MAL* CM9 .... **40** B8
Heybridge Dr *WICKW* SS12 .... **147** H6
Heybridge St *MAL* CM9 .... **40** C8
Heycroft Rd *HOC/HUL* SS5 .... **151** G8
  LOS SS9 .... **173** G6
Heycroft Wy *CHLM/GWD* CM2 ... **63** H8
Heygate Av *SOS* SS1 .... **9** D5
The Heythrop *CHLM/WR* CM1 ..... **5** F1
  ING CM4 .... **116** A2
Heywood Ct *MAL* CM9 .... **40** D7
Heywood Wy *MAL* CM9 .... **40** D7
Hickling Cl *LOS* SS9 .... **172** C7
Hickman Cl *BROX* EN10 .... **48** E2
Hickstars La *BCAYE* CM11 .... **144** D6
The Hides *HLW* CM20 .... **3** D2
Highams Cha *MAL* CM9 .... **42** D5
Highams Rd *HOC/HUL* SS5 .... **151** F8
Higham Vw *EPP* CM16 .... **54** B8
High Ash Cl *TIL* RM18 .... **216** B2
High Bank *VGE* SS16 .... **186** A1
Highbank Cl *LOS* SS9 .... **173** G8
High Beeches *SBF/HAD* SS7 ...... **190** A2
High Beech Rd *LOU* IG10 .... **107** G8
High Bridge Rd *CHLM/GWD* CM2 .. **5** D4
Highbridge St *WAB* EN9 .... **77** H7
Highcliff Crs *RCFD* SS4 .... **151** K6
Highcliff Rd *WICKE* SS11 .... **147** J6
Highcliffe Cl *WICKE* SS11 .... **147** J5
Highcliffe Rd *WICKE* SS11 .... **147** J6
Highcliffe Wy *WICKW* SS12 .... **146** C5
Highcliff Rd *SBF/HAD* SS7 .... **190** D4
High Cloister *BCAYE* CM11 .... **144** C3
High Easter Rd *GTDUN* CM6 ...... **16** C7
High Elms *CHIG* IG7 .... **135** H7
  UPMR RM14 .... **182** B2
  WFD IG8 .... **133** H8
High Elms Rd *HOC/HUL* SS5 ...... **149** K4
Highfield Ap *BCAYE* CM11 .... **144** E5
Highfield Av *SBF/HAD* SS7 .... **191** G1
Highfield Cl *RCHLM* CM3 .... **65** H7
  WOS/PRIT SS0 .... **8** A2
Highfield Crs *HCH* RM12 .... **181** G3
  RAYL SS6 .... **171** J3
  WOS/PRIT SS0 .... **8** A2
Highfield Dr *BROX* EN10 .... **48** E3
  WOS/PRIT SS0 .... **8** A2
Highfield Gdns *CDH/CHF* RM16 .. **214** C1
  WOS/PRIT SS0 .... **8** A1
Highfield Gn *EPP* CM16 .... **80** C5
Highfield Gv *WOS/PRIT* SS0 .... **8** A1
Highfield Pl *EPP* CM16 .... **80** C5
Highfield Ri *RCHLM* CM3 .... **126** E2
Highfield Rd *BCAYE* CM11 .... **144** E6
  CHLM/WR CM1 .... **62** A1
  HCH RM12 .... **181** G3
Highfields Md *RCHLM* CM3 .... **93** F5
Highfield Wy *WOS/PRIT* SS0 ...... **8** A1
Highgate *SBW* CM21 .... **11** H3
High House La *CDH/CHF* RM16 ... **215** J2
Highland Av *BRW* CM14 .... **141** F4
  LOU IG10 .... **134** C2
Highland Gv *BCAYE* CM11 .... **144** C2
Highland Rd *SLH/COR* SS17 .... **187** J4
  WAB EN9 .... **50** A4
Highlands Av *VGE* SS16 .... **188** A1
Highlands Bvd *LOS* SS9 .... **192** B3
Highlands Crs *PIT* SS13 .... **169** J7
Highlands Dr *MAL* CM9 .... **68** A3
Highlands Hl *RCHLM* CM3 .... **99** H7
Highlands Rd *PIT* SS13 .... **169** J7
  WICKE SS11 .... **149** G3
High La *RBSF* SM22 .... **12** E7
High Md *CHIG* IG7 .... **135** H5
  HOC/HUL SS5 .... **151** F8
Highmead *RAYL* SS6 .... **171** H3
High Meadow *BCAYE* CM11 .... **144** D3
High Mdw *CHIG* IG7 .... **135** G8
High Oaks *VGE* SS16 .... **186** C2
High Pastures *RBSF* CM22 .... **12** C5
High Rd *BKHH* IG9 .... **133** J5
  BROX EN10 .... **49** F2
  CDH/CHF RM16 .... **200** C8
  CDH/CHF RM16 .... **201** K5

CHIG IG7 .... **134** E6
EPP CM16 .... **53** F6
EPP CM16 .... **54** D6
EPP CM16 .... **80** A7
EPP CM16 .... **82** B1
HOC/HUL SS5 .... **150** B8
LAIN SS15 .... **166** CB
RAYL SS6 .... **171** H5
SBF/HAD SS7 .... **170** A8
SLH/COR SS17 .... **187** K4
SLH/COR SS17 .... **203** F2
SLH/COR SS17 .... **204** C4
VGE SS16 .... **186** D2
VGE SS16 .... **188** C1
High Road Broxbourne
  BROX EN10 .... **49** F3
High Rd North *LAIN* SS15 .... **6** A1
High Road Ongar
  (Chelmsford Road) *CHONG* CM5 .. **84** D1
High Road Turnford *BROX* EN10 .. **48** D8
High Road Woodford Gn *WFD* IG8 .. **133** H8
High Road Wormley *BROX* EN10 .. **49** F6
High Silver *LOU* IG10 .... **107** F8
High St *CHES/WCR* EN8 .... **76** E8
  BCAYW CM12 .... **144** B3
  BOC CM0 .... **74** C2
  BOC CM0 .... **128** D1
  BOC CM0 .... **155** G1
  BROX EN10 .... **48** E7
  BRW CM14 .... **141** F5
  CHLM/GWD CM2 .... **63** H6
  CHLM/WR CM1 .... **4** C3
  CHONG CM5 .... **84** C3
  CVI SS8 .... **208** C1
  EMPK RM11 .... **180** E2
  EPP CM16 .... **80** D5
  GRAYS RM17 .... **213** K4
  GVE DA12 .... **219** G4
  GVW DA11 .... **218** A4
  HLWE CM17 .... **25** C1
  HLWW/ROY CM19 .... **22** D4
  HOD EN11 .... **49** C1
  ING CM4 .... **88** C8
  ING CM4 .... **116** B2
  ING CM4 .... **118** A3
  LOS SS9 .... **192** D5
  MAL CM9 .... **44** C4
  MAL CM9 .... **68** B2
  RAYL SS6 .... **171** H4
  RCFD SS4 .... **153** G3
  SBF/HAD SS7 .... **190** C4
  SBF/HAD SS7 .... **191** J2
  SBN/FI SS3 .... **196** E1
  SBN/FI SS3 .... **197** F6
  SLH/COR SS17 .... **203** K4
  SOCK/AV RM15 .... **208** E8
  SOS SS1 .... **9** D4
  WICKW SS12 .... **147** G6
Hightrees *ING* CM4 .... **117** K3
High Vw *BOC* CM0 .... **72** C5
High View Av *GRAYS* RM17 .... **214** B4
Highview Av *VGE* SS16 .... **185** K1
High View Cl *LOU* IG10 .... **133** K1
Highview Crs *RBRW/HUT* CM13 .. **142** B2
High View Gdns *GRAYS* RM17 ... **214** B4
Highview Gdns *UPMR* RM14 .... **181** J3
High View Ri *BCAYE* CM11 .... **145** K8
Highview Rd *SBF/HAD* SS7 .... **171** F6
Highwood Cl *BRW* CM14 .... **140** E3
  LOS SS9 .... **193** G1
Highwood La *LOU* IG10 .... **134** D2
Highwood Rd *CHLM/WR* CM1 ..... **87** K1
High Wych La *SBW* CM21 .... **10** E3
High Wych Rd *HLW* CM20 .... **11** C7
  SBW CM21 .... **11** G7
Hilary Cl *HCH* RM12 .... **180** E6
  RCFD SS4 .... **152** B8
Hilary Crs *RAYL* SS6 .... **171** K3
Hilbery Rd *CVI* SS8 .... **208** C2
Hildaville Dr *WOS/PRIT* SS0 ...... **193** K3
Hilden Dr *ERITH* DA8 .... **210** C6
Hillary Av *GVW* DA11 .... **218** D8
Hillary Cl *CHLM/WR* CM1 .... **5** E1
  MAL CM9 .... **40** D8
Hillary Mt *BCAYW* CM12 .... **144** A4
Hill Av *WICKE* SS11 .... **147** J6
Hillborough Rd *WOS/PRIT* SS0 ... **8** A1
Hill Cl *SBF/HAD* SS7 .... **190** D1
Hill Crs *CHLM/GWD* CM2 .... **5** E5
  EMPK RM11 .... **160** D8
Hillcrest *RCHLM* CM3 .... **98** E4
Hillcrest Av *HOC/HUL* SS5 .... **149** K3
  WTHK RM20 .... **212** D5
Hillcrest Cl *SLH/COR* SS17 .... **203** F1
Hill Crest Rd *CHONG* CM5 .... **82** B1
Hillcrest Rd *EMPK* RM11 .... **180** B1
  HOC/HUL SS5 .... **151** F8
  LOU IG10 .... **134** A2
  RCHLM CM3 .... **122** C6
  SLH/COR SS17 .... **202** E2
  SOS SS1 .... **9** E4
Hillcrest Vw *VGE* SS16 .... **188** A2
Hillcrest Wy *EPP* CM16 .... **80** E5
Hillcroft *LOU* IG10 .... **107** J8
Hilldene Av *HARH* RM3 .... **160** D1

Hilldene Cl HARH RM3........................ 138 E8
Hillhouse WAB EN9 .... 78 B7
Hillhouse Cl BCAYW CM12 .... 144 C1
Hillhouse Dr BCAYW CM12 .... 144 C1
Hillingdon Rd GVW DA11 .... 219 G7
Hill La HOC/HUL SS5 .... 151 G8
Hillman Cl EMPK RM11 .... 160 E5
Hill Ri UPMR RM14 .... 181 H3
Hill Rd BRW CM14 .... 140 D6
CHLM/GWD CM2 .... 5 E3
EPP CM16 .... 108 C3
SBF/HAD SS7 .... 190 D2
SOSN SS2 .... 8 C1
Hill's Chace BRW CM14 .... 141 F7
Hillside GRAYS RM17 .... 214 C3
HLWE CM17 .... 25 G7
Hillside Av CHES/WCR EN8 .... 76 D5
GVE DA12 .... 219 J7
HOC/HUL SS5 .... 151 F8
WFD IG8 .... 133 K8
Hillside Cl BCAYE CM11 .... 144 C4 [2]
WFD IG8 .... 133 K8 [1]
Hillside Crs CHES/WCR EN8 .... 76 D5
LOS SS9 .... 193 H5 [1]
Hillside Dr GVE DA12 .... 219 J7
Hillside Gv CHLM/GWD CM2 .... 62 C7
Hillside Ms CHLM/GWD CM2 .... 4 B6 [1]
Hillside Rd BCAYW CM12 .... 144 C4
BOC CM0 .... 128 B8
BOC CM0 .... 128 C1
HOC/HUL SS5 .... 150 C8
LOS SS9 .... 172 D5
SBF/HAD SS7 .... 190 D5
Hillside Wk BRW CM14 .... 140 D6
Hill's Rd BKHH IG9 .... 133 J4
Hill Ter SLH/COR SS17 .... 187 K8
The Hill GVW DA11 .... 218 B4
HLWE CM17 .... 25 G1
Hill Top LOU IG10 .... 107 J7
Hilltop Av HOC/HUL SS5 .... 149 K4
Hill Top Av SBF/HAD SS7 .... 190 E3
Hill Top Cl LOU IG10 .... 107 J7
Hilltop Cl RAYL SS6 .... 171 H4
Hilltop Ri VGE SS16 .... 186 A1
Hilltop Rd WTHK RM20 .... 212 D5
Hill Tree Cl SBW CM21 .... 11 H4
Hill Vw RCHLM CM3 .... 93 K4
Hillview Av EMPK RM11 .... 160 D8
Hillview Gdns CHES/WCR EN8 .... 76 E1
SLH/COR SS17 .... 187 G8 [1]
Hill View Rd CHLM/WR CM1 .... 5 D1
Hillway BCAYE SS16 .... 144 E3
WOS/PRIT SS0 .... 193 H5
The Hill Wy BRW CM15 .... 115 J5
Hillwood Cl RBRW/HUT CM13 .... 142 A4
Hillwood Gv RBRW/HUT CM13 .... 142 A4
WICKE SS12 .... 147 H6
Hilly Fld HLWS CM18 .... 52 D1
Hilton Rd CVI SS8 .... 107 J6
Hilton Rd CVI SS8 .... 191 F8
Hilton Wk CVI SS8 .... 191 F8
Hiversum Wy CVI SS8 .... 191 G8 [1]
Hind Cl CHIG IG7 .... 135 J3
Hindles Rd CVI SS8 .... 208 D1
Hinguar St SBN/FI SS3 .... 196 E7
Hitchin Cl HARH RM3 .... 138 D7
Hither Blakers HLWS CM18 .... 122 D5 [5]
Hitherwood Cl HCH RM12 .... 180 E5 [1]
Hive La GVW DA11 .... 218 A3
Hobart Cl CHLM/WR CM1 .... 34 A8
Hobart Rd TIL RM18 .... 215 F7
Hobbiton Hi RCHLM CM3 .... 122 C7
Hobbs Cl CHES/WCR EN8 .... 76 F2
Hobbs Cross Rd EPP CM16 .... 81 G8
HLWE CM17 .... 25 K2
Hobhouse Rd SLH/COR SS17 .... 203 K1 [1]
Hobleythick La WOS/PRIT SS0 .... 8 A1
Hobtoe Rd HLW CM20 .... 2 A2
Hockley Cl BOC CM0 .... 74 E3
BSDN SS14 .... 168 A7
Hockley Dr GPK RM2 .... 160 A7
Hockley Gn BSDN SS14 .... 168 B7
Hockley Ri HOC/HUL SS5 .... 151 F8
Hockley Rd BOC CM0 .... 74 E2
RAYL SS6 .... 171 K2
Hodgson Ct WICKE SS12 .... 147 K8
Hodgson Wy WICKE SS12 .... 147 J7
Hodings Rd HLW CM20 .... 2 B2
Hoecroft WAB EN9 .... 50 B4 [1]
Hoe La ABR/ST RM4 .... 109 F7
EN EN1 .... 104 B4
PEND EN3 .... 104 C4
RCHLM CM3 .... 20 A7
RCHLM CM3 .... 120 D7
WAB EN9 .... 50 B4
Hoe Mill Rd MAL CM9 .... 66 D1
Hoestock Rd HLW CM21 .... 11 H3
Hoe St CHLM/WR CM1 .... 60 C1
The Hoe HLW CM20 .... 166 C1
Hogarth Av BRW CM14 .... 141 F6
Hogarth Dr SBN/FI SS3 .... 197 F5
Hogarth Reach LOU IG10 .... 134 C1
Hogarth Rd CDH/CHF RM16 .... 200 E8 [1]

Hogarth Wy RCFD SS4 .... 151 K7
Hogg La CDH/CHF RM16 .... 213 K2
GRAYS RM17 .... 213 K3
Hog La MEO DA13 .... 218 C8
Hogwell Cha RCHLM CM3 .... 123 H4
Holbech Rd BSDN SS14 .... 168 C5
Holbek Rd CVI SS8 .... 208 E2
Holbrook Cl BCAYE CM11 .... 144 E3 [3]
RCHLM CM3 .... 122 D6
Holdbrook Wy HARH RM3 .... 161 J4
BSDN SS14 .... 168 C4
Holden Gdns BRW CM14 .... 141 C8
BSDN SS14 .... 168 B4
Holden Rd BSDN SS14 .... 168 B4
Holden Wy UPMR RM14 .... 182 A2
Holecroft WAB EN9 .... 78 A8
Holford Rd CDH/CHF RM16 .... 215 K2
TIL RM18 .... 215 J3
Holgate PIT SS13 .... 169 F5
Holkham Av RCHLM CM3 .... 122 D8
Holland Av CVI SS8 .... 190 C8
Holland Rd WOS/PRIT SS0 .... 8 A5
Hollands Wk VGE SS16 .... 188 A3
Holliday Hl CHLM/GWD CM2 .... 119 G1
The Hollies SLH/COR SS17 .... 203 J4 [2]
Hollis Lock CHLM/GWD CM2 .... 63 J2
Hollis Pl GRAYS RM17 .... 213 K2
Holloway Crs GTDUN CM6 .... 16 A6
Holloway Rd MAL CM9 .... 40 B7
Hollowfield Av GRAYS RM17 .... 214 C3
Hollow La CHLM/WR CM1 .... 33 K6
The Hollow WFD IG8 .... 133 G7 [1]
Hollybush Rd GVE DA12 .... 219 H7
Hollybush Wy CHESW EN7 .... 76 A3
Holly Cl BKHH IG9 .... 134 A6
BOC CM0 .... 128 B7
Holly Dr CHING E4 .... 132 C3
SOCK/AV RM15 .... 200 B4
Holly Fld HLWW/ROY CM19 .... 2 C6
Hollyfields BROX EN10 .... 48 E8
Hollyford BCAYE CM11 .... 117 J3
Holly Gv VGE SS16 .... 166 A8
Hollymead SLH/COR SS17 .... 204 A1
Holly Rd PEND EN3 .... 104 D2
Hollytree Gdns RAYL SS6 .... 171 G5
Holly Wy CHLM/GWD CM2 .... 5 D6
Hollywood Cl CHLM/GWD CM2 .... 63 G7
Hollywood Wy ERITH DA8 .... 210 C7
Holmans RCHLM CM3 .... 36 C5
Holmbridge Gdns PEND EN3 .... 104 D8
Holme Cl CHES/WCR EN8 .... 76 E5 [1]
Holme Rd EMPK RM11 .... 181 H2
Holmes Cl SLH/COR SS17 .... 203 F2
Holmesdale CHES/WCR EN8 .... 104 C1
Holme Wk WICKE SS12 .... 147 J8
Holmsdale Rd WOS/PRIT SS0 .... 193 J1
Holmwood Cvi BRWN CM15 .... 191 K8 [1]
Holmwood Cl BRWN CM15 .... 141 K1
Holmwood Rd PEND EN3 .... 104 D2
Holst Av LAIN SS15 .... 6 A2
Holst Cl SLH/COR SS17 .... 203 J3
Holt Cl CHIG IG7 .... 135 J8
Holt Farm Wy RCFD SS4 .... 174 A1
Holton Rd CVI SS8 .... 209 F2
RAYL SS6 .... 172 B4 [4]
Holt Wy CHIG IG7 .... 135 J8
Holtynge SBF/HAD SS7 .... 190 B1
Holybread La RCHLM CM3 .... 65 C1
Holy Cross Hl BROX EN10 .... 48 A5
Holyfield Rd WAB EN9 .... 77 J3
Holyoak La HOC/HUL SS5 .... 173 F1
Holyrood Dr WOS/PRIT SS0 .... 193 J3
Holyrood Gdns CDH/CHF RM16 ...... 215 H3
Home Cl BROX EN10 .... 49 F6
HLW CM20 .... 3 F1
Homecroft Gdns LOU IG10 .... 107 K8
Home Farm Rd RBRW/HUT CM13 ... 163 H3
Homefield BOC CM0 .... 100 E8
WAB EN9 .... 78 C6
Homefield Cl BCAYE CM11 .... 144 E7 [1]
CHLM/WR CM1 .... 33 K8
EPP CM16 .... 80 E3
Homefields SBF/HAD SS7 .... 170 A8
Homelands Gv BCAYE CM11 .... 145 K1
Homeleight Ct CHES/WCR EN8 .... 76 B4 [1]
Home Md CHLM/GWD CM2 .... 90 E3
CHLM/WR CM1 .... 61 G4
LAIN SS15 .... 166 C5
Home Mead Cl GVE DA12 .... 219 G5
Home Mdw BCAYW CM12 .... 144 B3 [1]
Home Pastures RBSF CM22 .... 34 D6
Homestead CHLM/WR CM1 .... 34 D6
Homestead Dr VGE SS16 .... 186 D3
Homestead Gdns SBF/HAD SS7 ..... 191 J2
Homestead Rd BCAYE CM11 .... 146 A5
PIT SS13 .... 169 H6
SBF/HAD SS7 .... 191 J3
Homestead Wy SBF/HAD SS7 .... 191 J3
Homeway HARH RM3 .... 161 J1
Honey Brook WAB EN9 .... 78 A7
Honey Cl BRWN CM15 .... 114 B1
CHLM/GWD CM2 .... 63 F7
Honeycroft LOU IG10 .... 107 J9
Honey La CHES/WCR EN8 .... 77 F8
WAB EN9 .... 78 B8

Honeymeade HLW CM20 .... 11 G6
Honeypot La BRW CM14 .... 140 D5
BSDN SS14 .... 7 F4
ING CM4 .... 117 J4
Honey Pot La RCHLM CM3 .... 124 A2
Honeypots CHLM/GWD CM2 .... 62 E7
Honeysuckle Cl BRWN CM15 .... 140 E1
HARH RM3 .... 160 E1 [1]
Honiley Av WICKE SS12 .... 169 H3
Honington Cl WICKE SS11 .... 98 A7
Honiton Rd SOS SS1 .... 9 F4
Honywood Rd BSDN SS14 .... 168 C5
Hood Cl WICKW SS12 .... 147 H7
Hook End La BRW CM15 .... 86 A8
Hook End Rd BRWN CM15 .... 113 K1
Hook Fld HLWS CM18 .... 3 E5
Hookfields GVW DA11 .... 218 D8
Hook Ga EN EN1 .... 104 B3
Hook La ABR/ST RM4 .... 136 E2
Hooley Dr RAYL SS6 .... 149 H7
The Hoo HLWE CM17 .... 11 G8
Hoover Dr LAIN SS15 .... 166 A7
Hope Av SLH/COR SS17 .... 187 F5
Hope Cl BRWN CM15 .... 115 J5 [1]
CVI SS8 .... 208 D2
SBF/HAD SS7 .... 190 B4
Hop Gardens La MAL CM9 .... 67 F1
Hopkins Cl CHLM/GWD CM2 .... 63 J2 [1]
GPK RM2 .... 160 D5
Hopkins Md CHLM/GWD CM2 .... 63 H3
Hopkirk Cl RCHLM CM3 .... 65 K5
Hoppett Rd CHING E4 .... 133 F6
Hopping Jacks La RCHLM CM3 .... 65 K6
The Hoppitt CHONG CM5 .... 55 J2
Horace Rd BCAYE CM11 .... 144 C1
SOS SS1 .... 9 E5
Horkesley Wy WICKW SS12 .... 147 H7 [1]
Horksley Gdns
RBRW/HUT CM13 .... 142 B2 [1]
Hornbeam Av UPMR RM14 .... 181 H5
Hornbeam Cha SOCK/AV RM15 ...... 200 B3
Hornbeam Cl CHLM/GWD CM2 .... 62 C7
EPP CM16 .... 108 C3
RBRW/HUT CM13 .... 142 A6
Hornbeam Gv CHING E4 .... 133 F6
Hornbeam La CHING E4 .... 133 F1
Hornbeam Rd BKHH IG9 .... 134 A8
EPP CM16 .... 108 B3 [1]
Hornbeams SBF/HAD SS7 .... 170 A5
Hornbeams Av EN EN1 .... 104 C1
The Hornbeams HLW CM20 .... 2 C5
Hornbeam Wy LAIN SS15 .... 6 B1
Hornby Av WOS/PRIT SS0 .... 173 K8
Hornby Cl WOS/PRIT SS0 .... 174 A1
Hornchurch Cl WICKE SS11 .... 147 K7 [5]
Hornchurch Rd EMPK RM11 .... 180 C2
HCH RM12 .... 180 B2
Horndon Rd SLH/COR SS17 .... 203 G4
Horne Rw RCHLM CM3 .... 65 H8
Hornet Wy BOC CM0 .... 128 B8
Hornminster Gln EMPK RM11 .... 181 H3 [1]
Hornsby La CDH/CHF RM16 .... 202 A7
Hornsby Sq LAIN SS15 .... 165 K6
Hornsby Wy LAIN SS15 .... 166 A6
Hornsland Rd CVI SS8 .... 208 E2
Horn Yd GVE DA12 .... 219 G4 [8]
Horsecroft Rd HLWW/ROY CM19 ..... 23 G6
Horseman Side BRW CM14 .... 138 E2
Horseshoe Cl BCAYW CM12 .... 117 G8
Horseshoe Hl WAB EN9 .... 78 E7
Horsley Cross BSDN SS14 .... 7 F5
Horsley Rd CHING E4 .... 132 D5
Hospital Ap CHLM/WR CM1 .... 34 D2
Hospital Rd SBN/FI SS3 .... 196 E7
Houblons El EPP CM16 .... 81 H5
Houchin Dr CHONG CM5 .... 57 F3
Hove Cl GRAYS RM17 .... 213 K5
RBRW/HUT CM13 .... 142 B5
Hovefields Av PIT SS13 .... 169 G2
WICKW SS12 .... 169 G2
Hovefields Dr WICKW SS12 .... 169 G2 [1]
Howard Cha BSDN SS14 .... 7 D2
Howard Cl WAB EN9 .... 77 K8
Howard Crs PIT SS13 .... 169 F8
Howard Dr CHLM/GWD CM2 .... 63 J3
Howard Pl CVI SS8 .... 208 B3 [2]
Howard Rd CDH/CHF RM16 .... 213 F2
UPMR RM14 .... 181 K3
Howards Cha WOS/PRIT SS0 .... 8 B2
Howards Cl RCHLM CM3 .... 36 C5 [5]
Howard Wy HLW CM20 .... 3 F1
Howbury La ERITH DA8 .... 210 B8
Howard Rd DART DA1 .... 210 B8
Howe Green Rd RCHLM CM3 .... 96 A7
Howell Rd SLH/COR SS17 .... 187 G7
Hows Md EPP CM16 .... 54 D6
Hoylake Gdns HARH RM3 .... 161 H2 [1]
Hoynors RCHLM CM3 .... 66 A6
Hubbards Cha EMPK RM11 .... 161 H7
Hubbards Cl EMPK RM11 .... 161 H7
Hubert Rd BRW CM14 .... 140 E6
Hucknall Cl HARH RM3 .... 161 G1
Hudson Crs LOS SS9 .... 173 F7
Hudson Rd LOS SS9 .... 172 E7

Hudsons Cl *SLH/COR* SS17 .... 203 K2
Hudson Wy *CVI* SS8 .... 191 F7
Hughes Rd *CDH/CHF* RM16 .... 215 F2
Hugo Gdns *RAIN* RM13 .... 180 A7
Hullbridge Rd *RAYL* SS6 .... 149 J5
  RCHLM CM3 .... 122 D7
Hullett's La *BRWN* CM15 .... 113 H8
Hull Gn *HLWE* CM17 .... 27 K3
Hull Gv *HLW/ROY* CM19 .... 51 J2
Hull's La *CHLM/GWD* CM2 .... 64 C7
Hulton Cl *RCHLM* CM3 .... 36 C5
Humber Av *SOCN/AV* RM15 .... 199 H6
Humber Cl *RAYL* SS6 .... 171 H4
Humber Dr *UPMR* RM14 .... 162 A8
Humber Rd *CHLM/WR* CM1 .... 34 E8
Hume Av *TIL* RM18 .... 219 G1
Hume Cl *TIL* RM18 .... 219 F1
Humphrey's Farm La *RCHLM* CM3 .... 19 J6
Hungerdown *CHING* E4 .... 132 D4
Hunsdon Rd *WARE* SG12 .... 22 A1
Hunt Av *MAL* CM9 .... 40 D8
Hunter Av *BCAYW* CM12 .... 144 C6
Hunter Dr *HCH* RM12 .... 180 D5
  WICKW SS12 .... 147 H8
Hunters Av *CHING* E4 .... 132 B6
Hunters Cha *RBRW/HUT* CM13 .... 143 H4
Hunters Gv *CRW* RM5 .... 137 G8
Hunters Wy *CHLM/WR* CM1 .... 35 H6
Huntingdon Cl *BROX* EN10 .... 48 E6
Huntingdon Rd *SOS* SS1 .... 195 G5
Huntley Av *GVW* DA12 .... 218 A4
Huntridge Rd *GVW* DA12 .... 218 D8
Hunt's Cl *CHLM/WR* CM1 .... 61 H5
Hunt's Dr *CHLM/WR* CM1 .... 61 H5
Hunts Farm Cl *MAL* CM9 .... 44 D3
Huntsmans Dr *UPMR* RM14 .... 181 K6
Hunts Md *BCAYW* CM12 .... 144 A4
  PEND EN3 .... 104 D7
Hurlock Rd *BCAYE* CM11 .... 144 C3
Hurrell Down *RCHLM* CM3 .... 36 D4
Hurrells La *RCHLM* CM3 .... 64 E2
Hurricane Cl *WICKE* SS11 .... 148 A8
Hurricane Wy *EPP* CM16 .... 81 K1
  WICKE SS11 .... 147 K8
Hursley Rd *CHIG* IG7 .... 135 J8
Hurst Av *CHING* E4 .... 132 B6
Hurst Cl *CHING* E4 .... 132 B6
Hurst Dr *CHES/WCR* EN8 .... 76 B7
Hurstlands Cl *EMPK* RM11 .... 160 D8
Hurst Park Av *HCH* RM12 .... 181 F5
Hurst Rd *BKHH* IG9 .... 134 A4
Hurst Wy *CHLM/GWD* CM2 .... 63 H3
  LOS SS9 .... 193 G2
Hurstwood Av *BRWN* CM15 .... 140 F3
Hutchins Cl *HCH* RM12 .... 181 F4
Hutton Cl *RBRW/HUT* CM13 .... 142 C3
Hutton Ga *RBRW/HUT* CM13 .... 142 A3
Hutton Rd *BRWN* CM15 .... 141 J3
Hutton Village *RBRW/HUT* CM13 .... 142 D3
Hyacinth Cl *MAL* CM9 .... 44 E4
Hycliffe Gdns *CHIG* IG7 .... 135 F3
Hyde Cha *MAL* CM9 .... 94 C1
Hyde Gn *RCHLM* CM3 .... 66 B6
Hyde La *RCHLM* CM3 .... 94 B1
Hyde Md *WAB* EN9 .... 50 A5
Hyder Rd *CDH/CHF* RM16 .... 215 H2
The Hyde *VGE* SS16 .... 6 A6
Hydeway *SBF/HAD* SS7 .... 170 E8
Hyde Wy *WICKW* SS12 .... 147 G7
Hyde Wood La *RCFD* SS4 .... 152 C6
Hyland Cl *EMPK* RM11 .... 180 C1
  HOC/HUL SS5 .... 150 E8
Hyland Wy *EMPK* RM11 .... 180 C1
The Hythe *MAL* CM9 .... 68 D3

I

Ian Rd *BCAYW* CM12 .... 144 A4
Ibbetson Pth *LOU* IG10 .... 107 K7
Ia Butts Rd *SBN/FI* SS3 .... 197 H4
Ifracombe Av *PIT* SS13 .... 169 G8
  SOS SS1 .... 195 G5
Ifracombe Crs *HCH* RM12 .... 180 D5
Ifracombe Rd *SOSN* SS2 .... 9 F3
Ilgars Rd *WICKE* SS11 .... 147 H4
Ilmington Dr *PIT* SS13 .... 168 D4
Imperial Av *RCHLM* CM3 .... 98 C4
  WOS/PRIT SS0 .... 193 J4
Inchbonnie Rd *RCHLM* CM3 .... 122 E7
Ingatestone By-pass *ING* CM4 .... 88 B3
Ingatestone Rd *CHLM/WR* CM1 ...... 87 J3
  ING CM4 .... 86 D6
  ING CM4 .... 117 F4
Ingaway *VGE* SS16 .... 7 D5
Ingelrica Av *RCHLM* CM3 .... 38 B2
Ingels Md *EPP* CM16 .... 80 D3
Ingersoll Rd *PEND* EN3 .... 104 C4
Ingleby Gdns *CHIG* IG7 .... 136 A3
Ingleby Rd *CDH/CHF* RM16 .... 215 G2
Inglefield Rd *SLH/COR* SS17 .... 187 J5
Ingleglen *EMPK* RM11 .... 181 H1
Inglewood Cl *HCH* RM12 .... 180 E5

Ingoldsby Rd *GVE* DA12 .... 219 K6
Ingram Rd *GRAYS* RM17 .... 214 B3
Ingrave Cl *WICKW* SS12 .... 147 H7
Ingrave Rd *BRW* CM14 .... 141 H6
Ingrebourne Gdns *UPMR* RM14 ...... 181 K2
Ingreway *HARH* RM3 .... 161 J1
Inkerpole Pl *CHLM/GWD* CM2 .... 63 H1
Inks Gn *CHING* E4 .... 132 D8
Inmans Rw *WFD* IG8 .... 133 H7
Innes Cl *WICKW* SS12 .... 147 G8
Inskip Dr *EMPK* RM11 .... 181 F2
Institute Rd *EPP* CM16 .... 81 H3
Inverness Av *WOS/PRIT* SS0 .... 8 A2
Invicta Cl *BCAYW* CM12 .... 143 K1
Iona Wy *WICKW* SS12 .... 147 J8
Ipswich Ms *VGE* SS16 .... 166 A8
Ireton Pl *GRAYS* RM17 .... 213 K5
Iris Cl *BRWN* CM15 .... 140 E1
  CHLM/WR CM1 .... 35 H8
Ironwell La *HOC/HUL* SS5 .... 173 H2
  RCFD SS4 .... 174 A3
Irvine Gdns *SOCK/AV* RM15 .... 199 H6
Irvine Pl *WICKW* SS12 .... 147 J8
Irvine Wy *BCAYW* CM12 .... 144 B4
Irvington Cl *LOS* SS9 .... 192 E1
Irvon Hill Rd *WICKW* SS12 .... 147 F6
Irye Md *VGE* SS16 .... 6 A6
Isabel Ga *CHES/WCR* EN8 .... 49 F8
Isis Dr *UPMR* RM14 .... 162 B8
Ives Gdns *ROM* RM1 .... 160 A6
Ivy Barns La *ING* CM4 .... 88 A4
Ivybridge *BROX* EN10 .... 49 G1
Ivy Chimneys Rd *EPP* CM16 .... 80 C6
Ivy Lodge La *HARH* RM3 .... 161 K4
Ivy Rd *SBF/HAD* SS7 .... 169 K7

J

Jacaranda Cl *CHLM/WR* CM1 .... 35 H7
Jackdaw Cl *BCAYE* CM11 .... 144 D5
  SBN/FI SS3 .... 196 D5
Jack Evans Ct *SOCK/AV* RM15 ...... 199 J6
Jacks Cl *WICKE* SS11 .... 147 J6
Jackson Cl *EMPK* RM11 .... 161 G6
Jackson Pl *CHLM/GWD* CM2 .... 63 H7
Jacksons Cl *CHONG* CM5 .... 84 C5
Jacksons Dr *CHESW* EN7 .... 76 A2
Jacksons La *BCAYE* CM11 .... 144 C2
Jacksons Ms *BCAYE* CM11 .... 144 D3
Jack Stevens Cl *HLWE* CM17 .... 25 G7
Jacobs Av *HARH* RM3 .... 161 F4
Jacqueline Gdns *BCAYW* CM12 ...... 144 C1
James Cl *GPK* RM2 .... 160 B7
James Cft *CHLM/GWD* CM2 .... 90 B7
James St *EPP* CM16 .... 80 D2
James Watt Wy *ERITH* DA8 .... 210 A6
Janette Av *CVI* SS8 .... 207 J2
Jardine Rd *PIT* SS13 .... 169 F5
Jarndyce *CHLM/WR* CM1 .... 34 B7
Jarvis Fld *RCHLM* CM3 .... 37 H8
Jarvis Av *CVI* SS8 .... 191 F7
  SBF/HAD SS7 .... 190 D1
Jarvis Wy *HARH* RM3 .... 161 F4
Jasmine Cl *VGE* SS16 .... 186 A1
Jason Cl *CDH/CHF* RM16 .... 202 E6
  CVI SS8 .... 191 G8
Jasons Cl *BRW* CM14 .... 140 C7
Jasper Cl *PEND* EN3 .... 104 C4
Jefferson Av *LAIN* SS15 .... 166 B7
Jeffery Rd *CHLM/GWD* CM2 .... 63 J6
Jeffreys Rd *PEND* EN3 .... 105 F8
Jellicoe Av *GVE* DA12 .... 219 H6
Jena Cl *SBN/FI* SS3 .... 196 D6
Jenner Md *CHLM/GWD* CM2 .... 63 J2
Jenningham Dr *CDH/CHF* RM16 ...... 200 E8
Jenningtree Rd *ERITH* DA8 .... 210 C6
Jericho Pl *ING* CM4 .... 86 C5
Jermayns *LAIN* SS15 .... 6 C4
Jerounds *HLWW/ROY* CM19 .... 2 B5
Jersey Gdns *WICKE* SS11 .... 147 G5
Jersey Rd *MAL* CM9 .... 68 D4
  RAIN RM13 .... 180 B8
Jervis Av *PEND* EN3 .... 104 E1
Jesmond Rd *CDH/CHF* RM16 .... 201 H8
  CVI SS8 .... 208 B5
Jessel Dr *LOU* IG10 .... 108 A6
Jetty Wk *GRAYS* RM17 .... 213 K5
Jocelyns *HLWE* CM17 .... 25 G1
Jodrell Wy *WTHK* RM20 .... 212 C4
Johnby Cl *PEND* EN3 .... 104 E3
John Eliot Cl *WAB* EN9 .... 50 A4
Johnson Cl *GVW* DA11 .... 218 C3
  RCFD SS4 .... 152 A8
  WICKW SS12 .... 147 G8
Johnson Rd *CHLM/GWD* CM2 .... 63 H8
The Johns *CHONG* CM5 .... 84 C1
Johnstone Rd *SOS* SS1 .... 195 K6
Johnston Rd *WFD* IG8 .... 133 H8
Johnston Wy *MAL* CM9 .... 68 E3
John St *GRAYS* RM17 .... 214 B5
  SBN/FI SS3 .... 197 F7

Jones Cl *SOSN* SS2 .... 8 B1
Joslin Rd *PUR* RM19 .... 211 K4
Joslyn Cl *PEND* EN3 .... 105 G4
Josselin Ct *PIT* SS13 .... 169 F3
Josselin Rd *PIT* SS13 .... 169 F3
Jotmans La *SBF/HAD* SS7 .... 189 K2
Journeymans Wy *SOSN* SS2 .... 174 D8
Joyce Ct *WAB* EN9 .... 77 K8
Joyce Green La *DART* DA1 .... 210 E7
Joyce's Cha *MAL* CM9 .... 42 E5
Joyners Fld *HLWS* CM18 .... 52 A1
Joy Rd *GVE* DA12 .... 219 H6
Jubilee Av *CHLM/WR* CM1 .... 34 D3
Jubilee Cl *HOC/HUL* SS5 .... 151 F8
Jubilee Crs *GVE* DA12 .... 219 K7
Jubilee Dr *WICKW* SS12 .... 147 F5
Jubilee Ri *RCHLM* CM3 .... 65 K7
Jubilee Rd *BCAYE* CM11 .... 167 J1
  RAYL SS6 .... 171 K3
  WTHK RM20 .... 212 E5
Julian Cl *CHLM/WR* CM1 .... 34 D4
Juliers Cl *CVI* SS8 .... 208 D2
Juliers Rd *CVI* SS8 .... 208 D2
Juliette Wy *PUR* RM19 .... 211 G1
Junction Rd *BRW* CM14 .... 141 F7
  RCHLM CM3 .... 96 C7
  ROM RM1 .... 160 A6
  VGE SS16 .... 188 E1
Juniper Cl *BCAYE* CM11 .... 144 D1
  BROX EN10 .... 49 F7
Juniper Dr *CHLM/GWD* CM2 .... 62 D7
  SOCK/AV RM15 .... 200 C3
Juniper Rd *LOS* SS9 .... 193 G1
  RCHLM CM3 .... 36 C5
Juniper Wy *HARH* RM3 .... 161 F3
Jury St *GVE* DA12 .... 219 G4
Jute La *PEND* EN3 .... 104 E6

K

Kale Rd *SBF/HAD* SS7 .... 190 D1
Kamerwyk Av *CVI* SS8 .... 208 C1
Kandlewood *RBRW/HUT* CM13 ...... 142 A3
Karen Cl *BRWN* CM15 .... 141 F3
  SBF/HAD SS7 .... 190 C5
  SLH/COR SS17 .... 203 J4
  WICKW SS12 .... 147 F7
Karina Cl *CHIG* IG7 .... 135 H8
Katherine Cl *RAYL* SS6 .... 172 B4
Katherine Rd *PIT* SS13 .... 169 H6
Katherine's Wy *HLWW/ROY* CM19 .... 2 A6
Kathleen Cl *SLH/COR* SS17 .... 203 K1
Kathleen Dr *LOS* SS9 .... 193 G3
Kathleen Ferrier Crs *LAIN* SS15 ...... 6 C2
Katonia Av *RCHLM* CM3 .... 98 D4
Kavanaghs Rd *BRW* CM14 .... 140 D6
Kavanaghs Ter *BRW* CM14 .... 140 E6
Keats Av *HARH* RM3 .... 160 C2
Keats Cl *MAL* CM9 .... 68 C5
Keats Gdns *TIL* RM18 .... 215 G8
Keats Wk *RBRW/HUT* CM13 .... 142 C3
Keats Wy *WICKW* SS12 .... 147 F6
Kecksy's *SBW* CM21 .... 11 K1
Keeble Pk *MAL* CM9 .... 68 B5
Keegan Pl *CVI* SS8 .... 208 C1
Keelings La *BOC* CM0 .... 102 A5
Keelings Rd *BOC* CM0 .... 101 K5
Keene Wy *CHLM/GWD* CM2 .... 90 D2
Keer Av *CVI* SS8 .... 208 D3
Keighley Ms *SBN/FI* SS3 .... 196 C3
Keith Av *WICKE* SS11 .... 147 G4
Keith Wy *EMPK* RM11 .... 181 F1
  SOSN SS2 .... 174 B8
Kellington Rd *CVI* SS8 .... 191 H8
Kelly Rd *PIT* SS13 .... 169 H7
Kelman Cl *CHES/WCR* EN8 .... 76 D5
Kelvedon Cl *CHLM/WR* CM1 .... 34 C7
  RAYL SS6 .... 171 F2
  RBRW/HUT CM13 .... 142 D2
Kelvedon Gn *BRWN* CM15 .... 113 H5
Kelvedon Hall La *BRW* CM14 .... 84 E3
Kelvedon Rd *BCAYE* CM11 .... 144 D3
Kelvin Rd *SBF/HAD* SS7 .... 170 C6
  TIL RM18 .... 215 F8
Kelvinside *SLH/COR* SS17 .... 187 F8
Kembles *RAYL* SS6 .... 149 K8
Kempe Rd *EN* EN1 .... 104 B2
Kempton Av *HCH* RM12 .... 181 G5
Kempton Cl *SBF/HAD* SS7 .... 171 G5
Kendal Av *EPP* CM16 .... 80 E4
Kendal Cl *HOC/HUL* SS5 .... 149 K4
  RAYL SS6 .... 171 K3
  WFD IG8 .... 133 G5
Kendal Ct *WICKE* SS11 .... 147 K8
Kendal Cft *HCH* RM12 .... 180 B6
Kendale *CDH/CHF* RM16 .... 215 G2
Kendal Wy *LOS* SS9 .... 173 F6
Kenholme *LOS* SS9 .... 193 F1
Kenilworth Av *HARH* RM3 .... 139 J8
Kenilworth Cl *BCAYW* CM12 .... 143 K3
Kenilworth Gdns *HCH* RM12 .... 180 C4
  LOU IG10 .... 134 C2

RAYL SS6 .... 171 H2
WOS/PRIT SS0 .... 193 H2
Kenilworth Pl *LAIN* SS15 .... 6 C1 🔲
Kenley Cl *WICKE* SS11 .... 147 K7
Kenley Gdns *HCH* RM12 .... 181 G3
Kenmore Cl *CVI* SS8 .... 208 E3 🔲
Kennedy Av *LAIN* SS15 .... 166 A7
Kennedy Cl *CHES/WCR* EN8 .... 76 E2
RAYL SS6 .... 172 B5
SBF/HAD SS7 .... 170 A6
Kennel La *BCAYW* CM12 .... 144 C6
Kennet Cl *UPMR* RM14 .... 162 B8
Kenneth Gdns *SLH/COR* SS17 .... 187 G8 🔲
Kenneth Rd *PIT* SS13 .... 169 F6
SBF/HAD SS7 .... 170 E8
Kennington Av *SBF/HAD* SS7 .... 170 B8
Kensington Gdns *BCAYW* CM12 .... 144 B1 🔲
Kensington Rd *BRWN* CM15 .... 140 D2
SOS SS1 .... 195 G5
Kent Av *CVI* SS8 .... 191 G8 🔲
LOS SS9 .... 193 G3
Kent Cl *LAIN* SS15 .... 166 C7
Kent Dr *HCH* RM12 .... 180 E5
Kent Elms Cl *SOSN* SS2 .... 173 G8
Kent Green *HOC/HUL* SS5 .... 151 G8
Kenton Wy *VGE* SS16 .... 166 A8
Kent Rd *GRAYS* RM17 .... 214 A5
GVW RM16 .... 219 F6
Kents Farm La *CHLM/GWD* CM2 .... 119 F1
Kents Grass *MAL* CM9 .... 44 D3
Kents Hill Rd *SBF/HAD* SS7 .... 190 C1
Kents Hill Rd North *SBF/HAD* SS7 ...... 170 C8
Kents La *EPP* CM16 .... 54 D3
Kent Vw *SOCK/AV* RM15 .... 211 K1
Kent View Av *LOS* SS9 .... 193 H5
Kent View Rd *VGE* SS16 .... 168 C8
Kent Wy *RAYL* SS6 .... 172 B5
Kenway *SOSN* SS2 .... 9 D2
Kenwood Rd *SLH/COR* SS17 .... 204 D1
Kenworth Cl *CHES/WCR* EN8 .... 76 D7
Kerby Ri *CHLM/GWD* CM2 .... 65 H3
Kerril Crt *HLW* CM20 .... 2 A2
Kerry Av *PUR* RM19 .... 211 G1
Kerry Cl *UPMR* RM14 .... 182 C1
Kerry Dr *UPMR* RM14 .... 182 C1
Kerry Rd *CDH/CHF* RM16 .... 201 H8
Kersbrooke Wy *SLH/COR* SS17 .... 187 J8
Kersey Gdns *HARH* RM3 .... 161 F2
Kershaw Cl *CHLM/GWD* CM16 .... 213 F2
EMPK RM11 .... 180 E1
Kershaws Cl *WICKW* SS12 .... 147 F8
Kestrel Cl *BARK/HLT* IG6 .... 136 B7 🔲
RAIN RM13 .... 180 C8 🔲
Kestrel Gv *RAYL* SS6 .... 171 G5
Kestrel Rd *WAB* EN9 .... 78 C8
Keswick Av *EMPK* RM11 .... 180 E2
HOC/HUL SS5 .... 149 K3
Keswick Cl *RAYL* SS6 .... 171 K3 🔲
Keswick Dr *PEND* EN3 .... 104 C2
Keswick Rd *SBF/HAD* SS7 .... 170 D7
Ketleys *CHLM/GWD* CM2 .... 90 E2
Kettering Rd *HARH* RM3 .... 161 J4
PEND EN3 .... 104 D3
Kettlebury Wy *CHONG* CM5 .... 84 B4
Kevin Cl *BCAYE* CM11 .... 144 E6
Keyes Cl *SBN/FI* SS3 .... 196 D4
Keynsham Av *WFD* IG8 .... 133 K8
Keysers Rd *BROX* EN10 .... 49 G4
Keysland *SBF/HAD* SS7 .... 171 G6
Kibcaps *VGE* SS16 .... 7 D6 🔲
Kilmartin Wy *HCH* RM12 .... 180 C6
Kilmington Cl *RBRW/HUT* CM13 .... 142 A5
Kilnfield *CHONG* CM5 .... 84 B3 🔲
Kiln La *HLWE* CM17 .... 25 H6
Kiln Rd *EPP* CM16 .... 82 A1
SBF/HAD SS7 .... 191 F1
Kiln Wy *GRAYS* RM17 .... 213 J4
Kilnwood Rd *HOC/HUL* SS5 .... 150 E8
Kilowan Cl *VGE* SS16 .... 186 A1
Kilsmore La *CHES/WCR* EN8 .... 76 D2
Kilworth Av *BRWN* CM15 .... 141 K2
SOS SS1 .... 9 E4
Kimberley Rd *CHING* E4 .... 133 F4
SBF/HAD SS7 .... 190 B2
SBN/FI SS3 .... 176 D7
Kimberley Wy *CHING* E4 .... 133 G4
Kimberly Dr *LAIN* SS15 .... 167 G3
Kimpton Av *BRWN* CM15 .... 140 E3
Kimpton's Cl *CHONG* CM5 .... 56 B8 🔲
Kinfauns Av *EMPK* RM11 .... 160 D6
Kingaby Gdns *RAIN* RM13 .... 180 B8
King Alfred Rd *HARH* RM3 .... 161 G4
King Arthur Ct *CHES/WCR* EN8 .... 76 E5
King Edward Av *BOC* CM0 .... 128 C3
King Edward Dr *CDH/CHF* RM16 .... 214 D2
GRAYS RM17 .... 214 D3
King Edward Rd *CHES/WCR* EN8 .... 76 E7
BRW CM14 .... 141 F6 🔲
LAIN SS15 .... 166 C5
ROM RM1 .... 160 A8 🔲
King Edward's Rd *PEND* EN3 .... 104 D8
RCHLM CM3 .... 122 E5 🔲
SLH/COR SS17 .... 203 K5
Kingfisher Cl *MAL* CM9 .... 40 E8 🔲
RBRW/HUT CM15 .... 141 K3

SBN/FI SS3 .... 196 D4
Kingfisher Crs *RAYL* SS6 .... 171 G2 🔲
Kingfisher Dr *SBF/HAD* SS7 .... 190 B3
Kingfisher Rd *UPMR* RM14 .... 182 C2
Kingfishers *VGE* SS16 .... 187 K1 🔲
King George Rd *WAB* EN9 .... 77 J8 🔲
King George's Cl *RAYL* SS6 .... 171 J4
King George's Rd *BRWN* CM15 .... 140 C3
King George Vi Av *TIL* RM18 .... 216 C3
King Henry's Dr *RCFD* SS4 .... 174 C6
King Henry's Ms *PEND* EN3 .... 105 G3 🔲
Kingley Cl *WICKW* SS12 .... 146 E6
Kingley Dr *WICKW* SS12 .... 146 E6
King's Av *WFD* IG8 .... 133 K8
Kingsbridge Rd *HARH* RM3 .... 161 F1 🔲
King's Cha *BRW* CM14 .... 141 F6
Kings Cl *CVI* SS8 .... 207 G2
RAYL SS6 .... 171 K3
Kings Crs *LAIN* SS15 .... 166 C4
Kings Cft *BOC* CM0 .... 128 C1
Kingsdon La *HLWE* CM17 .... 25 G6
Kingsdown Ct *PIT* SS13 .... 169 F7
Kings Dr *GVE* DA12 .... 219 G8
Kings Farm *RAYL* SS6 .... 149 K8
Kingsfield *PEND* EN3 .... 104 D1 🔲
Kingsfield Wy *PEND* EN3 .... 104 D1 🔲
Kingsford Dr *CHLM/GWD* CM2 .... 63 K2
Kings Gdns *UPMR* RM14 .... 182 B1
King's Gn *LOU* IG10 .... 107 G7 🔲
Kings Gv *ROM* RM1 .... 160 B7
Kingshawes *SBF/HAD* SS7 .... 171 C7
Kings Head Hl *CHING* E4 .... 132 C3
Kingsland *HLWS* CM18 .... 2 C5
Kingsley Av *CHES/WCR* EN8 .... 76 B3
Kingsley Ct *EMPK* RM11 .... 160 C8 🔲
EMPK RM11 .... 160 E6
Kingsley Crs *SBF/HAD* SS7 .... 171 G5
Kingsley La *SBF/HAD* SS7 .... 171 G5
Kingsley Wy *CDH/CHF* RM16 .... 215 F3
King's Lynn Dr *HARH* RM3 .... 160 E1
Kingsman Dr *CDH/CHF* RM16 .... 201 F7 🔲
Kingsman Rd *SLH/COR* SS17 .... 203 H4
Kingsmans Farm Rd
  HOC/HUL SS5 .... 150 A1
Kingsmead Av *ROM* RM1 .... 160 A8 🔲
Kingsmead Cl *HLWW/ROY* CM19 .... 22 D6
Kingsmere *SBF/HAD* SS7 .... 171 H8
Kingsmoor Rd *HLWW/ROY* CM19 .... 2 B6
Kings Pk *SBF/HAD* SS7 .... 170 E8
Kings Pl *BKHH* IG9 .... 133 K5 🔲
King's Rd *CHES/WCR* EN8 .... 76 A1
BOC CM0 .... 128 D2
BOC CM0 .... 155 G1
BRW CM14 .... 141 F6
CHING E4 .... 132 E4
CLAN/WR CM7 .... 4 A1
CVI SS8 .... 207 G2
LAIN SS15 .... 166 C4
RAYL SS6 .... 171 K3
ROM RM1 .... 160 B7
SBF/HAD SS7 .... 190 D3
WOS/PRIT SS0 .... 193 J4
Kingsteignton *SBN/FI* SS3 .... 196 B4
Kingston Av *CHLM/GWD* CM2 .... 5 F2
SBN/FI SS3 .... 196 D3
Kingston Cha *MAL* CM9 .... 40 B7
Kingston Ct *GVW* DA11 .... 218 A4 🔲
Kingston Crs *CHLM/GWD* CM2 .... 5 F2
Kingston Hl *VGE* SS16 .... 186 E3
Kingston Rd *ROM* RM1 .... 160 A6
Kingston Wy *SBF/HAD* SS7 .... 170 D8
King St *CHONG* CM5 .... 85 K2
CVE DA12 .... 219 G4
MAL CM9 .... 68 C4
SLH/COR SS17 .... 203 J4
Kings Wk *MAL* CM9 .... 44 E4
Kings Wy *BCAYE* CM11 .... 144 E7
RCHLM CM3 .... 122 C4
Kingsway *HOC/HUL* SS5 .... 149 J4
WOS/PRIT SS0 .... 193 H3
Kingsway Ms *WOS/PRIT* SS0 .... 193 J3 🔲
Kingswood Cha *LOS* SS9 .... 192 E2
Kingswood Cl *BCAYE* CM11 .... 144 D2
Kingswood Cl *BOC* CM0 .... 74 C2
Kingswood Crs *RAYL* SS6 .... 171 G4
Kingswood Rd *VGE* SS16 .... 167 K8
Kipling Av *TIL* RM18 .... 215 H2
Kipling Cl *CHLM/WR* CM1 .... 34 C8
Kirby Cl *HARH* RM3 .... 139 H8
LOU IG10 .... 134 B3 🔲
Kirby Rd *BSDN* SS14 .... 168 B7
Kirkham Av *SLH/COR* SS17 .... 186 A6
Kirkham Rd *SLH/COR* SS17 .... 186 A6
Kirkham Shaw *SLH/COR* SS17 .... 186 A5
Kirkmans Rd *CHLM/GWD* CM2 .... 91 F2
Kirk Pl *CHLM/GWD* CM2 .... 63 H2 🔲
Kirton Cl *HCH* RM12 .... 180 D7
Kitchener Rd *RCHLM* CM3 .... 124 C4 🔲
Kitkatts Rd *CVI* SS8 .... 208 A2
Kitson Wy *HLW* CM20 .... 2 C2 🔲

Kittiwake Dr *MAL* CM9 .... 40 E8 🔲
Knapton Cl *CHLM/WR* CM1 .... 35 F6
The Knares *VGE* SS16 .... 6 C6 🔲
Knightbridge Wk *BCAYW* CM12 .... 144 B2
Knighton Cl *WFD* IG8 .... 133 J7
Knighton Dr *WFD* IG8 .... 133 J7
Knighton La *BKHH* IG9 .... 133 J5
Knights *LAIN* SS15 .... 6 B1 🔲
Knight St *RCHLM* CM3 .... 122 E6
SBW CM21 .... 11 J3
Knights Wk *ABR/ST* RM4 .... 109 F7
Knight's Wy *RBRW/HUT* CM13 .... 141 K7
Knightswick Rd *CVI* SS8 .... 208 B1
Knivet Cl *RAYL* SS6 .... 171 K4
Knollcroft *SBN/FI* SS3 .... 196 C5
The Knoll *BCAYW* CM12 .... 144 C1
RAYL SS6 .... 171 J3 🔲
The Knowle *VGE* SS16 .... 187 K1
Knox Cl *MAL* CM9 .... 68 C5
Knox Ct *WICKW* SS12 .... 147 J8 🔲
Kolburg Rd *CVI* SS8 .... 208 D3 🔲
Kollum Rd *CVI* SS8 .... 209 F2
Koln Cl *CVI* SS8 .... 207 G2
Komberg Crs *CVI* SS8 .... 191 H8
Konnybrook *SBF/HAD* SS7 .... 191 F1
Korndyk Av *CVI* SS8 .... 208 C1
Kursaal Wy *SOS* SS1 .... 9 F5
Kyme Rd *ROM* RM1 .... 160 A8
Kynance Cl *HARH* RM3 .... 138 D6
Kynoch Ct *SLH/COR* SS17 .... 204 A4

L

Laars Av *CVI* SS8 .... 208 C1
Laburnham Cl *UPMR* RM14 .... 182 D1
Laburnham Gdns *UPMR* RM14 .... 182 C1
Laburnum *RCHLM* CM3 .... 38 A2
Laburnum Av *HCH* RM12 .... 180 B3
WICKW SS12 .... 147 F7
Laburnum Cl *CHES/WCR* EN8 .... 76 D3 🔲
HOC/HUL SS5 .... 150 D7 🔲
WICKW SS12 .... 147 F6 🔲
Laburnum Dr *CHLM/GWD* CM2 .... 62 D7 🔲
SLH/COR SS17 .... 204 C2
Laburnum Gv *CVI* SS8 .... 207 H2 🔲
GVW DA11 .... 218 C5
HOC/HUL SS5 .... 150 C5
SOCK/AV RM15 .... 200 B4 🔲
Laburnum Rd *EPP* CM16 .... 81 G3
Laburnum Wk *HCH* RM12 .... 180 D6
Laburnum Wy *RAYL* SS6 .... 149 G7 🔲
Labworth Rd *CVI* SS8 .... 208 C3
Lackmore Rd *EN* EN1 .... 104 C1 🔲
Ladram Cl *SOS* SS1 .... 196 B5
Ladram Rd *SOS* SS1 .... 196 A5
Ladram Wy *SOS* SS1 .... 196 A5
Ladyfields *LOU* IG10 .... 107 K8
Lady La *CHLM/GWD* CM2 .... 4 C5
Ladyshot *HLW* CM20 .... 24 E4 🔲
Ladysmith Wy *LAIN* SS15 .... 7 D1 🔲
Ladywell La *CHLM/GWD* CM2 .... 63 K8
Ladywell Prospect *SBW* CM21 .... 11 K4
Laindon Common Rd
  BCAYW CM12 .... 144 A8
Laindon Link *LAIN* SS15 .... 6 B4 🔲
Laindon Rd *BCAYW* CM12 .... 144 B5
Laindon West *LAIN* SS15 .... 165 K7 🔲
Laird Av *CDH/CHF* RM16 .... 214 C1
Lake Av *BCAYW* CM12 .... 144 B2
Lake Dr *SBF/HAD* SS7 .... 170 D8
Lakeland Cl *CHIG* IG7 .... 136 A7
Lake Ri *ROM* RM1 .... 160 A5
WTHK RM20 .... 212 D3
Lake Rd *WAB* EN9 .... 50 A3
Lakeside *RAIN* RM13 .... 198 A2
RAYL SS6 .... 171 J1 🔲
Lakeside Cl *CHIG* IG7 .... 135 J7
Lakeside Crs *BRW* CM14 .... 141 C6
CVI SS8 .... 191 J8 🔲
Lakeside Rd *CHES/WCR* EN8 .... 76 C2
Lakeview *CVI* SS8 .... 191 F8
Lake Vw *VGE* SS16 .... 186 A1
Lakin Cl *CHLM/GWD* CM2 .... 63 J2
Lamb Cl *TIL* RM18 .... 215 H8
Lambeth Ms *HOC/HUL* SS5 .... 150 D7 🔲
Lambeth Rd *LOS* SS9 .... 173 J2
SBF/HAD SS7 .... 170 B7
Lambourne *CVI* SS8 .... 208 A3
Lambourne Cl *CHIG* IG7 .... 136 A6
Lambourne Crs *BSDN* SS14 .... 168 C8
CHIG IG7 .... 135 K7
Lambourne Dr *RBRW/HUT* CM13 .... 142 D2
Lambourne Gdns *CHING* E4 .... 132 B5
HCH RM12 .... 180 E3
Lambourne Gv *MAL* CM9 .... 68 B5
Lambourne Hall Rd *RCFD* SS4 .... 153 J4
Lambourne Rd *CHIG* IG7 .... 135 J7
Lambourni Cl *SBN/FI* SS3 .... 196 D3 🔲
Lambton Av *CHES/WCR* EN8 .... 76 D7 🔲
Lammasmead *BROX* EN10 .... 49 F5
Lamont Cl *WICKW* SS12 .... 147 H8 🔲
Lamorna Av *GVE* DA12 .... 219 J8

ampern Crs BCAYW CM12	117	J7
ampits Hl SLH/COR SS17	187	H7
ampits Hill Av SLH/COR SS17	187	H8
ampits La SLH/COR SS17	187	H8
amplighters Cl WAB EN9	78	C8
ancaster Cl BRWN CM15	140	D1
ancaster Dr HCH RM12	180	C6
LOU IG10	134	B2
VGE SS16	166	A3
ancaster Gdns RAYL SS6	172	B5
SOS SS1	9	E4
ancaster Rd EPP CM16	54	A8
RAYL SS6	172	B4
ancer Wy BCAYW CM12	144	A2
ancing Rd HARH RM3	161	F2
andau Wy BROX EN10	49	F8
ERITH DA8	210	E4
andermere BSDN SS14	171	F5
ander Rd GRAYS RM17	214	C4
andisdale HCH	66	A6
andmead Rd CHES/WCR EN8	76	E3
andsburg Rd CVI SS8	191	J3
andseer Av DA11	218	C8
andseer Cl HCH RM12	180	C2
andview Gdns CHONG CM5	84	B4
andwick La BOC CM0	102	B6
ane End HLWE CM17	25	J6
anes Av DA11	218	C7
angale Gdns CHLM/GWD CM2	5	D5
HCH RM12	180	B6
PEND EN3	104	D1
angdon Rd RAYL SS6	171	G2
angdon Wy SLH/COR SS17	187	J3
angemore Wy BCAYE CM11	144	C3
angenhoe WICKW SS12	147	H7
angfield Cl WAB EN9	50	A4
angford Crs SBF/HAD SS7	170	E7
angford Gn RBRW/HUT CM13	142	B2
angford Gv PIT SS13	169	F5
angford Rd MAL CM9	40	B7
WIT CM8	39	J2
angfords BKHH IG9	134	A3
angham Crs EMPK RM11	180	E1
angham Crs BCAYW CM12	144	C5
angham Dr RAYL SS6	170	E4
RAYL SS6	171	F2
angland SLH/COR SS17	204	C1
LOS SS9	192	D3
SOS SS1	9	F4
angley Cl HARH RM3	160	C2
LOS SS9	172	C6
SOS SS1	9	F4
angley Dr BRW CM14	140	D6
angleys VGE SS16	7	F6
angport Dr WOS/PRIT SS0	193	H1
angside Cl LAIN SS15	166	C5
angthorne Crs GRAYS RM17	214	B3
angton Av CHLM/WR CM1	34	A8
angton Wy CDH/CHF RM16	215	H1
anhams PIT SS13	168	E5
ansbury Rd PEND EN3	104	D5
anscombe Gdns BRWN CM15	140	D2
arch Cl LAIN SS15	166	C5
he Larches RCHLM CM3	36	C5
SBF/HAD SS7	170	A5
arch Wk MAL CM9	40	A4
archwood Cl LOS SS9	172	C9
archwood Gdns BRWN CM15	140	D2
arke Ri WOS/PRIT SS0	194	A1
arkfield SLH/COR SS17	187	J8
arkfield Cl RCFD SS4	174	A1
arkfields GVW DA11	218	D8
arkhill Av RCFD SS4	152	D3
ark Hill Rd RCFD SS4	152	C4
arsen Dr WAB EN9	77	K8
arup Av CVI SS8	191	H8
ascelles Cl BRWN CM15	140	E1
ascelles Gdns RCFD SS4	151	K8
atchetts Shaw VGE SS16	7	F6
atchford Pl CHIG IG7	136	A7
atchingdon Cl RAYL SS6	171	F2
atchingdon Rd RCHLM CM3	96	B8
Lathcoates Crs CHLM/GWD CM2	5	F5
Latimer Dr HCH RM12	180	E4
LAIN SS15	166	C4
Latton Gn HLWS CM18	52	D1
Latton Hall Cl HLW CM20	24	E4
Latton House HLWS CM18	25	F8
Latton St HLW CM20	25	F5
HLWE CM17	25	G8
Launceston Cl HARH RM3	160	D3
Launder's La RAIN RM13	198	A5
Laundry La BRWN CM15	115	H5
WAB EN9	50	B7
Laurel Av GVE DA12	219	H7
WICKW SS12	147	F6
Laurel Cl LOS SS9	192	E5
RBRW/HUT CM13	142	A1
Laurel Dr SOCK/AV RM15	200	B4
Laurel Gdns CHING E4	132	C3
Laurel Gv CHLM/GWD CM2	4	B5
The Laurels RAYL SS6	172	A5
RCHLM CM3	122	D5
Laurence Cft CHLM/WR CM1	61	H4
Lavender Av BRWN CM15	140	E1
Lavender Cl HARH RM3	160	E2
HLW CM20	3	E2
SOCK/AV RM15	200	C4
Lavender Ct CHLM/WR CM1	35	H8
Lavender Dr BOC CM0	128	C2
Lavender Gv WOS/PRIT SS0	8	A1
Lavender Ms WOS/PRIT SS0	194	A1
Lavender Wy WICKW SS12	147	F6
Lawford Cl HCH RM12	180	D5
Lawling Av MAL CM9	40	E8
Lawling Rd RCHLM CM3	97	K8
Lawn Av SOSN SS2	9	E2
Lawn La CHLM/WR CM1	35	F7
Lawn Rd GVW DA11	218	B4
Lawnscourt SBF/HAD SS7	170	A6
Lawns CHING E4	132	B8
Lawns GRAYS RM17	214	C5
The Lawns CHING E4	132	B8
CHLM/WR CM1	35	F8
SBF/HAD SS7	170	B6
Lawrance Gdns CHES/WCR EN8	76	D2
Lawrence Av SBW CM21	11	J1
Lawrence Gdns TIL RM18	215	G6
Lawrence Hl CHING E4	132	B5
Lawrence Moorings SBW CM21	11	K4
Lawrence Rd GPK RM2	160	C2
PIT SS13	169	J5
Lawson Rd PEND EN3	104	C5
Lawton Rd LOU IG10	107	K7
Laxtons SLH/COR SS17	203	K2
The Laxtons RCFD SS4	152	A8
Leach Cl CHLM/GWD CM2	63	K6
Leadale Cl CHING E4	132	B5
Leaden Cl GTDUN CM6	16	A5
Leaforis Rd CHESW EN7	76	A2
Leafy Wy RBRW/HUT CM13	142	C4
Lea Gv MAL CM9	39	F4
Leamington Rd HARH RM3	139	H8
HOC/HUL SS5	151	C6
SOS SS1	9	F4
Leapingwell Cl CHLM/GWD CM2	63	J2
Lea Rd CDH/CHF RM16	215	F4
SBF/HAD SS7	170	B8
WAB EN9	77	G8
Leas Cl WOS/PRIT SS0	193	J5
Leas Gdns WOS/PRIT SS0	193	J5
Leaside SLH/COR SS17	217	H1
The Leas BOC CM0	128	C7
ING CM4	116	A3
UPMR RM14	182	A1
WOS/PRIT SS0	193	K6
Leasway BRW CM14	141	G6
CDH/CHF RM16	215	H3
RAYL SS6	171	H3
Leaway RCHLM CM3	80	A1
WAB EN9	77	K8
WICKW SS12	146	E7
The Leasway WOS/PRIT SS0	193	J5
Leat Cl SBW CM21	11	K2
Leathart Cl HCH RM12	180	C8
Leatherbottle Hl ING CM4	118	C2
Leather La EMPK RM11	180	E2
Lea Valley Rd CHING E4	132	A2
Lea Valley Wk WAB EN9	49	C8
Leaview WAB EN9	77	H7
Lea Wy BCAYW CM12	144	C5
Lechmere Av CHIG IG7	135	G5
Leda Av PEND EN3	104	D5
Lede Rd CM4	208	B1
Lee Chapel La VGE SS16	186	D2
Leecon Wy RCFD SS4	174	A2
Lee Gardens Av EMPK RM11	181	H2
Lee Gv CHIG IG7	135	F1
Lee Lotts SBN/FI SS3	197	F1
Lee Rd PIT SS13	169	J7
Leeward Rd RCHLM CM3	122	E8
The Leeway RCHLM CM3	65	K6
Lee Woottens La VGE SS16	7	E5
Legg St CHLM/WR CM1	4	C2
Leicester Av RCFD SS4	174	C5
Leicester Rd TIL RM18	214	E2
Leige Av CVI SS8	191	F7
Leigham Court Dr LOS SS9	193	G3
Leighams Rd RCHLM CM3	93	J8
Leigh Beck La CVI SS8	208	E3
Leigh Beck Rd CVI SS8	209	F2
Leigh Cliff Rd LOS SS9	193	G5
Leighcroft Gdns LOS SS9	195	F1
Leigh Dr HARH RM3	138	E2
Leigh Fells PIT SS13	169	F7
Leighfields SBF/HAD SS7	171	G2
Leighfields Av LOS SS9	172	E7
Leighfields Rd LOS SS9	172	D7
Leigh Gdns LOS SS9	192	D4
Leigh Hall Rd LOS SS9	193	F4
Leigh Hts SBF/HAD SS7	192	A2
Leigh Hl LOS SS9	193	F5
Leigh Hill Cl LOS SS9	193	F5
Leighlands Rd RCHLM CM3	122	D6
Leigh Park Cl LOS SS9	192	D4
Leigh Park Rd LOS SS9	192	E5
Leigh Rd CVI SS8	208	B5
GVW DA11	219	C2
LOS SS9	193	G4
Leighs Rd RCHLM CM3	21	G7
Leighton Av LOS SS9	193	G3
Leighton Gdns TIL RM18	215	F6
Leighton Rd SBF/HAD SS7	170	B6
Leigh View Dr LOS SS9	193	G1
Leighville Gv LOS SS9	192	E4
Leighwood Av LOS SS9	172	E8
Leinster Cl LAIN SS15	6	A3
Leith Park Rd GVW DA11	219	G6
Leitrim Av SBN/FI SS3	196	B2
Lekoe Rd CVI SS8	190	E7
Lenham Wy PIT SS13	169	F7
Lenmore Av GRAYS RM17	214	B2
Lennox Av GVW DA11	219	F4
Lennox Cl ROM RM1	160	A8
Lennox Dr WICKW SS12	147	J8
Lennox East GVW DA11	218	E4
Lennox Rd East GVW DA11	219	F5
Lensbury Cl CHES/WCR EN8	76	E2
Lenthall Av GRAYS RM17	213	K1
Leonard Av RAYL SS6	171	F1
Leonard Rd VGE SS16	187	J3
WOS/PRIT SS0	8	A5
Leonard Wy BRW CM14	140	B7
Leon Dr VGE SS16	188	A3
Leslie Cl LOS SS9	172	E7
Leslie Dr LOS SS9	172	E7
Leslie Gdns RAYL SS6	172	A4
Leslie Pk BOC CM0	155	H1
Leslie Rd RAYL SS6	171	K4
Lesney Gdns RCFD SS4	174	A2
Lettons Cha RCHLM CM3	122	D7
Letzen Rd CVI SS8	208	A1
Leven Cl CHES/WCR EN8	76	D7
Leven Dr CHES/WCR EN8	76	D7
Lever La RCFD SS4	174	C4
Lever Sq CDH/CHF RM16	215	F5
Leverton Wy WAB EN9	77	J7
Leveson Rd CDH/CHF RM16	215	G2
Levett Rd SLH/COR SS17	204	A3
Lewes Cl GRAYS RM17	213	K5
Lewes Rd HARH RM3	138	E7
SOSN SS2	9	F1
Lewes Wy SBF/HAD SS7	171	G6
Lewin Pl RCHLM CM3	36	C5
Lewis Cl BRWN CM15	141	J3
Lewis Dr CHLM/GWD CM2	62	D7
Lewis Rd EMPK RM11	160	D8
Lexington Wy UPMR RM14	162	B8
Leybourne Dr CHLM/WR CM1	35	F6
Leyburn Crs HARH RM3	161	F2
Leyburn Gdns HARH RM3	161	F2
Leyburn Rd HARH RM3	161	F2
Leycroft Gdns ERITH DA8	210	C7
Leyland Av PEND EN3	104	E6
Leyland Cl CHES/WCR EN8	76	C2
Leysings VGE SS16	6	C6
Leys Rd East PEND EN3	104	E5
The Leys CHLM/GWD CM2	35	H8
VGE SS16	187	K1
Lichfield Cl CHLM/WR CM1	62	A1
The Lichfields BSDN SS14	168	C6
Lichfield Ter UPMR RM14	182	B3
UPMR RM14	182	C3
Lichfield Wy BROX EN10	49	F4
Lifstan Wy SOS SS1	195	H5
Lilac Av CVI SS8	191	H8
EN EN1	104	C2
WICKW SS12	147	F6
Lilac Cl BRWN CM15	140	E1
CHLM/GWD CM2	62	D7
CHESW EN7	76	B5
Lilford Rd BCAYE CM11	144	D1
Lilian Crs RBRW/HUT CM13	142	B5
Lilian Pl RAYL SS6	172	B5
Lilian Rd BOC CM0	128	C8
Lilley Cl BRW CM14	140	C7
Lilly Hall Rd RAYL SS6	172	B4
Lily Cl CHLM/WR CM1	35	H7
Limbourne Dr MAL CM9	40	E8
Limburg Rd CVI SS8	207	H1
Lime Av GVW DA11	218	C5
LOS SS9	192	D3
RBRW/HUT CM13	141	J6

UPMR RM14 ... 181 H5
Limebrook Wy MAL CM9 ... 68 C6
Lime CI BKHH IG9 ... 134 A5
SOCK/AV RM15 ... 200 A3
Lime Gv BRWN CM15 ... 114 A4
Lime PI LAIN SS15 ... 6 A1
Limerick Gdns UPMR RM14 ... 182 C1
Lime Rd SBF/HAD SS7 ... 190 D1
Limes Av CHIG IG7 ... 135 F8
The Limes CHLM/GWD CM2 ... 90 D3
ING CM4 ... 116 C1
PUR RM19 ... 211 H4
RAYL SS6 ... 172 A5
RBRW/HUT CM13 ... 141 J6
Limetree Av SBF/HAD SS7 ... 190 A1
Limetree Rd CVI SS8 ... 208 D1
Lime Wk CHLM/GWD CM2 ... 128 A7
Lime Wy BOC CM0 ...
Lincefield Vge SS16 ... 186 C2
Linclon CI ERITH DA8 ... 210 A8
Linclon CI SOCK SS2 ... 195 H2
Lincoln CI EMPK RM11 ... 161 H7
Lincoln Rd BSDN SS14 ... 168 C6
ERITH DA8 ... 210 A8
RCFD SS4 ... 151 J7
Lincolns Fld EPP CM16 ... 80 D3
Lincolns La BRW CM14 ... 139 K2
Lincoln Wy CVI SS8 ... 207 J1
RAYL SS6 ... 149 H8
Linda Gdns BCAYW CM12 ... 143 K1
Linden Av EN EN1 ... 104 A5
Linden CI CHLM/GWD CM2 ... 5 D6
CHESW EN7 ... 76 B4
PUR RM19 ... 211 K5
RAYL SS6 ... 172 A4
SBF/HAD SS7 ... 170 B8
Linden Gdns EN EN1 ... 104 A5
Linden Leas SBF/HAD SS7 ... 170 B7
Linden Ri BRW CM14 ... 141 G8
Linden Rd SBF/HAD SS7 ... 170 B7
The Lindens ING CM4 ... 118 A3
LOU IG10 ... 134 C1
VGE SS16 ... 166 B8
Linden Wy CVI SS8 ... 207 K1
Linde Rd CVI SS8 ... 208 B1
Lindfield Rd HARH RM3 ... 139 F8
Lindhill CI PEND EN3 ... 104 D6
Lindhurst Dr BCAYE CM11 ... 145 K1
Lindisfarne CI GVE DA12 ... 219 K7
Lindon Rd WICKE SS11 ... 147 F2
Lindsay PI CHESW EN7 ... 76 B4
Lindsell Gn BSDN SS14 ... 168 B8
Lindsell La BSDN SS14 ... 168 B8
Lindsey CI BRW CM14 ... 140 D7
Lindsey Rd SBN/FI SS3 ... 197 G1
Lindsey Vw EMPK RM11 ... 160 D7
Linford CI HLWW/ROY CM19 ... 2 C5
Linford Dr BSDN SS14 ... 168 B8
Linford End HLWW/ROY CM19 ... 2 C5
Linford Ms CHLM/GWD CM2 ... 68 A5
Linford Rd CDH/CHF RM16 ... 215 H4
Lingcroft Vge SS16 ... 181 G4
Lingfield Av UPMR RM14 ... 181 G4
Lingfield Dr RCFD SS4 ... 174 D2
Lingfield Rd GVE DA12 ... 219 G7
Lingmere CI CHIG IG7 ... 135 F5
Lingwood CI RCHLM CM3 ... 65 J6
Linkdale BCAYW CM12 ... 144 C5
Link Rd CVI SS8 ... 207 J1
RAYL SS6 ... 171 J2
SLH/COR SS17 ... 203 K2
Links Av GPK RM2 ... 160 C4
Links Dr CHLM/GWD CM2 ... 4 A6
Linkside CHIG IG7 ... 135 F8
Links Rd WFD IG8 ... 133 H8
The Links CHES/WCR EN8 ... 48 D8
BCAYW CM12 ... 143 K1
Linksway CID SS9 ... 192 D1
Links Wy SBF/HAD SS7 ... 192 A2
The Link PEND EN3 ... 104 E5
Linkway BSDN SS14 ... 7 F4
Linkway EMPK RM11 ... 181 J2
Linkway Rd BRW CM14 ... 140 C6
Linley CI TIL RM18 ... 216 E6
Linnet CI SBN/FI SS3 ... 196 D4
Linnet Dr CHLM/GWD CM2 ... 62 D7
SBF/HAD SS7 ... 190 D1
Linnets VGE SS16 ... 187 H2
Linnett CI CHING E4 ... 132 D7
Linnet Wy PUR RM19 ... 211 J4
Linroping Av CVI SS8 ... 209 F2
Linton Rd SBN/FI SS3 ... 196 D7
The Lintons CHLM/GWD CM2 ... 64 B7
Linwood SBW CM21 ... 11 J3
Linwood Crs EN EN1 ... 104 A5
Lionel Rd CVI SS8 ... 208 A2
Lion HI SLH/COR SS17 ... 205 F1
Lion La BCAYW CM12 ... 144 B3
Liphook CI HCH RM12 ... 180 A5
Lippitts HI VGE SS16 ... 186 D2
Lippitts HI LOU IG10 ... 106 A6

Lisa CI BCAYW CM12 ... 117 H7
Lisle PI GRAYS RM17 ... 213 K2
Lister Av HARH RM3 ... 160 E4
Lister Rd TIL RM18 ... 215 F8
Lister Tye CHLM/GWD CM2 ... 5 D6
Litchborough Pk RCHLM CM3 ... 65 K5
Littell Tweed CHLM/GWD CM2 ... 63 J2
Little & Great Sir Hughes La CHLM/GWD CM2 ... 91 J3
Little Aston Rd HARH RM3 ... 161 G3
Little Baddow Rd MAL CM9 ... 66 C2
RCHLM CM3 ... 65 J6
Little Belhus CI SOCK/AV RM15 ... 199 J4
Little Bentley BSDN SS14 ... 7 F3
Little Berry La VGE SS16 ... 186 B1
Littlebrook Gdns CHES/WCR EN8 ... 76 D4
Little Brook Rd HLWW/ROY CM19 ... 22 E5
Littlebury Ct BRWN CM15 ... 113 H3
PIT SS13 ... 168 D5
Littlebury Gn PIT SS13 ... 168 D5
Little Cattins HLWW/ROY CM19 ... 51 H1
Little Charlton PIT SS13 ... 169 H1
Little Chittock BSDN SS14 ... 168 B7
Littlecroft RCHLM CM3 ... 122 D7
Little Dorrit CHLM/WR CM1 ... 34 A6
Little Dragons LOU IG10 ... 107 F8
Little Flds RCHLM CM3 ... 66 A6
Little Friday Rd CHING E4 ... 133 F5
Little Garth PIT SS13 ... 168 D8
Little Gaynes Gdns UPMR RM14 ... 181 J5
Little Gaynes La UPMR RM14 ... 181 G5
Little Gerpins Rd UPMR RM14 ... 198 B1
Little Gregories La EPP CM16 ... 108 B1
Little Grove Fld HLWW/ROY CM19 ... 2 C3
Little Gypps CI CVI SS8 ... 207 K1
Little Gypps Rd CVI SS8 ... 207 K2
Little Hayes CI SS8 ... 123 J4
Little Hays LOS SS9 ... 172 C7
Little Heath RBSF CM22 ... 13 F2
Littlehurst La LAIN SS15 ... 167 G3
Little Hyde La ING CM4 ... 88 B7
HLWE CM17 ... 28 A3
Little Laver Rd CHONG CM5 ... 56 B2
Little London La MAL CM9 ... 38 C8
Little Lullaway LAIN SS15 ... 6 C3
Little Meadow CHLM/WR CM1 ... 61 G4
Little Mdw MAL CM9 ... 66 E7
Little Nell CHLM/WR CM1 ... 34 A6
Little Norsey Rd BCAYW CM12 ... 144 D1
Little Oaks BSDN SS14 ... 7 E4
Little Oxcroft LAIN SS15 ... 6 A5
Little Pluckett's La BKHH IG9 ... 134 A4
Little Pynchons HLWS CM18 ... 3 F6
Little Russets RBRW/HUT CM13 ... 142 D3
Little Searles PIT SS13 ... 168 E6
Little Spenders BSDN SS14 ... 168 A5
Little Stambridge Hall Rd RCFD SS4 ... 174 E3
Little Stile CHLM/WR CM1 ... 61 G5
Little Thorpe SOS SS1 ... 195 K5
Littlethorpe VGE SS16 ... 188 C1
Littleton Av CHING E4 ... 133 G4
Little Totham Rd MAL CM9 ... 42 A4
Little Wakering Hall La SBN/FI SS3 ... 177 F8
Little Wakering Rd SBN/FI SS3 ... 176 D6
Little Waltham Rd CHLM/WR CM1 ... 35 F4
Little Warley Hall La RBRW/HUT CM13 ... 163 H1
Little Wheatley Cha RAYL SS6 ... 171 F2
Llewellyn CI CHLM/GWD CM2 ... 5 E1
Lloyd Wise CI SOSN SS2 ... 195 G2
Lobelia CI CHLM/WR CM1 ... 35 H1
Locarno Av WICKE SS11 ... 147 H4
Locke CI RAIN RM13 ... 180 A7
SLH/COR SS17 ... 203 J2
Lockfield Av PEND EN3 ... 105 J1
Locks HI RCFD SS4 ... 174 C4
Locksley CI SOSN SS2 ... 195 J3
Lockyer Rd PUR RM19 ... 211 K4
Lodge Av CHLM/GWD CM2 ... 63 H6
GPK RM2 ... 160 B7
Lodge CI CHIG IG7 ... 135 K6
RAYL SS6 ... 171 K4
RBRW/HUT CM13 ... 142 D3
SBF/HAD SS7 ... 171 F8
Lodge Crs CHES/WCR EN8 ... 76 E8
RCHLM CM3 ... 36 C5
Lodge Farm CI LOS SS9 ... 172 E5
Lodge Hall HLWS CM18 ... 52 C1
Lodgelands CI RAYL SS6 ... 172 A4
Lodge La CDH/CHF RM16 ... 213 K1
GRAYS RM17 ... 214 B2
RCHLM CM3 ... 95 H3
WAB EN9 ... 105 K1
Lodge Rd CHLM/WR CM1 ... 61 F5
EPP CM16 ... 79 J8
MAL CM9 ... 76 B8
RCHLM CM3 ... 93 J7
RCHLM CM3 ... 95 C1
Lodwick SBN/FI SS3 ... 196 B8
Loewen Rd CDH/CHF RM16 ... 215 H4
Loftin Wy CHLM/GWD CM2 ... 5 E6
Logan CI PEND EN3 ... 104 D5

Logan Link WICKW SS12 ... 147 J8
Loman Pth SOCK/AV RM15 ... 199 H6
Lombard Av PEND EN3 ... 104 C5
Lombards Cha RBRW/HUT CM13 ... 164 C8
The Lombards EMPK RM11 ... 181 G
London HI CHLM/GWD CM2 ... 90 C3
RAYL SS6 ... 171 H2
London Rd ABR/ST RM4 ... 108 E2
BCAYE CM11 ... 146 B2
BCAYW CM12 ... 143 K3
BRW CM14 ... 140 D7
CHLM/GWD CM2 ... 4 A6
CHONG CM5 ... 83 K8
EPP CM16 ... 53 F4
GRAYS RM17 ... 213 H5
GVW DA11 ... 218 C4
HLWE CM17 ... 25 C2
MAL CM9 ... 67 H3
PIT SS13 ... 169 G8
RAYL SS6 ... 171 G7
SBF/HAD SS7 ... 169 K8
SBW CM21 ... 11 J3
SLH/COR SS17 ... 203 H4
SOCK/AV RM15 ... 211 H1
SOS SS1 ... 8 C4
TIL RM18 ... 215 G
VGE SS16 ... 188 A3
WICKE SS11 ... 148 C6
WOS/PRIT SS0 ... 8 A3
WTHK RM20 ... 213 G5
London Road Purfleet PUR RM19 ... 211 J1
London Road West Thurrock WTHK RM20 ... 212 C1
Londons CI UPMR RM14 ... 181 K6
Longacre BSDN SS14 ... 7 F
CHLM/WR CM1 ... 61 K
Long Acre HLWE CM17 ... 25 F
Longaford Wy RBRW/HUT CM13 ... 142 B
Long Banks HLWS CM18 ... 3 D
Longborough CI PIT SS13 ... 168 D4
Long Common MAL CM9 ... 40 B8
Long Ct PUR RM19 ... 211 H
Long Croft Dr CHES/WCR EN8 ... 77 F
Longcroft Ri LOU IG10 ... 134 E1
Long Deacon Rd CHING E4 ... 133 F
Longfellow Dr RBRW/HUT CM13 ... 142 B
Longfellow Rd MAL CM9 ... 68 C
Longfield HLWS CM18 ... 24 E
LOU IG10 ... 133 K1
Longfield Av EMPK RM11 ... 180 A
PEND EN3 ... 104 C
Longfield CI WICKE SS11 ... 147 K
Longfield La CHESW EN7 ... 76 B
Longfield Rd CHLM/GWD CM2 ... 5 F
RCHLM CM3 ... 122 D
WICKE SS11 ... 147 K
Long Flds CHONG CM5 ... 84 C
Long Gn CHIG IG7 ... 135 H
Long Gv HARH RM3 ... 161 F
Longhams Dr RCHLM CM3 ... 122 D5
Longhouse Rd CDH/CHF RM16 ... 215 G
Longlands CI CHES/WCR EN8 ... 76 D6
Long La CDH/CHF RM16 ... 201 K
HOC/HUL SS5 ... 150 A
Longleat CI CHLM/WR CM1 ... 34 B
Long Ley HLWW/ROY CM19 ... 3 F
Longmead Av CHLM/GWD CM2 ... 63 H
Longmead CI BRWN CM15 ... 141 H
Long Meadow RBRW/HUT CM13 ... 142 B
Long Meadow Dr WICKE SS11 ... 147 H
Longmeads CI CHLM/WR CM1 ... 61 F
Long Moor CHES/WCR EN8 ... 76 E
Longmore Av CHLM/GWD CM2 ... 5
Longreach Rd ERITH DA8 ... 210 C
Long Riding BSDN SS14 ... 7 F
Long Ridings Av RBRW/HUT CM13 ... 142 A
Longrise BCAYW CM12 ... 144 C
Long Rd CVI SS8 ... 207 K
Longsands SBN/FI SS3 ... 196 C6
Longshaw Rd CHING E4 ... 132 E
Longship Wy MAL CM9 ... 68 A
Longshots CI CHLM/WR CM1 ... 34 C
Longs La RCHLM CM3 ... 21 H
Longstomps Av CHLM/GWD CM2 ... 62 C
Long St WAB EN9 ... 79 G
Longtail BCAYE CM11 ... 117 J
Longtown Rd HARH RM3 ... 138 D
Longwick VGE SS16 ... 6 A
Long Wd HLWS CM18 ... 52 B
Longwood CI UPMR RM14 ... 181 K
The Loning PEND EN3 ... 104 C
Lonsdale Av RBRW/HUT CM13 ... 142 C
Lonsdale Rd SOSN SS2 ... 195 G
Loop Rd WAB EN9 ... 77 H
Lord Roberts Av LOS SS9 ... 193 C
Lordship CI RBRW/HUT CM13 ... 142 C
Lordship Rd CHLM/WR CM1 ... 61 F
CHESW EN7 ... 76 B
Lord St GVE DA12 ... 219 G
Lordswood Vw GTDUN CM6 ... 16 B
Lorien Gdns RCHLM CM3 ... 122 C
Lorne Rd BRW CM14 ... 141 F
Lornes CI SOSN SS2 ... 195 G

orraine Cl *BCAYE* CM11 .... 144 E7 🔲
orrimore Cl *BCAYW* CM12 ...... 117 F8 🔲
orton Cl *GVE* DA12 .... 219 K7
oten Rd *SBF/HAD* SS7 .... 190 A3
ottem Rd *CVI* SS8 .... 208 D3
oughton La *EPP* CM16 .... 108 B3
oughton Wy *BKHH* IG9 .... 134 A4
ouisa Av *SBF/HAD* SS7 .... 170 A7
ouis Dr *RAYL* SS6 .... 171 F1
ouis Dr East *RAYL* SS6 .... 171 G1
ouis Dr West *RAYL* SS6 .... 171 F1
ouise Rd *RAYL* SS6 .... 171 K3
ouvaine Av *SOS* SS1 .... 195 G5
ovelace Av *SOS* SS1 .... 195 G4
ovelace Gdns *SOSN* SS2 .... 195 G4
ove La *CHONG* CM5 .... 84 C2
  RAYL SS6 .... 171 H3
  SOCK/AV RM15 .... 211 K1
  TIL RM18 .... 216 D5
ovell Ri *LOS* SS9 .... 173 H7 🔲
ovell Rd *EN* EN1 .... 104 B1
ovell Wk *RAIN* RM13 .... 180 B7
ovens Cl *CVI* SS8 .... 208 C3
oves Wk *CHLM/WR* CM1 .... 61 H5
ovet Rd *HLWW/ROY* CM19 .... 2 A4
owe Cl *CHONG* CM5 .... 84 C2
ower Anchor St *CHLM/GWD* CM2 ... 4 D4
ower Av *PIT* SS13 .... 169 H5
ower Bedfords Rd *ROM* RM1 .. 160 B1
ower Burnham Rd *RCHLM* CM3 ... 125 F3
ower Bury La *EPP* CM16 .... 80 C5
ower Cha *RCHLM* CM3 .... 126 D1
ower Church St *SBF/HAD* SS7 .. 170 A7
ower Cloister *BCAYE* CM11 .... 144 C3 🔲
ower Crs *SLH/COR* SS17 .... 216 B2
ower Dunton Rd *RBRW/HUT* CM13 ... 143 J7
ower Gn *CHLM/GWD* CM2 ...... 90 D4
ower Island Wy *WAB* EN9 ...... 105 H1
ower Lambricks *RAYL* SS6 ...... 171 J1
ower Meadow *CHES/WCR* EN8 .. 76 D1
  HLWS CM18 .... 52 C1
ower Noke Cl *BRW* CM14 .... 139 F5
ower Park Rd *LOU* IG10 .... 134 A1
  WICKW SS12 .... 147 K6
ower Queen's Rd *BKHH* IG9 ... 134 B5
ower Range Rd *GVE* DA12 ...... 219 K3
ower Rd *CHLM/WR* CM15 .... 115 H7
  HOC/HUL SS5 .... 149 J4
  LOU IG10 .... 107 J5
  TIL RM18 .... 219 F2
ower Southend Rd *WICKE* SS11 .. 147 G5
ower Stock Rd *ING* CM4 .... 118 C2
ower St *LAIN* SS15 .... 6 C1
ower Swaines *EPP* CM16 .... 80 C4
he Lowe *SBW* CM21 .... 11 F4
owfield *SBW* CM21 .... 11 J4
ubbards Cl *RAYL* SS6 .... 149 J8
ucas Av *CHLM/GWD* CM2 .... 62 C7
ucas Rd *GRAYS* RM17 .... 213 K2
ucerne Dr *WICKE* SS11 .... 147 K6
ucerne Wk *WICKE* SS11 .... 147 K6
ucerne Wy *CHLM/WR* CM1 ..... 61 H5 🔲
  HARH RM3 .... 160 E1
uck's La *RCHLM* CM3 .... 20 D1
uckyn La *BSDN* SS14 .... 7 D2
uctons Av *BKHH* IG9 .... 133 K4
ucy Rd *SOS* SS1 .... 9 E5
udgores La *RCHLM* CM3 .... 65 H8
udgrove *RCHLM* CM3 .... 97 J7
uker Rd *SOS* SS1 .... 9 D4
ukin Crs *CHING* E4 .... 132 E6
ulworth Cl *SLH/COR* SS17 ..... 203 H5
ulworth Dr *CRW* RM5 .... 137 G8
uncies Rd *BSDN* SS14 .... 168 B3
undy Cl *LOU* IG10 .... 134 E1 🔲
upin Cl *CHLM/WR* CM1 .... 35 H7
uppits Ct *RBRW/HUT* CM13 .. 141 K4
ushes Ct *LOU* IG10 .... 134 E1
ushes Rd *LOU* IG10 .... 134 E1 🔲
utea Cl *LAIN* SS15 .... 6 B1
uther King Rd *HLW* CM20 .... 2 C3
uthers Cl *BRWN* CM15 .... 113 G3
uxborough La *CHIG* IG7 .... 134 C7
uxford Pl *SBW* CM21 .... 11 K4
ych Ga *LAIN* SS15 .... 6 A4 🔲
ydford Rd *WOS/PRIT* SS0 .... 8 B5 🔲
ydia Rd *ERITH* DA8 .... 210 A3 🔲
ylt Rd *CVI* SS8 .... 208 A2 🔲
yme Rd *SOSN* SS2 .... 9 F3
ymington Av *LOS* SS9 .... 193 F3
ympstone Cl *WOS/PRIT* SS0 .. 175 H8
ynceley Gra *EPP* CM16 .... 80 E3
yndale *BRWN* CM15 .... 113 H3 🔲
yndale Av *SOSN* SS2 .... 9 E1
yndene *SBF/HAD* SS7 .... 170 A4
yndhurst Dr *EMPK* RM11 ...... 180 C2
  RCHLM CM3 .... 93 J1
yndhurst Ri *CHIG* IG7 .... 134 D7
yndhurst Rd *SLH/COR* SS17 .. 204 B1

Lyndhurst Wy *RBRW/HUT* CM13 .... 142 B4
Lynfords Av *WICKE* SS11 .... 147 J2
Lynfords Dr *WICKE* SS11 .... 147 J2
Lynmouth Av *CHLM/GWD* CM2 .. 5 D5
Lynmouth Gdns *CHLM/GWD* CM2 .. 5 D4
Lynn View Cl *SBF/HAD* SS7 .... 170 B8
Lynross Cl *HARH* RM3 .... 161 F4
Lynstede *BSDN* SS14 .... 168 D8
Lynton Dr *CHLM/WR* CM1 ...... 35 G8
  GVW DA11 .... 219 F6
  SBF/HAD SS7 .... 191 H2
  SOS SS1 .... 195 J7
Lynton Rd South *GVW* DA11 ... 219 F6
Lynwood Gn *RAYL* SS6 .... 172 B5
Lyon Cl *CHLM/WR* CM2 .... 90 D2
Lyon Rd *ROM* RM1 .... 180 A1
Lyster Av *CHLM/GWD* CM2 ...... 63 J6
Lytton Av *PEND* EN3 .... 104 C4
Lytton Av *PEND* EN3 .... 104 E4
Lytton Rd *CDH/CHF* RM16 ..... 215 F3
  GPK RM2 .... 160 C7

M

Mabey's Wk *SBW* CM21 .... 11 F4
Macaulay Rd *VGE* SS16 .... 166 B8 🔲
Macdonald Av *EMPK* RM11 .... 161 F6
  WOS/PRIT SS0 .... 8 B2
Macdonald Wy *EMPK* RM11 ... 161 F6 🔲
Macer's La *BROX* EN10 .... 49 F6
Mace Wk *CHLM/WR* CM1 .... 4 A2
Macgregor Dr *WICKW* SS12 ... 147 H8
Macintyres Wk *RCFD* SS4 ..... 151 K7
Mackenzie Cl *WICKW* SS12 .... 147 H7 🔲
Mackley Dr *SLH/COR* SS17 .... 187 G8
Maclaren Wy *WICKW* SS12 .... 147 H8 🔲
Macleod Cl *GRAYS* RM17 .... 214 C5 🔲
Macmurdo Cl *LOS* SS9 .... 172 B5
Macmurdo Rd *LOS* SS9 .... 172 B6
Macon Wy *UPMR* RM14 .... 162 C8
Maddox Rd *HLW* CM20 .... 33 J7
Madeira Av *LOS* SS9 .... 193 F3
Madeline Pl *CHLM/WR* CM1 ..... 4 A2
Madells *EPP* CM16 .... 80 D5
Madies La *ING* CM4 .... 118 B4
Madrid Av *RAYL* SS6 .... 149 F6
Magazine Rd *SBN/FI* SS3 ...... 196 B5
Magdalen Gdns
  RBRW/HUT CM13 .... 142 D2 🔲
Magenta Cl *BCAYW* CM12 ...... 143 K2
Magna Md *SBN/FI* SS3 .... 176 C6
Magnet Rd *WTHK* RM20 .... 213 F5
Magnolia Cl *CHLM/GWD* CM2 .. 62 D7
  SOCK/AV RM15 .... 200 C4
Magnolia Rd *HOC/HUL* SS5 ... 151 J8
Magnolias *BCAYE* CM11 .... 144 D7 🔲
  RCFD SS4 .... 174 E5
Magpie Cl *EN* EN1 .... 104 A5
Magpie La *RBRW/HUT* CM13 .. 163 G4
Magpies *EPP* CM16 .... 51 J6
Magwitch Cl *CHLM/WR* CM1 ... 34 B6
Mahonia Dr *VGE* SS16 .... 166 B7
Maida Av *CHING* E4 .... 132 C3
Maida Wy *CHING* E4 .... 132 C3
Maidstone Rd *GRAYS* RM17 ... 213 K5
Maine Crs *RAYL* SS6 .... 171 G1
Main Rd *BOC* CM0 .... 72 C5
  CHLM/WR CM1 .... 34 D4
  GPK RM2 .... 160 D2
  HOC/HUL SS5 .... 150 E7
  RCHLM CM3 .... 64 B3
  ROM RM1 .... 160 A6
Maitland Pl *SBN/FI* SS3 .... 196 B5
Maitland Rd *WICKW* SS12 ..... 147 H8
Maizey Ct *BRWN* CM15 .... 140 D1
Malan Sq *RAIN* RM13 .... 180 C2
Maldon Rd *BOC* CM0 .... 73 J5
  BOC CM0 .... 127 J5
  ING CM4 .... 89 H5
  MAL CM9 .... 39 F5
  MAL CM9 .... 40 C3
  RCHLM CM3 .... 38 B1
  RCHLM CM3 .... 65 K6
  RCHLM CM3 .... 99 G5
  SOSN SS2 .... 9 D3
Malgraves *PIT* SS13 .... 168 E6
Malgraves Pl *PIT* SS13 .... 168 E6
Mallard Cl *MAL* CM9 .... 44 D3
  UPMR RM14 .... 182 C1 🔲
Mallard Rd *CHLM/GWD* CM2 ... 62 C8
Mallards *RCHLM* CM3 .... 98 E5
  SBN/FI SS3 .... 196 B5
Mallards Ri *HLWE* CM17 .... 25 G5
Mallard Wy *RBRW/HUT* CM13 .. 141 K3
Mallinson Cl *HCH* RM12 .... 180 D6 🔲
Mallion Ct *WAB* EN9 .... 78 B7
Mallory Wy *BCAYW* CM12 ..... 144 B4 🔲
Mallow Ct *GRAYS* RM17 .... 214 C5
Mallow Gdns *BCAYW* CM12 .... 117 F8
Mallows Gn *HLWW/ROY* CM19 .. 51 J2

The Mall *HCH* RM12 .... 180 C2
Malmsmead *SBN/FI* SS3 .... 196 B5
Malpas Rd *CDH/CHF* RM16 .... 215 H2
Malta Rd *TIL* RM18 .... 214 E8
Maltby Dr *EN* EN1 .... 104 B4
Maltese Rd *CHLM/WR* CM1 ...... 4 B1
Malting La *CDH/CHF* RM16 .... 202 A4
Malting Cha *ING* CM4 .... 116 B2
Maltings Hl *CHONG* CM5 .... 55 K2
Maltings La *EPP* CM16 .... 80 E3 🔲
Maltings Rd *CHLM/GWD* CM2 .. 63 J8 🔲
  WICKE SS11 .... 148 D5
The Maltings *BOC* CM0 .... 128 E1
  ROMW/RG RM7 .... 180 A1 🔲
Malting Villas Rd *RCFD* SS4 ... 174 C3
Malvern Av *CVI* SS8 .... 207 H2
Malvern Cl *RAYL* SS6 .... 171 J1
Malvern Dr *WFD* IG8 .... 133 K8
Malvern Gdns *LOU* IG10 .... 134 C2
Malvern Rd *EMPK* RM11 .... 160 B8
  GRAYS RM17 .... 214 D3
  HOC/HUL SS5 .... 151 G5
  PEND EN3 .... 104 E3
Malvina Av *GVE* DA12 .... 219 G7
Malwood Dr *SBF/HAD* SS7 ..... 170 A8
Malwood Rd *SBF/HAD* SS7 ..... 170 A8
Malyon Court Cl *SBF/HAD* SS7 .. 191 G1
Malyons *PIT* SS13 .... 168 E6
Malyons Cl *PIT* SS13 .... 168 E5
Malyons Gn *PIT* SS13 .... 168 E6
Malyons La *HOC/HUL* SS5 ..... 149 J5
Malyons Ms *PIT* SS13 .... 168 E6
Malyons Rd *PIT* SS13 .... 168 E5
The Malyons *SBF/HAD* SS7 .... 191 G1
Manchester Dr *LOS* SS9 .... 192 E3
Mandeville Cl *BROX* EN10 ...... 49 F2
Mandeville Rd *PEND* EN3 ...... 104 E3
Mandeville Wy *CHLM/WR* CM1 .. 34 D2
  SBF/HAD SS7 .... 170 B6 🔲
  VGE SS16 .... 6 A5
Manford Cl *CHIG* IG7 .... 136 A7
Manford Cross *CHIG* IG7 .... 135 K8
Manford Wy *CHIG* IG7 .... 135 K8
Mangapp Cha *BOC* CM0 .... 128 A5
Manilla Rd *SOS* SS1 .... 9 F5
Manly Dixon Dr *PEND* EN3 .... 104 E3
Mannering Gdns *WOS/PRIT* SS0 .. 193 J2
Manners Wy *SOSN* SS2 .... 174 B8
Manning Gv *VGE* SS16 .... 6 A6
Manning Rd *SOCK/AV* RM15 .. 198 E8
Mannock Dr *LOU* IG10 .... 108 A6
Manns Wy *RAYL* SS6 .... 149 H6
Manor Av *EMPK* RM11 .... 160 D7
  PIT SS13 .... 169 F7
Manor Cl *BCAYE* CM11 .... 145 K2
  RAYL SS6 .... 171 J5
  ROM RM1 .... 160 B7
  SOCK/AV RM15 .... 198 E8
Manor Ct *EN* EN1 .... 104 B2
Manor Crs *EMPK* RM11 .... 160 D7
  RCHLM CM3 .... 20 D8
Manor Dr *CHLM/GWD* CM2 ..... 63 H6
Manor Farm Dr *CHING* E4 ..... 133 H6
Manor Farm Rd *EN* EN1 .... 104 B1
Manor Hatch *HLWS* CM18 .... 24 E6
Manor Hatch Cl *HLWS* CM18 ... 25 F6
Manor Rd *ABR/ST* RM4 .... 136 C4
  BOC CM0 .... 101 K4
  CHIG IG7 .... 135 F8
  CHLM/GWD CM2 .... 4 C5
  ERITH DA8 .... 210 A8
  GRAYS RM17 .... 214 B5
  GVE DA12 .... 219 G4 🔲
  HLWE CM17 .... 11 G3
  HOC/HUL SS5 .... 150 D7
  LAIN SS15 .... 166 C6
  LOU IG10 .... 106 D5
  MAL CM9 .... 38 E8
  RCHLM CM3 .... 38 C4
  RCHLM CM3 .... 122 C5
  ROM RM1 .... 160 B7
  SBF/HAD SS7 .... 170 B7
  SLH/COR SS17 .... 203 K3
  TIL RM18 .... 215 F8
  WAB EN9 .... 77 K7
  WOS/PRIT SS0 .... 8 A5
  WTHK RM20 .... 213 F5
Manor Wy *BRW* CM14 .... 140 D6
  CHING E4 .... 132 E7
  GRAYS RM17 .... 214 B6
Manorway *WFD* IG8 .... 133 K8 🔲
The Manorway *SLH/COR* SS17 .. 203 J3
Mansard Cl *HCH* RM12 .... 180 B3
Manse Cha *MAL* CM9 .... 68 C4
Mansel Cl *LOS* SS9 .... 173 F7
Mansfield *SBW* CM21 .... 10 E4
Mansfield Gdns *HCH* RM12 ... 180 E3
Mansfield Hl *CHING* E4 .... 132 C4
Mansfields *CHLM/WR* CM1 ..... 61 F4 🔲
Mansted Gdns *RCFD* SS4 ...... 152 A8
Manston Cl *CHES/WCR* EN8 ... 76 C4 🔲
Manston Rd *HLW* CM20 .... 3 E3
Manston Wy *HCH* RM12 .... 180 C7
Maple Av *LOS* SS9 .... 193 G5
  MAL CM9 .... 40 C7

UPMR RM14 .... 181 J4
Maple CI BARK/HLT IG6 ...... 135 H8
  BKHH IG9 .... 134 A6
  HCH RM12 .... 180 C4
  RBRW/HUT CM13 ...... 141 H6
Maplecroft La WAB EN9 .... 50 A3
Mapledene Av HOC/HUL SS5 .. 149 K3
Maple Dr CHLM/GWD CM2 .... 62 D7
  RAYL SS6 .... 149 H6
  SOCK/AV RM15 ...... 200 B4
Mapleford Sweep VGE SS16 ... 188 J4
Maple Ga LOU IG10 ...... 107 J6
Mapleleaf CI HOC/HUL SS5 .... 151 G6
Mapleleaf Gdns WICKW SS12 .. 146 E7
Maple Ms BCAYW CM12 ...... 144 D5
Maple Rd GRAYS RM17 ...... 214 B5
Maplesfield SBF/HAD SS7 ...... 191 J1
Maple Springs WAB EN9 ...... 78 C7
Maple Sq SOS SS9 ...... 9 E2
Maplestead BSDN SS14 ...... 168 A5
The Maples HLWW/ROY CM19 .. 51 K2
Mapleton Crs PEND EN3 ...... 104 C4
Mapleton Rd CHING E4 ...... 132 D6
  EN EN1 .... 104 B6
Mapletree La ING CM4 ...... 87 K6
Maple Tree La VGE SS16 ...... 166 A8
  CVI SS8 .... 207 J2
Maplin CI SBF/HAD SS7 ...... 170 B6
Maplin Gdns BSDN SS14 ...... 168 B8
Maplin Wy SOS SS9 ...... 196 B6
Maplin Wy North SBN/FI SS3 .. 196 B6
Marchmant Rd HCH RM12 ...... 180 D4
Marconi Rd CHLM/WR CM1 .... 4 C2
  GVW DA11 .... 218 C8
Marcos Rd CVI SS8 ...... 208 D2
Marcus Av SOS SS1 ...... 196 A7
Marcus CI SOS SS1 ...... 196 A6
Marcus Gdns SOS SS1 ...... 196 A6
Marden Ash LAIN SS15 ...... 166 B7
Mardyke Rd HLW CM20 ...... 24 E3
Margaret Av BRWN CM15 ...... 141 J3
  CHING E4 .... 132 C2
Margaret CI GPK RM2 ...... 160 C7
  WAB EN9 .... 77 K7
Margaret Dr EMPK RM11 ...... 181 G2
Margaret Rd EPP CM16 ...... 80 E3
  GPK RM2 .... 160 C7
Margaretting CHLM/GWD CM2 .. 90 C3
  CHLM/WR CM1 ...... 61 G5
  ING CM4 .... 90 B4
Margarite Wy WICKW SS12 .... 146 E5
Margeth Rd BCAYW CM12 .... 166 D2
Margherita Pl WAB EN9 ...... 78 B8
Margraten Av CVI SS8 ...... 208 C2
Marguerite Dr LOS SS9 ...... 193 G4
Mariam Gdns HCH RM12 ...... 181 G3
Marian CI CDH/CHF RM16 .... 200 C8
  CHLM/WR CM1 ...... 35 H7
Marigold La ING CM4 ...... 118 A5
Marigold Pl HLWE CM17 ...... 25 F1
Marina Av RAYL SS6 ...... 171 H2
Marina CI SOSN SS1 ...... 194 B1
Marina Dr GVW DA11 ...... 218 E5
Marina Gdns CHES/WCR EN8 .. 76 C4
Marina Rd RCHLM CM3 ...... 38 A1
Marine Ap CVI SS8 ...... 208 B3
Marine Av CVI SS8 ...... 208 E2
  LOS SS9 .... 192 E3
  WOS/PRIT SS0 ...... 8 B5
Marine CI LOS SS9 ...... 192 E3
Marine Ct PUR RM19 ...... 211 G3
Marine Pde CVI1 SS8 ...... 209 F3
  LOS SS9 .... 192 B4
  RCHLM CM3 .... 98 C4
  SOS SS1 .... 9 E5
Mariners Ct SBN/FI SS3 ...... 197 H2
Mariners Ms MAL CM9 ...... 68 C5
Marion Gv WFD IG8 ...... 133 F8
Marisco CI CDH/CHF RM16 .... 215 G3
Mariskals PIT SS13 ...... 168 D8
Maritime Av MAL CM9 ...... 69 G2
Marjorams Av LOU IG10 ...... 107 J6
Mark Av CHING E4 ...... 132 C2
Market Av WICKW SS12 ...... 147 F5
Market HI MAL CM9 ...... 68 C5
Market PI ING CM4 ...... 116 B1
  SOS SS1 .... 9 D5
Market Rd CHLM/WR CM1 .... 4 C3
  WICKW SS12 ...... 147 F5
Market Sq BSDN SS14 ...... 7 E5
Market St HLWE CM17 ...... 25 G1
Markfield Gdns CHING E4 .... 132 C3
Mark Hall Moors HLW CM20 .. 25 F2
Markhams SLH/COR SS17 .... 204 B2
Markhams Cha LAIN SS15 .... 6 B3
  LAIN SS15 .... 6 C3
Markland Dr MAL CM9 ...... 68 A4
Mark La GVE DA12 ...... 219 K5
Markay Dr RCHLM CM3 ...... 122 C4
Mark Rd BOC CM0 ...... 74 B7
Mark's Av CHONG CM5 ...... 84 B1
Marks CI BCAYW CM12 ...... 143 K1
  ING CM4 .... 115 K4
Marks Hall La GTDUN CM6 .... 30 C2

Marks La RCHLM CM3 ...... 120 D5
Markwell Wd EPP CM16 ...... 51 K3
Marlborough Av BOC CM0 .... 102 A2
Marlborough CI CDH/CHF RM16 .. 214 B1
  SBF/HAD SS7 ...... 170 C6
  UPMR RM14 ...... 182 B2
Marlborough Gdns UPMR RM14.. 182 B2
Marlborough Rd BRWN CM15 .. 140 D2
  CHLM/GWD CM2 ...... 4 B5
  SOS SS1 .... 195 C5
Marlborough Wk HOC/HUL SS5 .. 150 D7
Marlborough Wy BCAYW CM12 .. 117 C8
Marle Gdns HLW CM20 ...... 77 J6
Marlescroft Wy LOU IG10 .... 134 E1
Marlin CI SBF/HAD SS7 ...... 171 K7
Marlow Av PUR RM19 ...... 211 H3
Marlowe CI BCAYW CM12 .... 117 H8
  MAL CM9 .... 68 C5
Marlow Gdns SOSN SS2 .... 194 B1
Marlpits Rd MAL CM9 ...... 94 E1
Marriyon Ap CHING E4 ...... 136 A8
Marmion Ap CHING E4 ...... 132 B7
Marmion CI CHING E4 ...... 132 A7
Marmion Ct CHING E4 ...... 132 A7
Marney CI CHLM/GWD CM2 .... 5 F5
Marney Dr BSDN SS14 ...... 168 C8
Marrilyne Av PEND EN3 ...... 105 F4
Mar Rd SOCK/AV RM15 ...... 200 A4
Marryat Rd EN EN1 ...... 104 B1
Marshall CI LOS SS9 ...... 192 B2
Marshalls RCFD SS4 ...... 174 A1
Marshalls CI RAYL SS6 ...... 172 A3
Marsh CI CHES/WCR EN8 .... 77 F7
Marshcroft Dr CHES/WCR EN8 .. 76 E4
Marsh Farm Rd RCHLM CM3 .. 122 D8
Marshfoot Rd GRAYS RM17 .. 214 A4
Marsh HI WAB EN9 ...... 78 A1
Marsh La HLWE CM17 ...... 11 J8
  RBRW/HUT CM13 ...... 116 A6
  SLH/COR SS17 ...... 188 A7
Marsh Rd BOC CM0 ...... 74 C8
  BOC CM0 .... 128 C7
Marsh St DART DA1 ...... 211 H8
Marsh View Ct VGE SS16 .... 188 B2
Marston Beck CHLM/GWD CM2 .. 63 J3
Martin CI BCAYW CM12 ...... 144 C4
Martindale Av LAIN SS15 .... 166 E3
Martingale CI SBF/HAD SS7 .. 171 G8
Martingale CI BCAYW CM12 .. 117 K8
Martingale Dr CHLM/WR CM1 .. 35 H6
Martingale Rd BCAYW CM11 .. 143 K6
Martin Rd SOCK/AV RM15 .... 199 F8
Martins CI SLH/COR SS17 .... 203 K2
Martins Dr CHES/WCR EN8 .. 76 E2
Martins Ms SBF/HAD SS7 .... 190 B1
Martin Wk HOC/HUL SS5 .... 173 G1
Martlesham CI HCH RM12 .... 180 D6
Martock Av WOS/PRIT SS0 .. 173 H8
Martyns Gv WOS/PRIT SS0 .. 193 J3
Marvens CHLM/GWD CM2 .... 91 F7
Marwell CI ROM RM1 ...... 160 B8
Marylands Av HOC/HUL SS5 .. 150 E6
Mascalls Gdns BRW CM14 .... 140 C7
Mascalls La BRW CM14 ...... 140 C7
Mascalls Wy CHLM/GWD CM2 .. 5 F5
Masefield CI ERITH DA8 ...... 210 A7
  HARH RM3 .... 160 C3
Masefield Crs GPK RM2 ...... 160 D3
Masefield Dr UPMR RM14 .... 181 K1
Masefield Rd CDH/CHF RM16 .. 214 D1
  GVW DA11 .... 218 C8
  MAL CM9 .... 68 C4
Mashbury Rd RCHLM CM3 .... 19 F6
Mason Dr HARH RM3 ...... 161 F4
Mason Wy WFD IG8 ...... 133 F7
Masons Rd EN EN1 ...... 104 B2
Mason Wy WAB EN9 ...... 78 A7
Matching Fld BRWN CM15 .... 113 H3
Matching Gn BSDN SS14 .... 168 A4
Matching Rd HLWE CM17 .... 26 B1
  RBSF CM22 .... 13 H4
Matfield CI CHLM/WR CM1 .. 35 H6
Matlock Gdns HCH RM12 .... 181 F4
Matlock Rd CVI SS8 ...... 207 K2
Maugham CI WICKW SS12 .... 147 G8
Maunds Hatch HLWS CM18 .. 52 B1
Maurice Rd CVI SS8 ...... 208 D2
Mavis Gv HCH RM12 ...... 181 F3
Maya CI SBN/FI SS3 ...... 196 D6
May Av CVI SS8 ...... 208 C1
  GVW DA11 .... 218 E6
Maybank Av HCH RM12 ...... 180 D6
Maybrick Rd EMPK RM11 .... 160 D7
Maybury Av CHES/WCR EN8 .. 76 B2
  CHESW EN7 .... 76 B2
Maybush Rd EMPK RM11 .... 181 F1
Maycroft Av SBF/HAD SS7 .. 214 C4
Maycroft Gdns GRAYS RM17 .. 214 C4
Maydells PIT SS13 ...... 168 E8
Mayes CI CHLM/GWD CM2.. 64 C7
  RCHLM CM3 ...... 65 J7
Mayfair Av PIT SS13 ...... 169 F5
Mayfield Av HOC/HUL SS5 .... 149 K5
  SOSN SS2 .... 194 B1
Mayfield CI HLWE CM17 .... 25 K1

Mayfield Gdns BRW CM14 .... 140 E4
  BRW CM14 .... 141 F4
Mayfield Rd CHING E4 ...... 132 E2
  CHLM/WR CM1 ...... 61 G7
  GVW DA11 .... 218 E6
  PEND EN3 .... 104 D7
Mayfields CDH/CHF RM16 .... 214 B
Mayflower CI SOCK/AV RM15 .. 200 A
  SOSN SS2 .... 173 J
  WAB EN9 .... 50 A
Mayflower Dr MAL CM9 ...... 68 C
Mayflower Rd BCAYE CM11 .. 144 C3
Mayflowers SBF/HAD SS7 .... 170 A6
Mayflower Wy CHONG CM5 .. 84 C
Maygreen Crs EMPK RM11 .. 180 B
Mayhew CI CHING E4 ...... 132 B
Mayland Av CVI SS8 ...... 207 K
Mayland CI MAL CM9 ...... 69 F
  RCHLM CM3 .... 98 E
Mayland Gn RCHLM CM3 .... 99 F
Mayland HI RCHLM CM3 .... 99 G
Maylands Av HCH RM12 .... 180 C
Maylands Wy HARH RM3 .... 161 K
Maylins Dr SBW CM21 ...... 11 H
Maynard CI ERITH DA8 ...... 210 A
Maynards EMPK RM11 ...... 181 F
Mayne Crest CHLM/WR CM1 .. 35 G
Mayo CI CHES/WCR EN8 .... 76 C
Maypole Crs ERITH DA8 .... 210 E
Maypole Dr CHIG IG7 ...... 135 K
Maypole Rd MAL CM9 ...... 40 B
May Wk CHLM/GWD CM2 .... 5 D6
Maywin Dr EMPK RM11 ...... 181 G
The Maze LOS SS9 ...... 172 E
Mccalmont Dr RAYL SS6 .... 149 H
Mcdivitt Wk LOS SS9 ...... 173 H7
Mead Barn EPP CM16 ...... 108 C
Mead CI CDH/CHF RM16 .... 214 A
  GPK RM2 .... 160 B
  LOU IG10 .... 107 K
Mead Ct WAB EN9 ...... 77 H
Mead Crs CHING E4 ...... 132 D
Meade Rd BCAYE CM11 ...... 117 K
Meadgate PIT SS13 ...... 169 F5
Meadgate Av CHLM/GWD CM2 .. 5 E
  WFD IG8 .... 134 B
Meadgate Rd HOD EN11 .... 49 K
Mead Monks RCHLM CM3 .... 93 K
Meadow CI CHING E4 ...... 132 C4
  PEND EN3 .... 104 E
  SBF/HAD SS7 ...... 171 G
  SLH/COR SS17 ...... 216 B
Meadow Ct WICKE SS11 .... 147 H
Meadowcross WAB EN9 .... 78 A
Meadow Dr SOS SS9 ...... 195 H
  VGE SS16 .... 186 C
Meadowgate ING CM4 ...... 118 B
Meadowland Rd WICKE SS11 .. 147 K
Meadowlands EMPK RM11 .. 181 F1
Meadow La WICKW SS11 .... 147 H
Meadow Ms RCHLM CM3 .... 122 B5
Meadow RI BCAYE CM11 .... 144 D
  ING CM4 .... 86 C
Meadow Rd CDH/CHF RM16 .. 201 C
  EPP CM16 .... 80 D
  GVW DA11 .... 218 D
  GVW DA11 .... 219 F
  HOC/HUL SS5 ...... 149 K
  LOU IG10 .... 134 B
  RCHLM CM3 .... 121 G
  SBF/HAD SS7 ...... 191 K
Meadows CI RBRW/HUT CM13 .. 164 B1
Meadows Gn RCHLM CM3 .... 66 A
Meadowside CHLM/GWD CM2 .. 5 D
  RAYL SS6 .... 171 J5
Meadowside Rd UPMR RM14 .. 181 K
The Meadows RBRW/HUT CM13.. 164 B
  SBW CM21 .... 12 A
Meadow Vw EPP CM16 ...... 80 E3
  VGE SS16 .... 185 K
Meadow Vw BOC CM0 ...... 128 A
  CHIC IG7 .... 135 F
  HOC/HUL SS5 ...... 151 F
  RCHLM CM3 .... 97 J
  SBW CM21 .... 12 A
  UPMR RM14 ...... 181 K
  WICKW SS12 ...... 169 G
The Meadow Wy BCAYE CM11 .. 144 D
Mead Pastures MAL CM9 .... 66 D
Mead Pth CHLM/GWD CM2 .... 4 A
Mead Rd GVW DA11 ...... 219 G
Meads CI ING CM4 ...... 116 B
Meads Rd PEND EN3 ...... 104 E
The Meads ING CM4 ...... 116 B
  UPMR RM14 ...... 182 B3
  VGE SS16 .... 188 D
Meadsway RBRW/HUT CM13 .. 163 F1
The Mead ABR/ST RM4 ...... 109 F
  CHES/WCR EN8 ...... 76 C
  LAIN SS15 .... 166 C
Mead Wk CHONG CM5 ...... 84 B
Meadway CVI SS8 ...... 208 C
  GPK RM2 .... 160 B
  GRAYS RM17 214

HOD EN11	49 G1
MAL CM9	68 D4
PEND EN3	104 D2
RAYL SS6	172 A6
SBF/HAD SS7	170 B6
WFD IG8	133 K8 🅑
he Meadway BKHH IG9	134 A4
WOS/PRIT SS0	193 J5
eakins Cl LOS SS9	173 C7
earns Pl CHLM/GWD CM2	63 H1
edcalf Rd PEND EN3	105 F3
edebridge Rd CDH/CHF RM16	200 D3
edick Ct GRAYS RM17	214 D5
edina Rd GRAYS RM17	214 C4
edlar Dr SOCK/AV RM15	200 C4 🅑
edlar Rd GRAYS RM17	214 C5
edoc Cl PIT SS13	169 F5
edway Cl CHLM/WR CM1	61 K1
edway Crs LOS SS9	192 E1
eeson Mdw MAL CM9	68 A5
eesons La GRAYS RM17	213 J3
eesons Md RCFD SS4	174 A2
eggison Wy SBF/HAD SS7	190 B2
elba Ct CHLM/WR CM1	61 J4
elba Gdns TIL RM18	215 F6
elbourne Av CHLM/WR CM1	33 K8
elbourne Rd TIL RM18	214 D7
elcombe Rd SBF/HAD SS7	190 B2
elksham Cl HARH RM3	161 G2 🅑
elksham Gdns HARH RM3	161 F2
elksham Gn HARH RM3	161 F2 🅑
elling Gn EN1	104 A5
ellish Gdns WFD IG8	133 H8
ellor Cl ING CM4	116 B1 🅑
ellow Purgess Cl LAIN SS15	6 A4
ellow Purgess End LAIN SS15	6 A4
ell Rd MAL CM9	68 D5
elstock Av UPMR RM14	181 K5
elton Gdns ROM RM1	180 A1
elville Dr WICKW SS12	147 G8
elville Heath RCHLM CM3	122 E7
emory Cl MAL CM9	68 C6 🅑
endip Cl RAYL SS6	171 J2
WICKE SS11	147 H6 🅑
endip Crs WOS/PRIT SS0	173 H8
endip Rd CHLM/WR CM1	33 K7
EMPK RM11	180 B1
LOS SS9	193 H5
endoza Cl EMPK RM11	161 F7
entmore VGE SS16	186 C1
enzies Av LAIN SS15	166 A7
eon Cl CHLM/WR CM1	35 F7
eppel Av CVI SS8	191 F7
ercer Av SBN/FI SS3	197 F1
ercer Rd BCAYE CM11	117 K8
erchant St RCHLM CM3	122 E6 🅑
ercia Cl CHLM/GWD CM2	63 J8
ercury Cl WICKE SS11	147 J5
ercury Gdns ROM RM1	160 A7
eredene BSDN SS14	168 C8
eredith Rd CDH/CHF RM16	215 F3
erefield SBW CM21	11 J4 🅑
eriadoc Dr RCHLM CM3	122 D7
erilies Cl WOS/PRIT SS0	193 J5
erilies Gdns WOS/PRIT SS0	193 J2
erlin Cl WAB EN9	78 C8
erlin Ct CVI SS8	208 B2 🅑
erlin Pl CHLM/WR CM1	34 B8 🅑
erlin Wy EPP CM16	54 A7
WICKE SS11	147 J5
ermagen Rd RAIN RM13	180 C8
ermaid Wy MAL CM9	68 D5 🅑
erriam Cl CHING E4	132 D8 🅑
erricks La VGE SS16	188 B3
errivale SBF/HAD SS7	190 B3
erryfield Ap LOS SS9	193 F1
erryfields Av HOC/HUL SS5	150 E6
erryhill Cl CHING E4	132 C3
errylands LAIN SS15	166 B6
ersea Crs WICKW SS12	147 J7
ersey Av UPMR RM14	162 A8
erton Pl CDH/CHF RM16	215 F3
RCHLM CM3	123 J7
erton Rd HOC/HUL SS5	150 B5
SBF/HAD SS7	190 B1
essant Cl GPK RM2	160 E4 🅑
eteor Rd WOS/PRIT SS0	8 A4
eteor Wy CHLM/WR CM1	4 A3
ethersgate BSDN SS14	167 K6
etsons La CHLM/WR CM1	87 H3
etz Av CVI SS8	208 A1
eux Cl CHESW EN7	76 A5
ews Ct CHLM/GWD CM2	4 C4
ews Pl WFD IG8	133 H7
he Mews HOC/HUL SS5	150 D1
SBW CM21	11 J2 🅑
eyel Av CVI SS8	191 H8
eyer Gn EN EN1	104 A4
eynell Av CVI SS8	208 C3
eynell Rd HARH RM3	160 C1
ey Wk HOC/HUL SS5	150 D7
icawber Wy CHLM/WR CM1	33 K6
ichael Gdns EMPK RM11	160 E6

Middle Boy ABR/ST RM4	109 F7
Middle Dr SLH/COR SS17	187 J4
Middle Gn BRWN CM15	114 A3
Middlemead CHLM/GWD CM2	119 H1 🅑
Middle Md RCFD SS4	174 C3 🅑
Middlemead RCHLM CM3	120 A5
Middle Mead Cl	
CHLM/GWD CM2	119 H1 🅑
Middle Rd RBRW/HUT RM13	142 B7
WAB EN9	77 H6
Middlesburg CVI SS8	190 C8
Middlesex Av LOS SS9	193 G3
Middle St WAB EN9	50 B5
Middleton Av CHING E4	132 A7
Middleton Cl CHING E4	132 A6
Middleton Hall La BRWN CM15	141 H5
Middleton Rd BRWN CM15	141 H4
Middleton Rw RCHLM CM3	122 E7
Midguard Wy MAL CM9	68 A5
Midhurst Av WOS/PRIT SS0	194 A1
Midhurst Cl HCH RM12	180 B5 🅑
Midsummer Meadow	
SBN/FI SS3	196 D4 🅑
Milbanke Cl SBN/FI SS3	196 D4 🅑
Milburn Crs CHLM/WR CM1	61 K4
Mildmayes VGE SS16	6 A6
Mildmay Rd BOC CM0	128 C8
CHLM/GWD CM2	4 C5
Mildmays RCHLM CM3	65 C5
Mile Cl WAB EN9	77 J7 🅑
Miles Cl HLWW/ROY CM19	2 B4
Miles Gray Rd BSDN SS14	6 C2
Milford Rd CDH/CHF RM16	201 H6
Millais Pl TIL RM18	215 F6
Millars Cl RCHLM CM3	122 E5 🅑
The Millars CHLM/WR CM1	34 C2 🅑
Millbank Av CHONG CM5	84 B3
Mill Cl BOC CM0	102 A1
CHLM/WR CM1	32 A8
Millers Cl CHIG IG7	136 A5
Millers Cft CHLM/GWD CM2	63 H7
Millersdale HLWW/ROY CM19	51 K1
Millers Green Rd CHONG CM5	57 K1
Miller's La CHIG IG7	136 A4
Millfield CHONG CM5	84 E2
Millfield Cl RAYL SS6	171 K2
Millfield Dr GVW DA11	218 D7
Mill Flds RCHLM CM3	66 A7
Millfields CHLM/WR CM1	61 C4
SBW CM21	11 K2
Mill Gra BOC CM0	128 B6
Mill Gn PIT SS13	168 D7
Mill Green Pl PIT SS13	168 D6
Mill Green Rd ING CM4	87 K5
Millmead Wy RCFD SS4	174 E4
Mill Hi BRWN CM15	141 H5
CHLM/GWD CM2	90 B3
RCHLM CM3	95 J5
SBF/HAD SS7	190 D4
Mill Hill Dr BCAYW CM12	117 H8
Millhurst Ms CHLM/WR CM17	25 J1
Milligans Cha CHLM/GWD CM2	90 D4
Mill La ABR/ST RM4	111 J6
CHES/WCR EN8	76 E2
BCAYE CM11	118 D8
BROX EN10	49 F5
BRWN CM15	113 G3
CDH/CHF RM16	202 A6
CHING E4	105 H7
CHLM/WR CM1	34 D4
CHONG CM5	27 J8
CHONG CM5	82 E3
CHONG CM5	84 E5
HLWE CM17	25 J1
ING CM4	88 A1
ING CM4	118 B3
MAL CM9	42 C2
MAL CM9	68 B2
RBSF CM22	13 F1
RCFD SS4	174 E4
RCHLM CM3	95 J4
SBW CM21	11 K2
SLH/COR SS17	187 J6
SLH/COR SS17	203 F2
WFD IG8	133 G8
WTHK RM20	213 G4
Mill Lane Cl BROX EN10	49 F5
Millmarsh La PEND EN3	104 E6
Mill Park Av HCH RM12	181 F5
Mill Rd BCAYE CM11	144 E7
BOC CM0	102 A1
BOC CM0	128 B6
CHLM/WR CM1	17 H8
GVW DA11	218 A3
ING CM4	118 A3
MAL CM9	68 D4
PUR RM19	211 J5
RCHLM CM3	99 F5
SOCK/AV RM15	198 E2
Mills Ct PIT SS13	169 F4
Millson Bank CHLM/GWD CM2	63 J1 🅑
Mill St HLWE CM17	25 J8
Mills Wy RBRW/HUT CM13	142 B4

Millview Mdw RCFD SS4	174 C4
Mill Vue Rd CHLM/GWD CM2	5 F3
Millways MAL CM9	40 D1
Millwell Crs CHIG IG7	135 G8
Milner Pl BCAYW CM12	117 F8
Milroy Av GVW DA12	218 D7
Milton Av GVE DA12	219 J6
HCH RM12	180 A3
VGE SS16	185 K1
WOS/PRIT SS0	8 B5
Milton Cl RAYL SS6	172 A5
Milton Ct WAB EN9	77 J8 🅑
Milton Crs CHONG CM5	56 B8
Milton Gdns TIL RM18	215 G7
Milton Hall Cl SBN/FI SS3	196 E2
Milton Hall Rd GVE DA12	219 J6
Milton Pl CHLM/WR CM1	34 B8
GVE DA12	219 H4
SOS SS1	8 C5 🅑
Milton Rd BRW CM14	140 E6
GRAYS RM17	214 A3
GVE DA12	219 H4 🅑
MAL CM9	68 C5
ROM RM1	160 B8
SLH/COR SS17	187 G7
WOS/PRIT SS0	8 B4
Milton St SOSN SS2	9 D5
Miltsin Av CVI SS8	191 H8
Milwards HLWW/ROY CM19	51 K1 🅑
Mimosa Cl BRWN CM15	140 E1 🅑
CHLM/WR CM1	35 H7
HARH RM3	160 D2
Minchen Rd HLW CM20	24 E4
Minster Rd LAIN SS15	6 A4
Minster Wy EMPK RM11	181 G2
MAL CM9	68 A5
Minton Hts RCFD SS4	151 K7
Minton Cl HLWE CM17	25 G5
Miramar Av CVI SS8	207 J2
Miramar Wy HCH RM12	180 E6 🅑
Mirosa Dr MAL CM9	68 D5
Mirosa Reach MAL CM9	68 C5
Mistley End VGE SS16	167 K8
Mistley Pth VGE SS16	167 K8
Mistley Rd HLW CM20	24 E3
Mistley Side VGE SS16	167 K8
Mitchell Av GVW DA11	218 C7
Mitchells Av CVI SS8	208 D1
Mitchell Wy RCHLM CM3	122 D5
Mitton V CHLM/GWD CM2	63 H3 🅑
Moat Cl BCAYE CM11	145 K2
Moat Edge Gdns BCAYW CM12	144 B1
Moat End SOS SS1	196 A4
Moat Fld BSDN SS14	167 K5
Moat La ERTH DA8	210 B7
Moat Ri RAYL SS6	171 J4
Moat Side PEND EN3	104 C8
Mollands VGE SS16	188 C1
Mollands La SOCK/AV RM15	200 C4
Mollands La SOCK/AV RM15	200 A4
Mollison Av PEND EN3	104 E7
Molrams La CHLM/GWD CM2	63 K7
Momples Rd HLW CM20	24 E4
Monarch Cl TIL RM18	215 G8
Monarch Wy BKHH IG9	133 K5
Monarch's Wy CHES/WCR EN8	76 D7 🅑
Monastery Rd LAIN SS15	6 A4
Monkchester Cl LOU IG10	107 J5 🅑
Monkham's Av WFD IG8	133 J8
Monkham's Dr WFD IG8	133 J8
Monkham's La WFD IG8	133 J7
Monksbury HLWS CM18	24 E8
Monks Cl BRWN CM15	142 B8
Monks Cl BROX EN10	49 G2
Monksford Dr HOC/HUL SS5	149 K4
Monksgrove LOU IG10	134 D1
Monks Hvn SLH/COR SS17	204 A2
Monks Wk MAL CM9	44 E5
Monkswick Rd HLW CM20	3 F1
Monkswood Dr WAB EN9	77 K7
Monmouth Ms VGE SS16	166 A8 🅑
Monnow Rd SOCK/AV RM15	198 E2
Monoux Cl BCAYE CM11	144 E4
Monroe Crs EN EN1	104 B5
Mons Av BCAYE CM11	144 E3
Monson Rd BROX EN10	49 F2 🅑
Montague Av LOS SS9	192 C3
Montague Pl CVI SS8	207 J2
Montague Wy BCAYW CM12	117 G8
Montalt Rd WFD IG8	133 G8
Montayne Rd CHES/WCR EN8	76 D6
Montefiore Av RAYL SS6	149 H5
Montfort Av SLH/COR SS17	204 C1
Montgomery Cl CHLM/WR CM1	35 G8
Montgomery Ct SBN/FI SS3	196 D4 🅑
Montgomery Crs HARH RM3	138 E8
Montgomery Dr CHES/WCR EN8	76 E2
Montpelier Cl BCAYW CM12	117 C8 🅑
Montreal Rd TIL RM18	219 F1
Montrose Av GPK RM2	160 D4
Montrose Cl WFD IG8	133 H7
Montrose Rd CHLM/GWD CM2	63 H1
Montsale PIT SS13	169 F5
Moons Cl RCFD SS4	152 A6

Moorcroft *RCFD* SS4 .... 151 K7
Moorcroft Av *SBF/HAD* SS7 .... 171 K7
Moore Av *TIL* RM18 .... 215 G8
  WTHK RM20 .... 213 H4
Moore Cl *BCAYE* CM11 .... 117 K8 🔟
Moores Av *SLH/COR* SS17 .... 187 K4
Moorescroft *BRWN* CM15 .... 113 G3 🔟
Moorfield Rd *PEND* EN3 .... 104 C5
Moorfields *HLWS* CM18 .... 52 A2
Moor Hall La *RCHLM* CM3 .... 93 J2
Moor Hall Rd *HLW* CM17 .... 25 K1
Moorhen Av *BOC* CM0 .... 72 C5
Moorhen Cl *ERITH* DA8 .... 210 C6 🔟
Moor La *UPMR* RM14 .... 182 C2
Moor Park Cl *LOS* SS9 .... 172 D8
Moor Park Gdns *LOS* SS9 .... 172 D8
Moor's Farm Cha *MAL* CM9 .... 41 J2
Mopsies Rd *BSDN* SS14 .... 168 B7
Moran Cl *CHLM/GWD* CM1 .... 34 D6
Morant Gdns *CRW* RM5 .... 137 G8
Morant Rd *CDH/CHF* RM16 .... 215 G2
Morecambe Cl *HCH* RM12 .... 180 C6
Moreland Av *SBF/HAD* SS7 .... 170 B6
Moreland Cl *SBF/HAD* SS7 .... 170 B6
  SBN/FI SS3 .... 197 F1 🔟
Moreland Rd *WICKE* SS11 .... 147 F3
Morelands Av *CDH/CHF* RM16 .... 214 B1 🔟
Moreland Wy *CHING* E4 .... 132 C6
Moremead *WAB* EN9 .... 77 K7
Mores La *UPMR* RM14 .... 113 F7
Moreton Br *CHONG* CM5 .... 55 J3
Moreton Cl *CHESW* EN7 .... 76 B1
Moreton Gdns *WFD* IG8 .... 134 B8
Moreton Rd *CHONG* CM5 .... 55 G5
Moretons *CHLM/GWD* CM2 .... 90 D3
  PIT SS13 .... 168 D7
Morgan Crs *EPP* CM16 .... 108 C2
Morland Wy *CHES/WCR* EN8 .... 76 E2
Morley Gv *HLW* CM20 .... 2 C2
Morley Hl *SLH/COR* SS17 .... 187 G7
Morley Lnk *SLH/COR* SS17 .... 187 G8 🔟
Morley Sq *CDH/CHF* RM16 .... 215 F3
Mornington Av *RCFD* SS4 .... 174 D3
Mornington Crs *CVI* SS8 .... 208 C1 🔟
  SBF/HAD SS7 .... 192 A2
Mornington Rd *CHING* E4 .... 132 E3
  CVI SS8 .... 191 G8
Morningtons *HLWW/ROY* CM19 .... 51 K3
Morrells *VGE* SS16 .... 7 D6
Morrin's Cha *SBN/FI* SS3 .... 197 J2
Morrins Cl *SBN/FI* SS3 .... 197 J2
Morris Av *BCAYE* CM11 .... 144 E4
Morris Ct *CHING* E4 .... 132 C6
  LAIN SS15 .... 166 C6
  WAB EN9 .... 78 B3
Morris Cl *CHLM/GWD* CM2 .... 5 E3 🔟
  HARH RM3 .... 160 C2
Mortimer Ga *CHES/WCR* EN8 .... 77 F1
Mortimer Rd *RAYL* SS6 .... 149 J8
  RCHLM CM3 .... 38 A1
Morton Rd *MAL* CM9 .... 40 C1
Mosbach Gdns *RBRW/HUT* CM13 ...... 142 A5
Moseley St *SOSN* SS2 .... 195 G4
Moss Bank *GRAYS* RM17 .... 213 J3
Moss Cl *VGE* SS16 .... 188 B3
Moss Dr *VGE* SS16 .... 188 B2
Moss La *ROM* RM1 .... 160 A8
Moss Rd *SOCK/AV* RM15 .... 200 A5
Motehill *WICKE* SS16 .... 6 A6
Motherwell Wy *WTHK* RM20 .... 212 D4
Mott St *CHING* E4 .... 106 A5
Moulsham Cha *CHLM/GWD* CM2 .... 5 D5
Moulsham Dr *CHLM/GWD* CM2 .... 4 C6
Moulsham Thrift *CHLM/GWD* CM2 ...... 62 C7
Moultrie Wy *UPMR* RM14 .... 182 B1
Mountain Ash Cl *SBF/HAD* SS7 .... 172 C7
Mount Av *CHING* E4 .... 132 B6
  HARH RM3 .... 161 K1
  HOC/HUL SS5 .... 150 E7
  RBRW/HUT CM13 .... 142 A3
  WOS/PRIT SS0 .... 193 H5
Mountbatten Ct *BKHH* IG9 .... 134 A5
Mountbatten Dr *SBN/FI* SS3 .... 196 D4
Mountbatten Wy *CHLM/WR* CM1 .... 35 F6
Mount Bovers La *HOC/HUL* SS5 .... 175 F2
Mount Cl *RAYL* SS6 .... 171 H3
  WICKE SS11 .... 147 H5
Mount Crs *BRW* CM14 .... 141 G7
  HOC/HUL SS5 .... 151 F7
  SBF/HAD SS7 .... 190 D1
Mountdale Gdns *LOS* SS9 .... 193 G5
Mount Echo Av *CHING* E4 .... 132 C4
Mount Echo Dr *CHING* E4 .... 132 C3
Mountfield Cl *SLH/COR* SS17 .... 204 A2
Mountfields *PIT* SS13 .... 188 E5
Mounthill Av *CHLM/GWD* CM2 .... 5 J2
Mountnessing *SBF/HAD* SS7 .... 191 J3
Mountnessing La *BRWN* CM15 .... 114 C4
Mountnessing Rd *BCAYW* CM12 .... 116 D6
  BRWN CM15 .... 114 E2
Mountney Cl *INC* CM4 .... 115 K4
Mount Pleasant *MAL* CM9 .... 68 B3
Mount Pleasant Av
  RBRW/HUT CM13 .... 142 D2

Mount Pleasant Rd *CHIG* IG7 .... 135 C7
  RCHLM CM3 .... 122 D6
Mount Rd *EPP* CM16 .... 81 J6
  SBF/HAD SS7 .... 190 E1
  WICKE SS11 .... 147 H5
The Mount *BCAYE* CM11 .... 145 F2
  BRW CM14 .... 141 F6 🔟
  HARH RM3 .... 138 D6
  MAL CM9 .... 44 D4
  SLH/COR SS17 .... 204 B2
Mount Vw *WICKE* SS11 .... 147 H5
Mountview Cl *VGE* SS16 .... 188 B2
Mountview Crs *BOC* CM0 .... 72 C4
Mount View Rd *CHING* E4 .... 132 D3
Mount Wy *WICKE* SS11 .... 147 H5
Mowbray Rd *HLW* CM20 .... 3 F1
Mowbrey Gdns *LOU* IG10 .... 108 A5 🔟
Moxom Av *CHES/WCR* EN8 .... 76 E4
Muckingford Rd *TIL* RM18 .... 216 A3
Mucking Hall Rd *SBN/FI* SS3 .... 176 B5
Mucking Wharf Rd *SLH/COR* SS17 ... 203 J6
Muirway *SBF/HAD* SS7 .... 170 A6
Mulberry Cl *BROX* EN10 .... 49 F6
  CHING E4 .... 132 B5
  GPK RM2 .... 160 C6
Mulberry Dr *PUR* RM19 .... 211 G3
Mulberry Gdns *HLWE* CM17 .... 25 H1
Mulberry Hl *BRWN* CM15 .... 141 J3
Mulberry Rd *CVI* SS8 .... 207 G2
Mulberry Wy *CHLM/WR* CM1 .... 35 F8
Mullberry Gdns *VGE* SS16 .... 166 C8 🔟
Mullein Ct *GRAYS* RM17 .... 214 C5
The Mullions *BCAYW* CM12 .... 144 A2
Multon Lea *CHLM/WR* CM1 .... 35 J6
Mundells *CHESW* EN7 .... 76 A1
Mundon Rd *MAL* CM9 .... 68 C4
Mungo Park Rd *RAIN* RM13 .... 180 C8 🔟
Munro Ct *WICKW* SS12 .... 147 H8 🔟
Munsons Av *BOC* CM0 .... 128 D1
Munsterburg Rd *CVI* SS8 .... 191 J8
Murchison Cl *CHLM/WR* CM1 .... 34 A8
Murfitt Wy *UPMR* RM14 .... 181 H5 🔟
Murrell Lock *CHLM/GWD* CM2 .... 63 J1
Murrells La *HOC/HUL* SS5 .... 150 B6
Murthering La *ABR/ST* RM4 .... 111 G8
Muskalls Cl *CHESW* EN7 .... 76 A1 🔟
Musket Gv *LOS* SS9 .... 172 C6
Muskham Rd *HLW* CM20 .... 24 E2
Mutton Rw *CHONG* CM5 .... 83 J4
Mylne Cl *CHES/WCR* EN8 .... 76 C1
Myln Meadow *INC* CM4 .... 118 B3
Mynchens *LAIN* SS15 .... 6 C4
Myrtle Gv *SOCK/AV* RM15 .... 211 K1
Myrtle Rd *BRW* CM14 .... 141 F7
  HARH RM3 .... 160 D1

N

Nabbott Rd *CHLM/WR* CM1 .... 62 A3
Naffenton Ri *LOU* IG10 .... 134 A1 🔟
Nag's Head La *UPMR* RM14 .... 161 K5
Nags Head Rd *PEND* EN3 .... 104 C8
Nalla Gdns *CHLM/WR* CM1 .... 62 A4
Namur Rd *CVI* SS8 .... 191 H8
Nansen Av *RCFD* SS4 .... 152 A7
Napier Av *SOS* SS1 .... 8 C4
Napier Cl *RCH* RM12 .... 180 C2 🔟
Napier Crs *WICKW* SS12 .... 147 H8
Napier Gdns *SBF/HAD* SS7 .... 171 H7
Napier Rd *GVW* DA11 .... 218 E6
  RAYL SS6 .... 172 A2
Narboro Ct *ROM* RM1 .... 160 B8 🔟
Nare Rd *SOCK/AV* RM15 .... 198 E7
Narvik Cl *MAL* CM9 .... 68 A5
Nash Dr *CHLM/WR* CM1 .... 34 C2
Nathan Cl *UPMR* RM14 .... 182 D2
Nathan's La *CHLM/WR* CM1 .... 60 D8
Nation Wy *CHING* E4 .... 132 D4 🔟
Naunton Wy *HCH* RM12 .... 180 E1 🔟
Navestock Cl *CHING* E4 .... 132 D6 🔟
  RAYL SS6 .... 171 F2 🔟
Navestock Gdns *SOS* SS1 .... 195 J4
Navestock Side *BRW* CM14 .... 112 E6
Navigation Rd *CHLM/GWD* CM2 .... 5 D3
Nayland Cl *WICKW* SS12 .... 147 H6 🔟
Nazeingbury Cl *WAB* EN9 .... 49 K4 🔟
Nazeing Common *WAB* EN9 .... 50 E5
The Nazeing *BSDN* SS14 .... 168 B7
Neave Crs *HARH* RM3 .... 160 D3
Neil Armstrong Wy *LOS* SS9 .... 173 H6
Nelmes Cl *EMPK* RM11 .... 161 G2
Nelmes Crs *EMPK* RM11 .... 161 G1
Nelmes Rd *EMPK* RM11 .... 161 F1
Nelmes Wy *EMPK* RM11 .... 161 G1
Nelson Cl *BRW* CM14 .... 141 G8
  RAYL SS6 .... 172 A1
Nelson Dr *LOS* SS9 .... 193 G4
Nelson Gdns *RAYL* SS6 .... 172 A1
Nelson Gv *CHLM/WR* CM1 .... 4 A2
Nelson Ms *SOS* SS1 .... 9 D5
Nelson Pl *RCHLM* CM3 .... 122 E7

Nelson Rd *BSDN* SS14 .... 168 A7
  CDH/CHF RM16 .... 202 D6
  CVW DA11 .... 218 E2
  RAYL SS6 .... 172 A1
  RCFD SS4 .... 152 A4
  SOCK/AV RM15 .... 200 A5
  WOS/PRIT SS0 .... 193 H4
Nelson St *SOS* SS1 .... 9 D7
Nelwyn Av *EMPK* RM11 .... 161 G2
Ness Rd *SBN/FI* SS3 .... 196 D6
Nestuda Wy *WOS/PRIT* SS0 .... 173 J7
Nethan Dr *SOCK/AV* RM15 .... 198 E7
Netherfield *SBF/HAD* SS7 .... 191 F7
Netherhall Rd *HLWW/ROY* CM19 .... 22 B7
Nether Mayne *VGE* SS16 .... 7 F6
Nether Priors *BSDN* SS14 .... 7 F6
Netherpark Dr *GPK* RM2 .... 160 A4
Nettleswellbury Farm *HLWS* CM18 ..... 3 F4 🔟
Netteswell Orch *HLW* CM20 .... 3 D4
Netteswell Rd *HLW* CM20 .... 3 E4
Nevada Rd *CVI* SS8 .... 191 H6
Nevell Rd *CDH/CHF* RM16 .... 215 G2
Nevendon Ms *PIT* SS13 .... 168 D3 🔟
Nevendon Rd *PIT* SS13 .... 168 D7
  WICKW SS12 .... 147 F7
Nevern Cl *RAYL* SS6 .... 172 A4
Nevern Rd *RAYL* SS6 .... 171 K4
Neville Shaw *BSDN* SS14 .... 7 F6
Nevill Wy *LOU* IG10 .... 134 B3
Nevin Dr *CHING* E4 .... 132 C2
New Av *VGE* SS16 .... 186 B4
New Barns Wy *CHIG* IG7 .... 134 E6 🔟
Newberry Side *CHLM/GWD* CM1 .... 35 H1
Newbery Av *PEND* EN3 .... 105 F7
Newbury Cl *HARH* RM3 .... 160 D2
Newbury Gdns *HARH* RM3 .... 160 E1
  UPMR RM14 .... 181 G2
Newbury Rd *HARH* RM3 .... 138 D2
Newbury Wk *HARH* RM3 .... 138 E8
New Century Rd *LAIN* SS15 .... 166 C6
Newcourt Rd *CHLM/GWD* CM2 .... 5 E4
New Dukes Wy *CHLM/GWD* CM2 .... 63 H3 🔟
Newell Av *SBN/FI* SS3 .... 197 F2
New England Cl *RCHLM* CM3 .... 93 K4
New England Crs *SBN/FI* SS3 .... 197 H3
New Farm Dr *ABR/ST* RM4 .... 109 G2
New Ford Rd *CHES/WCR* EN8 .... 77 F2
Newgate St *CHING* E4 .... 133 F6 🔟
Newhall *RCFD* SS4 .... 151 K5
New Hall Dr *HARH* RM3 .... 161 F1
New Hall La *MAL* CM9 .... 97 G2
Newhouse Av *WICKW* SS12 .... 146 C3
Newhouse La *CHONG* CM5 .... 55 J5
New House La *GVW* DA11 .... 218 E2
Newington Av *SOSN* SS2 .... 195 H4
Newington Cl *SOSN* SS2 .... 195 H4
Newland Dr *EN* EN1 .... 104 B3
Newlands Cl *BCAYW* CM12 .... 144 C3
  RBRW/HUT CM13 .... 142 C3
Newlands End *LAIN* SS15 .... 166 C6
Newlands Rd *BCAYW* CM12 .... 144 C3
  CVI SS8 .... 191 J8 🔟
  WFD IG8 .... 133 G2
  WICKW SS12 .... 147 H6
New Lodge Cha *RCHLM* CM3 .... 69 F7
New London Rd *CHLM/WR* CM1 .... 4 C3
Newman Cl *EMPK* RM11 .... 161 F2
Newmans Dr *RBRW/HUT* CM13 .... 142 B9
Newmans La *LOU* IG10 .... 120 J7
Newman's Rd *GVW* DA11 .... 218 E2
Newmarket Wy *HCH* RM12 .... 181 F1
New Meadgate Ter
  CHLM/GWD CM2 .... 5 E5
New Moor Cl *BOC* CM0 .... 128 E
New Moor Crs *BOC* CM0 .... 128 E
New Nabbotts Wy *CHLM/WR* CM1 ..... 35 G
Newnham Cl *LOU* IG10 .... 134 A
Newnham Gn *MAL* CM9 .... 68 A2
Newnham Pl *CDH/CHF* RM16 .... 215 F3
New Park Rd *HOC/HUL* SS5 .... 151 H
  SBF/HAD SS7 .... 170 B
Newpiece *LOU* IG10 .... 107 V
New Place Gdns *UPMR* RM14 .... 182 A
Newport Av *RCHLM* CM3 .... 96 D
Newport Cl *CHLM/GWD* CM2 .... 63 H
  PEND EN3 .... 104 E3
Newports *SBW* CM21 .... 11 G
New Rd *ABR/ST* RM4 .... 136 C
  BCAYW CM12 .... 166 B
  BOC CM0 .... 128 D
  BROX EN10 .... 49 F
  BRW CM14 .... 142 C
  CHING E4 .... 132 C
  CHLM/GWD CM2 .... 63 J
  CHLM/WR CM1 .... 34 D
  CVI SS8 .... 207 J
  GRAYS RM17 .... 213 K
  GVW DA11 .... 219 F4
  HLWE CM17 .... 25 H
  INC CM4 .... 116 C
  LOS SS9 .... 192 E
  MAL CM9 .... 44 D
  RAIN RM13 .... 198 D
  RCHLM CM3 .... 38 A

SBF/HAD SS7 .... 191 J2
SBN/FI SS3 .... 197 H2
ewstead Rd *SBN/FI* SS5 ...... 197 G1
SBW CM21 .... 11 J2
MAL CM9 .... 68 B3
ew St *CHLM/WR* CM1 .... 4 C3
SBW CM21 .... 11 J2
ewton Abbot Rd *GVW* DA11 ... 218 E7
ewton Dr *WAB* EN9 .... 77 K6
ewton Hall Gdns *RCFD* SS4 ... 152 A7
ewton Park Rd *SBF/HAD* SS7 171 G6
ewton Rd *TIL* RM18 .... 215 F8
ew Waverley Rd *LAIN* SS15 ...... 6 C1
ew Way La *HLWE* CM17 .... 26 D4
ew Writtle St *CHLM/GWD* CM2 .. 4 C4
iagara La *CHES/WCR* EN8 ..... 76 D3
icholas Cl *CHLM/WR* CM1 ..... 61 H5
SOCK/AV RM15 .... 200 A3
icholl St *EPP* CM16 .... 80 D5
LAIN SS15 .... 166 C6
icholls Fld *HLWS* CM18 .... 25 F6
icholson Crs *SBF/HAD* SS7 ... 191 G2
icholson Gv *WICKW* SS12 .... 147 H8
icholson Pl *RCHLM* CM3 .... 93 F6
ickleby Rd *CHLM/WR* CM1 .... 33 K6
HARH RM3 .... 138 E6
obel Sq *PIT* SS13 .... 169 F3
obles Green Cl *LOS* SS9 ...... 173 F6
obles Green Gdns *LOS* SS9 .. 173 F6
orbury Rd *CHING* E4 .... 132 B8
ordland Rd *CVI* SS8 .... 208 D1
ordmann Pl *SOCK/AV* RM15 .. 200 B4
oredale *SBN/FI* SS3 .... 196 C7
ore Rd *LOS* SS9 .... 172 D5
orfolk Av *LOS* SS9 .... 193 G2
orfolk Cl *CVI* SS8 .... 191 F3
LAIN SS15 .... 166 B7
MAL CM9 .... 68 A4
orfolk Dr *CHLM/WR* CM1 ...... 34 C6
orfolk Rd *GVE* DA12 .... 219 J3
MAL CM9 .... 68 A4
UPMR RM14 .... 181 H4
orfolk Wy *CVI* SS8 .... 190 E8
orman Cl *WAB* EN9 .... 77 K7
orman Crs *RAYL* SS6 .... 149 K8
RBRW/HUT CM13 .... 141 K6
ormandy Av *BOC* CM0 .... 128 C8
ormanhurst *RBRW/HUT* CM13 . 142 B2
orman Rd *EMPK* RM11 .... 180 B1
ormans Cl *GVW* DA11 .... 219 F5
ormanshire Dr *CHING* E4 ..... 132 B7
ormans Rd *CVI* SS8 .... 208 D1
ormanton Pk *CHING* E4 .... 133 F6
orris Gv *BROX* EN10 .... 48 E2
orsey Cl *BCAYE* CM11 .... 144 C2
orsey Dr *BCAYE* CM11 .... 144 D2
orsey Rd *BCAYE* CM11 .... 144 C2
orsey View Dr *BCAYW* CM12 . 117 H7
orthallerton Wy *HARH* RM3 .. 138 E8
orthampton Gv *VGE* SS16 .... 186 A1
orthampton Rd *PEND* EN3 .... 104 E2
orth Av *CHLM/WR* CM1 .... 34 B8
CVI SS8 .... 207 K1
SOSN SS2 .... 9 E3
orth Barn *BROX* EN10 .... 49 H4
orth Benfleet Hall Rd
WICKW SS12 .... 169 J4
orthbrooks *HLWW/ROY* CM19 .. 2 B4
orth Cl *CHIG* IG7 .... 135 K8
orth Colne *VGE* SS16 .... 188 A1
orthcote Rd *GVW* DA11 .... 218 E6
orth Crs *SOSN* SS2 .... 173 K8
WICKW SS12 .... 147 G6
orth Crockerford *VGE* SS16 .. 168 B8
orth Dell *CHLM/WR* CM1 .... 35 F6
orthdene *CHIG* IG7 .... 135 G8
orthdown Rd *EMPK* RM11 ..... 180 C1
orth Dr *CHLM/GWD* CM2 .... 63 H6
GPK RM2 .... 160 D5
RBRW/HUT CM13 .... 143 D2
RCHLM CM3 .... 98 D3
orth End *BKHH* IG9 .... 133 K3
BOC CM0 .... 100 D8
orthend *RBRW/HUT* CM13 .... 141 F8
orthend Rd *ERITH* DA8 .... 210 A7

Northern Av *SBF/HAD* SS7 ..... 170 B8
Northfalls Rd *CVI* SS8 .... 209 F2
North Farm *LOU* IG10 .... 133 K2
Northfield Cl *BCAYE* CM11 .... 144 D3
Northfield Rd *CHES/WCR* EN8 . 76 E6
SBW CM21 .... 11 J1
Northfields *GRAYS* RM17 ...... 214 B3
North Ga *HLWS* CM18 .... 24 E6
North Gunnels *BSDN* SS14 ..... 7 F4
North Hl *RCHLM* CM5 .... 37 H7
SLH/COR SS17 .... 203 F1
North Hill Dr *HARH* RM3 .... 138 E7
North Kent Av *GVW* DA11 ...... 218 B4
North Kent Aveune *GVW* DA11 218 B4
Northlands Ap *VGE* SS16 .... 186 D4
Northlands Cl *SLH/COR* SS17 . 187 F8
Northlands Farm Cha
SLH/COR SS17 .... 187 F6
Northolme Cl *CDH/CHF* RM16 . 214 B2
Northolt Wy *HCH* RM12 .... 180 D6
North Pl *HLW* CM20 .... 10 E8
WAB EN9 .... 77 H7
Northridge Rd *GVE* DA12 ...... 219 H8
North Rd *ABR/ST* RM4 .... 137 K5
CHES/WCR EN8 .... 76 E7
BCAYE CM11 .... 146 A8
BRW CM14 .... 141 F4
MAL CM9 .... 44 C3
PUR RM19 .... 211 K3
SOCK/AV RM15 .... 183 G8
WOS/PRIT SS0 .... 8 B3
North Road Av *BRW* CM14 ..... 141 F4
North Service Rd *BRW* CM14 .. 141 F5
North Shoebury Rd *SBN/FI* SS3 196 C4
North St *BOC* CM0 .... 74 A8
BOC CM0 .... 128 D1
EMPK RM11 .... 180 E1
GVE DA12 .... 219 G5
LOS SS9 .... 193 F5
MAL CM9 .... 68 D3
RCFD SS4 .... 174 A3
SBN/FI SS3 .... 197 G1
WAB EN9 .... 50 A4
Northumberland Av *EMPK* RM11 160 D7
EN EN1 .... 104 B4
LAIN SS15 .... 6 A5
SOS SS1 .... 9 F5
Northumberland Ct
CHLM/GWD CM2 .... 63 H1
Northumberland Crs *SOS* SS1 . 195 G6
Northumberland Rd
SLH/COR SS17 .... 216 A1
North View Av *TIL* RM18 .... 215 F7
Northview Dr *WOS/PRIT* SS0 .... 8 A2
Northville Dr *WOS/PRIT* SS0 .. 193 K1
North Weald Cl *WICKE* SS11 .. 148 A7
Northwick Rd *CVI* SS8 .... 206 E1
Northwood *CDH/CHF* RM16 ... 215 G1
Northwood Av *HCH* RM12 ...... 180 B5
Norton Av *CVI* SS8 .... 208 E2
Norton Cl *CHING* E4 .... 132 B8
SLH/COR SS17 .... 204 B1
Norton Heath Rd *CHONG* CM5 . 58 B5
Norton La *CHONG* CM5 .... 57 J7
Norton Rd *CHLM/WR* CM1 ..... 116 B1
ING CM4 .... 86 D1
Norwich Av *SOSN* SS2 .... 9 F1
Norwich Cl *SOSN* SS2 .... 9 F3
Norwich Crs *RAYL* SS6 .... 149 H8
Norwood Dr *SBF/HAD* SS7 ..... 190 D4
Norwood Rd *BSDN* SS14 .... 168 A6
CHONG CM5 .... 28 E6
Norwood Rd *CHES/WCR* EN8 .. 76 E6
Nottage Cl *SLH/COR* SS17 .... 204 B1
Nottingham Wy *VGE* SS16 .... 166 A8
Nounsley Rd *RCHLM* CM3 .... 38 B4
Nunns Wy *GRAYS* RM17 .... 214 B4
Nunsbury Dr *BROX* EN10 .... 48 E2
Nursery Cl *PEND* EN3 .... 104 D5
RAYL SS6 .... 171 J4
SOCK/AV RM15 .... 200 A4
WFD IG8 .... 133 J8
Nursery Flds *SBW* CM21 .... 11 J3
Nursery Gdns *LAIN* SS15 .... 6 A2
PEND EN3 .... 104 D5
Nursery La *RCHLM* CM3 .... 65 K5
Nursery Rd *BROX* EN10 .... 48 E2
BRWN CM15 .... 86 A8
CHLM/GWD CM2 .... 4 C5
LOU IG10 .... 107 F8
SLH/COR SS17 .... 203 K2
WAB EN9 .... 49 K4
The Nursery *ERITH* DA8 .... 210 A6
Nutberry Av *CDH/CHF* RM16 .. 213 K1
Nutberry Cl *CDH/CHF* RM16 .. 213 K1
Nutcombe Crs *RCFD* SS4 ...... 174 A1
Nuthatch Cl *BCAYE* CM11 ..... 144 D5
Nyth Cl *UPMR* RM14 .... 162 A8

O

Oak Av *BCAYE* CM11 .... 167 K1
UPMR RM14 .... 181 J4
WICKE SS11 .... 148 B6
Oakbank *RBRW/HUT* CM13 ... 142 D1
Oak Cha *WICKW* SS12 .... 146 D6
Oak Cl *MAL* CM9 .... 68 D5
WAB EN9 .... 77 K8
Oakdale Gdns *CHING* E4 .... 132 D8
Oakdene *CHES/WCR* EN8 .... 76 E4
Oak Dene Cl *ROM* RM1 .... 160 C8
Oakdene Rd *PIT* SS13 .... 168 E5
Oak Dr *SBW* CM21 .... 11 G5
Oak End *HLWS* CM18 .... 3 F5
Oaken Grange Dr *SOSN* SS2 ... 174 B8
Oak Farm Rd *MAL* CM9 .... 66 D3
Oakfield *CHING* E4 .... 132 C8
Oakfield Cl *SBF/HAD* SS7 ...... 190 B2
Oakfield Rd *HOC/HUL* SS5 ..... 151 H5
SBF/HAD SS7 .... 190 B2
Oak Gld *EPP* CM16 .... 81 H3
Oak Gln *EMPK* RM11 .... 161 F5
Oakham Cl *VGE* SS16 .... 166 A8
Oak Hill Rd *ABR/ST* RM4 .... 137 J3
Oakhill Rd *PUR* RM19 .... 211 J4
Oakhurst Cl *WICKW* SS12 ..... 147 F8
Oakhurst Dr *WICKW* SS12 ..... 146 E7
Oakhurst Gdns *CHING* E4 ...... 133 G4
Oakhurst Rd *PEND* EN3 .... 104 D2
RAYL SS6 .... 172 A5
SOSN SS2 .... 9 D2
Oakland Gdns *RBRW/HUT* CM13 142 B1
Oakland Pl *BKHH* IG9 .... 133 H5
Oaklands Crs *CHLM/GWD* CM2 . 4 C5
Oaklands Dr *HLWE* CM17 .... 25 G6
SOCK/AV RM15 .... 200 A5
Oaklands Gv *BROX* EN10 .... 48 E6
Oaklands Ms *RCFD* SS4 .... 173 K1
Oaklands Wy *RCHLM* CM3 ..... 65 J5
Oak La *BCAYE* CM11 .... 167 K2
WFD IG8 .... 133 G7
Oaklea Av *CHLM/GWD* CM2 ..... 5 F1
Oakleigh Av *HOC/HUL* SS5 .... 149 K3
SOS SS1 .... 195 G5
Oakleigh Park Dr *LOS* SS9 .... 193 F4
Oakleighs *SBF/HAD* SS7 .... 190 B1
Oakley Av *RAYL* SS6 .... 170 E2
Oakley Cl *CHING* E4 .... 132 D6
WTHK RM20 .... 213 F5
Oakley Dr *BCAYW* CM12 .... 117 F8
HARH RM3 .... 139 H8
Oak Lodge Av *CHIG* IG7 .... 135 G8
Oak Lodge Tye *CHLM/WR* CM1 . 35 J7
Oakmoor Wy *CHIG* IG7 .... 135 H8
Oak Piece *EPP* CM16 .... 54 C7
Oak Ri *BKHH* IG9 .... 134 A6
Oak Rd *BCAYE* CM11 .... 119 F8
BCAYE CM11 .... 167 K1
CVI SS8 .... 208 C2
EPP CM16 .... 80 D4
ERITH DA8 .... 210 B7
GRAYS RM17 .... 214 B5
GVE DA12 .... 219 G8
HARH RM3 .... 140 D7
MAL CM9 .... 40 D7
RCFD SS4 .... 174 A3
Oak Rd North *SBF/HAD* SS7 .. 191 K3
Oak Rd South *SBF/HAD* SS7 .. 191 K3
Oaks Gv *CHING* E4 .... 133 F5
The Oaks *BCAYE* CM11 .... 144 D7
Oak Tree Cl *LOU* IG10 .... 108 A5
Oaktree Cl *RBRW/HUT* CM13 . 141 J6
Oakview Cl *CHESW* EN7 .... 76 C1
Oak Wk *HOC/HUL* SS5 .... 151 F6
SBF/HAD SS7 .... 170 A5
Oakway *CDH/CHF* RM16 .... 201 F8
Oakwood Av *LOS* SS9 .... 193 H1
RBRW/HUT CM13 .... 142 D2
Oakwood Cha *EMPK* RM11 .... 181 G1
Oakwood Cl *SBF/HAD* SS7 .... 170 A8
Oakwood Cl *RCHLM* CM3 ...... 126 E2
Oakwood Dr *BCAYW* CM12 .... 117 J8
Oakwood Gv *PIT* SS13 .... 168 E7
Oakwood Hl *LOU* IG10 .... 134 D2
Oakwood Hill Industrial Est
LOU IG10 .... 134 E1
Oakwood Rd *RAYL* SS6 .... 171 H1
SLH/COR SS17 .... 204 D1
Oast Wy *RCFD* SS4 .... 174 C3
Oates Rd *CRW* RM5 .... 137 G8
Oatlands Rd *PEND* EN3 .... 104 C5
Oban Ct *WICKE* SS11 .... 148 A8
Oban Rd *SOSN* SS2 .... 9 F3
Ockelford Av *CHLM/WR* CM1 .. 34 B8
Ockendon Rd *UPMR* RM14 .... 182 A7
Odessa Rd *CVI* SS8 .... 208 C2
Ogilvie Cl *WICKW* SS12 .... 147 H8
Okehampton Sq *HARH* RM3 ... 160 D1
Old Barn La *RCHLM* CM3 .... 120 D4
Old Barns La *ING* CM4 .... 59 F7
Old Bell La *RCHLM* CM3 .... 121 F4
Oldbury Rd *CHLM/GWD* CM2 .. 63 H6

Oldbury Rd *EN* EN1 .... 104 A6
Old Church Hl *VGE* SS16 .... 186 A4
Old Church La *RBRW/HUT* CM13 .... 115 J8
Old Church Rd *CHING* E4 .... 132 B6
  PIT SS13 .... 169 J8
  RBRW/HUT CM13 .... 115 K6
  RCHLM CM3 .... 93 F8
Old Ct *CHLM/WR* CM1 .... 5 E2
Old Crown La *BRW* CM14 .... 113 F6
Old Forge Rd *RCHLM* CM3 .... 36 C5
Old Hall La *MAL* CM9 .... 44 C1
Old Hall Ri *HLWE* CM17 .... 25 J5
Old Heath Rd *BOC* CM0 .... 128 A3
Old Hill Av *VGE* SS16 .... 186 C5
Oldhouse Cft *HLW* CM20 .... 3 E1
Old House La *RBRW/HUT* CM19 .... 23 F8
Old Jenkins Cl *SLH/COR* SS17 .... 203 H4 🔢
Old Leigh Rd *LOS* SS9 .... 193 H4
Old London Rd *MAL* CM9 .... 66 D5
  WICKE SS11 .... 148 C2
Old Md *LOS* SS9 .... 173 H6
Old Nazeing Rd *BROX* EN10 .... 49 G3
  WAB EN9 .... 49 J4
Old Oaks *WAB* EN9 .... 78 A6 🔢
Old Orch *HLWS* CM18 .... 3 C5
Old Perry St *GVW* DA11 .... 218 D7
Old Rd *ABR/ST* RM4 .... 111 K6
  HLWE CM17 .... 11 G7
  PEND EN3 .... 104 C5
Old Rd East *GVE* DA12 .... 219 J6
Old Rd West *GVE* DA12 .... 218 E6
Old School Cr *RCHLM* CM3 .... 38 B2 🔢
Old School Fld *CHLM/WR* CM1 ...... 5 F1
Old School Meadow *SBN/FI* SS3 .. 196 D1
Old Ship La *RCFD* SS4 .... 174 C3 🔢
Old Shire La *WAB* EN9 .... 78 C8
Old Southend Rd *CHLM/GWD* CM2 .. 92 B4
  SOS SS1 .... 9 E5
Old Station Rd *LOU* IG10 .... 134 B3
Old Vicarage Cl *CHLM/WR* CM1 .... 17 G3
Old Wickford Rd *RCHLM* CM3 .... 122 B5
Oldwyk *VGE* SS16 .... 188 B1
Olive Av *LOS* SS9 .... 192 B3
Oliver Cl *WTHK* RM20 .... 212 C6
Oliver Rd *BRWN* CM15 .... 141 K1
  WTHK RM20 .... 212 C7
Olivers Crs *SBN/FI* SS3 .... 197 F1
Oliver Wy *CHLM/WR* CM1 .... 34 B6
Olivia Dr *LOS* SS9 .... 193 G3
Ollard's Gv *LOU* IG10 .... 107 F8
One Tree Hl *SLH/COR* SS17 .... 187 G4
Ongark Rd *CHLM/WR* CM1 .... 61 H4 🔢
Ongar Pl *BRW* CM14 .... 141 G5
Ongar Rd *ABR/ST* RM4 .... 109 G6
  BRWN CM15 .... 141 J4
  CHLM/WR CM1 .... 59 K6
  CHONG CM5 .... 56 D6
  GTDUN CM6 .... 30 B3
Onslow Cl *CHING* E4 .... 132 B2
Onslow Gdns *CHONG* CM5 .... 84 C1
Orange Rd *LOS* SS9 .... 208 D1
Orange Tree Cl *CHLM/GWD* CM2 .. 62 E2
Orange Tree Hl *ROM* RM1 .... 137 J8
Orchard Av *BCAYE* CM11 .... 146 A3
  BCAYE CM11 .... 117 J8
  HOC/HUL SS5 .... 151 F6
  RAYL SS6 .... 171 H5
  RBRW/HUT CM13 .... 141 J6
Orchard Cl *CHING* E4 .... 132 B7
  CHLM/GWD CM2 .... 62 E7
  CHLM/WR CM1 .... 5 F1
  HOC/HUL SS5 .... 151 G6 🔢
  MAL CM9 .... 44 E4
  MAL CM9 .... 68 B3
  RBSF CM22 .... 12 C5
  RCHLM CM3 .... 93 H5
  SBN/FI SS3 .... 197 F1
  SOCK/AV RM15 .... 200 A4
Orchard Side *LOS* SS9 .... 173 G7
Orchard Sq *BROX* EN10 .... 49 F6 🔢
The Orchards *EPP* CM16 .... 80 E6
  SBW CM21 .... 11 J3 🔢
Orchard St *CHLM/GWD* CM2 .... 4 C4
The Orchard *WICKW* SS12 .... 146 E6
Orchard Wy *CHIC* IG7 .... 135 K6
Orchill Dr *SBF/HAD* SS7 .... 191 K1

Orchis Gv *GRAYS* RM17 .... 213 J3
Orchis Wy *HARH* RM3 .... 161 G1
Ordnance Rd *GVE* DA12 .... 219 H4
Orford Crs *CHLM/WR* CM1 .... 34 E8
Orlando Dr *PIT* SS13 .... 169 F4 🔢
Ormesby Chine *RCHLM* CM3 .... 122 D8
Ormonde Av *RCFD* SS4 .... 174 B2 🔢
  SBF/HAD SS7 .... 192 B5
Ormonde Gdns *LOS* SS9 .... 192 B3
Ormonde Ri *BKHH* IG9 .... 133 K4
Ormonds Crs *RCHLM* CM3 .... 122 B1
Ormsby Rd *CVI* SS8 .... 207 H3
Ormo Rd *CVI* SS8 .... 209 F2
Orrett Av *LOS* SS9 .... 172 D8
Orsett End *BSDN* SS14 .... 167 K6
Orsett Heath Crs *CHLM/CHF* RM16 .. 215 F2
Orsett Rd *CDH/CHF* RM16 .... 202 D4
  GRAYS RM17 .... 214 A4
Orton Cl *ING* CM4 .... 89 C5
Orwell St *WICKE* SS11 .... 148 A8
Osborne Cl *EMPK* RM11 .... 160 C8 🔢
  BKHH IG9 .... 133 J4
  BROX EN10 .... 49 C1
  BRWN CM15 .... 140 E2
  EMPK RM11 .... 160 C8
  PEND EN3 .... 104 E6
  PIT SS13 .... 169 H5
  WOS/PRIT SS0 .... 8 B5
Osbourne Av *HOC/HUL* SS5 .... 150 D7
Osea Rd *MAL* CM9 .... 69 K2
Osea Wy *CHLM/WR* CM1 .... 35 H8
Osprey Cl *SBN/FI* SS3 .... 196 D4 🔢
Osprey Rd *WAB* EN9 .... 78 C8
Osprey Wy *CHLM/GWD* CM2 ...... 62 C8 🔢
Osterley Dr *VGE* SS16 .... 166 A8 🔢
Osterley Pl *RCHLM* CM3 .... 122 D8
Ottawa Rd *TIL* RM18 .... 215 F8
Otterbourne Rd *CHING* E4 .... 132 E6 🔢
Ouida Rd *CVI* SS8 .... 208 D2
Ousden Cl *CHES/WCR* EN8 .... 76 E4
Ousden Dr *CHES/WCR* EN8 .... 76 E4
Outing Cl *SOS* SS1 .... 9 F5
Outing's La *BRWN* CM15 .... 113 K2
Outwood Common Rd
  BCAYE CM11 .... 144 D6
Outwood Farm Cl *BCAYE* CM11 .. 145 F3
Outwood Farm Rd *BCAYE* CM11 .. 145 F5
Oval Gdns *GRAYS* RM17 .... 214 B2
The Oval *BROX* EN10 .... 48 E7
Overcliffe *GVW* DA11 .... 219 F4
Overcliff Rd *GRAYS* RM17 .... 214 C4
Overlord Cl *BROX* EN10 .... 48 E2 🔢
Overmead Dr *RCHLM* CM3 .... 93 J1
Overshot Br *RCHLM* CM3 .... 122 E5
Overton Cl *SBF/HAD* SS7 .... 170 B7
Overton Dr *SBF/HAD* SS7 .... 170 B7
Overton Rd *SBF/HAD* SS7 .... 170 A6 🔢
Overton Wy *SBF/HAD* SS7 .... 170 A7
Ovington Gdns *BCAYW* CM12 ...... 117 G8
Owlets Hall La *HARH* RM3 .... 161 G5 🔢
Oxford Av *CDH/CHF* RM16 .... 215 F3
  EMPK RM11 .... 161 H6
Oxford Cl *CHES/WCR* EN8 .... 76 C3
  VGE SS16 .... 166 A8 🔢
Oxford Ct *BRW* CM14 .... 141 J6 🔢
  CHLM/GWD CM2 .... 5 F1 🔢
  HARH RM3 .... 161 G1
  RCFD SS4 .... 174 B1
  SLH/COR SS17 .... 202 E1
  SLH/COR SS17 .... 203 H5
  WFD IG8 .... 134 A3
Oxley Cl *GPK* RM2 .... 160 D4 🔢
Oxley Gdns *SLH/COR* SS17 .... 203 K1
Oxleys Rd *WAB* EN9 .... 78 C1
The Oxleys *HLWE* CM17 .... 25 H1
Oxney Md *CHLM/WR* CM1 .... 61 F5
Oxwich Cl *SLH/COR* SS17 .... 204 C1
Oyster Pl *CHLM/GWD* CM2 .... 63 H1
Ozonia Av *WICKW* SS12 .... 147 F8
Ozonia Cl *WICKW* SS12 .... 146 E8
Ozonia Wy *WICKW* SS12 .... 147 F8

P

Paarl Rd *CVI* SS8 .... 208 A1
Packham Rd *GVW* DA11 .... 218 E8
Paddock Cl *BCAYE* CM11 .... 144 D6 🔢
  CDH/CHF RM16 .... 202 B5 🔢
  LOS SS9 .... 173 F6
Paddock Dr *CHLM/WR* CM1 .... 35 C6
Paddock Md *HLWS* CM18 .... 52 A2
The Paddocks *ABR/ST* RM4 .... 138 A2
  CDH/CHF RM16 .... 202 B5 🔢
  ING CM4 .... 116 B2
  MAL CM9 .... 40 C1 🔢
  RAYL SS6 .... 172 A3
The Paddock *BROX* EN10 .... 49 G2
  ING CM4 .... 118 A3

Padgetts Wy *HOC/HUL* SS5 149
Padham's Green Rd *ING* CM4 ...... 116 C
Pageant Cl *TIL* RM18 .... 215 H
Page Crs *ERITH* DA8 .... 210 A
Page Rd *PIT* SS13 .... 169 J
Pages La *MAL* CM9 .... 43 K
Paget Dr *BCAYW* CM12 .... 117 C
Pagette Wy *GRAYS* RM17 .... 213 K
Paglesfield *RBRW/HUT* CM13 ..... 142 B2
Paglesham Rd *RCFD* SS4 .... 153 J
Paignton Av *CHLM/WR* CM1 .... 35 F
Paignton Cl *RAYL* SS6 .... 149 J8
Paines Brook Wy *HARH* RM3 ..... 161 G
Painswick Av *SLH/COR* SS17 ..... 187 G
Painters Ash La *GVW* DA11 .... 218 C
Painters La *PEND* EN3 .... 104 E
Pakes Wy *EPP* CM16 .... 108 C
Palace Gdns *BKHH* IG9 .... 134 A
Palace Gv *LAIN* SS15 .... 6 C2
Palace View Rd *CHING* E4 .... 132 C
Palatine Pk *LAIN* SS15 .... 166 A7
Paley Gdns *LOU* IG10 .... 107 K
Palins Wy *CDH/CHF* RM16 .... 200 E
Pall Ml *LOS* SS9 .... 193 H
Palm Cl *CHLM/GWD* CM2 .... 62 E
Palmeira Av *WOS/PRIT* SS0 .... 8 A
Palmer Cl *LAIN* SS15 .... 6 B4
Palmers *SLH/COR* SS17 .... 204 B2
Palmer's Av *GRAYS* RM17 .... 214 B
Palmers Cft *CHLM/GWD* CM2 ...... 63 J3
Palmers Dr *GRAYS* RM17 .... 214 B
Palmers Gv *WAB* EN9 .... 50 B
Palmers Hl *EPP* CM16 .... 80 E
Palmers La *PEND* EN3 .... 104 C
Palmerstone Rd *CVI* SS8 .... 207 H2
Palmerston Gdns *WTHK* RM20 ... 213 G
Palmerston Ldg *CHLM/GWD* CM2 .. 63 H
Palmerston Rd *BKHH* IG9 .... 133 K
  WOS/PRIT SS0 .... 8 A
  WTHK RM20 .... 213 C
Palmers Wy *CHES/WCR* EN8 ...... 76 E
Palm Ms *LAIN* SS15 .... 6 E
Panadown *LAIN* SS15 .... 7 C
Pancroft *ABR/ST* RM4 .... 109 F
Panfields *LAIN* SS15 .... 166 B
Pan La *RCHLM* CM3 .... 92 E
Pantile Av *SOSN* SS2 .... 9 F
Pantile Hl *BOC* CM0 .... 128 C
Papenburg Rd *CVI* SS8 .... 191 F
Paper Mill Br *RCHLM* CM3 .... 37 H
Paprilis *VGE* SS16 .... 66 B
Paradise Cl *CHESW* EN7 .... 76 C
Paradise Rd *CHLM/WR* CM1 .... 61 H
  WAB EN9 .... 77 J8
Pargat Dr *LOS* SS9 .... 172 D
Pargetters Hyam *HOC/HUL* SS5 .. 151 C7
Paringdon Rd *HLWW/ROY* CM19 .. 51 K
Parish Cl *HCH* RM12 .... 180 C3
Parish Wy *LAIN* SS15 .... 6 A
Parkanaur Av *SOS* SS1 .... 196 A
Park Av *CHLM/WR* CM1 .... 4 A
  CVI SS8 .... 209 F
  GVE DA12 .... 219 H
  GVW DA11 .... 218 D
  HLWE CM17 .... 25 C
  LOS SS9 .... 173 F
  RBRW/HUT CM13 .... 142 B
  UPMR RM14 .... 182 B
  WFD IG8 .... 133 J
  WTHK RM20 .... 212 D
Park Bvd *GPK* RM2 .... 160 A
Park Cha *SBF/HAD* SS7 .... 191 K
Park Cl *EPP* CM16 .... 82 A
  WICKW SS12 .... 147 F7
Park Ct *HLW* CM20 .... 3 D
Park Crs *EMPK* RM11 .... 180 B
  WOS/PRIT SS0 .... 8 C
Parkdale *RCHLM* CM3 .... 65 C
Park Dr *ING* CM4 .... 116 C
  MAL CM9 .... 68 D
  RBSF CM22 .... 13 H
  UPMR RM14 .... 181 K
  WICKW SS12 .... 147 C
Parker Av *TIL* RM18 .... 215 F
Parker Rd *CHLM/GWD* CM2 .... 5 C
  GRAYS RM17 .... 213 C
Parker's Farm Rd *UPMR* RM14 ... 184 C5
Parkes Rd *CHIG* IG7 .... 135 J
Park Farm Rd *UPMR* RM14 .... 181 C
Park Flds *HLWW/ROY* CM19 .... 22 D
Parkfields *SBF/HAD* SS7 .... 191 H
Park Gdns *HOC/HUL* SS5 .... 151 C
Park Gate Rd *SLH/COR* SS17 ..... 187 H
Park Hl *HLWE* CM17 .... 25 F
  LOU IG10 .... 134 A
Parkhill Cl *HCH* RM12 .... 180 D
Parkhill Rd *CHING* E4 .... 132 D
Parkhurst Dr *RAYL* SS6 .... 188 D
Parkhurst Rd *PIT* SS13 .... 169 H
Parkland Av *UPMR* RM14 .... 181 J
Parklands *BCAYE* CM11 .... 144 C2
  CHIG IG7 .... 135 F
  CVI SS8 .... 191 F8
  RCFD SS4 .... 174 A
  WAB EN9 78

arklands Av *RAYL* SS6 .... 171 K3
arklands Dr *CHLM/WR* CM1 .... 5 E2 🔲
ark La *CHES/WCR* EN8 .... 76 D7
  BCAYE CM11 .... 145 K1
  BROX EN10 .... 48 E1
  CVI SS8 .... 209 F2
  CHESW EN7 .... 76 A1
  EMPK RM11 .... 180 B1
  HLW CM20 .... 3 D1
  RAIN RM13 .... 180 C7
  RBRW/HUT CM13 .... 164 C2
  RCHLM CM3 .... 19 F1
  SOCK/AV RM15 .... 199 F8
  SOS SS1 .... 9 F4
  WOS/PRIT SS0 .... 8 C5
ark Lane Paradise *BROX* EN10 .... 48 A6
ark Md *HLW* CM20 .... 2 B2
arkmead *LOU* IG10 .... 134 D1
ark Meadow *BRWN* CM15 .... 114 B4
arknmill Ct *SLH/COR* SS17 .... 204 C1
ark Pl *GVE* DA12 .... 219 H6
ark Rd *CHES/WCR* EN8 .... 76 D7 🔲
  BOC CM0 .... 155 C1
  BRW CM14 .... 140 E4
  CHLM/GWD CM2 .... 4 C3
  CVI SS8 .... 209 F3
  GVW DA11 .... 219 C7
  LOS SS9 .... 192 C4
  MAL CM9 .... 68 B4
  PEND EN3 .... 104 E2
  SBF/HAD SS7 .... 170 E7
  SLH/COR SS17 .... 203 H4
  SLH/COR SS17 .... 204 C2
  UPMR RM14 .... 181 H5 🔲
  WOS/PRIT SS0 .... 8 C4
ark Side *BCAYE* CM11 .... 144 D3 🔲
  BKHH IG9 .... 133 J5
  PIT SS13 .... 168 D6
  WOS/PRIT SS0 .... 193 H4
arkside *CHES/WCR* EN8 .... 76 E8
  CDH/CHF RM16 .... 214 C2
arkside Av *TIL* RM18 .... 215 G8
arkstone Av *EMPK* RM11 .... 161 F8
  SBF/HAD SS7 .... 191 G1
  WICKW SS12 .... 146 C5
arkstone Dr *SOSN* SS2 .... 8 B1
ark St *WOS/PRIT* SS0 .... 8 C4
ark Ter *WOS/PRIT* SS0 .... 8 C4
ark Vw *SOCK/AV* RM15 .... 199 F8
ark View Crs *CHLM/GWD* CM2 .... 63 H8
ark View Dr *LOS* SS9 .... 172 C8
ark View Gdns *GRAYS* RM17 .... 214 A4 🔲
ark Wy *BRWN* CM15 .... 141 J4
arkway *CDH/CHF* RM16 .... 202 A5
  CHLM/WR CM1 .... 4 B2
  GPK RM2 .... 160 A4
  HLWW/ROY CM19 .... 23 C5
  RAYL SS6 .... 171 K5
  SBW CM21 .... 11 J4
  SLH/COR SS17 .... 187 K8
  WFD IG8 .... 133 K8 🔲
arkway Cl *SOSN* SS9 .... 173 G6
ne Parkway *CVI* SS8 .... 208 B3
arkwood Cl *HOD* EN11 .... 48 E1
ark Wood La *HLW* CM20 .... 3 J2
arnall Rd *HLW* CM20 .... 52 B1
arndon Mill La *HLW* CM20 .... 23 K2
arndon Wood Rd
  HLWW/ROY CM19 .... 52 A2
arrock Av *GVE* DA12 .... 219 H6
arrock Rd *GVE* DA12 .... 219 H5
arrock St *GVE* DA12 .... 219 G4 🔲
arry Cl *SLH/COR* SS17 .... 203 K2
arsloe Rd *EPP* CM16 .... 51 J3
arsonage Cha *MAL* CM9 .... 97 F5
arsonage Cl *CHLM/WR* CM1 .... 34 C4 🔲
arsonage Fld *BRWN* CM15 .... 114 B3
arsonage La *ING* CM4 .... 89 G6
  LAIN SS15 .... 6 A4
  RCHLM CM3 .... 20 C3 🔲
  RCHLM CM3 .... 65 H3
arsonage Leys *HLW* CM20 .... 3 F3
arsonage Rd *WTHK* RM20 .... 213 F5 🔲
arsons Lawn *SBN/FI* SS3 .... 196 C4
arsons Rd *SBF/HAD* SS7 .... 170 C6
artridge Av *CHLM/WR* CM1 .... 34 B7
artridge Ct *HLWS* CM18 .... 3 E5
artridge Rd *HLWS* CM18 .... 3 D5
arvills *HLW* CM20 .... 77 K6
aschal Wy *CHLM/GWD* CM2 .... 5 F5
asfield *WAB* EN9 .... 77 K7 🔲
aslowes *VGE* SS16 .... 188 C1
assingham Av *BCAYE* CM11 .... 144 D7
assingham Cl *BCAYE* CM11 .... 144 D6 🔲
asteur Dr *HARH* RM3 .... 160 E4
aston Cl *RCHLM* CM3 .... 122 C4
asture High *RCHLM* CM3 .... 65 H2
aternoster St *WAB* EN9 .... 78 B7
aternoster Rw *WAB* EN9 .... 78 B6
aternoster Rw *MAR/ST* RM4 .... 138 C7
athways *BSDN* SS14 .... 168 B8 🔲
atmore Rd *WAB* EN9 .... 78 A8 🔲
atmore Wy *CRW* RM5 .... 137 G8

Patricia Dr *EMPK* RM11 .... 181 F2
  SLH/COR SS17 .... 187 K7
Patricia Gdns *BCAYE* CM11 .... 144 E6 🔲
Patterdale *SBF/HAD* SS7 .... 170 A6
Pattiswick Cnr *BSDN* SS14 .... 168 B6 🔲
Pattiswick Sq *BSDN* SS14 .... 168 B6
Pattocks *BSDN* SS14 .... 168 B6
Pauline Gdns *BCAYW* CM12 .... 144 A7 🔲
Paul's Rd *LAIN* SS15 .... 6 A2
Pavilion Dr *SOSN* SS2 .... 195 H4 🔲
Pavilion Dr *LOS* SS9 .... 193 G3
The Pavilions *EPP* CM16 .... 54 C7
Pavillion Pl *BCAYW* CM12 .... 144 A1 🔲
Pavitt Meadow *CHLM/GWD* CM2 .... 60 E3
Pawle Cl *CHLM/GWD* CM2 .... 63 J6
Paxfords *LAIN* SS15 .... 166 A7 🔲
Paycocke Rd *BSDN* SS14 .... 168 C3
Paycocke Rd *BSDN* SS14 .... 168 B5
Payne Pl *RCHLM* CM3 .... 93 F7
Paynes La *WAB* EN9 .... 49 J6
Paynters Md *VGE* SS16 .... 188 B2
Peach Av *HOC/HUL* SS5 .... 151 F6
Peach Cft *GVW* DA11 .... 218 D8
Peacock Cl *EMPK* RM11 .... 161 F6 🔲
Peacocks *HLWW/ROY* CM19 .... 23 H7
Peacock St *GVE* DA12 .... 219 H5
Pea La *UPMR* RM14 .... 182 D7
Pearce Mnr *CHLM/GWD* CM2 .... 4 A5
Peareswood Rd *ERITH* DA8 .... 210 A7
Pearmain Cl *WICKE* SS11 .... 147 G4
Pearsons *SLH/COR* SS17 .... 204 B2 🔲
Pearsons Av *RAYL* SS6 .... 171 C1
Peartree Cl *BRWN* CM15 .... 114 B4
  MAL CM9 .... 42 C7
  SOCK/AV RM15 .... 200 A2 🔲
  SOSN SS2 .... 9 F1
Peartree La *BRWN* CM15 .... 114 A3
  RCHLM CM3 .... 93 K2
  UPMR RM14 .... 184 E4
Pear Tree Md *HLWS* CM18 .... 24 E7
Peartrees *RBRW/HUT* CM13 .... 164 B1
Pear Trees *SBF/HAD* SS7 .... 190 E1 🔲
Pease Pl *HCH* RM12 .... 180 C1
Pease Pl *RCHLM* CM3 .... 93 F7
Pebmarsh Dr *WICKW* SS12 .... 147 H7
Peck's Hl *WAB* EN9 .... 50 A3
Pedlars Cl *RCHLM* CM3 .... 66 A7
Pedlars End *CHONG* CM5 .... 55 H3
Pedlars Pth *RCHLM* CM3 .... 66 A7
Peel Av *SBN/FI* SS3 .... 197 F6
Peel Cl *CHING* E4 .... 132 C5
Peel Rd *CHLM/GWD* CM2 .... 5 F1
Peel Wy *HARH* RM3 .... 161 F1
Peerage Wy *EMPK* RM11 .... 161 F1
Pegasus Ct *GVE* DA12 .... 219 H8
Pegelm Gdns *EMPK* RM11 .... 181 G1
Peggotty Cl *CHLM/WR* CM1 .... 34 B7
Pegrams Rd *HLWS* CM18 .... 2 C6
Peldon Pavement *BSDN* SS14 .... 168 A5 🔲
Peldon Rd *HLWW/ROY* CM19 .... 2 A5
Pelham Pl *SLH/COR* SS17 .... 204 A1
Pelham Rd *GVW* DA11 .... 218 E5
  SOSN SS2 .... 195 H4
Pelham Rd South *GVW* DA11 .... 218 E6
Pelly Ct *EPP* CM16 .... 80 D5
Pemberton Av *GPK* RM2 .... 160 C5
  ING CM4 .... 116 B1
Pemberton Fld *RCFD* SS4 .... 151 J1
Pembrey Wy *HCH* RM12 .... 180 D7 🔲
Pembroke Av *EN* EN1 .... 104 B5
  MAL CM9 .... 68 B4
  SLH/COR SS17 .... 204 C1
Pembroke Cl *BCAYW* CM12 .... 117 G8 🔲
  BROX EN10 .... 48 E6
  EMPK RM11 .... 161 H6 🔲
Pembroke Ms *PIT* SS13 .... 169 F5 🔲
Pembroke Pl *CHLM/WR* CM1 .... 34 C6
Pembury Rd *WOS/PRIT* SS0 .... 193 K6
Pendle Cl *BSDN* SS14 .... 168 D4
Pendle Dr *BSDN* SS14 .... 168 C4
Pendlestone *SBF/HAD* SS7 .... 191 H1
Pendower *RAYL* SS6 .... 171 C5
Pengelly Cl *CHESW* EN7 .... 76 B1
Penhurst Av *SOSN* SS2 .... 8 C2 🔲
Penhurst Dr *RCHLM* CM3 .... 122 D8 🔲
Penlow Rd *HLWS* CM18 .... 2 C6
Penn Cl *CDH/CHF* RM16 .... 202 B4
Pennial Rd *CVI* SS8 .... 208 A1
Pennine Rd *CHLM/WR* CM1 .... 33 K7
Pennine Wy *GVW* DA11 .... 218 D8
Penny Flds *BRW* CM14 .... 141 F7
Pennymead *HLW* CM20 .... 24 E5
Penny Royal Rd *RCHLM* CM3 .... 65 H7
Penny's La *ING* CM4 .... 89 F5
Penrith Crs *RAIN* RM13 .... 180 B6
Penrith Rd *HARH* RM3 .... 161 H1
Penrose Md *CHLM/WR* CM1 .... 61 H5
Penshurst *HLWE* CM17 .... 25 F2
Penson's La *CHONG* CM5 .... 83 G2
Pentire Cl *UPMR* RM14 .... 162 B8
Pentland Av *CHLM/WR* CM1 .... 34 C7
  SBN/FI SS3 .... 196 B7
Pentlow Wy *BXHH* IG9 .... 134 B3
Pentney Rd *CHING* E4 .... 132 C4 🔲

Penton Dr *CHES/WCR* EN8 .... 76 D3
Pentrich Av *EN* EN1 .... 104 A4
Penzance Cl *CHLM/WR* CM1 .... 35 G8
Penzance Gdns *HARH* RM3 .... 161 H1 🔲
Penzance Rd *HARH* RM3 .... 161 H1
Pepper Hl *GVW* DA11 .... 218 B8
Pepys Cl *GVW* DA11 .... 218 C8
  TIL RM18 .... 215 H7
Percival Rd *EMPK* RM11 .... 160 D8
Percy Cottis Rd *RCFD* SS4 .... 174 B2
Percy Rd *LOS* SS9 .... 192 E3
Percy St *GRAYS* RM17 .... 214 B5
Peregrine Cl *SBN/FI* SS3 .... 196 D4
  VGE SS16 .... 7 F6 🔲
Peregrine Dr *CHLM/GWD* CM2 .... 62 C8
  SBF/HAD SS7 .... 190 B3
Peregrine Gdns *RAYL* SS6 .... 171 G2 🔲
Peregrine Rd *BARK/HLT* IG6 .... 136 A8
Peregrin Rd *WAB* EN9 .... 78 C8
Perram Cl *BROX* EN10 .... 48 E8 🔲
Perriclose *CHLM/WR* CM1 .... 35 F6 🔲
Perriors Cl *CHESW* EN7 .... 76 A1
Perryfield *HLWE* CM17 .... 27 J3
Perry Gn *BSDN* SS14 .... 7 F2
Perry Hl *CHLM/WR* CM1 .... 5 E2
  WAB EN9 .... 50 B5
Perry Rd *HLWS* CM18 .... 2 C6
  SBF/HAD SS7 .... 190 A2
Perrysfield Rd *CHES/WCR* EN8 .... 76 E1
Perry Spring *HLWE* CM17 .... 25 G7
Perry St *BCAYW* CM12 .... 144 A2
  GVW DA11 .... 218 D6
Perry Wy *SOCK/AV* RM15 .... 198 E7
ertwee Dr *CHLM/GWD* CM2 .... 63 H7
  RCHLM CM3 .... 122 C6
Peterborough Av *UPMR* RM14 .... 182 B2
Peterborough Wy *BSDN* SS14 .... 168 C5
Petersfield *CHLM/WR* CM1 .... 34 D7
Petersfield Av *HARH* RM3 .... 161 F1
Petersfield Cl *HARH* RM3 .... 161 H1
Peter St *ING* CM4 .... 118 B4
Peterswood *HLWS* CM18 .... 52 B1
Petrebrook *CHLM/GWD* CM2 .... 63 J2
Petre Cl *ING* CM4 .... 116 A3
  RBRW/HUT CM13 .... 164 B8
Petrel Wy *CHLM/GWD* CM2 .... 62 E7
Petresfield Wy *RBRW/HUT* CM13 .... 164 B8
Pett Cl *HCH* RM12 .... 180 C3
Pettits La *BRWN* CM15 .... 114 C3
Pettys Cl *CHES/WCR* EN8 .... 76 D5
Petunia Crs *CHLM/WR* CM1 .... 34 B7
Petworth Gdns *SOSN* SS2 .... 195 J3
Petworth Wy *HCH* RM12 .... 180 A5
Pevensey Gdns *HOC/HUL* SS5 .... 150 A5
Pevensey Wy *PIT* SS13 .... 168 E7 🔲
Peverel Av *RCHLM* CM3 .... 38 C4
Pewsey Cl *CHING* E4 .... 132 B8 C4
Phelips Rd *EPP* CM16 .... 51 J2
Philbrick Crs West *RAYL* SS6 .... 171 G2
Philip Cl *BRWN* CM15 .... 140 E2
Phillida Rd *HARH* RM3 .... 161 H4
Philmead Rd *SBF/HAD* SS7 .... 190 A3
Philpott Av *SOSN* SS2 .... 195 G3
Phoenix Wy *SBF/HAD* SS7 .... 171 H6
Picasso Wy *SBN/FI* SS3 .... 197 F4
Picketts *CVI* SS8 .... 207 H1
Picketts Av *LOS* SS9 .... 193 F1
Picketts Cl *LOS* SS9 .... 193 F1
Pick Hl *WAB* EN9 .... 78 D6
Pickwick Av *CHLM/WR* CM1 .... 33 K7
Pickwick Cl *LAIN* SS15 .... 6 B3 🔲
Pickwick Gdns *GVW* DA11 .... 218 C8
Picton Cl *RAYL* SS6 .... 171 K4
Picton Gdns *RAYL* SS6 .... 171 J4
Piercing Hl *EPP* CM16 .... 108 B1
Piercys *PIT* SS13 .... 168 D8
Pier Hl *SOS* SS1 .... 9 D5
Pier Rd *GVW* DA11 .... 218 E4
Pigstye Green Rd *CHONG* CM5 .... 58 D5
Pike La *UPMR* RM14 .... 182 C6
Pike Wy *EPP* CM16 .... 82 A1
Pilgrims Cl *BCAYE* CM11 .... 144 C3 🔲
  BRWN CM15 .... 140 C1
  SOS SS1 .... 195 H4
Pilgrim's La *BRW* CM14 .... 113 G8
  CDH/CHF RM16 .... 200 A8
Pilgrims Wy *SBF/HAD* SS7 .... 192 A2 🔲
Pilgrim Wy *LAIN* SS15 .... 6 A4
Pilkingtons *HLWE* CM17 .... 25 H5
Pilots Pl *GVE* DA12 .... 219 H4
Pinceybrook Rd *HLWS* CM18 .... 52 A1
Pine Av *GVE* DA12 .... 219 J6
Pine Cl *CHES/WCR* EN8 .... 76 C2
  CVI SS8 .... 207 J2
  LOS SS9 .... 172 C8
Pine Ct *UPMR* RM14 .... 181 H5
Pine Crs *RBRW/HUT* CM13 .... 142 C1
Pinecroft *GPK* RM2 .... 160 D6
  RBRW/HUT CM13 .... 142 A3
Pine Dr *ING* CM4 .... 116 C1
Pine Rd *SBF/HAD* SS7 .... 191 J3
Pines Av *EN* EN1 .... 104 C2
Pines Rd *CHLM/WR* CM1 .... 33 K8
The Pines *CDH/CHF* RM16 .... 201 F8 🔲
  LAIN SS15 .... 6 A1

yrles La *LOU* IG10 .... 107 K6
ytt Fld *HLWE* CM17 .... 25 F6

Q

he Quadrant *PUR* RM19 .... 211 K3
uaker La *WAB* EN9 .... 77 J3
uale Rd *CHLM/GWD* CM2 .... 63 K1
uarry La *GRAYS* RM17 .... 213 K4
uarry Ms *PUR* RM19 .... 211 H3
uarry Springs *HLW* CM20 .... 24 E5
uarry Wy *WTHK* RM20 .... 212 C5
uarter Ga *RCHLM* CM3 .... 122 E8
he Quay *BOC* CM0 .... 155 H1
uebec Av *SOS* SS1 .... 9 D4
uebec Cl *SOS* SS1 .... 9 E4
uebec Rd *TIL* RM18 .... 215 F8
ueen Anne's Dr *WOS/PRIT* SS0 .... 193 K3
ueen Anns Gv *HOC/HUL* SS5 ...... 149 J5
ueen Mary Av *TIL* RM18 .... 216 D3
ueen Mary Cl *ROM* RM1 .... 160 A8
ueen's Av *LOS* SS9 .... 193 F4
  MAL CM9 .... 68 C4
  WFD IG8 .... 133 J8
ueen's Cl *SBW* CM21 .... 11 K1
ueen's Dr *CHES/WCR* EN8 .... 77 G8
ueens Gdns *UPMR* RM14 .... 162 C3
ueen's Gate Ms *BCAYW* CM12 .... 117 F8
ueens Grove Rd *CHING* E4 .... 132 E4
ueensland Av *RCFD* SS4 .... 174 C6
ueensland Crs *CHLM/WR* CM1 ..... 33 K8
ueensmere *SBF/HAD* SS7 .... 171 G8
ueens Park Av *BCAYW* CM12 ..... 117 E8
ueens Park Rd *HARH* RM3 .... 161 G3
ueen's Wy *CHES/WCR* EN8 .... 76 E3
  BCAYE CM11 .... 167 J1
  BKHH IG9 .... 133 J5
  BOC CM0 .... 128 B8
  BRW CM14 .... 141 F6
  CHLM/GWD CM2 .... 5 E3
  EPP CM16 .... 54 C7
  GVE DA12 .... 219 H8
  LAIN SS15 .... 142 C6
  LOS SS9 .... 193 F5
  LOU IG10 .... 107 H7
  RAYL SS6 .... 171 J4
  SBF/HAD SS7 .... 190 C3
  WOS/PRIT SS0 .... 8 C4
ueen St *BOC* CM0 .... 128 B1
  BRW CM14 .... 141 F8
  CHLM/GWD CM2 .... 4 B4
  CHONG CM5 .... 57 G3
  GVE DA12 .... 219 G4
  MAL CM9 .... 68 C3
ueens Wy *CHING* E4 .... 132 C2
uendon Dr *WAB* EN9 .... 77 K7
uennell Wy *RBRW/HUT* CM13 .... 142 B3
uilp Dr *CHLM/WR* CM1 .... 34 B6
uilters Cl *BSDN* SS14 .... 168 A5
uilters Dr *BCAYW* CM12 .... 144 A5
uilters Straight *BSDN* SS14 .... 168 A5
uince Tree Cl *SOCK/AV* RM15 .... 200 A4
uinion Cl *CHLM/WR* CM1 .... 33 K6
uinton Wy *WAB* EN9 .... 105 J1
uorn Gdns *LOS* SS9 .... 192 B4
he Quorn *CHLM* CM4 .... 116 A3

R

achael Clarke Cl
  SLH/COR SS17 .... 204 A1
ackenford *SBN/FI* SS3 .... 196 C5
adburn Cl *HLWS* CM18 .... 52 E1
adford Ct *BCAYW* CM12 .... 144 C2
adford Crs *BCAYW* CM12 .... 144 B2
adford Wy *BCAYW* CM12 .... 144 B3
adley Green Rd *ING* CM4 .... 59 C7
adstocks *BCAYW* CM12 .... 144 C4
adwinter Av *WICKW* SS12 .... 147 G8
aglan Av *CHES/WCR* EN8 .... 76 D1
ahn Rd *EPP* CM16 .... 80 E5
ailway Ap *LAIN* SS15 .... 166 B7
ailway Pl *GVE* DA12 .... 219 G4
ailway Rd *CHES/WCR* EN8 .... 77 F7
ailway Sq *CHLM/WR* CM1 .... 4 B2
ailway St *CHLM/WR* CM1 .... 4 B2
ailway Ter *SOSN* SS2 .... 9 D1

Rainbow Av *CVI* SS8 .... 208 C1
Rainbow La *SLH/COR* SS17 .... 204 B4
Rainbow Ms *MAL* CM9 .... 40 B8
Rainbow Rd *CDH/CHF* RM16 .... 213 G5
  CVI SS8 .... 208 C1
  HLWE CM17 .... 26 E2
Rainer Cl *CHES/WCR* EN8 .... 76 D3
Rainham Rd *RAIN* RM13 .... 180 A8
Rainsford Av *CHLM/WR* CM1 .... 4 A2
Rainsford Rd *CHLM/WR* CM1 .... 4 A2
Rainsford Wy *HCH* RM12 .... 180 A3
Raleigh Cl *ERITH* DA8 .... 210 A5
Raligh Dr *LAIN* SS15 .... 6 B5
Ramblers Wy *BOC* CM0 .... 155 J1
Ram Gorse *HLW* CM20 .... 2 B1
Ramney Dr *PEND* EN3 .... 104 E2
The Ramparts *RAYL* SS6 .... 171 K3
Rampart St *SBN/FI* SS3 .... 196 E7
Rampart Ter *SBN/FI* SS3 .... 197 F7
Rampton Cl *CHING* E4 .... 132 B6
Ramsay Cl *BROX* EN10 .... 48 E3
Ramsay Dr *VGE* SS16 .... 188 B2
Ramsay Gdns *GPK* RM2 .... 160 C3
Ramsden Park Rd *BCAYE* CM11 .. 145 K4
Ramsden View Rd *WICKW* SS12 .. 146 C7
Ramsey Cha *RCHLM* CM3 .... 97 J7
  WICKW SS12 .... 147 J8
Ramsey Cl *MAL* CM9 .... 69 F1
Ramshaw Dr *CHLM/GWD* CM2 .... 63 H2
Ramuz Dr *WOS/PRIT* SS0 .... 8 A2
Randall Dr *HCH* RM12 .... 180 D5
Randalls Dr *RBRW/HUT* CM13 .... 142 D2
Randolph Cl *LOS* SS9 .... 193 F2
  MAL CM9 .... 68 B5
Randway *RAYL* SS6 .... 171 J4
Ranelagh Gdns *GVW* DA11 .... 218 E5
Range Rd *GVE* DA12 .... 219 J5
Ransomes Wy *CHLM/WR* CM1 .... 4 C1
Rantree Fold *VGE* SS16 .... 7 D6
Ranulf Cl *HLWE* CM17 .... 11 G7
Ranulph Wy *RCHLM* CM3 .... 38 B2
Raphael Cl *ROM* RM1 .... 160 A5
  TIL RM18 .... 215 F7
Raphael Dr *CHLM/WR* CM1 .... 35 H6
  SBN/FI SS3 .... 197 F5
Raphaels *LAIN* SS15 .... 6 C5
Rapier Cl *PUR* RM19 .... 211 G3
Rathmore Rd *GVW* DA11 .... 219 F5
Rat La *SBF/HAD* SS7 .... 171 H5
Ratsborough Cha *BOC* CM0 .... 128 C3
Rat's La *LOU* IG10 .... 106 A1
Rattwick Dr *CVI* SS8 .... 209 F2
Ravel Gdns *SOCK/AV* RM15 .... 198 E6
Ravel Rd *SOCK/AV* RM15 .... 199 F6
Raven Cl *BCAYW* CM12 .... 144 A1
Raven Crs *BCAYW* CM12 .... 144 A1
Ravencroft *CDH/CHF* RM16 .... 215 C3
Ravendale Wy *SBN/FI* SS3 .... 196 C3
Raven Dr *SBF/HAD* SS7 .... 190 A3
Raven La *BCAYW* CM12 .... 144 A1
Ravenoak Wy *CHIG* IG7 .... 135 H8
Ravensbourne Cres *HARH* RM3 .. 161 G5
Ravensbourne Dr *CHLM/WR* CM1 .. 62 A3
Ravenscourt Cl *CRW* RM5 .... 149 H7
Ravenscourt Dr *HCH* RM12 .... 181 F4
Ravenscourt Gv *HCH* RM12 .... 181 F3
  VGE SS16 .... 7 F6
Ravensfield *SBN/FI* SS14 .... 168 C7
Ravensmere *EPP* CM16 .... 80 E4
Ravenswood Cha *RCFD* SS4 .... 174 C6
Ravenswood Cl *CRW* RM5 .... 149 H7
  WICKW SS12 .... 147 F5
Rawreth La *RAYL* SS6 .... 149 F6
Rayburn Rd *EMPK* RM11 .... 181 J4
Ray Cl *CVI* SS8 .... 208 A3
  LOS SS9 .... 192 C4
Rayfield *EPP* CM16 .... 80 D4
Ray Lamb Wy *ERITH* DA8 .... 210 C5
Rayleigh Av *LOS* SS9 .... 172 C5
  WOS/PRIT SS0 .... 8 B3
Rayleigh Cl *RBRW/HUT* CM13 .... 142 B3
Rayleigh Downs Rd *RAYL* SS6 ... 172 B6
Rayleigh Dr *LOS* SS9 .... 192 E2
Rayleigh Rd *LOS* SS9 .... 172 D6
  RBRW/HUT CM13 .... 142 B2
  SBF/HAD SS7 .... 171 G6
  SLH/COR SS17 .... 203 H4
Rayley La *EPP* CM16 .... 54 A6
Ray Md *RCHLM* CM3 .... 20 B6
Rayment Av *CVI* SS8 .... 208 D2
Raymond Gdns *CHIG* IG7 .... 135 A6
Raymonds Dr *RCHLM* CM3 .... 122 C6
Raymonds Dr *SBF/HAD* SS7 .... 170 E7
Rayonton Av *PEND* EN3 .... 104 D3
Ray Rd *CRW* RM5 .... 137 G8
Rayside *BSDN* SS14 .... 167 K8
The Ray *CHLM/WR* CM1 .... 35 G8
Ray Wk *LOS* SS9 .... 192 C4
Read Cl *HOC/HUL* SS5 .... 173 H4
Read Ct *WAB* EN9 .... 78 C7
Readers Ct *CHLM/GWD* CM2 .... 63 J1
Reading Cl *VGE* SS16 .... 166 A8
The Readings *HLWS* CM18 .... 3 F6

Rebels La *SBN/FI* SS3 .... 195 J1
Recreation Av *HARH* RM3 .... 161 G4
  LOS SS9 .... 193 G3
  SLH/COR SS17 .... 187 J8
Recreation Wk *BCAYE* CM11 ...... 118 E8
Rectory Av *RCFD* SS4 .... 151 K7
Rectory Cha *BRWN* CM15 .... 114 A3
  RBRW/HUT CM13 .... 163 H6
  SOS SS1 .... 195 H4
Rectory Cl *CHING* E4 .... 132 B6
  ING CM4 .... 116 B1
  ING CM4 .... 117 K3
  RCHLM CM3 .... 20 E7
  SBF/HAD SS7 .... 191 K2
Rectory Fld *HLWW/ROY* CM19 .... 2 B5
Rectory Gdns *PIT* SS13 .... 169 F8
  UPMR RM14 .... 182 A3
Rectory Garth *RAYL* SS6 .... 171 J2
Rectory Gv *LOS* SS9 .... 192 E5
  WICKE SS11 .... 147 J6
Rectory La *CHLM/WR* CM1 .... 4 C1
  HLWW/ROY CM19 .... 2 B6
  LOU IG10 .... 107 J5
  MAL CM9 .... 67 F7
  RBRW/HUT CM13 .... 164 D2
  RCHLM CM3 .... 125 K1
Rectory Park Dr *PIT* SS13 .... 168 E8
Rectory Rd *BCAYW* CM12 .... 166 A1
  CDH/CHF RM16 .... 202 B5
  CHLM/WR CM1 .... 61 H5
  GRAYS RM17 .... 214 C2
  HOC/HUL SS5 .... 173 H2
  MAL CM9 .... 66 D2
  PIT SS13 .... 169 F6
  RCHLM CM3 .... 124 C5
  SBF/HAD SS7 .... 191 K2
  SLH/COR SS17 .... 203 J4
  TIL RM18 .... 215 J5
Rectory Wd *HLW* CM20 .... 2 C1
Redcar Rd *HARH* RM3 .... 139 G8
Redcliff Dr *LOS* SS9 .... 193 G5
Redcliffe Rd *CHLM/GWD* CM2 .... 4 B4
Redden Court Rd *HARH* RM3 ...... 161 F5
Reddings La *BOC* CM0 .... 101 J2
Reddy Rd *ERITH* DA8 .... 210 A5
Redfern Gdns *GPK* RM2 .... 160 E4
Redgate Cl *WICKE* SS11 .... 147 K5
Redgates Pl *CHLM/WR* CM1 .... 5 F1
Redgrave Rd *VGE* SS16 .... 188 B1
Redhills Rd *RCHLM* CM3 .... 122 E5
The Redinge *BCAYE* CM11 .... 144 E6
Redlands Rd *PEND* EN3 .... 104 E5
Redlie Cl *SLH/COR* SS17 .... 203 K1
Red Lion Crs *HLWE* CM17 .... 25 G7
Red Lion La *HLWE* CM17 .... 25 G7
Redmayne Dr *CHLM/GWD* CM2 ..... 4 A6
Redricks La *HLW* CM20 .... 10 D7
Red Rd *BRW* CM14 .... 140 E7
Redrose La *ING* CM4 .... 86 D4
Redruth Cl *CHLM/WR* CM1 .... 35 G8
Redruth Rd *HARH* RM3 .... 139 G8
Redshank Crs *RCHLM* CM3 .... 122 D4
Redshank Dr *MAL* CM9 .... 40 E8
Redstock Rd *SOSN* SS2 .... 9 D2
Red Willow *HLWW/ROY* CM19 ..... 23 H8
Redwing Dr *BCAYE* CM11 .... 144 D5
Redwood Cha *SOCK/AV* RM15 ... 200 B4
Redwood Dr *CHLM/WR* CM1 .... 61 F4
  LAIN SS15 .... 6 B1
Redwood Gdns *CHING* E4 .... 132 C2
The Redwoods *CVI* SS8 .... 207 J2
Reedings Wy *SBW* CM21 .... 11 K1
Reed Pond Wk *GPK* RM2 .... 160 A4
  VGE SS16 .... 186 C1
Reeds Wy *WICKW* SS12 .... 147 F5
Reeves Cl *BRWN* CM15 .... 85 K8
  VGE SS16 .... 186 A1
Reeves La *HLWW/ROY* CM19 .... 50 E1
Reeves Wy *RCHLM* CM3 .... 122 E6
Regal Cl *CHLM/GWD* CM2 .... 5 E5
Regan Cl *SLH/COR* SS17 .... 204 A1
Regarder Rd *CHIG* IG7 .... 136 A8
Regency Cl *CHIG* IG7 .... 135 F8
  CHLM/GWD CM2 .... 5 E2
  RCFD SS4 .... 174 B3
  WICKE SS11 .... 147 G3
Regency Ct *BRW* CM14 .... 141 F5
  HLWS CM18 .... 24 E8
  MAL CM9 .... 40 C8
Regency Gdns *EMPK* RM11 .... 180 D1
Regency Gn *SOSN* SS2 .... 8 C2
Regent Cl *CDH/CHF* RM16 .... 214 B1
  RAYL SS6 .... 171 G1
Regent Rd *EPP* CM16 .... 80 D4
Regents Cl *BOC* CM0 .... 128 D1
Regents Pl *LOU* IG10 .... 134 A3
Reginald Rd *HARH* RM3 .... 161 H3
Regina Rd *CHLM/WR* CM1 .... 5 D2
Rembrandt Cl *CVI* SS8 .... 208 A2
  SBN/FI SS3 .... 197 F5
Rembrandt Dr *GVW* DA11 .... 218 C8
Rembrandt Gv *CHLM/WR* CM1 ..... 35 G7
Remembrance Av *BOC* CM0 .... 155 G1
  RCHLM CM3 .... 38 A2
Renacres *VGE* SS16 .... 7 D6

Rennie Pl *CHLM/GWD* CM2 .... 63 K2
Rennie Rd *CHLM/GWD* CM2 .... 5 E4
Renoir Pl *CHLM/WR* CM1 .... 35 H6
Repton Av *GPK* RM2 .... 160 B5
Repton Ct *PIT* SS13 .... 168 D4
Repton Dr *GPK* RM2 .... 160 B6
Repton Gdns *GPK* RM2 .... 160 B5
Repton Gv *LOS* SS9 .... 173 H6
Retford Cl *HARH* RM3 .... 161 H1
Retford Pth *HARH* RM3 .... 161 H1
Retford Rd *HARH* RM3 .... 161 H2
Retingham Wy *CHING* E4 .... 132 C5 🔢
Retreat Rd *HOC/HUL* SS5 .... 151 F7
WOS/PRIT SS0 .... 8 B5
The Retreat *BRW* CM14 .... 140 E4
GRAYS RM17 .... 214 A5 🔢
RBRW/HUT CM13 .... 142 A2
Retreat Wy *CHIG* IG7 .... 136 A6
Rettendon Cl *RAYL* SS6 .... 171 F2 🔢
Rettendon Gdns *WICKE* SS11 .... 147 H4
Rettendon Vw *WICKE* SS11 .... 147 J5
Reubens Rd *RBRW/HUT* CM13 .... 142 A2
Reynolds Ga *RCHLM* CM3 .... 122 E7 🔢
Rhoda Rd *SBF/HAD* SS7 .... 190 C11
Rhoda Rd North *SBF/HAD* SS7 .... 170 D8
Richardson Pl *CHLM/WR* CM1 .... 4 A2
Richmond Av *CHING* E4 .... 132 E8
SBF/HAD SS7 .... 190 C11
SBN/FI SS3 .... 196 C7
WOS/PRIT SS0 .... 8 B4 🔢
Richmond Ct *BROX* EN10 .... 49 F2 🔢
Richmond Crs *CHING* E4 .... 132 E8
Richmond Dr *RAYL* SS6 .... 171 J5
WOS/PRIT SS0 .... 193 K1 🔢
Richmond Rd *CHING* E4 .... 132 E4 🔢
CHLM/GWD CM2 .... 63 J1
GRAYS RM17 .... 214 B4
ROM RM1 .... 160 A8 🔢
WICKE SS11 .... 147 F3
Richmond St *SOSN* SS2 .... 195 G4
Ricketts Dr *CHLM/WR* CM1 .... 144 A2
Rickling *VGE* SS16 .... 188 C1
Riddiford Dr *CHLM/WR* CM1 .... 4 A1
Riddings La *HLWS* CM18 .... 52 E1
The Ride *PEND* EN3 .... 104 C7
Ridgemount *SBF/HAD* SS7 .... 190 D1 🔢
The Ridge *RCHLM* CM3 .... 122 E8
Ridgeway *BCAYW* CM12 .... 144 B5
GRAYS RM17 .... 214 B6
ING CM4 .... 116 A4
MAL CM9 .... 68 C5 🔢
RAYL SS6 .... 171 J4
RBRW/HUT CM13 .... 142 A4
WFD IG8 .... 133 K7
Ridgeway Av *GVE* DA12 .... 219 G8
Ridgeway Gdns *WOS/PRIT* SS0 .... 193 J5 🔢
Ridgeways *HLWE* CM17 .... 25 J5
The Ridgeway *CHING* E4 .... 132 D4
GPK RM2 .... 160 B6
HARH RM3 .... 161 F3
LOS SS9 .... 193 H5
WOS/PRIT SS0 .... 193 J5
Ridgewell Av *CHLM/WR* CM1 .... 4 A1
Ridgwell Av *CDH/CHF* RM16 .... 202 A4
The Ridings *CHLM/GWD* CM2 .... 5 E6
CVI SS8 .... 191 F8 🔢
RCFD SS4 .... 174 C4
Ridley Cl *HARH* RM3 .... 160 C3
Ridley Rd *CHLM/WR* CM1 .... 34 D5
PIT SS13 .... 169 F4
Riffams Ct *PIT* SS13 .... 169 F5 🔢
Riffams Dr *PIT* SS13 .... 169 F5
Riffhams Cha *RCHLM* CM3 .... 123 K8
Riffhams Dr *CHLM/GWD* CM2 .... 63 H6
Riffhams La *RCHLM* CM3 .... 65 C5
Rigby Gdns *CDH/CHF* RM16 .... 215 G3
Rignals La *CHLM/GWD* CM2 .... 91 F2
Riley Rd *PEND* EN3 .... 104 C3
Ringwood Av *HCH* RM12 .... 180 E3
Ringwood Dr *LOS* SS9 .... 172 C6
Ripley Vw *LOU* IG10 .... 107 K4
Ripley Wy *CHESW* EN7 .... 76 B4
Rippleside *BSDN* SS14 .... 168 C8
Risdens *HLWS* CM18 .... 2 C6 🔢
Risebridge Cha *ROM* RM1 .... 160 A2
Risebridge Rd *GPK* RM2 .... 160 A4
Rise Pk *LAIN* SS15 .... 7 D4
Rise Park Bvd *GPK* RM2 .... 160 A3
Riseway *BRWN* CM15 .... 141 H6
The Rising *BCAYE* CM11 .... 144 B4
Rivendell V *RCHLM* CM3 .... 122 C7
Rivenhall *SBF/HAD* SS7 .... 171 G5
WICKE SS11 .... 147 K7
River Cl *CHES/WCR* EN8 .... 77 G8
Riverdale *LOS* SS9 .... 172 E6
River Dr *UPMR* RM14 .... 161 KB
Riverfield La *SBW* CM21 .... 11 J2 🔢
Rivermill *WLW* CM20 .... 2 C1
River Rd *BKHH* IG9 .... 134 B4
BRW CM14 .... 140 B7
Riversdale *GVW* DA11 .... 218 D7
Riverside Av *BROX* EN10 .... 49 G4
Riverside Ct *CHING* E4 .... 132 C2 🔢

HLW CM20 .... 11 G7
Riverside Rd *BOC* CM0 .... 155 H1 🔢
Riverside Wk *WICKW* SS12 .... 146 E5
Riverton Dr *BOC* CM0 .... 72 B4
Rivertons *VGE* SS16 .... 188 C1
Riverview *VGE* SS16 .... 188 D1
Riverview Gdns *HOC/HUL* SS5 .... 149 H2
River View Rd *SBF/HAD* SS7 .... 190 C3
River View Ter *RCHLM* CM3 .... 126 C3
River Wy *HLW* CM20 .... 10 E8
LOU IG10 .... 134 D2
Riviera Dr *SOS* SS1 .... 9 F4
Roach Av *RAYL* SS6 .... 171 H4
Roach V *LOS* SS9 .... 173 G6
Roach Valley Wy *HOC/HUL* SS5 .... 172 D2
RCFD SS4 .... 173 H5
RCFD SS4 .... 176 B1
Robert Cl *BCAYW* CM12 .... 144 A3
CHIG IG7 .... 135 J8
CHLM/GWD CM2 .... 63 H1
HARH RM3 .... 160 C3
Roberts Cl *CHES/WCR* EN8 .... 76 E4 🔢
Robertson Cl *BROX* EN10 .... 48 E8 🔢
Robertson Dr *WICKW* SS12 .... 147 H8 🔢
Roberts Rd *LAIN* SS15 .... 166 C6 🔢
RCHLM CM3 .... 124 C6
Robin Cl *BCAYW* CM12 .... 117 J7
Robin Hood Rd *BRWN* CM15 .... 140 E3
Robinia Av *GVW* DA11 .... 218 C5
Robinia Cl *LAIN* SS15 .... 6 B1
Robinson Cl *HCH* RM12 .... 180 C8 🔢
Robinson Rd *CDH/CHF* RM16 .... 202 D1
The Robins *SWH* CM15 .... 114 B1
Robin W *CHLM/GWD* CM2 .... 62 D8
Robjohns Rd *CHLM/WR* CM1 .... 62 A5
Robsons Cl *CHES/WCR* EN8 .... 76 C3 🔢
Robyns Cft *GVW* DA11 .... 218 D8
Roche Av *RCFD* SS4 .... 174 B3
Rochefort Dr *RCFD* SS4 .... 174 C5
Rochehall Wy *RCFD* SS4 .... 174 C5
Rochester Dr *WOS/PRIT* SS0 .... 193 K1
Rochester Ms *WOS/PRIT* SS0 .... 193 K1
Rocheway *RCFD* SS4 .... 174 D3
Rochford Av *BRWN* CM15 .... 141 K1
WAB EN9 .... 77 K8
WOS/PRIT SS0 .... 8 B3
Rochford Cl *BROX* EN10 .... 48 B3
HCH RM12 .... 180 C7 🔢
WICKE SS11 .... 147 J7 🔢
Rochford Garden Wy *RCFD* SS4 .... 174 B2
Rochford Gn *LOU* IG10 .... 108 A7
Rochford Hall *RCFD* SS4 .... 174 C4
Rochford Rd *CHLM/GWD* CM2 .... 5 D4 🔢
CVI SS8 .... 208 D2
SOSN SS2 .... 194 A1
Rockall *SOSN* SS2 .... 173 H6
Rockchase Gdns *EMPK* RM11 .... 161 F8 🔢
Rockingham Av *EMPK* RM11 .... 160 C8
Rockleigh Av *LOS* SS9 .... 193 H4
Rockleigh Ct *BRWN* CM15 .... 141 K3
Rockwood Gdns *LOU* IG10 .... 108 A7
Rodbridge Dr *SOS* SS1 .... 195 J4
Roden Cl *HLWE* CM17 .... 25 K1
Rodeo Cl *ERITH* DA8 .... 210 C7
Roding Cl *CHONG* CM5 .... 57 F5 🔢
SBN/FI SS3 .... 197 J3 🔢
Roding Dr *BRWN* CM15 .... 113 H3
Roding Gdns *LOU* IG10 .... 134 C1
Roding La *BKHH* IG9 .... 134 B4
CHIG IG7 .... 134 D4
Roding Leigh *RCHLM* CM3 .... 122 E6 🔢
Roding Rd *LOU* IG10 .... 134 C1
Rodings Av *SLH/COR* SS17 .... 203 K1
The Rodings *LOS* SS9 .... 172 E6
UPMR RM14 .... 162 A8
Roding Vw *WICKW* SS12 .... 147 H6
CHONG CM5 .... 84 D1
Rodney Rd *CHONG* CM5 .... 84 B3
Rodney Rd *CHLM/WR* CM1 .... 62 A1
Roebuck La *BKHH* IG9 .... 133 K4
Roedean Av *PEND* EN3 .... 104 C5
Roedean Cl *PEND* EN3 .... 104 C5
SOSN SS2 .... 195 J4
Roedean Gdns *SOSN* SS2 .... 195 J4
Roehampton Cl *GVE* DA12 .... 219 K5
Rogers Rd *GRAYS* RM17 .... 214 B4
Roggel Rd *CVI* SS8 .... 208 D4
Rokells *BSDN* SS14 .... 7 E3
Rokescroft *PIT* SS13 .... 168 D8
Roland La *CVI* SS8 .... 208 B1 🔢
Rollestons *CHLM/WR* CM1 .... 61 F4
Rolls Park Rd *CHING* E4 .... 132 A1
Romagne Cl *SLH/COR* SS17 .... 203 F2
Romainville Wy *CVI* SS8 .... 207 G2
Roman Cl *BRWN* CM15 .... 115 J5
MAL CM9 .... 68 B1 🔢
Roman Ri *SBW* CM21 .... 11 H3
Roman Rd *BRWN* CM15 .... 115 K4
GVW DA11 .... 218 B8
ING CM4 .... 88 E7
RCHLM CM3 .... 20 D7
Romans Pl *CHLM/WR* CM1 .... 61 H3 🔢
Romans Wy *CHLM/WR* CM1 .... 61 H4

Roman V *HLWE* CM17 .... 11 G7
Roman Wy *BCAYW* CM12 .... 144 B
BOC CM0 .... 128 B
Romeland *WAB* EN9 .... 77 J
Romford Rd *CHIG* IG7 .... 136 A
CHONG CM5 .... 84 A
SOCK/AV RM15 .... 198 E
Romney Cha *EMPK* RM11 .... 161 H8
Romney Rd *BCAYW* CM12 .... 144 A
GVW DA11 .... 218 D
Romsey Cl *HOC/HUL* SS5 .... 150 E
SLH/COR SS17 .... 203 H4
Romsey Crs *SBF/HAD* SS7 .... 170 A
Romsey Dr *SBF/HAD* SS7 .... 169 K
Romsey Rd *SBF/HAD* SS7 .... 169 K
Romsey Wy *SBF/HAD* SS7 .... 170 A
Ronald Dr *RAYL* SS6 .... 171 F
Ronald Hill Gv *LOS* SS9 .... 192 E
Ronald Park Av *WOS/PRIT* SS0 .... 193 K
Ronald Rd *HARH* RM3 .... 161 H
Roneo Cnr *ROMW/RG* RM7 .... 180 A
Roneo Link *HCH* RM12 .... 180 A2
Roodegate *BSDN* SS14 .... 7 E
Rookery Cl *RAYL* SS6 .... 171 H
SLH/COR SS17 .... 203 H
Rookery Hl *SLH/COR* SS17 .... 204 E
Rookery La *RCHLM* CM3 .... 124 A
Rookery Md *RCHLM* CM3 .... 122 D5
Rookery Rd *ING* CM4 .... 86 A
The Rookery *WTHK* RM20 .... 212 D
Rookery Vw *GRAYS* RM17 .... 214 C
Rookwood Av *LOU* IG10 .... 108 A
Rookwood Cl *GRAYS* RM17 .... 214 A
Rookwood Gdns *CHING* E4 .... 133 C5
Rookyards *VGE* SS16 .... 168 B8
Roosevel Av *CVI* SS8 .... 208 A
Roosevelt Rd *LAIN* SS15 .... 166 B7
Roots Hall Av *SOSN* SS2 .... 8 C
Roots Hall Dr *SOSN* SS2 .... 8 B
Roots La *WIT* CM8 .... 40 A
Ropers Av *CHING* E4 .... 132 D
Rope Wk *MAL* CM9 .... 68 C
Rosary Gdns *WOS/PRIT* SS0 .... 193 J
Rosbach Rd *CVI* SS8 .... 208 D
Rosberg Rd *CVI* SS8 .... 208 E2
Roscommon Wy *CVI* SS8 .... 207 G
Rose Acre *BSDN* SS14 .... 168 C
Roseacre *EMPK* RM11 .... 181 C
Roseacres *SBW* CM21 .... 11 H
Rose Av *GVE* DA12 .... 219 K
Rose Bank *BRW* CM14 .... 141 G
Rosebank *WAB* EN9 .... 78 A
Rosebank Av *HCH* RM12 .... 180 D
Rosebank Gdns *GVW* DA11 .... 218 D
Rosebay Av *BCAYW* CM12 .... 117 F
Roseberry Av *SBF/HAD* SS7 .... 170 F
VGE SS16 .... 186 C
Roseberry Cl *UPMR* RM14 .... 162 C
Roseberry Gdns *UPMR* RM14 .... 182 C
Rosebery Ct *GVW* DA11 .... 218 E
Rosebery Rd *CHLM/GWD* CM2 .... 4 C
GRAYS RM17 .... 213 H
Rose Cl *WICKW* SS12 .... 147 H6 🔢
Rose Ct *CHESW* EN7 .... 76 A
Rosecroft *VGE* SS16 .... 186 B
Rosedale Rd *GRAYS* RM17 .... 214 C
Rosedale Wy *CHESW* EN7 .... 76 A
Rose Dr *BOC* CM0 .... 128 C
Rose Gln *CHLM/GWD* CM2 .... 5 D
Roselaine *BSDN* SS14 .... 7 F
Rose La *BCAYW* CM12 .... 144 B
Rosemary Av *ROM* RM1 .... 160 A
Rosemary Cl *SOCK/AV* RM15 .... 200 A
Rosemead *SBF/HAD* SS7 .... 170 B
Rosemead Gdns *RBRW/HUT* CM13 .... 115 H
Rosemount *HLWW/ROY* CM19 .... 2 B
Roserna Rd *CVI* SS8 .... 208 D
Rose Rd *CVI* SS8 .... 208 A
Rose St *GVW* DA11 .... 218 A
Rose Va *BRW* CM14 .... 141 F6
Rose Valley Crs *SLH/COR* SS17 .... 203 K
Rose Wy *RCFD* SS4 .... 174 D
Rosewood Av *HCH* RM12 .... 180 B6
Rosewood Cl *SOCK/AV* RM15 .... 200 C5
Rosewood La *SBN/FI* SS3 .... 196 E
Rosherville Wy *GVW* DA11 .... 218 D
Rosilian Dr *HOC/HUL* SS5 .... 150 D
Roslings Cl *CHLM/WR* CM1 .... 33 K
Roslyn Cl *BROX* EN10 .... 48 E
Roslyn Gdns *GPK* RM2 .... 160 A
Rossall Cl *EMPK* RM11 .... 160 B
Rossdene Gdns *GTDUN* CM6 .... 16 B
Rossell Rd *TIL* RM18 .... 214 E8
Rossendale *CHLM/WR* CM1 .... 62 A
Rossiter Rd *SBN/FI* SS3 .... 197 G
Rosslyn Av *CHING* E4 .... 133 G
HARH RM3 .... 161 F
Rosslyn Cl *HOC/HUL* SS5 .... 150 A
Rosslyn Rd *BCAYW* CM12 .... 144 A
HOC/HUL SS5 .... 151 F
Ross Wy *VGE* SS16 .... 186 C
Roswell Cl *CHES/WCR* EN8 .... 76 E4 🔢
Rothbury Rd *CHLM/WR* CM1 .... 61 K
Roth Dr *RBRW/HUT* CM13 .... 142 K5
Rotherfield Rd *PEND* EN3 .... 104 D3

othesay Av *CHLM/GWD* CM2 .... 4 B5
othmans Av *CHLM/GWD* CM2 .... 63 G7
othwell Cl *LOS* SS9 .... 172 D7
ouge La *GVE* DA12 .... 219 G6
oughtallys *EPP* CM16 .... 81 K1
oughtons *CHLM/GWD* CM2 .... 90 E2
oundacre *LAIN* SS15 .... 7 E5
oundbush Rd *MAL* CM9 .... 96 C5
ound Hl Rd *SBF/HAD* SS7 .... 191 F3
oundhills *WAB* EN9 .... 78 A8
oundmead *LOU* IG10 .... 107 J7
oundmead Cl *LOU* IG10 .... 107 J6
oundmead Dr *CHES/WCR* EN8 ..... 76 E3
oundwood *RBRW/HUT* CM13 ...... 141 K4
oundwood Cl *RBRW/HUT* CM13 ... 142 B3
ounton Rd *WAB* EN9 .... 78 A7
ous Cha *CHLM/GWD* CM2 .... 90 D4
ous Rd *BKHH* IG9 .... 134 B3
owan Cl *RAYL* SS6 .... 149 G7
owan Dr *BROX* EN10 .... 49 F6
MAL CM9 .... 44 B4
owan Gn East
RBRW/HUT CM13 .... 141 J6
owan Gn West
RBRW/HUT CM13 .... 141 J6
owan Gv *SOCK/AV* RM15 .... 198 E2
he Rowans *BCAYE* CM11 .... 144 E5
BROX EN10 .... 48 E1
SOCK/AV RM15 .... 198 E8
owans Wy *LOU* IG10 .... 107 H8
WICKE SS11 .... 147 H5
owan Wk *EMPK* RM11 .... 160 E6
LOS SS9 .... 172 E7
SBW CM21 .... 11 C5
owan Wy *RCFD* SS4 .... 153 H4
RCHLM CM3 .... 38 A2
SOCK/AV RM15 .... 200 B4
owenhall *LAIN* SS15 .... 166 A7
owhedge *RBRW/HUT* CM13 ...... 141 K6
owhedge Cl *PIT* SS13 .... 169 G3
owland Crs *CHIG* IG7 .... 135 H7
owlands *CHES/WCR* EN8 .... 76 D4
he Rowlands *SBF/HAD* SS7 .... 190 D1
owley Md *EPP* CM16 .... 53 G2
owley Rd *CDH/CHF* RM16 .... 202 A5
owmarsh *GVW* DA11 .... 218 C3
owney Gdns *SBW* CM21 .... 11 C5
owney Wd *SBW* CM21 .... 11 C4
oxburgh Av *UPMR* RM14 .... 181 K4
oxwell Av *CHLM/WR* CM1 .... 61 C2
oxwell Gdns *RBRW/HUT* CM13 .. 142 B1
oxwell Rd *CHLM/WR* CM1 .... 31 K5
oyal Artillery Wy *SOSN* SS2 ...... 195 H2
oyal Av *CHES/WCR* EN8 .... 76 E2
oyal Cl *RCFD* SS4 .... 152 A8
oyal Ct *MAL* CM9 .... 68 C4
oyal Ms *LOS* SS9 .... 9 D5
oyal Oak Dr *WICKE* SS11 .... 147 K5
oyal Pier Rd *GVE* DA12 .... 219 C4
oyal Ter *LOS* SS9 .... 9 D5
oyce Cl *BROX* EN10 .... 49 G5
oydon Br *BSDN* SS14 .... 168 A5
oydon Cl *LOU* IG10 .... 134 B3
oydon Rd *HLWW/ROY* CM19 .... 23 C4
oyer Rd *HOC/HUL* SS5 .... 173 H1
oyle Cl *GPK* RM2 .... 160 C7
oyston Av *CHING* E4 .... 132 B8
LAIN SS15 .... 6 B1
SOSN SS2 .... 9 E1
oyston Rd *HARH* RM3 .... 161 H2
ubens Cl *SBN/FI* SS3 .... 197 F5
ubens Ga *CHLM/WR* CM1 .... 35 H6
ubicon Av *WICKE* SS11 .... 147 J5
ue De St Lawrence *WAB* EN9 ...... 77 J8
uffles Cl *RAYL* SS6 .... 171 K2
umbullion La *BCAYW* CM12 .... 144 A2
umsey Flds *RCHLM* CM3 .... 65 K6
umsley *CHESW* EN7 .... 76 A1
undells *HLWS* CM18 .... 7 K4
undells Wk *BSDN* SS14 .... 168 B6
he Rundels *SBF/HAD* SS7 .... 171 F8
unning Mare La *CHLM/GWD* CM2 ... 90 C2
unning Waters
RBRW/HUT CM13 .... 141 K7
unnymede Cha *SBF/HAD* SS7 .... 191 F1
unnymede Rd *SLH/COR* SS17 .... 208 B2
SLH/COR SS17 .... 203 J4
unsell Cl *RCHLM* CM3 .... 65 K6
unsell La *RCHLM* CM3 .... 65 K5
unsell Vw *RCHLM* CM3 .... 65 K6
unsell Gdns *WICKE* SS11 .... 147 G3
unwell Rd *WICKE* SS11 .... 147 G5
unwell Ter *LOS* SS9 .... 8 C5
upert Rd *BOC* CM0 .... 128 C1
ural Cl *HCH* RM12 .... 180 C2
ural V *GVW* DA11 .... 218 D5
urik Ct *MAL* CM9 .... 68 A3
ushbottom La *SBF/HAD* SS7 ..... 170 A7
WICKW SS12 .... 170 A5
ush Cl *SBF/HAD* SS7 .... 170 A7
ushdene Rd *BCAYW* CM12 .... 144 A5
BRWN CM15 .... 141 F3
ushdon Cl *CDH/CHF* RM16 .... 213 K2
ROM RM1 .... 160 B7
ushes La *BOC* CM0 .... 101 G4

Rushes Md *HLWS* CM18 .... 3 E5
Rushfield *SBW* CM21 .... 11 J3
Rushleigh Av *CHES/WCR* EN8 ...... 76 D4
Rushley *PIT* SS13 .... 169 G5
Rushley Cl *CDH/CHF* RM16 .... 201 H8
SBN/FI SS3 .... 197 F1
Rushleydale *CHLM/WR* CM1 .... 35 G8
Rushton Gv *HLWE* CM17 .... 25 H5
Ruskin Av *SOSN* SS2 .... 9 D2
UPMR RM14 .... 181 K1
WAB EN9 .... 78 A8
Ruskin Dene *BCAYW* CM12 .... 144 B2
Ruskin Gdns *HARH* RM3 .... 160 C3
Ruskin Rd *CDH/CHF* RM16 .... 215 F5
CHLM/GWD CM2 .... 5 F3
SLH/COR SS17 .... 203 J4
Ruskoi Rd *CVI* SS8 .... 190 E8
Russell Cl *BRWN* CM15 .... 140 E3
LAIN SS15 .... 166 C7
Russell Gdns *CHLM/GWD* CM2 ..... 90 C1
WICKE SS11 .... 147 H6
Russell Gv *RCFD* SS4 .... 174 D3
Russell Rd *BKHH* IG9 .... 133 K4
CHING E4 .... 132 A7
GVE DA12 .... 219 J4
RCHLM CM3 .... 124 D4
TIL RM18 .... 214 D7
Russell's Dr *CHES/WCR* EN8 .... 76 E5
Russell's Ride *CHES/WCR* EN8 .... 76 E5
Russel Rd *GRAYS* RM17 .... 213 K3
Russet Cl *SLH/COR* SS17 .... 203 K2
Russets *EMPK* RM11 .... 161 F6
Russets Cl *CHING* E4 .... 132 E6
The Russets *RCFD* SS4 .... 152 A8
Russetts *VGE* SS16 .... 166 B8
Russet Wy *BOC* CM0 .... 128 C7
HOC/HUL SS5 .... 151 F5
Rustic Cl *UPMR* RM14 .... 182 B2
Rutherford Cl *BCAYW* CM12 ...... 117 C8
LOS SS9 .... 172 D7
Rutherfords *CHLM/WR* CM1 .... 34 D4
Ruthven Av *CHES/WCR* EN8 .... 76 E5
Ruthven Cl *WICKW* SS12 .... 147 G7
Rutland Ap *EMPK* RM11 .... 161 H7
Rutland Av *SOS* SS1 .... 195 H5
Rutland Cl *LAIN* SS15 .... 166 B7
Rutland Dr *EMPK* RM11 .... 161 H7
RAYL SS6 .... 149 G6
Rutland Gdns *RCFD* SS4 .... 151 K8
Rutland Rd *CHLM/WR* CM1 .... 34 C7
RCHLM CM3 .... 124 C6
Rydal *HOC/HUL* SS5 .... 149 J3
RAYL SS6 .... 171 K3
Ryde Cl *LOS* SS9 .... 172 C8
Ryde Dr *SLH/COR* SS17 .... 203 J5
Ryder Gdns *RAIN* RM13 .... 180 A7
Ryde Wy *PIT* SS13 .... 169 G3
The Ryde *LOS* SS9 .... 172 C8
Rye Cl *HCH* RM12 .... 180 D6
RCHLM CM3 .... 38 A2
Ryecroft *HLWW/ROY* CM19 .... 2 B3
Ryedene *VGE* SS16 .... 188 B3
Ryedene Cl *VGE* SS16 .... 188 B2
Ryedene Pl *VGE* SS16 .... 188 B2
The Rye Fld *RCHLM* CM3 .... 65 H2
Rye Hill Rd *HLWS* CM18 .... 52 B2
Rye Wk *ING* CM4 .... 116 A3
Rykhill *CDH/CHF* RM16 .... 215 G2
Rylands Rd *SOS* SS1 .... 9 F2
The Ryle *CHLM/WR* CM1 .... 61 G5
Rysley *RCHLM* CM3 .... 65 H1

Sabina Rd *CDH/CHF* RM16 .... 215 H3
Sabines Rd *ABR/ST* RM4 .... 112 B7
Sackville Cl *CHLM/WR* CM1 .... 62 A2
Sackville Crs *HARH* RM3 .... 161 F3
Sackville Rd *SOSN* SS2 .... 195 H4
Saddington St *GVE* DA12 .... 219 C5
Saddle Ri *RCHLM* CM3 .... 35 C5
Saddleworth Sq *HARH* RM3 .... 160 D1
Sadlers *SBF/HAD* SS7 .... 170 A6
Sadlers Cl *BCAYE* CM11 .... 117 K8
Sadlers Md *HLWS* CM18 .... 24 E6
Saffory Cl *LOS* SS9 .... 172 D6
Saffron *CDH/RHUT* CM13 .... 164 C8
SLH/COR SS17 .... 203 G2
Saffron Gdns *SLH/COR* SS17 ..... 203 F4
Saffron Rd *CDH/CHF* RM16 .... 215 F3
Saffron Wk *BCAYE* CM11 .... 144 C3
St Agnes Cl *CVI* SS8 .... 207 H2
St Agnes Rd *BCAYW* CM12 .... 166 D2
St Aidan's Wy *GVE* DA12 .... 219 K8
St Albans Av *UPMR* RM14 .... 182 B2
St Alban's Cl *GVE* DA12 .... 219 J8
St Alban's Gdns *GVE* DA12 .... 219 J8
St Alban's Rd *EPP* CM16 .... 81 H3
St Andrews Av *HCH* RM12 .... 180 A6
St Andrews Cl *CVI* SS8 .... 207 H1
EPP CM16 .... 54 C6

St Andrews La *LAIN* SS15 .... 6 A3
St Andrews Pl *BRWN* CM15 .... 141 J5
St Andrew's Rd *GVE* DA12 .... 219 G5
RCFD SS4 .... 174 B3
RCHLM CM3 .... 36 D4
RCHLM CM3 .... 38 A1
SBN/FI SS3 .... 196 B7
TIL RM18 .... 214 D8
St Annes Cl *CDH/CHF* RM16 ...... 201 F8
CHESW EN7 .... 76 A2
St Anne's Pk *BROX* EN10 .... 49 G2
St Anne's Rd *BRWN* CM15 .... 115 G5
CVI SS8 .... 208 D2
St Ann's Rd *SOSN* SS2 .... 9 D3
St Anthony's Dr *CHLM/GWD* CM2 .. 5 D6
St Augustine Rd *CDH/CHF* RM16 .. 215 G3
St Augustine's Av *SOS* SS1 .... 196 A7
St Augustines Cl *BROX* EN10 ...... 49 F2
St Augustines Dr *BROX* EN10 ...... 49 F2
St Benedict's Av *GVE* DA12 .... 219 K8
St Benet's Rd *SOSN* SS2 .... 8 C1
St Botolph Rd *GVW* DA11 .... 218 C8
St Catharine's Rd *BROX* EN10 ..... 49 G1
St Catherines Cl *WICKE* SS11 ..... 147 J5
St Catherines Rd *CHING* E4 .... 132 B5
CHLM/WR CM1 .... 62 A3
St Cecilia Rd *CDH/CHF* RM16 .... 215 G3
St Chads Cl *LAIN* SS15 .... 6 A3
St Chad's Dr *GVE* DA12 .... 219 K8
St Chad's Rd *TIL* RM18 .... 215 F7
St Charles Dr *WICKE* SS11 .... 147 H6
St Charles Rd *BRW* CM14 .... 140 E5
St Christophers Ct *CVI* SS8 .... 207 H1
St Clare Meadow *RCFD* SS4 .... 174 C2
St Clement's Av *LOS* SS9 .... 193 F3
WTHK RM20 .... 212 D5
St Clements Cl *GVW* DA11 .... 218 B2
HOC/HUL SS5 .... 173 H1
SBF/HAD SS7 .... 170 B8
St Clements Ct *PUR* RM19 .... 211 H3
St Clement's Crs *SBF/HAD* SS7 .. 170 C8
St Clement's Dr *LOS* SS9 .... 193 F2
St Clement's Rd *SBF/HAD* SS7 ... 170 B8
WTHK RM20 .... 213 F6
St Cleres Crs *WICKE* SS11 .... 147 J6
St Cleres Wy *RCHLM* CM3 .... 65 H7
St Columba's Cl *GVE* DA12 .... 219 K8
St Cross Ct *HOD* EN11 .... 49 G1
St David's Dr *BROX* EN10 .... 49 F1
SBF/HAD SS7 .... 192 B2
St David's Rd *LOS* SS9 .... 186 C1
St David's Ter *LOS* SS9 .... 192 B2
St David's Wy *WICKE* SS11 .... 147 J6
St Dunstan's Dr *GVE* DA12 .... 219 K8
St Edith's Cl *BCAYW* CM12 .... 144 B4
St Ediths La *BCAYW* CM12 .... 144 B4
St Edmund's Cl *SOSN* SS2 .... 9 F1
St Edmund's Wy *HLWE* CM17 ...... 25 G1
St Egberts Wy *CHING* E4 .... 132 D4
St Fabian's Dr *CHLM/WR* CM1 ..... 62 A1
St Francis Dr *CDH/CHF* RM16 .... 215 H3
St Gabriels Ct *PIT* SS13 .... 168 E8
Saint George's Av *EMPK* RM11 .. 181 G1
St George's Av *GRAYS* RM17 ..... 214 B3
St Georges Cl *BRWN* CM15 .... 113 K1
St George's Dr *WOS/PRIT* SS0 ..... 8 B1
St George's La *SBN/FI* SS3 .... 196 E7
St George's Park Av
WOS/PRIT SS0 .... 193 J3
St Georges Wk *SBF/HAD* SS7 .... 170 A7
St Giles Cl *CDH/CHF* RM16 .... 202 A5
MAL CM9 .... 68 A3
St Giles Crs *MAL* CM9 .... 68 A3
St Gregory's Ct *GVE* DA12 .... 219 K7
St Guilberts Rd *CVI* SS8 .... 190 D8
St Helen's Rd *WOS/PRIT* SS0 .... 8 B4
St Helens Wk *BCAYW* CM12 ...... 144 A1
St Hilda's Wy *GVE* DA12 .... 219 K8
St Ives Cl *HARH* RM3 .... 161 G2
St Ivians Dr *GPK* RM2 .... 160 B5
St James' Av *CHONG* SM5 .... 84 B4
SOS SS1 .... 196 A7
St James Av East *SLH/COR* SS17 .. 204 A2
St James Av West *SLH/COR* SS17 .. 204 A2
St James Cl *CVI* SS8 .... 207 H1
WOS/PRIT SS0 .... 193 H2
St James Gdns *WOS/PRIT* SS0 ... 193 H2
St James Ms *BCAYW* CM12 .... 144 B3
St James Pk *CHLM/WR* CM1 .... 61 K1
St James's Av *GVE* DA11 .... 168 B8
St James's Av *GVW* DA11 .... 219 F5
St James's Rd *BRW* CM14 .... 141 F6
GVW DA11 .... 219 F5
St James's Cl *GVW* DA11 .... 219 F4
St James's Wk *HOC/HUL* SS5 .... 150 D7
St John's Av *BRW* CM14 .... 141 G7
CHLM/GWD CM2 .... 4 C5
HLWE CM17 .... 25 G1
St Johns Cl *LAIN* SS15 .... 6 A3
RAIN RM13 .... 180 B8
St John's Crs *BKHH* IG9 .... 133 J4
MAL CM9 .... 44 C4
St Johns Crs *CVI* SS8 .... 207 H1
St Johns Dr *RAYL* SS6 .... 170 E1
St John's Gn *CHLM/WR* CM1 .... 61 H4

St Johns Ms *SLH/COR* SS17 ..... 204 B1 ⊞
St John's Rd *BCAYE* CM11 ..... 144 C2
  CDH/CHF RM16 ..... 215 G4
  CHING E4 ..... 132 C6
  CHLM/GWD CM2 ..... 4 C4
  CHLM/WR CM1 ..... 61 H4
  CRW RM5 ..... 137 H8
  EPP CM16 ..... 80 D4
  GVE DA12 ..... 219 J3
  LOU IG10 ..... 107 H6
  SBF/HAD SS7 ..... 191 H2
  SBN/FI SS3 ..... 197 G2
  WOS/PRIT SS0 ..... 8 B4
St John's St *MAL* CM9 ..... 44 C4
St John's Wk *HLWE* CM17 ..... 25 G1 ⊞
St Kilda's Rd *BARW* CM15 ..... 140 E3
St Laurence Dr *BROX* EN10 ..... 48 E5
St Lawrence Dr *BOC* CM0 ..... 72 B5
St Lawrence Gdns *ING* CM4 ..... 86 C5 ⊞
  LOS SS9 ..... 173 F7
St Lawrence Hl *BOC* CM0 ..... 72 E8
St Lawrence Rd *BOC* CM0 ..... 73 H8
  UPMR RM14 ..... 181 K3
St Leonard's Rd *SOS* SS1 ..... 9 E5
  WAB EN9 ..... 49 K6
St Leonards Wy *HCH* RM12 ..... 180 C7
St Lukes Cl *CVI* SS8 ..... 207 H1 ⊞
St Luke's Rd *SOSN* SS2 ..... 9 F1
St Margaret's Av *SLH/COR* SS17 ..... 203 J5
St Margaret's Crs *GVE* DA12 ..... 219 K8
St Margaret's Rd *CHLM/GWD* CM2 ..... 5 F2
St Mark's Av *GVW* DA11 ..... 218 E5
St Mark's Fld *GRAYS* RM17 ..... 174 C3
St Marks Rd *CVI* SS8 ..... 207 H1
  SBF/HAD SS7 ..... 191 H2
St Martin's Cl *EN* EN1 ..... 104 B5
  CTDUN CM6 ..... 14 E6
  RAYL SS6 ..... 171 H5
  SBF/HAD SS7 ..... 170 A6
St Mary's Av *BCAYW* CM12 ..... 144 B3
  BRWN CM15 ..... 141 K1
St Mary's Cl *CHLM/GWD* CM2 ..... 63 H7 ⊞
  GRAYS RM17 ..... 214 C5 ⊞
  GVE DA12 ..... 219 H7
  SBF/HAD SS7 ..... 190 C4 ⊞
  SBN/FI SS3 ..... 196 C4
St Mary's Crs *PIT* SS13 ..... 169 F6
St Mary's Dr *SBF/HAD* SS7 ..... 190 D4
St Mary's La *MAL* CM9 ..... 68 D3
  UPMR RM14 ..... 181 H3
St Marys Md *CHLM/WR* CM1 ..... 34 C4 ⊞
St Mary's Rd *CHES/WCR* EN8 ..... 76 C3
  BOC CM0 ..... 128 B7
  CDH/CHF RM16 ..... 215 G3
  SBF/HAD SS7 ..... 190 C5
  SOSN SS2 ..... 8 C2
  WICKW SS12 ..... 146 E8
St Matthew's Pl *RAIN* RM13 ..... 134 D8 ⊞
St Michaels Av *PIT* SS13 ..... 188 E1
St Michael's Cl *HLW* CM20 ..... 5 E2
  RCHLM CM3 ..... 97 J8
  SOCK/AV RM15 ..... 198 E2
St Michael's Dr *CHLM/WR* CM1 ..... 32 A8
St Michael's Rd *BROX* EN10 ..... 49 F2
  CDH/CHF RM16 ..... 215 G4
  CVI SS8 ..... 207 H2
  SBF/HAD SS7 ..... 172 A7
St Mildreds Rd *CHLM/GWD* CM2 ..... 4 C5
St Nazaire Rd *CHLM/WR* CM1 ..... 34 A7
St Neot's Rd *HARH* RM3 ..... 161 C2
St Nicholas Av *HCH* RM12 ..... 180 B4
St Nicholas Gv *RBRW/HUT* CM13 ..... 142 B8
St Nicholas La *LAIN* SS15 ..... 6 B3
St Nicholas Rd *BOC* CM0 ..... 102 A1
St Omar Cl *WICKW* SS12 ..... 147 G7 ⊞
St Patrick's Pl *CDH/CHF* RM16 ..... 215 G3
St Paul's Cl *SOCK/AV* RM15 ..... 198 E7 ⊞
St Pauls Gdns *BCAYW* CM12 ..... 144 B1 ⊞
St Paul's Pl *SOCK/AV* RM15 ..... 198 E7 ⊞
St Pauls Rd *CVI* SS8 ..... 207 H1
St Pauls Wy *WAB* EN9 ..... 77 K7 ⊞
St Peter's Av *CHONG* CM5 ..... 56 B8
  MAL CM9 ..... 68 B3
St Peters Fld *BOC* CM0 ..... 128 A6
St Peter's Pavement
  BSDN SS14 ..... 168 C4 ⊞
St Peter's Rd *BRW* CM14 ..... 140 E7 ⊞
  CDH/CHF RM16 ..... 215 G3
  CHLM/WR CM1 ..... 62 A3
  CVI SS8 ..... 207 H1 ⊞
  HOC/HUL SS5 ..... 150 C6
St Peter's Ter *WICKW* SS12 ..... 147 F6
St Peters Wk *BCAYW* CM12 ..... 144 A1
St Stephens Crs *RBRW/HUT* CM13 ..... 141 K7
St Stephen's Rd *PEND* EN3 ..... 104 D3
  RCHLM CM3 ..... 124 B1
Saint's Wk *CDH/CHF* RM16 ..... 215 H3
St Teresa Wk *CDH/CHF* RM16 ..... 215 G3
St Thomas Rd *GVW* DA11 ..... 218 D6 ⊞
  RCFD SS4 .....
St Thomas's Av *GVW* DA11 ..... 219 C7
St Thomas's Cl *WAB* EN9 ..... 78 D7
St Thomas's Pl *GRAYS* RM17 ..... 214 B5 ⊞

St Vincents Rd *CHLM/GWD* CM2 ..... 4 C5 ⊞
  WOS/PRIT SS0 ..... 8 B5
St Winifred's Cl *CHIG* IG7 ..... 135 F8
Sairard Cl *LOS* SS9 ..... 172 E6
Sairard Gdns *LOS* SS9 ..... 172 E6
Sakins Cft *HLWS* CM18 ..... 3 F6
Saladin Dr *PUR* RM19 ..... 211 H3
Salcott Crs *WICKW* SS12 ..... 147 H6
Salem Pl *GVW* DA11 ..... 218 C5 ⊞
Salerno Wy *CHLM/WR* CM1 ..... 34 A7
Salesbury Dr *BCAYE* CM11 ..... 144 E3
Salforal Cl *RCHLM* CM3 ..... 121 F4
Saling Gn *LAIN* SS15 ..... 167 G3 ⊞
Salisbury Av *SLH/COR* SS17 ..... 203 K4 ⊞
  WOS/PRIT SS0 ..... 8 A4
Salisbury Crs *CHES/WCR* EN8 ..... 76 D6
Salisbury Rd *CHING* E4 ..... 132 B6
  GPK RM2 ..... 160 C7
  GRAYS RM17 ..... 214 B5
  GVW DA11 ..... 218 E6
  LOS SS9 ..... 192 D4
  PEND EN3 ..... 105 F3
Salix Rd *GRAYS* RM17 ..... 214 C5
Salmond's Gv *RBRW/HUT* CM13 ..... 142 B8
Saltcoats *RCHLM* CM3 ..... 122 D5
Saltcote Maltings *MAL* CM9 ..... 69 G1 ⊞
Salter Pl *CHLM/GWD* CM2 ..... 63 H3 ⊞
Salter's Meadow *MAL* CM9 ..... 43 H1
The Saltings *SBF/HAD* SS7 ..... 191 J2
Salt's Gn *CHLM/WR* CM1 ..... 31 H3
Salwey Dr *BROX* EN10 ..... 49 F3
Samphire Ct *GRAYS* RM17 ..... 214 D5
Samuel Mnr *CHLM/GWD* CM2 ..... 63 H2 ⊞
Samuel Rd *VGE* SS16 ..... 186 C1
Samuels Dr *SOS* SS1 ..... 196 A5
Sanctuary Gdn *SLH/COR* SS17 ..... 204 A3 ⊞
Sanctuary Rd *LOS* SS9 ..... 192 B2
Sandbanks *SBF/HAD* SS7 ..... 191 J3
Sanderling Gdns *MAL* CM9 ..... 40 E8 ⊞
Sanderlings *SBF/HAD* SS7 ..... 190 B3 ⊞
Sanderson Cl *RBRW/HUT* CM13 ..... 164 B8 ⊞
Sanders Rd *GVE* SS16 ..... 191 F7
Sandford Av *LOU* IG10 ..... 108 A7
Sandford Mill Rd *CHLM/GWD* CM2 ..... 65 J3
Sandford Rd *CHLM/GWD* CM2 ..... 5 E2
Sandhill Rd *LOS* SS9 ..... 172 C5
Sandhurst *CVI* SS8 ..... 207 G2
Sandhurst Cl *LOS* SS9 ..... 193 G1
Sandhurst Crs *LOS* SS9 ..... 193 G1
Sandhurst Rd *TIL* RM18 ..... 215 H8
Sandleigh Rd *LOS* SS9 ..... 193 H4
Sandon Br *CHLM/GWD* CM2 ..... 64 D6
Sandon Cl *BSDN* SS14 ..... 168 C8
  RCFD SS4 ..... 174 A2 ⊞
Sandon Ct *BSDN* SS14 ..... 168 C8 ⊞
Sandon Hall Bridleway
  CHLM/GWD CM2 ..... 92 B2
Sandon Pl *CHONG* CM5 ..... 84 C4
  BSDN SS14 ..... 168 C8
Sandon Rd *CHES/WCR* EN8 ..... 76 C4
Sandown Av *HCH* RM12 ..... 180 E3
  WOS/PRIT SS0 ..... 193 J3
Sandown Cl *WICKE* SS11 ..... 147 K6 ⊞
Sandown Rd *CDH/CHF* RM16 ..... 202 E5
  SBF/HAD SS7 ..... 171 G4
  WICKE SS11 ..... 147 K6
Sandpiper Cl *SBN/FI* SS3 ..... 196 D5
Sandpiper Dr *ERITH* DA8 ..... 210 C6
The Sandpipers *GVE* DA12 ..... 219 J7
Sandpit La *BOC* CM0 ..... 128 C8
  BRW CM14 ..... 140 C2
Sandpit Rd *SBN/FI* SS3 ..... 197 G5
Sandringham Av
  HLWW/ROY CM19 ..... 23 G5
  HOC/HUL SS5 ..... 150 D7 ⊞
Sandringham Cl *SLH/COR* SS17 ..... 204 A2
Sandringham Pl *CHLM/GWD* CM2 ..... 5 D3 ⊞
Sandringham Rd *BRWN* CM15 ..... 140 E1
  LAIN SS15 ..... 6 C2
  SOS SS1 ..... 195 G5
Sandringham Wy *CHES/WCR* EN8 ..... 76 C8
Sandy Bank Rd *GVE* DA12 ..... 219 G6
Sandy La *CDH/CHF* RM16 ..... 215 G5
  SOCK/AV RM15 ..... 198 C7
  WTHK RM20 ..... 212 E5
San Remo Pde *WOS/PRIT* SS0 ..... 8 B5
San Remo Rd *CVI* SS8 ..... 208 D2
Sappers Cl *SBW* CM21 ..... 11 K3
Sarre Av *HCH* RM12 ..... 180 D7 ⊞
Sassoon Wy *MAL* CM9 ..... 68 C4 ⊞
Satanita Rd *WOS/PRIT* SS0 ..... 193 K5
Saunders Cl *CHES/WCR* EN8 ..... 76 C2
  GVW DA11 ..... 218 D7
Saunton Rd *HCH* RM12 ..... 180 B3
Savernake Rd *CHLM/WR* CM1 ..... 62 A4
Savoy Cl *VGE* SS16 ..... 166 B8
Savoy Wd *EPP* CM16 ..... 51 K3 ⊞
Sawbridgeworth Rd *SBW* CM21 ..... 12 C2
Sawells *BROX* EN10 .....
Sawkins Av *CHLM/GWD* CM2 ..... 63 F7
Sawkins Cl *CHLM/GWD* CM2 ..... 63 F7
Sawkins Gdns *CHLM/GWD* CM2 ..... 63 F7
Sawney Brook *CHLM/WR* CM1 ..... 61 G4
Sawyer's Hall La *BRWN* CM15 ..... 141 F3
Sawyer's Rd *MAL* CM9 ..... 42 A1

Saxlingham Rd *CHING* E4 ..... 132 E6 ⊞
Saxon Cl *GVW* DA11 ..... 218 B3
  HARH RM3 ..... 161 G4
  RAYL SS6 ..... 149 K1
  RBRW/HUT CM13 ..... 141 K8
  WICKE SS11 ..... 147 H4
Saxon Gdns *SBN/FI* SS3 ..... 196 B8
Saxon Shore Wy *GVE* DA12 ..... 219 H4
Saxonville *SBF/HAD* SS7 ..... 190 A4
Saxon Wy *CHLM/WR* CM1 ..... 34 D8
  MAL CM9 ..... 68 D4
  SBF/HAD SS7 ..... 190 B3
Sayers *SBF/HAD* SS7 ..... 171 F7
Sayesbury Av *SBW* CM21 ..... 11 H2
Sayesbury Rd *SBW* CM21 ..... 11 J2
Sayes Gdns *SBW* CM21 ..... 11 K3
Saywell Brook *CHLM/GWD* CM2 ..... 63 J5 ⊞
Scalby Rd *BOC* CM0 ..... 128 A3
Scaldhurst *PIT* SS13 ..... 169 F5 ⊞
Scarborough Rd *BOC* CM0 ..... 128 A3
  LOS SS9 ..... 193 F7
Scarletts *BSDN* SS14 ..... 167 K1
Sceptre Cl *MAL* CM9 ..... 44 D1
Scholars Rd *CHING* E4 ..... 132 D4
Schoolfield Rd *WTHK* RM20 ..... 212 D1
School Green La *EPP* CM16 ..... 54 C2
School La *CDH/CHF* RM16 ..... 202 A5
  CHIG IG7 ..... 135 J2
  CHLM/WR CM1 ..... 17 F2
  CHONG CM5 ..... 26 D7
  CHONG CM5 ..... 29 G2
  HLW CM20 ..... 3 E2
  ING CM4 ..... 117 K3
  RBRW/HUT CM13 ..... 164 B7
  SBF/HAD SS7 ..... 190 C5
  WICKW SS12 ..... 169 K3
School Rd *BCAYE* CM11 ..... 119 H8
  BCAYW CM12 ..... 144 C5 ⊞
  BRWN CM15 ..... 113 G3
  CHLM/WR CM1 ..... 17 G8
  CHONG CM5 ..... 83 F4
  GVE DA12 ..... 219 H8
  MAL CM9 ..... 40 D2
  MAL CM9 ..... 41 K3
School View Rd *CHLM/WR* CM1 ..... 4 A2
School Wy *LOS* SS9 ..... 195 G2
Scimitar Pk *PIT* SS13 ..... 169 G3
Scotland Green Rd North
  PEND EN3 ..... 104 D6
Scotland Rd *BKHH* IG9 ..... 133 K4
Scott Crs *ERITH* DA8 ..... 210 A2
Scott Dr *WICKW* SS12 ..... 147 G8
Scott Rd *CDH/CHF* RM16 ..... 215 F3
Scotts Cl *HCH* RM12 ..... 180 D6 ⊞
Scotts Hall Rd *RCFD* SS4 ..... 153 G3
Scraley Rd *MAL* CM9 ..... 40 E2
Scratton Rd *SLH/COR* SS17 ..... 203 K3
  SOS SS1 ..... 8 C5
Scrub La *SBF/HAD* SS7 ..... 191 K2
Scrub Ri *BCAYW* CM12 ..... 144 A8
Scurvy Hall La *RCHLM* CM3 ..... 20 D4
Scylla Cl *MAL* CM9 ..... 40 E2
Seabrough Rd *CDH/CHF* RM16 ..... 215 H2
Seabrook Gdns *RCHLM* CM3 ..... 56 D4
Seabrook Rd *CHLM/GWD* CM2 ..... 63 J2
Seaforth Av *SOSN* SS2 ..... 9 F2
Seaforth Dr *CHES/WCR* EN8 ..... 76 D4
Seaforth Gdns *WFD* IG8 ..... 133 K8
Seaforth Gv *SOSN* SS2 ..... 195 G3
Seaforth Rd *WOS/PRIT* SS0 ..... 8 A5
Seagers *MAL* CM9 ..... 40 D7
Seamans La *ING* CM4 ..... 118 D3
Seamer Rd *BOC* CM0 ..... 128 A3
Seamore Av *SBF/HAD* SS7 ..... 170 B2
Seamore Cl *SBF/HAD* SS7 ..... 170 A2
Sea Reach *LOS* SS9 ..... 193 F5 ⊞
Seaview *VGE* SS16 ..... 188 A2
Seaview Dr *SBN/FI* SS3 ..... 197 H3
Sea View Pde *BOC* CM0 ..... 72 C4
  RCHLM CM3 ..... 98 D3
Sea View Prom *BOC* CM0 ..... 72 B4
Seaview Rd *CVI* SS8 ..... 208 E3
  LOS SS9 ..... 193 F5
  SBN/FI SS3 ..... 196 C2
Seaview Ter *SBF/HAD* SS7 ..... 191 J2
Seaway *BOC* CM0 ..... 72 C1
  CVI SS8 ..... 208 B3
  SOS SS1 ..... 9 E5
Seax Ct *LAIN* SS15 ..... 166 A6
Seax Wy *LAIN* SS15 ..... 166 A6
Sebastian Av *BRWN* CM15 ..... 141 K2
Sebert Cl *BCAYE* CM11 ..... 144 E6 ⊞
Second Av *BCAYW* CM12 ..... 143 K6
  BRWN CM15 ..... 86 A4
  CHLM/WR CM1 ..... 34 C5
  CVI SS8 ..... 207 H7
  HLWE CM17 ..... 25 F6
  HLWS CM18 ..... 3 F3
  HOC/HUL SS5 ..... 150 A5
  SLH/COR SS17 ..... 203 K2
  WICKE SS11 ..... 147 K2
  WOS/PRIT SS0 ..... 193 J6
  WTHK RM20 ..... 212 D5
Seddons Wk *HOC/HUL* SS5 ..... 151 F7 ⊞
Sedgefield Cl *HARH* RM3 ..... 139 G7

dgefield Crs *HARH* RM3 .... 139 C8
dge Gn *HLWW/ROY* CM19 .... 50 B1
WAB EN9 .... 50 A2
dgemoor *SBN/FI* SS3 .... 196 C4
dley Ri *LOU* IG10 .... 25 C1
lbourne Rd *HOC/HUL* SS5 .... 151 F7
SBF/HAD SS7 .... 170 C8
SOSN SS2 .... 9 F2 🔲
ldon Cl *WOS/PRIT* SS0 .... 193 J2
lwood Rd *BRW* CM14 .... 140 C6
lworthy Cl *BCAYE* CM11 .... 144 D6
lwyn Rd *SOSN* SS2 .... 9 F2
TIL RM18 .... 214 E8
mper Rd *CDH/CHF* CM16 .... 215 H1 🔲
mples *SLH/COR* SS17 .... 204 B3 🔲
ttle Rd *HARH* RM3 .... 139 H7
ven Acres *WICKE* SS11 .... 147 H5
ven Arches Rd *BRW* CM14 ...... 141 H6
ven Ash Gn *CHLM/WR* CM1 ..... 34 E8
venth Av *CHLM/WR* CM1 .... 34 D7
CVI SS8 .... 207 J1
vern *TIL* RM18 .... 216 C2
vern Av *GPK* RM2 .... 160 C5
vern Dr *EN* EN1 .... 104 A4
UPMR RM14 .... 162 A8
vern Rd *SOCK/AV* RM15 .... 198 E6
verns Fld *EPP* CM16 .... 80 E3
wards End *WICKE* SS12 .... 147 H7 🔲
wardstone Rd *CHING* E4 .... 105 H8
WAB EN9 .... 77 J8
wardstone St *WAB* EN9 .... 77 J8
wardstone Wy *WAB* EN9 .... 105 J2
well Harris Cl *HLW* CM20 ...... 3 F2
xton *TIL* RM18 .... 214 E7 🔲
ymour Rd *CDH/CHF* CM16 ...... 213 F2
CHING E4 .... 132 C4
GVW DA11 .... 218 E6
SBF/HAD SS7 .... 192 A2
TIL RM18 .... 214 E7
WOS/PRIT SS0 .... 193 K4
ymours *HLWW/ROY* CM19 ...... 2 A6
ymour St *CHLM/GWD* CM2 ..... 4 B3
aftesbury *LOU* IG10 .... 107 F7 🔲
aftesbury Av *PEND* EN3 .... 104 D6 🔲
aftesbury Rd *CHING* E4 .... 132 E4 🔲
EPP CM16 .... 80 D3
aron Rd *ROM* RM1 .... 160 A8
akespeare Av *BCAYE* CM11 .... 144 D5 🔲
RAYL SS6 .... 172 A3
TIL RM18 .... 215 C8
VGE SS16 .... 166 B8
WOS/PRIT SS0 .... 8 A2
akespeare Dr *MAL* CM9 .... 68 C5
WOS/PRIT SS0 .... 8 B2
akespeare Rd *ROM* RM1 .... 160 A8 🔲
akeston Cl *CHLM/WR* CM1 ..... 61 H5
akletons *CHONG* CM5 .... 84 C7
alcross Dr *CHLM/WR* CM1 ..... 77 F4
alford Rd *BCAYE* CM11 .... 144 E3 🔲
amrock Cl *MAL* CM9 .... 44 D3
amrock Rd *GVE* DA12 .... 219 K5
anklin Cl *BCAYE* CM11 .... 144 B3
anklin Dr *WOS/PRIT* SS0 .... 193 H3
annon Av *RAYL* SS6 .... 171 H4
annon Cl *LOS* SS9 .... 193 F1
annon Wy *CVI* SS8 .... 207 H2
SOCK/AV RM15 .... 198 E6 🔲
arland Rd *GVE* DA12 .... 219 H7
arlands Cl *WICKE* SS11 .... 147 J5
ambrook *SBN/FI* SS3 .... 196 C3
aron Rd *PEND* EN3 .... 104 E6
arpecroft *HLWW/ROY* CM19 ... 2 C3
arpington Cl *CHLM/GWD* CM2 .. 90 E2
awbridge *HLWW/ROY* CM19 ... 2 C6
aw Cl *CHES/WCR* EN8 .... 76 C3
HCH RM12 .... 180 C2 🔲
WICKW SS12 .... 147 G8
aw Crs *RBRW/HUT* CM13 ...... 142 C5
eldon Cl *HLWE* CM17 .... 25 J5
SLH/COR SS17 .... 187 J3
eldon Rd *CVI* SS8 .... 208 E2
ellbeach Rd *CVI* SS8 .... 208 D3
elley Av *HCH* RM12 .... 180 A3 🔲
elley Cl *CHONG* CM5 .... 56 B8
MAL CM9 .... 68 C5 🔲
elley Gv *LOU* IG10 .... 107 H3
elley Pl *RAYL* SS6 .... 171 F2
TIL RM18 .... 215 C7

Shelley Rd *CHLM/GWD* CM2 ... 5 E3
RBRW/HUT CM13 .... 142 C3
Shelley Sq *SOSN* SS2 .... 9 E2
Shellow Rd *CHONG* CM5 ...... 58 B1
Shelly Av *VGE* SS16 .... 166 B8 🔲
Shelsley Dr *VGE* SS16 .... 186 D2
Shenfield Ct *HLWS* CM18 ...... 2 C6 🔲
Shenfield Crs *BRWN* CM15 .... 141 H5
Shenfield Gdns *RBRW/WR* CM1 . 35 F8
Shenfield Gn *BRWN* CM15 .... 141 H3
Shenfield Pl *BRWN* CM15 ...... 141 H3
Shenfield Rd *BRWN* CM15 .... 141 H4
Shenstone Gdns *HARH* RM3 ... 160 D3
Shepard Cl *LOS* SS9 .... 173 H7
Shepeshall *LAIN* SS15 .... 6 C4
Shepherds Cl *SBF/HAD* SS7 ... 191 K1
Shepherds Hl *HARH* RM3 .... 161 K1
Shepherd St *CVI* SS8 .... 218 C5
Shepherds Wk *SBF/HAD* SS7 . 191 K1
Shepley Cl *HCH* RM12 .... 180 E4 🔲
Sheppard Cl *EN* EN1 .... 104 B4
Sheppard Rd *CHLM/GWD* CM2 . 63 J1
Shepparts *HLWW/ROY* CM19 .. 23 H8
Sheppey Cl *ERITH* DA8 .... 210 C6
Sheppy Pl *GVE* DA12 .... 219 C5
Sherborne Av *PEND* EN3 .... 104 C6
Sherborne Rd *CHLM/WR* CM1 . 35 F8
Sherbourne Cl *SOSN* SS2 ...... 174 E7 🔲
Sherbourne Dr *PIT* SS13 .... 168 D4
Sherbourne Gdns *SOSN* SS2 .. 174 C7
Sheredan Rd *CHING* E4 .... 132 C4
Sheredes Dr *HOD* EN11 .... 49 F1
Sherfield Rd *GRAYS* RM17 .... 214 A5
Sheridan Av *SBF/HAD* SS7 .... 191 C2
Sheridan Cl *HARH* RM3 .... 160 C2
RAYL SS6 .... 172 A3
Sheriden Wk *BROX* EN10 ...... 48 E2
Sheringham Cl *SLH/COR* SS17 . 204 A2
Sheriton Sq *RAYL* SS6 .... 171 J1
Shernbroke Rd *WAB* EN9 ...... 78 B8
Sherry Wy *SBF/HAD* SS7 ...... 171 K7
Sherwood Cl *VGE* SS16 .... 186 D1 🔲
Sherwood Crs *SBF/HAD* SS7 .. 191 K1
Sherwood Dr *CHLM/WR* CM1 .. 61 K4
Sherwood Dr *SOSN* SS2 .... 195 H3
Shevon Wy *BRW* CM14 .... 140 C7
Shillibeer Wk *CHIG* IG7 .... 135 J6
Shillingstone *SBN/FI* SS3 ...... 196 C4
Shingle Ct *WAB* EN9 .... 78 C7
Ship La *SOCK/AV* RM15 .... 212 A1
Ship Rd *BOC* CM0 .... 155 H1
CHLM/GWD CM2 .... 90 D8
Shipwrights Cl *SBF/HAD* SS7 .. 191 G3
Shipwrights Dr *SBF/HAD* SS7 . 191 G3
Shirebourn V *RCHLM* CM3 ..... 122 D7
Shire Cl *BCAYE* CM11 .... 144 E1
BROX EN10 .... 49 F8 🔲
CHLM/WR CM1 .... 35 H6
Shirley Cl *CHES/WCR* EN8 .... 76 C3
BROX EN10 .... 49 F6 🔲
Shirley Gdns *HCH* RM12 .... 180 C3
PIT SS13 .... 169 F5
Shirley Rd *LOS* SS9 .... 173 F8
Shoebury Av *SBN/FI* SS3 ...... 196 E6
Shoebury Common Rd
SBN/FI SS3 .... 196 B8
Shoebury Rd *SBN/FI* SS3 ...... 197 G2
SOS SS1 .... 195 K4
Shonks Mill Rd *ABR/ST* RM4 .. 111 H4
Shooters Dr *WAB* EN9 .... 50 A4
Shopland Hall Rd *RCFD* SS4 .. 175 G7
Shopland Rd *RCFD* SS4 .... 175 F6
Shorefield *SBF/HAD* SS7 ...... 190 A2
Shorefield Gdns *WOS/PRIT* SS0 . 8 B5 🔲
Shorefield Rd *WOS/PRIT* SS0 . 8 A5
Shore Rd *BOC* CM0 .... 155 H1 🔲
The Shore *GVW* DA11 .... 218 B3
Shortacre *BSDN* SS14 .... 167 K7
Short Cft *BRWN* CM15 .... 113 H3 🔲
Shorter Av *BRWN* CM15 .... 141 J2
Shortlands Av *CHONG* CM5 ... 56 B8
Short La *BCAYE* CM11 .... 145 K2
Shortmead Dr *CHES/WCR* EN8 . 76 E5
Short Rd *CVI* SS8 .... 208 B1
SBF/HAD SS7 .... 191 J3
Short St *SOSN* SS2 .... 9 D5
Shrewsbury Cl *VGE* SS16 ...... 166 A8 🔲
Shrewsbury Dr *SBF/HAD* SS7 . 170 C6 🔲
Shropshire Cl *CHLM/GWD* CM2 . 63 H8 🔲
CHLM/GWD CM2 .... 63 J8 🔲
The Shrubberies *CHIG* IG7 .... 135 F8
CHLM/WR CM1 .... 61 F5 🔲
Shrubbery Cl *LAIN* SS15 .... 6 B2 🔲
Shrubbery Rd *GVE* DA12 .... 219 G6
The Shrubbery *UPMR* RM14 .. 181 K4
Shrublands Cl *CHLM/GWD* CM2 . 5 D3
Sibneys Gn *HLWS* CM18 .... 52 C2
The Sidings *BROX* EN10 .... 49 F8 🔲
Sidmouth Av *WOS/PRIT* SS0 .. 174 A8
Sidmouth Rd *CHLM/WR* CM1 .. 35 G7 🔲
Sidney Rd *EPP* CM16 .... 108 B2
Sidwell Av *SBF/HAD* SS7 ...... 190 D4
Sidwell Cha *SBF/HAD* SS7 .... 190 D4
Sidwell La *SBF/HAD* SS7 ...... 190 D4

Sidwell Pk *SBF/HAD* SS7 ...... 190 D4
Silva Island Wy *WICKW* SS12 . 147 J8 🔲
Silver Birch Av *CHING* E4 ...... 132 A8
EPP CM16 .... 81 J1
Silver Birches *RBRW/HUT* CM13 . 141 K4
Silverdale *RAYL* SS6 .... 171 K5
Silverdale Av *WOS/PRIT* SS0 .. 170 E6
SLH/COR SS17 .... 203 K1
Silverdale Av *WOS/PRIT* SS0 .. 8 B2
Silverdale Dr *HCH* RM12 .... 180 C6
Silverdale East *SLH/COR* SS17 . 203 K1
Silverfield *BROX* EN10 .... 49 F4
Silver La *CHONG* CM5 .... 58 C5
Silverlocke Rd *GRAYS* RM17 .. 214 C5
Silvermere *VGE* SS16 .... 166 B8 🔲
Silverpoint Marine *CVI* SS8 .... 209 G2
Silver Rd *BOC* CM0 .... 155 H1
GVE DA12 .... 219 K7
Silversea Dr *WOS/PRIT* SS0 ... 193 H3
Silver St *ABR/ST* RM4 .... 109 F7
MAL CM9 .... 68 B2 🔲
WAB EN9 .... 77 J8 🔲
Silverthorn Cl *RCFD* SS4 .... 174 A1
Silverthorne *CVI* SS8 .... 207 K2
Silverthorn Gdns *CHING* E4 .... 132 B5
Silvertown Av *SLH/COR* SS17 . 203 K3
Silvertree Cl *HOC/HUL* SS5 ... 150 C7 🔲
Silver Wy *WICKE* SS11 .... 147 F5
Silverwood Cl *CDH/CHF* CM16 . 200 E7 🔲
Simmonds La *MAL* CM9 .... 96 C4
Simmonds Wy *RCHLM* CM3 ... 65 K5
Simmons La *CHING* E4 .... 132 C5
Simmons Pl *CDH/CHF* CM16 ... 200 E8 🔲
Simpson Rd *RAIN* RM13 .... 180 A7
Sims Cl *ROM* RM1 .... 160 A6
Sinclair Rd *CHING* E4 .... 132 A8
Sinclair Wk *WICKW* SS12 ...... 147 G8
Singleton Cl *HCH* RM12 .... 180 A5 🔲
Singlewell Rd *GVW* DA11 ...... 219 G8
Sirdar Rd *RAYL* SS6 .... 171 J5
Sir Francis Wy *BRW* CM14 .... 140 E5
Sir Walter Raleigh Dr *RAYL* SS6 . 171 H1
Sixth Av *CHLM/WR* CM1 .... 34 D7
CVI SS8 .... 207 J1
Skarnings Ct *WAB* EN9 .... 78 C7
Skerry Ri *CHLM/WR* CM1 .... 34 D6
Skinner's La *CHLM/GWD* CM2 . 90 D2
Skreens Ct *CHLM/WR* CM1 .... 61 K1 🔲
Skylark Cl *BCAYE* CM11 .... 144 D4
Slade End *EPP* CM16 .... 108 C2
Slade Gdns *ERITH* DA8 .... 210 A7
Slade Green Rd *ERITH* DA8 ... 210 C2
Slade's La *CHLM/GWD* CM2 ... 90 C2
The Slades *VGE* SS16 .... 188 B3
Sleepers Farm Rd *CDH/CHF* CM16 . 215 G1
Slewins Cl *EMPK* RM11 .... 160 D7
Slewins La *EMPK* RM11 .... 160 D7
Slipe La *BROX* EN10 .... 49 F6
Slough Rd *CHLM/WR* CM1 ..... 17 F3
RCHLM CM3 .... 94 C3
Smallgains Av *CVI* SS8 .... 208 C3
Small Gains La *ING* CM4 .... 117 K5
Smallgains La *ING* CM4 .... 118 A5
Smart Cl *HARH* RM3 .... 160 C3
Smart's La *LOU* IG10 .... 107 G8
Smarts Rd *GVE* DA12 .... 219 G8
Smartt Av *CVI* SS8 .... 208 A1 🔲
Smeaton Cl *WAB* EN9 .... 78 A6 🔲
Smeaton Rd *WAB* EN9 .... 105 C4
WFD IG8 .... 134 C8
Smither's Cha *SOSN* SS2 ...... 174 E8
Smithers Cl *CHLM/GWD* CM2 . 63 J7
Smiths Av *RCHLM* CM3 .... 98 E5
Smith St *SBN/FI* SS3 .... 196 E5
Smyatts Cl *BOC* CM0 .... 128 D2
Smythe Rd *BCAYE* CM11 ...... 117 K8
Snakes Hl *BRW* CM14 .... 112 E7
Snakes La *SOSN* SS2 .... 173 H8
Snelling Av *GVW* DA11 .... 218 E7
Snelling Gv *CHLM/GWD* CM2 . 63 H7
Snipe Cl *ERITH* DA8 .... 210 C6
Snoreham Gdns *RCHLM* CM3 . 97 J8
Snowdonia Cl *PIT* SS13 .... 169 F5
Snowdrop Cl *CHLM/WR* CM1 .. 35 G6 🔲
Soames Md *BRWN* CM15 ...... 85 J7
Soane St *PIT* SS13 .... 168 E5
Softwater La *SBF/HAD* SS7 ... 191 J2
Soham Rd *PEND* EN3 .... 105 F3
Solid La *BRWN* CM15 .... 113 H5
Solway *TIL* RM18 .... 216 D2
Somby Rd *BROX* EN10 .... 49 C3
Somerset Av *RCFD* SS4 .... 174 B2
WOS/PRIT SS0 .... 193 J1
Somerset Crs *WOS/PRIT* SS0 . 193 J1
Somerset Gdns *EMPK* RM11 .. 181 H2
PIT SS13 .... 168 E7 🔲
Somerset Pl *CHLM/WR* CM1 ... 34 C6
Somerset Rd *LAIN* SS15 .... 166 C2
PEND EN3 .... 104 D5
SLH/COR SS17 .... 216 B1
Somerton Av *WOS/PRIT* SS0 .. 193 H1
Somerville Gdns *LOS* SS9 ..... 193 C5
Somnes Av *CVI* SS8 .... 190 D7
Sonning Wy *SBN/FI* SS3 .... 196 C4
Sonters Down *RCHLM* CM3 ... 121 G8

Soper Cl *CHING* E4 .... 132 A8
Soper Ms *PEND* EN3 .... 105 G4 🔲
Sorrell Cl *MAL* CM9 .... 42 C6
  RCHLM CM3 .... 20 D7
The Sorrells *SLH/COR* SS17 .... 204 B3
The Sorrels *SBF/HAD* SS7 .... 170 C6
Sorrel Wk *ROM* RM1 .... 160 A5
Southall Wy *BRW* CM14 .... 140 C7
South Av *CHING* E4 .... 132 C3
  HOC/HUL SS5 .... 149 K4
  SOSN SS2 .... 9 E3
  VGE SS16 .... 186 C6
South Beech Av *WICKE* SS11 .... 147 G6 🔲
Southborough Dr *WOS/PRIT* SS0 ...... 193 J3
Southborough Rd *CHLM/GWD* CM2 ... 4 B5
Southbourne Gdns *WOS/PRIT* SS0 .... 193 J1
Southbourne Gv *HOC/HUL* SS5 .... 151 G7
  WICKW SS12 .... 146 D5
  WOS/PRIT SS0 .... 193 J2
Southbrook *SBW* CM21 .... 11 J4
Southbrook Dr *CHES/WCR* EN8 ...... 76 D2 🔲
Southbury Av *EN* EN1 .... 104 A8
Southbury Cl *HCH* RM12 .... 180 E6 🔲
Southbury Rd *EN* EN1 .... 104 B8
Southchurch Av *SBN/FI* SS3 .... 197 F6 🔲
  SOS SS1 .... 9 F5
Southchurch Bvd *SOS* SS1 .... 195 H4
Southchurch Hall Cl *SOS* SS1 .... 9 F4
Southchurch Rd *SOS* SS1 .... 9 D4
Southcliff *SBF/HAD* SS7 .... 190 B1
South Colne *VGE* SS16 .... 188 A1
Southcote Crs *BSDN* SS14 .... 168 B5
Southcote Rw *BSDN* SS14 .... 168 C5
South Crs *BSDN* SS14 .... 168 B5
South Crockerford *VGE* SS16 .... 188 B1
Southdown Rd *EMPK* RM11 .... 180 C1
South Dr *BRW* CM14 .... 141 G7
  GPK RM2 .... 160 D5
Southend Arterial Rd *BSDN* SS14 ... 167 J3
  EMPK RM11 .... 161 F5
  LAIN SS15 .... 161 F5
  RAYL SS6 .... 171 F5
  RBRW/HUT CM13 .... 162 E7
  SBF/HAD SS7 .... 171 H5
Southend Rd *WAB* EN9 .... 78 D8
  BCAYE CM11 .... 144 D6
  BCAYW CM12 .... 144 C4
  CHLM/GWD CM2 .... 92 B4
  GRAYS RM17 .... 214 B3
  MAL CM9 .... 66 C8
  RCFD SS4 .... 174 C6
  SBN/FI SS3 .... 196 B2
  SLH/COR SS17 .... 187 H7
  WICKE SS11 .... 147 K6
Southend Road Main Rd
  HOC/HUL SS5 .... 150 E8
Souther Cross Rd *CHLM/WR* CM1 ... 17 H8
Southern Dr *LOU* IG10 .... 134 C2
  RCHLM CM3 .... 122 C6
Southernhay *BSDN* SS14 .... 7 F4 🔲
  LOS SS9 .... 172 A4
  LOU IG10 .... 134 A1 🔲
Southern Wy *HLWE* CM17 .... 25 C7
  HLWS CM18 .... 3 D6
  HLWW/ROY CM19 .... 2 A6
Southey Cl *MAL* CM9 .... 68 C5 🔲
Southey Wk *TIL* RM18 .... 215 F7
Southfalls Rd *CVI* SS8 .... 209 F2
Southfield Cha *BCAYW* CM12 .... 165 K4
Southfield Cl *SBF/HAD* SS7 .... 171 K8
Southfield Dr *SBF/HAD* SS7 .... 171 K8
Southfield Rd *CHES/WCR* EN8 .... 76 C6
Southfield Wy *GVW* DA11 .... 218 E6 🔲
Southfleet Rd *GVW* DA11 .... 218 E6 🔲
South Ga *HLW* CM20 .... 3 D3
  PUR RM19 .... 211 K3
South Hanningfield Rd
  RCHLM CM3 .... 120 A5
South Hanningfield Wy
  WICKE SS11 .... 147 J2
South Hill Crs *SLH/COR* SS17 .... 203 G2
South Hill Rd *GVE* DA12 .... 219 G6
South House Cha *MAL* CM9 .... 68 D6
South Kent Av *GVW* DA11 .... 218 B4
Southlands Cha *CHLM/GWD* CM2 ... 92 C3
Southlands Rd *BCAYE* CM11 .... 146 A7
South Mayne *PIT* SS13 .... 168 D7
Southmead Crs *CHES/WCR* EN8 ...... 76 E4
Southminster Rd *BOC* CM0 .... 101 F2
Southminster Road Button's Hl
  RCHLM CM3 .... 126 E1
Southminster Road Scotts Hl
  BOC CM0 .... 128 A1
South Ordnance Rd *PEND* EN3 ...... 105 G3
South Pde *CVI* SS8 .... 208 E3
South Pl *HLW* CM20 .... 24 E2
South Primrose Hl *CHLM/WR* CM1 ... 4 A5
South Rdg *BCAYE* CM11 .... 144 D4
South Riding *BSDN* SS14 .... 168 B7
South Rd *BCAYE* CM11 .... 146 A8
  ERITH DA8 .... 210 A5
  HLW CM20 .... 24 E5
  SOCK/AV RM15 .... 200 A3
Southsea Av *LOS* SS9 .... 192 E3

South St *BOC* CM0 .... 74 C3
  BOC CM0 .... 102 A2
  BRW CM14 .... 141 F5
  GVE DA12 .... 219 G5
  MAL CM9 .... 43 H1
  RCFD SS4 .... 174 C4
  RCHLM CM3 .... 20 A6
South Vw *CDH/CHF* RM16 .... 202 B5
South View Av *TIL* RM18 .... 215 F7
South View Cl *RAYL* SS6 .... 172 A5
Southview Cl *RCHLM* CM3 .... 122 D5
South View Dr *UPMR* RM14 .... 181 H4
Southview Dr *WOS/PRIT* SS0 .... 193 K3
South View Rd *LOU* IG10 .... 134 C2
  RCHLM CM3 .... 121 G8
  SBF/HAD SS7 .... 190 B2
  WTHK RM20 .... 213 F5
Southview Rd *HOC/HUL* SS5 .... 151 G6
  RCHLM CM3 .... 65 H7
  VGE SS16 .... 168 A8
Southwalters *CVI* SS8 .... 207 K1
South Wash Rd *LAIN* SS15 .... 167 F5
South Wy *PUR* RM19 .... 212 B2
  WAB EN9 .... 105 H3
Southway *VGE* SS16 .... 186 E5
South Weald Dr *WAB* EN9 .... 77 K7
South Weald Rd *BRW* CM14 .... 140 D6
Southwell Rd *SBF/HAD* SS7 .... 190 D1
South Wharf Rd *GRAYS* RM17 .... 213 J5
Southwick Gdns *CVI* SS8 .... 207 K2
Southwick Rd *CVI* SS8 .... 207 K2
Southwold Crs *SBF/HAD* SS7 .... 170 B8
Southwood Cha *RCHLM* CM3 .... 94 A1
Southwood Gdns *RAYL* SS6 .... 172 C5
Sovereign Cl *RCFD* SS4 .... 174 B3 🔲
Sowerberry Cl *CHLM/WR* CM1 .... 34 B6
Sowrey Av *RAIN* RM13 .... 180 A7
Spa Cl *HOC/HUL* SS5 .... 151 F7
Spa Dr *BOC* CM0 .... 72 B7 🔲
Spains Hall Pl *VGE* SS16 .... 167 K8
Spains Hall Rd *CHONG* CM5 .... 58 B2
Spalding Av *CHLM/WR* CM1 .... 34 A8
Spalding Wy *CHLM/GWD* CM2 .... 63 H5
Spalt Cl *RBRW/HUT* CM13 .... 141 K5
Spanbeek Rd *CVI* SS8 .... 191 G8 🔲
Spareleaze Hl *LOU* IG10 .... 107 H8
Sparkbridge *LAIN* SS15 .... 166 B7 🔲
Spar La *RCHLM* CM3 .... 95 J3
Spa Rd *HOC/HUL* SS5 .... 150 E7
Sparrows Cl *ING* CM4 .... 60 A8
Sparrows Herne *VGE* SS16 .... 187 H2
Sparrow's La *HLWE* CM17 .... 14 A8
  RBSF CM22 .... 14 A6
Spellbrook La *WICKW* SS12 .... 147 J7
Spells Cl *BOC* CM0 .... 128 D1
Spencer Cl *MAL* CM9 .... 68 C5 🔲
  WFD IG8 .... 133 K8
Spencer Ct *RCHLM* CM3 .... 122 E6
Spencer Gdns *RCFD* SS4 .... 152 A8
Spencer Rd *SBF/HAD* SS7 .... 170 C7
Spencers Cft *HLWS* CM18 .... 24 E7
Spencer St *GVW* DA11 .... 219 F5
Spenlow Dr *CHLM/WR* CM1 .... 33 K6
Spenser Crs *UPMR* RM14 .... 181 K1
Spicersfield *CHESW* EN7 .... 76 A1
Spillbutters *BRWN* CM15 .... 113 K2
Spilsby Rd *HARH* RM3 .... 161 F2
Spindle Beams *RCFD* SS4 .... 174 C4
Spindles *TIL* RM18 .... 215 F6
Spingate Cl *HCH* RM12 .... 180 E6 🔲
Spinnaker Dr *MAL* CM9 .... 69 G8 🔲
The Spinnakers *SBF/HAD* SS7 .... 170 A8
The Spinnaker *RCHLM* CM3 .... 122 E8
Spinney Cl *WICKE* SS11 .... 147 J6
The Spinneys *HOC/HUL* SS5 .... 150 E8
  LOS SS9 .... 173 G6
  RAYL SS6 .... 172 B4
The Spinney *BCAYW* CM12 .... 144 C1
  BROX EN10 .... 49 F1 🔲
  CDH/CHF RM16 .... 202 A4 🔲
  CHONG CM5 .... 84 B4
  RBRW/HUT CM13 .... 142 B2
Spinning Wheel Md *HLWS* CM18 ...... 24 E8
Spire Cl *GVE* DA12 .... 219 H5
Spire Rd *LAIN* SS15 .... 6 A3
The Spires *CHLM/GWD* CM2 .... 63 H7
Spital La *BRW* CM14 .... 140 C6
Spital Rd *MAL* CM9 .... 67 K6
Sporehams La *CHLM/GWD* CM2 .... 92 D1
Sporhams *VGE* SS16 .... 7 F2
Sportsmans La *RCHLM* CM3 .... 38 A3
Spriggs La *ING* CM4 .... 86 D2
Springbank Av *HCH* RM12 .... 180 D6 🔲
Spring Cl *RCHLM* CM3 .... 37 H8
Spring Elms La *RCHLM* CM3 .... 65 J2
Springfield *EPP* CM16 .... 80 D6
  SBF/HAD SS7 .... 191 J1
Springfield Av *RBRW/HUT* CM13 ... 142 D3
Springfield Cl *CHONG* CM5 .... 56 B8
Springfield Dr *WOS/PRIT* SS0 .... 8 A1
Springfield Gdns *UPMR* RM14 .... 181 K4
Springfield Gn *CHLM/WR* CM1 .... 5 F1

Springfield Lyons Ap
  CHLM/GWD CM2 .... 35 J8
Springfield Park Av
  CHLM/GWD CM2 .... 5 E▢
Springfield Park La
  CHLM/GWD CM2 .... 5 F▢
Springfield Park Pde
  CHLM/GWD CM2 .... 5 E3
Springfield Park Rd
  CHLM/GWD CM2 .... 5 E▢
Springfield Pl *CHLM/WR* CM1 .... 35 F8
Springfield Rd *CHES/WCR* EN8 ...... 76 E▢
  BCAYW CM12 .... 117 H▢
  BOC CM0 .... 128 A▢
  CDH/CHF RM16 .... 214 D▢
  CHING E4 .... 133 H▢
  CHLM/GWD CM2 .... 5 D3
  CVI SS8 .... 209 H▢
  WICKE SS11 .... 147 ▢
Springfields *BROX* EN10 .... 49 F▢
Spring Gdns *HCH* RM12 .... 180 C▢
  RAYL SS6 .... 171 H▢
Spring Gv *GVE* DA12 .... 219 ▢
  LOU IG10 .... 134 A▢
Springhall La *SBW* CM21 .... 11 ▢
Springhall Rd *SBW* CM21 .... 11 ▢
Springhead Rd *ERITH* DA8 .... 210 A▢
  GVW DA11 .... 218 E▢
Spring Hills *HLW* CM20 .... 2 F▢
Springhouse La *SLH/COR* SS17 ...... 204 C▢
Springhouse Rd *SLH/COR* SS17 ...... 204 ▢
Spring La *MAL* CM9 .... 68 ▢
  RCHLM CM3 .... 39 ▢
Spring Pond Cl *CHLM/GWD* CM2 .... 5 ▢
Spring Pond Meadow *BRWN* CM15 .. 86 ▢
The Springs *BROX* EN10 .... 48 ▢
Spring Wk *BROX* EN10 .... 48 C▢
Springwater Cl *LOS* SS9 .... 172 C▢
Springwater Gv *LOS* SS9 .... 172 C▢
Springwater Rd *LOS* SS9 .... 172 C▢
Springwood Wy *ROM* RM1 .... 160 B7 ▢
Spruce Cl *LAIN* SS15 .... 6 ▢
Spruce Hl *HLWS* CM18 .... 52 C▢
Sprundel Av *CVI* SS8 .... 208 ▢
Spur Cl *ABR/ST* RM4 .... 109 F▢
Spurgate *RBRW/HUT* CM13 .... 141 K▢
The Spur *CHES/WCR* EN8 .... 76 D2
Squadrons Ap *HCH* RM12 .... 180 ▢
The Square *BOC* CM0 .... 102 ▢
  BROX EN10 .... 49 F5
  ING CM4 .... 118 ▢
  SBW CM21 .... 11 J3
  WFD IG8 .... 133 ▢
Squire St *RCHLM* CM3 .... 122 ▢
Squirrells Ct *CHLM/GWD* CM1 .... 34 B8
Squirrels *VGE* SS16 .... 186 ▢
Squirrel's Heath Av *GPK* RM2 .... 160 ▢
Squirrels Heath La *EMPK* RM11 ...... 160 ▢
Squirrels Heath Rd *HARH* RM3 .... 161 ▢
Stablecroft *CHLM/WR* CM1 .... 35 ▢
Stacey Dr *VGE* SS16 .... 186 ▢
Stacey's Mt *BCAYE* CM11 .... 145 ▢
Stackfield *HLW* CM20 .... 25 F▢
Stadium Rd *SOSN* SS2 .... 9 ▢
Stadium Wy *HLWW/ROY* CM19 .... 23 ▢
  SBF/HAD SS7 .... 171 ▢
Staffa Cl *WICKW* SS12 .... 147 ▢
Stafford Av *EMPK* RM11 .... 160 ▢
Stafford Cl *CHES/WCR* EN8 .... 76 ▢
  CDH/CHF RM16 .... 213 ▢
  LOS SS9 .... 173 ▢
  SLH/COR SS17 .... 216 ▢
Stafford Dr *BROX* EN10 .... 49 G2
Stafford Gn *VGE* SS16 .... 186 ▢
Staffords *HLWE* CM17 .... 25 ▢
Stagden Cross *BSDN* SS14 .... 168 ▢
Stag La *BKHH* IG9 .... 133 ▢
Stains Cl *CHES/WCR* EN8 .... 76 ▢
Stainton Rd *PEND* EN3 .... 105 ▢
Stairs Rd *SBN/FI* SS3 .... 197 ▢
Stambridge Rd *RCFD* SS4 .... 153 ▢
Stanbrook Rd *GVW* DA11 .... 218 ▢
Standard Rd *PEND* EN3 .... 104 ▢
Standen Av *HCH* RM12 .... 180 ▢
Standingford *EPP* CM16 .... 51 K2
Staneway *VGE* SS16 .... 186 ▢
Stanfield Rd *SOSN* SS2 .... 9 ▢
Stanford Cl *WFD* IG8 .... 134 ▢
Stanford Ct *WAB* EN9 .... 78 C7
Stanford Gdns *SOCK/AV* RM15 .... 199 ▢
Stanford-le-Hope By-pass
  CDH/CHF RM16 .... 202 ▢
  SLH/COR SS17 .... 187 ▢
Stanford Rivers Rd *CHONG* CM5 ...... 84 C▢
Stanford Rd *CDH/CHF* RM16 .... 201 ▢
  CVI SS8 .... 208 ▢
  SLH/COR SS17 .... 203 ▢
Stanhope Rd *CHES/WCR* EN8 .... 76 ▢
Stanier Cl *SOS* SS1 .... 9 F4
Stanley Av *GPK* RM2 .... 160 ▢
Stanley Cl *GPK* RM2 .... 160 ▢
  HCH RM12 .... 180 ▢
Stanley Pl *CHONG* CM5 .... 84 ▢

...anley Ri *CHLM/GWD* CM2 ...... 63 H2 🔲
...anley Rd *CHING* E4 ...... 132 E4
...CVI *CVI* SS8 ...... 208 C1
...GRAYS RM17 ...... 214 A4
...RCFD SS4 ...... 151 K6
...SBF/HAD SS7 ...... 170 C8
...SOS SS1 ...... 9 E5
...UPMR RM14 ...... 184 E5
...anley Ter *BCAYW* CM12 ...... 144 B4
...anmore Rd *WICKE* SS11 ...... 148 A7 🔲
...anmore Wy *LOU* IG10 ...... 107 J5
...annetts *LAIN* SS15 ...... 166 C5 🔲
...ansfield Rd *SBF/HAD* SS7 ...... 170 A6
...ansgate Rd *BOC* CM0 ...... 71 K8
...CHLM/WR* CM1 ...... 62 A4
...HCH RM12 ...... 180 D7 🔲
...anway Cl *CHIG* IG7 ...... 135 H8
...anway Rd *SBF/HAD* SS7 ...... 170 B8
...WAB EN9 ...... 78 C7
...anwyck Gdns *HARH* RM3 ...... 138 C8
...apleford Cl *CHING* E4 ...... 132 D6 🔲
...CHLM/GWD* CM2 ...... 4 B4 🔲
...apleford End *WICKE* SS11 ...... 148 A8 🔲
...apleford Rd *ABR/ST* RM4 ...... 110 B8
...aplegrove *SBN/FI* SS3 ...... 196 B5
...aplers Cl *MAL* CM9 ...... 40 D1 🔲
...aplers Heath *MAL* CM9 ...... 40 D1
...aples Rd *LOU* IG10 ...... 107 G7
...apleton Crs *RAIN* RM13 ...... 180 C5
...arboard Wy *RCHLM* CM3 ...... 122 E8 🔲
...ING CM4 ...... 80 E4
...SBN/FI* SS3 ...... 196 D2
...arling Cl *BKHH* IG9 ...... 133 H4
...arling Rd *LOU* IG10 ...... 107 J5
...HOC/HUL* SS5 ...... 151 F7 🔲
...LAIN SS15 ...... 6 A5
...RCHLM CM3 ...... 122 C5
...RCHLM CM3 ...... 124 D5
...SOS SS1 ...... 9 D4 🔲
...SOSN SS2 ...... 8 C2
...VGE SS16 ...... 188 E1
...WICKE SS11 ...... 147 C5 🔲
...ation Approach Rd *TIL* RM18 ...... 219 F2
...ation Av *RAYL* SS6 ...... 171 H2
...SOSN SS2 ...... 9 D1
...WICKE SS11 ...... 147 H4
...ation Crs *RAYL* SS6 ...... 171 J2
...RCHLM CM3 ...... 96 B8
...ation La *HCH* RM12 ...... 181 F5
...ING CM4 ...... 116 B2
...PIT SS13 ...... 169 F8
...ation Pde *HCH* RM12 ...... 180 D5 🔲
...ation Rd *CHES/WCR* EN8 ...... 77 C8
...BCAYW CM12 ...... 144 A3
...BOC CM0 ...... 128 B8
...BOC CM0 ...... 155 G1
...BROX EN10 ...... 49 F2
...CHIG IG7 ...... 134 C6
...CHING E4 ...... 132 E4
...CVI SS8 ...... 208 E3
...EPP CM16 ...... 80 B5
...EPP CM16 ...... 82 B1
...GPK RM2 ...... 160 C6
...GVW DA11 ...... 218 A4
...HARH RM3 ...... 161 G3 🔲
...HLWE CM17 ...... 25 G1
...HOC/HUL* SS5 ...... 151 F7
...LOS SS9 ...... 193 F2
...LOU IG10 ...... 44 D3
...MAL CM9 ...... 68 C7
...RAYL SS6 ...... 171 H2
...RBRW/HUT* CM13 ...... 164 D8
...RCHLM CM3 ...... 96 C8
...RCHLM CM3 ...... 126 D4
...SBF/HAD* SS7 ...... 190 C5
...SBW CM21 ...... 11 K2
...SOS SS1 ...... 196 A5
...TIL RM18 ...... 216 C6
...UPMR RM14 ...... 181 K3
...WAB EN9 ...... 78 A1
...WICKE SS11 ...... 147 F3
...WIT CM8 ...... 39 J1
...WOS/PRIT* SS0 ...... 193 K5
...ation Wy *BKHH* IG9 ...... 134 A7
...VGE SS16 ...... 7 E5
...averton Rd *EMPK* RM11 ...... 160 E8 🔲
...ays La *CHONG* CM5 ...... 8 E2
...ebbings *VGE* SS16 ...... 5 J4
...eed Cl *HCH* RM12 ...... 180 C3 🔲
...eeds Cl *LOU* IG10 ...... 107 C7
...eeds Cl *ING* CM4 ...... 116 B1
...eeple Cl *MAL* CM9 ...... 69 F1
...RCFD SS4 ...... 174 A2
...eeplefield *LOS* SS9 ...... 173 F7
...eeplehall *PIT* SS13 ...... 168 D8
...eeple Hts *SBF/HAD* SS7 ...... 170 A7 🔲
...eeple Mdw *BOC* CM0 ...... 128 B7
...eeple Rd *BOC* CM0 ...... 100 B7
...BOC CM0 ...... 100 C1

BOC CM0 ...... 128 B1
RCHLM CM3 ...... 97 K7
RCHLM CM3 ...... 98 D6
Steeple Wy *BRWN* CM15 ...... 113 K3 🔲
Steerforth St *CHLM/WR* CM1 ...... 33 K6 🔲
Steli Av *CVI* SS8 ...... 190 E8
Stella Maris Cl *CVI* SS8 ...... 209 F2
Stenning Av *TIL* RM18 ...... 216 C5
Stephen Av *RAIN* RM13 ...... 180 B7
Stephens Cl *HARH* RM3 ...... 138 D8
Stephens Crs *SLH/COR* SS17 ...... 203 F2 🔲
Stephenson Av *TIL* RM18 ...... 215 F7
Stephenson Rd *LOS* SS9 ...... 124 C5
RCHLM CM3 ...... 97 H3
Sterling Av *CHES/WCR* EN8 ...... 76 D8
Stevens Cl *CVI* SS8 ...... 208 D1
Stevenson Cl *ERITH* DA8 ...... 210 C6 🔲
Stevenson Wy *WICKW* SS12 ...... 147 F8
Steward Cl *CHES/WCR* EN8 ...... 76 E4
Stewards Cl *EPP* CM16 ...... 80 E7
Stewards Elm Farm La *RCFD* SS4 ...... 175 D3
Stewards Green Rd *EPP* CM16 ...... 81 F6
Stewart Pl *WICKW* SS12 ...... 147 J8 🔲
Stewart Rd *CHLM/GWD* CM2 ...... 62 C7
Steyning Av *SOSN* SS2 ...... 195 H3
Stifford Clays Rd
 CDH/CHF RM16 ...... 200 E7 🔲
 CDH/CHF RM16 ...... 201 F7
Stifford Hl *CHLM/CHF* RM16 ...... 200 B8
 SOCK/AV RM15 ...... 200 A7
Stifford Rd *SOCK/AV* RM15 ...... 199 K7
 SOCK/AV RM15 ...... 200 A7 🔲
Stile Cft *HLWS* CM18 ...... 24 E7
Stile La *RAYL* SS6 ...... 171 J3
Stilemans *WICKE* SS11 ...... 147 C5 🔲
The Stiles *MAL* CM9 ...... 69 D8
Stirling Av *LOS* SS9 ...... 192 C3
Stirling Cl *RAYL* SS6 ...... 149 G8
Stirling Pl *PIT* SS13 ...... 168 E5
Stirrup Cl *CHLM/WR* CM1 ...... 35 G6
Stivvy's Rd *MAL* CM9 ...... 66 C2
Stock Cha *MAL* CM9 ...... 40 D8
Stock Cl *SOSN* SS2 ...... 194 C1
Stockingswater La *PEND* EN3 ...... 104 E7
Stock La *ING* CM4 ...... 116 C7
Stock Rd *BCAYE* CM11 ...... 144 C1
 BCAYW CM12 ...... 144 C3
 CHLM/GWD CM2 ...... 90 C2
 ING CM4 ...... 118 B2
 SOSN SS2 ...... 194 D1
Stocksfield *BRWN* CM15 ...... 113 H3
Stocks La *BRWN* CM15 ...... 113 H3
Stockwell Cl *BCAYE* CM11 ...... 144 E7 🔲
 CHESW EN7 ...... 76 A2
Stockwood *SBF/HAD* SS7 ...... 171 F6
Stokefelde *PIT* SS13 ...... 168 E6
Stonards Hl *EPP* CM16 ...... 81 G5
 LOU IG10 ...... 134 C2
Stondon Rd *CHONG* CM5 ...... 84 D4
Stonechat Rd *BCAYW* CM12 ...... 144 D5
Stonehill Cl *LOS* SS9 ...... 193 G4
Stonehill Rd *CHLM/WR* CM1 ...... 59 K1
 LOS SS9 ...... 193 F1
Stonehouse La *PUR* RM19 ...... 212 B4
Stoneleigh *SBW* CM21 ...... 11 H2 🔲
Stoneleigh Av *EN* EN1 ...... 104 B4
Stoneleigh Cl *CHES/WCR* EN8 ...... 76 D7 🔲
Stoneleighs *SBF/HAD* SS7 ...... 170 E7
Stoneness Rd *WTHK* RM20 ...... 212 E5
Stone Path Dr *RCHLM* CM3 ...... 37 K1
Stone St *GVE* DA12 ...... 219 G4
Stoney Hills *BCAYE* CM11 ...... 118 D8
 BOC CM0 ...... 128 C5
Stonycroft Cl *PEND* EN3 ...... 104 E6
Stony La *CHONG* CM5 ...... 55 H5
Stony Pth *LOU* IG10 ...... 107 H5
Stonyshotts *WAB* EN9 ...... 78 A8
Stony Wd *HLWS* CM18 ...... 3 D4
Stormonts Wy *VGE* SS16 ...... 186 D5
Stornoway Rd *SOSN* SS2 ...... 9 F3
Storr Gdns *RBRW/HUT* CM13 ...... 142 C1
Stortford Rd *GTDUN* CM6 ...... 15 J7
 RBSF RM22 ...... 12 E1
Stort Ml *HLW* CM20 ...... 11 J7
Stort Valley Wy *HLW* CM20 ...... 11 H6
 HLWE CM17 ...... 26 E5
 HLWW/ROY CM19 ...... 22 B5
 SBW CM21 ...... 12 C5
Stour Cl *SBN/FI* SS3 ...... 196 D7 🔲
Stour Rd *CDH/CHF* RM16 ...... 215 F4
Stour Wy *UPMR* RM14 ...... 162 B8
Stowe's La *BOC* CM0 ...... 101 J1
Stow Rd *RCHLM* CM3 ...... 123 K1
The Stow *CHLM* CM20 ...... 3 F1
St Peter's Wy *BOC* CM0 ...... 74 C8
 CHLM/GWD CM2 ...... 91 J8
 CHONG CM5 ...... 84 D2
 CHONG CM5 ...... 85 G3
 ING CM4 ...... 86 C5
 ING CM4 ...... 117 J1
 ING CM4 ...... 118 C3
 RCHLM CM3 ...... 94 E4
 RCHLM CM3 ...... 98 E1
Stradbroke Gv *BKHH* IG9 ...... 134 A4

Straight Rd *HARH* RM3 ...... 138 C8
The Straits *WAB* EN9 ...... 77 H6
Strangman La *SBF/HAD* SS7 ...... 191 G1
Strasbourg Rd *CVI* SS8 ...... 191 J8
Stratfield Dr *BROX* EN10 ...... 48 E1
Stratford Gdns *SLH/COR* SS17 ...... 203 K3
Strathmore *TIL* RM18 ...... 216 D5 🔲
Strathmore Gdns *HCH* RM12 ...... 180 A2
Strathmore Rd *RCHLM* CM3 ...... 124 D5
Stratton Rd *HARH* RM3 ...... 139 H8
Stratton Wk *HARH* RM3 ...... 139 H8 🔲
Strawbrook Hl *RCHLM* CM3 ...... 21 G1
The Street *BOC* CM0 ...... 99 J3
 CHLM/GWD CM2 ...... 90 D7
 CHLM/WR CM1 ...... 32 A7
 CHONG CM5 ...... 58 B2
 CHONG CM5 ...... 85 F1
 MAL CM9 ...... 66 D3
 RBSF RM22 ...... 12 D5
 RCHLM CM3 ...... 18 A3
 RCHLM CM3 ...... 20 D7
 RCHLM CM3 ...... 37 K1
 RCHLM CM3 ...... 97 H8
 RCHLM CM3 ...... 122 B1
 RCHLM CM3 ...... 123 J1
Stroma Gdns *SBN/FI* SS3 ...... 196 C7
Stromburg Rd *CVI* SS8 ...... 190 D8
Stromness Pl *SOSN* SS2 ...... 9 F4
Stromness Rd *SOSN* SS2 ...... 9 F3
Struan Av *SLH/COR* SS17 ...... 187 F8
Strutt Cl *RCHLM* CM3 ...... 38 A1 🔲
Struttons Av *GVW* DA11 ...... 218 C2
Stuart Cl *BRWN* CM15 ...... 140 E1
 CHLM/GWD CM2 ...... 63 K7
 CVI SS8 ...... 208 B1
 SBN/FI SS3 ...... 196 E1
 SOSN SS2 ...... 9 D1
Stuart Rd *GRAYS* RM17 ...... 214 A4 🔲
 GVW DA11 ...... 219 F4
 SOSN SS2 ...... 9 D2
Stuart St *SOSN* SS2 ...... 9 D1 🔲
Stuart Wy *BCAYE* CM11 ...... 145 F4 🔲
 CHESW EN7 ...... 76 B5
Stubbers La *UPMR* RM14 ...... 182 B7
Stublands *BSDN* SS14 ...... 168 C7
Studland Av *WICKW* SS12 ...... 146 C5
Stump La *CHLM/WR* CM1 ...... 5 E1
Sturlas Wy *CHES/WCR* EN8 ...... 76 D7
Sturrocks *VGE* SS16 ...... 188 B2
Sudbrook Cl *WICKW* SS12 ...... 147 G7 🔲
Sudbury Cl *HOC/HUL* SS5 ...... 173 C3
Sudbury Rd *BCAYE* CM11 ...... 119 J8
Sudburys Farm Rd *BCAYW* CM12 ...... 143 G2
Sudeley Gdns *HOC/HUL* SS5 ...... 150 E7
Sudicamps Ct *WAB* EN9 ...... 78 C7 🔲
Suez Rd *PEND* EN3 ...... 104 E8
Suffield Rd *CHING* E4 ...... 132 C6
Suffolk Av *LOS* SS9 ...... 193 G2
Suffolk Crs *MAL* CM9 ...... 68 A4
Suffolk Dr *LAIN* SS15 ...... 166 C7
Suffolk Rd *GVE* DA12 ...... 219 J4
 MAL CM9 ...... 68 A4
Suffolk Wy *CVI* SS8 ...... 207 J1
 EMPK RM11 ...... 161 H6 🔲
Sugden Av *WICKW* SS12 ...... 146 D6
Sullivan Rd *TIL* RM18 ...... 215 F7
Sullivan Wy *VGE* SS16 ...... 166 B8
Summercourt Rd *WOS/PRIT* SS0 ...... 8 B4 🔲
Summerdale *BCAYW* CM12 ...... 144 B3
 RCHLM CM3 ...... 126 E2 🔲
Summerfield Rd *LOU* IG10 ...... 134 A2
Summerfields *ING* CM4 ...... 116 C2 🔲
Summerwood Cl *SBF/HAD* SS7 ...... 191 H2 🔲
The Summit *LOU* IG10 ...... 107 H5
Sumners Farm Cl *EPP* CM16 ...... 51 J2 🔲
Sumpters Wy *SOSN* SS2 ...... 174 C7
Sunbury Ct *SBN/FI* SS3 ...... 196 D3
Sunbury Wy *MAL* CM9 ...... 68 B5
Sun Ct *ERITH* DA8 ...... 210 A8
Sunflower Wy *HARH* RM3 ...... 160 E3
Sun La *GVE* DA12 ...... 219 H7
Sunnedon *VGE* SS16 ...... 168 A8
Sunningdale *VGE* SS16 ...... 208 C1 🔲
Sunningdale Av *LOS* SS9 ...... 193 H4
Sunningdale Fall *RCHLM* CM3 ...... 38 B1 🔲
Sunningdale Rd *CHLM/WR* CM1 ...... 62 A1
 RAIN RM13 ...... 180 B6
 RCHLM CM3 ...... 126 C3
Sunninghill *GVW* DA11 ...... 218 D7 🔲
Sunnings La *UPMR* RM14 ...... 182 A7
Sunnybank Cl *LOS* SS9 ...... 173 C9
Sunny Cft *HLWS* CM18 ...... 3 F6 🔲
Sunnycroft Rd *UPMR* RM14 ...... 182 E1
Sunnydene Av *CHING* E4 ...... 132 E8
Sunnydene Cl *HARH* RM3 ...... 161 G2
Sunnyfield Gdns *HOC/HUL* SS5 ...... 150 C7
Sunnymede *CHIG* IG7 ...... 136 A6
Sunnymede Cl *SBF/HAD* SS7 ...... 171 F7
Sunny Rd *HOC/HUL* SS5 ...... 151 F8
The Sunny Rd *PEND* EN3 ...... 104 D5
Sunnyside *VGE* SS16 ...... 186 A1 🔲
 WAB EN9 ...... 50 B4
Sunnyside Dr *CHING* E4 ...... 132 D3
Sunnyside Gdns *UPMR* RM14 ...... 181 K4
Sunnyside Rd *EPP* CM16 ...... 80 D6

Sunny Wy BOC CM0 ... 72 C5
Sun Ray Av RBRW/HUT CM13 ... 142 D2
Sunrise Cl CHLM/WR CM1 ... 34 C8
  HCH RM12 ... 180 D4
Sunset Av CHING E4 ... 132 C4
  WFD IG8 ... 133 H8
Sunset Cl ERITH DA8 ... 210 C6
Sun St BCAYW CM12 ... 144 B4
  SBW CM21 ... 11 K4
  WAB EN9 ... 77 J7
Surbiton Av SOS SS1 ... 195 G5
Surbiton Rd SOSN SS2 ... 195 G4
Surig Rd CVI SS8 ... 208 A1
Surman Crs RBRW/HUT CM13 ... 142 B3
Surrey Av LOS SS9 ... 193 G2
Surrey Dr EMPK RM11 ... 161 H1
Surrey Wy LAIN SS15 ... 166 B7
Sussex Av HARH RM3 ... 161 G2
Sussex Cl CVI SS8 ... 191 F8
  LAIN SS15 ... 166 C7
  RCHLM CM3 ... 36 C5
Sussex Rd BRW CM14 ... 140 E2
Sussex Wy BCAYW CM12 ... 117 H5
  CVI SS8 ... 191 F8
Sutcliffe Cl WICKW SS12 ... 147 G7
Sutherland Bvd LOS SS9 ... 192 C5
Sutherland Pl WICKW SS12 ... 147 G8
Sutton Cl BROX EN10 ... 48 E2
  LOU IG10 ... 134 B3
Sutton Court Rd RCFD SS4 ... 174 C6
Sutton Md CHLM/GWD CM2 ... 63 J1
Sutton Rd RCFD SS4 ... 174 D5
  SOSN SS2 ... 9 D2
Suttons Av HCH RM12 ... 180 C4
Suttons Gdns HCH RM12 ... 180 E4
Suttons La HCH RM12 ... 180 E6
Suttons Rd SBN/FI SS3 ... 197 C5
Swale Cl SOCK/AV RM15 ... 198 E6
Swale Rd SBF/HAD SS7 ... 171 C8
Swallowcliffe SBN/FI SS3 ... 196 C4
Swallow Cl CDH/CHF RM16 ... 213 F3
  RAYL SS6 ... 171 G2
Swallow Dl VGE SS16 ... 7 F6
Swallow Rd SBF/HAD SS7 ... 190 A3
Swallow Rd WICKE SS11 ... 147 F3
Swallows HLWE CM17 ... 25 C5
The Swallows BCAYE CM11 ... 144 D8
Swanage Rd SOSN SS2 ... 9 E5
Swan And Pike Rd PEND EN3 ... 105 C4
Swan Av UPMR RM14 ... 182 C2
Swanbourne Dr HCH RM12 ... 180 C1
Swan Cl LAIN SS15 ... 6 C4
  RCHLM CM3 ... 37 K1
Swan Ct MAL CM9 ... 68 D1
Swanfield Cl CHES/WCR EN8 ... 76 E7
Swan La BRWN CM15 ... 113 G3
  INC CM4 ... 117 K2
  LOU IG10 ... 133 K3
  WICKE SS11 ... 147 G4
Swan Md VGE SS16 ... 188 A4
Swansea Rd PEND EN3 ... 104 C8
Swans Green Cl SBF/HAD SS7 ... 171 F7
Swanshope LOU IG10 ... 107 K6
Swans Rd CHES/WCR EN8 ... 76 D8
Swanstead VGE SS16 ... 188 B1
Swan Wy PEND EN3 ... 104 D6
Sweet Briar SBF/HAD SS7 ... 190 C3
Sweet Briar Dr LAIN SS15 ... 6 B1
Sweyne HLWE CM17 ... 25 C8
Sweyne Av RCD/HUL SS5 ... 173 H1
  WOS/PRIT SS0 ... 8 C3
Sweyne Cl RAYL SS6 ... 171 G1
Swift Cl UPMR RM14 ... 182 B2
Swiftsure Rd CDH/CHF RM16 ... 213 F3
Swinborne Rd PIT SS13 ... 168 E3
Swinborne Rd RAYL SS6 ... 169 F4
Swinburne Gdns TIL RM18 ... 215 C8
Swindon Gdns HARH RM3 ... 139 G8
Swindon La HARH RM3 ... 139 G8
Swiss Av CHLM/WR CM1 ... 4 A1
Sycamore Av UPMR RM14 ... 181 H4
Sycamore Cl CVI SS8 ... 207 K2
  GVE DA12 ... 219 G5
  RAYL SS6 ... 149 G7
  TIL RM18 ... 214 E7
Sycamore Dr BRW CM14 ... 141 F4
Sycamore Fld HLWW/ROY CM19 ... 51 J1
Sycamore Gv SOSN SS2 ... 9 E2
Sycamore Rd MAL CM9 ... 40 D7
Sycamore Wy CHLM/GWD CM2 ... 62 E2
  RCFD SS4 ... 153 G4
  SOCK/AV RM15 ... 200 B4
Sydenham Cl ROM RM1 ... 160 A6
Sydervelt Rd CVI SS8 ... 208 A1
Sydner Cl CHLM/GWD CM2 ... 63 J8
Sydney Rd LOS SS9 ... 192 C5
  SBF/HAD SS7 ... 190 B1
  TIL RM18 ... 215 F8
Sykes Md RAYL SS6 ... 171 J4
Sylvan Av EMPK RM11 ... 161 G8
Sylvan Cl CDH/CHF RM16 ... 213 H5
  CHLM/GWD CM2 ... 62 D7
  CVI SS8 ... 208 B3
  LAIN SS15 ... 166 C7
Sylvan Tryst BCAYW CM12 ... 144 C1

Sylvan Wy CHIG IG7 ... 136 A6
  LAIN SS15 ... 166 A6
  LOS SS9 ... 192 B1
Sylvesters HLWW/ROY CM19 ... 23 H7
Sylvia Av RBRW/HUT CM13 ... 142 D2
Symonds Ct CHES/WCR EN8 ... 76 D2
Symons Av LOS SS9 ... 173 F6

T

Tabora Av CVI SS8 ... 190 E8
Tabors Av CHLM/GWD CM2 ... 65 H6
Tabrum's La HARH RM3 ... 122 B6
The Tabrums RCHLM CM3 ... 122 C4
Tabrums Wy UPMR RM14 ... 182 B1
Tadlows Cl UPMR RM14 ... 181 J6
Tadworth Pde HCH RM12 ... 180 C5
Taffrail Gdns RCHLM CM3 ... 122 E8
Tailors Ct SOSN SS2 ... 174 C4
Tailors Wy SOSN SS2 ... 174 C8
Taits SLH/COR SS17 ... 177 G4
Takeley Cl WAB EN9 ... 77 K7
Takely End VGE SS16 ... 7 E5
Takely Ride VGE SS16 ... 7 E5
Talbot Av RAYL SS6 ... 171 H2
Talbrook BRW CM14 ... 140 C6
Tallis Cl SLH/COR SS17 ... 203 J2
Tallis Rd LAIN SS15 ... 6 B2
Tallon Rd RBRW/HUT CM13 ... 143 G4
Tallow Ga RCHLM CM3 ... 122 E6
Tall Trees TIL RM18 ... 160 E8
Tally-ho Dr RBRW/HUT CM13 ... 143 G4
Talus Dr PUR RM19 ... 212 A3
Talza Wy SOSN SS2 ... 174 C8
Tamar Cl UPMR RM14 ... 162 B8
Tamar Dr SOCK/AV RM15 ... 198 E6
Tamarisk SBF/HAD SS7 ... 190 B1
Tamarisk Rd SOCK/AV RM15 ... 200 A3
  SOCK/AV ... 200 A4
  SOCK/AV ... 200 A4
Tamar Ri CHLM/WR CM1 ... 34 E2
Tanfield Cl CHESW EN7 ... 76 A1
Tanfield Dr BCAYW CM12 ... 144 B3
Tangent Link HARH RM3 ... 160 E5
Tangent Rd HARH RM3 ... 160 E5
Tangham Wk BSDN SS14 ... 7 J3
Tangmere Cl WICKE SS11 ... 148 A7
Tanners Wy RCHLM CM3 ... 122 C5
Tankerville Dr LOS SS9 ... 192 E2
Tank Hill Rd PUR RM19 ... 211 H3
Tank La PUR RM19 ... 211 H3
Tanswell Av PIT SS13 ... 168 E6
Tanswell Ct PIT SS13 ... 168 E7
Tansy Cl HARH RM3 ... 161 F1
Tany's Dell HLW CM20 ... 24 E2
Tapley Rd CHLM/WR CM1 ... 34 B7
Taranto Rd CVI SS8 ... 208 D2
Tarnworth Rd HARH RM3 ... 139 H8
Tarpan Wy BROX EN10 ... 49 F8
Tasker Rd CDH/CHF RM16 ... 215 G2
Tasman Cl SLH/COR SS17 ... 204 B1
Tatsfield Av WAB EN9 ... 49 K5
Tattenham Rd LAIN SS15 ... 166 C6
Tattersall Gdns LOS SS9 ... 192 B4
Tattersalls Cha DOC CM0 ... 128 E1
Taunton Dr WOS/PRIT SS0 ... 193 J7
Taunton Rd CHLM/WR CM1 ... 35 G8
  HARH RM3 ... 138 D7
Taunton V GVE DA12 ... 219 J8
Taveners Green Cl WICKW SS12 ... 147 H7
Taverners Cl CHING E4 ... 133 F4
Tavistock Cl HARH RM3 ... 160 B8
Tavistock Dr BCAYW CM12 ... 117 F8
Tavistock Rd CHLM/WR CM1 ... 35 F8
  LAIN SS15 ... 6 A2
  LAIN SS15 ... 6 A3
Tawney Common EPP CM16 ... 82 A6
Tawney La ABR/ST RM4 ... 110 C5
  EPP CM16 ... 82 C6
Tawneys Rd HLWS CM18 ... 24 B4
Tawny Av UPMR RM14 ... 181 J6
Taylifers HLWW/ROY CM19 ... 51 J2
Taylor Av CHLM/WR CM1 ... 34 A8
Tay Wy ROM RM1 ... 160 A3
Teagles LAIN SS15 ... 6 C4
Teal Av RCHLM CM3 ... 98 E5
Tees Cl UPMR RM14 ... 162 B8
Tees Dr HARH RM3 ... 138 E6
Tees Rd CHLM/WR CM1 ... 34 E7
Teigngrace SBN/FI SS3 ... 196 C5
Teignmouth Dr RAYL SS6 ... 149 J8
Tempest Wy RAIN RM13 ... 180 E2
Temple Bank HLW CM20 ... 11 F8
Temple Cl CHESW EN7 ... 76 A5
  LAIN SS15 ... 6 A3
  SBF/HAD SS7 ... 192 A2
Temple Md HLWW/ROY CM19 ... 22 D5
Templer Cl CDH/CHF RM16 ... 215 F3
Templeton Av CHING E4 ... 132 B7
Temple Wy MAL CM9 ... 40 B8

Templewood Ct SBF/HAD SS7 ... 191
Templewood Rd PIT SS13 ... 168 E
  SBF/HAD SS7 ... 191
Temptin Av CVI SS8 ... 208 E
Ten Acre Ap MAL CM9 ... 40 E
Tenby Rd PEND EN3 ... 104 C
Tendring Av RAYL SS6 ... 171 F
Tendring Rd HLWS CM18 ... 2 C5
Tennyson Av GRAYS RM17 ... 214 A
  SOSN SS2 ... 9 E
  WAB EN9 ... 78 A
Tennyson Cl LOS SS9 ... 192 E
Tennyson Dr PIT SS13 ... 188 E
Tennyson Rd CHLM/WR CM1 ... 34
  HARH RM3 ... 160 C
  MAL CM9 ... 68 C
  RBRW/HUT CM13 ... 142 E
Tennyson Wk CVW DA11 ... 218 C
  TIL RM18 ... 215 C
Tennyson Wy HCH RM12 ... 180 A
Tensing Av CVW DA11 ... 218 D8
Tensing Gdns BCAYW CM12 ... 144 A
Tenterfield Rd MAL CM9 ... 68 C
Tenterfields PIT SS13 ... 169 E
Teramo Rd CVI SS8 ... 208 D2
Tercel Pth CHIG IG7 ... 136 A
Terence Webster Rd WICKW SS12 ... 147 C
Teresa Gdns CHES/WCR EN8 ... 76 A
Terling VGE SS16 ... 7 E
The Terlings BRW CM14 ... 140 C
Terminal Cl SBN/FI SS3 ... 196 E
Terminus Dr VGE SS16 ... 188 E
Terminus St HLW CM20 ... 3 C
Terms Av CVI SS8 ... 191 F8
Tern Cl RCHLM CM3 ... 98 C
Tern Gdns UPMR RM14 ... 182 B2
Terni Rd CVI SS8 ... 208 C
Tern Wy BRW CM14 ... 140 E
Terrace St GVE DA12 ... 219 C
The Terrace GVE DA12 ... 219 C
  SBN/FI SS3 ... 196 E
Teviot Av SOCK/AV RM15 ... 198 E
Tewkes Rd CVI SS8 ... 191
Thackeray Av TIL RM18 ... 215 C
Thackerey Rw WICKW SS12 ... 147 G8
Thal Massing Cl RBRW/HUT CM13 ... 142 A
Thames Av CHLM/WR CM1 ... 33
Thames Cl LOS SS9 ... 192 E
  RAYL SS6 ... 171 F
  SLH/COR SS17 ... 204 E
Thames Crs SLH/COR SS17 ... 187 E
Thames Dr CDH/CHF RM16 ... 215 F
  LOS SS9 ... 192 E
Thames Haven Rd SLH/COR SS17 ... 204 C
Thameside Crs CVI SS8 ... 207 K
Thames Rd CVI SS8 ... 207 K
  GRAYS RM17 ... 214 A
Thames Vw GRAYS RM17 ... 215 F
  VGE SS16 ... 186 C
Thames Wy BOC CM0 ... 128 A
  CVW DA11 ... 218 C
Thamley PUR RM19 ... 211 H
Thatchers Dr LOU IG10 ... 108 A
Thatchers Cft RCHLM CM3 ... 97 C
Thaxted Gn RBRW/HUT CM13 ... 142 E
Thaxted Rd BKHH IG9 ... 134 E
Thaxted Wy WAB EN9 ... 77 H
Thear Cl WOS/PRIT SS0 ... 193 H
Thelma Av CVI SS8 ... 208 A
Theobalds Av GRAYS RM17 ... 214 E
Theobalds Gv CHES/WCR EN8 ... 76 D6
Theobald's La CHES/WCR EN8 ... 76 E
Theobalds Rd LOS SS9 ... 192 C
Thetford Pl LAIN SS15 ... 6 E
Theydon Cl WAB EN9 ... 78 C
Theydon Crs BSDN SS14 ... 168 C
Theydon Gdns RAIN RM13 ... 180 A8
Theydon Ga EPP CM16 ... 108 C2
Theydon Gv EPP CM16 ... 80 E
Theydon Park Rd EPP CM16 ... 108 C
Theydon Pk EPP CM16 ... 80 D
Theydon Rd EPP CM16 ... 80 E
Thielen Rd CVI SS8 ... 191 H
Thieves Cnr CHLM/WR CM1 ... 61 H
Third Av CHLM/WR CM1 ... 34 C
  CVI SS8 ... 207
  HLWS CM18 ... 3 C
  HLWW/ROY CM19 ... 2 E
  SLH/COR SS17 ... 204 A
  WICKE SS11 ... 147 H
  WTHK RM20 ... 212 C
Thirlmere Rd SBF/HAD SS7 ... 170 C
Thirslet Dr MAL CM9 ... 68 E
Thisselt Rd CVI SS8 ... 191 F
Thistle Cl LAIN SS15 ... 7 C
Thistledene Av CRW RM5 ... 137 C
Thistledown BSDN SS14 ... 167 K7
Thistle Md LOU IG10 ... 107 J7
Thistle Rd GVE DA12 ... 219 H
Thistley Cl LOS SS9 ... 193 C
  MAL CM9 ... 114 C
Thoby La BRWN CM15 ... 114 C
Thomas Bata Av TIL RM18 ... 216 C
Thomas Cl BRWN CM15 ... 141 H
  CHLM/GWD CM2 ... 63 H3

...omas Dr CVI SS8 .... 190 D8
GVE DA12 .... 219 J7
...omasin Rd PIT SS13 .... 169 H4
...omasin Rd PIT SS13 .... 169 H6
...omas Rochford Wy CHES/WCR EN8 77
F1
...ompson Av SBF/HAD SS7 .... 209 F2
...orington Av SBF/HAD SS7 .... 171 J7
...orington Rd RAYL SS6 .... 172 B4 ☐
...orin's Ga RCHLM CM3 .... 122 C7
...orley Rd CDH/CHF RM16 .... 200 E8
...ornborough Av RCHLM CM3 .... 122 E6
...ornbush LAIN SS15 .... 6 C4
...orncroft EMPK RM11 .... 160 C4
...orndale SBF/HAD SS7 .... 171 G6 ☐
...orndales BRW CM14 .... 141 D7
...orndon Ap RBRW/HUT CM13 .... 164 C2
...orndon Av RBRW/HUT CM13 .... 164 B7
...orndon Ga RBRW/HUT CM13 .... 142 B8
...orndon Park Cl LOS SS9 .... 172 D8
...orndon Park Crs LOS SS9 .... 172 C8
...orndon Park Dr LOS SS9 .... 172 C8
...orney Bay Rd CVI SS8 .... 207 K3
...ornford Gdns SOSN SS2 .... 174 C8
...ornhill EPP CM16 .... 54 C8
LOS SS9 .... 193 F1
RCHLM CM3 .... 95 K4 ☐
...ornridge BRW CM14 .... 140 E4 ☐
...ornton Pl ING CM4 .... 118 A3
...ornton Wy LAIN SS15 .... 166 B8
...ornwood Rd EPP CM16 .... 81 F2
...orolds VGE SS16 .... 188 B2
...orpe Bay Gdns SOS SS1 .... 195 K7
...orpe CI HOC/HUL SS5 .... 173 G1
...orpedene Av HOC/HUL SS5 .... 149 K3
...orpedene Gdns SBN/FI SS3 .... 196 C6
...orpe Esp SOS SS1 .... 195 K7
...orpe Hall Av SOS SS1 .... 195 K5 ☐
...orpe Hall CI SOS SS1 .... 195 K5
...orpe Rd HOC/HUL SS5 .... 173 G1
...orp Leas CVI SS8 .... 208 B3
...ors Oak SLH/COR SS17 .... 204 A3
...ree Forests Wy ABR/ST RM4 .... 110 D3
CHONG CM5 .... 29 F5
...ree forests Wy CHONG CM5 .... 57 H1
...ree Forests Wy GTDUN SS16 .... 15 F5
...HLWW/ROY CM19 .... 22 B5
LOU IG10 .... 107 F5
SBW CM21 .... 11 J4
WAB EN9 .... 51 F3
WAB EN9 .... 106 E2
...ree Horseshoes Rd
HLWW/ROY CM19 .... 2 B5
...reshelford VGE SS16 .... 7 D6 ☐
...rifts Md EPP CM16 .... 108 C3
...rift Wd RCHLM CM3 .... 93 J4
...rowley CI PIT SS13 .... 169 F8
...undersley Church Rd
SBF/HAD SS7 .... 170 C8
...undersley Gv SBF/HAD SS7 .... 170 E8
...undersley Park Rd
SBF/HAD SS7 .... 190 C2
...urlby U WFD IG8 .... 134 C8 ☐
...urlow Vw GRAYS RM17 .... 213 K2
...urlow Dr SOS SS1 .... 195 J5
...urlstone SBF/HAD SS7 .... 171 H8
...urrock Park Wy GRAYS RM17 .... 214 C6
...urso CI HARH RM3 .... 161 J1
...urstable CI MAL CM9 .... 44 D3
...urstable Rd MAL CM9 .... 44 D3
...urstable Wy MAL CM9 .... 44 E3
...urstans HLWW/ROY CM19 .... 51 K2
...urston Av SOSN SS2 .... 195 H4
...ynne Rd BCAYE CM11 .... 144 D3
...ury Gdns TIL RM18 .... 219 F2
...ury Md HLWS CM18 .... 24 E7
...ury Rd RBRW/HUT CM13 .... 164 D6
...egate Rd CHONG CM5 .... 54 C1
...HLWS CM18 .... 3 F5
...lingham St WAB EN9 .... 78 C7 ☐
...lingham Gn LAIN SS15 .... 166 D7
...lingham Rd BOC CM0 .... 101 F8
...lingham Wy RAYL SS6 .... 171 F2
...lwicks Rd HLWS CM18 .... 3 F4
...ney Turn VGE SS16 .... 188 C3
...mberlog St BSDN SS14 .... 168 B7
...mberlog La BSDN SS14 .... 168 B8
...mbermans Vw VGE SS16 .... 188 C2
...ndall CI HARH RM3 .... 161 G4
...ndal St CHLM/WR CM1 .... 4 C3
...ne Rd CHIG IG7 .... 135 H6
...nker's La RCFD SS4 .... 174 C4
...nnocks La BOC CM0 .... 72 B4
...ntagel Wy MAL CM9 .... 68 A5
...ntern Av WOS/PRIT SS0 .... 193 K3
...tiers Br BCAYE CM11 .... 118 D8
...ppersfield SBF/HAD SS7 .... 190 D1 ☐

Tipps Cross La BRWN CM15 .... 85 K8
Tips Cross Md BRWN CM15 .... 113 K1
Tiptree CI CHING E4 .... 132 D6
EMPK RM11 .... 181 H2
LOS SS9 .... 193 G1
Tiptree Ct RBRW/HUT CM13 .... 142 C1
Tiptree Gv WICKW SS12 .... 147 G6 ☐
Tiree Cha WICKW SS12 .... 147 J8
Titan Rd GRAYS RM17 .... 213 K4
Titchfield Rd PEND EN3 .... 104 E3
Tithelands HLWW/ROY CM19 .... 23 H8
The Tithe HLWW/ROY CM19 .... 146 E7
Titley Cl CHING E4 .... 132 B8
Tiverton Gv HARH RM3 .... 139 H8
Tobruk Rd CHLM/WR CM1 .... 34 B7
Toddbrook HLWW/ROY CM19 .... 2 B4
Toft Av GRAYS RM17 .... 214 C3
Tofts Cha HARH RM3 .... 37 J8
Toledo Cl SOS SS1 .... 9 E4
Toledo Rd SOS SS1 .... 9 E4
Tollesbury Cl WICKW SS12 .... 147 H7 ☐
Tollesbury Rd MAL CM9 .... 43 J1
Tolleshunt D'arcy Rd MAL CM9 ..... 42 D2
Tollgate SBF/HAD SS7 .... 171 H7
Tollgate Rd CHES/WCR EN8 .... 104 D1
Tomkins CI SLH/COR SS17 .... 203 J3
Tomkyns La UPMR RM14 .... 162 A5
Tomlyns CI RBRW/HUT CM13 .... 142 D2
Tom Tit La MAL CM9 .... 66 E5
Tonbridge Rd HARH RM3 .... 160 E2
HOC/HUL SS5 .... 151 G6
Tongres Rd CVI SS8 .... 208 A1
Took Dr RCHLM CM3 .... 122 C7
Tooley St GVW DA11 .... 218 C5
Toot Hill Rd CHONG CM5 .... 83 F3
Top House Ri CHING E4 .... 132 E3 ☐
Toplands AV SOCK/AV RM15 .... 198 D8
Toppesfield AV WICKW SS12 .... 147 F8
Top Rd MAL CM9 .... 66 D3
Tor Bryan ING CM4 .... 116 B3
Torney CI VGE SS16 .... 186 A1
Toronto Rd TIL RM18 .... 215 F3
Torquay CI RAYL SS6 .... 149 J8 ☐
Torquay Dr LOS SS9 .... 193 F4
Torquay Rd CHLM/WR CM1 .... 35 F8 ☐
Torrance CI HCH RM12 .... 180 D2 ☐
Torrington SBN/FI SS3 .... 196 C5
Torrington CI CHLM/WR CM1 .... 35 G8
Torrington Dr LOU IG10 .... 108 A8
Torrington Gdns LOU IG10 .... 108 A8
Torsi Rd CVI SS8 .... 208 D2 ☐
Totman CI RAYL SS6 .... 171 J5
Totman Crs RAYL SS6 .... 171 H5
Totnes Wk CHLM/WR CM1 .... 35 G7
Totteridge Rd PEND EN3 .... 104 D3
Toucan Cl SBN/FI SS3 .... 196 D4 ☐
Toucan Wy VGE SS16 .... 187 H2
Toulmin Rd RCHLM CM3 .... 38 A1
Tovey Cl WAB EN9 .... 50 A5
Tower Av CHLM/WR CM1 .... 4 A2
LAIN SS15 .... 6 A3
Tower Cl EPP CM16 .... 54 D6
Tower Ct BRW CM14 .... 140 E5
Tower Court Ms WOS/PRIT SS0 ...... 8 B5
Towerfield Cl SBN/FI SS3 .... 196 B5
Towerfield Rd SBN/FI SS3 .... 196 A5
Tower HI BRW CM14 .... 141 F5
Tower Rd CHLM/WR CM1 .... 61 F4
EPP CM16 .... 80 C4
Towers Rd GRAYS RM17 .... 214 B4
MAL CM9 .... 40 E8
Town Cft CHLM/WR CM1 .... 34 C8
Townfield Cnr GVE DA12 .... 219 H6
Townfield Rd RCFD SS4 .... 174 C4
Townfield St CHLM/WR CM1 .... 4 B2
Townfield Wk SBN/FI SS3 .... 196 D1 ☐
Towngate BSDN SS14 .... 7 E4
Town Mead Rd WAB EN9 .... 77 J8
Tracyes Rd HLWS CM18 .... 25 F7
Traddles Ct CHLM/WR CM1 .... 34 B7 ☐
Trafalgar Rd BROX EN10 .... 49 F3
Trafalgar Rd GVW DA11 .... 219 H5
SBN/FI SS3 .... 196 C6
Trafalgar Wy BCAYW CM12 .... 117 H8
Trap's HI LOU IG10 .... 107 H8
Travers Wy PIT SS13 .... 168 D7
Treebeard Copse RCHLM CM3 ..... 122 B7 ☐
Treecot Ct LOS SS9 .... 193 H1
Treelawn Dr LOS SS9 .... 193 G1
Treelawn Gdns LOS SS9 .... 193 G1
Tree Tops BRWN CM15 .... 141 F4
Trenchard Crs CHLM/WR CM1 .... 35 F6
Trenders Av RAYL SS6 .... 149 G7
Trenham Av PIT SS13 .... 169 G6
Trent TIL RM18 .... 216 D3
Trent Av UPMR RM14 .... 162 A8
Trent Cl BOC CM0 .... 128 A7
WICKW SS12 .... 147 G7
Trent Rd BKHH IG9 .... 33 J3
CHLM/WR CM1 .... 33 J8
Trescoe Gdns CRW RM5 .... 137 H8
Tresco Wy WICKW SS12 .... 147 J8
Trevor CI BCAYW CM12 .... 144 A6
Trimble CI ING CM4 .... 116 B1
Trimley CI BSDN SS14 .... 167 K6

Trindehay LAIN SS15 .... 6 C5
Trinder Wy WICKW SS12 .... 146 D7
Tring CI HARH RM3 .... 139 G7
Tring Gdns HARH RM3 .... 139 F7
Trinity Av WOS/PRIT SS0 .... 8 B5
Trinity CI BCAYE CM11 .... 144 D7
LAIN SS15 .... 6 A4
RAYL SS6 .... 171 K4
Trinity La CHES/WCR EN8 .... 76 E6
Trinity Rd BCAYE CM11 .... 144 D7
CHLM/GWD CM2 .... 5 E3
GVE DA12 .... 219 H5
RAYL SS6 .... 171 K4
SOSN SS2 .... 9 F3
Trinity Wood Rd HOC/HUL SS5 ... 151 H5
Tripat CI SLH/COR SS17 .... 188 A3
Tripton Rd HLWS CM18 .... 3 E4
Triton Wy SBF/HAD SS7 .... 171 G7
Triumph CI CDH/CHF RM16 .... 213 F3
Troopers Dr HARH RM3 .... 138 E7
Trosley Av GVW DA11 .... 219 G2
Trotter's Gap WARE SG12 .... 22 A1
Trotters Rd HLWS CM18 .... 24 E8
Trotwood CHIG IG7 .... 135 G8
Trotwood CI CHLM/WR CM1 .... 34 A6
Troubridge CI RCHLM CM3 .... 123 F6
Trowbridge Rd HARH RM3 .... 160 E1
Trueloves La ING CM4 .... 115 J3
Truman CI LAIN SS15 .... 166 B7 ☐
The Trunnions RCFD SS4 .... 174 C4
Truro Crs RAYL SS6 .... 149 H8
Truro Rd GVE DA12 .... 219 J8
Trusses Rd BOC CM0 .... 74 B2
Trustons Gdns EMPK RM11 .... 180 B1
Trust Rd CHES/WCR EN8 .... 76 E8 ☐
Tuck Rd RAIN RM13 .... 180 B7
Tudor Av CHESW EN7 .... 76 B5
GPK RM2 .... 160 B5
SLH/COR SS17 .... 204 A1
Tudor CI BRWN CM15 .... 141 J2
CHIG IG7 .... 37 J8
CHESW EN7 .... 76 B5
GVW DA11 .... 218 D6
ING CM4 .... 116 A3
LOS SS9 .... 172 D6
RAYL SS6 .... 172 A3
SBF/HAD SS7 .... 170 E8
WFD IG8 .... 133 J8
Tudor Ct LAIN SS15 .... 167 G3 ☐
Tudor Dr GPK RM2 .... 160 B6
Tudor Gdns GPK RM2 .... 160 B6
LOS SS9 .... 192 E2
SBN/FI SS3 .... 196 C7
UPMR RM14 .... 181 K3
Tudor Ri BROX EN10 .... 48 E3
Tudor Rd CVI SS8 .... 207 H2
LOS SS9 .... 172 D6
WOS/PRIT SS0 .... 8 B2
Tudor Wy HOC/HUL SS5 .... 173 G1
WAB EN9 .... 77 K7
WICKW SS12 .... 146 D6
Tufter Rd CHIG IG7 .... 135 J8
Tufton Rd CHING E4 .... 132 B7
Tugby PI CHLM/WR CM1 .... 34 A7
Tulip CI BRWN CM15 .... 140 E1
CHLM/WR CM1 .... 35 G6 ☐
HARH RM3 .... 160 D1
Tumbler Rd HLWS CM18 .... 24 E6
Tunbridge Rd SOSN SS2 .... 8 C2
Tunnmeade HLW CM20 .... 24 E4
Tunstall CI PIT SS13 .... 169 F8
Turkey Oaks CHLM/WR CM1 ..... 5 E2 ☐
Turkey St EN EN1 .... 104 B3
Turner CI SBN/FI SS3 .... 196 E5
Turners CI CHONG CM5 .... 84 B3
Turner's HI CHES/WCR EN8 ...... 76 D4
Turnors HLWW/ROY CM19 .... 2 C3
Turnpike La CDH/CHF RM16 ..... 215 J4
The Turnstones CVI SS8 .... 219 J7
Turold Rd SLH/COR SS17 .... 204 A1
Turp Av CDH/CHF RM16 .... 214 B1
Turpin La ERITH DA8 .... 210 B5
Turpin's La WFD IG8 .... 134 C8
The Turpins BSDN SS14 .... 167 K6
Tutors Wy RCHLM CM3 .... 122 E6 ☐
Tweed TIL RM18 .... 216 D3
Twentyman CI WFD IG8 .... 133 H8 ☐
Twin Oaks CHLM/GWD CM2 .... 63 J1
Twinstead WICKW SS12 .... 147 H7
Twitten La CHLM/GWD CM2 ...... 90 D3 ☐
Twitty Fee RCHLM CM3 .... 66 A4
Twizzlefoot Br BOC CM0 .... 129 H6
Twyford Av SBN/FI SS3 .... 197 F1
Twyzel Rd CVI SS8 .... 191 H8 ☐
Tyberry Rd EN EN1 .... 104 B7
The Tyburns RBRW/HUT CM13 .. 142 B5
Tyechurst HI LOU IG10 .... 107 H8
Tye Common Rd BCAYW CM12 .. 143 K8
Tyefields PIT SS13 .... 169 F6
Tye Green Village HLWS CM18 .. 3 F6 ☐
Tyelands BCAYW CM12 .... 144 A5
The Tye RCHLM CM3 .... 93 G6
Tyfield CI CHES/WCR EN8 ...... 76 C4 ☐
Tyle Gn EMPK RM11 .... 161 F7
Tyler Av LAIN SS15 .... 6 A4

Tylers Av BCAYW CM12 .... 117 H8
SOS SS1 .... 9 D5
Tylers CI CHLM/GWD CM2 .... 62 D7
Tylers Crs HCH RM12 .... 180 D6
Tylers Ride RCHLM CM3 .... 122 E6
Tyler Wy BRW CM14 .... 140 E4
Tylewood SBF/HAD SS7 .... 191 H3
Tylney Av RCFD SS4 .... 174 B2
Tylney Cft HLWE/ROY CM19 .... 2 B5
Tyms Wy RAYL SS6 .... 171 K1 🔟
Tyndale CI HOC/HUL SS5 .... 149 J2
Tyndales La RCHLM CM3 .... 66 B8
Tyne CI UPMR RM14 .... 162 A8
Tyne Gdns RCFD SS4 .... 174 B3
Tyne Gdns ARW RM15 .... 198 E7 🔟
Tynemouth Dr EN EN1 .... 104 A4
Tyrel Dr SOS SS1 .... 9 E4
Tyrells HOC/HUL SS5 .... 172 E1
Tyrells CI CHLM/WR CM1 .... 5 F1
UPMR RM14 .... 181 J3 🔟
Tyrells Wy CHLM/GWD CM2 .... 63 H6
Tyrone Av BCAYE CM11 .... 144 D7
Tyrone Rd BCAYE CM11 .... 144 D7
SOS SS1 .... 195 K7
Tyrrell Rd SBF/HAD SS7 .... 190 A3
Tyrrells Hall CI GRAYS RM17 .... 214 C5
Tyrrells Rd BCAYE CM11 .... 144 E7
Tysea CI HLWS CM18 .... 3 F6
Tysea HI ABR/ST RM4 .... 138 A4
Tysea Rd HLWS CM18 .... 3 F6
Tysoe Av PEND EN3 .... 105 F2
Tyssen Md RCHLM CM3 .... 36 C5
Tyssen PI SOCK/AV RM15 .... 200 A3 🔟
Tythe Barn Wy RCHLM CM3 .... 122 C5 🔟
Tythe CHLM/WR CM1 .... 35 G5

U

Uckfield Rd PEND EN3 .... 104 D3
Ullswater Rd SBF/HAD SS7 .... 170 E6
Ullswater Wy HCH RM12 .... 180 B6
Ulster Av SBN/FI SS3 .... 196 B7
Ulting Hall Rd MAL CM9 .... 38 E6
Ulting La MAL CM9 .... 38 D7
Ulting Rd RCHLM CM3 .... 38 C4
Ulting Wy WICKE SS11 .... 147 K5
Una Rd PIT SS13 .... 169 J7
Underhill Rd SBF/HAD SS7 .... 190 D2
Underwood Rd CHING E4 .... 132 C8
Underwood Sq LOS SS9 .... 192 D3
Union La RCFD SS4 .... 174 B3
Unity Rd PEND EN3 .... 104 C3
Upland CI BCAYW CM12 .... 144 A1 🔟
Upland Court Rd HARH RM3 .... 161 G4
Upland Dr BCAYW CM12 .... 144 A1
Upland Rd BCAYW CM12 .... 144 A1
EPP CM16 .... 193 H5 🔟
LOS SS9 .... 193 H5 🔟
Uplands CI HOC/HUL SS5 .... 151 G8
SBF/HAD SS7 .... 190 A1
Uplands Dr CHLM/WR CM1 .... 35 F6
Uplands Park Rd RAYL SS6 .... 171 J1
Uplands Rd HOC/HUL SS5 .... 151 G8
SBF/HAD SS7 .... 190 A2
The Uplands LOU IG10 .... 107 H7
Upminster Rd HCH RM12 .... 181 G3
Upminster Rd North RAIN RM13 .... 198 A3
Upney CI HCH RM12 .... 180 E6 🔟
Upper Av PIT SS13 .... 169 H5
Upper Brentwood Rd GPK RM2 .... 160 D6
Upper Bridge Rd CHLM/GWD CM2 .... 4 B4
Upper Cha CHLM/GWD CM2 .... 4 B5
RCHLM CM3 .... 126 D3
Upper Cornsland BRW CM14 .... 141 G6
Upper Hook HLWS CM18 .... 3 F5
Upper Lambricks RAYL SS6 .... 171 K1
Upper Market Rd WICKW SS12 .... 147 G5 🔟
WICKW SS12 .... 147 F5 🔟
Upper Mayne LAIN SS15 .... 7 D3
Upper Mealines HLWS CM18 .... 24 E8
Upper Moors RCHLM CM3 .... 20 B6
Upper Pk HLW CM20 .... 2 B2
LOU IG10 .... 134 A1
Upper Park Rd WICKW SS12 .... 169 G1
Upper Rainham Rd HCH RM12 .... 180 A5
Upper Rd BCAYE CM11 .... 146 A8
Upper Roman Rd CHLM/GWD CM2 .... 4 C4
Upper Ryle BRW CM14 .... 140 E3
Upper Stonyfield
HLWE/ROY CM19 .... 22 B4
Upper Swaines EPP CM16 .... 80 D4
Upshire Rd WAB EN9 .... 78 B6
Upton CI SLH/COR SS17 .... 203 K3
Upway RAYL SS6 .... 171 J2
The Upway BSDN SS14 .... 7 F5
Urban Av HCH RM12 .... 180 A5
Urmond Rd LOS SS9 .... 208 A1
Usk Rd SOCK/AV RM15 .... 198 E6
Uttons Av LOS SS9 .... 192 E5
Uxbridge CI WICKE SS11 .... 147 J7

V

Vaagen Rd CVI SS8 .... 208 B1
Vadsoe Rd CVI SS8 .... 191 G8 🔟
Valance Av CHING E4 .... 133 C4
Vale Av SOSN SS2 .... 9 D2
Vale CI BRWN CM15 .... 140 C1
Vale End CHLM/GWD CM2 .... 90 E2
Valence Dr CHESW EN7 .... 76 A2
Valence Wy VGE SS16 .... 6 A6
Valentines ING CM4 .... 118 B3
Vale Rd GVW DA11 .... 218 D6
The Vale BRW CM14 .... 141 K6
ING CM4 .... 117 K6
VGE SS16 .... 188 A2
Valkyrie Rd MAL CM9 .... 44 D3
Valkyrie Rd WOS/PRIT SS0 .... 8 A4
Vallance CI SOSN SS2 .... 195 H2
Valletta CI CHLM/WR CM1 .... 4 B2
Valley Br CHLM/WR CM1 .... 34 D7
Valley CI LOU IG10 .... 134 C2
WAB EN9 .... 77 J6
Valley Dr CVE DA12 .... 219 J8
Valley HI LOU IG10 .... 134 B3 🔟
Valley Rd BCAYE CM11 .... 144 C3
Valley Side CHING E4 .... 132 B4
Valmar Av SLH/COR SS17 .... 203 H4
Vanderbilt Av RAYL SS6 .... 149 H5
Vanderbilt Av CVI SS8 .... 208 B1
Van Dieman's La CHLM/GWD CM2 .... 5 D5 🔟
Vange Corner Dr SLH/COR SS17 .... 187 J4
Vange Hill Dr VGE SS16 .... 168 A8
Vange Park Rd SLH/COR SS17 .... 187 J4
The Vanguards SBN/FI SS3 .... 196 E6
Vanguard Wy SBN/FI SS3 .... 196 E5
Vantorts CI SBW CM21 .... 11 J3
Vantorts Rd SBW CM21 .... 11 J4
Varden CI CHLM/WR CM1 .... 34 B7
Vardon Dr LOS SS9 .... 192 C2
Varney CI CHESW EN7 .... 76 A1
Vaughan Av HCH RM12 .... 180 E5
Vaughan CI RCFD SS4 .... 152 B8
Vaughan Williams Rd LAIN SS15 .... 6 A2 🔟
Vaulx Rd CVI SS8 .... 208 B1
Vauxhall Av CVI SS8 .... 208 D2 🔟
Vauxhall Rd GVW DA11 .... 218 E5
Velizy Av HLW CM20 .... 3 D2
Vellacotts CHLM/WR CM1 .... 34 D6
Venables CI CVI SS8 .... 208 C2
Venlo Rd CVI SS8 .... 191 G8 🔟
Veny Crs HCH RM12 .... 180 E6
Vera Av BCAYE CM11 .... 146 D3
Verbena CI SOCK/AV RM15 .... 200 A6 🔟
Verderers Rd CHIG IG7 .... 135 K8
Vere Rd LOU IG10 .... 134 B3
Vermeer Crs SBN/FI SS3 .... 197 F5
Vermeer Ride CHLM/WR CM1 .... 35 H6 🔟
Vermont CI PIT SS13 .... 169 J6
Vernon Av PEND EN3 .... 104 E2
RAYL SS6 .... 171 G1
Vernon Cnr ING CM4 .... 117 K3
Vernon Crs RBRW/HUT CM13 .... 141 K6
Vernon Rd CRW RM5 .... 137 H8
LOS SS9 .... 192 D4
RCHLM CM3 .... 124 C4
Veronica CI HARH RM3 .... 160 D2
Vestry CI LAIN SS15 .... 6 A3
Vexil CI PUR RM19 .... 212 A3
Viaduct Rd CHLM/WR CM1 .... 4 B5 🔟
Vian Av PEND EN3 .... 104 E1
Viborg Gdns MAL CM9 .... 68 A5 🔟
Vicarage CI BRW CM14 .... 140 B7
CVI SS8 .... 207 H2
LAIN SS15 .... 6 A4 🔟
MAL CM9 .... 43 H1 🔟
Vicarage Crs RCHLM CM3 .... 38 B1
Vicarage Dr GVW DA11 .... 218 B4 🔟
Vicarage HI SBF/HAD SS7 .... 190 E3
Vicarage La BOC CM0 .... 102 A1
CHIG IG7 .... 135 G6
CHLM/GWD CM2 .... 91 H2
EPP CM16 .... 54 B6
MAL CM9 .... 97 G2
Vicarage Meadow BOC CM0 .... 128 D2
Vicarage Rd CHLM/GWD CM2 .... 90 E8
CHLM/WR CM1 .... 32 C8
EPP CM16 .... 81 G3
HCH RM12 .... 180 B2
RCHLM CM3 .... 18 E3
Vicarage Sq GRAYS RM17 .... 213 K5 🔟
Vicarage Wd HLW CM20 .... 3 F2
Vickers Rd SOSN SS2 .... 174 A7
Victor Ap HCH RM12 .... 180 E2
Victor CI PIT SS13 .... 169 G7
Victor CI HCH RM12 .... 180 E2
Victor Dr LOS SS9 .... 195 G5
Victor Gdns HCH RM12 .... 180 E2
HOC/HUL SS5 .... 151 G8
Victoria Av CDH/CHF RM16 .... 214 B1
RAYL SS6 .... 149 G8
VGE SS16 .... 186 D2 🔟
WICKW SS12 .... 146 E5
Victoria CI CDH/CHF RM16 .... 214 B1

Victoria Crs CHLM/WR CM1 .... 4 C
LAIN SS15 .... 6 A2 🔟
RBRW/HUT CM13 .... 142 A
WICKW SS12 .... 146 E
Victoria Dr LOS SS9 .... 193 F
SBN/FI SS3 .... 197 H
Victoria Ga HLWE CM17 .... 25 F
Victoria Rd BKHH IG9 .... 134 A
BRW CM14 .... 141 F
CHING E4 .... 133 F
CHLM/WR CM1 .... 4 C
CHLM/WR CM1 .... 60 E
GVW DA11 .... 218 E
LAIN SS15 .... 166 C6 🔟
LOS SS9 .... 193 F
MAL CM9 .... 68 C
RAYL SS6 .... 171 K
RCHLM CM3 .... 96 B
RCHLM CM3 .... 122 D
ROM RM1 .... 160 A
SLH/COR SS17 .... 203 J
SOS SS1 .... 9 F
UPMR RM14 .... 184 E
VGE SS16 .... 188 A
WAB EN9 .... 77 J
Victor Mew CI WICKW SS12 .... 147 C
Victor's Crs RBRW/HUT CM13 .... 142 A
View CI CHIG IG7 .... 135 C
Vigerons Wy CDH/CHF RM16 .... 215 C
Viking Rd GVW DA11 .... 218 B
MAL CM9 .... 68 A
Vikings Wy CVI SS8 .... 207 H
Viking Wy BRWN CM15 .... 140 E
WICKE SS11 .... 147 C
Village CI CHING E4 .... 132 D
Village Dr CVI SS8 .... 207 J
Village Ga CHLM/GWD CM2 .... 63 J
Village Hall CI CVI SS8 .... 207 H2 🔟
Villa Rd SBF/HAD SS7 .... 190 B
Villiers PI RCHLM CM3 .... 36 C
Villiers Wy SBF/HAD SS7 .... 170 E
Vincent Av SLH/COR SS17 .... 203 F
Vincent CI CHES/WCR EN8 .... 76 E
SBN/FI SS3 .... 196 D
SLH/COR SS17 .... 204 D
Vincent Wy BCAYW CM12 .... 117 F
Vine Gv HLW CM20 .... 10 B
Vineway BRW CM14 .... 141 F
The Vintners SOSN SS2 .... 174 C
Viola CI SOCK/AV RM15 .... 200 A
Violet CI CHLM/WR CM1 .... 35 G
Virgil Dr BROX EN10 .... 49 F5 🔟
Virginia CI SBF/HAD SS7 .... 170 A
Virley CI MAL CM9 .... 69 F
Vista Av PEND EN3 .... 104 D
Vista Rd WICKE SS11 .... 147 J
Volwycke Av MAL CM9 .... 68 B
Voorburg Rd CVI SS8 .... 208 D1
Vowler Rd VGE SS16 .... 186 C
Voysey Gdns PIT SS13 .... 168 E

W

Waalwyk Dr CVI SS8 .... 208 C
Waarden Rd CVI SS8 .... 208 A
Waarem Av CVI SS8 .... 208 A
Wacketts CHESW EN7 .... 76 A1
Wadham CI ING CM4 .... 116 B
Wadham Park Av HOC/HUL SS5 .... 150 B
Wagon Md RBSF CM22 .... 13 C
Wagtail Dr MAL CM9 .... 40 E
Wainwright Av RBRW/HUT CM13 .... 142 C
Wakelin Cha ING CM4 .... 116 A
Wakefield CI EMPK RM11 .... 161 C6
Wakering Av SBN/FI SS3 .... 196 E
Wakering Rd SBN/FI SS3 .... 195 K
Wakescolne WICKE SS11 .... 147 K
Walcot Rd PEND EN3 .... 105 F
Waldegrave VGE SS16 .... 7 F
Waldegrave Gdns UPMR RM14 .... 181 J
Walden CI MAL CM9 .... 40 C
Walden Rd EMPK RM11 .... 160 E
Walden Wy EMPK RM11 .... 160 E
Waldon TIL RM18 .... 111 J
Waldringfield BSDN SS14 .... 7 F
Walford PI CHLM/GWD CM2 .... 63 H
Walfords CI HLWE CM17 .... 25 C
Walker Av CHONG CM5 .... 57 F
Walker CI LOS SS9 .... 192 B
Walkers CI CHLM/WR CM1 .... 35 F
Walkers Sq SLH/COR SS17 .... 203 K
Walkey Wy SBN/FI SS3 .... 197 C
The Walk EMPK RM11 .... 181 C
HOC/HUL SS5 .... 149 J
Wallace Binder CI MAL CM9 .... 68 B
Wallace CI HOC/HUL SS5 .... 149 J
Wallace Crs CHLM/GWD CM2 .... 5 D
Wallace Dr WICKW SS12 .... 147 H
Wallace Rd GRAYS RM17 .... 213 H
Wallace's La RCHLM CM3 .... 36 E

Wallace St *SBN/FI* SS3 .... 196 E6
Wallasea Gdns *CHLM/WR* CM1 .... 35 H8 ☐
Wallenger Av *GPK* RM2 .... 160 C5
Waller's Hoppet *LOU* IG10 .... 107 H6
Wallflower Ct *CHLM/WR* CM1 .... 35 H7 ☐
Wallhouse Rd *ERITH* DA8 .... 210 D6
Wallis Av *SOSN* SS2 .... 8 C2 ☐
Wallis Cl *HCH* RM12 .... 180 C2 ☐
Wall Rd *CVI* SS8 .... 209 F2
Walmer Ct *CHING* E4 .... 132 C5
Walnut Ct *HOC/HUL* SS5 .... 151 F6 ☐
Walnut Tree Av *SBW* CM21 .... 11 J1
Walnut Tree Cl *CHES/WCR* EN8 ... 76 D5
Walnut Tree Crs *SBW* CM21 ...... 11 J2 ☐
Walnut Wy *BKHH* IG9 .... 134 A6
Walpole Cl *GRAYS* RM17 .... 214 B5 ☐
Walsingham Cl *LAIN* SS15 .... 6 A3 ☐
Walsingham Rd *SOSN* SS2 .... 9 E1
Walsingham Wy *BCAYW* CM12 .... 117 H8 ☐
Waltham Av *CHLM/GWD* CM2 ..... 90 C2
                LOS SS9 .... 173 F7
Waltham Ct *RBRW/HUT* CM13 .... 142 B2 ☐
Waltham Crs *SOSN* SS2 .... 9 E1
Waltham Gdns *PEND* EN3 .... 104 C5 ☐
Waltham Gln *CHLM/GWD* CM2 ..... 5 D6
Waltham Rd *RAYL* SS6 .... 171 G2
                RCHLM CM3 .... 36 D1
                WAB EN9 .... 50 A8
Walthams *SBN/FI* SS3 .... 196 C4
Walthams Pl *PIT* SS13 .... 168 E6
Walthams Pl *PIT* SS13 .... 168 E6
Walton Wy *CHING* E4 .... 132 B5
Walton Ct *LAIN* SS15 .... 6 A2 ☐
Walton Gdns *RBRW/HUT* CM13 .... 142 B1
                WAB EN9 .... 77 H7
Walton Rd *LAIN* SS15 .... 195 J7
Walton's Hall Rd *SLH/COR* SS17 .. 203 H8
Wambrook *SBN/FI* SS3 .... 196 C4
Wambrook Cl *RBRW/HUT* CM13 ... 142 B5
Wamburg Rd *CVI* SS8 .... 208 D1
Wansfeld Gdns *SOS* SS1 .... 195 J4
Wansford Cl *BRW* CM14 .... 140 C6
Wantz Cha *MAL* CM9 .... 68 C3
Wantz Hvn *MAL* CM9 .... 68 C3 ☐
Wantz Rd *ING* CM4 .... 89 F4
                MAL CM9 .... 68 C3
Warboys Crs *CHING* E4 .... 132 D8
Warburtons *SLH/COR* SS17 ...... 204 B2
Ward Av *GRAYS* RM17 .... 214 A4
Ward Cl *CHESW* EN7 .... 76 A1 ☐
Warden Av *CRW* RM5 .... 137 H8
Wardle Wy *CHLM/WR* CM1 .... 34 A6 ☐
Ward Pth *CHLM/GWD* CM2 .... 63 K1
Warescot Cl *BRWN* CM15 .... 140 E3
Warescot Rd *BRWN* CM15 .... 140 E3
Wares Rd *CHLM/WR* CM1 .... 17 K8
Warley Gap *RBRW/HUT* CM13 .... 162 E2
Warley Hl *RBRW/HUT* CM13 ...... 141 F8
Warley Mt *BRW* CM14 .... 141 F7
Warley Rd *RBRW/HUT* CM13 ...... 162 B4
Warley St *UPMR* RM14 .... 183 C1
Warner Cl *BCAYE* CM11 .... 144 E2 ☐
Warners Av *HOD* EN11 .... 49 F1
Warners Bridge Cha *RCFD* SS4 ... 174 C7
Warners Gdns *SOSN* SS2 .... 174 B7
Warren Cha *SBF/HAD* SS7 .... 191 F1
                RAYL SS6 .... 171 H5
Warren Ct *CHIG* IG7 .... 135 C7
Warren Dr *HCH* RM12 .... 180 B4
                WICKE SS11 .... 147 K5
Warrene Cl *SLH/COR* SS17 .... 203 K4
Warren Fld *EPP* CM16 .... 80 E6
Warrenfield *CHESW* EN7 .... 76 A5 ☐
Warren Hl *LOU* IG10 .... 133 K1
Warren La *BRWN* CM15 .... 113 C5
                CDH/CHF RM16 ..... 213 G3
Warren Pond Rd *CHING* E4 .... 133 C3
Warren Rd *CHING* E4 .... 132 D5
                LOS SS9 .... 192 B3
                RCHLM CM3 .... 119 K7
The Warren *BCAYW* CM12 .... 143 K1
Warriner Av *HCH* RM12 .... 180 B5
Warrington Gdns *RBRW* RM11 ... 160 D8
Warrior Sq *BCAYW* CM12 .... 144 C5 ☐
Warrior Sq *SOS* SS1 .... 9 D4 ☐
Warrior Sq East *SOS* SS1 .... 9 D4 ☐
Warrior Sq North *SOS* SS1 .... 9 D4 ☐
Warrior Square *SBN/FI* SS3 ...... 196 E8
Warwick Cl *CVI* SS8 .... 208 C4
                MAL CM9 .... 68 C4 ☐
                RAYL SS6 .... 172 A4
                SBF/HAD SS7 .... 170 C6
Warwick Crs *MAL* CM9 .... 68 C4
Warwick Dr *CHES/WCR* EN8 ..... 76 D2
                MAL CM9 .... 68 B4
                RCFD SS4 .... 174 C6
Warwick Gdns *GPK* RM2 .... 160 D5
                RAYL SS6 .... 172 A4
Warwick Gn *RAYL* SS6 .... 172 B4
Warwick La *RAIN* RM13 .... 198 B2
Warwick Pl *BRW* CM14 .... 112 E8
                CVW DA11 .... 218 A3
                VGE SS16 .... 186 A1
Warwick Rd *CHING* E4 .... 132 B8
                PEND EN3 .... 105 F5
                RAYL SS6 .... 172 A4
                SOS SS1 .... 195 J7
Warwick Sq *CHLM/WR* CM1 .... 4 A1
Washington Av *LAIN* SS15 .... 166 B7
Washington Cl *MAL* CM9 .... 68 A4 ☐
Washington Rd *MAL* CM9 .... 68 B4
Wash La *MAL* CM9 .... 41 K4
Wash Rd *LAIN* SS15 .... 6 A1
                RBRW/HUT CM13 ... 142 D1
Watchfield La *RAYL* SS6 .... 171 H4
Watchouse Rd *CHLM/GWD* CM2 ... 90 D3
Waterdales *CVW* DA11 .... 218 C6
Waterdene *CVI* SS8 .... 190 D8
The Waterfalls *VGE* SS16 .... 186 C2 ☐
Waterford Rd *SBN/FI* SS3 .... 196 C7
Waterfront Wk *BSDN* SS14 .... 7 F1
Waterhale *SOS* SS1 .... 195 K4
Waterhall Av *CHING* E4 .... 133 F7 ☐
Waterhouse Moor *HLWS* CM18 .... 3 K4
Waterhouse La *CHLM/WR* CM1 ... 62 A4
Waterhouse St *CHLM/WR* CM1 ... 4 A5
Water La *HLWW/ROY* CM19 .... 51 C1
                PUR RM19 .... 211 H3
Waterloo La *CHLM/WR* CM1 ...... 4 C3
Waterloo Rd *BRW* CM14 .... 141 F4
                SBN/FI SS3 .... 196 C6
Waterloo St *GVE* DA12 .... 219 H5 ☐
Watermans Wy *EPP* CM16 .... 82 A1
Watermeadow Cl *ERITH* DA8 ..... 210 C7 ☐
Waterside Cl *BCAYE* CM11 .... 144 A4
Waterside Rd *BOC* CM0 .... 74 B2
                RCFD SS4 .... 155 F8
Watersmeet *HLWW/ROY* CM19 ... 51 K1
Waterson Rd *CDH/CHF* RM16 .... 215 C3
Waterson V *CHLM/GWD* CM2 ..... 5 D6
Waterton Av *GVE* DA12 .... 219 K5
Waterville Dr *VGE* SS16 .... 188 D1
Waterworks La *SLH/COR* SS17 ... 187 K7
Watery La *CHONG* CM5 .... 27 K5
                WICKE SS11 .... 149 H4
Wates Wy *BRWN* CM15 .... 141 G4
Watkins Cl *PIT* SS13 .... 169 G4
Watkins Wy *SBN/FI* SS3 .... 196 E4
Watling St *MEO* DA13 .... 218 A8
Watlington Rd *HLWE* CM17 ...... 25 H1
                SBF/HAD SS7 .... 190 C2
Watson Cl *SBN/FI* SS3 .... 196 C6
                WTHK RM20 .... 212 D7
Watts Crs *PUR* RM19 .... 211 K3
Wavell Cl *CHES/WCR* EN8 .... 76 E1
                CHLM/WR CM1 ...... 35 F5 ☐
Waveney Dr *CHLM/WR* CM1 ...... 34 E7
Waverley Av *CHING* E4 .... 132 A7
Waverley Crs *HARH* RM3 .... 160 C1
                WICKE SS11 .... 147 F2
Waverley Gdns *CDH/CHF* RM16 .. 213 K1
Waverley Rd *LAIN* SS15 .... 6 C1 ☐
                SBF/HAD SS7 .... 170 B8
Wavertree Rd *SBF/HAD* SS7 ..... 190 A1
Waxwell Rd *HOC/HUL* SS5 .... 149 K5
Waycross Rd *UPMR* RM14 .... 162 B8
Wayfarer Gdns *BOC* CM0 .... 128 A8 ☐
Wayfaring Gn *GRAYS* RM17 ...... 213 J4 ☐
Wayletts *LAIN* SS15 .... 166 B6 ☐
                LOS SS9 .... 172 C7
Wayre St *HLWE* CM17 .... 25 G1
Wayside *RCHLM* CM3 .... 65 J5
Wayside Av *HCH* RM12 .... 180 B4
Wayside Cl *ROM* RM1 .... 160 A5
Weald Br *EPP* CM16 .... 54 E4
Weald Bridge Rd *EPP* CM16 ...... 54 E4
Weald Cl *BRW* CM14 .... 140 D6
Weald Hall La *EPP* CM16 .... 53 C7
Weald Park Wy *BRW* CM14 ...... 140 B6
Weald Rd *BRW* CM14 .... 139 H4
The Weald *CVI* SS8 .... 207 J1
Weale Dr *CHING* E4 .... 132 E6
Wear Dr *CHLM/WR* CM1 .... 35 F7
Weare Gifford *SBN/FI* SS3 .... 196 B5
Weaverdale *SBN/FI* SS3 .... 196 D4 ☐
Weavers *VGE* SS16 .... 188 C1
Weavers Cl *BCAYE* CM11 .... 144 C3 ☐
                CVW DA11 .... 219 F6 ☐
Webber Cl *ERITH* DA8 .... 210 C6 ☐
Webster Cl *HCH* RM12 .... 180 E4 ☐
                WAB EN9 .... 78 C7 ☐
Webster Pl *ING* CM4 .... 118 A3 ☐
Webster Rd *SLH/COR* SS17 ...... 204 A3
Websters Wy *RAYL* SS6 .... 171 J3
Wedds Wy *SBN/FI* SS3 .... 197 J3
Wedgewood Cl *EPP* CM16 .... 80 E4
Wedgewood Dr *HLWE* CM17 ...... 25 H6
Wedgwood Wy *RCFD* SS4 .... 151 K7
Wedhey *HLWW/ROY* CM19 .... 2 C3
Wedlake Cl *EMPK* RM11 .... 181 F2 ☐
Wednesbury Gdns *HARH* RM3 .... 161 G2
Wednesbury Gn *HARH* RM3 ...... 161 G2 ☐
Wednesbury Rd *HARH* RM3 ...... 161 G2
Weelkes Cl *SLH/COR* SS17 .... 203 J2
Weel Rd *CVI* SS8 .... 208 D3
Weight Rd *CHLM/GWD* CM2 ...... 5 D3
Weir Farm Rd *RAYL* SS6 .... 171 H5
Weir Gdns *RAYL* SS6 .... 171 H5

Weir Pond Rd *RCFD* SS4 .... 174 C3
Weir Wynd *BCAYW* CM12 .... 144 B4
Welbeck Cl *HOC/HUL* SS5 .... 173 C1
Welbeck Dr *VGE* SS16 .... 186 B1
Welbeck Ri *VGE* SS16 .... 186 B1 ☐
Welbeck Rd *CVI* SS8 .... 208 A3
Welch Cl *SOSN* SS2 .... 195 H2
Welland Av *CHLM/WR* CM1 .... 33 J8
Welland Rd *BOC* CM0 .... 128 A7
Weller Gv *CHLM/WR* CM1 .... 34 A6
Wellers Gv *CHESW* EN7 .... 76 A2 ☐
Wellesley *EPP* CM16 .... 51 J2
Wellesley Rd *BRW* CM14 .... 141 F4
Well Fld *CHLM/WR* CM1 .... 61 C4
Wellfields *LOU* IG10 .... 107 J7
Wellingbury *SBF/HAD* SS7 .... 170 B8 ☐
Welling Rd *CDH/CHF* RM16 ...... 202 D6
Wellington Av *CHING* E4 .... 132 B5
                HOC/HUL SS5 .... 149 J4
                WOS/PRIT SS0 ...... 193 H4
Wellington Cl *CHLM/WR* CM1 .... 33 K8
Wellington Hl *LOU* IG10 .... 106 D4
Wellington Av *ABR/ST* RM4 ...... 137 K6
Wellington Ms *BCAYW* CM12 .... 117 F8
Wellington Pl *BRW* CM14 .... 141 F8
Wellington Rd *EPP* CM16 .... 82 A1
                MAL CM9 .... 68 B3
                RAYL SS6 .... 172 A2
                TIL RM18 .... 219 F1
The Wellingtons *BOC* CM0 .... 128 D2 ☐
Wellington St *GVE* DA12 .... 219 H5 ☐
Well La *BRWN* CM15 .... 113 H7
                CDH/CHF RM16 ..... 200 C8
                CHLM/GWD CM2 .... 90 D3
                HLW CM20 .... 2 A3
                HLWW/ROY CM19 ... 2 A2
                ING CM4 .... 118 A4
                RCHLM CM3 .... 65 G7
Well Md *BCAYW* CM12 .... 144 D6 ☐
Wells Av *SOSN* SS2 .... 174 A7
Wells Ct *CHLM/WR* CM1 .... 35 F8
Wellsfield *RAYL* SS6 .... 171 K1
Wells Gdns *RAIN* RM13 .... 180 A7
Well's St *CHLM/WR* CM1 .... 4 B2 ☐
Wellstead Gdns *WOS/PRIT* SS0 .. 193 J2
Wellstye Gn *BSDN* SS14 .... 168 B5
Welsummer Wy *CHES/WCR* EN8 .. 76 D1
Wembley Av *RCHLM* CM3 .... 98 D5
Wendene *VGE* SS16 .... 188 C1
Wendon Cl *RCFD* SS4 .... 173 K1 ☐
Wendover Gdns *RBRW/HUT* CM13.. 142 A5
Wendover Wy *HCH* RM12 .... 180 D6 ☐
Wenham Dr *WOS/PRIT* SS0 .... 8 B2
Wenlocks La *ING* CM4 .... 86 C7
Wennington Gn *RAIN* RM13 ...... 198 A7
Wensley Cl *CRW* RM5 .... 137 F8
Wensley Rd *SBF/HAD* SS7 .... 191 C1
Wentworth Cl *RCHLM* CM3 ...... 38 B1
Wentworth Mdw *MAL* CM9 .... 68 B3
Wentworth Pl *CDH/CHF* RM16 ... 214 C2 ☐
Wentworth Rd *SOSN* SS2 .... 9 D1
Wesley Gdns *BCAYW* CM12 ...... 117 F8 ☐
Wesley Rd *SOS* SS1 .... 9 E5
Wessem Rd *CVI* SS8 .... 191 C8 ☐
Westall Rd *LOU* IG10 .... 107 K7
West Av *CHLM/WR* CM1 .... 34 B8
                HOC/HUL SS5 .... 149 H2
                RCHLM CM3 .... 98 C4
                VGE SS16 .... 185 K1
West Beech Av *WICKE* SS11 ..... 147 C6
West Beech Cl *WICKE* SS11 ..... 147 H6
West Belvedere *RCHLM* CM3 ..... 65 K6
Westborough Rd *WOS/PRIT* SS0 .. 193 J5
Westbourne Cl *HOC/HUL* SS5 .... 151 H6 ☐
                SBF/HAD SS7 .... 171 H8
Westbourne Dr *BRW* CM14 .... 140 C7
Westbourne Gdns
                BCAYW CM12 .... 117 H8 ☐
                WOS/PRIT SS0 ...... 193 J1
West Bowers Rd *MAL* CM9 .... 66 C1
Westbury *CHES/WCR* EN8 .... 76 D4 ☐
                RCFD SS4 .... 173 K1
Westbury Dr *BRW* CM14 .... 140 E6
Westbury La *BKHH* IG9 .... 133 K5
Westbury Ri *HLWE* CM17 .... 25 H6
Westbury Rd *BKHH* IG9 .... 133 K4
                BRW CM14 .... 141 F5
                SOSN SS2 .... 9 F2
Westbury Ter *UPMR* RM14 .... 182 B3
West Cha *MAL* CM9 .... 68 B2
                MAL CM9 .... 97 G4
Westcliff Av *WOS/PRIT* SS0 ...... 8 B5
Westcliff Dr *LOS* SS9 .... 192 E4
Westcliff Gdns *CVI* SS8 .... 208 E2
Westcliff Pde *WOS/PRIT* SS0 .... 8 B5
Westcliff Park Dr *WOS/PRIT* SS0 .. 8 A2
West Cloister *BCAYE* CM11 ...... 144 C3 ☐
Westcott Av *CVW* DA11 .... 219 F8
West Crs *CVI* SS8 .... 207 K1
West Crescent Rd *GVE* DA12 .... 219 G4
West Cft *BCAYE* CM11 .... 144 C4 ☐
Westcroft Cl *PEND* EN3 .... 104 C4 ☐
Westcroft Ct *BROX* EN10 .... 49 G1 ☐
West Dene Dr *HARH* RM3 .... 138 E8

Westerdale *CHLM/WR* CM1 .... 35 F6
Westerings *RCHLM* CM3 .... 93 K3
  RCHLM CM3 .... 95 K4
The Westerings *CHLM/GWD* CM2 .. 63 H8
  HOC/HUL SS5 .... 151 F8
Westerland Av *CVI* SS8 .... 208 D1
Western Approaches *LOS* SS9 ..... 173 H6
Western Av *BRW* CM14 .... 141 F4
  EPP CM16 .... 80 D6
  GPK RM2 .... 160 D4
Western Esp *CVI* SS8 .... 208 B3
  SOS SS1 .... 8 C5
  WOS/PRIT SS0 .... 8 A5
Western Ms *BCAYW* CM12 .... 144 B3
Western Rd *BCAYW* CM12 .... 144 B3
  BOC CM0 .... 155 G1
  BRW CM14 .... 141 F5
  LOS SS9 .... 192 B4
  RAYL SS6 .... 171 G4
  ROM RM1 .... 160 A7
  SBF/HAD SS7 .... 171 K7
  WAB EN9 .... 50 A4
Westfield *HLWS* CM18 .... 3 E4
  LAIN SS15 .... 166 B5
Westfield Av *CHLM/WR* CM1 .... 4 B1
Westfield Cl *CHES/WCR* EN8 ...... 77 F5
  PEND EN3 .... 104 E7
  RAYL SS6 .... 149 G8
  WICKE SS11 .... 147 J5
Westgate *BSDN* SS14 .... 7 E4
West Ga *HLW* CM20 .... 2 C3
West Gn *SBF/HAD* SS7 .... 170 A8
West Hanningfield Rd
  CHLM/GWD CM2 .... 91 F7
West Hayes *RBSF* CM22 .... 13 G2
Westhill Cl *GVE* DA12 .... 219 G6
West Hook *VGE* SS16 .... 186 A2
West House Est *BOC* CM0 .... 128 C1
Westlake Av *PIT* SS13 .... 169 H7
Westland Av *EMPK* RM11 .... 181 F2
Westland Vw *CDH/CHF* RM16 ... 200 E8 @
Westlea Cl *BROX* EN10 .... 49 F6 @
Westlea Rd *BROX* EN10 .... 49 F5
Westleigh Av *LOS* SS9 .... 192 E3
West Ley *BOC* CM0 .... 128 C8
Westley Rd *VGE* SS16 .... 186 D3
Westman Rd *CVI* SS8 .... 208 E2
Westmarch *RCHLM* CM3 .... 122 C7
West Mayne *LAIN* SS15 .... 166 B7
Westmeade Cl *CHESW* EN7 .... 76 B3
Westmede *VGE* SS16 .... 6 A6 @
Westminster Dr *HOC/HUL* SS5 ... 150 D7
  WOS/PRIT SS0 .... 193 J3
Westminster Gdns *CHING* E4 .... 133 F4
Westmoor Gdns *PEND* EN3 ...... 104 D6
Westmoor Rd *PEND* EN3 .... 104 D6
Westmoreland Av *EMPK* RM11 .. 160 D7 @
Weston Av *WTHK* RM20 .... 212 C3
Weston Cl *RBRW/HUT* CM13 .... 142 B3
Weston Rd *SOS* SS1 .... 9 D5
West Park Av *BCAYW* CM12 ..... 144 B3
West Park Dr *BCAYW* CM12 ..... 144 B3
West Park Hl *BRW* CM14 .... 140 D6
West Point Pl *CVI* SS8 .... 207 G2
West Rdg *BCAYW* CM12 .... 144 B5
West St *GRAYS* CM1 .... 213 K5
  GVW DA11 .... 218 E4
  LOS SS9 .... 193 F5
  MAL CM9 .... 44 B4
  RCFD SS4 .... 174 B3
  WOS/PRIT SS0 .... 8 B2
West Side *BROX* EN10 .... 48 E7
West Vw *LOU* IG10 .... 107 H7
West View Dr *RAYL* SS6 .... 171 G4
Westward Rd *CHING* E4 .... 132 A8
Westwater *SBF/HAD* SS7 .... 190 A1
West Wy *BRW* CM14 .... 140 D6
  WAB EN9 .... 105 H3
Westway *CHLM/WR* CM1 .... 62 A5
  RCHLM CM3 .... 122 C6
Westwood Av *BRW* CM14 .... 140 D7
West Wood Cl *SBF/HAD* SS7 .... 191 H1 @
Westwood Gdns *SBF/HAD* SS7 .. 191 J1
Westwood Ldg *SBF/HAD* SS7 ... 171 H8
Westwood Rd *CVI* SS8 .... 208 B2
Wetherland *VGE* SS16 .... 7 D5 @
Wetherly Cl *HLWE* CM17 .... 25 G2
Wethersfield Cl *RAYL* SS6 .... 171 F2 @
Wethersfield Wy *WICKE* SS11 .. 148 A8
Weybourne Cl *SOSN* SS2 .... 9 E1
Weybourne Gdns *SOSN* SS2 .... 9 E1
Weybridge Wk *SBF/HAD* SS7 ... 196 C4
Weydale *SLH/COR* SS17 .... 187 J8
Weymarks *LAIN* SS15 .... 6 B3

Weymouth Rd *CHLM/WR* CM1 ... 35 G7
Whadden Cha *ING* CM4 .... 116 A2
Wharf Cl *SLH/COR* SS17 .... 203 K4 @
Wharf Rd *BROX* EN10 .... 49 F6
  BRW CM14 .... 141 F6
  CHLM/GWD CM2 .... 5 D3
  GRAYS RM17 .... 213 J5
  GVE DA12 .... 219 K4
  MAL CM9 .... 69 H1
  SLH/COR SS17 .... 204 A6
Wharley Hook *HLWS* CM18 .... 3 F6
Wheatear Pl *BCAYE* CM11 ...... 144 D4 @
Wheatfields *HLWE* CM17 .... 11 H7 @
  PEND EN3 .... 104 E5
  RCFD SS4 .... 175 G1
Wheatfield Wy *CHLM/WR* CM1 ... 4 A2
  VGE SS16 .... 186 B1
Wheatley Cl *EMPK* RM11 .... 160 E7
  RCFD SS4 .... 174 A1
  SBW CM21 .... 11 G4
Wheatley Rd *SLH/COR* SS17 .... 187 J8
Wheatley Terrace Rd *ERITH* DA8 .. 210 A5
Wheatsheaf Rd *ROM* RM1 .... 160 A8 @
Wheelers *EPP* CM16 .... 80 E3 @
Wheelers Cl *WAB* EN9 .... 50 A4
Wheelers Farm Gdns *EPP* CM16 . 54 B8 @
Wheeler's Hl *RCHLM* CM3 .... 20 E7
Wheelers La *BRW* CM14 .... 112 D8
  SLH/COR SS17 .... 188 A8
The Wheelwrights *SOSN* SS2 .... 174 D8
Whernside Av *CVI* SS8 .... 191 H8
Whinhams Wy *BCAYW* CM12 ... 144 A2
Whist Av *WICKE* SS11 .... 147 J4
Whistler Ri *SBN/FI* SS3 .... 197 F5
Whitakers Wy *LOU* IG10 .... 107 H5
Whitbreads Farm La *RCHLM* CM3 .. 21 F1
Whitby Av *RBRW/HUT* CM13 ... 164 C5
Whitby Rd *BOC* CM0 .... 128 B3
Whitchurch Rd *HARH* RM3 ...... 139 F7 @
Whitcroft *VGE* SS16 .... 186 D2
White Av *GVW* DA11 .... 218 E8
Whitebeam Cl *CHLM/GWD* CM2 .. 4 A4
Whitebeam Dr *SOCK/AV* RM15 . 200 A3 @
White Elm Rd *RCHLM* CM3 .... 94 A3
Whitefields Rd *CHES/WCR* EN8 .. 76 C2
Whitefriars Crs *WOS/PRIT* SS0 . 193 K6
Whitegate Rd *SOS* SS1 .... 9 D4
White Gates *HCH* RM12 .... 180 D3 @
  WAB EN9 .... 50 A4 @
Whitehall Cl *CHIG* IG7 .... 135 K6 @
  WAB EN9 .... 50 A4 @
Whitehall Gdns *CHING* E4 .... 132 E4
Whitehall La *BKHH* IG9 .... 133 H5
  ERITH DA8 .... 210 A8
  GRAYS RM17 .... 214 B5
  SLH/COR SS17 .... 187 K6
Whitehall Rd *CHING* E4 .... 133 F5
  GRAYS RM17 .... 214 B3
White Hall Rd *SBN/FI* SS3 .... 197 G1
White Hart La *HOC/HUL* SS5 ... 151 F8
Whitehill La *GVE* DA12 .... 219 J8
Whitehill Pde *GVE* DA12 .... 219 H8
Whitehill Rd *GVE* DA12 .... 219 H7
Whitehills Rd *LOU* IG10 .... 107 J7
White Horse La *MAL* CM9 .... 68 B3
White House Cha *RAYL* SS6 .... 171 K5
Whitehouse Crs *CHLM/GWD* CM2 .. 5 E5
Whitehouse Mdw *LOS* SS9 .... 173 H7
Whitehouse Rd *LOS* SS9 .... 173 G7
Whitelands Rd *RCHLM* CM3 ..... 122 D5
Whitelands *BRWN* CM15 .... 114 B1
Whitelands Cl *WICKE* SS11 ..... 147 H4 @
Whitelands Wy *HARH* RM3 .... 160 E3
White Lyons Rd *BRW* CM14 ..... 141 F6 @
White Mdd *CHLM/WR* CM1 .... 4 A3
White Post Fld *SBW* CM21 .... 11 H3
Whitesbridge La *ING* CM4 .... 89 K4
White's Hl *ING* CM4 .... 118 B3
Whiteshott *VGE* SS16 .... 7 E6
Whitesmith Dr *BCAYW* CM12 ... 143 K2
Whitethorn Gdns *CHLM/GWD* CM2 .. 5 D6
  EMPK RM11 .... 160 D8 @
White Tree Ct *RCHLM* CM3 ...... 122 B7 @
Whiteways *HLW* CM20 .... 3 E2
Whiteways *BCAYE* CM11 .... 144 E3
  CVI SS8 .... 208 D3
  LOS SS9 .... 173 G7
Whitfields *SLH/COR* SS17 .... 204 B3
Whit Hern Ct *CHES/WCR* EN8 ... 76 C4
Whitmore Av *SOSN* SS2 .... 195 H3
Whitmore Ct *BSDN* SS14 .... 168 B4
Whitmore Cl *CHLM/GWD* CM2 ... 63 K2
Whitmore Wy *BSDN* SS14 .... 7 F3
  BSDN SS14 .... 168 A6
Whittingham Av *SOSN* SS2 ...... 195 H3
Whittington Rd *RBRW/HUT* CM13 .. 142 C2
Whybrews *SLH/COR* SS17 .... 204 B3 @
Whytewaters *VGE* SS16 .... 188 C2
Whyverne Cl *CHLM/WR* CM1 .... 35 G7
Wick Beech Av *WICKE* SS11 .... 147 H6
Wick Cha *SOSN* SS2 .... 195 H4
Wick Crs *WICKW* SS12 .... 147 H8
Wick Dr *WICKW* SS12 .... 147 G6
Wick Farm Rd *BOC* CM0 .... 72 C5

Wickfield Ash *CHLM/WR* CM1 ... 33 K
Wickford Av *PIT* SS13 .... 168 D
Wickford Dr *HARH* RM3 .... 139 G
Wickford Rd *RCHLM* CM3 .... 122 A
  WOS/PRIT SS0 .... 8 B5
Wick Gln *BCAYW* CM12 .... 144 A
Wickham Bishop Rd *RCHLM* CM3 .. 38 D
Wickham Cl *EN* EN1 .... 104 B
Wickham Crs *CHLM/WR* CM1 ... 34 B
Wickham Hall La *WIT* CM8 .... 39 J
Wickham Pl *VGE* SS16 .... 167 K
Wickham Rd *CDH/CHF* RM16 ... 215 H
Wickham's Cha *RCHLM* CM3 .... 94 C
Wickhay *LAIN* SS15 .... 7 D
Wick La *WICKE* SS11 .... 147 H
Wicklow Av *CHLM/WR* CM1 ...... 33 K
Wicklow Wk *SBN/FI* SS3 .... 196 B
Wickmead Cl *SOSN* SS2 .... 195 H
Wick Rd *BOC* CM0 .... 155 J
Widbrook *BRWN* CM15 .... 114 A
Wid Cl *RBRW/HUT* CM13 .... 142 C1
Widecombe Cl *HARH* RM3 .... 160 E3
Widford Cha *CHLM/GWD* CM2 ... 4 A
Widford Cl *CHLM/GWD* CM2 ...... 4 A6
Widford Gv *CHLM/GWD* CM2 ...... 4 A
Widford Park Pl *CHLM/GWD* CM2 . 4 A6
Widford Rd *CHLM/GWD* CM2 ...... 4 A
Widgeon Rd *ERITH* DA8 .... 210 C
Widgeons *PIT* SS13 .... 169 F
Widworthy Hayes
  RBRW/HUT CM13 .... 142 A
  BCAYW CM12 .... 143 K
Wiggin's La *BCAYW* CM12 ...... 143 K
Wigley Bush La *BRW* CM14 ..... 140 B
Wigton Rd *HARH* RM3 .... 139 F
Wigton Wy *HARH* RM3 .... 139 F
Wilde Cl *TIL* RM18 .... 215 G
Wilfred St *GVE* DA12 .... 219 G4 @
Wilkes Rd *RBRW/HUT* CM13 ... 142 C
Wilkinsons Md *CHLM/GWD* CM2 . 63 J1
William Rd *PIT* SS13 .... 169 H
Williamsons Wy *SLH/COR* SS17 . 187 G
Williams Rd *CHLM/WR* CM1 ..... 34 D
William St *GRAYS* RM17 .... 214 B5
  GVE DA12 .... 219 G
Willingale Av *RAYL* SS6 .... 171 F
Willingale Cl *RBRW/HUT* CM13 . 142 D2
Willingale Rd *CHONG* CM5 .... 57 J
  LOU IG10 .... 108 A
The Willingales *LAIN* SS15 ...... 166 B7 @
Willingale Wy *SOS* SS1 .... 195 K
Willinghall Cl *WAB* EN9 .... 77 K6
Willmott Rd *SOSN* SS2 .... 174 A
Willoughby Cl *BROX* EN10 .... 48 E3
Willoughby Dr *CHLM/GWD* CM2 . 63 H3
Willowbank *CHLM/GWD* CM2 .... 90 D2
Willow Cl *BKHH* IG9 .... 134 A
  BOC CM0 .... 128 B
  BRWN CM15 .... 114 B
  CHLM/WR CM1 .... 34 D
  CVI SS8 .... 207 K
  HCH RM12 .... 180 C4
  HOC/HUL SS5 .... 151 G
  LOS SS9 .... 173 G
  RBRW/HUT CM13 .... 142 A2
Willow Crs *RCHLM* CM3 .... 38 A
Willowdene *CHES/WCR* EN8 ...... 76 E
  BRWN CM15 .... 140 C1
Willowdene Ct *BRW* CM14 ...... 141 F
Willow Dr *RAYL* SS6 .... 171 H
Willowfield *HLWS* CM18 .... 3 D
Willowfields *LAIN* SS15 .... 6 A
Willow Gn *ING* CM4 .... 116 B
Willow Gv *RCHLM* CM3 .... 122 A
Willowhill *SLH/COR* SS17 .... 187 F
Willowmead *BCAYE* CM11 .... 118 E8
  CHIG IG7 .... 135 K
Willow Md *SBW* CM21 .... 11 J
Willow Pl *HLWE* CM17 .... 53 K
Willow Rd *ERITH* DA8 .... 210 B
The Willows *BCAYE* CM11 .... 144 E6
  GRAYS RM17 .... 214 C
  RCHLM CM3 .... 36 C
  SBF/HAD SS7 .... 190 A
  SOS SS1 .... 195 K
Willow St *CHING* E4 .... 132 E
Willow Wk *HOC/HUL* SS5 .... 151 G
  RCFD SS4 .... 153 G
  SBF/HAD SS7 .... 191 J
  UPMR RM14 .... 182 B
Willow Wy *HARH* RM3 .... 161 J
Wills Hl *SLH/COR* SS17 .... 205 K
Wilmot Gn *RBRW/HUT* CM13 ... 163 F1
Wilmslowe *CVI* SS8 .... 191 J
Wilrich Av *CVI* SS8 .... 208 D
Wilshire Av *CHLM/GWD* CM2 ... 63 H
Wilsman Rd *SOCK/AV* RM15 .... 200 A
Wilsner *PIT* SS13 .... 169 F
Wilson Cl *SLH/COR* SS17 .... 203 J5
Wilson Rd *WOS/PRIT* SS0 .... 8 C
Wiltshire Av *EMPK* RM11 .... 161 G
Wimarc Crs *RAYL* SS6 .... 171 G
Wimbish End *PIT* SS13 .... 168 E
Wimborne Cl *BKHH* IG9 .... 133 K
  SBW CM21 .... 11 H3

Jimborne Rd SOSN SS2 .... 9 E3
Jimbourne LAIN SS15 .... 166 B6
Jimhurst Cl RCHLM CM3 .... 151 F6
Jinbrook Cl RAYL SS6 .... 171 K5
Jinbrook Rd RAYL SS6 .... 171 K5
Jincanton Rd HARH RM3 .... 138 E6
Jinchcombe Cl LOS SS9 .... 193 F2
Jinchelsea Dr CHLM/GWD CM2 .... 5 E6
Jinchester Av UPMR RM14 .... 182 C2
Jinchester Cl LOS SS9 .... 173 C6
Jinchester Crs GVE DA12 .... 219 J8
Jinchester Gdns LAIN SS15 .... 6 A1
Jinch Vw EPP CM16 .... 81 F3
Jinckford Cl RCHLM CM3 .... 20 D7
Jincoat Cl SBF/HAD SS7 .... 190 B2
Jincoat Dr SBF/HAD SS7 .... 190 A2
Jindermere Av HCH RM12 .... 180 B6
    HOC/HUL SS5 .... 149 J3
Jindermere Rd SBF/HAD SS7 .... 170 D6
    SOS SS1 .... 5 K4
Jind HI CHONG CM5 .... 55 C1
Jindmill Cl UPMR RM14 .... 181 H3
    WAB EN9 .... 78 A8
Jindmill Flds HLWE CM17 .... 25 K1
Jindmill Hts BCAYW CM12 .... 144 C5
Jindmill La CHES/WCR EN8 .... 76 E4
Jindmill Mdw GTDUN CM6 .... 16 A2
The Windmills CHLM/WR CM1 .... 34 C2
Jindmill St GVE DA12 .... 219 C5
Jindmill Wy RCHLM CM3 .... 113 C5
Jindrush Dr CHLM/WR CM1 .... 34 E7
    SLH/COR SS17 .... 187 H8
Jindsor Cl CVI SS8 .... 208 B2
    CHESW EN7 .... 76 A4
Jindsor Gdns HOC/HUL SS5 .... 173 J1
    SBF/HAD SS7 .... 191 H1
    WICKE SS11 .... 147 G2
Jindsor Rd BCAYE CM11 .... 119 F8
    CHEMC15 .... 140 E2
    CHING E4 .... 132 C7
    EMPK RM11 .... 180 D1
    PEND EN3 .... 104 D2
    PIT SS13 .... 169 H5
    WOS/PRIT SS0 .... 8 B3
The Windsors BKHH IG9 .... 134 B5
Jindsor Wy RAYL SS6 .... 171 K4
Jindsor Wd WAB EN9 .... 78 A7
Jindward Cl PEND EN3 .... 104 D1
Jindward Wy RCHLM CM3 .... 123 F7
Jindy HI RBRW/HUT CM13 .... 142 B4
Jinfields PIT SS13 .... 169 F5
Jinford Dr BROX EN10 .... 49 F4
Jingfield GRAYS RM17 .... 213 J4
Jingfield Rd RBRW/HUT CM13 .... 141 K1
Jingfield Gdns UPMR RM14 .... 162 C8
Jingfield Rd GVW DA11 .... 219 G5
Jingletye La EMPK RM11 .... 181 G2
Jingrave Crs BRW CM14 .... 140 B7
Jingway BRWN CM15 .... 141 K4
Jinifred Av HCH RM12 .... 180 E5
Jinifred Rd PIT SS13 .... 168 E7
Jinnington Rd PEND EN3 .... 104 C4
Jinsford Gdns WOS/PRIT SS0 .... 193 H1
Jinsford Wy CHLM/GWD CM2 .... 35 K7
Jinslow Gv CHING E4 .... 133 F5
Jinstone Churchill Wy CHES/WCR EN8 .... 76 C7
Jinstree PIT SS13 .... 168 E5
Jinstree Rd BOC CM0 .... 128 B8
Jinter Folly LAIN SS15 .... 6 C5
Jinter Gardens Pth CVI SS8 .... 190 D6
Jinters Wy WAB EN9 .... 78 C7
Jinterswyk Av CVI SS8 .... 208 E2
Jinton Av WICKW SS12 .... 146 D5
    WOS/PRIT SS0 .... 8 B5
Jinton Dr CHES/WCR EN8 .... 76 E3
Jiscombe HI VGE SS16 .... 186 D2
Jisemans Gdns SBW CM21 .... 11 C4
Jistaria Cl BRWN CM15 .... 140 E1
Jitchards VGE SS16 .... 7 F5
Jitcham Cl LOU IG10 .... 134 B2
Jitham Gdns RBRW/HUT CM13 .... 164 C8
Jitham Rd GPK RM2 .... 160 C7
The Witherings EMPK RM11 .... 161 F7
Jithy Md CHING E4 .... 132 C5
Jithypool SBN/FI SS3 .... 196 C4
Jitney Rd BOC CM0 .... 155 H1
Jittem Rd CHING E4 .... 132 E6
The Witterings CVI SS8 .... 191 F8
Joburn Av EPP CM16 .... 108 C3
    HCH RM12 .... 180 B5
Joburn Pl BCAYW CM12 .... 117 F8
Jokindon Rd CDH/CHF RM16 .... 215 G2
Jollaston Crs PIT SS13 .... 169 C3
Jollaston Wy PIT SS13 .... 169 F4
Jolmers Hey RCHLM CM3 .... 20 B6
Jolseley Rd CHLM/GWD CM2 .... 4 B3
Jolsey Rd EN EN1 .... 104 B6
Jombwell Gdns GVW DA11 .... 218 C7
Jonston Rd BOC CM0 .... 128 C1
Jood Av HOC/HUL SS5 .... 151 F5
    PUR RM19 .... 211 K3

Woodberry Cl CVI SS8 .... 191 F7
    LOS SS9 .... 172 D8
Woodberry Down EPP CM16 .... 80 E5
Woodberry Rd WICKE SS11 .... 147 K7
Woodberry Wy CHING E4 .... 132 D3
Woodbine Cl HLWW/ROY CM19 .... 2 C5
Woodbridge Cl HARH RM3 .... 138 E7
Woodbridge La HARH RM3 .... 138 E6
Woodbrooke Wy SLH/COR SS17 .... 187 J8
Woodburn Cl SBF/HAD SS7 .... 191 C1
Woodbury HI LOU IG10 .... 107 C6
Woodcote Ap SBF/HAD SS7 .... 170 A6
Woodcote La CHLM/WR CM12 .... 180 B5
Woodcote Crs PIT SS13 .... 169 G7
Woodcote Ms LOU IG10 .... 134 A3
Woodcote Rd LOS SS9 .... 193 H3
Woodcotes SBN/FI SS3 .... 196 C4
Woodcote Wy SBF/HAD SS7 .... 170 A6
Woodcroft HLWS CM18 .... 2 C5
Woodcroft Cl SBF/HAD SS7 .... 191 H1
Woodcutters Av
    CDH/CHF RM16 .... 214 D3
    LOS SS9 .... 172 D8
Wood DI CHLM/GWD CM2 .... 63 C7
Woododge Cl CHING E4 .... 133 C4
Wood End Av HOC/HUL SS5 .... 150 C8
Woodend Cl SBF/HAD SS7 .... 191 H1
Wood Farm Cl LOS SS9 .... 192 E1
Woodfield Av GVW DA11 .... 219 G2
Woodfield Cl GPK RM2 .... 160 B6
Woodfield Gdns LOS SS9 .... 193 H4
Woodfield Park Dr LOS SS9 .... 193 H4
    SBF/HAD SS7 .... 192 B2
Woodfield Wy HCH RM12 .... 180 E2
    RCHLM CM3 .... 38 A1
The Woodfines EMPK RM11 .... 160 E8
Woodford Cl WAB EN9 .... 78 C7
Woodgrange Cl SOS SS1 .... 195 H5
Woodgrange Dr SOS SS1 .... 9 F5
Wood Gn PIT SS13 .... 168 E4
Woodgreen Rd WAB EN9 .... 78 E7
Woodhall Crs EMPK RM11 .... 181 G1
Woodhall HI CHLM/WR CM1 .... 33 H2
Woodhall Rd CHLM/WR CM1 .... 34 C6
Woodham Dr RCHLM CM3 .... 38 B1
Woodham Halt RCHLM CM3 .... 122 C5
Woodham Mortimer Rd MAL CM9 .... 66 E5
Woodham Park Dr SBF/HAD SS7 .... 190 A3
Woodham Rd RCHLM CM3 .... 123 C3
    RCHLM CM3 .... 124 D2
    SBF/HAD SS7 .... 190 A3
Woodhill HLWS CM18 .... 3 E6
Woodhill Common Rd RCHLM CM3 .... 65 F8
Woodhill Rd CHLM/GWD CM2 .... 64 A7
Woodhouse La CHLM/WR CM1 .... 34 C1
Woodhurst Rd CVI SS8 .... 207 J2
Wooding Gv HLWW/ROY CM19 .... 2 B3
Woodland Av RBRW/HUT CM13 .... 142 B1
Woodland Cl RBRW/HUT CM13 .... 142 B1
    SBF/HAD SS7 .... 192 A2
    WFD IG8 .... 133 H6
Woodland Park Cha RCHLM CM3 .... 98 E6
Woodland Rd CHING E4 .... 132 D4
    CHLM/WR CM1 .... 4 B1
    LOU IG10 .... 107 C7
Woodlands RCHLM CM3 .... 126 E2
Woodlands Av EMPK RM11 .... 160 E8
    RAYL SS6 .... 171 J5
Woodlands Cl CDH/CHF RM16 .... 214 D2
    HOC/HUL SS5 .... 116 C1
    ING CM4 .... 89 F2
    RAYL SS6 .... 171 J5
    VGE SS16 .... 188 C1
Woodlands Dr HOD EN11 .... 49 C1
    SLH/COR SS17 .... 187 K4
Woodlands Pk LOS SS9 .... 192 B2
Woodlands Rd HARH RM3 .... 161 H5
    HOC/HUL SS5 .... 150 B8
    ROM RM1 .... 160 A5
    WICKW SS12 .... 147 C6
The Woodlands SBN/FI SS3 .... 196 E5
Woodland Wy CHONG CM5 .... 84 B4
    EPP CM16 .... 108 C2
    WFD IG8 .... 133 H6
Wood La CHONG CM5 .... 58 B2
    GTDUN CM6 ....
    HCH RM12 .... 180 B6
    MAL CM9 .... 40 D4
    MAL CM9 .... 97 C4
    WFD IG8 .... 133 C8
Woodleigh Av LOS SS9 .... 192 E2
Woodley Wk SBN/FI SS3 .... 196 D3
Woodlow SBF/HAD SS7 .... 171 C7
Woodmanhurst Rd
    SLH/COR SS17 .... 187 G8
Woodman La CHING E4 .... 132 E1
Woodman Pth BARK/HLT IG6 .... 135 H8
Woodman Rd BRW CM14 .... 141 F8
Wood Meads EPP CM16 .... 80 E3
Woodpond Av HOC/HUL SS5 .... 150 E8
Woodredon Cl HLWW/ROY CM19 .... 22 D6
Woodridden HI WAB EN9 .... 107 F1

Wood Rd MAL CM9 .... 40 D7
Woodroffe Cl CHLM/GWD CM2 .... 63 J2
Woodrolfe Farm La MAL CM9 .... 44 E4
Woodrolfe Pk MAL CM9 .... 45 F5
Woodrolfe Rd MAL CM9 .... 44 E4
Woodside BKHH IG9 .... 133 K5
    CHESW EN7 .... 76 A5
    EPP CM16 .... 81 H1
    LOS SS9 .... 172 C8
    MAL CM9 .... 40 D2
    RCHLM CM3 .... 65 J4
Woodside Av SBF/HAD SS7 .... 170 A5
Woodside Cha SLH/COR SS17 .... 173 F1
Woodside Cl RBRW/HUT CM13 .... 142 C1
    SBF/HAD SS7 .... 172 B7
Woodside Gdns CHING E4 .... 132 C8
Woodside Rd HOC/HUL SS5 .... 150 C8
    WFD IG8 .... 133 H7
Woodside Vw SBF/HAD SS7 .... 170 B5
The Woods SBF/HAD SS7 .... 192 A2
Woodstock LAIN SS15 .... 166 A7
Woodstock Av HARH RM3 .... 139 J8
Woodstock Crs HOC/HUL SS5 .... 150 E7
    LAIN SS15 .... 166 A7
Woodstock Rd BROX EN10 .... 48 E1
Wood St CHLM/GWD CM2 .... 4 A6
    GRAYS 214 B5
Wood Vw GRAYS RM17 .... 214 D3
Woodview VGE SS16 .... 185 K1
Woodview Av CHING E4 .... 132 D7
Woodville Cl RCFD SS4 .... 174 A1
Woodville Pl GVE DA12 .... 219 G5
Woodville Rd CVI SS8 .... 208 A3
Woodward Cl GRAYS RM17 .... 214 A3
Woodward Hts GRAYS 214 A3
Woodwards HLWW/ROY CM19 .... 2 C5
Woodway RBRW/HUT CM13 .... 141 K4
Woodyards BOC CM0 .... 74 B2
Woolards Wy RCHLM CM3 .... 122 D6
Woolhampton Wy CHIG IG7 .... 136 A6
Woolifers Av SLH/COR SS17 .... 204 D1
Woollard St WAB EN9 .... 77 J8
Woollard Wy ING CM4 .... 86 C4
Woolmans Cl BROX EN10 .... 49 F4
Woolmergreen LAIN SS15 .... 6 C3
Woolmers Md RCHLM CM3 .... 18 E3
Woolmonger's La ING CM4 .... 85 J5
Woolshotts Rd WICKW SS12 .... 146 C6
Wootton Cl EMPK RM11 .... 160 E7
Worcester Av UPMR RM14 .... 182 C2
Worcester Cl RCHLM CM3 .... 98 K4
    SLH/COR SS17 .... 203 K2
    VGE SS16 .... 166 A4
Worcester Ct CHLM/GWD CM2 .... 63 J8
Worcester Crs WFD IG8 .... 133 J8
Worcester Dr RAYL SS6 .... 172 A4
Worcester Rd BOC CM0 .... 128 C7
Worcesters Av EN EN1 .... 104 A4
Wordsworth Av MAL CM9 .... 68 C5
    SOSN SS2 .... 9 C2
    TIL RM18 .... 215 H8
Workhouse La RCHLM CM3 .... 122 A3
Wormley Ct WAB EN9 .... 78 C7
Wormley Lodge Cl BROX EN10 .... 49 F5
Wormyngford Ct WAB EN9 .... 78 C7
Worrin Cl BRWN CM15 .... 141 J4
Worrin Rd BRWN CM15 .... 141 J5
Worthing Rd LAIN SS15 .... 166 B7
Wouldham Rd WTHK RM20 .... 213 H5
Wrangley Ct WAB EN9 .... 78 C7
Wray Cl EMPK RM11 .... 180 E1
Wraysbury Dr LAIN SS15 .... 6 B1
Wren Av LOS SS9 .... 172 D6
Wren Cl BCAYE CM11 .... 144 D4
    LOS SS9 .... 172 E6
    SBF/HAD SS7 .... 170 A7
Wren Dr WAB EN9 .... 78 C8
Wren Gdns HCH RM12 .... 180 A2
Wren Pl BRW CM14 .... 141 G6
The Wrens HLWW/ROY CM19 .... 2 B3
Wren Ter LOU IG10 .... 107 K5
Wren Wk TIL RM18 .... 215 G6
Wrexham Rd HARH RM3 .... 138 E7
    LAIN SS15 .... 166 C4
Wrightsbridge Rd BRW CM14 .... 139 C4
Wrights La BRWN CM15 .... 114 B2
Writtle Rd CHLM/GWD CM2 .... 4 B5
    CHLM/WR CM1 ....
    ING CM4 .... 89 F2
Wrotham Rd GVW DA11 .... 219 F8
Wroths Pth LOU IG10 .... 107 H5
Wroxham Ct SBF/HAD SS7 .... 172 C7
Wyatts Dr SOS SS1 .... 195 J6
Wyatts Green La BRWN CM15 .... 114 B2
Wyatts Green Rd BRWN CM15 .... 114 B2
Wyatt's Green Rd BRWN CM15 ....
Wyburn Rd SBF/HAD SS7 .... 171 J7
Wyburns Av RAYL SS6 .... 171 K5
Wyburns Av East RAYL SS6 .... 171 K5
Wych Elm HLW 2 C2
Wych Elm Cl EMPK RM11 .... 161 H8
Wych Elm Rd EMPK RM11 .... 161 H6
Wychford Dr SBW CM21 .... 11 C4
Wycke HI MAL CM9 .... 67 K5
Wycke La MAL CM9 .... 44 E5

Wychford Dr SBW CM21	11	G4
Wycke Hl MAL CM9	67	K5
Wycke La MAL CM9	44	E5
Wycliffe Rw GVW DA11	218	E6
Wycombe Av SBF/HAD SS7	169	K7 1
Wyemead Crs CHING E4	133	F5
Wye Rd GVE DA12	219	J7
Wykeham Av EMPK RM11	160	E8
Wykeham Rd CHLM/WR CM1	61	H4
Wykes Gn BSDN SS14	167	K6
Wyldwood Cl HLWE CM17	11	G7
Wynters VGE SS16	7	F6
Wyse's Rd ING CM4	59	K7
Wythefield PIT SS13	168	D7

Yarwood Rd CHLM/GWD CM2	5	F3
Yeldham Lock CHLM/GWD CM2	63	J3 3
Yellowpine Wy CHIG IG7	136	A7
Yelverton Cl HARH RM3	160	D3
Yeomans Wy EN EN1	104	B6 2
Yeovil Cha WOS/PRIT SS0	193	J1
Yevele Wy EMPK RM11	181	F1
Yew Cl BKHH IG9	134	A5 2
LAIN SS15	6	A1
Yewlands SBW CM21	11	J4 3
Yews Av EN EN1	104	B2
The Yews GVE DA12	219	J7
Yew Tree Cl RBRW/HUT CM13	142	A2
Yew Tree Gdns CHLM/GWD CM2	62	E7 3
York Av SLH/COR SS17	187	H8
York Cl BRWN CM15	141	J3
RAYL SS6	172	B5
York Crs LOU IG10	107	G7
Yorkes HLWS CM18	3	F5
York Hl LOU IG10	107	G7
York Pl GRAYS RM17	213	K5 3
York Ri RAYL SS6	172	B5
York Rd CHES/WCR EN8	76	E8
BCAYW CM12	117	G8

BOC CM0	155	H
BRWN CM15	141	J
CHING E4	132	B
CHLM/GWD CM2	4	B
EPP CM16	82	A
GVE DA12	219	H
GVW DA11	218	C
RAYL SS6	172	B
RCFD SS4	151	K
SLH/COR SS17	203	F
SOS SS1	9	D
Young Cl LOS SS9	173	H

Z

Zandi Rd CVI SS8	208	D3
Zealand Dr CVI SS8	208	E
Zelham Dr CVI SS8	209	F
Zider Pass CVI SS8	209	F
Zion Pl GVE DA12	219	G6

Index - featured places

Aaron House Clinic of Physiotherapy WOS/PRIT SS0	193	J2
Abbey Mead Industrial Park WAB EN9	77	H8
Abbey Road Surgery CHES/WCR EN8	76	E8
Abbotsweld Primary School HLWS CM18	3	D5
Abbotts Hall Infant School SLH/COR SS17	204	A2
A B C Cinema GVE DA12	219	G4
Acorn Trading Centre WTHK RM20	213	G5
Adams Business Centre BSDN SS14	168	C4
Adult Community College Chelmsford CHLM/WR CM1	62	A3
Ainslie Wood Primary School CHING E4	132	C8
Airborne Industrial Estate LOS SS9	173	F8
Airport Business Park SOSN SS2	174	B7
Albany School Grant Maintained PEND EN3	104	D4
The Albany School HCH RM12	180	C3
Alderton County Junior & Infant School LOU IG10	134	D1
Alleyn Court & Eton House School SBN/FI SS3	195	K2
Alleyn Court Preparatory School WOS/PRIT SS0	193	K4
Ambresbury Banks Fort EPP CM16	79	K8
Andrews Lane Junior & Infant School CHESW EN7	76	A2
Anglia Polytechnic University BRWN CM15	141	G4
Anglia Polytechnic University CHLM/GWD CM2	4	B3
Anglia Polytechnic University CHLM/WR CM1	4	A2
Anglia Polytechnic University CHLM/WR CM1	34	C2
Anglia University CHLM/WR CM1	4	C1
Annandale Clinic WOS/PRIT SS0	193	J2
Appleton School SBF/HAD SS7	190	B1
Ardleigh Green Junior School EMPK RM11	160	E5
The Art Gallery LOS SS9	193	F5
Arthur Bugler Junior & Infant School SLH/COR SS17	204	A2
Ash Industrial Estate HLWW/ROY CM19	23	H6
Ashingdon School RCFD SS4	151	J4
Ashingdon Surgery RCFD SS4	151	K8
Ash Tree Surgery SLH/COR SS17	204	D1

Asquith School PEND EN3	104	C8
Aveley Football Club SOCK/AV RM15	198	E7
Aveley Medical Centre SOCK/AV RM15	200	A4
Aveley Primary School SOCK/AV RM15	199	G8
The Aveley School SOCK/AV RM15	199	F7
Avenue Industrial Estate GPK RM2	160	E4
Avenue Road Surgery BRW CM14	141	F7
Avon Bradbury School WFD IG8	133	H7
Aylands School PEND EN3	104	C2
Ayloff Primary School HCH RM12	180	C5
Baddow Hall Junior & Infant School CHLM/GWD CM2	63	J7
Balfour Medical Centre GRAYS RM17	214	B3
Ballards Gore Golf Club RCFD SS4	153	H7
Ballards Walk Surgery LAIN SS15	6	C3
Bancrofts School WFD IG8	133	H6
Barbara Castle Health Centre HLWW/ROY CM19	51	J1
Barling Magna Primary School SBN/FI SS3	176	D6
Barnes Farm County Junior School CHLM/GWD CM2	63	J2
Barons Court Infant School WOS/PRIT SS0	8	C4
Barstable School BSDN SS14	168	C7
Basildon College VGE SS16	187	G2
Basildon District Council BCAYE CM11	167	F1
Basildon District Council BCAYW CM12	144	B4
Basildon District Council BSDN SS14	7	E4
Basildon District Council LAIN SS15	6	A4
Basildon District Council WICKW SS12	147	F6
Basildon Hospital VGE SS16	187	G2
Basildon Rugby Football Club BSDN SS14	168	A4
Basildon & Thurrock Community Health Council BSDN SS14	7	F4
Basildon United Football Club BSDN SS14	167	K4
Basildon Zoo VGE SS16	187	K3
Bata Medical Centre TIL RM18	216	D3
Bates Industrial Estate HARH RM3	161	H2

Battlesbridge Motorcycle Museum WICKE SS11	148	C
Beacon Hill Industrial Estate PUR RM19	211	J
Beauchamps High School WICKE SS11	147	K
Beckingham Business Park MAL CM9	42	B
Beech Avenue Surgery UPMR RM14	181	J
Beecroft Art Gallery WOS/PRIT SS0	8	B
Beehive Lane County Primary School CHLM/GWD CM2	62	E
Belfairs Community College LOS SS9	192	D
Belfairs Swimming Pool LOS SS9	192	D
Belhus Golf Club & Leisure Centre SOCK/AV RM15	199	G
Benbridge Industrial Estate MAL CM9	40	C
Benfleet Business Centre SBF/HAD SS7	190	C
Benhurst Jmi School HCH RM12	180	C
Bentalls Industrial Estate MAL CM9	40	C
Bentalls Shopping Centre MAL CM9	40	D
Bentley Street Industrial Estate GVE DA12	219	H
Benyon CP School SOCK/AV RM15	200	A
The Billericay School BCAYW CM12	144	C
Billericay Swimming Pool BCAYW CM12	144	B
Billericay Town Council BCAYW CM12	144	B
Billericay Town Football Club BCAYW CM12	143	H
The Bishops C of E & RC Primary School CHLM/WR CM1	35	H
Bishop Stopford School EN EN1	104	B
Blackall Industrial Estate RCHLM CM3	123	F
Blackmore CP School ING CM4	86	C
Blackshots Leisure Centre CDH/CHF RM16	214	C
Blackwater Leisure Centre MAL CM9	68	C
Blackwater Sailing Club MAL CM9	69	H
Blackwater Trading Estate MAL CM9	68	C
Blenheim County Primary School LOS SS9	193	C
Bluehouse County Infant School LAIN SS15	6	A
Bonneygrove Junior & Infant School CHESW EN7	76	A

Church Langley Primary School
HLWE CM17 .... 25 G5

Church Trading Estate
ERITH DA8 .... 210 B6

Church View Surgery
RAYL SS6 .... 171 J3

Civic Centre
CHLM/WR CM1 .... 4 B2

Civic Centre
GWW DA11 .... 219 G5

Civic Halls
CVI SS8 .... 208 B2

Civic Theatre
CHLM/WR CM1 .... 4 B2

Clair Gallery
BRWN CM15 .... 141 K2

Clements Hall Leisure Centre
HOC/HUL SS5 .... 173 H1

Clements House Surgery
RCHLM CM3 .... 122 E6

Cockridden Farm Industrial
Estate
RBRW/HUT CM13 .... 164 E4

The Colin Dove Practice
ROM RM1 .... 160 A7

College of Teachers
EPP CM16 .... 108 B2

College St Pierre
LOS SS9 .... 193 H4

Collingwood Primary School
RCHLM CM3 .... 122 E7

Commonside School
HLWS CM18 .... 52 D1

Community Clinic
HLWS CM18 .... 3 F6

Coopersale Hall School
EPP CM16 .... 81 F7

Coopersale & Theydon Garnon
C of E Primary School
EPP CM16 .... 81 H3

Co-ordinated Industrial Estate
SBF/HAD SS7 .... 171 J6

Coppice Primary School
CHIG IG7 .... 135 K8

Corbets Tey School
UPMR RM14 .... 181 J6

Cornelius Vermuyden School
CVI SS8 .... 190 D8

Cornell Estate
CHLM/GWD CM2 .... 5 D3

Cornwallis Business Centre
BSDN SS14 .... 7 E2

Corringham County Primary
School
SLH/COR SS17 .... 204 E1

Corringham Health Centre
SLH/COR SS17 .... 204 D2

County Hall
CHLM/WR CM1 .... 4 C3

County Junior & Infant School
BRWN CM15 .... 140 D2

County Junior School
CHLM/WR CM1 .... 61 G5

County Primary School
CHLM/WR CM1 .... 88 A1

County Primary School
RCHLM CM3 .... 96 B8

County Primary School
RCHLM CM3 .... 121 G8

Coward Industrial Estate
CDH/CHF RM16 .... 215 G4

Cramphorn Theatre
CHLM/WR CM1 .... 4 B3

Cranes Industrial Centre
BSDN SS14 .... 168 C3

Cranham Health Centre
UPMR RM14 .... 182 B1

Craylands Clinic
BSDN SS14 .... 168 B6

Crays Hill County Primary School
BCAYE CM11 .... 146 A7

Cricket Club
EPP CM16 .... 108 C3

Cricketers Retail Park
PIT SS13 .... 168 D2

Cricketers Retail Park
WICKW SS12 .... 169 G2

Criton Industrial Estate
CDH/CHF RM16 .... 202 E6

Crouch Yacht Club
BOC CM0 .... 155 G1

Crown Club
WOS/PRIT SS0 .... 8 B3

Crown & County Court
BSDN SS14 .... 7 E4

Crown Hall
RAYL SS6 .... 171 H3

Crowstone Preparatory School
RCFD SS4 .... 174 E5

Crowstone Preparatory School
WOS/PRIT SS0 .... 193 J5

Cygnet Leisure Centre
GWW DA11 .... 218 D7

Dacre Industrial Estate
CHES/WCR EN8 .... 76 E3

Dame Tipping School
ABR/ST RM4 .... 137 J6

Danbury Clinic
RCHLM CM3 .... 65 K6

Danbury Park School
RCHLM CM3 .... 65 G6

Darlinghurst School
LOS SS9 .... 193 G3

Davenant Foundation School
LOU IG10 .... 108 A4

Deanes Secondary School
SBF/HAD SS7 .... 171 H7

Debden Sports Club
LOU IG10 .... 135 F1

De La Salle RC School
BSDN SS14 .... 7 F2

Deneholm CP School
CDH/CHF RM16 .... 214 B1

Dewhurst St Mary Junior
Middle & Infant School
CHESW EN7 .... 76 B3

Dickens Place Surgery
CHLM/WR CM1 .... 33 K7

Dilkes CP School
SOCK/AV RM15 .... 199 H6

Dipple Medical Centre
PIT SS13 .... 168 E8

District Council Offices
RAYL SS6 .... 171 J3

Doddinghurst C of E
Junior School
BRWN CM15 .... 113 K3

Doddinghurst County
Infant School
BRWN CM15 .... 113 K3

Doggetts CP School
RCFD SS4 .... 174 C2

Dominoes Health Centre
GRAYS RM17 .... 213 K5

Dover Road Primary School
GWW DA11 .... 218 D6

Downfield School
CHES/WCR EN8 .... 76 E5

Downhall Primary School
RAYL SS6 .... 149 J8

Downham C of E
Primary School
BCAYE CM11 .... 145 K1

The Downs CP School
HLW CM20 .... 3 D3

Drakes Lane Industrial Estate
RCHLM CM3 .... 21 K6

Drapers Sports Club
MAL CM9 .... 41 F8

Dry Ski Slope
RBRW/HUT CM13 .... 163 F2

Dukes Park Industrial Estate
CHLM/GWD CM2 .... 63 H1

The Dukes Priory Hospital
CHLM/WR CM1 .... 5 E1

Dunningford Primary School
HCH RM12 .... 180 A6

Durants School
EN EN1 .... 104 C5

Dycorts School
HARH RM3 .... 139 H7

Eagle House Surgery
PEND EN3 .... 104 C8

Earls Hall Infant School
WOS/PRIT SS0 .... 194 A1

Earthworks Gallery
HCH RM12 .... 181 F2

East Essex Adult Community
College
MAL CM9 .... 68 B3

Eastfield Primary
& Infant School
PEND EN3 .... 104 D4

Eastgate Business Centre
BSDN SS14 .... 7 F4

East Hanningfield C of E
Primary School
RCHLM CM3 .... 93 F6

East Herts District Council
SBW CM21 .... 11 J3

East Thurrock Football Club
SLH/COR SS17 .... 204 D2

East Tilbury Surgery
TIL RM18 .... 216 C3

Eastwood Gm Infant School
LOS SS9 .... 173 G8

Eastwood Gm Junior School
LOS SS9 .... 173 G7

Eastwood High School
LOS SS9 .... 173 G8

Eastwood Industrial Estate
LOS SS9 .... 172 D7

Edward Francis
Community Junior School
RAYL SS6 .... 171 K

Edwards Hall Junior
& Infant School
LOS SS9 .... 172 D

Edwin Lambert Schooll
EMPK RM11 .... 160 B

Eldon Way Industrial Estate
HOC/HUL SS5 .... 151 F

Eleanor Estate
CHES/WCR EN8 .... 77 F

Elm Green School
RCHLM CM3 .... 65 H

Elms Business Park
WICKW SS12 .... 169 H

The Elmwood CP School
RCHLM CM3 .... 122 D

Emerson Park School
EMPK RM11 .... 181 J

Endeavour School
BRWN CM15 .... 141 J

Enfield Business Centre
PEND EN3 .... 104 C

Enfield College
PEND EN3 .... 104 C

Enfield Football Club Ltd
EN EN1 .... 104 A

Engayne Junior School
UPMR RM14 .... 162 B

Epping County Infant School
EPP CM16 .... 80 C

Epping County Junior School
EPP CM16 .... 80 D

Epping Forest District Council
CHIG IG7 .... 135 G

Epping Forest District Council
EPP CM16 .... 80 D

Epping Forest District Council
EPP CM16 .... 80 E

Epping Forest District Council
LOU IG10 .... 108 A

Epping Forest District Council
LOU IG10 .... 135 F

Epping & Ongar Rural District
Council
EPP CM16 .... 81 H

Theydon Bois Golf Club
EPP CM16 .... 80 D

Theydon Bois Golf Club
EPP CM16 .... 80 E

Theydon Bois Golf Club
EPP CM16 .... 80 D

Epping Upland Cofe
Primary School
EPP CM16 .... 51 H

Erith Small Business Centre
ERITH DA8 .... 210 A

Erith Theatre Guild
ERITH DA8 .... 210 A

Essex County Council
BKHH IG9 .... 134 A

Essex County Council
BRW CM14 .... 140 A

Essex County Council
BRW CM14 .... 141 G

Essex County Council
BSDN SS14 .... 168 E

Essex County Council
CHIG IG7 .... 135 F

Essex County Council
CHONG CM5 .... 56 C

Essex County Council
CVI SS8 207

Essex County Council
EPP CM16 .... 80 D

Essex County Council
GRAYS RM17 .... 214 A

Essex County Council
LOU IG10 107

Essex County Council
PIT SS13 .... 169 F

Essex County Council
RAYL SS6 171

Essex County Council
RBRW/HUT CM13 .... 162 F

Essex County Council
RCFD SS4 .... 174 B

Essex County Council
SBF/HAD SS7 .... 190 A

Essex County Council
SOSN SS2 .... 174 C

Essex County Council
TIL RM18 .... 215 F

Essex County Council
WAB EN9 .... 77 H

Essex County Cricket Club
CHLM/GWD CM2 .... 4 C

The Essex Nuffield Hospital
BRWN CM15 .... 141 H

Europa Trading Estate
WTHK RM20.................... 213 G4
Everest Sports Club
CHES/WCR EN8.............. 76 B3
Everik Business Centre
RBRW/HUT CM13............ 142 D1
Eversley College
SBW CM21...................... 11 H3
Eversley CP School
PIT SS13........................ 169 F7
The Eye Clinic
LOS SS9.......................... 192 B3
The Eye Clinic
SBN/FI SS3.................... 196 C7
Fairfield Clinic
BKHH IG9........................ 133 J4
Fairfields Junior Middle &
Infant School
CHESW EN7...................... 76 A1
Fairhouse Junior & Infant School
BSDN SS14...................... 168 A7
Fairways Primary School
LOS SS9.......................... 192 D1
The Fairways
CHES/WCR EN8................ 48 D8
Fawbert & Barnards (UNDL)
Primary School
HLWE CM17...................... 25 G2
Felmore County Infant School
PIT SS13........................ 168 E5
Fitzwimarc Secondary School
RAYL SS6........................ 171 K2
Flamstead End Junior School
CHESW EN7...................... 76 A1
Fledglings Pre-school
CHLM/GWD CM2................ 62 C8
Fleetway Sports Club
GVE DA12........................ 219 H6
Florance Nightingale
Health Centre
HLWE CM17...................... 25 G6
Fondu Sports Club
PUR RM19........................ 211 K3
Forest Medical Centre
LOU IG10........................ 134 B1
Forty Hill C of E School
EN EN1............................ 104 A3
Four Hands Gallery
ING CM4.......................... 116 C1
The Four Swanns Jmi School
CHES/WCR EN8................ 76 E7
Frances Bardsley School for Girls
ROM RM1........................ 160 B8
Franklin Way Practice
RCHLM CM3.................... 120 D8
Franklin Way Practice
WICKE SS11.................... 147 H5
Friars County Junior School
SBN/FI SS3.................... 196 C6
The Fryerns Medical Centre
BSDN SS14...................... 168 B5
Fyfield Dr Walkers C of E Primary
School
CHONG CM5...................... 57 F3
Gable Hall Gm School
SLH/COR SS17................ 187 G8
The Gallery at Lakeside
WTHK RM20.................... 212 E3
The Gallery
BOC CM0........................ 155 H1
The Gallery
CHLM/GWD CM2................ 4 C4
The Gallery
SBF/HAD SS7.................. 190 C4
Galleywood County
Infant School
CHLM/GWD CM2................ 90 D3
Garfield Gallery
RAYL SS6........................ 171 J3
Gateway
BSDN SS14........................ 7 F4
Gaynes School
UPMR RM14.................... 181 K6
Ghyllgrove County
Junior School
BSDN SS14........................ 7 E3
Gidea Park College
GPK RM2........................ 160 B5
Gidea Park Primary School
GPK RM2........................ 160 A6
Gidea Park Sports Ground
GPK RM2........................ 160 D4
Giffards County Junior &
Infant School
SLH/COR SS17................ 204 B1
The Glade Business Centre
WTHK RM20.................... 212 C4
Glebe Infant School & U H I
RAYL SS6........................ 171 H2
Glenwood School
WICKW SS12.................. 169 K6

Globe Industrial Estate
GRAYS RM17.................. 214 B5
Globe Works Industrial Estate
GRAYS RM17.................. 214 C4
Goffs School
CHESW EN7...................... 76 A3
Goldings Hill Clinic
LOU IG10........................ 107 J6
The Gowan Gallery
SBW CM21........................ 11 J3
Grange Primary School
WICKW SS12.................. 146 E7
Gravesend County Court
GVW DA11...................... 219 G4
Gravesend Cricket Club
GVW DA11...................... 219 F5
Gravesend Grammar
School for Boys
GVE DA12........................ 219 J5
Gravesend Grammar
School for Girls
GVW DA11...................... 219 F6
Gravesend Museum
GVW DA11...................... 219 G4
Gravesend & Northfleet
Football Club
GVW DA11...................... 218 B4
Gravesend & North
Kent Hospital
GVW DA11...................... 219 F4
Gravesend Rowing Club
GVW DA11...................... 219 H4
Gravesend Yacht Club
GVE DA12........................ 219 J4
Gravesham Borough Council
GVW DA11...................... 218 B6
Gravesham Borough Council
GVW DA11...................... 219 G5
Grays Athletic Football Club
GRAYS RM17.................. 214 A5
Grays Business Centre
GRAYS RM17.................. 214 B2
Grays Convent High School
GRAYS RM17.................. 214 A3
Grays County Court
GRAYS RM17.................. 213 K5
The Grays Gm School
GRAYS RM17.................. 214 A2
Grays Health Centre
GRAYS RM17.................. 213 K4
Great Baddow High School
CHLM/GWD CM2................ 63 F7
Great Berry CP School
VGE SS16........................ 186 A1
Great Oaks Clinic
BSDN SS14........................ 7 E4
Great Stony School
CHONG CM5...................... 84 C1
The Great Wakering
Health Centre
SBN/FI SS3.................... 196 E1
Great Wakering Primary School
SBN/FI SS3.................... 197 F2
Great Wakering Sports Centre
SBN/FI SS3.................... 196 E1
Great Waltham C of E School
RCHLM CM3...................... 20 A6
Greensted County Infant School
BSDN SS14...................... 168 B7
Greensward College
HOC/HUL SS5.................. 151 F6
Greensward Surgery
HOC/HUL SS5.................. 151 G6
Greenwood Surgery
RCHLM CM3.................... 122 E6
Grove Junior & Infant School
RAYL SS6........................ 172 B4
Grove Tennis Club
CHLM/GWD CM2................ 4 O6
Grundy Park Leisure Centre
CHES/WCR EN8................ 76 E4
Guardian Business Centre
HARH RM3...................... 160 E2
Guru Gobind Singh
Khalsa College
CHIG IG7........................ 134 C4
Guru Nanak Sports Club
GVE DA12........................ 219 H5
GX
CHLM/WR CM1.................. 62 B1
GX Superbowl
CHLM/WR CM1.................. 62 B1
Hacton Infant School
HCH RM12...................... 181 F5
Hadleigh Business Centre
SBF/HAD SS7.................. 191 K3
Hadleigh Castle
SBF/HAD SS7.................. 191 K4
Hadleigh Clinic
SBF/HAD SS7.................. 191 H2

Hadleigh Junior School
SBF/HAD SS7.................. 191 K2
Hainault Forest High School
CHIG IG7........................ 135 K8
Hainault Industrial Estate
BARK/HLT IG6................ 136 B8
Hallmark Industrial Estate
BOC CM0........................ 128 E1
Hall Mead School
UPMR RM14.................... 182 A1
Hall Road Industrial Estate
BOC CM0........................ 128 E2
Hallsford Bridge
Industrial Estate
CHONG CM5...................... 84 E5
Hallsford Business Centre
CHONG CM5...................... 84 E5
Hamstel Primary School
SOSN SS2...................... 195 G3
Hare Street County
Junior & Infant School
HLWW/ROY CM19.............. 2 C3
Harlowbury School
HLWE CM17...................... 25 H1
Harlow Business Park
HLWW/ROY CM19............ 23 G6
Harlow College
HLW CM20........................ 2 C3
Harlow College
HLW CM20........................ 3 E2
Harlow Museum
HLWS CM18...................... 2 C4
Harlow Rugby Football Club
HLW CM20........................ 2 B1
Harlow Sailing Club
RCHLM CM3...................... 98 D3
Harlow Sports Centre
HLW CM20........................ 2 C1
Harlow Sports Centre
HLW CM20........................ 3 D1
Harlow Urban District
Swimming Pool
HLW CM20........................ 3 E1
Harold Court School
HARH RM3...................... 161 H2
Harold Wood Clinic
HARH RM3...................... 161 G4
Harold Wood Jmi School
HARH RM3...................... 161 H5
The Hartswood Clinic
RBRW/HUT CM13............ 162 E1
Harvey Centre
HLW CM20........................ 2 C3
Haslemere Business Centre
EN EN1.......................... 104 B8
Haslemere Industrial Estate
HLWW/ROY CM19.............. 2 A4
Hassenbrook School
SLH/COR SS17................ 204 A3
Hassengate Medical Centre
SLH/COR SS17................ 203 J2
Hatfield Heath CP School
RBSF CM22...................... 13 G2
Hatfield Peverel County Infant
School
RCHLM CM3...................... 38 B2
Havering College of Further &
Higher Education
EMPK RM11.................... 161 F6
Havering College of Further &
Higher Education
EMPK RM11.................... 180 C1
Havering College of Further &
Higher Education
HARH RM3...................... 139 G7
Havering Court Nursing Home
ROM RM1........................ 137 K8
Havering Cricket Club
ABR/ST RM4.................... 111 F7
Havering Hospitals N H S Trust
HARH RM3...................... 161 F3
Havering Sixth Form College
EMPK RM11.................... 181 G2
Hawkesbury Road
Doctors Surgery
CVI SS8.......................... 207 J2
Hawkswood School & Centre
CHING E4........................ 132 D1
The Hayward School
CHLM/WR CM1.................. 4 B1
Heathcote School
CHING E4........................ 133 F5
The Heathcote School
RCHLM CM3...................... 65 J6
Heavitrees Surgery
CHLM/GWD CM2................ 4 B5
Hedgerows Business Park
CHLM/WR CM1................ 35 J7
Hedley Walter High School
BRWN CM15.................... 141 F3

The Hereward County School
LOU IG10 .... 108 B5
Herington House Preparatory
School
BRWN CM15 .... 141 K2
Herons Gate Trading Estate
BSDN SS14 .... 168 D3
Herringham County
Infant School
CDH/CHF RM16 .... 215 G3
Heybridge CP School
MAL CM9 .... 40 E8
Heybridge House
Industrial Estate
MAL CM9 .... 68 D1
Heybridge Swifts Football Club
MAL CM9 .... 41 F7
High Beech C of E
Primary School
LOU IG10 .... 106 C5
Highlands Surgery
LOS SS9 .... 192 C3
High Ongar CP School
CHONG CM5 .... 84 E1
High Street Surgery & Medical
Centre
EPP CM16 .... 80 E4
Highwood Hospital
BRWN CM15 .... 140 E4
Hilldene Junior School
HARH RM3 .... 160 D1
Hillgrove Business Park
WAB EN9 .... 49 J4
Hilltop Junior & Infant School
WICKE SS11 .... 147 K5
Hinguar Primary School
SBN/FI SS3 .... 196 E6
Hockley Primary School
HOC/HUL SS5 .... 150 D7
Hogarth Primary School
BRWN CM15 .... 141 J6
Holdbrook Junior Middle &
Infant School
CHES/WCR EN8 .... 77 F8
Holly House Private Hospital
BKHH IG9 .... 133 J5
The Holly Trees County Infant
School
BRW CM14 .... 140 E7
Hollytrees Junior School
BRW CM14 .... 140 E7
Hollywood Bowl
BSDN SS14 .... 7 F1
Holt Farm Infant School
RCFD SS4 .... 174 A2
Holy Cross RC Primary School
HLWS CM18 .... 24 E7
Holy Cross RC School
SOCK/AV RM15 .... 199 K7
Holy Family School
SBF/HAD SS7 .... 190 C1
Holy Trinity C of E
Primary School
CHES/WCR EN8 .... 76 D6
Holy Trinity C of E School
GVE DA12 .... 219 H5
Honilands Junior
& Infant School
EN EN1 .... 104 B2
Hornchurch Clinic
EMPK RM11 .... 181 F2
Hornchurch Sports Centre
HCH RM12 .... 180 D3
Horndon Industrial Park
RBRW/HUT CM13 .... 164 B8
Horndon-on-the-Hill C of E
Primary School
SLH/COR SS17 .... 203 F1
Howard Business Park
WAB EN9 .... 77 K8
Hullbridge Clinic
HOC/HUL SS5 .... 149 J3
Hullbridge Parochial Church
Council
HOC/HUL SS5 .... 149 J3
Hullbridge Sports Club
HOC/HUL SS5 .... 149 K4
Hurst Drive Jmi School
CHES/WCR EN8 .... 76 D8
Hutton All Saints C of E Primary
School
RBRW/HUT CM13 .... 142 C2
Hutton Clinic
RBRW/HUT CM13 .... 142 C2
Hyland House & Park
CHLM/WR CM1 .... 61 J8
Hylands School
CHLM/WR CM1 .... 61 K4
Ilford Trading Estate
BSDN SS14 .... 168 B3

Imperial Retail Park
GWW DA11 .... 219 F4
Industrial Estate
EPP CM16 .... 53 G7
Industrial Estate
RCHLM CM3 .... 93 F7
Industrial Estate
RCHLM CM3 .... 99 F5
Industrial Park
CHES/WCR EN8 .... 77 G8
Ingatestone County
Infant School
ING CM4 .... 116 A1
Ingatestone & Fryerning C of E
Primary School
ING CM4 .... 116 A1
Ingrave Johnstone
C of E School
RBRW/HUT CM13 .... 164 B1
Ingrebourne CP School
HARH RM3 .... 138 D7
International Business Centre
CVI SS8 .... 207 H2
International Business Park
CVI SS8 .... 207 G2
Island Golf
CVI SS8 .... 190 E7
Island Surgery
CVI SS8 .... 208 C3
Ivy Chimneys Primary School
EPP CM16 .... 80 D6
Janet Duke County
Infant School
LAIN SS15 .... 6 B4
Jerounds Junior & Infant School
HLWW/ROY CM19 .... 2 B6
John Cotgrove Gallery
LOS SS9 .... 193 F5
The Jones Family Practice
HOC/HUL SS5 .... 150 E8
Jotmans Hall Primary School
SBF/HAD SS7 .... 190 A1
Joyce Green Hospital
DART DA1 .... 211 G8
Jubilee Sports Ground
CHING E4 .... 132 E7
Katherines Primary School
HLWW/ROY CM19 .... 23 H7
Kelrose Swimming Pool Centre
RBRW/HUT CM13 .... 163 H7
Kelvedon Hatch CP School
BRWN CM15 .... 113 G2
Kenningtons Primary School
SOCK/AV RM15 .... 198 E6
Kent County Council
GWW DA11 .... 218 D8
Kent County Council
GWW DA11 .... 219 F5
Kents Hill Junior School
SBF/HAD SS7 .... 190 C1
Kents Hill Road Surgery
SBF/HAD SS7 .... 170 C8
King Edmunds School
RCFD SS4 .... 152 B8
King Edward Grammer Sports
Ground
CHLM/WR CM1 .... 34 B1
King Edward VI Grammar
School
CHLM/WR CM1 .... 4 B2
King Harold Comprehensive
School
WAB EN9 .... 78 A7
The King John School
SBF/HAD SS7 .... 191 G2
Kingsdale Industrial Estate
CHLM/WR CM1 .... 4 C2
Kingsdown School
LOS SS9 .... 173 H7
Kings Estate
HCH RM12 .... 180 B5
Kingsmead School
EN EN1 .... 104 A8
Kingsmoor Junior
& Infant School
HLWW/ROY CM19 .... 52 A1
Kingsmoor Recreation Centre
HLWW/ROY CM19 .... 51 K1
Kings Road Junior School
CHLM/WR CM1 .... 4 A1
Kingston CP School
SBF/HAD SS7 .... 170 D7
Kingswood County
Junior & Infant School
VGE SS16 .... 7 F5
Kingswood Medical Centre
VGE SS16 .... 7 F6
Kings Wood School
HARH RM3 .... 139 H7
Kingswood Surgery
VGE SS16 .... 7 F5

Knightsmead School
SOCK/AV RM15 .... 199 J7
Lady of Lourdes RC School
LOS SS9 .... 193 H3
Laindon Health Centre
LAIN SS15 .... 166 C7
Laindon Park CP School
LAIN SS15 .... 6 C2
Laindon Road Clinic
BCAYW CM12 .... 144 B5
The Laindon School
LAIN SS15 .... 166 C5
Lakeside Shopping Centre
WTHK RM20 .... 212 E2
Lambourne CP School
ABR/ST RM4 .... 109 F8
Langtons Junior
& Infant School
EMPK RM11 .... 181 F2
Lansdowne County
Primary School
TIL RM18 .... 214 E8
Larkswood Junior
& Infant School
CHING E4 .... 132 C7
Laser Clinic
CHESW EN7 .... 76 B4
Latchingdon C of E
Primary School
RCHLM CM3 .... 97 K7
Latton Bush Business Centre
HLWS CM18 .... 3 F6
Latton Bush Recreation Centre
HLWS CM18 .... 3 E6
The Laurels Surgery
RCHLM CM3 .... 36 D5
Laurence Industrial Estate
SOSN SS2 .... 173 J7
Lawn CP School
GWW DA11 .... 218 B4
Lea Valley High School
PEND EN3 .... 104 C1
Lee Chapel CP School
VGE SS16 .... 7 D6
Leigh Beck Primary School
CVI SS8 .... 208 E2
Leigh Junior & Infant School
LOS SS9 .... 193 F5
Leigh Parish Council
LOS SS9 .... 193 F4
The Leventhorpe School
SBW CM21 .... 11 J1
Ley Park CP School
BROX EN10 .... 49 F4
The Limes Medical Centre
EPP CM16 .... 54 B8
The Limes Medical Centre
EPP CM16 .... 81 F3
Lincewood County Junior
& Infant School
VGE SS16 .... 186 C2
Lingwood Clinic
SLH/COR SS17 .... 203 J4
Lionmede Bowling Club &
Tennis Courts
CHLM/GWD CM2 .... 5 E2
Lister Medical Centre
HLWS CM18 .... 2 C6
Little Margraves
Industrial Estate
UPMR RM14 .... 186 A4
Little Thurrock County
Primary School
GRAYS RM17 .... 214 C2
Little Waltham C of E Primary
School
RCHLM CM3 .... 20 D6
Llewelyn Surgery
WAB EN9 .... 77 J7
London Road Surgery
RAYL SS6 .... 171 G2
London Road Surgery
WICKW SS12 .... 147 F6
Longfield Medical Centre
MAL CM9 .... 40 D8
Longfield Medical Centre
MAL CM9 .... 68 C3
Long Gallery
BSDN SS14 .... 7 F5
Longlands Junior Middle &
Infant School
BROX EN10 .... 48 E7
Long Ridings Junior
& Infant School
RBRW/HUT CM13 .... 142 A1
Long Road Surgery
CVI SS8 .... 207 J2
Longshaw Primary School
CHING E4 .... 132 E6
Loughton Cricket Club
LOU IG10 .... 107 H7

Loughton Hall Clinic
LOU IG10 .... 107 K7
Loughton Health Centre
LOU IG10 .... 107 G7
Loughton Mental Health Centre
LOU IG10 .... 134 B1
Loyola Preparatory School
BKHH IG9 .... 133 K4
Lubbins Park Primary School
CVI SS8 .... 208 C3
Lychgate Industrial Estate
SBF/HAD SS7 .... 170 D4
Lynn Tait Gallery
LOS SS9 .... 192 E5
Magnet Estate
WTHK RM20 .... 213 F4
Malden All Saints C of E Primary
School
MAL CM9 .... 68 A3
Maldon Agricultural Museum
MAL CM9 .... 42 O6
Maldon Court School
MAL CM9 .... 68 B2
Maldon District Council
MAL CM9 .... 68 C3
Maldon Museum
MAL CM9 .... 68 D3
Maldon Primary School
MAL CM9 .... 68 C3
Maldon Town Council
MAL CM9 .... 68 C2
The Maltings Industrial Estate
BOC CM0 .... 128 E1
The Maltings Industrial Estate
SBW CM21 .... 11 K3
Manford Industrial Estate
ERITH DA8 .... 210 C5
Mangapps Farm
Railway Museum
BOC CM0 .... 128 A5
Manor County Junior
& Infant School
BSDN SS14 .... 167 K5
Manor Gallery
GVE DA12 .... 219 G5
The Manor of Groves
SBW CM21 .... 10 D3
The Manor Primary School
ROM RM1 .... 160 A7
Manor Trading Estate
SBF/HAD SS7 .... 170 O6
Manor Way Industrial Estate
GRAYS RM17 .... 214 B6
Maple River Industrial Estate
HLW CM20 .... 11 F7
Mardyke Surgery
PUR RM19 .... 211 H3
Margaretting C of E
Primary School
ING CM4 .... 88 E5
Marillac Hospital
RBRW/HUT CM13 .... 163 G1
Mark Hall Comprehensive School
HLWE CM17 .... 25 G2
Mark Hall Cycle Museum
HLWE CM17 .... 25 F2
Markhams Chase Leisure Centre
LAIN SS15 .... 6 B4
Matching Green C of E
Primary School
HLWE CM17 .... 27 K3
Matching Green Surgery
BSDN SS14 .... 168 A5
Maunds Wood CP School
HLWS CM18 .... 52 B1
May Avenue Industrial Estate
GVW DA11 .... 218 E6
Mayfair Industrial Estate
RCHLM CM3 .... 97 H7
Mayfield County Infant School
CHES/WCR EN8 .... 76 E1
Mayflower
Comprehensive School
BCAYW CM12 .... 117 J8
Mayflower Retail Park
BSDN SS14 .... 168 A3
Mayland Branch Surgery
RCHLM CM3 .... 98 D4
Maylandsea CP School
RCHLM CM3 .... 98 D5
Maylandsea Medical Centre
RCHLM CM3 .... 98 C4
Maylands Golf Club
HARH RM3 .... 139 J8
Meadgate CP School
CHLM/GWD CM2 .... 5 F5
Mead Industrial Park
HLW CM20 .... 24 D1
Mead Infant School
HARH RM3 .... 161 G1

The Mead School
HLWS CM18 .... 3 E5
Melbourne House Surgery
CHLM/WR CM1 .... 34 A8
Merrylands Junior School
LAIN SS15 .... 166 B7
Mid Essex Adult Community
College
RBRW/HUT CM13 .... 142 A2
Mid Essex Magistrates Courts
CHLM/WR CM1 .... 4 C3
Mildmay Industrial Estate
BOC CM0 .... 128 B8
Milehams Industrial Estate
PUR RM19 .... 211 H2
Millbrook Junior Middle &
Infant School
CHES/WCR EN8 .... 76 E3
Millhouse County Junior &
Infant School
LAIN SS15 .... 6 A2
Millwards CP School
HLWW/ROY CM19 .... 51 K1
Milton Hall Junior School
WOS/PRIT SS0 .... 8 B4
Milton Road Business Park
GVE DA12 .... 219 H5
Mitchell Junior School
HCH RM12 .... 180 C7
Monro Industrial Estate
CHES/WCR EN8 .... 76 E8
Montgomerie Infant School
SBF/HAD SS7 .... 170 A6
Moreton Bay Industrial Estate
GPK RM2 .... 160 E4
Moreton C of E Primary School
CHONG CM5 .... 55 J2
Mosque
WOS/PRIT SS0 .... 8 B4
Moulsham High School
CHLM/GWD CM2 .... 4 O6
Moulsham Infant School
CHLM/GWD CM2 .... 4 O6
Moulsham Lodge Clinic
CHLM/GWD CM2 .... 62 D7
Mountnessing C of E
Primary School
BRWN CM15 .... 115 H5
Museum
WAB EN9 .... 77 J8
Nabbotts County Junior School
CHLM/WR CM1 .... 35 G6
Nazeing CP School
WAB EN9 .... 50 A5
Nazeing Golf Club
WAB EN9 .... 50 E6
Nazeing Parish Council
WAB EN9 .... 50 D7
Nazeing Park (Sch)
WAB EN9 .... 50 E4
Neil Graham Gallery
BRWN CM15 .... 141 G5
Nelmes Primary & Junior School
EMPK RM11 .... 161 G6
Nevendon Trading Estate
PIT SS13 .... 168 E4
New Court Business Park
HLWW/ROY CM19 .... 52 A1
Newlands Spring Primary School
CHLM/WR CM1 .... 33 K6
The New Surgery
BCAYW CM12 .... 144 C2
Nicholas Comprehensive School
LAIN SS15 .... 6 B3
Noak Bridge Medical Centre
LAIN SS15 .... 167 G3
Noak Bridge Primary School
LAIN SS15 .... 7 D1
Normanhurst School
CHING E4 .... 132 E3
Northcourt County
Primary School
GVE DA12 .... 219 K6
North Crescent School
WICKW SS12 .... 147 G6
Northend CP School
ERITH DA8 .... 210 A7
North Fambridge Yacht Club
RCHLM CM3 .... 124 B6
Northfleet Boys' School
GVW DA11 .... 218 O6
Northfleet School for Girls
GVW DA11 .... 218 C7
Northgate Business Centre
EN EN1 .... 104 B7
North Hill Business Park
SLH/COR SS17 .... 203 F1
North Shoebury Surgery
SBN/FI SS3 .... 196 C4
North Weald Golf Club
EPP CM16 .... 54 A5

North & West Essex Adult
Community College
HLW CM20 .... 2 C1
Northwick Park Junior &
Infant School
CVI SS8 .... 207 H1
Oaklands County Infant School
CHLM/GWD CM2 .... 4 C5
Oaklands Farm Industrial Estate
BCAYE CM11 .... 118 A7
Oaklands School
LOU IG10 .... 134 A1
The Oaks Industrial Estate
HLW CM20 .... 24 D2
Oakwood Estate
HLW CM20 .... 24 E2
Oakwood Hill Industrial Estate
LOU IG10 .... 134 E1
Ockendon School
SOCK/AV RM15 .... 199 J5
Odeon Cinema
CHLM/GWD CM2 .... 5 D3
Odeon Cinema
HLW CM20 .... 2 C2
Odeon Cinema
ROM RM1 .... 160 A7
Oglethorpe County
Junior & Infant School
UPMR RM14 .... 182 C3
Old Bancroftians F C
BKHH IG9 .... 134 A7
Old Chigwellians Sports Club
CHIG IG7 .... 134 E4
Old Club House
BOC CM0 .... 155 H2
The Old Guild Theatre
GVW DA11 .... 218 O6
Old Harlow Health Centre
HLWE CM17 .... 25 G1
Old Westcliffians Rugby
Football Club
RCFD SS4 .... 173 K5
Olympic Business Centre
BSDN SS14 .... 168 C3
Ongar & District Sports Club
CHONG CM5 .... 84 C2
Ongar Health Centre
CHONG CM5 .... 84 C2
Ongar Leisure Centre
CHONG CM5 .... 56 C8
Ongar Parish Council
CHONG CM5 .... 84 C2
Ongar War Memorial Hospital
CHONG CM5 .... 56 C8
Oriental Galleries
BCAYE CM11 .... 118 B7
Orsett Church
of England Primary School
CDH/CHF RM16 .... 202 A5
Orsett Hospital
CDH/CHF RM16 .... 202 A5
Orsett Industrial Estate
CDH/CHF RM16 .... 203 F5
Painters Ash Primary School
GVW DA11 .... 218 C8
Palace Theatre
WOS/PRIT SS0 .... 8 A3
Palmers College
GRAYS RM17 .... 214 E3
Park Lane Surgery
BROX EN10 .... 49 F2
Park School
RAYL SS6 .... 149 G7
Parndoni Mill Gallery
HLW CM20 .... 23 K2
Parrock Street Surgery
GVE DA12 .... 219 G4
Passmores Comprehensive
School
HLWS CM18 .... 3 D5
Peartree Surgery
SOCK/AV RM15 .... 200 B2
Pembroke Business Centre
BSDN SS14 .... 168 B3
Perryfields County Junior &
Infant School
CHLM/WR CM1 .... 35 F7
Peterswood Junior & Infant
School
HLWS CM18 .... 52 B1
Phillips Gallery
CHLM/GWD CM2 .... 5 D3
The Picture House
HLW CM20 .... 2 C2
Pinewood Primary School
CRW RM5 .... 137 G8
Pipps Hill Retail Park
LAIN SS15 .... 6 C2
Pitsea County Junior &
Infant School
PIT SS13 .... 168 D8

t Marys RC Primary School
CHING E4 .... 132 E4

t Marys RC Primary School
PEND EN3 .... 104 D8

t Marys School C of E
Primary School
BOC CM0 .... 128 C7

t Michaels C of E Junior School
CHLM/GWD CM2 .... 90 E3

t Michaels Preparatory School
LOS SS9 .... 192 D4

t Nicholas C of E
Primary School
WICKE SS11 .... 148 D6

t Nicholas School
HLWE CM17 .... 25 K2

t Nicholas School
SOSN SS2 .... 195 H3

t Pauls C of E Primary School
BRW CM14 .... 113 F7

t Pauls Roman Catholic
Jmi School
CHESW EN7 .... 76 B1

t Peters C of E Primary School
BRW CM14 .... 140 B5

t Peters C of E School
CHLM/GWD CM2 .... 119 H1

t Peters High School
BOC CM0 .... 128 B7

t Peters Hospital
MAL CM9 .... 68 B3

t Peters RC Primary School
BCAYE CM11 .... 145 F7

t Pius RC Primary School
CHLM/WR CM1 .... 34 B7

t Teresa RC School
RCFD SS4 .... 174 A2

t Thomas More High
School for Boys
WOS/PRIT SS0 .... 193 H2

t Thomas of Canterbury
Junior & Infant School
BRWN CM15 .... 141 G3

t Thomas RC Primary School
GRAYS RM17 .... 214 A3

t Ursulas Junior School
HARH RM3 .... 160 C1

he Sanders Draper
Secondary School
HCH RM12 .... 180 D5

andon School
CHLM/GWD CM2 .... 63 K7

arbir Industrial Park
HLW CM20 .... 11 G8

awbridge Health Clinic
SBW CM21 .... 11 J3

choolhouse
ABR/ST RM4 .... 138 E5

chool House Aveley School
SOCK/AV RM15 .... 199 G8

chooling Licensed
Conveyancers
GRAYS RM17 .... 214 A4

scimitar Park Industrial Estate
PIT SS13 .... 169 G3

cott Park Surgery
LOS SS9 .... 173 G6

cotts Primary School
HCH RM12 .... 180 D6

eedbed Business Centre
SBN/FI SS3 .... 196 E6

haw County Junior
& Infant School
SOCK/AV RM15 .... 199 K6

hears Green CP School
GVW DA11 .... 218 E8

hears Green Infant School
GVW DA11 .... 218 E8

heering C of E Primary School
RBSF CM22 .... 12 D4

helley County Primary School
CHONG CM5 .... 56 A8

henfield Cricket Club
BRWN CM15 .... 141 J2

henfield High School
BRWN CM15 .... 141 K1

henfield Sports Centre
BRWN CM15 .... 141 K1

henval Industrial Park
HLW CM20 .... 24 E1

hoeburyness High School
SBN/FI SS3 .... 196 C6

ikh Temple
GVE DA12 .... 219 G6

killion Business Centre
BSDN SS14 .... 7 E2

lade Green Football Club
ERITH DA8 .... 210 C7

lade Green Infant School
ERITH DA8 .... 210 B6

Smilers Industrial Estate
PIT SS13 .... 169 J5

Somers Heath School
SOCK/AV RM15 .... 199 J7

Sooriakumaran Surgery
SOSN SS2 .... 194 B1

Sopwith Crescent
WICKE SS11 .... 148 A8

South Benfleet GM
Primary School
SBF/HAD SS7 .... 190 B3

Southbourne Grove Surgery
WOS/PRIT SS0 .... 193 J1

Southbury Primary
& Infant School
PEND EN3 .... 104 C8

Southbury Primary School
PEND EN3 .... 104 B8

South East Essex College
SOSN SS2 .... 8 C3

South East Essex
Sixth Form College
SBF/HAD SS7 .... 171 F8

Southend Adult
Community College
SOS SS1 .... 9 F4

Southend Borough Council
SOSN SS2 .... 8 C3

Southend Borough Football Club
WOS/PRIT SS0 .... 173 J7

Southend County Court
SOS SS1 .... 9 D4

Southend High School for Boys
SOSN SS2 .... 8 B1

Southend Hospital N H S Trust
WOS/PRIT SS0 .... 193 K2

Southend Rugby Football Club
SOSN SS2 .... 174 C7

Southend United Football Club
SOSN SS2 .... 8 B2

South Essex Clinical Trials Centre
LOS SS9 .... 192 C3

South Essex Health Authority
RAYL SS6 .... 171 H4

South Essex Health Authority
RBRW/HUT CM13 .... 141 F8

Southfields Industrial Park
LAIN SS15 .... 166 A6

South Green County
Infant & Junior School
BCAYW CM12 .... 144 C6

South Green Surgery
BCAYE CM11 .... 144 D6

Southminster Infant School
BOC CM0 .... 128 D2

Southminster Medical Centre
BOC CM0 .... 128 D1

Southview Park Surgery
VGE SS16 .... 188 A2

South West Essex
Magistrates Court
BSDN SS14 .... 7 E4

South Woodham Ferrers
Leisure Centre
RCHLM CM3 .... 122 E6

Sovereign Business Centre
PEND EN3 .... 105 F7

The Spinney Junior School
HLW CM20 .... 24 E4

Springfield Cricket Club
CHLM/GWD CM2 .... 5 F1

Springfield Industrial Estate
BOC CM0 .... 127 K8

Springfield Medical Centre
CHLM/WR CM1 .... 35 F7

Springfield School
CHONG CM5 .... 84 E4

Squirrels Heath Junior School
ROM RM1 .... 160 B7

Stadium Trading Estate
SBF/HAD SS7 .... 171 H6

Stafford Industrial Estate
EMPK RM11 .... 160 E5

Stambridge Primary School
RCFD SS4 .... 175 G3

Stanford Industrial Estate
SLH/COR SS17 .... 203 J4

Stapleford Abbotts
County Primary School
ABR/ST RM4 .... 137 G1

Staples Road Junior
& Infant School
LOU IG10 .... 107 G7

Staple Tye Shopping Centre
HLWS CM18 .... 3 D6

Star Lane Industrial Estate
SBN/FI SS3 .... 196 E2

Stewards Comprehensive
School
HLWS CM18 .... 52 A1

Stifford Clays County
Junior School
CDH/CHF RM16 .... 201 F8

Stifford Clays Health Centre
CDH/CHF RM16 .... 201 F8

Stifford County Primary School
GRAYS RM17 .... 213 H4

Stock C of E Primary
ING CM4 .... 117 K2

Stock Industrial Park
SOSN SS2 .... 194 D1

Stockwell Lodge Medical Centre
CHESW EN7 .... 76 A2

Strand Gallery
SOSN SS2 .... 195 G4

The Street Industrial Estate
MAL CM9 .... 40 D8

Stuarts Industrial Estate
CHLM/GWD CM2 .... 5 E4

Suffolks Junior & Infant School
EN EN1 .... 104 B6

Sumners Community
Recreation Centre
HLWW/ROY CM19 .... 51 J1

Sunnymede County
Junior School
BCAYE CM11 .... 144 E4

Sutherland Lodge Surgery
CHLM/GWD CM2 .... 5 E5

Suttons Jmi School
HCH RM12 .... 180 E5

Suttons Manor Clinic
ABR/ST RM4 .... 110 E4

Swaines Industrial Estate
RCFD SS4 .... 174 B2

Swan Mead Junior School
VGE SS16 .... 168 A8

The Sweyne Park School
RAYL SS6 .... 171 H1

Swimming Pool
SLH/COR SS17 .... 204 B1

Swimming Pool Centre
BCAYE CM11 .... 145 K1

Tanys Dell Junior School
HLW CM20 .... 24 E2

Temple Sutton Primary
& Infant School
SOSN SS2 .... 9 F1

Tennyson House Surgery
CHLM/WR CM1 .... 34 B7

Thameside Community
Health Care
VGE SS16 .... 168 A8

Thameside Community
Healthcare N H S Trust
BCAYW CM12 .... 144 C2

Thameside County Infant School
GRAYS RM17 .... 214 B5

Thameside Theatre
GRAYS RM17 .... 213 K4

Theydon Bois CP School
EPP CM16 .... 108 C2

Theydon Gallery
EPP CM16 .... 108 B3

Thomas Rivers Medical Centre
HLW CM20 .... 11 G6

The Thomas Rivers
Medical Centre
SBW CM21 .... 11 G4

Thomas Tallis School
WAB EN9 .... 78 B7

The Thomas Willingale
Gm School
LOU IG10 .... 108 A7

Thorpe Bay School
SOS SS1 .... 195 J4

Thorpe Bay Surgery
SOS SS1 .... 195 K6

Thorpedene Gm Junior School
SBN/FI SS3 .... 196 B6

Thorpe Hall School
SBN/FI SS3 .... 195 K3

Three Rivers Golf Club
RCHLM CM3 .... 96 A8

Thriftwood School
CHLM/GWD CM2 .... 90 C2

Thundersley Junior
& Infant School
SBF/HAD SS7 .... 171 F7

Thurrock Borough Council
GRAYS RM17 .... 214 A5

Thurrock Borough Council
SOCK/AV RM15 .... 199 J6

Thurrock Business Centre
WTHK RM20 .... 212 C5

Thurrock College
CDH/CHF RM16 .... 214 E3

Thurrock Council
PUR RM19 .... 211 G3

Thurrock Council
for Voluntary Services
GRAYS RM17 .... 214 A4
Thurrock Council Office
GRAYS RM17 .... 214 A4
Tilbury Fort
TIL RM18 .... 219 H2
Tilbury Manor Infant School
TIL RM18 .... 215 G6
Tilbury Surgery
TIL RM18 .... 215 F8
The Tile Gallery
LOS SS9 .... 193 H4
Tile House Surgery
BRWN SM15 .... 141 G4
Tillingham Medical Centre
BOC CM0 .... 102 A2
Tillingham St Nicholas
C of E Primary School
BOC CM0 .... 101 K1
Titan Industrial Estate
GRAYS RM17 .... 213 K3
Tollesbury CP School
MAL CM9 .... 44 D4
Tollesbury Sailing Club
MAL CM9 .... 45 F3
Tolleshunt Darcy C of E Primary
School
MAL CM9 .... 43 H1
Toot Hill Golf Club
CHONG CM5 .... 83 F5
Torells County Secondary
School for Girls
CDH/CHF RM16 .... 214 E1
Towers Infant School
EMPK RM11 .... 180 D1
Towers Junior School
EMPK RM11 .... 180 D1
Trading Estate
WTHK RM20 .... 212 D4
Trafalgar Trading Estate
PEND EN3 .... 105 F8
Treetops School
GRAYS RM17 .... 214 A3
Tricor Business Park
CHES/WCR EN8 .... 76 E8
Tricor Trading Estate
CHES/WCR EN8 .... 76 E8
Trinity Catholic Lower
High School
WFD IG8 .... 133 H7
Trinity Catholic Upper
High School
WFD IG8 .... 133 H7
Trinity Road Primary School
CHLM/GWD CM2 .... 5 E2
Tudor Court CP School
CDH/CHF RM16 .... 213 J1
Tunnel Industrial Estate
WTHK RM20 .... 212 C3
Tunnel Industrial Estate
WTHK RM20 .... 212 C5
Turnford School
CHES/WCR EN8 .... 76 E2
The Tyrrells CP School
CHLM/WR CM1 .... 35 G8
UCI Cinema
BSDN SS14 .... 7 F1
UCI Cinema
WTHK RM20 .... 212 C3
University of London
ENC/FH EN2 .... 104 A2
Upminster Infant School
UPMR RM14 .... 181 J4
Upminster Primary School
UPMR RM14 .... 181 K4
Upper Clapton Rugby
Football Club
EPP CM16 .... 53 F6
Upshire CP School
WAB EN9 .... 78 D6
Van & Car Surgery
PEND EN3 .... 104 D8

Virgin Cinemas
HLW CM20 .... 24 D1
Waltham Abbey Swimming Pool
WAB EN9 .... 105 K1
Waltham Holy Cross Council
WAB EN9 .... 77 H7
Waltham Holy Cross
Junior School
WAB EN9 .... 77 K7
Wansfell College
EPP CM16 .... 108 B1
Warden Lodge Surgery
CHES/WCR EN8 .... 76 D5
Warley County Junior School
BRW CM14 .... 141 F8
Warley Hill Business Park
RBRW/HUT CM13 .... 163 F1
Warley Hospital
BRW CM14 .... 140 E8
Warley Lodge Hospital
RBRW/HUT CM13 .... 163 G3
Warner Brothers Cinema
WTHK RM20 .... 212 D2
Warren Golf Club
MAL CM9 .... 66 C4
Warren Primary School
CDH/CHF RM16 .... 213 F2
Watermill Business Centre
PEND EN3 .... 105 F6
Waterside Farm Sports Centre
CVI SS8 .... 190 D7
Waverley School
PEND EN3 .... 104 C8
Wellesley Hospital
SOSN SS2 .... 9 F1
Well Lane Industrial Estate
RCHLM CM3 .... 65 G6
Wells Park School
CHIG IG7 .... 135 J7
Wells Primary School
WFD IG8 .... 133 J7
Wennington Hall Farm Business
Centre
RAIN RM13 .... 198 A6
Wentworth Primary School
MAL CM9 .... 68 B5
Westborough Primary School
WOS/PRIT SS0 .... 8 B2
Westcliff High School for Boys
WOS/PRIT SS0 .... 193 H2
Westcliff High School for Girls
LOS SS9 .... 193 H2
Westcliff Leisure Centre
WOS/PRIT SS0 .... 8 B5
Westcourt County
Primary School
GVE DA12 .... 219 K7
Westerings Primary School
HOC/HUL SS5 .... 172 E1
Western Road Surgery
BCAYW CM12 .... 144 B3
Westfleet Trading Estate
WICKE SS11 .... 147 J7
West Hatch High School
CHIG IG7 .... 134 C8
West Horndon CP School
RBRW/HUT CM13 .... 164 C7
Westlands County Secondary
School
CHLM/WR CM1 .... 61 K4
Westlands CP School
CHLM/WR CM1 .... 62 A3
West Leigh Junior
& Infant School
LOS SS9 .... 192 E3
Westmayne Industrial Park
LAIN SS15 .... 165 K7
West Road Mosque
WOS/PRIT SS0 .... 8 B2
West Station Industrial Estate
MAL CM9 .... 68 A4
West Station Yard
MAL CM9 .... 68 A4

West Thurrock CP School
WTHK RM20 .... 212 D8
Westwood Primary School
SBF/HAD SS7 .... 191 J4
The White Bridge County
Infant & Junior School
LOU IG10 .... 134 B3
Whitehall Estate
HLWW/ROY CM19 .... 23 G6
Whitehall Primary School
CHING E4 .... 133 F5
Whitehill Junior School
GVE DA12 .... 219 H8
Whitmore County Junior &
Infant School
BSDN SS14 .... 168 B8
Wickford Health Centre
WICKW SS12 .... 147 F5
Wickford Junior School
WICKW SS12 .... 147 F6
Wickford Swimming Pool
WICKW SS12 .... 147 F5
Widford Industrial Estate
CHLM/WR CM1 .... 62 A6
Widford Lodge
Preparatory School
CHLM/GWD CM2 .... 4 A6
William De Ferrers School
RCHLM CM3 .... 122 E6
William Edwards Gm School
CDH/CHF RM16 .... 201 G1
William Read CP School
CVI SS8 .... 207 K2
Windsor Trading Estate
BCAYE CM11 .... 146 A1
Winter Gardens Junior School
CVI SS8 .... 190 E6
Woodacre School
SOCK/AV RM15 .... 199 J6
Woodford Medical Clinic
RCHLM CM3 .... 65 G6
Woodham Ley CP School
SBF/HAD SS7 .... 170 A2
Woodham Walter C of E
Primary School
MAL CM9 .... 66 D6
Woodlands
Comprehensive School
VGE SS16 .... 7 E8
Woodlands Preparatory School
RBRW/HUT CM13 .... 163 G6
Woodlands School
CHLM/WR CM1 .... 34 B1
Wood Lane Surgery
HCH RM12 .... 180 B6
Woodside County
Primary School
CDH/CHF RM16 .... 214 E2
Woodville Primary School
RCHLM CM3 .... 122 C4
Wormley Jmi School
BROX EN10 .... 48 E8
Writtle College
CHLM/WR CM1 .... 61 H2
Writtle Junior School
CHLM/WR CM1 .... 61 G8
The Writtle Surgery
CHLM/WR CM1 .... 61 H1
Wrotham Road CP School
GWW DA11 .... 219 G8
Wrotham Road Health Clinic
GWW DA11 .... 219 G6
Wyburns City Junior School
RAYL SS6 .... 172 A5
Wycke Hill Business Park
MAL CM9 .... 68 A5
Wykeham Junior School
HCH RM12 .... 180 B2
Wyncroft Surgery
RCHLM CM3 .... 65 K6
Yardley Primary School
CHING E4 .... 132 C1

Page 6

A2
1 Arne Ct
2 Arne Ms
3 Bramley Gdns
4 Tavistock Rd
5 Vaughan Williams Rd
6 Victoria Crs
7 Walton Cl

Page 62

C4
1 Belle Vue
2 Haig Cl
3 Redcliffe Rd
4 Stapleford Cl

E3
1 Provident Sq
2 Sandringham Pl
3 Springfield Rd

E5
1 Amcotes Pl
2 Langdale Gdns
3 Van Dieman's La

Page 63

F2
1 Brookhurst Cl
2 Chelmer Pl
3 Parklands Dr
4 Regency Cl
5 Turkey Oaks

G1
1 Bishopscourt Gdns
2 The Heythrop
3 Oxford Ct
4 Redgates Pl

Page 68

C5
1 Dryden Cl
2 Johnston Wy
3 Ridgeway
4 Shelley Cl
5 Spencer Cl

Page 76

A2
1 Betjeman Cl
2 St Anne's Cl
3 Wellers Gv

B5
1 Ermine Cl
2 Greenwood Cl
3 Hargreaves Cl
4 Lilac Cl

D2
1 Campine Cl
2 The Colonnade
3 Drakes Cl
4 Faverolle Gn
5 Hamburgh Ct
6 Southbrook Dr
7 The Spur
8 Symonds Ct

D7
1 Lambton Av
2 Leven Cl
3 Monarch's Wy
4 Park Rd
5 Stoneleigh Cl

E2
1 Bromleigh Cl
2 Cordell Cl
3 Fraser Rd
4 Goodwin Ct
5 Lensbury Cl

E4
1 Foster Cl
2 Guinevere Gdns
3 Roberts Cl
4 Roswell Cl

E5
1 Acton Cl
2 Garland Cl
3 Holme Cl
4 Russell's Dr

E8
1 Abbey Rd
2 Lodge Crs
3 Station Ap
4 Trust Rd

Page 78

C7
1 Bromefield Ct
2 Stanford Cl
3 Sudicamps Ct
4 Tillingham Ct
5 Webster Cl
6 Wormley Cl
7 Wormyngford Ct
8 Wrangley Ct

Page 104

C6
1 Archers Dr
2 Ashdown Rd
3 Ashley Rd
4 Burncroft Av
5 Carterhatch La
6 Edington Rd
7 Hertford Rd

D1
1 Abridge Cl
2 Dewgrass Gv
3 The Greenway
4 Hawksmead Cl
5 Kingsfield Wy

D5
1 Addis Cl
2 Dison Cl
3 Logan Cl

D6
1 Burncroft Av
2 Lindhill Cl
3 Shaftesbury Av

E3
1 Coldham Gv
2 Cornhill Cl
3 The Generals Wk
4 Johnby Cl
5 Newport Cl

E8
1 Fairfield Cl
2 Northampton Rd

F8
1 Beresford Ct
2 Colville Ms
3 Dolphin Gdns
4 Edward Cl
5 Granville Cl
6 Lorrimore Cl
7 Oakley Dr
8 Queen's Gate Ms
9 Tavistock Dr
10 Wesley Gdns
11 Woburn Pl

G8
1 Berkeley Dr
2 Boleyn Cl
3 Brompton Cl
4 Dorchester Rd
5 Eccleston Gdns
6 Farriers Dr
7 Montpelier Cl
8 Pembroke Cl
9 Rutherford Cl

Page 122

D8
1 Drywoods
2 Penhurst Dr

E7
1 Reynolds Ga

Page 132

B5
1 Belle Staines
Pleasaunce
2 Dove House Gdns

B8
1 Burley Cl
2 Garden Cl
3 The Lawns
4 Pewsey Cl

D6
1 Ashingdon Cl
2 Daphne Gdns
3 Navestock Cl
4 Oakley Cl
5 Stapleford Cl

E4
1 Cambridge Rd
2 Carbis Cl
3 Cranworth Crs
4 Glendower Rd
5 The Green Wk
6 Pentney Rd
7 Queens Wk
8 Richmond Rd
9 Shaftesbury Rd

E5
1 Fairlight
2 The Four Wents
3 Onslow Cl

E8
1 Belmont Cl
2 Greenwood Dr

Page 133

G4
1 Littleton Av

H8
1 Butterworth Gdns
2 Colwall Gdns
3 Elrington Rd
4 Gardenia Wy
5 High Elms
6 Johnston Rd
7 Twentyman Cl

K8
1 Ewanrigg Ter
2 Frankland Cl
3 Hillside Cl
4 Manorway
5 Meadway
6 Parkway

Page 144

A1
1 Buckwyns Ct
2 Celandine Cl
3 Crescent Cl
4 Crescent Gdns
5 The Foxgloves
6 Hallam Ct
7 Pauline Gdns
8 Pavillion Pl
9 St Helens Wk
10 Upland Cl

C3
1 High Cloister
2 Hurlock Rd
3 Lower Cloister
4 Mayflower Rd
5 Pilgrims Cl
6 Saffron Wk
7 Weavers Cl
8 West Cloister

D3
1 Abbots Ride
2 The Chase
3 Copford Rd
4 David's Wk
5 Felsted Rd
6 Heather Bank
7 High Meadow
8 Jacksons Ms
9 Kelvedon Rd
10 Northfield Cl
11 Park Side
12 Shakespeare Av

D6
1 Carvers Wd
2 Foys Wk
3 Ganels Cl
4 Hammonds La
5 Hickstars La
6 Paddock Cl
7 Passingham Cl
8 Well Mead

E3
1 Gascoigne Wy
2 Hatfield Dr
3 Henham Cl
4 Holbrook Cl
5 Shalford Rd
6 Stansted Cl

E7
1 Anthony Cl
2 Copperfield
3 Homefield Cl
4 Lorraine Cl
5 Stockwell Cl

Page 147

F5
1 Upper Market Rd

G5
1 Beccles Ct
2 Station Ap
3 Stilemans
4 Upper Market Rd

G7
1 Champion Cl
2 Donald Thorn Cl
3 St Omar Cl
4 Sudbrook Cl

H4
1 Whitelands Cl

H7
1 Bannister Gn
2 Beazley End
3 Erskine Pl
4 Horkesley Wy
5 Ingrave Cl
6 Mackenzie Cl
7 Pleshey Cl
8 Sewards End
9 Taveners Green Cl
10 Tollesbury Cl

H8
1 Balfour Cl
2 Buchanan Gdns
3 Caladonia La
4 Chatton Cl
5 Chisholm Ct
6 Drummond Pl
7 Grant Cl
8 Lamont Cl
9 Madaren Wy
10 Munro Cl
11 Nicholson Gv
12 Ogilvie Ct
13 Robertson Dr
14 Rose Cl

Page 160

E3
1 Buttercup Cl
2 Copperfields Wy
3 Hatherleigh Wy
4 Widecombe Cl

E4
1 Chadwick Dr
2 Fleming Gdns
3 Messant Cl

Page 161

F2
1 Melksham Gn

F6
1 Banyards
2 Macdonald Wy
3 Peacock Cl
4 Russels

H6
1 Cornwall Cl
2 Hampshire Rd
3 Pembroke Cl
4 Suffolk Wy

Page 166

A8
1 Alnwick Cl
2 Amersham Av
3 Cambridge Cl
4 Flint Cl
5 Ipswich Ms
6 Lancaster Dr
7 Maple Tree La
8 Monmouth Wy
9 Oakham Cl
10 Osterley Dr
11 Oxford Cl
12 Reading Cl
13 Shrewsbury Cl
14 Worcester Cl

B7
1 Becketts
2 Brampstead
3 Braxteds
4 The Chignalls
5 Cumberland Dr
6 Easton End
7 Eisenhower Rd
8 Marden Ash
9 Roosevelt Rd
10 Sparkbridge
11 Truman Cl
12 The Willingales

B8
1 The Lindens
2 Macaulay Rd
3 Shelly Av
4 Silvermere

C7
1 Byron Ct
2 Ferndale Cl
3 Sylvan Cl

D5
1 Arne Cl
2 Arne Ms
3 Bramley Gdns
4 Tavistock Rd
5 Vaughan Williams Rd
6 Victoria Crs
7 Walton Ct

D6
1 Altar Pl
2 Chantry Pl
3 Copperfields
4 St Chads Cl
5 St Johns Cl
6 Tavistock Rd
7 Temple Cl
8 Walsingham Cl

D8
1 Little Oxcroft
2 Northumberland Av

E4
1 Box Cl
2 Doves Ms
3 Sweet Briar Dr
4 Wraysbury Dr

E6
1 Markhams Cha
2 Pickwick Cl

Page 167

F5
1 Buckingham Rd
2 Palace Gv

Page 168

C4
1 St Peter's Pavement

E7
1 Carisbrooke Cl
2 Pevensey Wy
3 Somerset Gdns

Page 171

F2
1 Bromley Ms
2 Broomfield Av
3 Denham V
4 Goldhanger Cl
5 Gosfield Cl
6 Hanningfield Cl
7 Kelvedon Cl
8 Langham Dr
9 Latchingdon Cl
10 Navestock Cl
11 Newsum Gdns
12 Rettendon Cl
13 Sheering Cl
14 Wethersfield Cl

Page 180

A8
1 Theydon Gdns

Page 181

F2
1 Bowden Dr
2 Brendans Cl
3 Chaplaincy Gdns
4 Inskip Dr
5 Wedlake Cl

Page 191

G8
1 Climmen Rd
2 Cropenburg Wk
3 Hilversum Wy
4 Kent Av
5 Spanbeek Rd
6 Vadsoe Rd
7 Venlo Rd
8 Wessem Rd

Page 196

D4
1 Barrington Cl
2 Blackwater Cl
3 Dovecote
4 Midsummer Meadow
5 Milbanke Cl
6 Montgomery Ct
7 Osprey Cl
8 Toucan Cl
9 Weaverdale

Page 208

C1
1 Aylett Cl
2 Herbert Rd
3 Keegan Pl
4 Mornington Crs
5 Rainbow Av
6 Sunningdale

C3
1 Ashingdale Cl
2 Atherstone Cl
3 Bruges Rd

Page 219

F6
1 Weavers Cl

Page 6

A2
1 Adnams Wk
2 Beaumont Crs
3 Freeborne Gdns
4 Tempest Wy

C2
1 Landseer Cl
2 Napier Cl
3 Prescott Cl
4 Priory Ms
5 Shaw Cl

C4
1 Beech Cl
2 Hazel Cl
3 Maple Cl
4 Willow Cl

C6
1 Derwent Wy

C8
1 Dawson Dr
2 Esmond Cl
3 Heron Flight Av
4 Hesselyn Dr
5 Kestrel Cl
6 Leathart Cl
7 Mungo Park Rd
8 Pease Cl
9 Robinson Cl

D5
1 Canberra Cl
2 Chestnut Cl
3 Lawford Cl

D6
1 Detling Cl
2 Griggs Gdns
3 Mallinson Cl
4 Martlesham Cl
5 Rye Cl
6 Scotts Cl
7 Springbank Av
8 Wendover Wy

D7
1 Craword Compton Cl
2 Franklin Rd
3 Gosport Dr
4 Hawkinge Wy
5 Pembrey Wy
6 Sarre Av
7 Stansted Cl

E4
1 Naunton Wy
2 Webster Cl

E6
1 Berry Cl
2 Bonington Rd
3 Edridge Cl
4 Hatfield Cl
5 Hilary Cl
6 Miramar Wy
7 Shepley Cl
8 Southbury Cl
9 Spingate Cl
10 Upney Cl

E7
1 Bennions Cl

Page 181

Page 191

Page 196

Page 208

Page 219

G4
1 Bank St
2 Bath St
3 Berkley Rd
4 Bernard St
5 Brewhouse Yd
6 Chase Sq
7 Carrick St
8 Horn Yd
9 Jury St
10 Manor Rd
11 New Swan Yd
12 Parrock St
13 Railway St
14 Wilfred St

G5
1 North St
2 St Andrew's Rd
3 Woodville Pl
4 Zion Cl

Notes

Notes